CONTENTS

INTRODUCTION

Our aim in this book has been to provide a complete and up-to-date set of colour illustrations of British wild flowers, together with a text concentrating on the natural history of the plants rather than on long technical descriptions. The book covers the whole of the British Isles (the United Kingdom, Ireland and the Channel Islands), and it is our hope that it will stimulate the ordinary lover of the countryside to a greater enjoyment and interest in our wild flowers as well as being used by the more serious botanist to complement the formal descriptions and keys in the standard floras.

Some decisions inevitably had to be made about the taxonomic scope of the book. Every species of wild flower native to the British Isles, except for the grasses, sedges and rushes, trees and some shrubs, is illustrated. In addition, most alien species that have become well established in the wild or turn up as casuals with a fair degree of regularity have been included, although the choice of such a list is inevitably highly subjective. In all, 1,454 different species and subspecies are illustrated.

Certain groups of plants present especial difficulties as they reproduce apomictically; that is, they produce viable seed without fertilisation, resulting in a large number of species differing only slightly from each other. For instance, there are more than 300 such 'micro-species' of bramble in Britain, and no attempt has been made to deal with these. The hawkweeds (*Hieracium*) and the dandelions (*Taraxacum*), the other two big apomictic genera, have been treated by illustrating representative species from each of the Sections into which the genera are usually divided. On the other hand, all the species of the other 'difficult' genera, such as lady's-mantles (*Alchemilla*) and the eyebrights, (*Euphrasia*) are illustrated.

A choice also had to be made about which shrubs to include and which to leave out, partly because there is no real difference between a small tree and a large shrub. The result is inevitably somewhat arbitrary. Holly, box, spindle, buckthorn, blackthorn, hawthorn and the willows are excluded, while most other shrubs, together with the woody climbers, are included.

Identification

The aim of the text has been to provide an account of the natural history of the various species – their distribution, ecology, method of pollination and flowering time, together with any other information of particular interest, such as poisonous properties or economic importance. All species that are considered to have been introduced either accidentally or deliberately by man are designated 'alien'. The native distribution of alien species is summarised but, for the sake of brevity, the extra-British distribution of native species is omitted. An attempt has been made to keep technical terms to a minimum, but the needs of precision and conciseness have ensured that some remain. Those that are used are explained in the Glossary.

There are no formal descriptions or technical keys, but in order to help with identification short notes are added in the text. These should be used in conjunction with the plates, and draw attention to critical differences between similar species and to characteristics that are not easy to illustrate. The combination of the plates and the notes should enable all but the more difficult groups to be identified with confidence. No attempt has been made to provide identification notes for some of the more critical groups such as the lady's-mantles (*Alchemilla*) and the eyebrights (*Euphrasia*), when naming should only be attempted using the more technical keys and descriptions in the references given. The same is true for other groups like the pondweeds (*Potamogeton*), starworts (*Callitriche*) and fumitories (*Fumaria*), and in any cases of doubt the keys in one of the standard floras should be consulted.

The most recent standard work on the British flora is *New Flora of the British Isles* by Clive Stace (2nd edition 1997). The *Excursion Flora of the British Isles* by Clapham, Tutin and Warburg (1981) has a good set of keys, but the text is abbreviated and some of the names have since been revised.

Names

Over the centuries many of our wild flowers have collected a prodigious number of local or vernacular names in different parts of the country. Lords-and-ladies (*Arum maculatum*), for instance, has about 100, and several species are universally known by more than one name. In an attempt to standardise English names used in publications, the Botanical Society of the British Isles has produced a list of recommended names, *English Names of Wild Flowers* by Dony, Rob and Perring. We have listed this recommended name first, followed by any others that are in widespread use.

THE WILD FLOWERS of the British Isles

THE WILD FLOWERS of the British Isles

Illustrations by IAN GARRARD
Text by DAVID STREETER

MIDSUMMER BOOKS

Published by:
Midsummer Books Ltd
179 Dalling Road
London W6 0ES
England
Telephone: 0181-749 2425
Fax: 0181-749 6249

Artist: **Ian Garrard**
Author: **David Streeter**
Editor: **Trisha Palmer**
Design: **Maggi Howells**
Editorial contributor: **Dr J.M. Lock**

First published 1983
Revised and updated edition published 1998

ISBN 1 900732 03 3

Printed in Italy

Taxonomists have a depressing habit of changing familiar Latin names with irritating frequency. The reasons for these changes, although often obscure, are usually perfectly good and are governed by international rules which, theoretically at least, ensure that the frequency of such changes should decrease as time goes on. The completion of the monumental five volumes of *Flora Europaea* in 1980 provides the most recent view of the taxonomy of the European flora, but is not a work that is likely to be widely read. The Latin names in this book follow those of the *New Flora of the British Isles*. Synonyms used in other recent standard floras have also been included where appropriate.

Conservation

We live in one of the most densely populated parts of the world, and the pressures on the countryside are enormous. Industry and developments in agricultural technology such as cleaner seed corn, the introduction of the phenoxyacetic acid herbicides, stubble burning, the enlargement of fields by the removal of hedges, the improvement of old pastures by chemical fertilisers and the reclamation of wetlands by drainage schemes have had an inevitable effect on the abundance of a large number of species, about 20 of which have actually become extinct in the last 100 years. To this must be added the pressures from informal recreation, especially around popular beauty spots, water habitats and the coast.

When visiting the countryside and studying plants, great care should always be taken not to trample and compact the soil around plants and to avoid drawing attention to rare species. On the other hand, the discovery of a new locality of a rare species should be reported to the local County Wildlife Trust so that moves can be made to safeguard it. Especial care should be taken when photographing plants, and plants should never be picked on nature reserves or nature trails. The Botanical Society of the British Isles has published a Code of Conduct for the conservation of wild plants which can be obtained from the Society (see below for address).

The Wildlife and Countryside Act 1981 makes it illegal to uproot any wild plant without the permission of the owner or the occupier of the land, and it is illegal to pick, uproot, collect the seed from or sell any of 107 particularly rare or vulnerable species. These specially protected plants are indicated by ** in the text. The Royal Society for Nature Conservation has published a list of 317 species and subspecies that are thought to be endangered or threatened with extinction, and a detailed account of these can be found in the *British Red Data Book: 1. Vascular Plants* by Perring and Farrell. Red Data Book species are indicated by * in the text, and copies of the book can be obtained from the Society (see below for address).

Anyone wishing to develop their interest in our wild plants should join the Botanical Society of the British Isles (B.S.B.I.). The Society publishes a journal, *Watsonia*, and the *B.S.B.I. News*, and holds regular field excursions and exhibitions. Details can be obtained from the Society, c/o Department of Botany, Natural History Museum, Cromwell Road, London SW7 5BD. Plantlife, the only charity solely devoted to the conservation of wild plants, produces a quarterly magazine, *Plantlife*, and details of membership can also be obtained from the Natural History Museum.

The leading organisations concerned with all aspects of wildlife conservation are the 44 County Wildlife Trusts, which between them manage over 2,000 nature reserves. The addresses of the various Trusts can be obtained from the parent organisation, the Royal Society for Nature Conservation, The Green, Witham Park, Waterside South, Lincoln LN5 7JR.

Acknowledgements

A book of this kind is not possible without the generous help, time and encouragement of a large number of people. For assistance, with particular plant groups we are especially grateful to Mr D. Lang (orchids), Dr S.M. Walters (*Alchemilla*) and Dr P. Yeo (*Euphrasia*). In addition, Mr T. Bennett, Mrs M. Briggs, Mr K. Butler, Mrs M. Harvey, Mr E. Jackson, Dr P. MacPherson, Mr L. Margetts, Prof. I. Mercer, Dr C. Nelson, Dr T. Rich, Dr F. Rose, the Field Studies Council, the National Trust, English Nature and the Sussex Wildlife Trust have assisted in a number of invaluable ways.

We would also like to thank Ron and Christine Foord, who generously provided extensive photographic references; Mrs S. Kippax for typing the original manuscript; Pat Gibbs and Suzanne Shepherd for retyping the text for revision; and Dr J.M. Lock of the Royal Botanic Gardens, Kew, for his assistance in updating and revising the text.

DAVID STREETER

BIBLIOGRAPHY

Clapham, A.R, Tutin, T.G. and Warburg, E.F. (1961)
Flora of the British Isles (second edition) (C.U.P.)

Clapham, A.R, Tutin, T.G. and Warburg, E.F. (1981)
Excursion Flora of the British Isles (third edition) (C.U.P.)

Dony, J.G., Rob, C.M. and Perring, F.H. (1974)
English Names of Wild Flowers (Butterworths)

Graham, G.C. and Primavesi, A.L. (1993)
Roses of Great Britain and Ireland (B.S.B.I.)

Haslam, S.M., Sinker, C.A. and Wolsey, P.M. (1975)
British Water Plants (Field Studies Council)

Holmes, N.T.H. (1979) A Guide to the Identification of Batrachium
Ranunculus Species in Britain (Nature Conservancy Council)

Lousley, J.E. and Kent, D.H. (1981)
Docks and Knotweeds of the British Isles (B.S.B.I.)

Perring, F.H. (editor) (1978)
Critical Supplement to the Atlas of the British Flora (E.P. Publishing)

Perring, F.H. and Farrell, L. (1983)
British Red Data Book: 1. Vascular Plants
(Royal Society For Nature Conservation)

Perring, F.H. and Walters, S.M. (editors) (1976)
Atlas of the British Flora (E.P. Publishing)

Preston, C.D. (1995)
Pondweeds of Great Britain and Ireland (B.S.B.I.)

Rich, T.C.G. (1991)
Crucifers of Great Britain and Ireland (B.S.B.I.)

Richards, A.J. and Dudman, A.A. (1997)
Dandelions of Britain and Ireland (B.S.B.I.)

Stace, C. (2nd edition 1997)
New Flora of the British Isles (C.U.P.)

Stewart, A. Pearman, D.A. and Preston, C.D. (1994)
Scarce Plants in Britain (Joint Nature Conservation Committee)

Tutin, T.G. (1980)
Umbellifers of the British Isles (B.S.B.I.)

Tutin, T.G. *et al* (editors) (1964-1980)
Flora Europaea (5 volumes) (C.U.P.)

Yeo, P.F. (1978)
A taxonomic revision of *Euphrasia* in Europe.
Bot. J. Linn. Soc. 77, 223-334

Wildlife and Countryside Act 1981 (H.M.S.O.)

The Plates

PLATE 1
RANUNCULACEAE *(see text page 217)*

Creeping Spearwort
Ranunculus reptans
Goldilocks Buttercup
Ranunculus auricomus
Greater Spearwort
Ranunculus lingua
Celery-leaved Buttercup
Celery-leaved Crowfoot
Ranunculus sceleratus
Lesser Spearwort
Ranunculus flammula
Adder's-tongue Spearwort
Snake-tongue Crowfoot
Ranunculus ophioglossifolius
Lesser Celandine
Ranunculus ficaria

PLATE 2

RANUNCULACEAE *(see text page 218)*

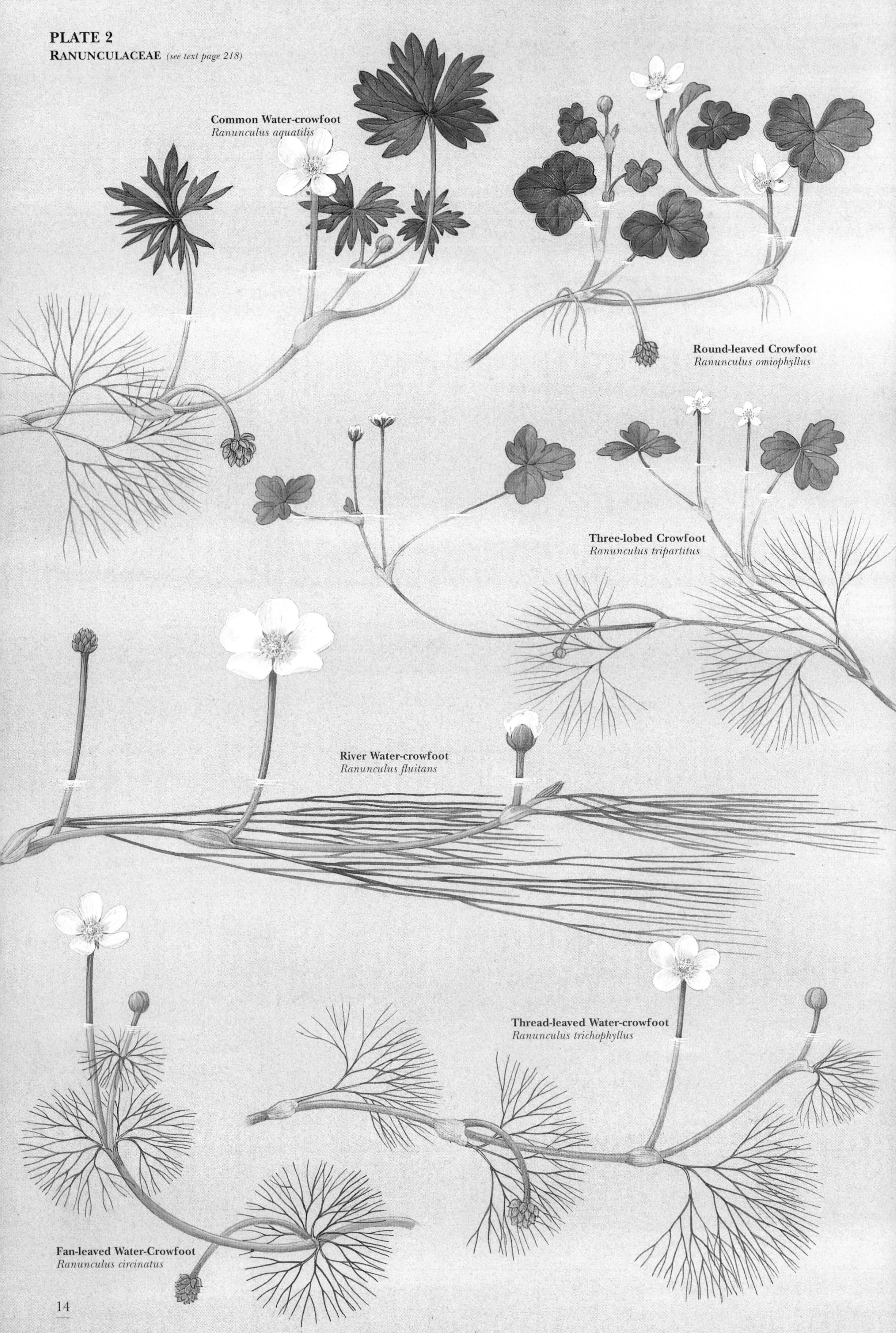

RANUNCULACEAE *(see text page 218)*

Ivy-leaved Crowfoot
Ranunculus hederaceus
Wood Anemone
Anemone nemorosa
Yellow Anemone
Anemone ranunculoides
Pond Water-crowfoot
Ranunculus peltatus
Blue Anemone
Anemone apennina
Brackish Water-crowfoot
Ranunculus baudotii
Stream Water-crowfoot
Ranunculus penicillatus
Larkspur
Consolida ajacis

PLATE 3
RANUNCULACEAE *(see text page 219)*

Pasque-flower
Pulsatilla vulgaris

Marsh-marigold
Kingcup
Caltha palustris

Globeflower
Trollius europaeus

Monk's-hood
Aconitum napellus

Stinking Hellebore
Helleborus foetidus

Winter Aconite
Eranthis hyemalis

Baneberry
Herb Christopher
Actaea spicata

Green Hellebore
Helleborus viridis

Mousetail
Myosurus minimus
Columbine
Aquilegia vulgaris
Lesser Meadow-rue
Thalictrum minus
Alpine Meadow-rue
Thalictrum alpinum
Pheasant's-eye
Adonis annua
Traveller's-joy
Old Man's Beard
Clematis vitalba
Common Meadow-rue
Thalictrum flavum

PLATE 4

PAEONIACEAE • BERBERIDACEAE • PAPAVERACEAE *(see text page 220)*

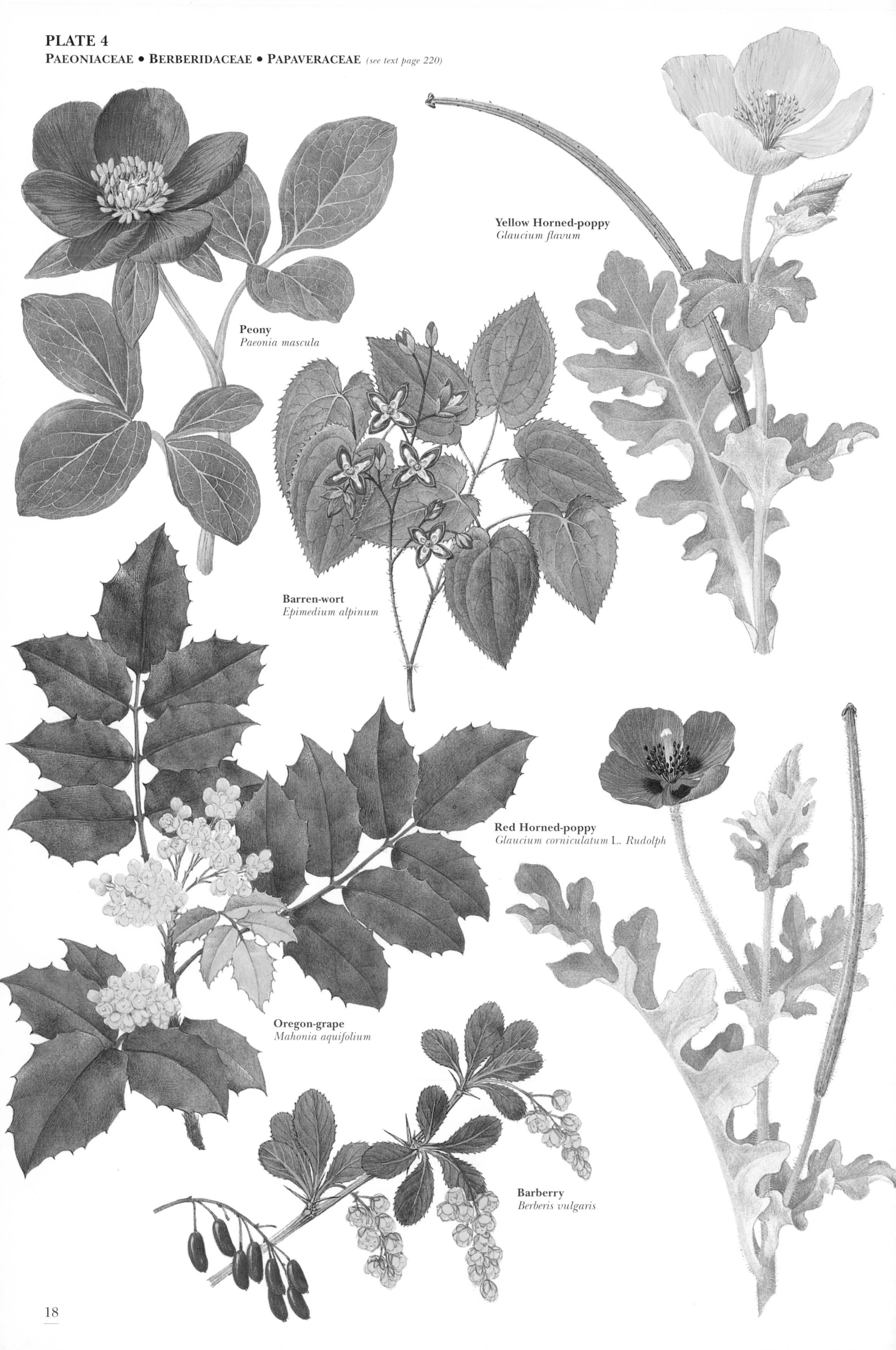

 (see text page 220)

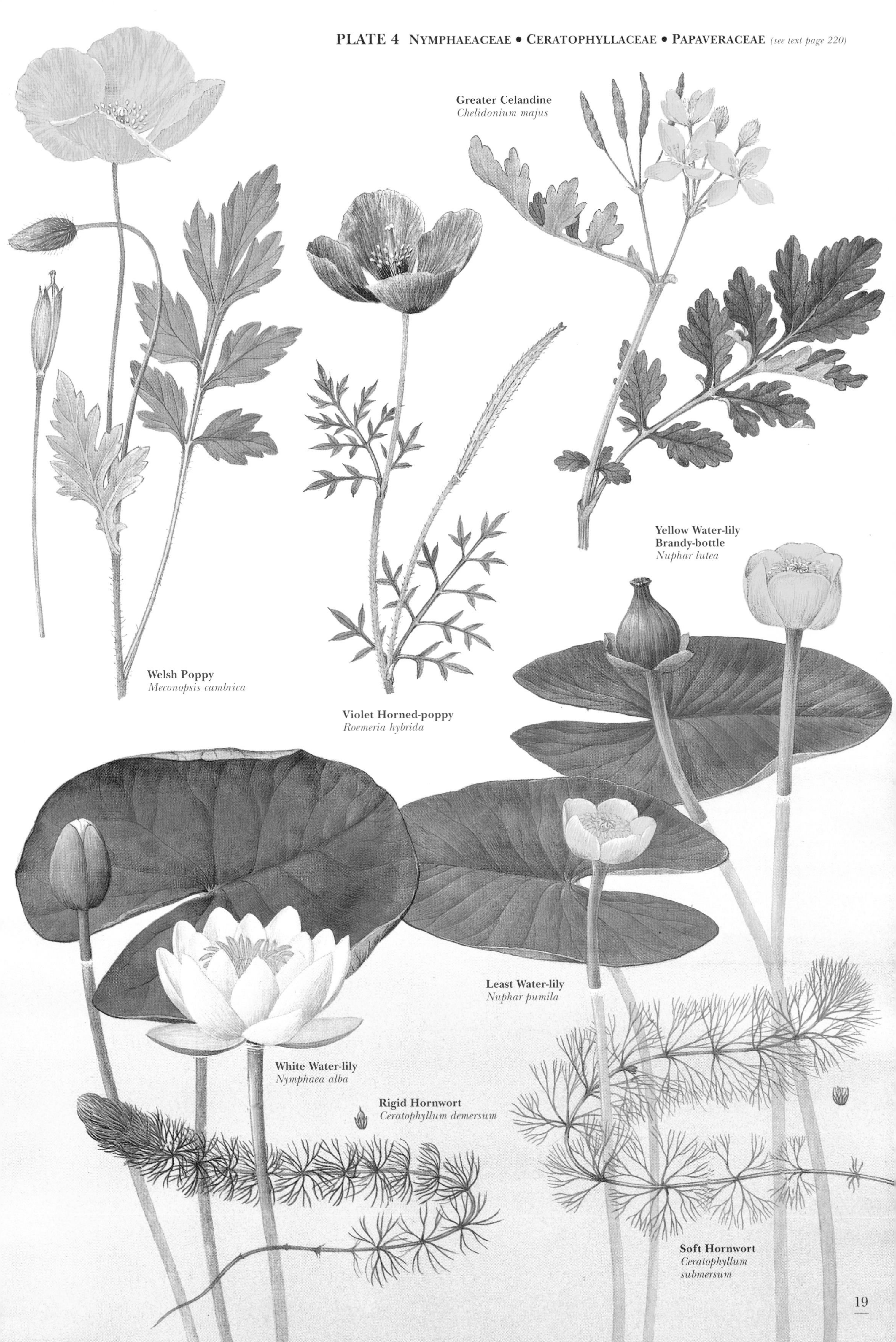
Greater Celandine
Chelidonium majus
Yellow Water-lily
Brandy-bottle
Nuphar lutea
Welsh Poppy
Meconopsis cambrica
Violet Horned-poppy
Roemeria hybrida
Least Water-lily
Nuphar pumila
White Water-lily
Nymphaea alba
Rigid Hornwort
Ceratophyllum demersum
Soft Hornwort
Ceratophyllum submersum

PLATE 5

PAPAVERACEAE *(see text page 221)*

Californian Poppy
Eschscholzia californica

Common Poppy
Papaver rhoeas

Long-headed Poppy
Papaver dubium subsp. *dubium*

Prickly Poppy
Papaver argemone

Yellow-juiced Poppy
Papaver dubium subsp. *lecoquii*

Rough Poppy
Papaver hybridum

PLATE 5

PAPAVERACEAE • FUMARIACEAE *(see text page 221)*

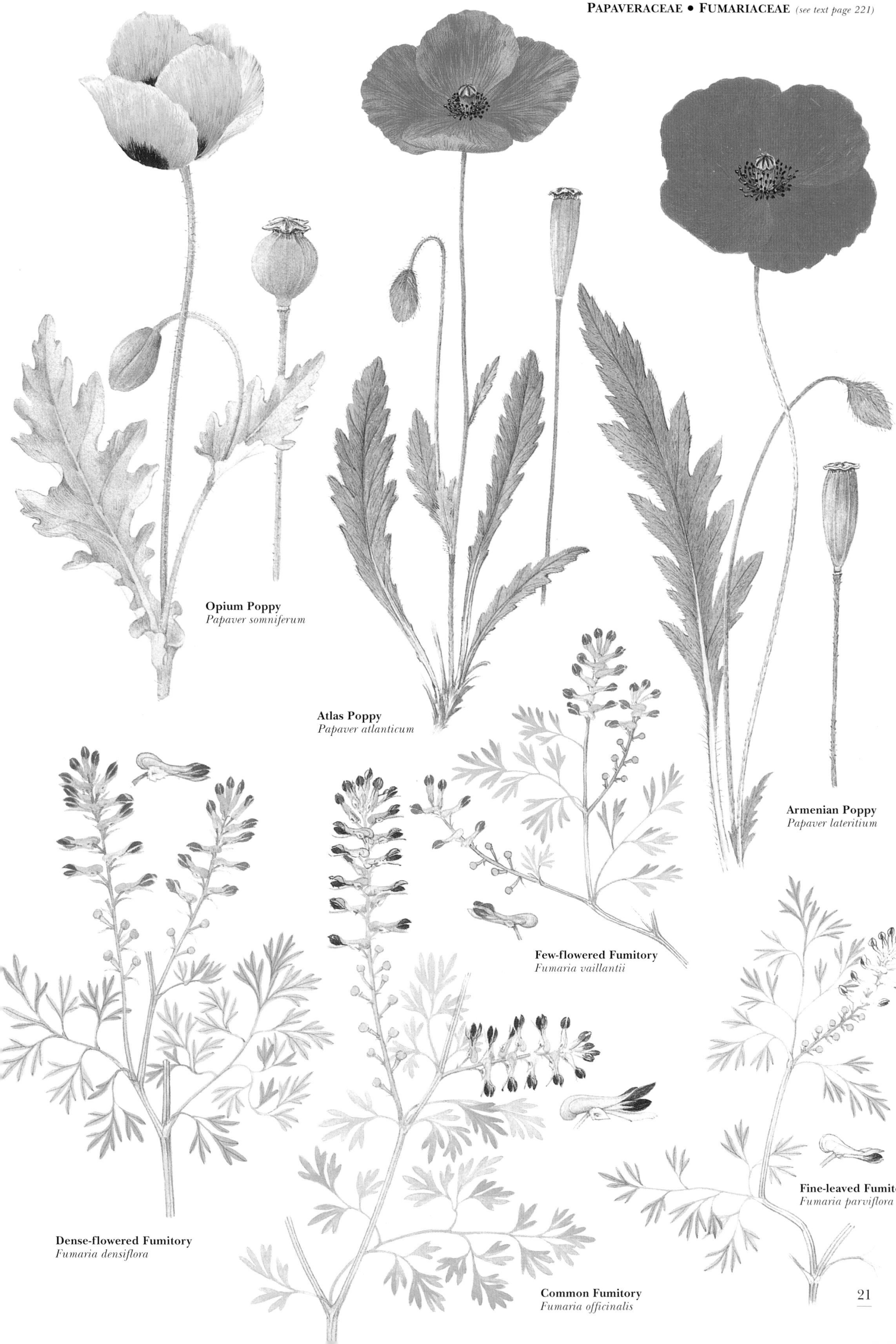

Opium Poppy
Papaver somniferum

Atlas Poppy
Papaver atlanticum

Armenian Poppy
Papaver lateritium

Few-flowered Fumitory
Fumaria vaillantii

Dense-flowered Fumitory
Fumaria densiflora

Fine-leaved Fumitory
Fumaria parviflora

Common Fumitory
Fumaria officinalis

PLATE 6
FUMARIACEAE *(see text page 222)*

Western Ramping-fumitory
Fumaria occidentalis Pugsley
White Ramping-fumitory
Fumaria capreolata
Purple Ramping-fumitory
Fumaria purpurea
Tall Ramping-fumitory
Fumaria bastardii
Martin's Ramping-fumitory
Fumaria reuteri
Common Ramping-fumitory
Fumaria muralis
Climbing Corydalis
White Climbing Fumitory
Ceratocapnos claviculata
Yellow Corydalis
Yellow Fumitory
Pseudofumaria lutea

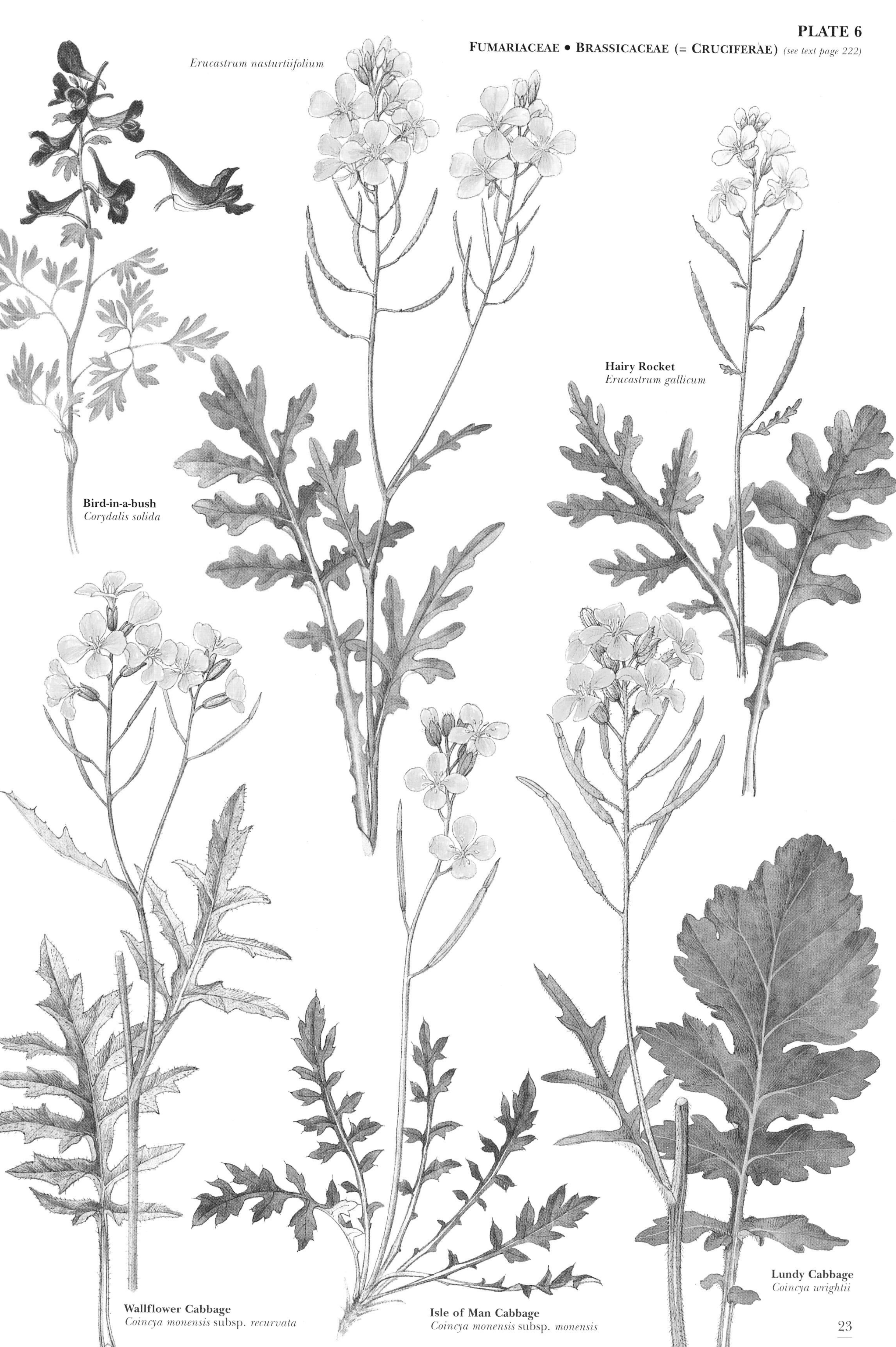
Erucastrum nasturtiifolium
Hairy Rocket
Erucastrum gallicum
Bird-in-a-bush
Corydalis solida
Wallflower Cabbage
Coincya monensis subsp. *recurvata*
Isle of Man Cabbage
Coincya monensis subsp. *monensis*
Lundy Cabbage
Coincya wrightii

PLATE 7
BRASSICACEAE (= CRUCIFERAE) *(see text page 223)*

 (see text page 223)

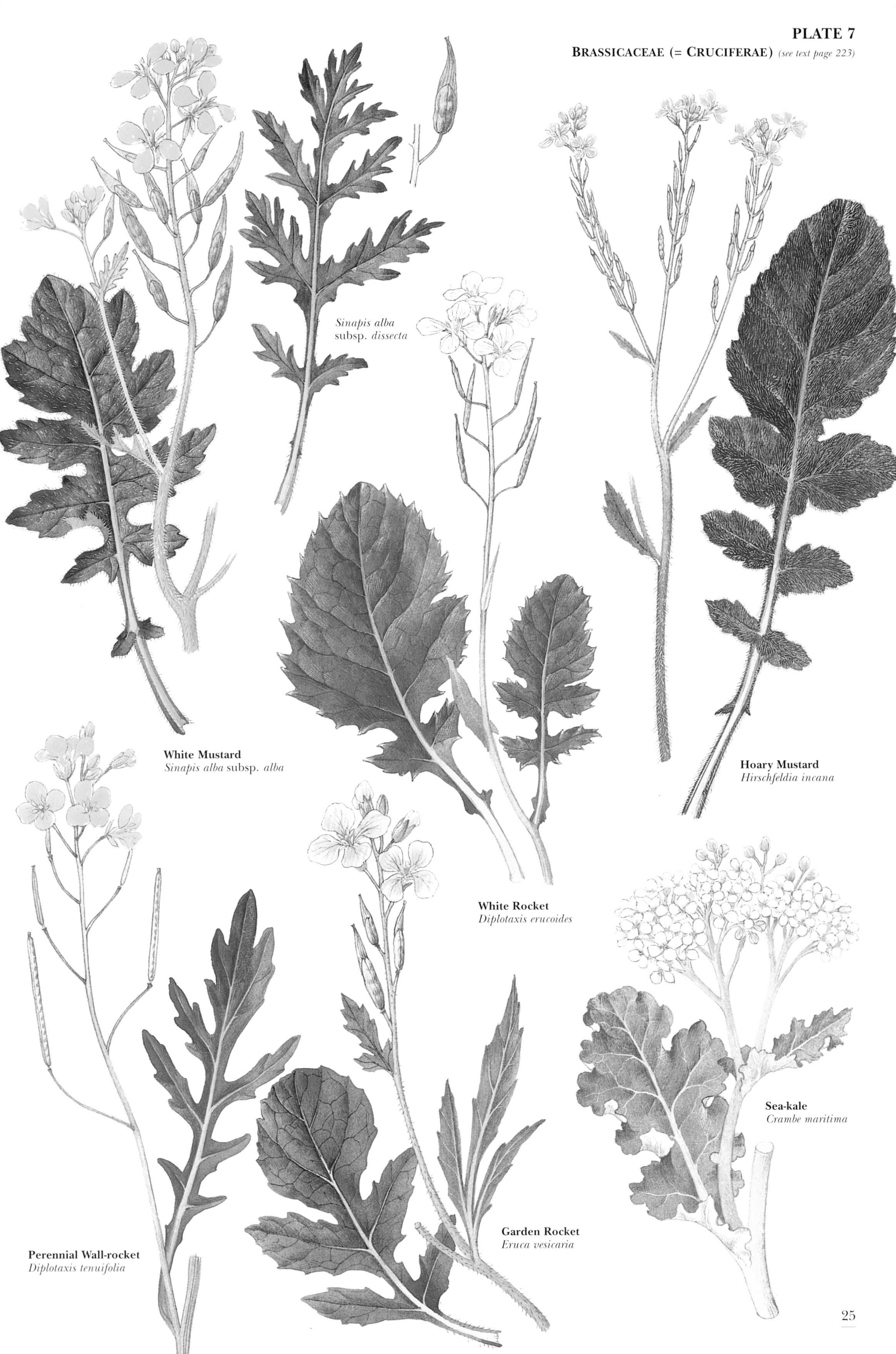
Sinapis alba
subsp. *dissecta*
White Mustard
Sinapis alba subsp. *alba*
Hoary Mustard
Hirschfeldia incana
White Rocket
Diplotaxis erucoides
Sea-kale
Crambe maritima
Garden Rocket
Eruca vesicaria
Perennial Wall-rocket
Diplotaxis tenuifolia

PLATE 8

BRASSICACEAE (= CRUCIFERAE) *(see text page 224)*

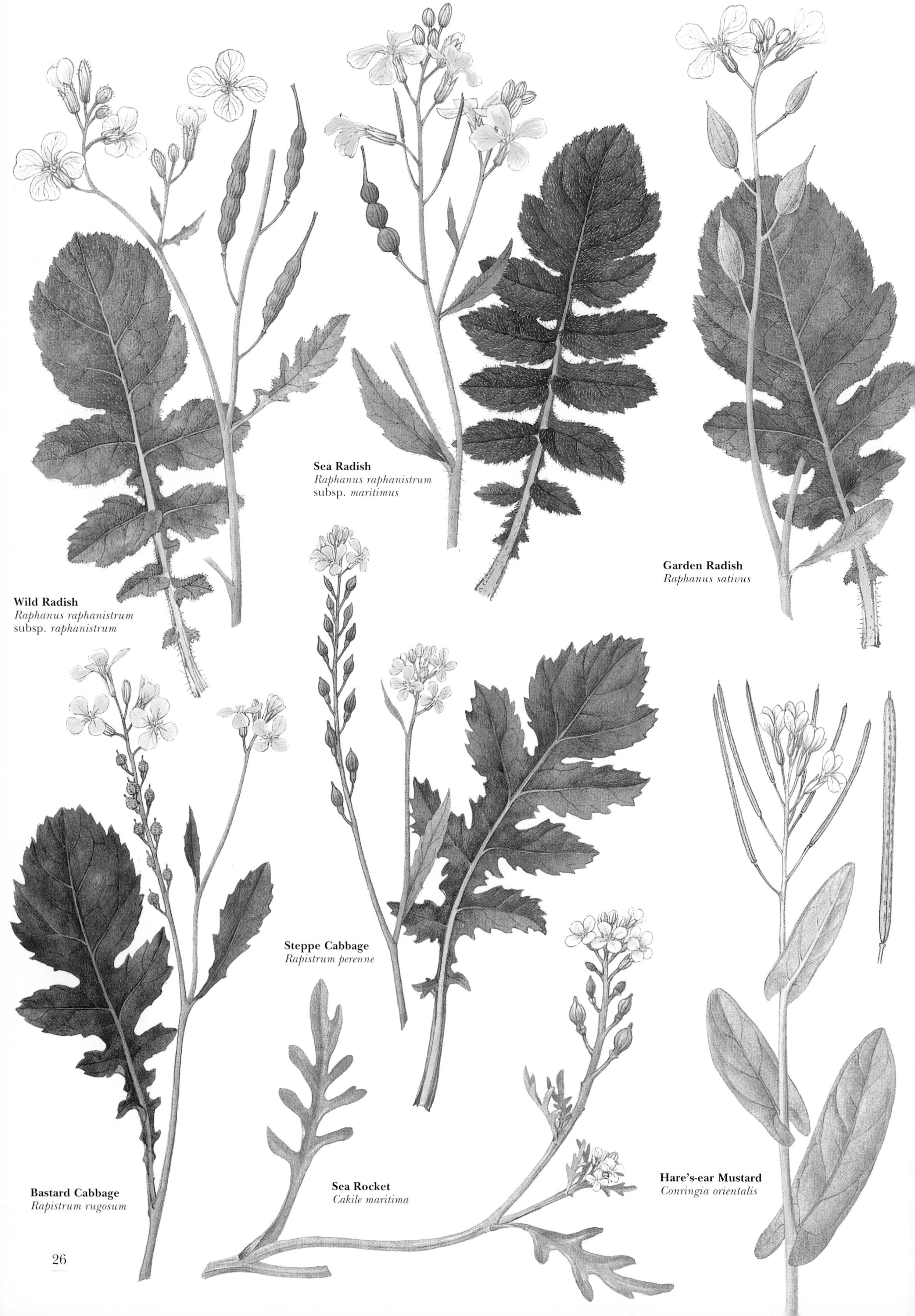

Sea Radish
Raphanus raphanistrum
subsp. *maritimus*

Garden Radish
Raphanus sativus

Wild Radish
Raphanus raphanistrum
subsp. *raphanistrum*

Steppe Cabbage
Rapistrum perenne

Hare's-ear Mustard
Conringia orientalis

Bastard Cabbage
Rapistrum rugosum

Sea Rocket
Cakile maritima

BRASSICACEAE (= CRUCIFERAE) *(see text page 224)*

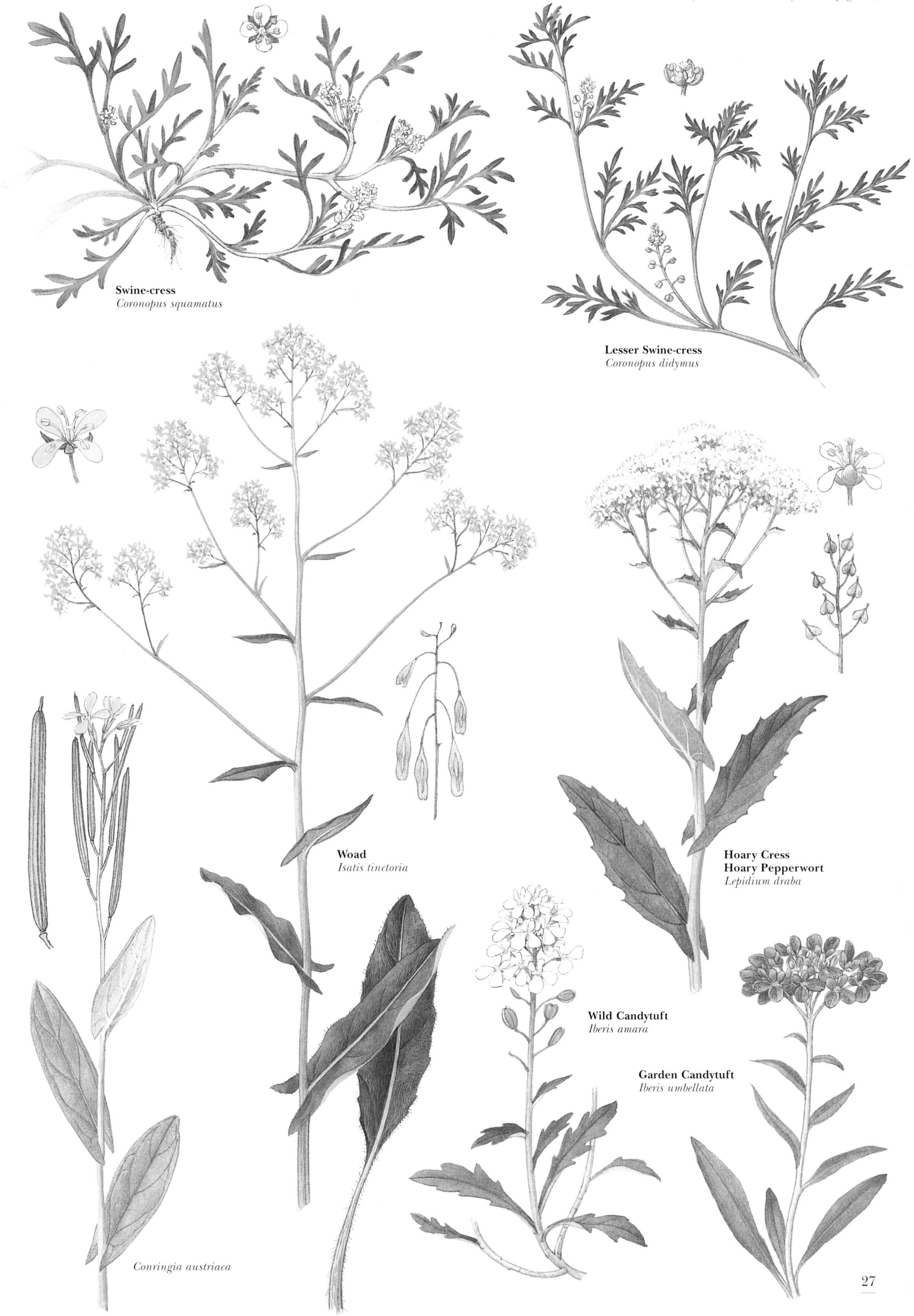

Swine-cress
Coronopus squamatus

Lesser Swine-cress
Coronopus didymus

Woad
Isatis tinctoria

Hoary Cress
Hoary Pepperwort
Lepidium draba

Wild Candytuft
Iberis amara

Garden Candytuft
Iberis umbellata

Conringia austriaca

PLATE 9

BRASSICACEAE (= CRUCIFERAE) *(see text page 225)*

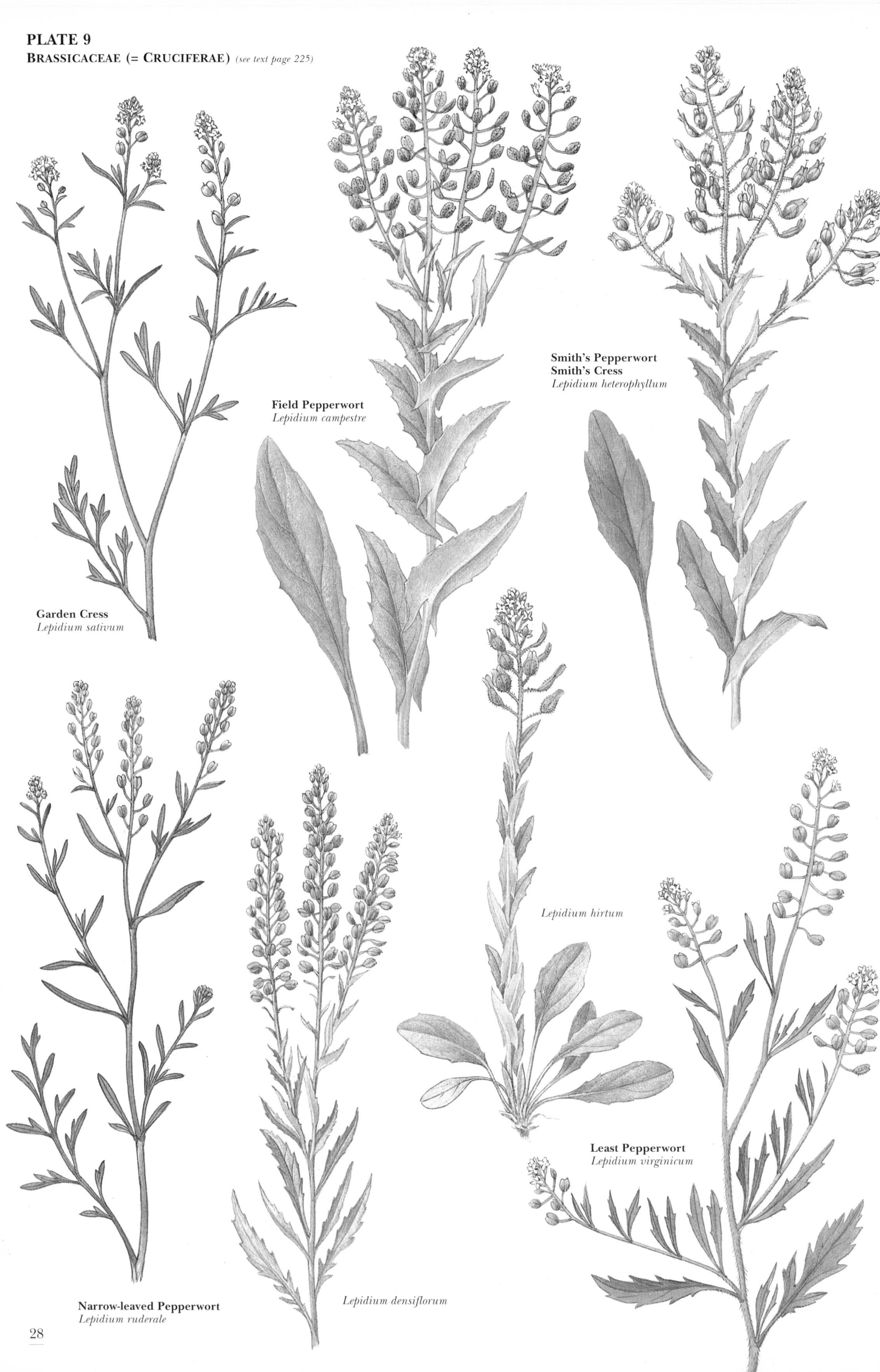

BRASSICACEAE (= CRUCIFERAE) *(see text page 225)*

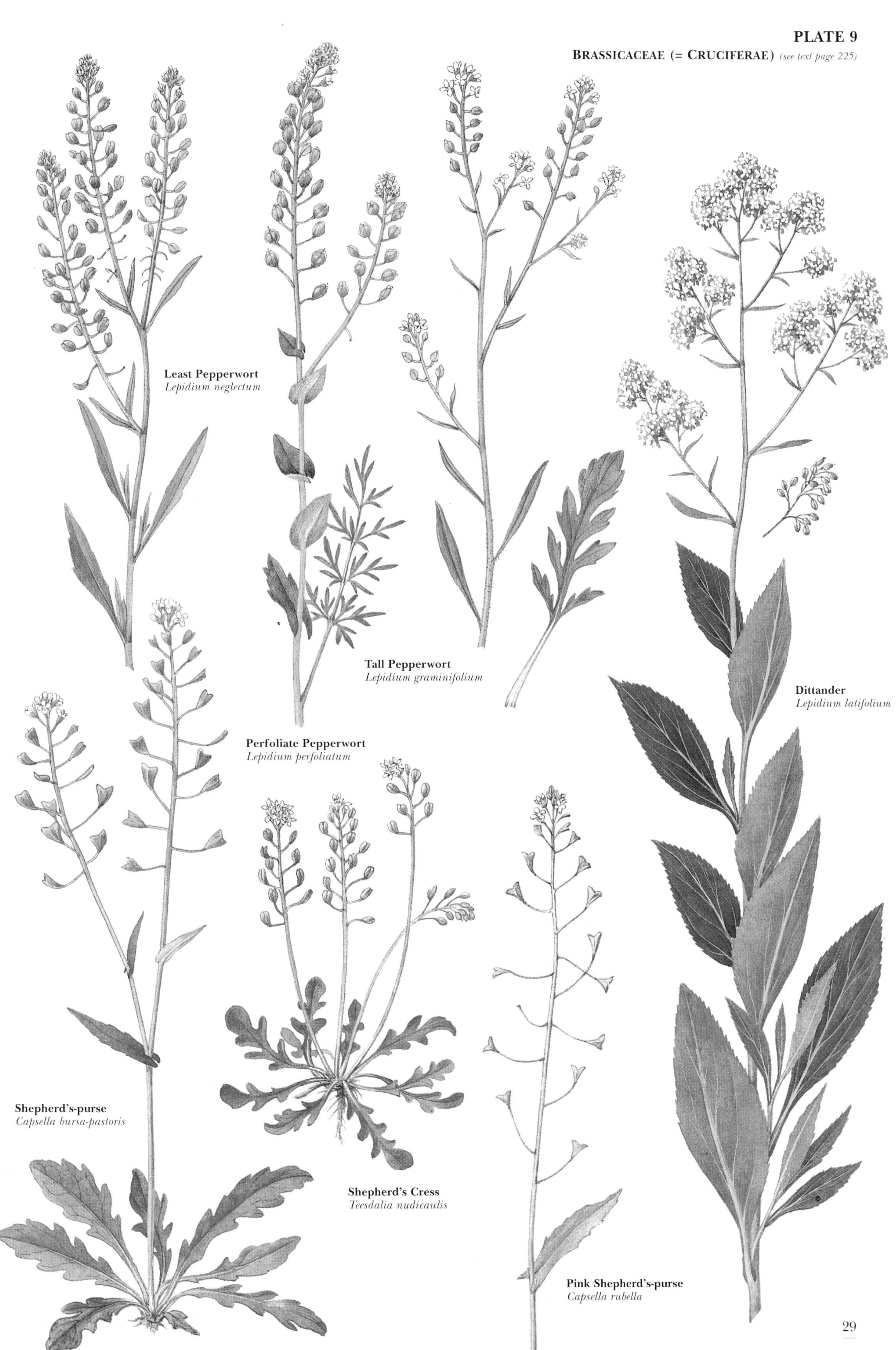

PLATE 10

BRASSICACEAE (= CRUCIFERAE) *(see text page 225)*

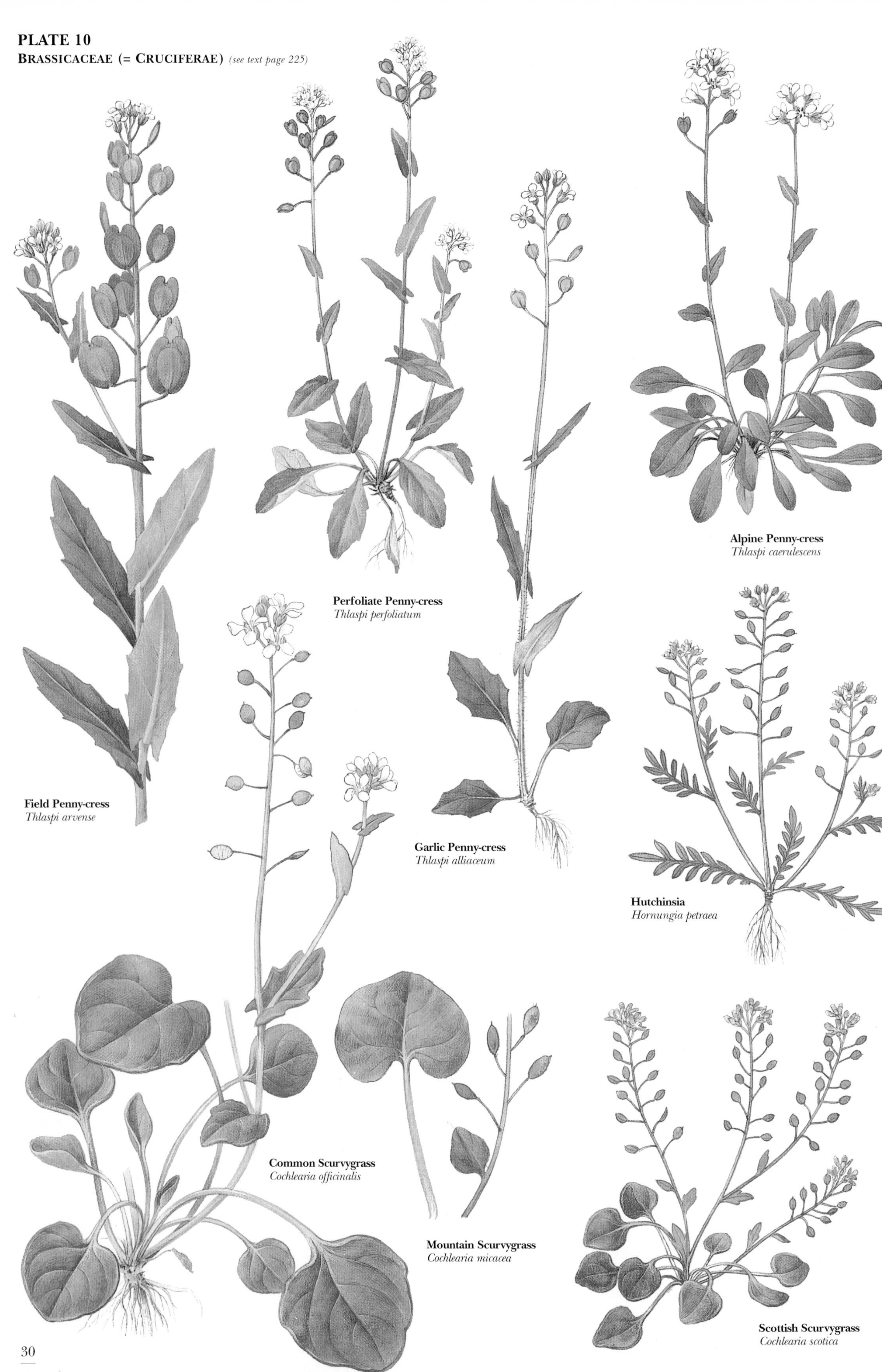

Field Penny-cress
Thlaspi arvense

Perfoliate Penny-cress
Thlaspi perfoliatum

Garlic Penny-cress
Thlaspi alliaceum

Alpine Penny-cress
Thlaspi caerulescens

Hutchinsia
Hornungia petraea

Common Scurvygrass
Cochlearia officinalis

Mountain Scurvygrass
Cochlearia micacea

Scottish Scurvygrass
Cochlearia scotica

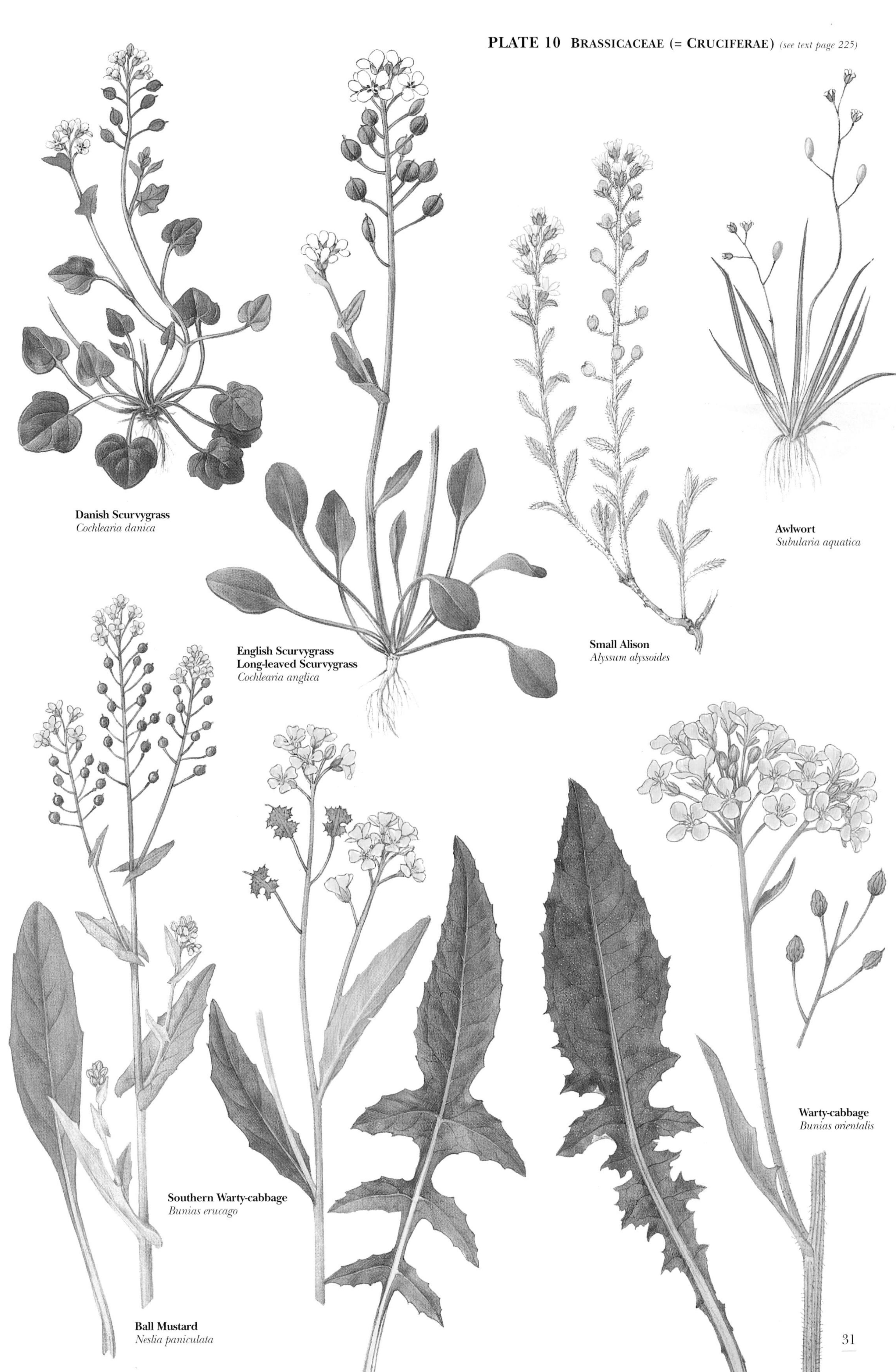
Danish Scurvygrass
Cochlearia danica
English Scurvygrass
Long-leaved Scurvygrass
Cochlearia anglica
Small Alison
Alyssum alyssoides
Awlwort
Subularia aquatica
Ball Mustard
Neslia paniculata
Southern Warty-cabbage
Bunias erucago
Warty-cabbage
Bunias orientalis

PLATE 11
BRASSICACEAE (= CRUCIFERAE) *(see text page 227)*

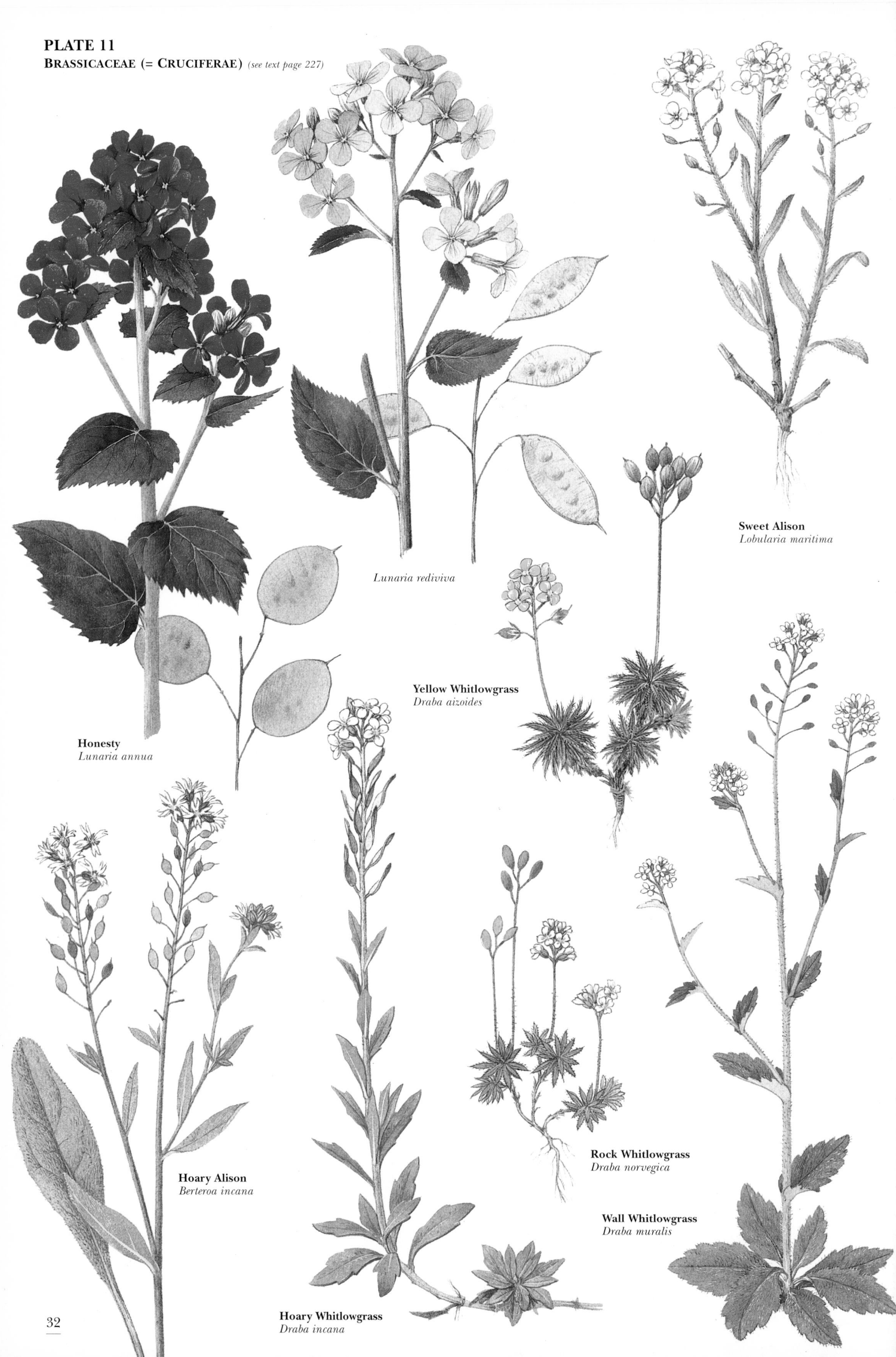

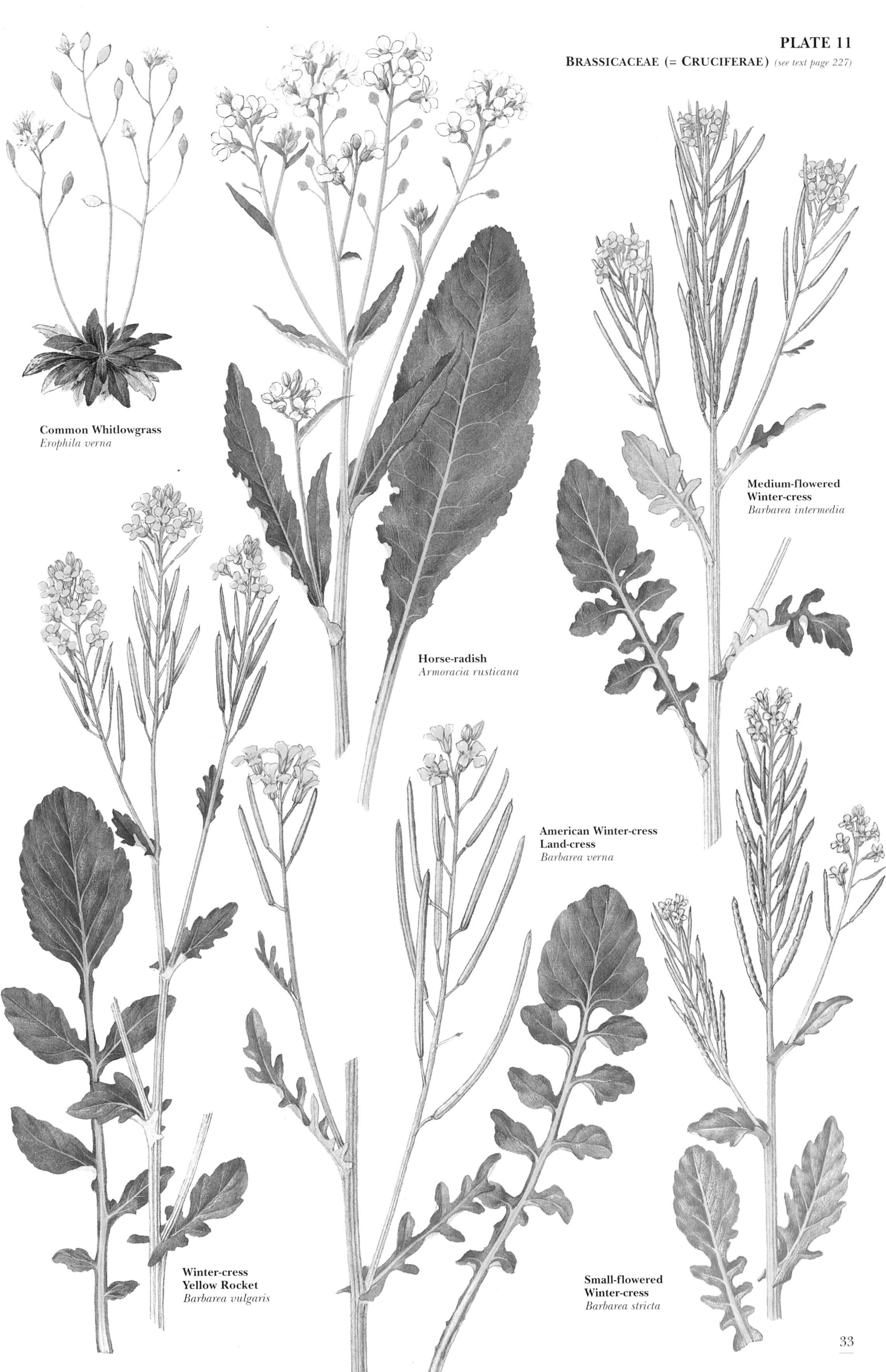

Common Whitlowgrass
Erophila verna

Horse-radish
Armoracia rusticana

Medium-flowered Winter-cress
Barbarea intermedia

American Winter-cress Land-cress
Barbarea verna

Winter-cress Yellow Rocket
Barbarea vulgaris

Small-flowered Winter-cress
Barbarea stricta

PLATE 12

BRASSICACEAE (= CRUCIFERAE) *(see text page 228)*

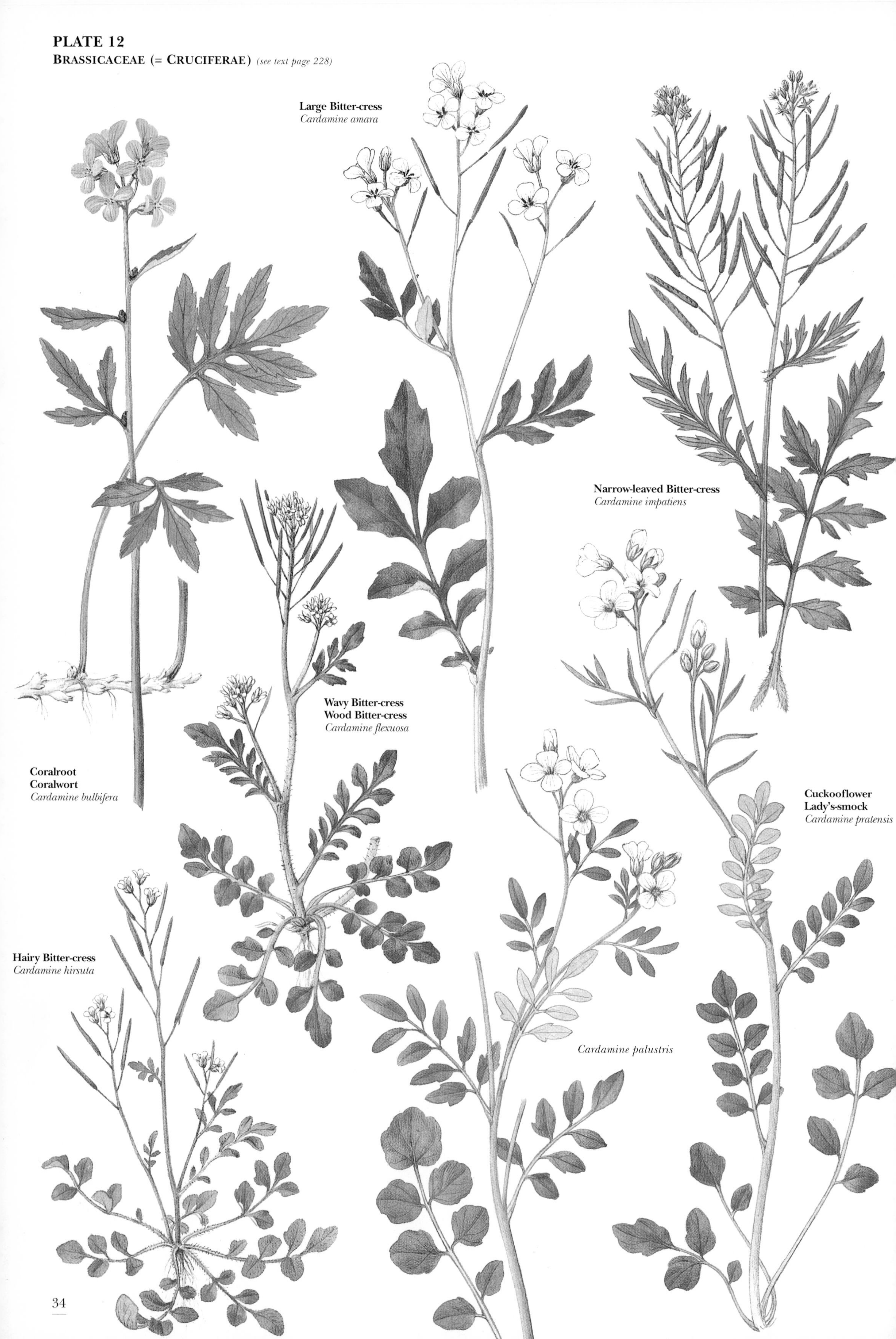

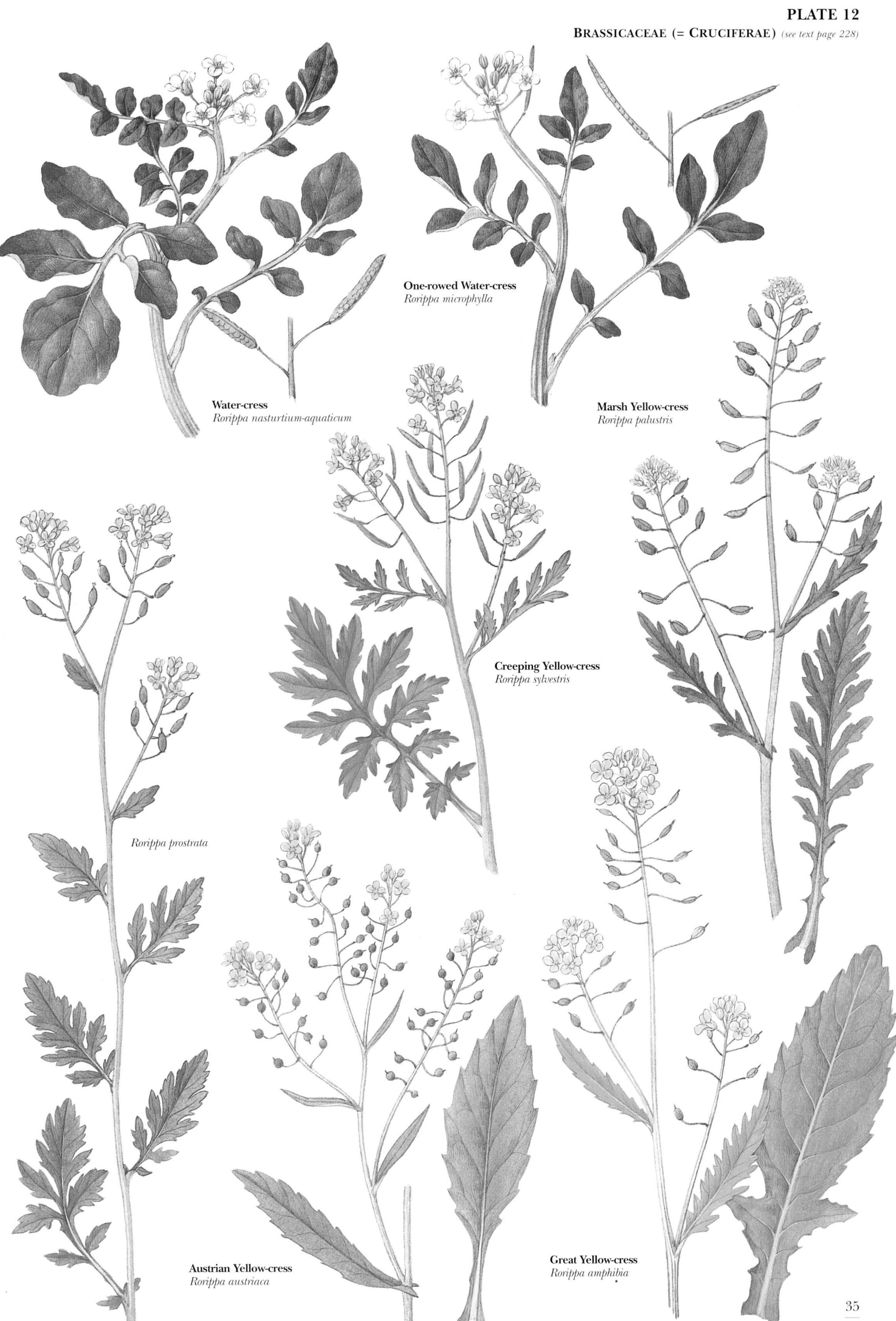
Water-cress
Rorippa nasturtium-aquaticum
One-rowed Water-cress
Rorippa microphylla
Marsh Yellow-cress
Rorippa palustris
Creeping Yellow-cress
Rorippa sylvestris
Rorippa prostrata
Austrian Yellow-cress
Rorippa austriaca
Great Yellow-cress
Rorippa amphibia

PLATE 13

BRASSICACEAE (= CRUCIFERAE) *(see text page 229)*

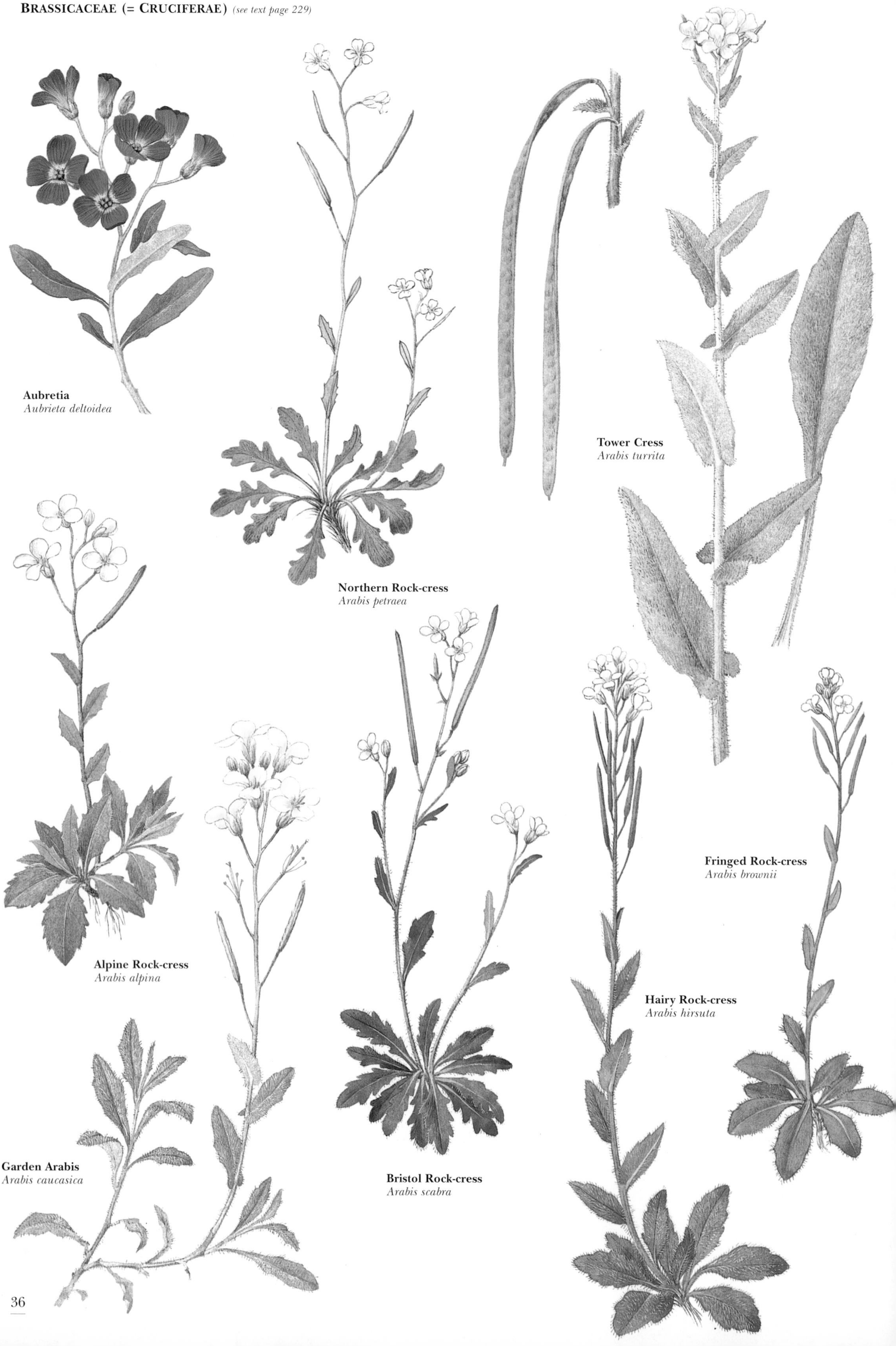

Aubretia
Aubrieta deltoidea

Northern Rock-cress
Arabis petraea

Tower Cress
Arabis turrita

Alpine Rock-cress
Arabis alpina

Fringed Rock-cress
Arabis brownii

Hairy Rock-cress
Arabis hirsuta

Garden Arabis
Arabis caucasica

Bristol Rock-cress
Arabis scabra

Tower Mustard
Arabis glabra
Sea Stock
Matthiola sinuata
Wallflower
Erysimum cheiri
Hoary Stock
Matthiola incana
Treacle Mustard
Erysimum cheiranthoides
Dame's-violet
Hesperis matronalis

PLATE 14

BRASSICACEAE (= CRUCIFERAE) *(see text page 230)*

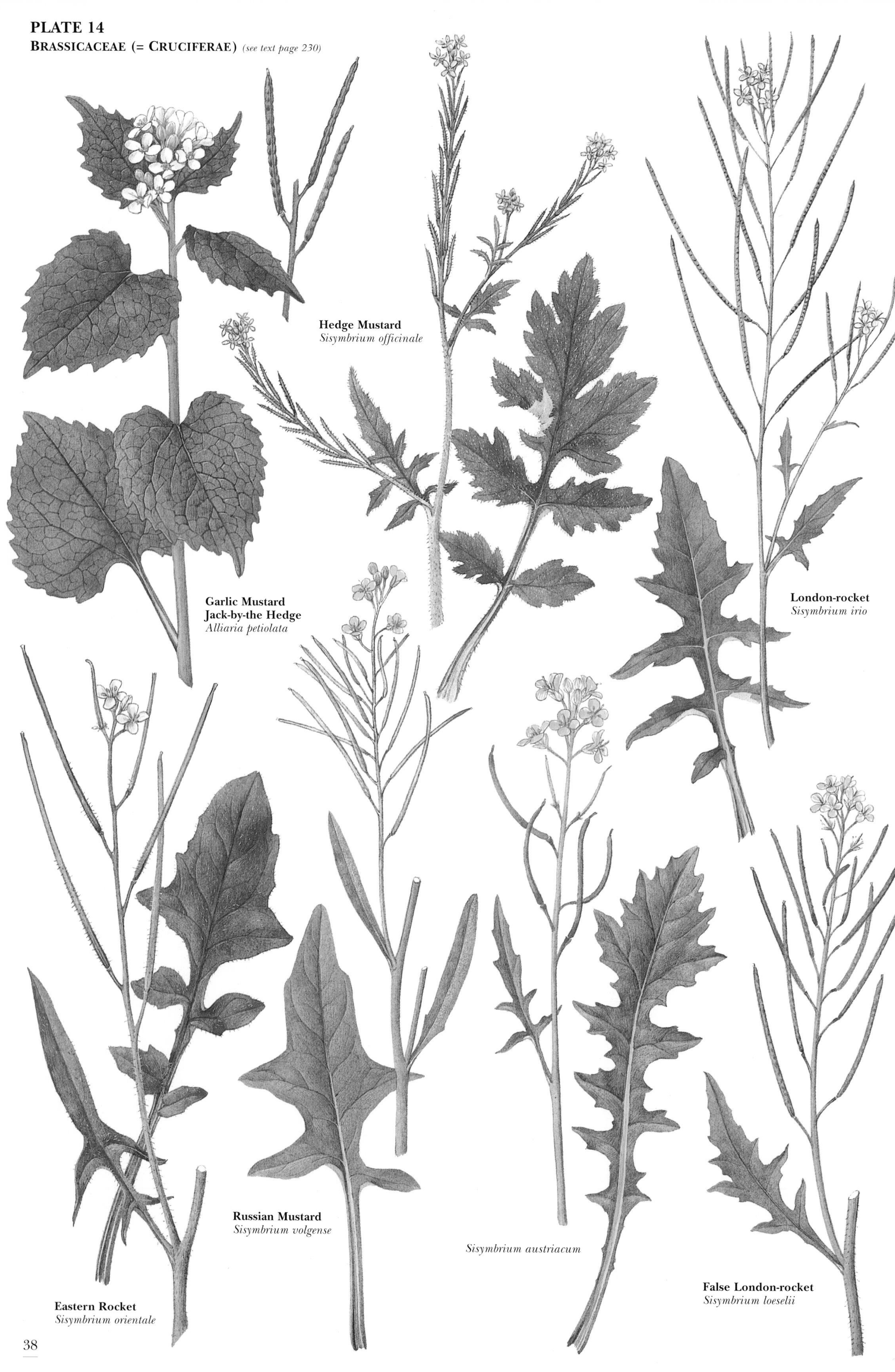

BRASSICACEAE (= CRUCIFERAE) *(see text page 230)*

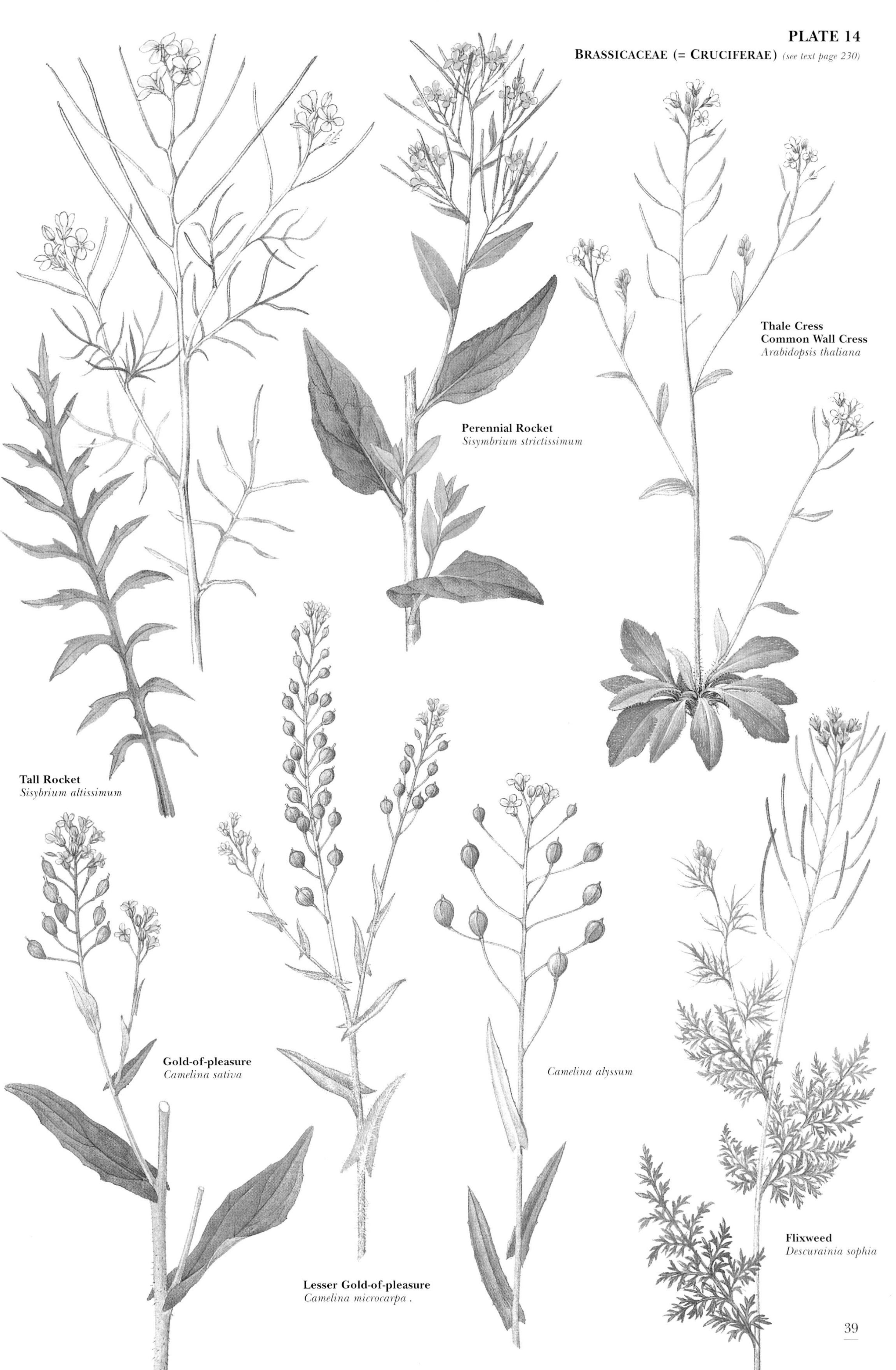

PLATE 15

RESEDACEAE • VIOLACEAE *(see text page 231)*

Weld
Dyer's Rocket
Reseda luteola

Wild Mignonette
Reseda lutea

Corn Mignonette
Reseda phyteuma

White Mignonette
Upright Mignonette
Reseda alba

Sweet Violet
Viola odorata

Hairy Violet
Viola hirta

Teesdale Violet
Viola rupestris

Common Dog-violet
Viola riviniana

Early Dog-violet
Pale Wood-violet
Viola reichenbachiana

Viola canina subsp. *montana*

Heath Dog-violet
Heath Violet
Viola canina subsp. *canina*

Pale Dog-violet
Pale Heath-violet
Viola lactea

Viola palustris
subsp. *juressii*

Fen Violet
Viola persicifolia

Horned Pansy
Viola cornuta

Marsh Violet
Viola palustris

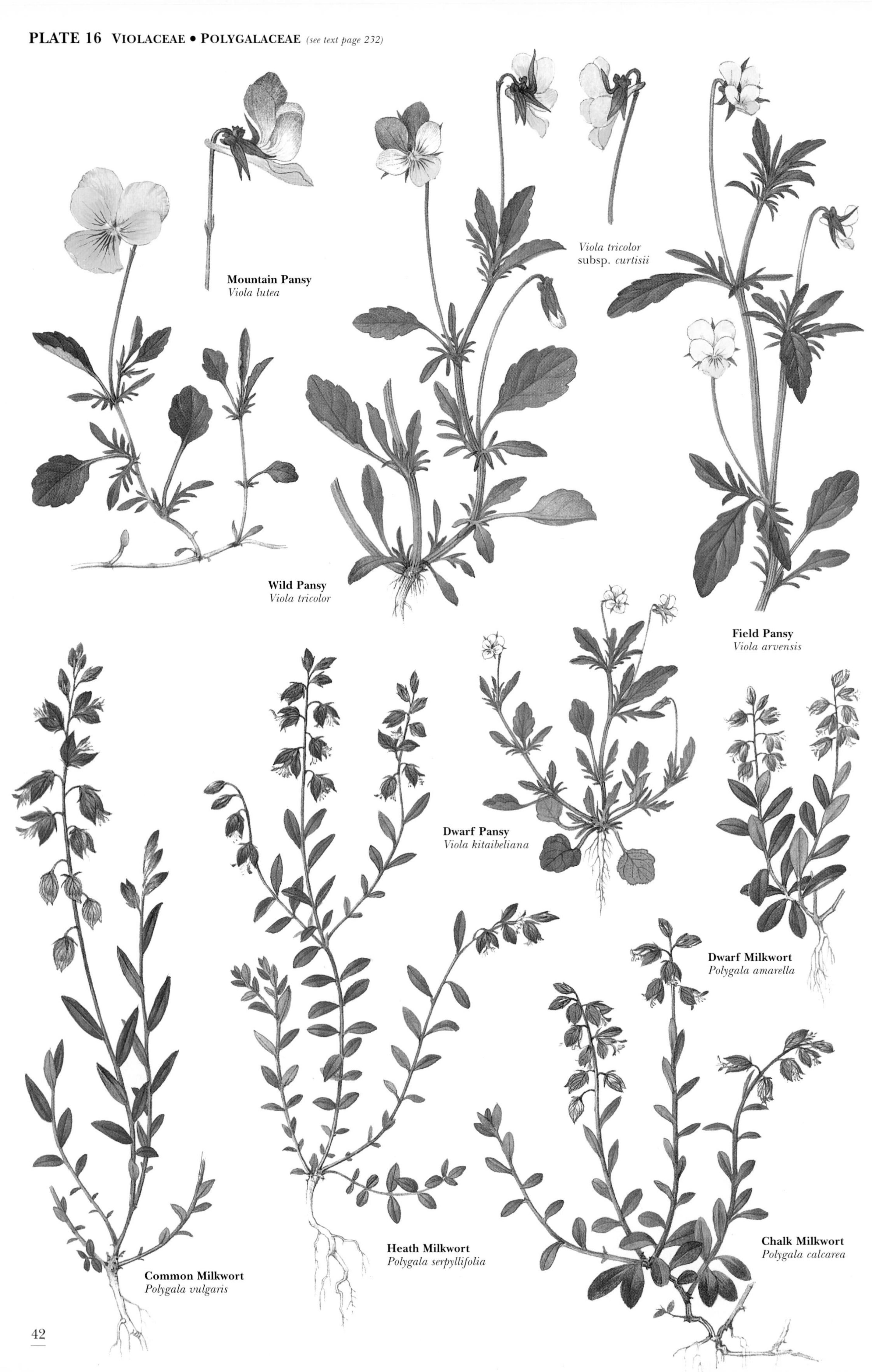
Mountain Pansy
Viola lutea
Viola tricolor
subsp. *curtisii*
Wild Pansy
Viola tricolor
Field Pansy
Viola arvensis
Dwarf Pansy
Viola kitaibeliana
Dwarf Milkwort
Polygala amarella
Heath Milkwort
Polygala serpyllifolia
Chalk Milkwort
Polygala calcarea
Common Milkwort
Polygala vulgaris

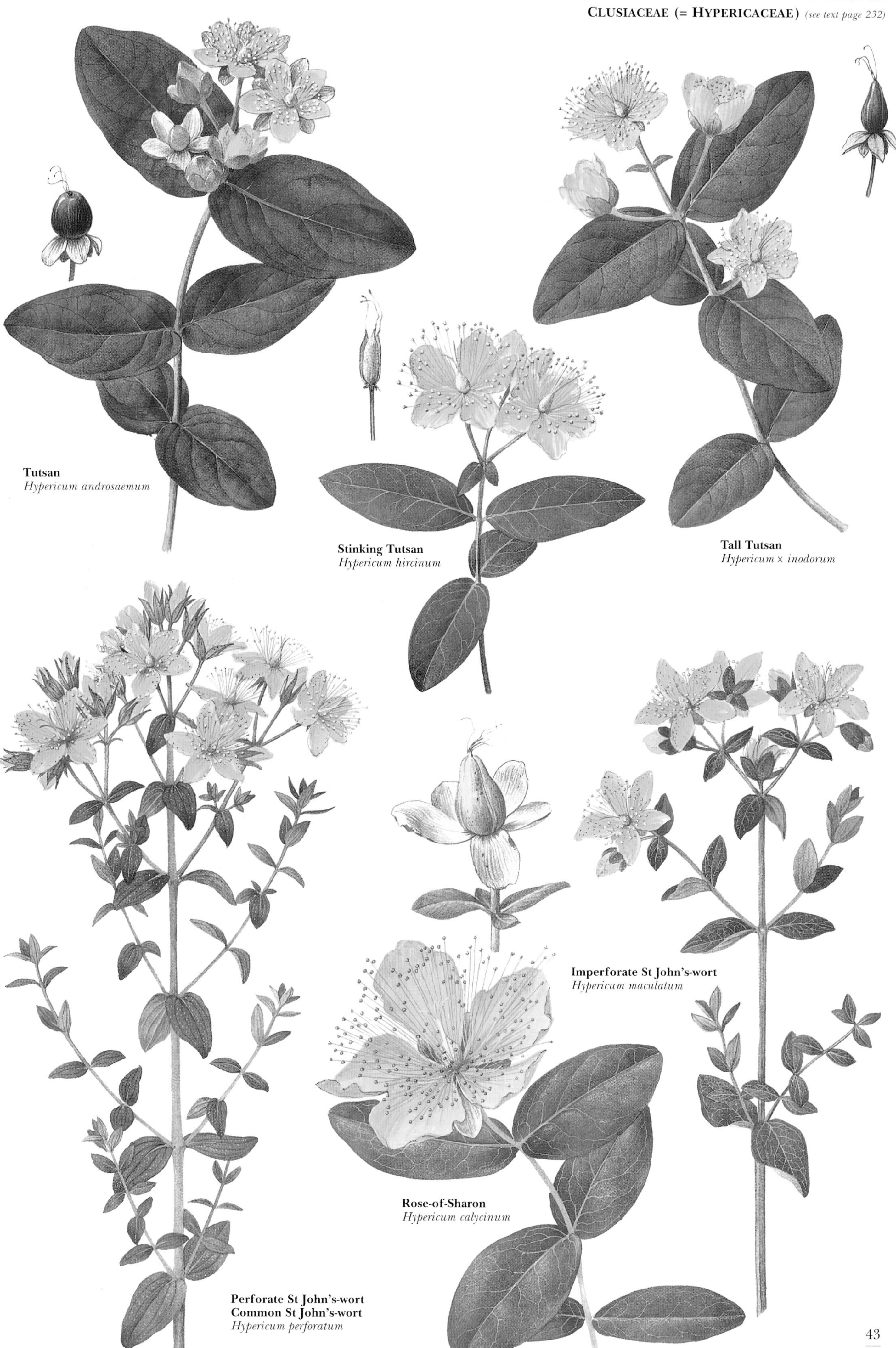

Tutsan
Hypericum androsaemum

Stinking Tutsan
Hypericum hircinum

Tall Tutsan
Hypericum × inodorum

Imperforate St John's-wort
Hypericum maculatum

Rose-of-Sharon
Hypericum calycinum

Perforate St John's-wort
Common St John's-wort
Hypericum perforatum

PLATE 17

CLUSIACEAE (= HYPERICACEAE) *(see text page 233)*

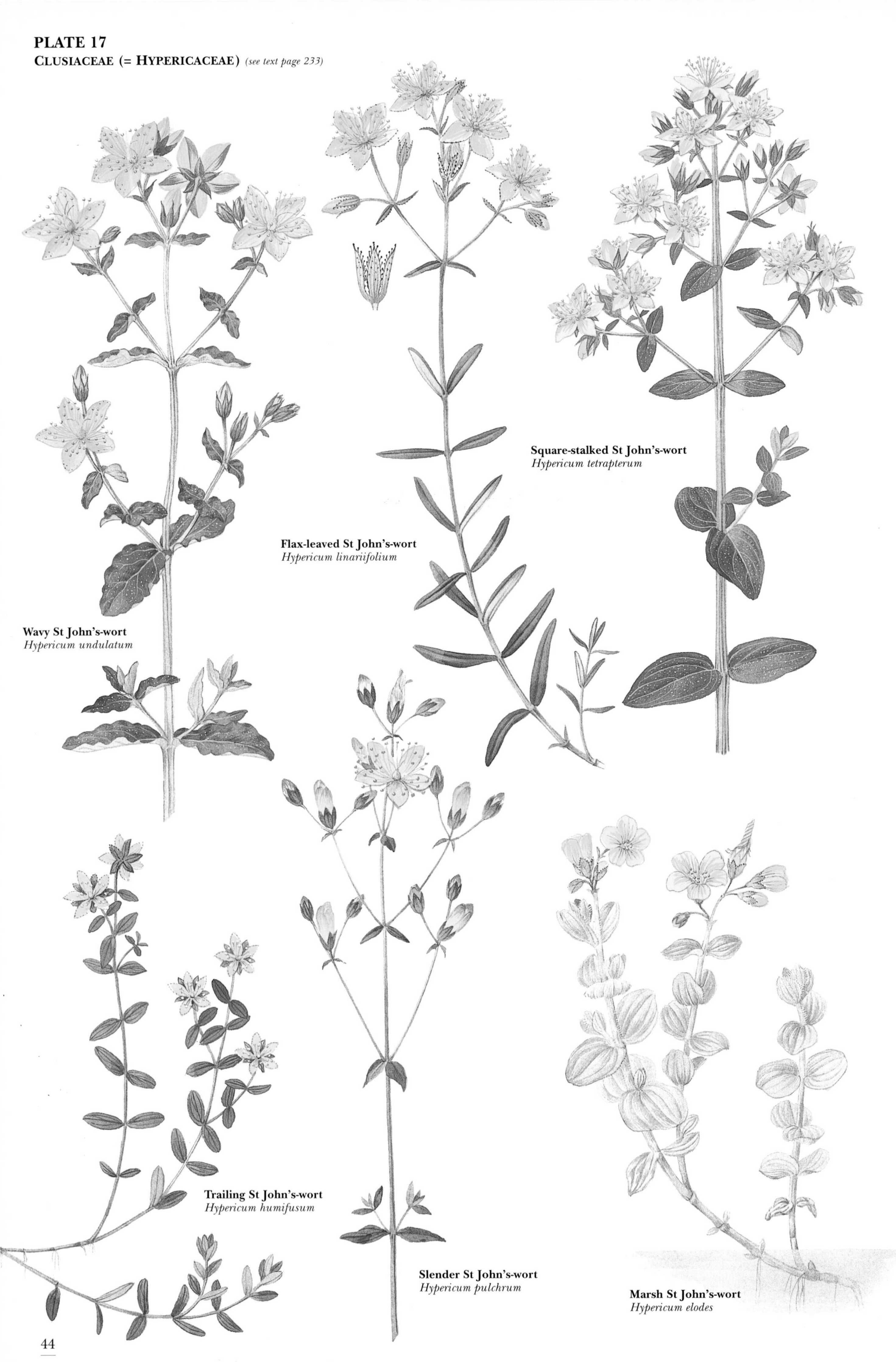

Irish St John's-wort
Hypericum canadense
Hairy St John's-wort
Hypericum hirsutum
Pale St John's-wort
Hypericum montanum
Cistus incanus
Common Rock-rose
Helianthemum nummularium
Spotted Rock-rose
Annual Rock-rose
Tuberaria guttata
Hoary Rock-rose
Helianthemum canum
White Rock-rose
Helianthemum apenninum
Helianthemum canum
subsp. *levigatum*

PLATE 18

TAMARICACEAE • FRANKENIACEAE • ELATINACEAE • CARYOPHYLLACEAE *(see text page 234)*

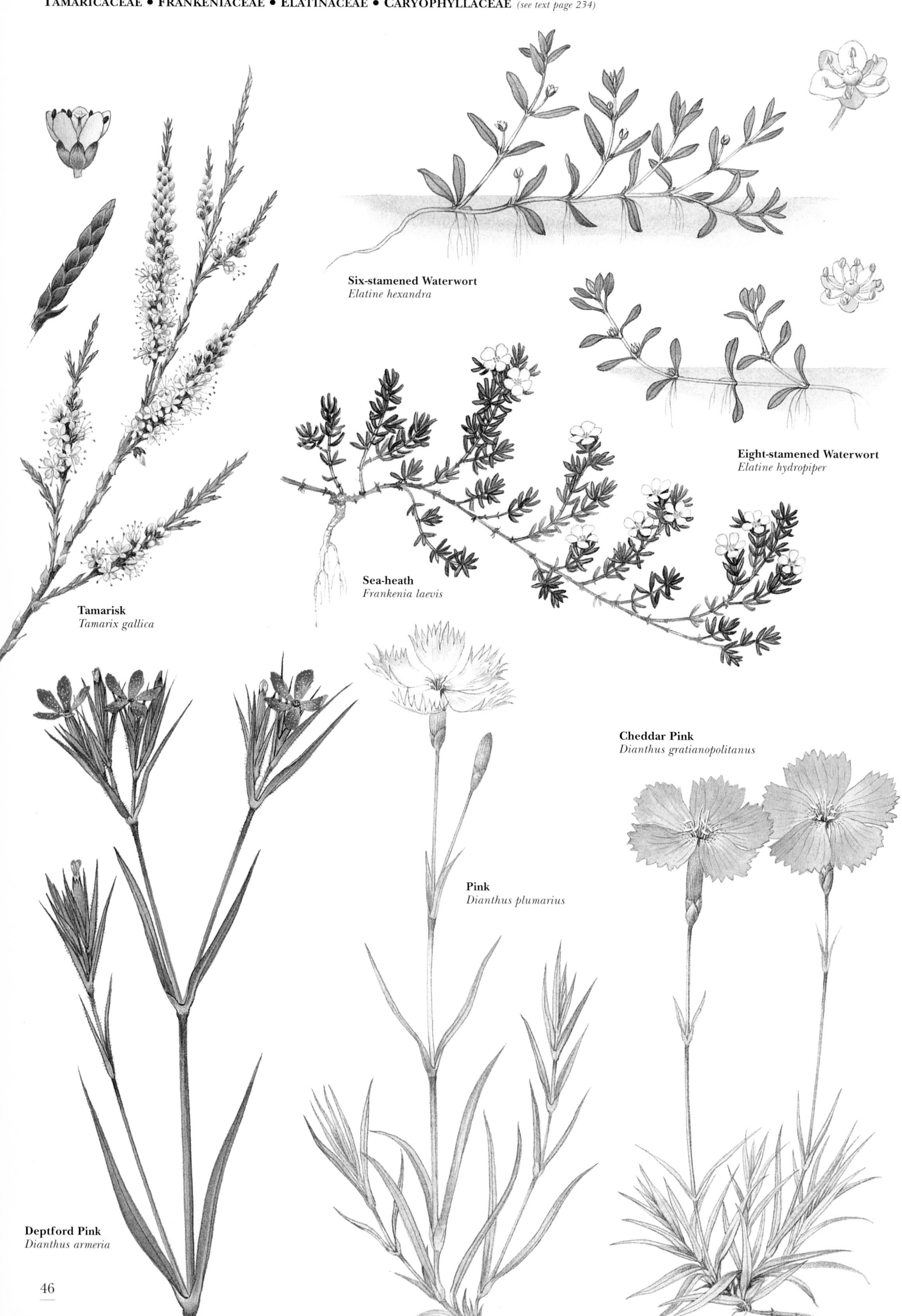

Six-stamened Waterwort
Elatine hexandra

Eight-stamened Waterwort
Elatine hydropiper

Sea-heath
Frankenia laevis

Tamarisk
Tamarix gallica

Cheddar Pink
Dianthus gratianopolitanus

Pink
Dianthus plumarius

Deptford Pink
Dianthus armeria

 (see text page 234)

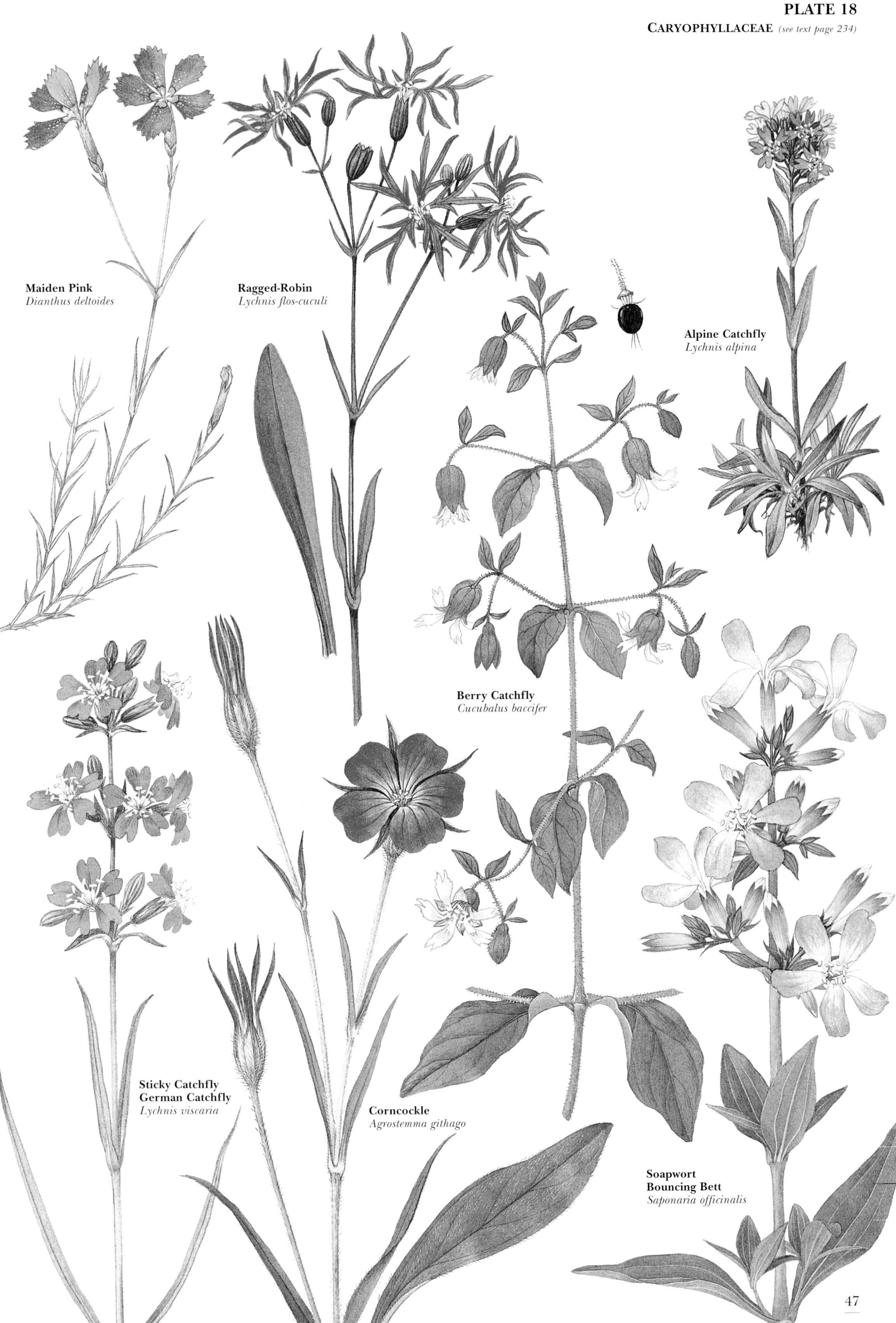
Maiden Pink
Dianthus deltoides
Ragged-Robin
Lychnis flos-cuculi
Alpine Catchfly
Lychnis alpina
Berry Catchfly
Cucubalus baccifer
Sticky Catchfly
German Catchfly
Lychnis viscaria
Corncockle
Agrostemma githago
Soapwort
Bouncing Bett
Saponaria officinalis

PLATE 19
CARYOPHYLLACEAE *(see text page 235)*

Red Campion
Silene dioica

White Campion
Silene latifolia

Night-flowering Catchfly
Silene noctiflora

Bladder Campion
Silene vulgaris

Silene vulgaris subsp. macrocarpa

Sea Campion
Silene uniflora

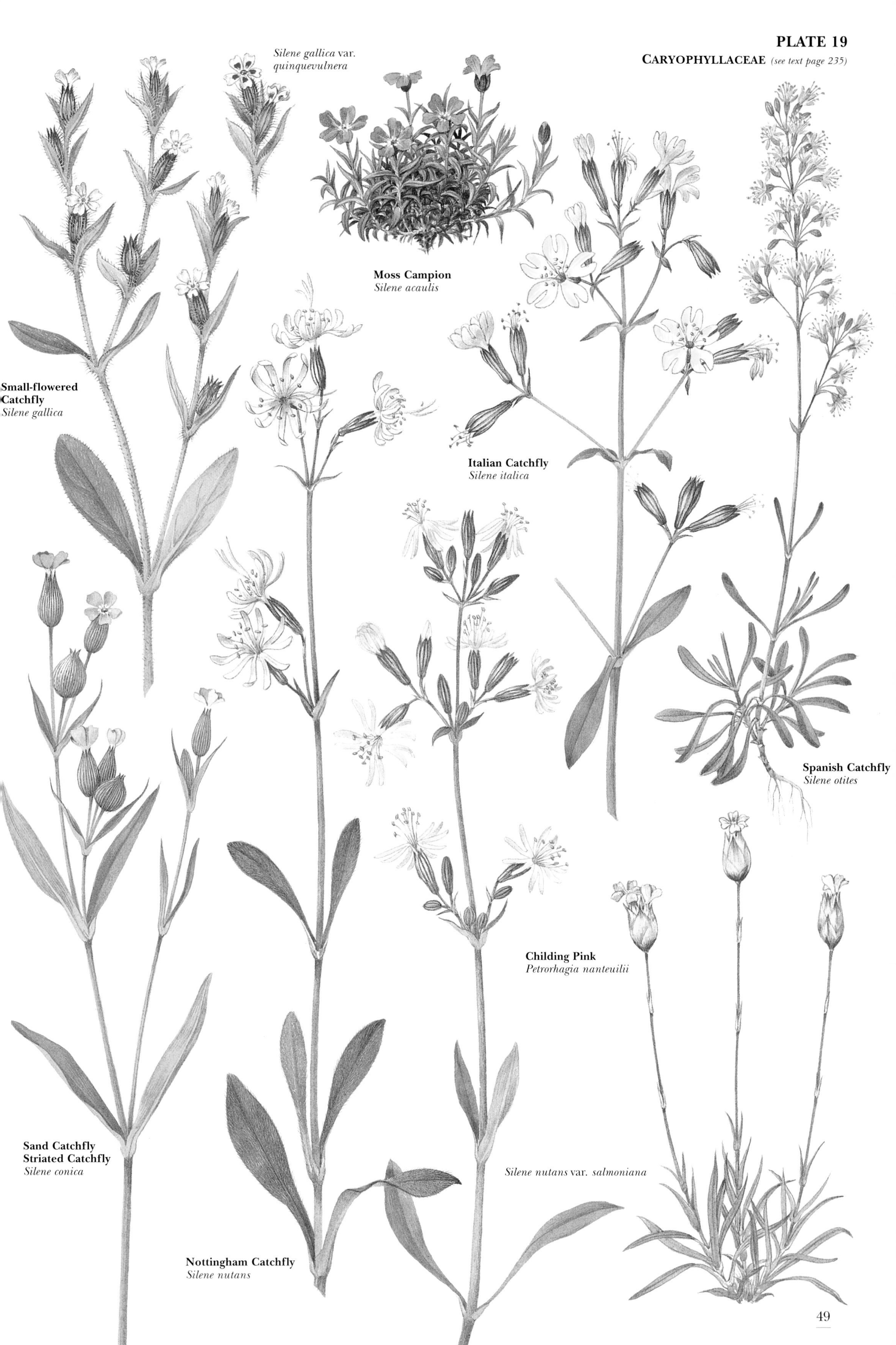
Silene gallica var. *quinquevulnera*
Moss Campion
Silene acaulis
Small-flowered Catchfly
Silene gallica
Italian Catchfly
Silene italica
Spanish Catchfly
Silene otites
Childing Pink
Petrorhagia nanteuilii
Sand Catchfly
Striated Catchfly
Silene conica
Silene nutans var. *salmoniana*
Nottingham Catchfly
Silene nutans

PLATE 20

CARYOPHYLLACEAE *(see text page 236)*

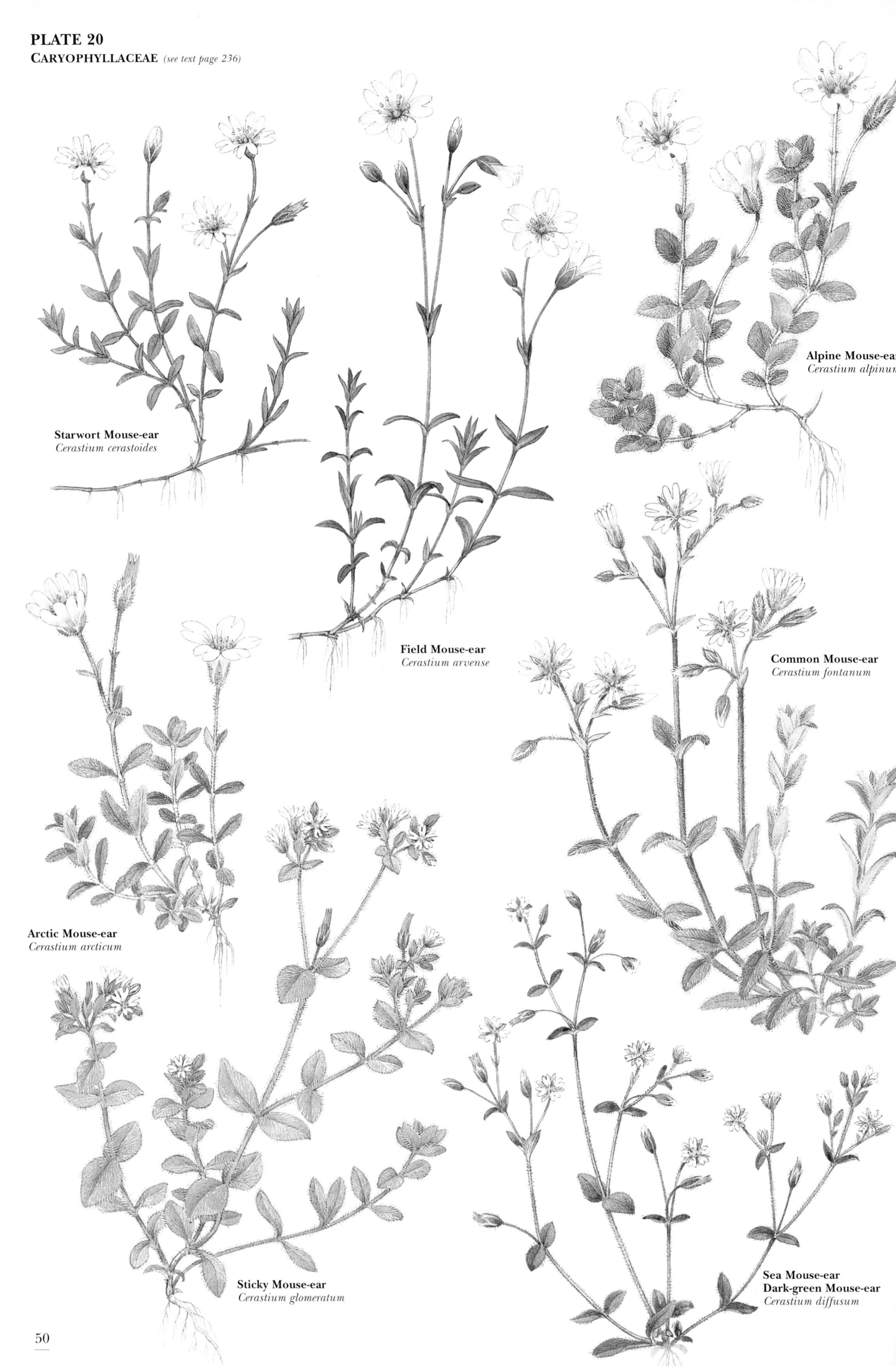

PLATE 20

CARYOPHYLLACEAE *(see text page 236)*

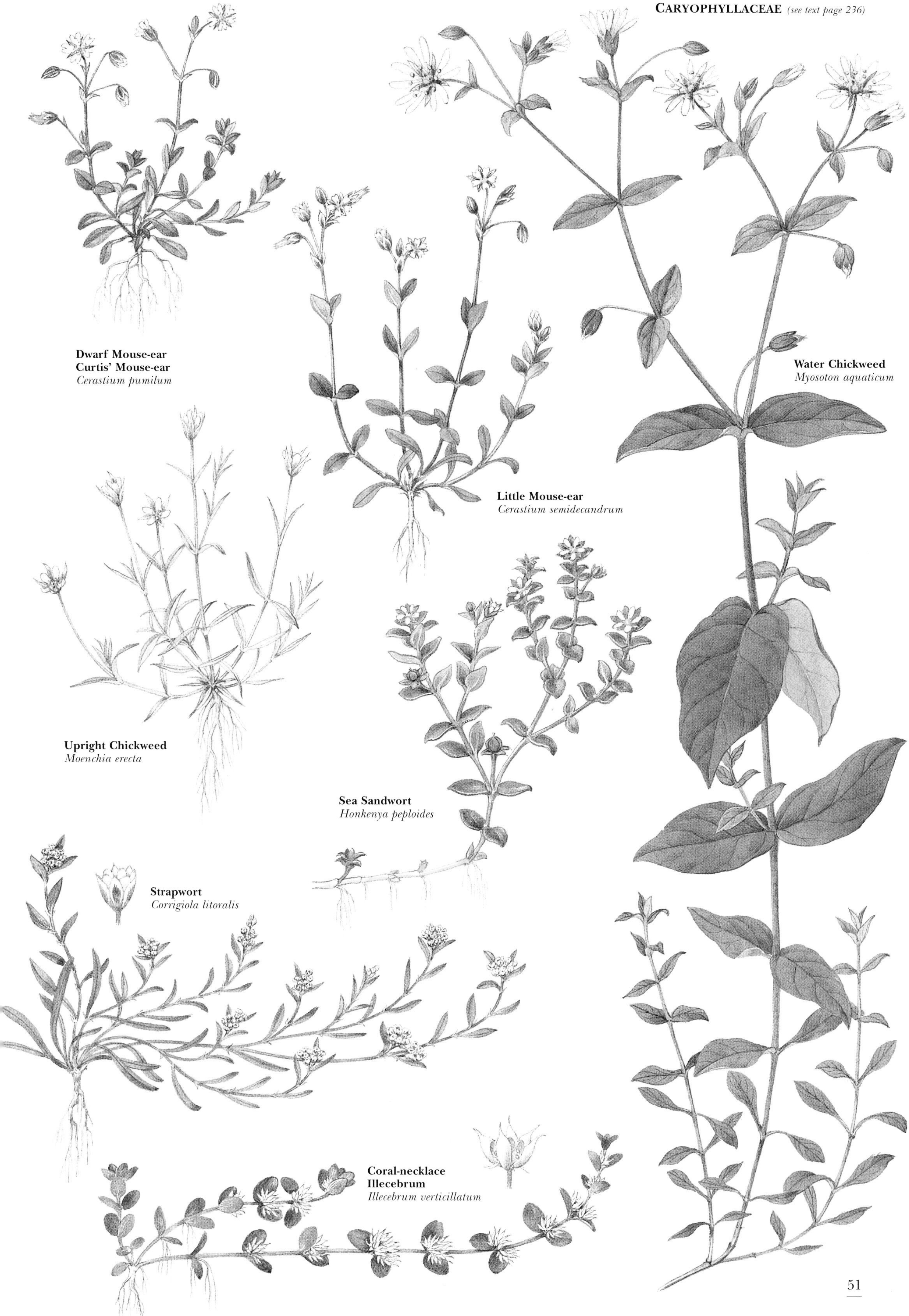

Dwarf Mouse-ear
Curtis' Mouse-ear
Cerastium pumilum
Little Mouse-ear
Cerastium semidecandrum
Water Chickweed
Myosoton aquaticum
Upright Chickweed
Moenchia erecta
Sea Sandwort
Honkenya peploides
Strapwort
Corrigiola litoralis
Coral-necklace
Illecebrum
Illecebrum verticillatum

PLATE 21
CARYOPHYLLACEAE *(see text page 237)*

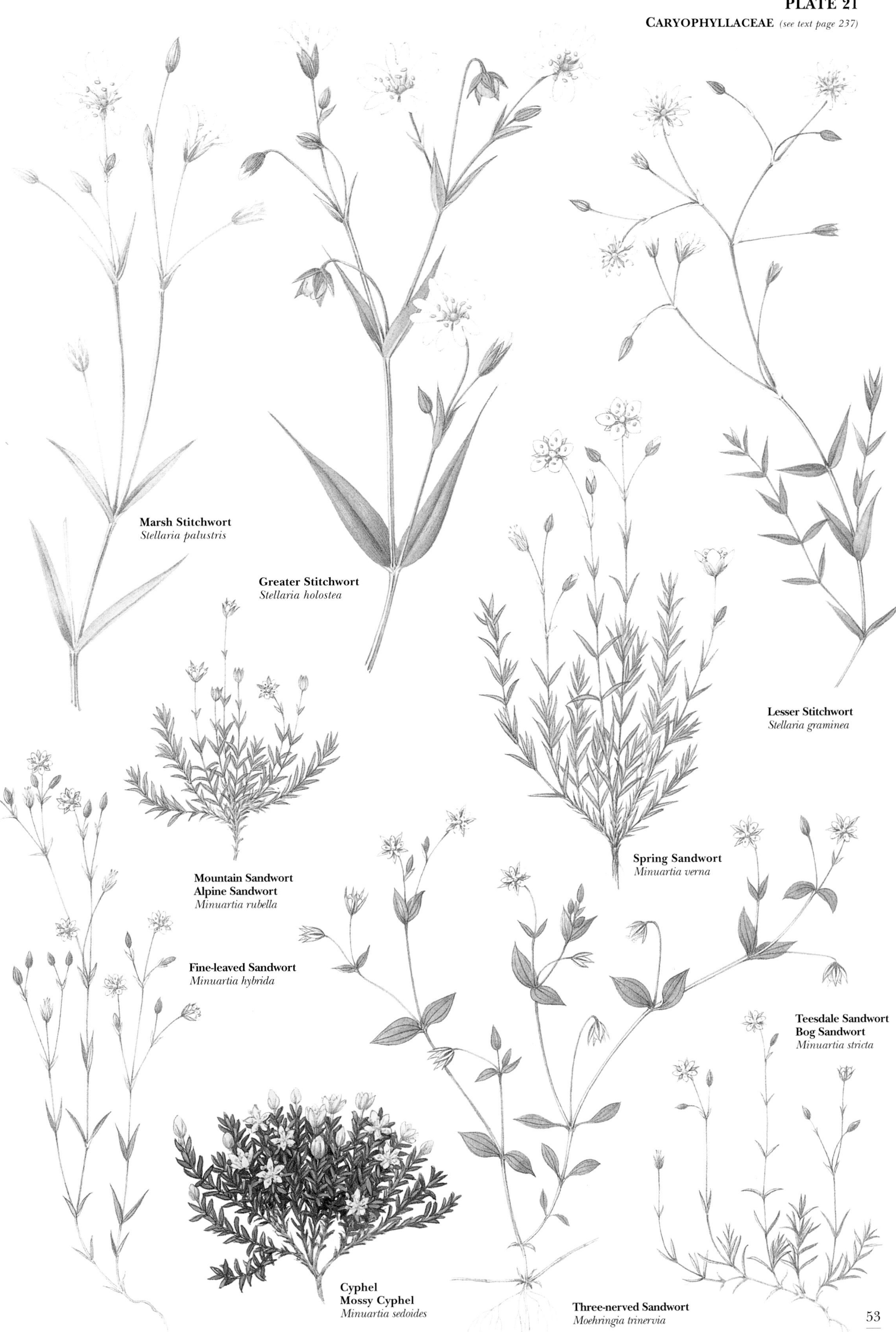
Marsh Stitchwort
Stellaria palustris
Greater Stitchwort
Stellaria holostea
Lesser Stitchwort
Stellaria graminea
Mountain Sandwort
Alpine Sandwort
Minuartia rubella
Spring Sandwort
Minuartia verna
Fine-leaved Sandwort
Minuartia hybrida
Teesdale Sandwort
Bog Sandwort
Minuartia stricta
Cyphel
Mossy Cyphel
Minuartia sedoides
Three-nerved Sandwort
Moehringia trinervia

PLATE 22

CARYOPHYLLACEAE *(see text page 237)*

Heath Pearlwort
Awl-leaved Pearlwort
Sagina subulata

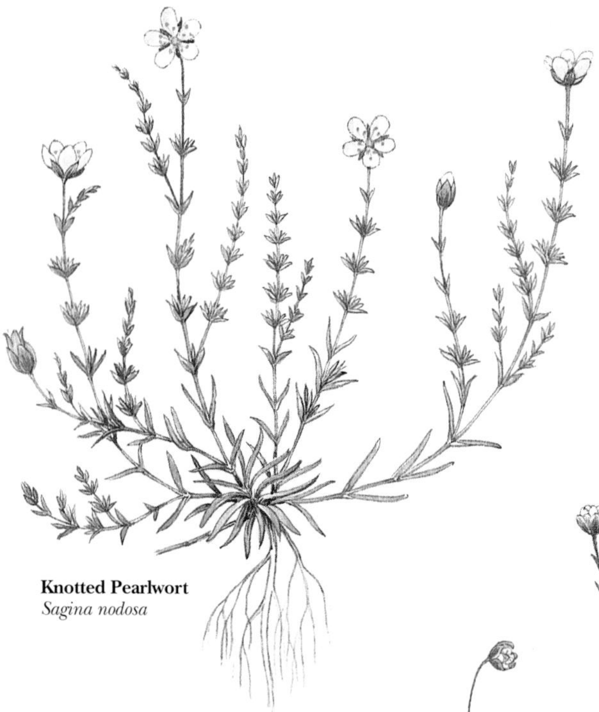

Knotted Pearlwort
Sagina nodosa

Snow Pearlwort
Lesser Alpine Pearlwort
Sagina nivalis

Alpine Pearlwort
Sagina saginoides

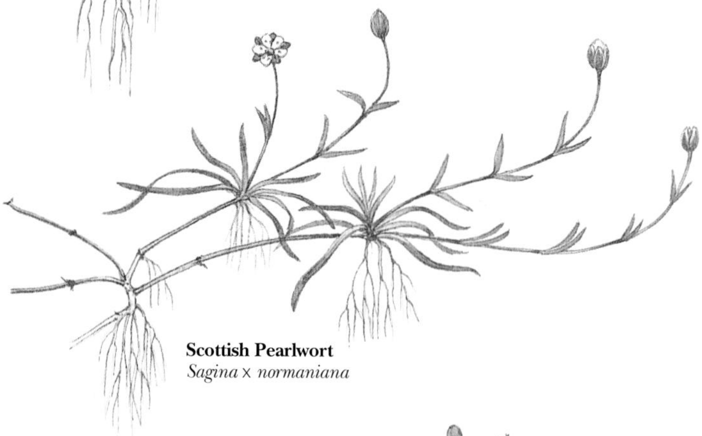

Scottish Pearlwort
Sagina × normaniana

Procumbent Pearlwort
Sagina procumbens

Annual Pearlwort
Common Pearlwort
Sagina apetala

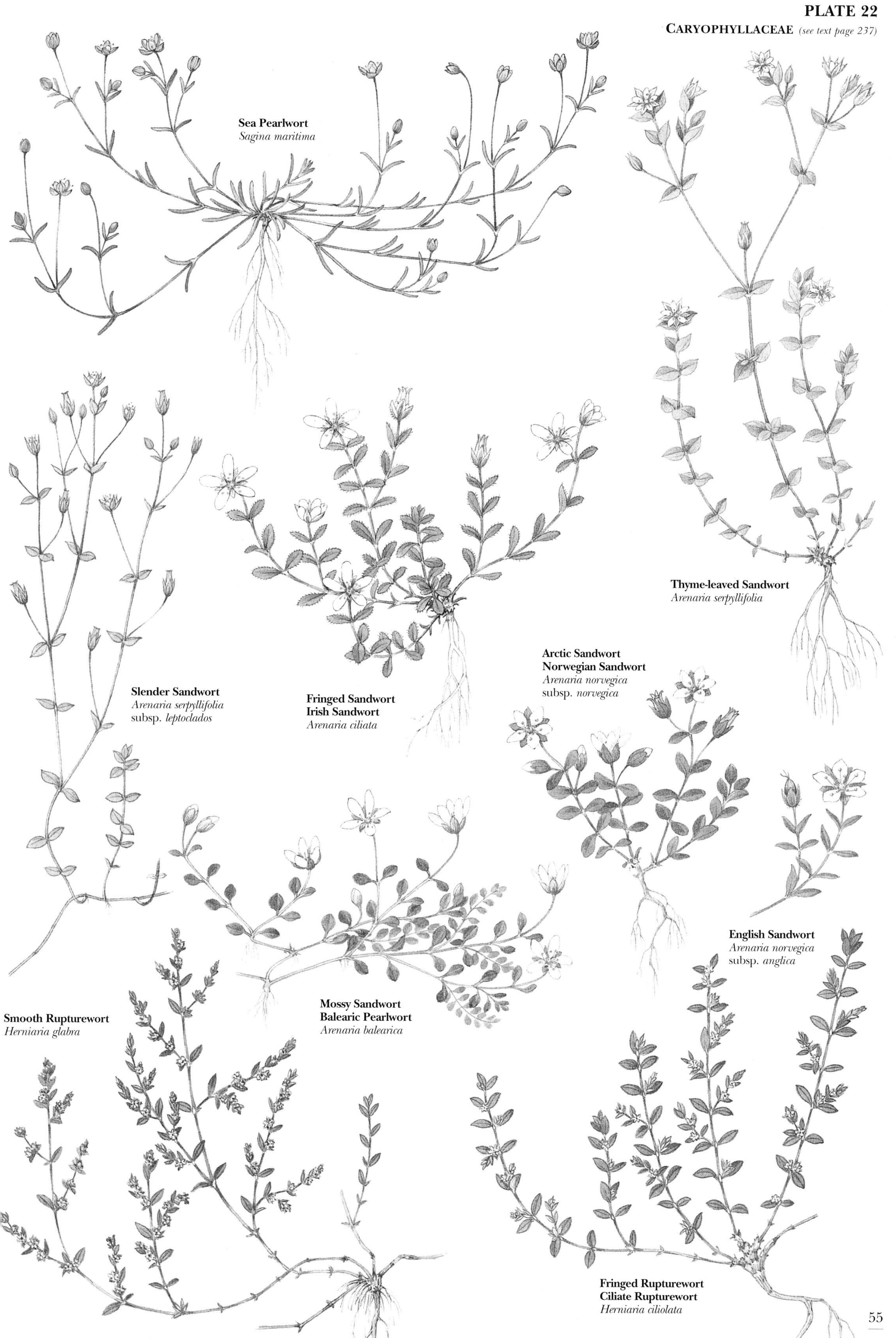
Sea Pearlwort
Sagina maritima
Thyme-leaved Sandwort
Arenaria serpyllifolia
Slender Sandwort
Arenaria serpyllifolia
subsp. *leptoclados*
Fringed Sandwort
Irish Sandwort
Arenaria ciliata
Arctic Sandwort
Norwegian Sandwort
Arenaria norvegica
subsp. *norvegica*
English Sandwort
Arenaria norvegica
subsp. *anglica*
Mossy Sandwort
Balearic Pearlwort
Arenaria balearica
Smooth Rupturewort
Herniaria glabra
Fringed Rupturewort
Ciliate Rupturewort
Herniaria ciliolata

PLATE 23

CARYOPHYLLACEAE *(see text page 239)*

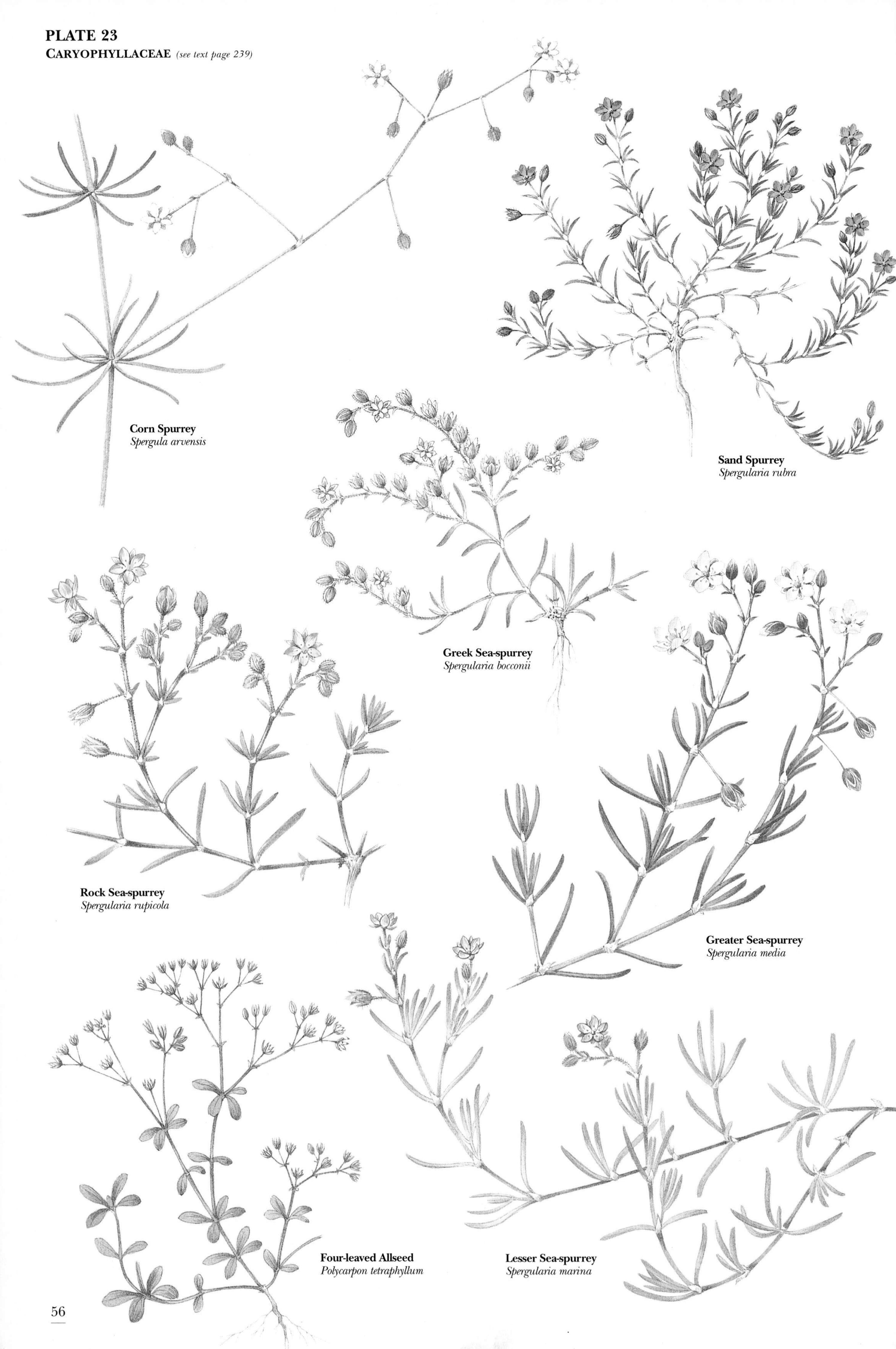

CARYOPHYLLACEAE • PORTULACACEAE • AIZOACEAE • CHENOPODIACEAE *(see text page 239)*

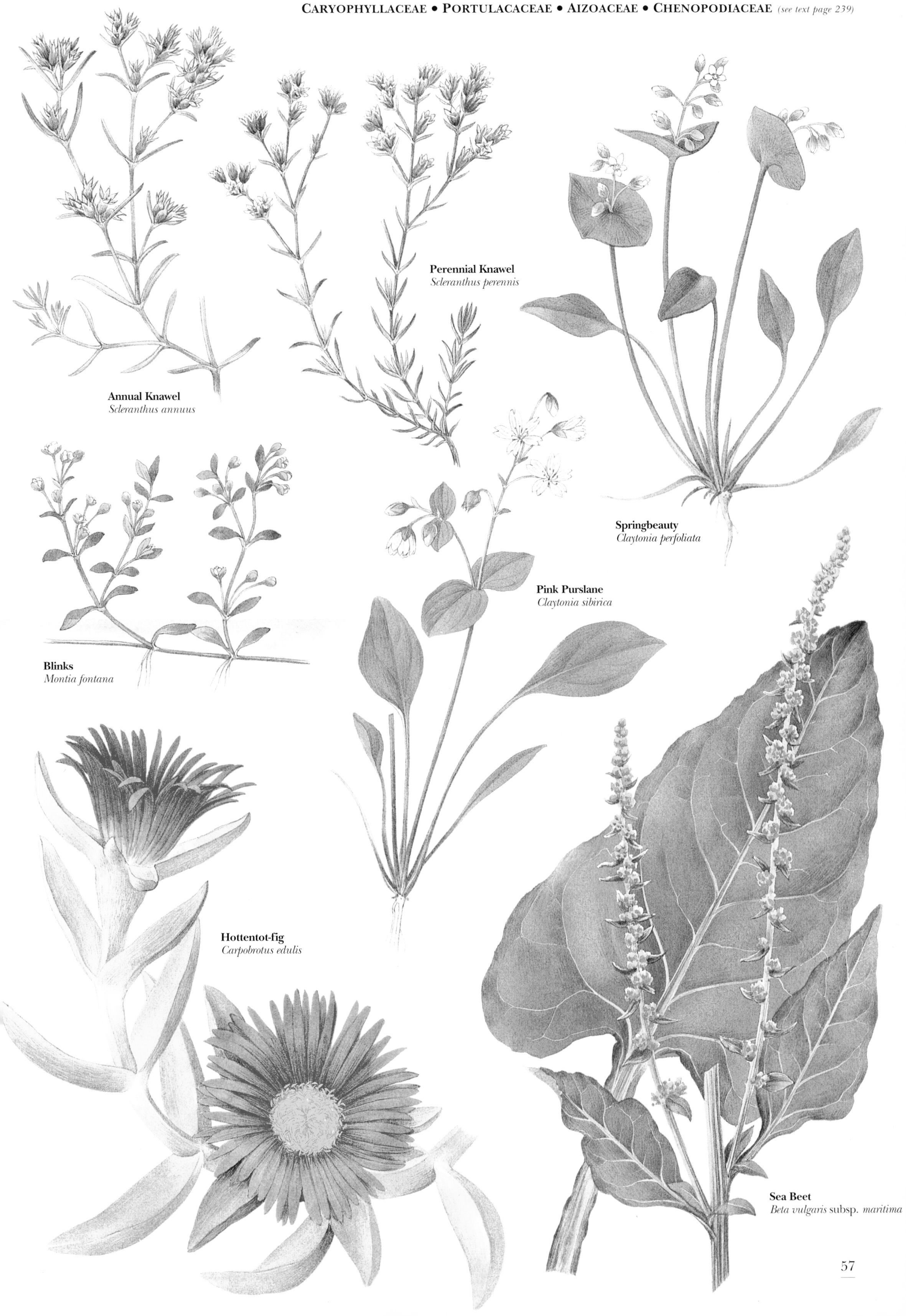

Perennial Knawel
Scleranthus perennis

Springbeauty
Claytonia perfoliata

Annual Knawel
Scleranthus annuus

Pink Purslane
Claytonia sibirica

Blinks
Montia fontana

Hottentot-fig
Carpobrotus edulis

Sea Beet
Beta vulgaris subsp. *maritima*

PLATE 24

CHENOPODIACEAE *(see text page 240)*

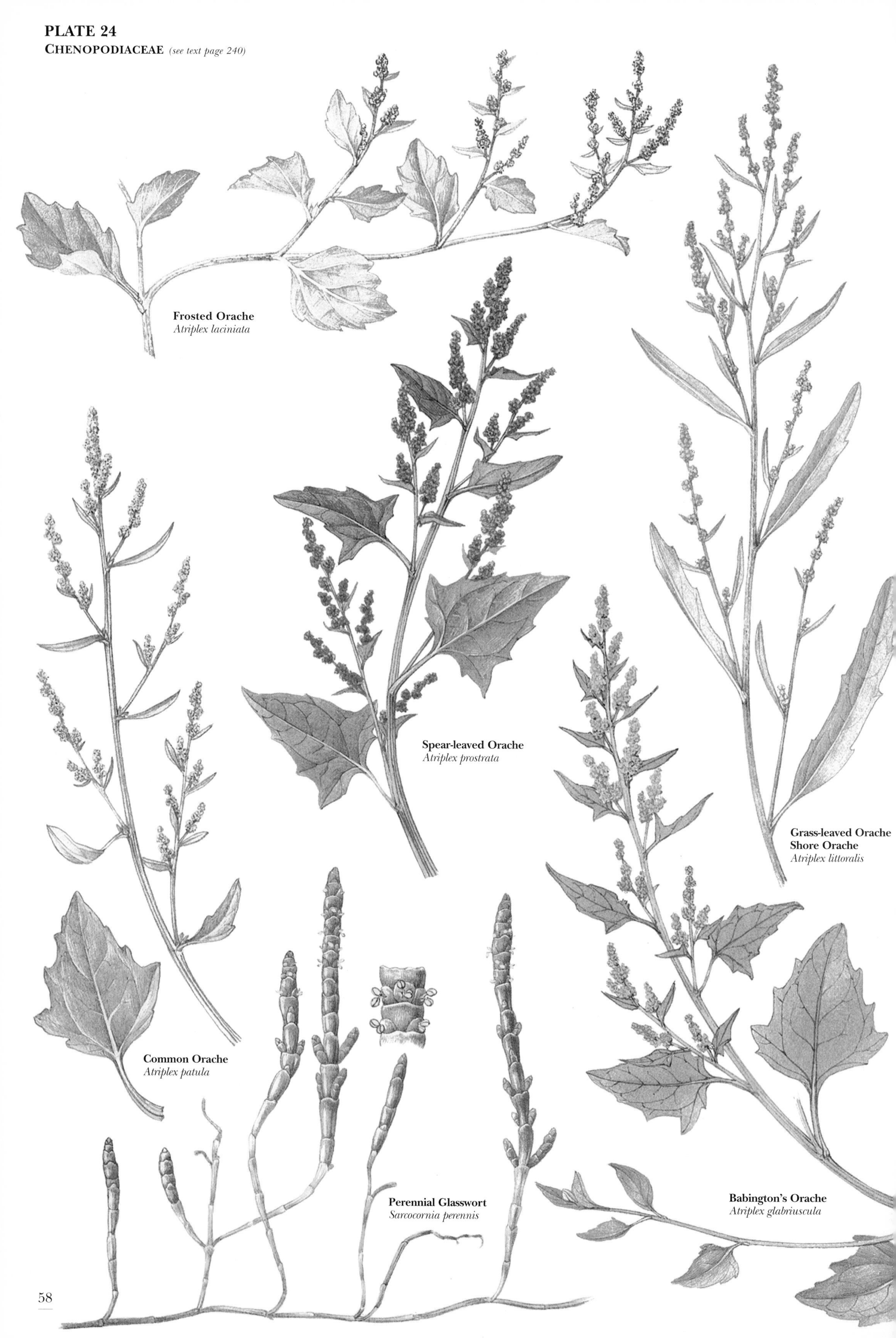

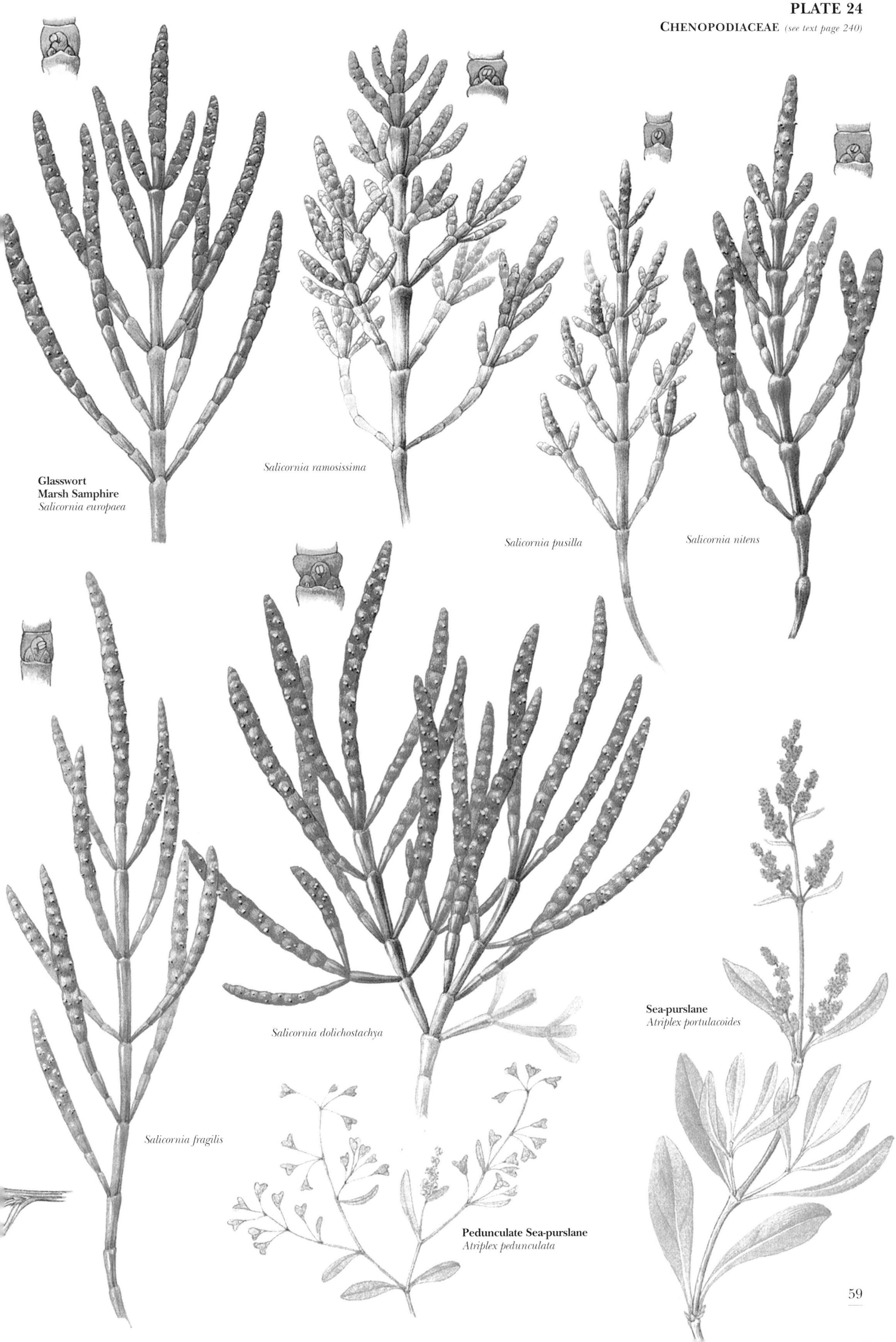

 (see text page 240)

Glasswort
Marsh Samphire
Salicornia europaea

Salicornia ramosissima

Salicornia pusilla

Salicornia nitens

Salicornia dolichostachya

Salicornia fragilis

Sea-purslane
Atriplex portulacoides

Pedunculate Sea-purslane
Atriplex pedunculata

(see text page 241)

Good-King-Henry
Chenopodium bonus-henricus
Oak-leaved Goosefoot
Glaucous Goosefoot
Chenopodium glaucum
Red Goosefoot
Chenopodium rubrum
Strawberry-blite
Chenopodium capitatum
Saltmarsh Goosefoot
Chenopodium chenopodioides
Maple-leaved Goosefoot
Sowbane
Chenopodium hybridum
Many-seeded Goosefoot
Allseed
Chenopodium polyspermum

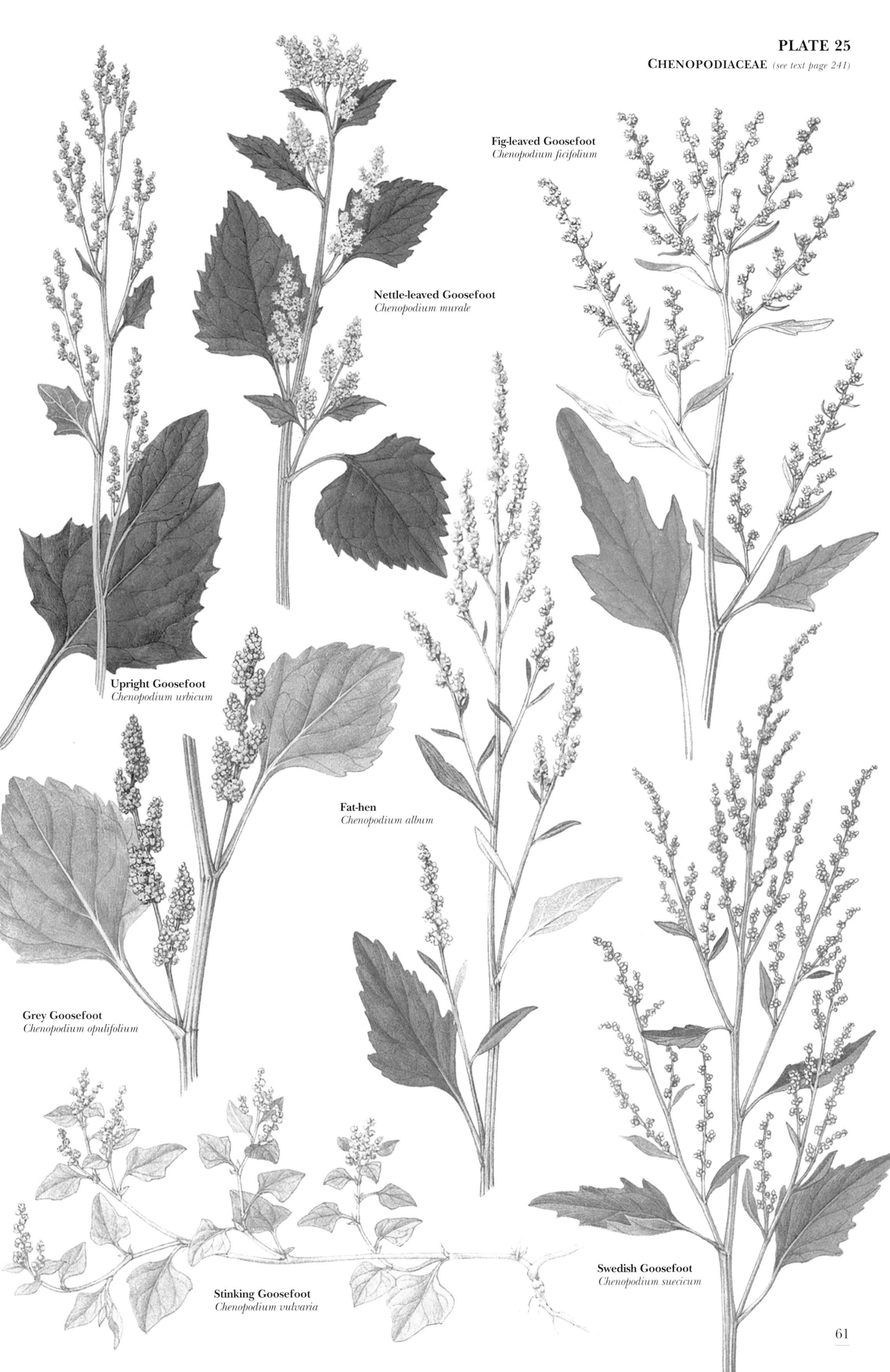
Fig-leaved Goosefoot
Chenopodium ficifolium
Nettle-leaved Goosefoot
Chenopodium murale
Upright Goosefoot
Chenopodium urbicum
Fat-hen
Chenopodium album
Grey Goosefoot
Chenopodium opulifolium
Stinking Goosefoot
Chenopodium vulvaria
Swedish Goosefoot
Chenopodium suecicum

PLATE 26

CHENOPODIACEAE • MALVACEAE *(see text page 242)*

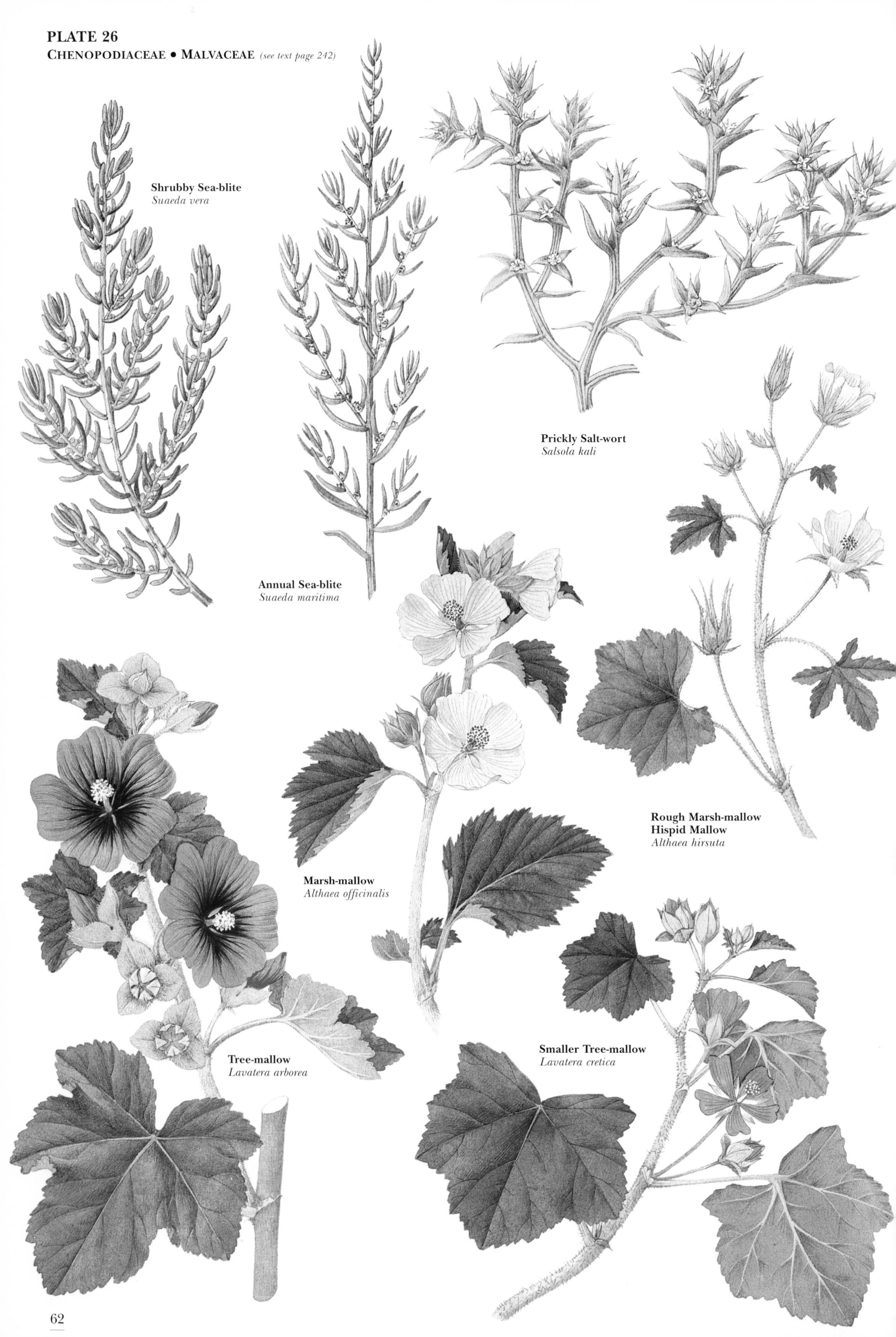

 (see text page 242)

Musk Mallow
Malva moschata
Common Mallow
Malva sylvestris
Small Mallow
Malva pusilla
Dwarf Mallow
Malva neglecta
Perennial Flax
Linum perenne
Pale Flax
Linum bienne
Fairy Flax
Purging Flax
Linum catharticum

PLATE 27
LINACEAE • GERANIACEAE *(see text page 243)*

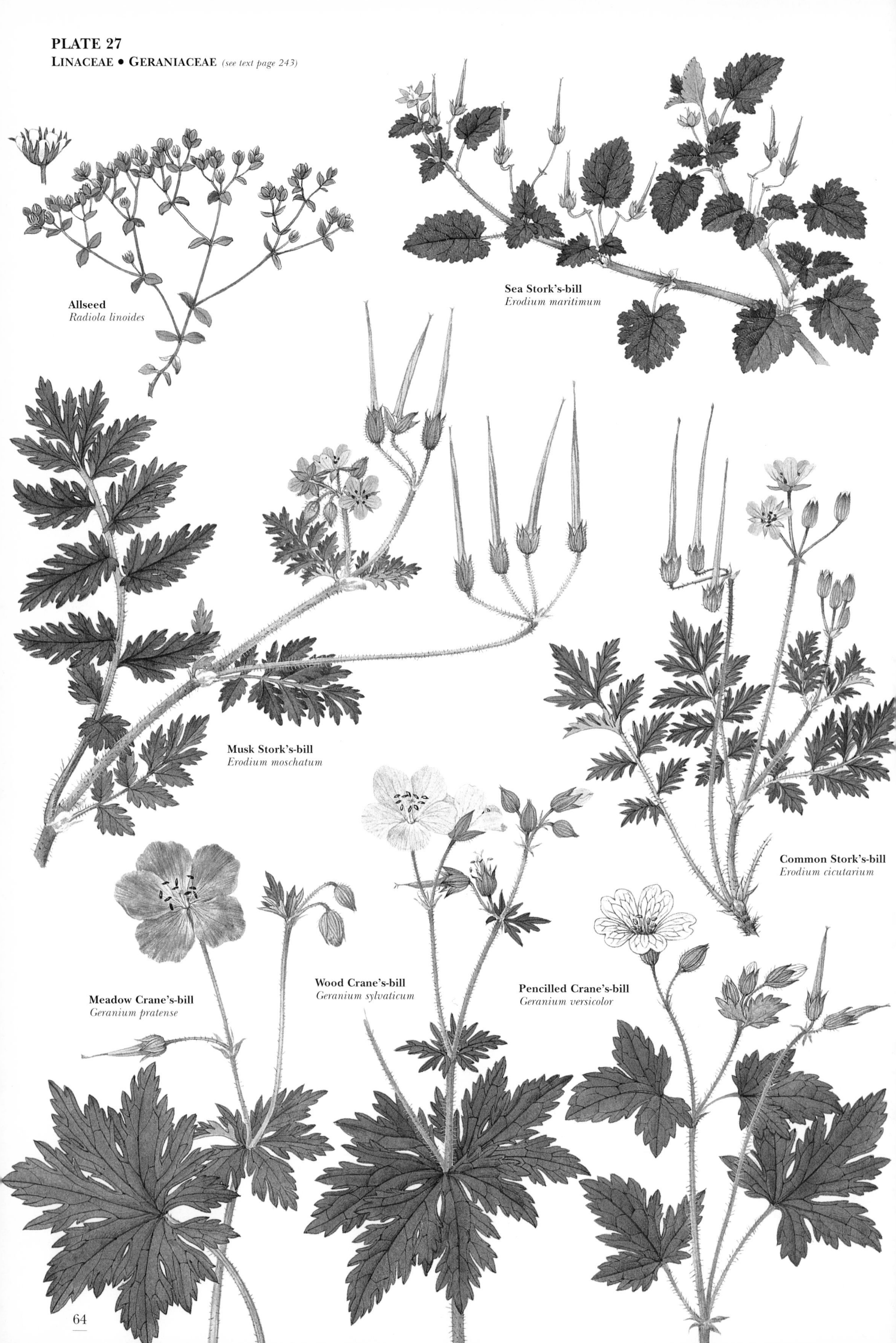

GERANIACEAE *(see text page 243)*

Dusky Crane's-bill
Geranium phaeum
Bloody Crane's-bill
Geranium sanguineum
Hedgerow Crane's-bill
Mountain Crane's-bill
Geranium pyrenaicum
Long-stalked Crane's-bill
Geranium columbinum
Cut-leaved Crane's-bill
Geranium dissectum
Dove's-foot Crane's-bill
Geranium molle
Round-leaved Crane's-bill
Geranium rotundifolium

PLATE 28

GERANIACEAE • OXALIDACEAE *(see text page 244)*

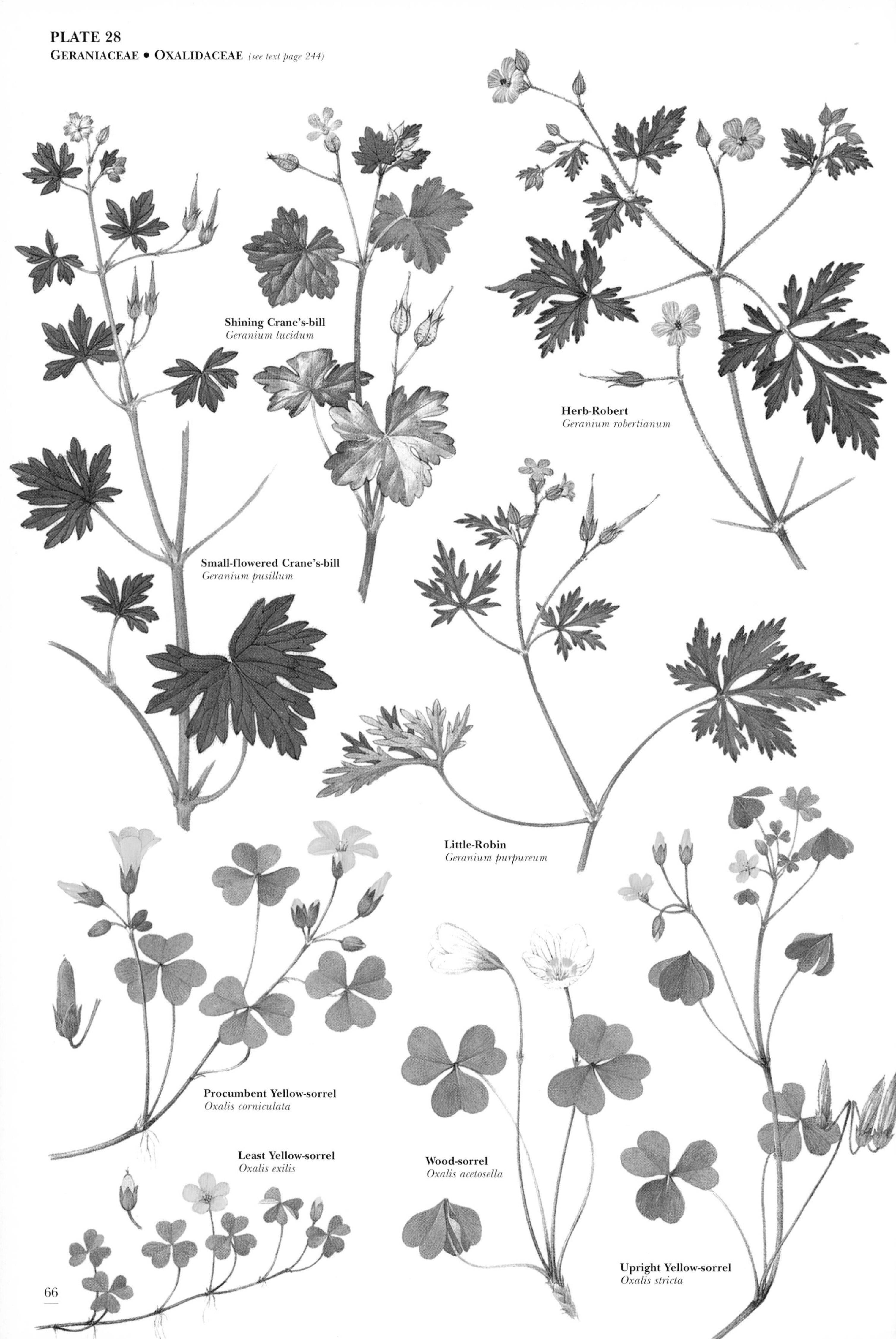

Garden Pink-sorrel
Oxalis latifolia
Pink-sorrel
Oxalis articulata
Large-flowered Pink-sorrel
Oxalis debilis
Pale Pink-sorrel
Oxalis incarnata
Touch-me-not
Impatiens noli-tangere
Bermuda-buttercup
Oxalis pes-caprae
Orange Balsam
Impatiens capensis

PLATE 29
BALSAMINACEAE • FABACEAE (= LEGUMINOSAE) *(see text page 245)*

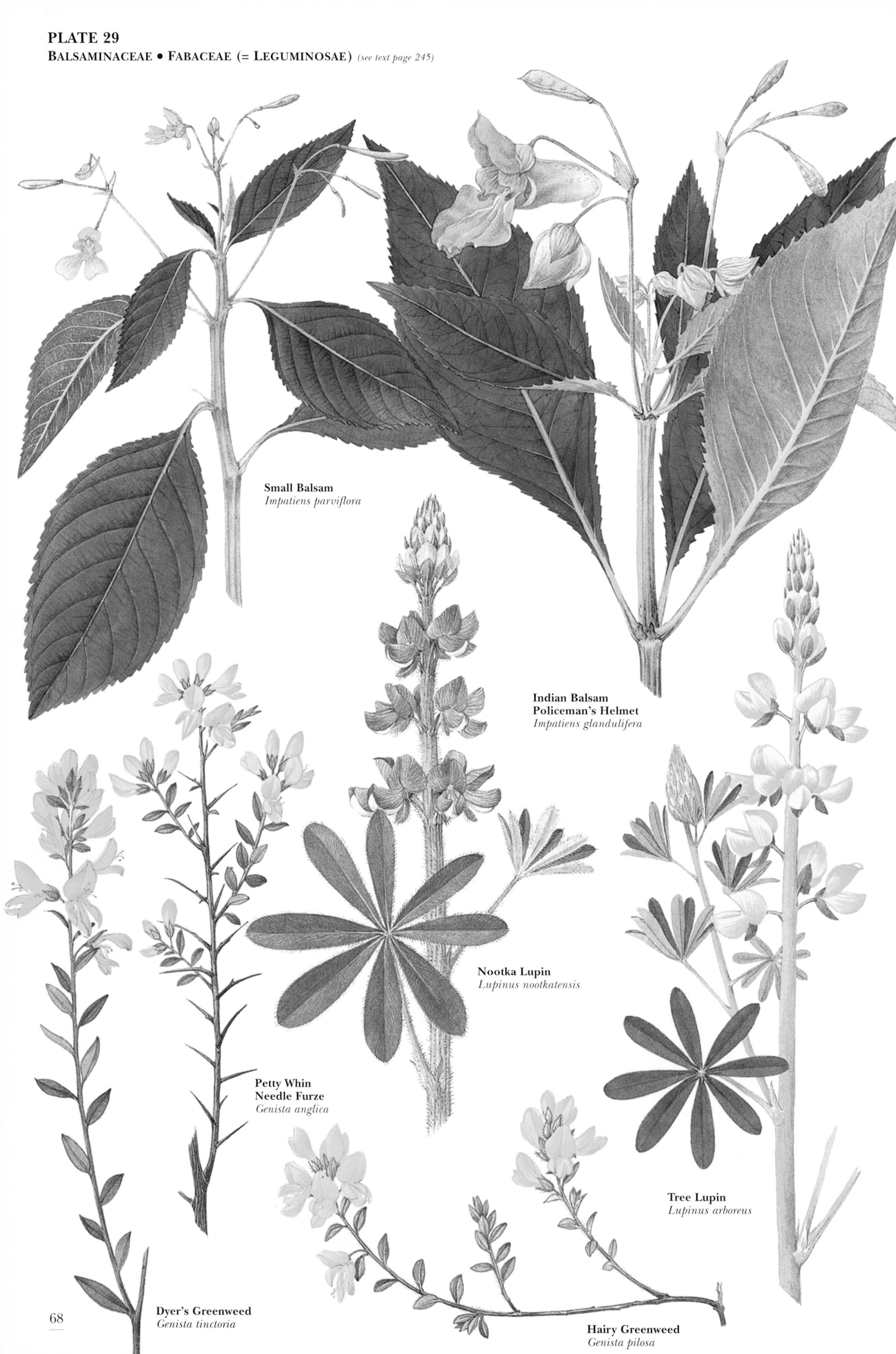

FABACEAE (= LEGUMINOSAE) *(see text page 245)*

Bur Medick
Small Medick
Medicago minima

Spotted Medick
Medicago arabica

Toothed Medick
Hairy Medick
Medicago polymorpha

Black Medick
Medicago lupulina

Goat's-rue
Galega officinalis

Kidney Vetch
Anthyllis vulneraria

Sickle Medick
Medicago sativa subsp. *falcata*

PLATE 30

FABACEAE (= LEGUMINOSAE) *(see text page 246)*

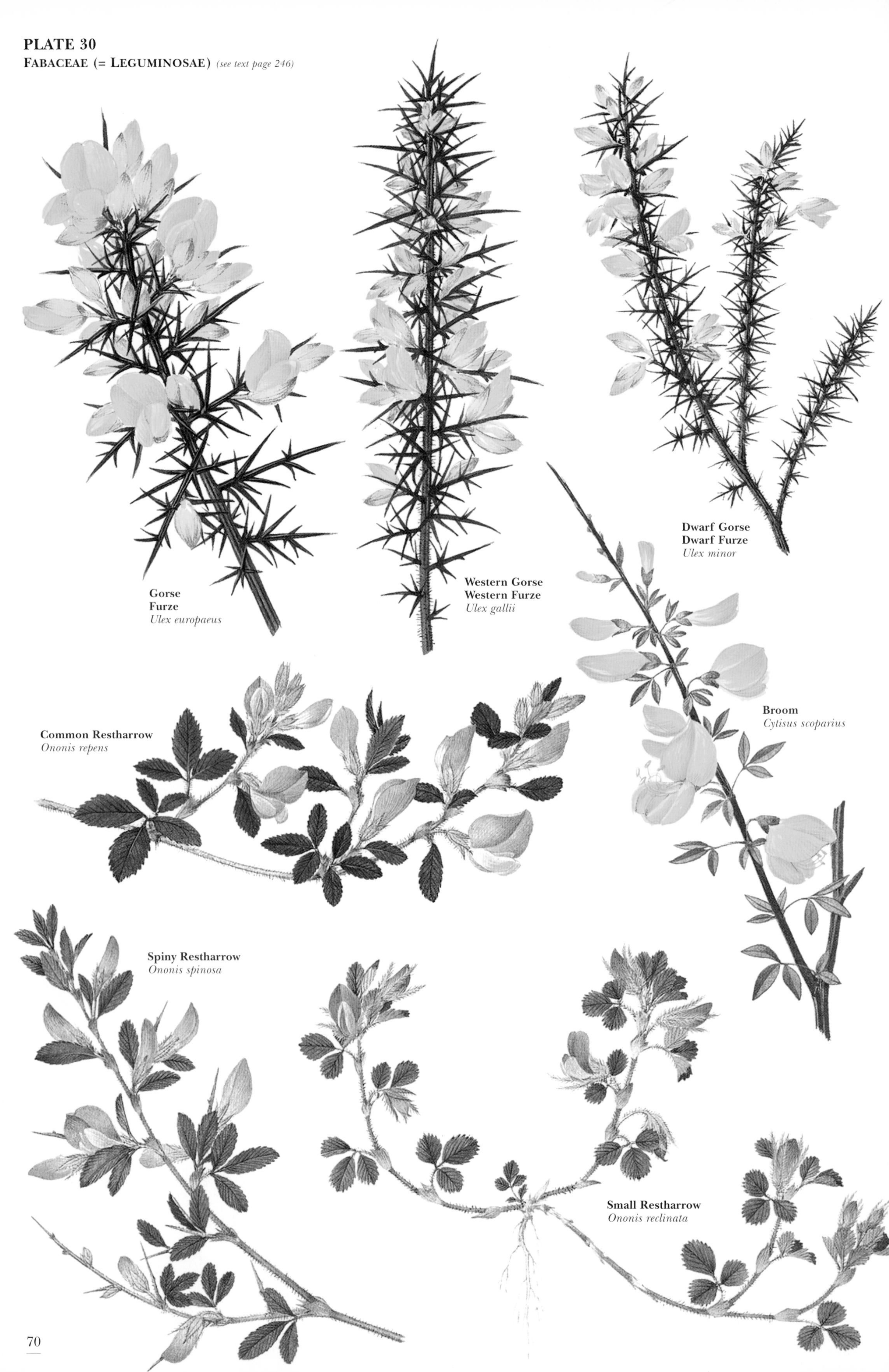

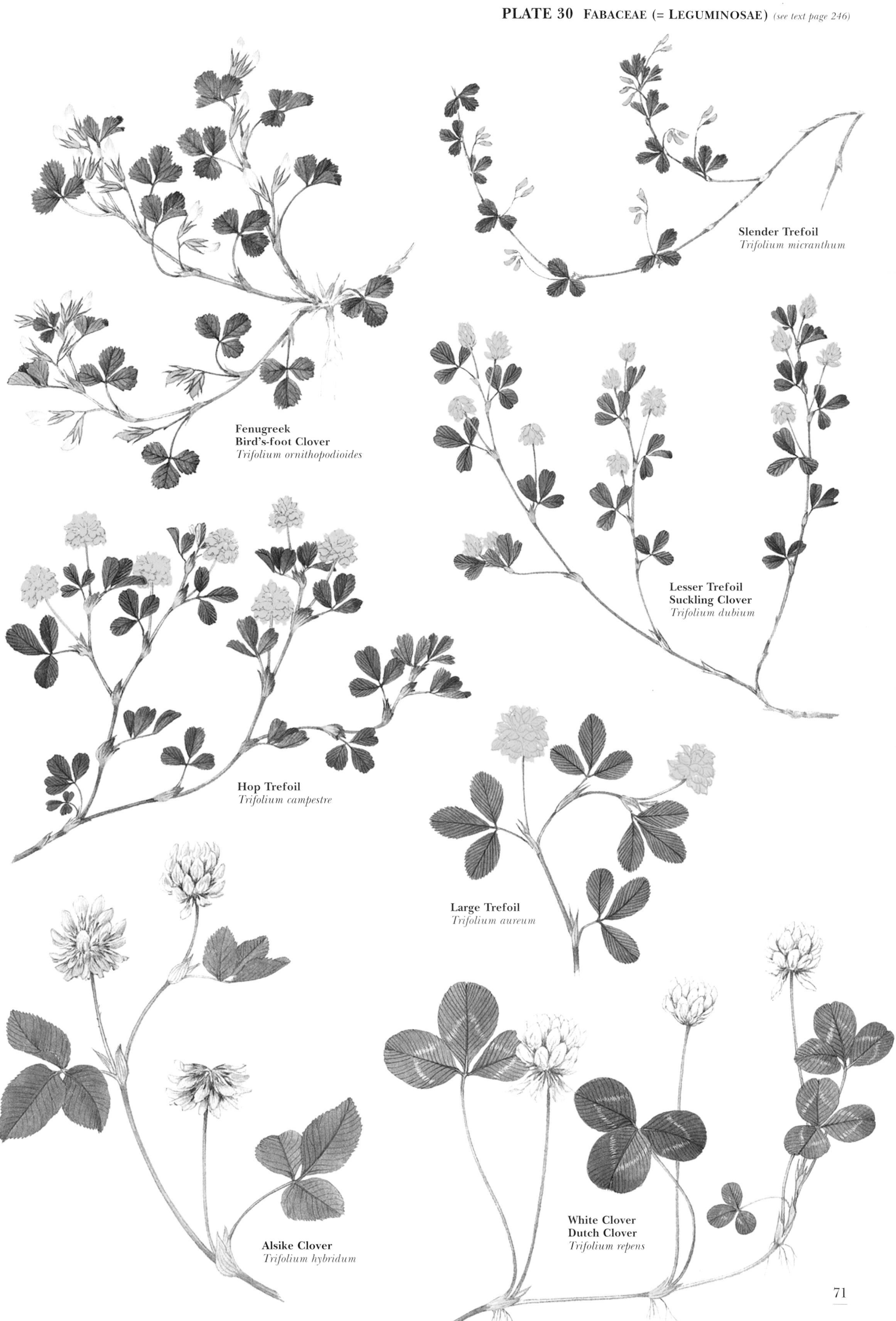

Fenugreek
Bird's-foot Clover
Trifolium ornithopodioides

Slender Trefoil
Trifolium micranthum

Lesser Trefoil
Suckling Clover
Trifolium dubium

Hop Trefoil
Trifolium campestre

Large Trefoil
Trifolium aureum

Alsike Clover
Trifolium hybridum

White Clover
Dutch Clover
Trifolium repens

Clustered Clover
Trifolium glomeratum
Suffocated Clover
Trifolium suffocatum
Strawberry Clover
Trifolium fragiferum
Upright Clover
Trifolium strictum
Zigzag Clover
Trifolium medium
Rough Clover
Rough Trefoil
Trifolium scabrum
Hare's-foot Clover
Trifolium arvense

 (see text page 247)

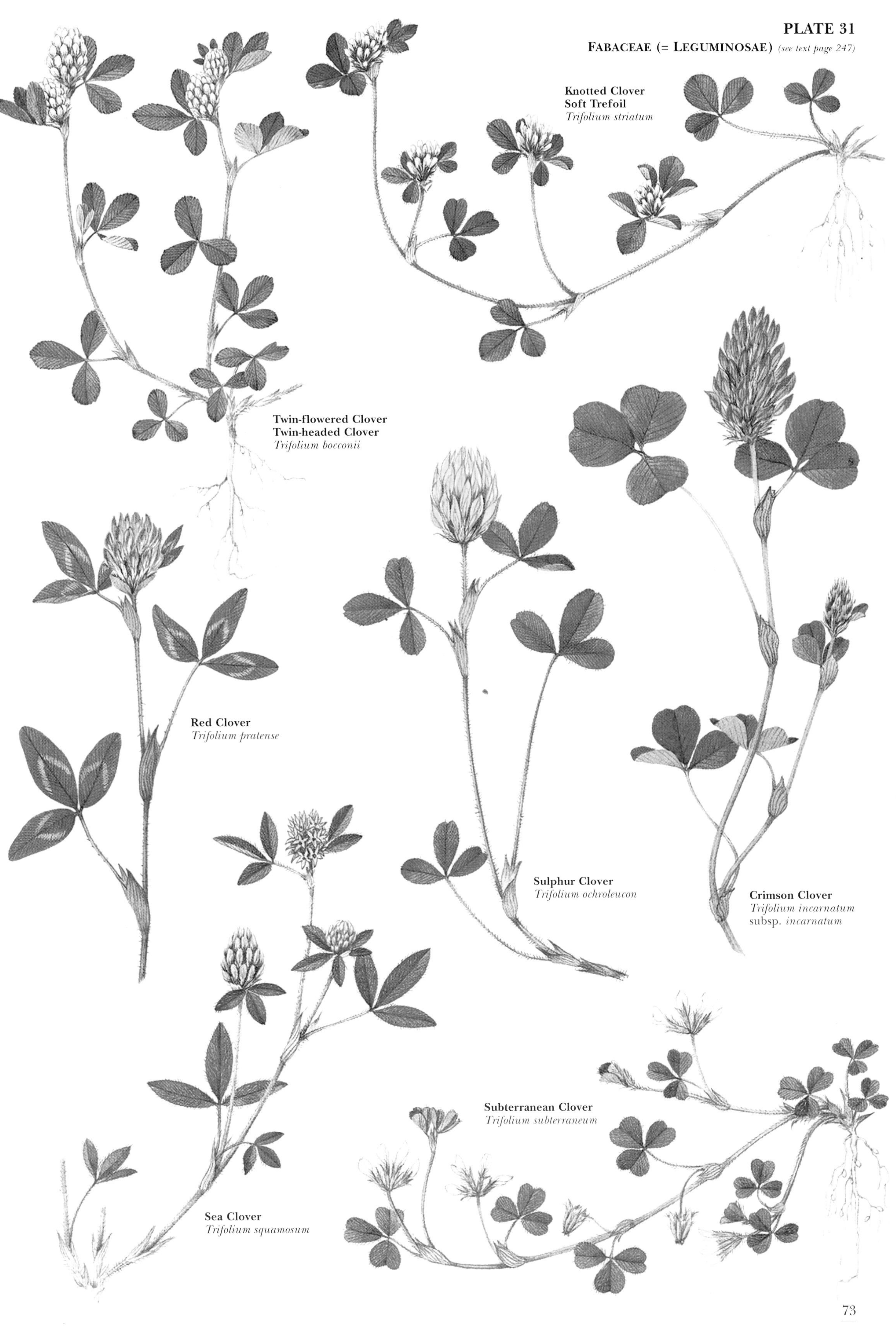
Knotted Clover
Soft Trefoil
Trifolium striatum
Twin-flowered Clover
Twin-headed Clover
Trifolium bocconii
Red Clover
Trifolium pratense
Sulphur Clover
Trifolium ochroleucon
Crimson Clover
Trifolium incarnatum
subsp. incarnatum
Subterranean Clover
Trifolium subterraneum
Sea Clover
Trifolium squamosum

PLATE 32

FABACEAE (= LEGUMINOSAE) *(see text page 248)*

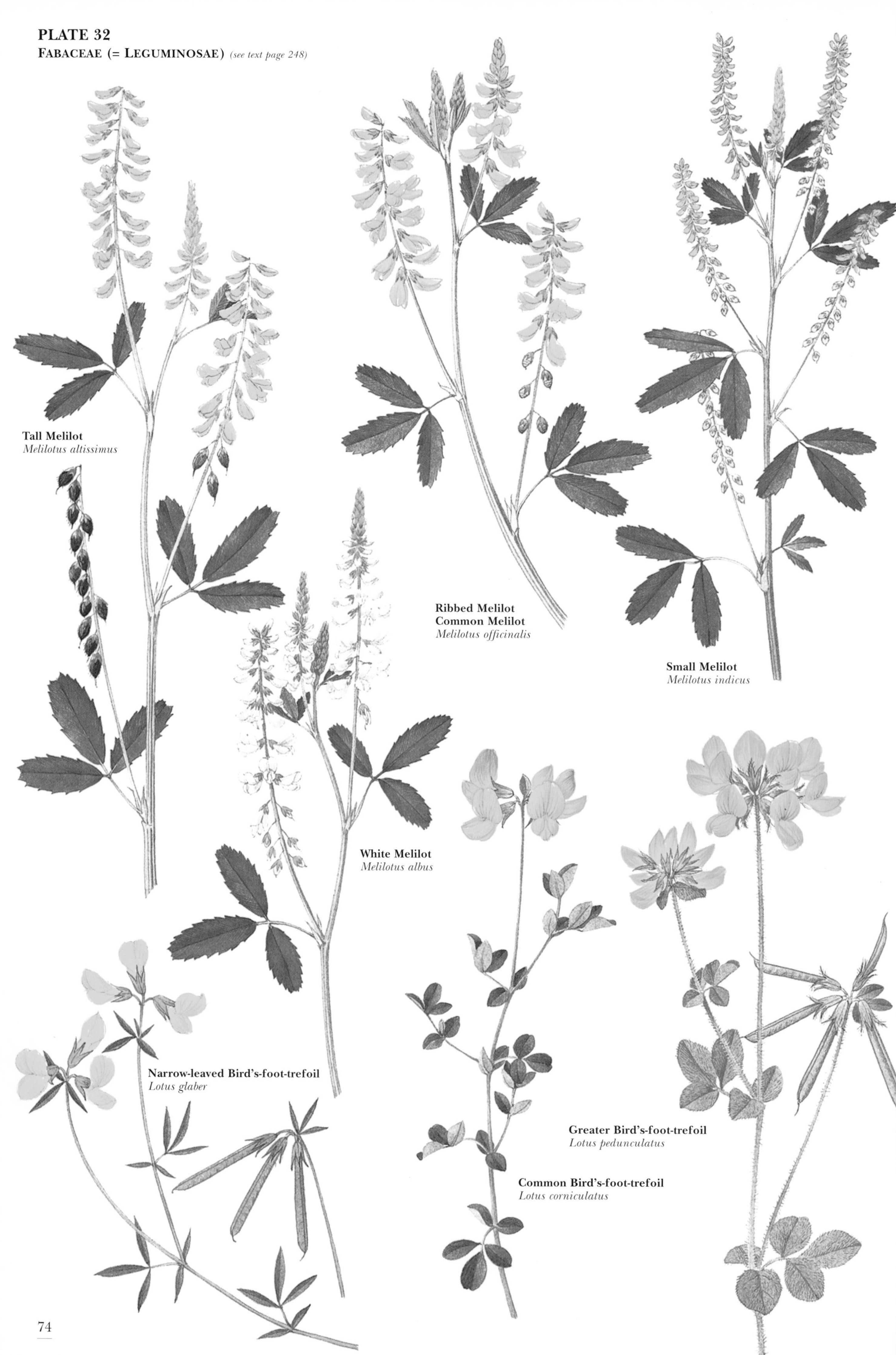

Tall Melilot
Melilotus altissimus

Ribbed Melilot
Common Melilot
Melilotus officinalis

Small Melilot
Melilotus indicus

White Melilot
Melilotus albus

Narrow-leaved Bird's-foot-trefoil
Lotus glaber

Greater Bird's-foot-trefoil
Lotus pedunculatus

Common Bird's-foot-trefoil
Lotus corniculatus

 (see text page 248)

Hairy Bird's-foot-trefoil
Lotus subbiflorus
Slender Bird's-foot-trefoil
Lotus angustissimus
Purple Milk-vetch
Astragalus danicus
Alpine Milk-vetch
Astragalus alpinus
Purple Oxytropis
Oxytropis halleri
Wild Liquorice
Astragalus glycyphyllos
Yellow Oxytropis
Oxytropis campestris

PLATE 33
FABACEAE (= LEGUMINOSAE) *(see text page 249)*

Wood Vetch
Vicia sylvatica
Bush Vetch
Vicia sepium
Yellow-vetch
Vicia lutea
Bithynian Vetch
Vicia bithynica
Common Vetch
Vicia sativa
subsp. *sativa*
Bird's-foot
Ornithopus perpusillus
Spring Vetch
Vicia lathyroides
Orange Bird's-foot
Ornithopus pinnatus

PLATE 34

FABACEAE (= LEGUMINOSAE) *(see text page 250)*

 (see text page 250)

Meadow Vetchling
Lathyrus pratensis

Marsh Pea
Lathyrus palustris

Tuberous Pea
Earth-nut Pea
Lathyrus tuberosus

Bitter Vetch
Lathyrus linifolius

Black Pea
Lathyrus niger

Sea Pea
Lathyrus japonicus

Bridewort
Willow Spiraea
Spiraea salicifolia

 (see text page 251)

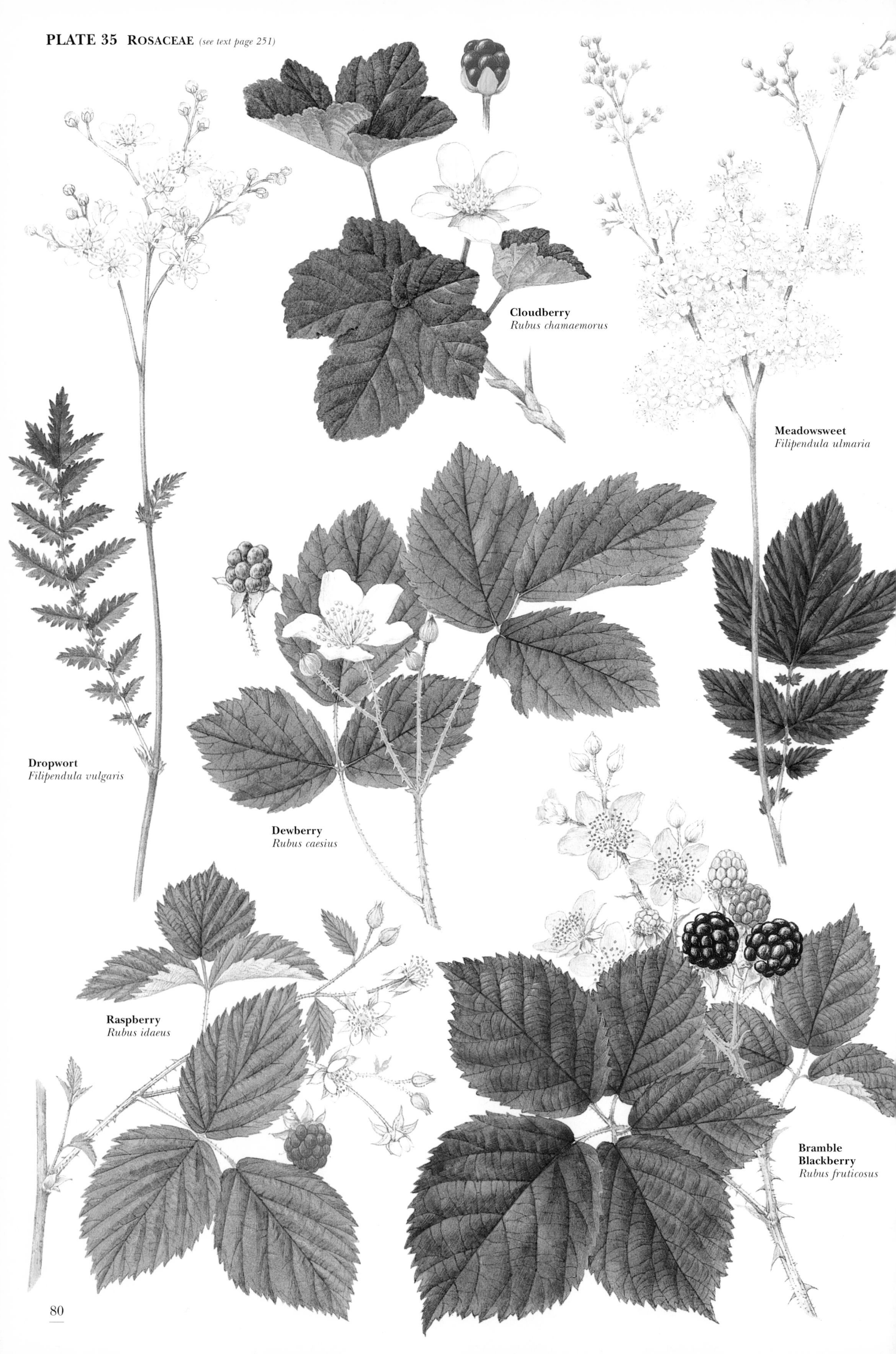
Cloudberry
Rubus chamaemorus
Meadowsweet
Filipendula ulmaria
Dropwort
Filipendula vulgaris
Dewberry
Rubus caesius
Raspberry
Rubus idaeus
Bramble
Blackberry
Rubus fruticosus

 (see text page 251)

Stone Bramble
Rubus saxatilis

Wood Avens
Geum urbanum

Water Avens
Geum rivale

Sibbaldia
Sibbaldia procumbens

Wild Strawberry
Fragaria vesca

Mountain Avens
Dryas octopetala

Pirri-pirri-bur
Acaena novae-zelandiae

Bastard Agrimony
Aremonia agrimonoides

Shrubby Cinquefoil
Potentilla fruticosa
Marsh Cinquefoil
Potentilla palustris
Ternate-leaved Cinquefoil
Potentilla norvegica
Rock Cinquefoil
Potentilla rupestris
Barren Strawberry
Potentilla sterilis
Silverweed
Potentilla anserina
Hoary Cinquefoil
Potentilla argentea

 (see text page 252)

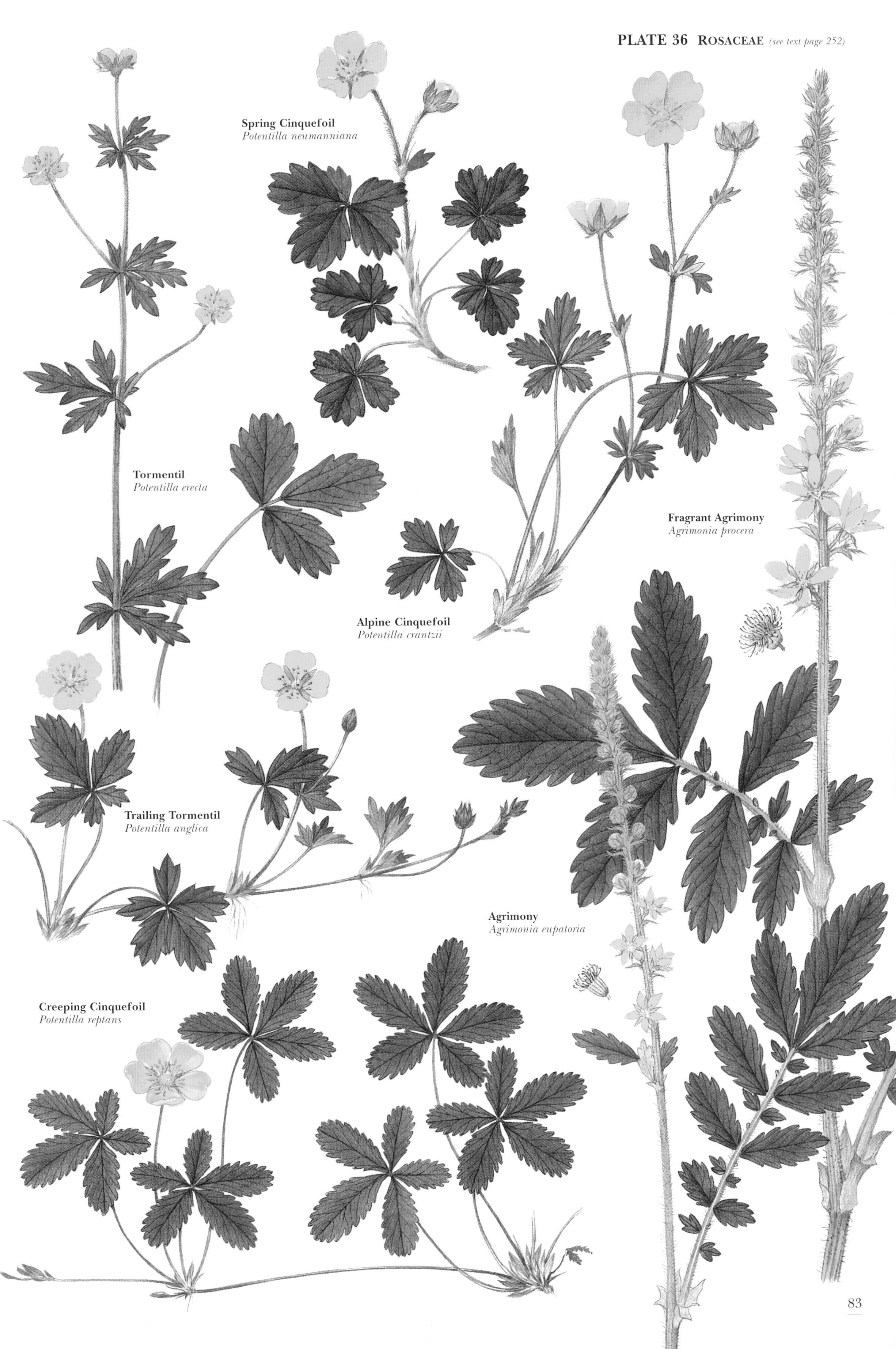
Spring Cinquefoil
Potentilla neumanniana
Tormentil
Potentilla erecta
Alpine Cinquefoil
Potentilla crantzii
Fragrant Agrimony
Agrimonia procera
Trailing Tormentil
Potentilla anglica
Agrimony
Agrimonia eupatoria
Creeping Cinquefoil
Potentilla reptans

PLATE 37
ROSACEAE *(see text page 253)*

 (see text page 253)

PLATE 38
ROSACEAE *(see text page 254)*

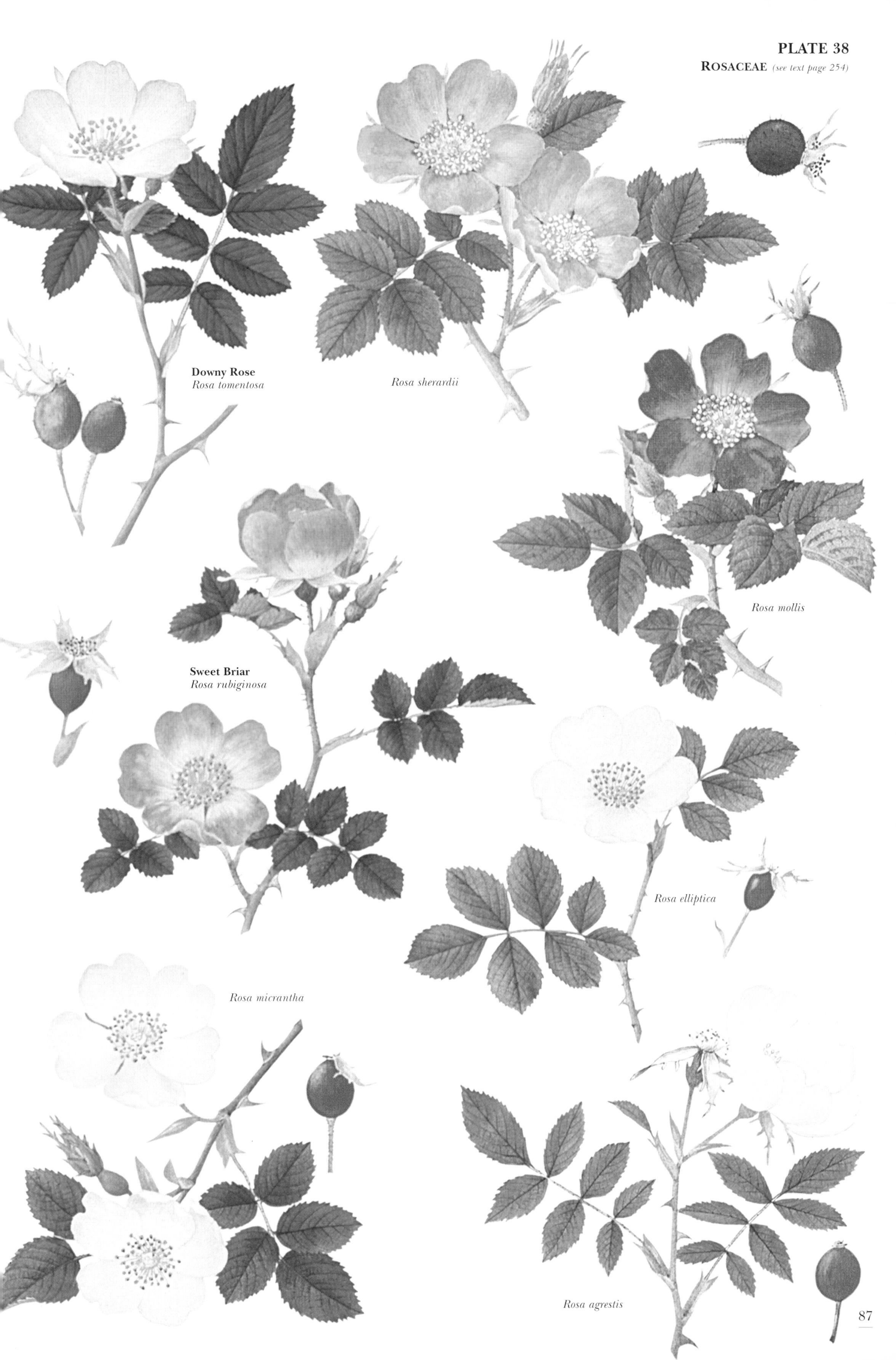
Downy Rose
Rosa tomentosa
Rosa sherardii
Rosa mollis
Sweet Briar
Rosa rubiginosa
Rosa elliptica
Rosa micrantha
Rosa agrestis

 (see text page 255)

Great Burnet
Sanguisorba officinalis
Salad Burnet
Sanguisorba minor subsp. *minor*
Fodder Burnet
Sanguisorba minor
subsp. *muricata*
Wild Cotoneaster
Cotoneaster integerrimus
Orpine
Livelong
Sedum telephium
Himalayan Cotoneaster
Cotoneaster simonsii
Small-leaved Cotoneaster
Cotoneaster integrifolius

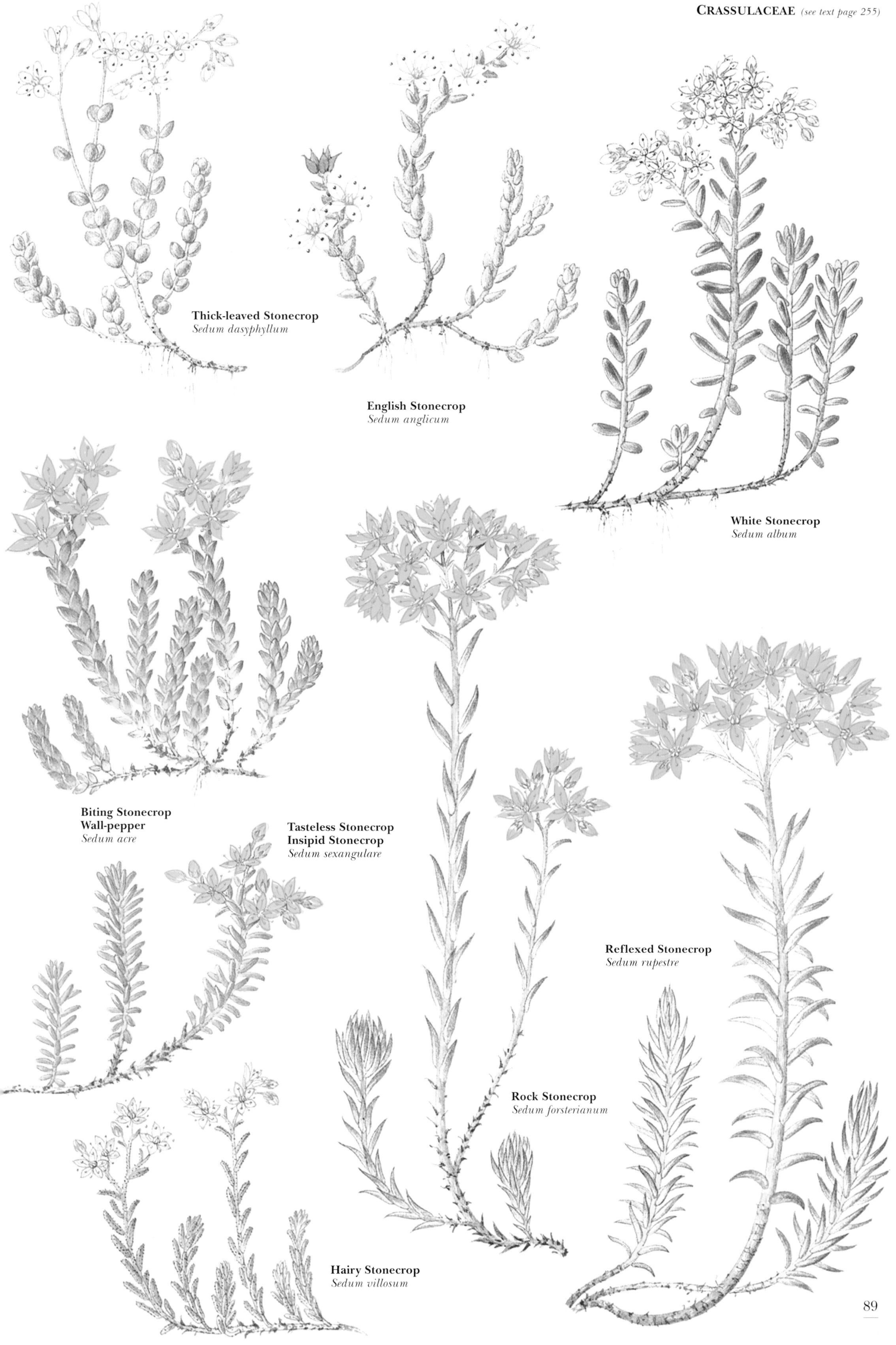

Thick-leaved Stonecrop
Sedum dasyphyllum

English Stonecrop
Sedum anglicum

White Stonecrop
Sedum album

Biting Stonecrop
Wall-pepper
Sedum acre

Tasteless Stonecrop
Insipid Stonecrop
Sedum sexangulare

Reflexed Stonecrop
Sedum rupestre

Rock Stonecrop
Sedum forsterianum

Hairy Stonecrop
Sedum villosum

PLATE 40

CRASSULACEAE • SAXIFRAGACEAE *(see text page 256)*

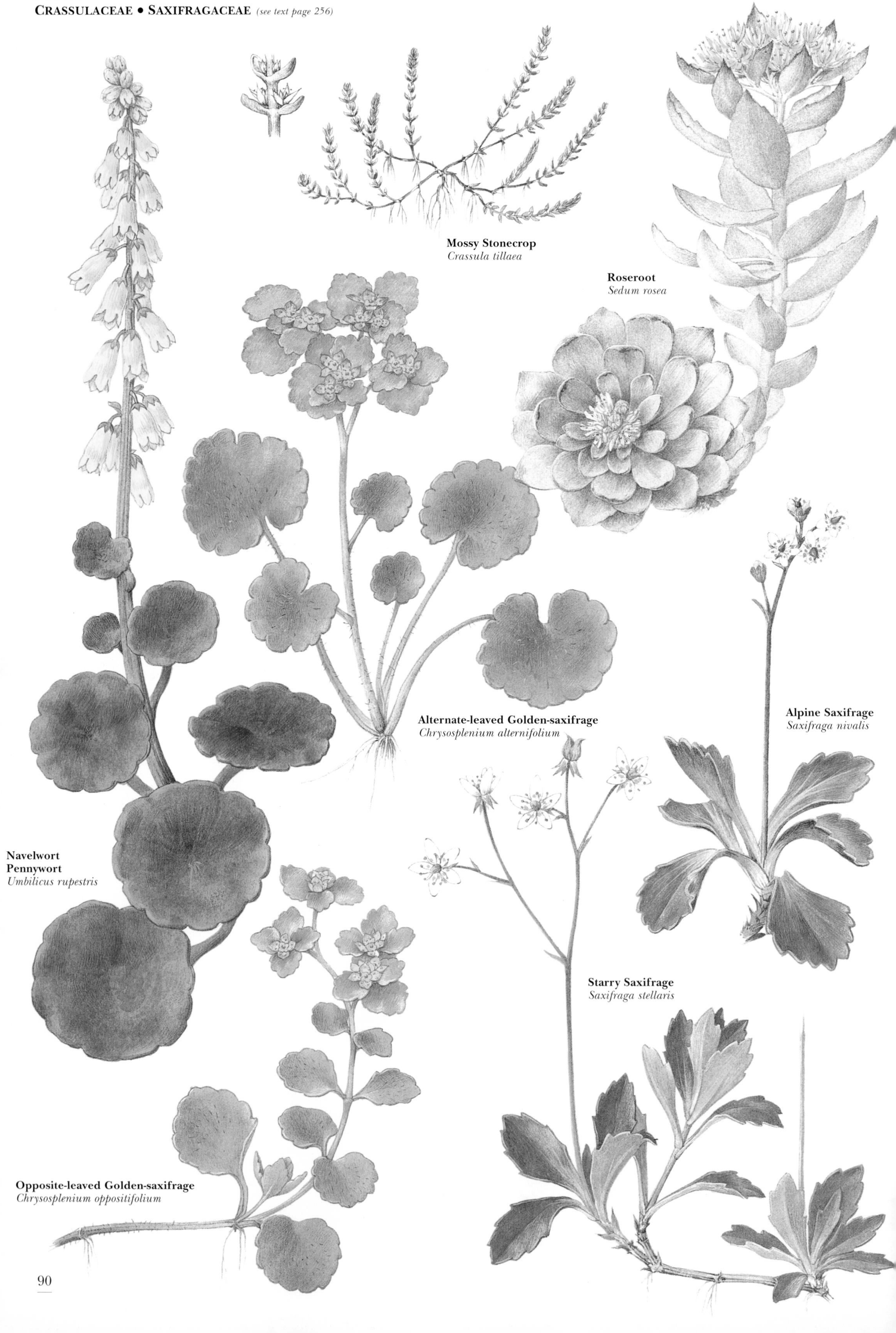

Mossy Stonecrop
Crassula tillaea

Roseroot
Sedum rosea

Alternate-leaved Golden-saxifrage
Chrysosplenium alternifolium

Alpine Saxifrage
Saxifraga nivalis

Navelwort
Pennywort
Umbilicus rupestris

Starry Saxifrage
Saxifraga stellaris

Opposite-leaved Golden-saxifrage
Chrysosplenium oppositifolium

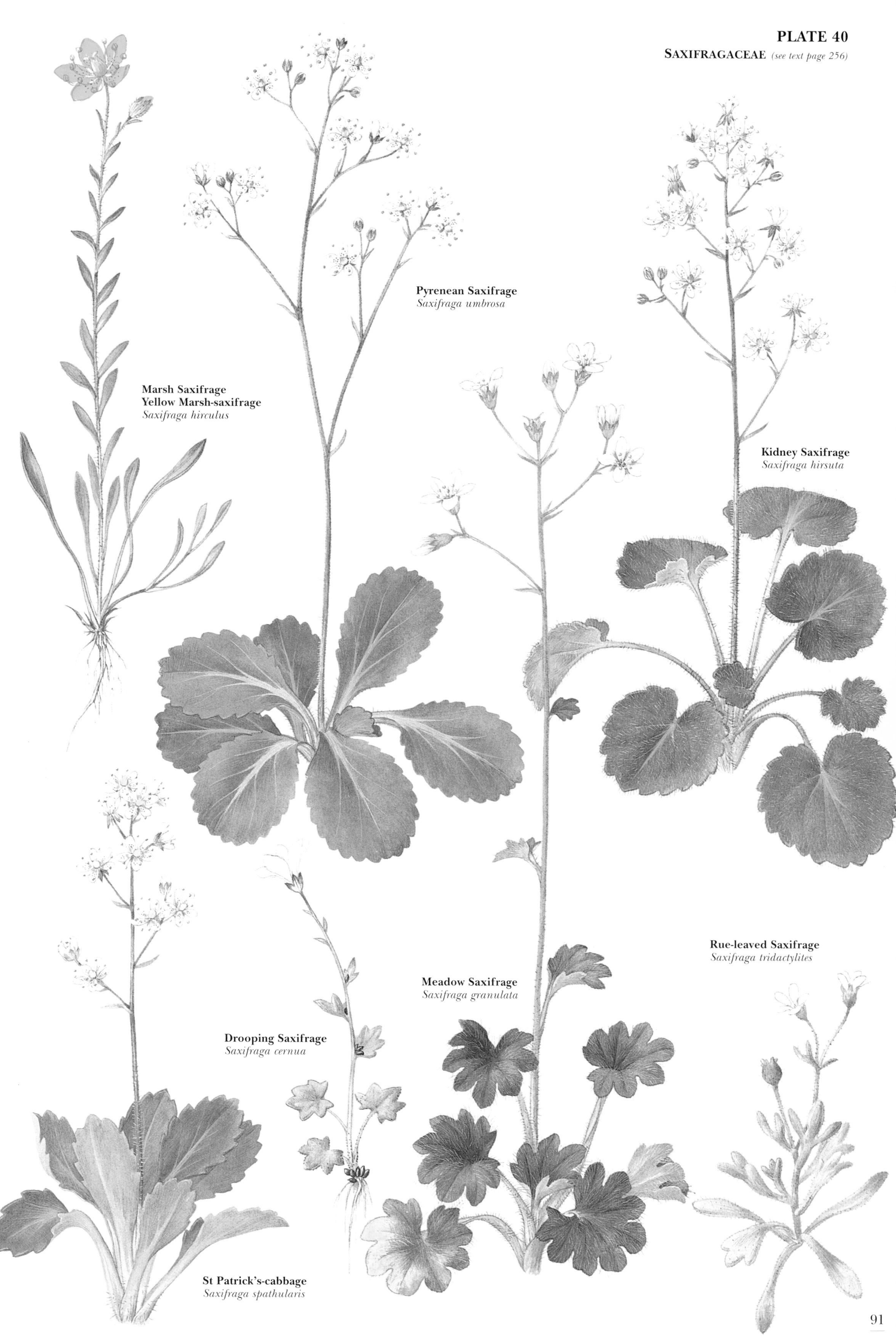
Marsh Saxifrage
Yellow Marsh-saxifrage
Saxifraga hirculus
Pyrenean Saxifrage
Saxifraga umbrosa
Kidney Saxifrage
Saxifraga hirsuta
Rue-leaved Saxifrage
Saxifraga tridactylites
Meadow Saxifrage
Saxifraga granulata
Drooping Saxifrage
Saxifraga cernua
St Patrick's-cabbage
Saxifraga spathularis

PLATE 41

SAXIFRAGACEAE *(see text page 257)*

Highland Saxifrage
Brook Saxifrage
Saxifraga rivularis

Saxifraga rosacea subsp. *hartii*

Tufted Saxifrage
Saxifraga cespitosa

Irish Saxifrage
Saxifraga rosacea subsp. *rosacea*

Mossy Saxifrage
Dovedale Moss
Saxifraga hypnoides

Purple Saxifrage
Saxifraga oppositifolia

Yellow Saxifrage
Yellow Mountain-saxifrage
Saxifraga aizoides

Grass-of-Parnassus
Parnassia palustris

 (see text page 257)

Downy Currant
Ribes spicatum
Black Currant
Ribes nigrum
Gooseberry
Ribes uva-crispa
Mountain Currant
Ribes alpinum
Red Currant
Ribes rubrum
Pitcherplant
Sarracenia purpurea

PLATE 42

DROSERACEAE • LYTHRACEAE • THYMELAEACEAE *(see text page 257)*

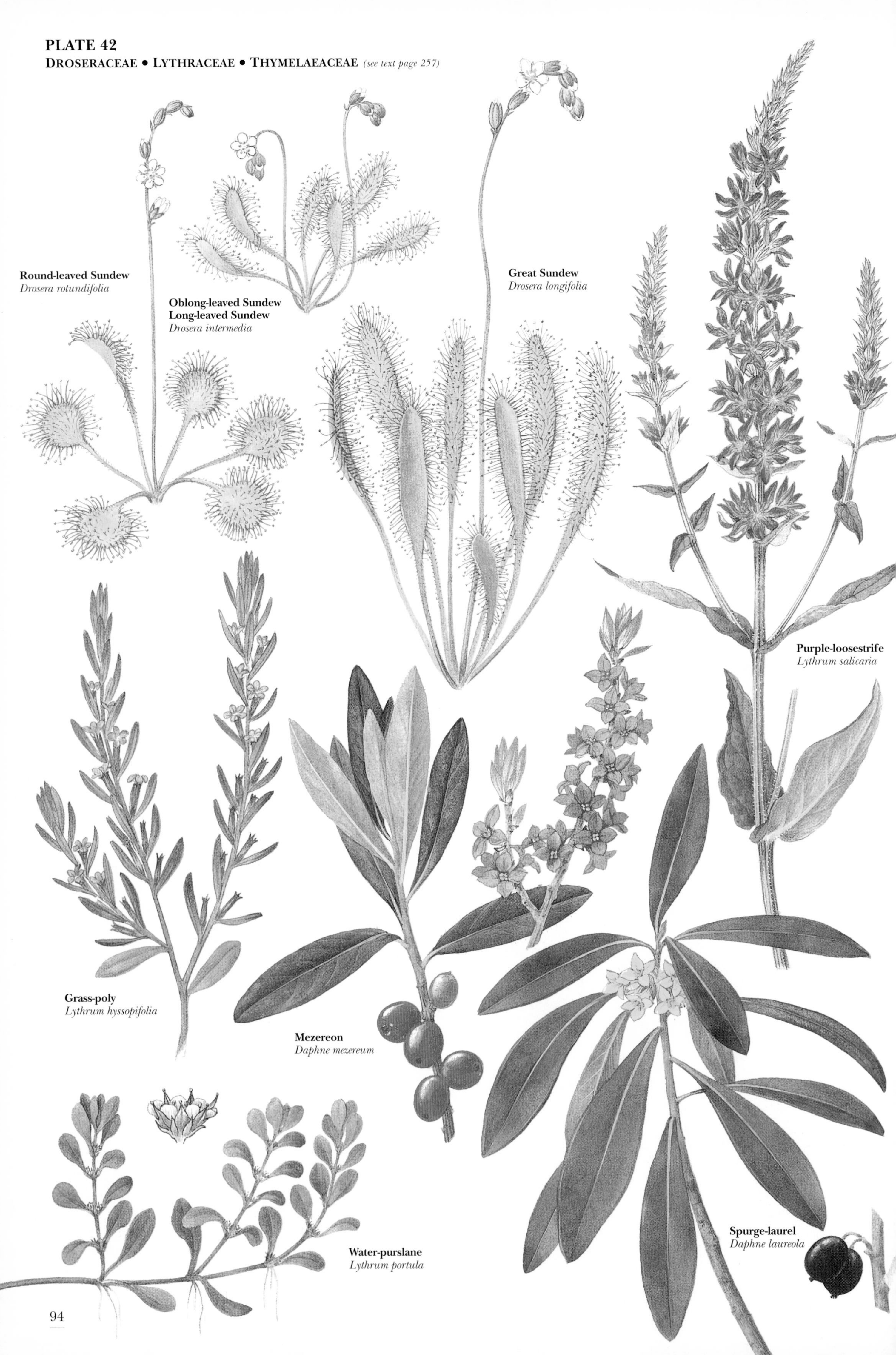

 (see text page 257)

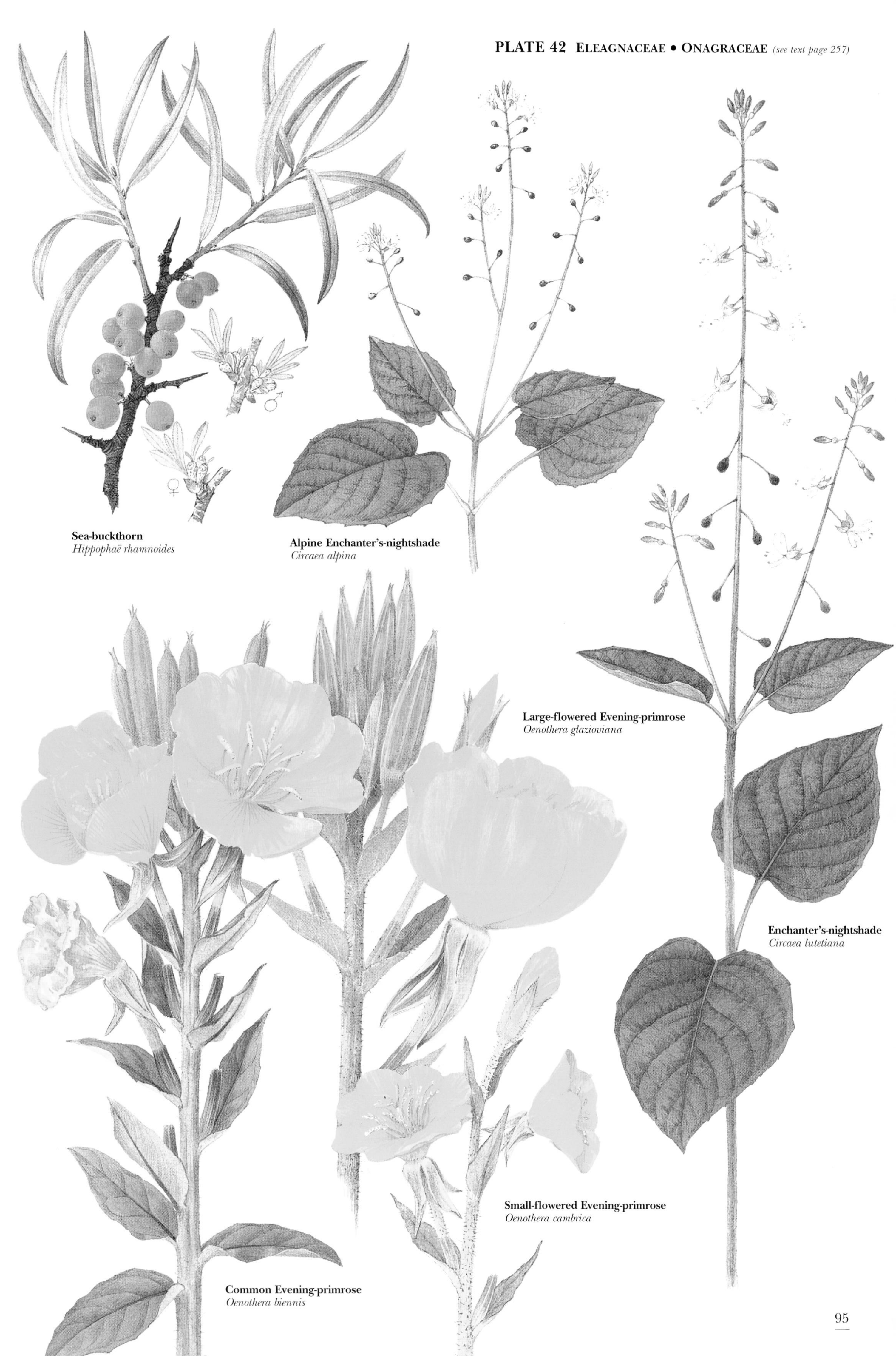

Sea-buckthorn
Hippophaë rhamnoides

Alpine Enchanter's-nightshade
Circaea alpina

Large-flowered Evening-primrose
Oenothera glazioviana

Enchanter's-nightshade
Circaea lutetiana

Small-flowered Evening-primrose
Oenothera cambrica

Common Evening-primrose
Oenothera biennis

PLATE 43

ONAGRACEAE *(see text page 259)*

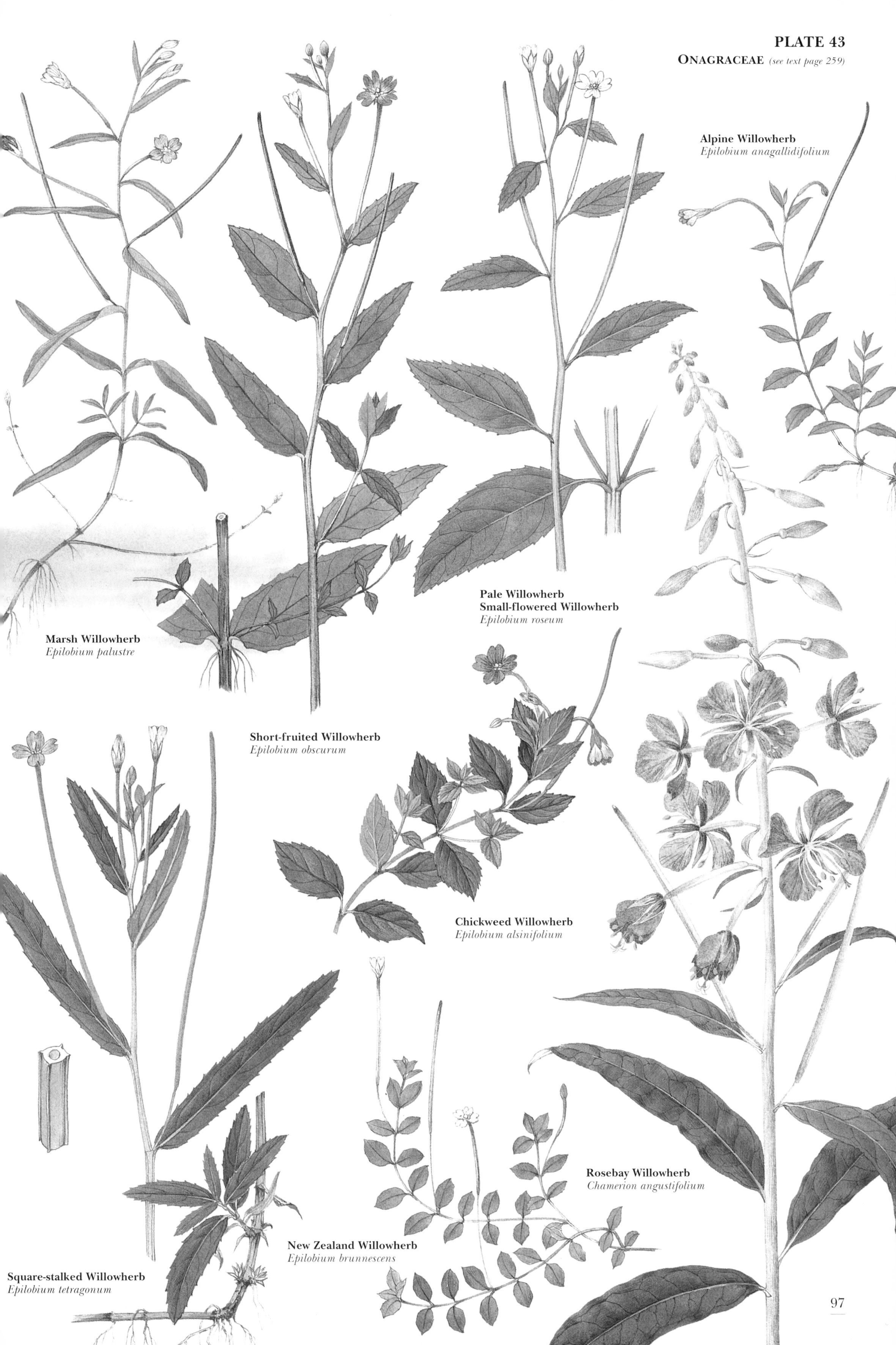
Alpine Willowherb
Epilobium anagallidifolium
Marsh Willowherb
Epilobium palustre
Pale Willowherb
Small-flowered Willowherb
Epilobium roseum
Short-fruited Willowherb
Epilobium obscurum
Chickweed Willowherb
Epilobium alsinifolium
Rosebay Willowherb
Chamerion angustifolium
New Zealand Willowherb
Epilobium brunnescens
Square-stalked Willowherb
Epilobium tetragonum

PLATE 44

Viscaceae • Santalaceae • Araliaceae • Callitrichaceae *(see text page 260)*

Various-leaved Water-starwort
Long-styled Water-starwort
Callitriche platycarpa

Mistletoe
Viscum album

Bastard-toadflax
Thesium humifusum

Common Water-starwort
Callitriche stagnalis

Blunt-fruited Water-starwort
Callitriche obtusangula

Ivy
Hedera helix

Autumnal Water-starwort
Callitriche hermaphroditica

HALORAGACEAE • HIPPURIDACEAE • CALLITRICHACEAE • APIACEAE (= UMBELLIFERAE) *(see text page 260)*

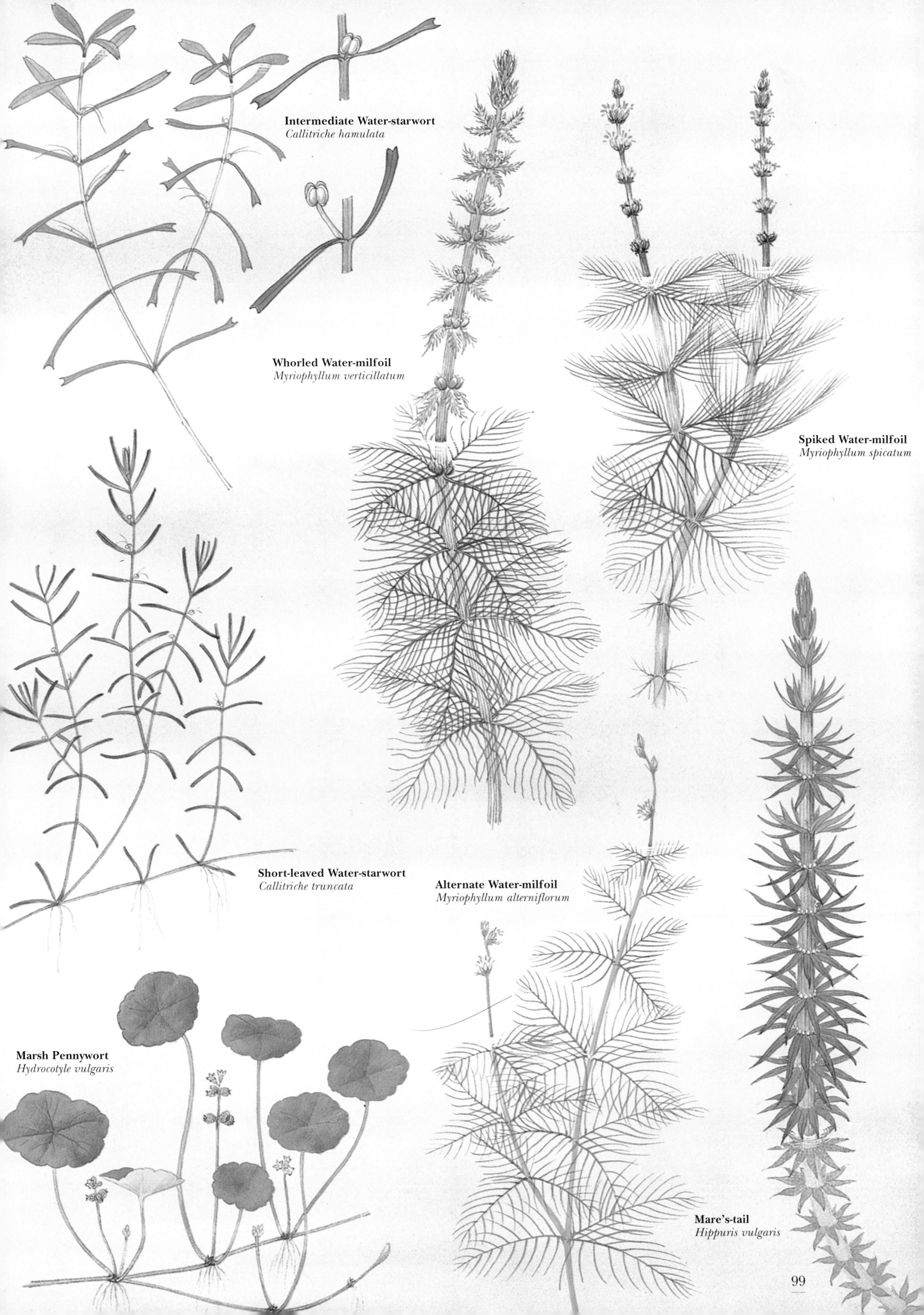

Intermediate Water-starwort
Callitriche hamulata

Whorled Water-milfoil
Myriophyllum verticillatum

Spiked Water-milfoil
Myriophyllum spicatum

Short-leaved Water-starwort
Callitriche truncata

Alternate Water-milfoil
Myriophyllum alterniflorum

Marsh Pennywort
Hydrocotyle vulgaris

Mare's-tail
Hippuris vulgaris

PLATE 45

CORNACEAE • APIACEAE (= UMBELLIFERAE)

(see text page 261)

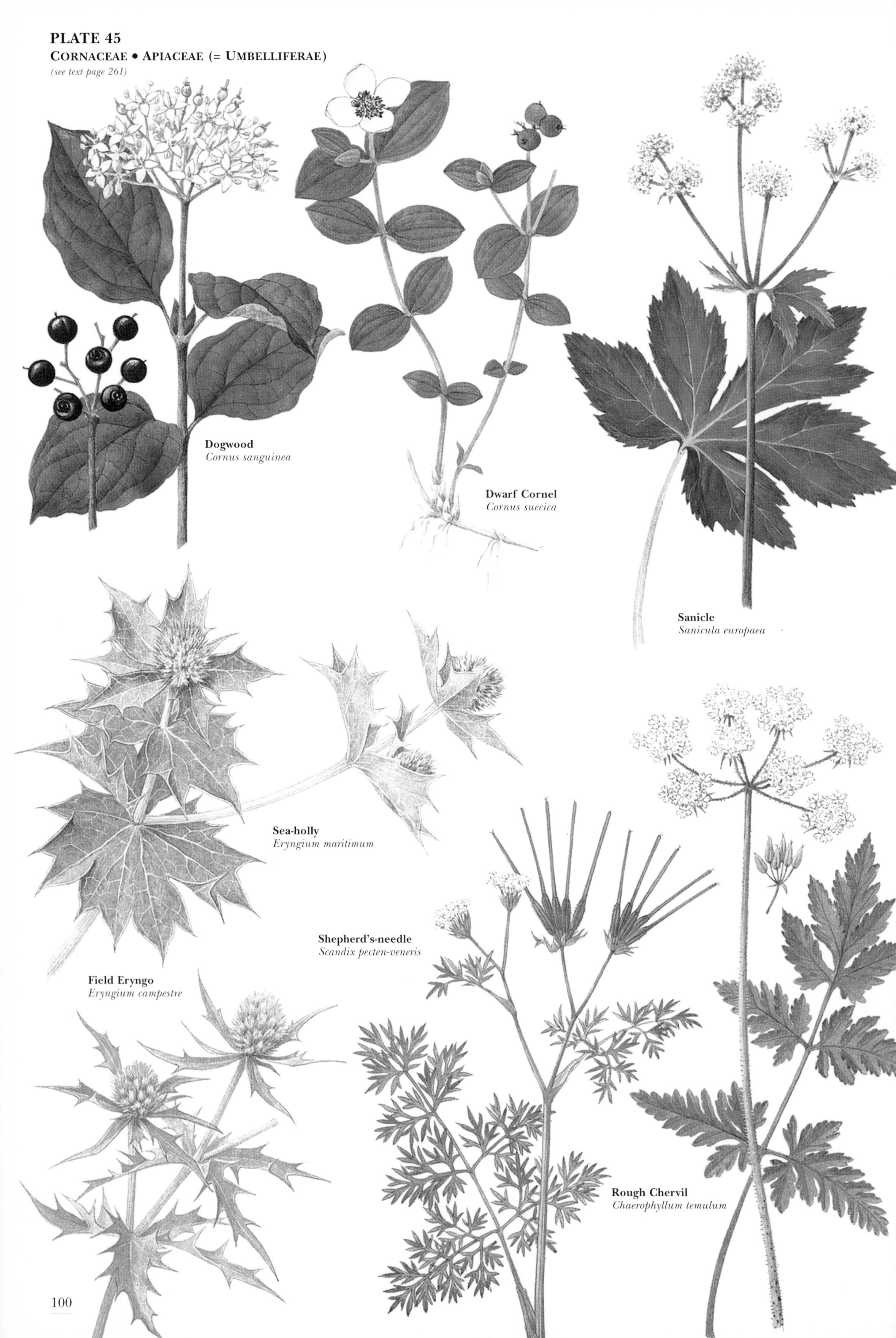

APIACEAE (= UMBELLIFERAE) *(see text page 261)*

Bur Chervil
Bur Parsley
Anthriscus caucalis

Astrantia
Astrantia major

Cow Parsley
Anthriscus sylvestris

Golden Chervil
Chaerophyllum aureum

Knotted Hedge-parsley
Torilis nodosa

Spreading Hedge-parsley
Torilis arvensis

Upright Hedge-parsley
Torilis japonica

PLATE 46

APIACEAE (= UMBELLIFERAE) *(see text page 262)*

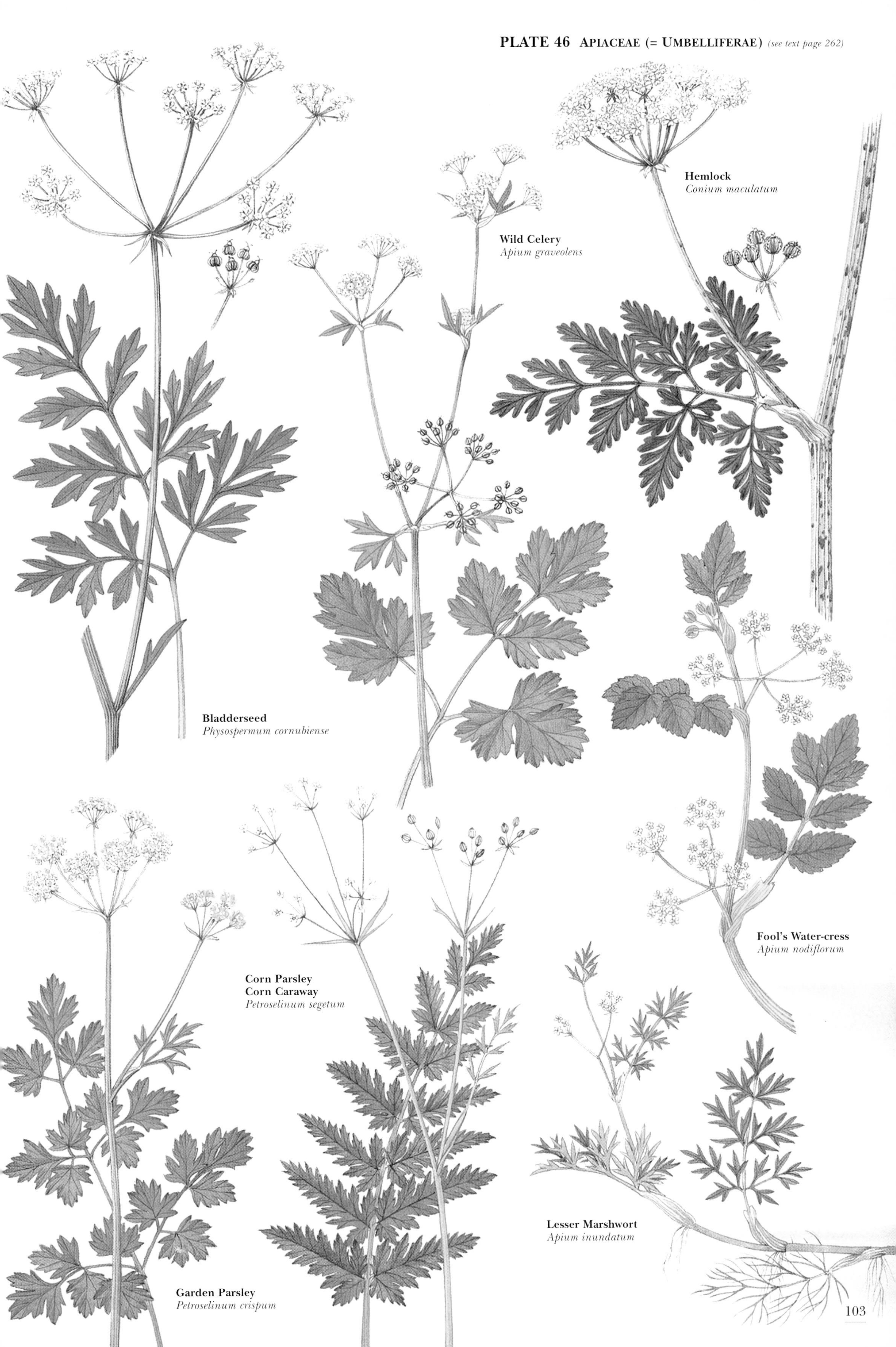
Hemlock
Conium maculatum
Wild Celery
Apium graveolens
Bladderseed
Physospermum cornubiense
Fool's Water-cress
Apium nodiflorum
Corn Parsley
Corn Caraway
Petroselinum segetum
Lesser Marshwort
Apium inundatum
Garden Parsley
Petroselinum crispum

PLATE 47

Apiaceae (= Umbelliferae) *(see text page 263)*

(see text page 263)

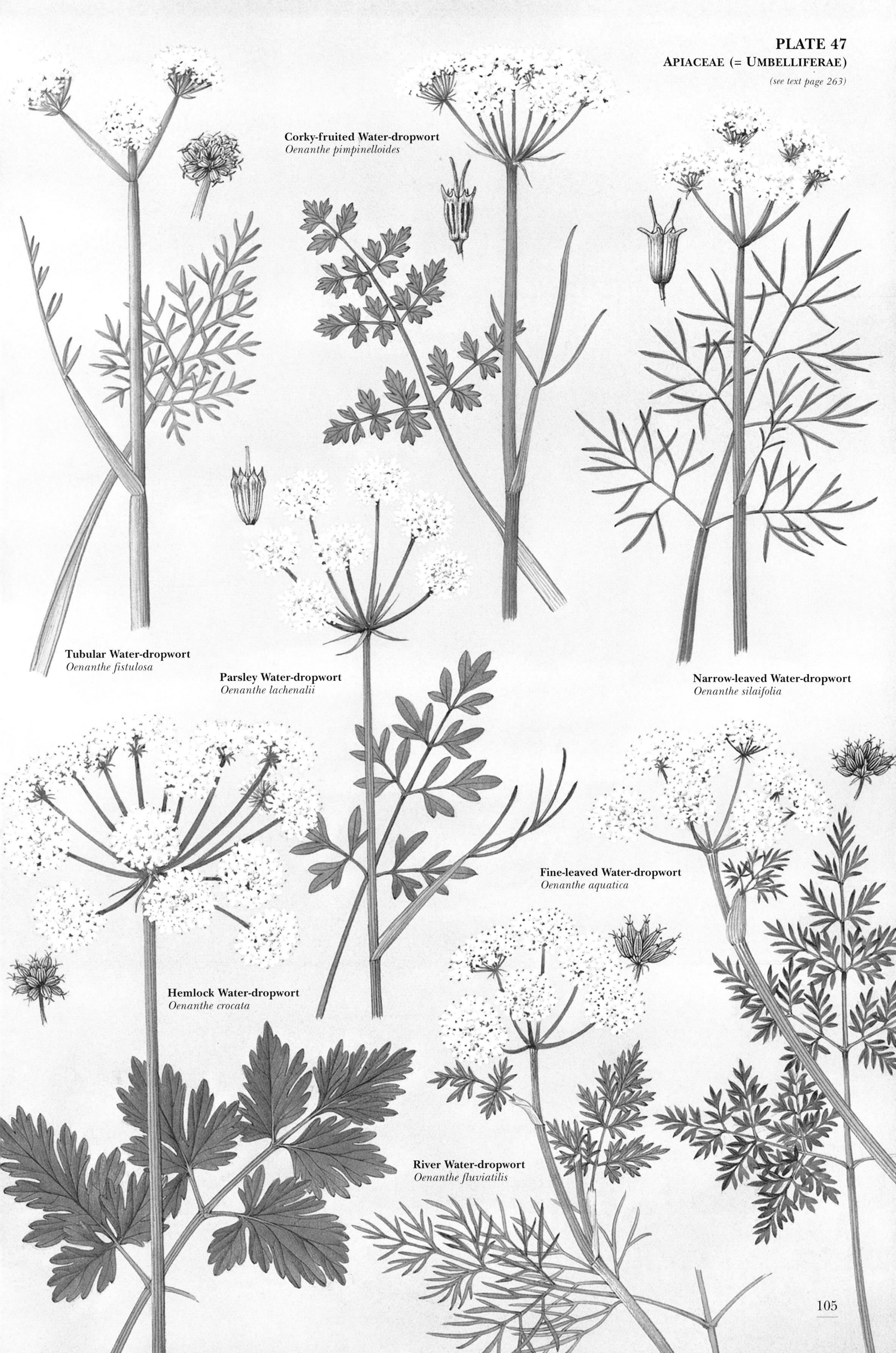
Corky-fruited Water-dropwort
Oenanthe pimpinelloides
Tubular Water-dropwort
Oenanthe fistulosa
Parsley Water-dropwort
Oenanthe lachenalii
Narrow-leaved Water-dropwort
Oenanthe silaifolia
Fine-leaved Water-dropwort
Oenanthe aquatica
Hemlock Water-dropwort
Oenanthe crocata
River Water-dropwort
Oenanthe fluviatilis

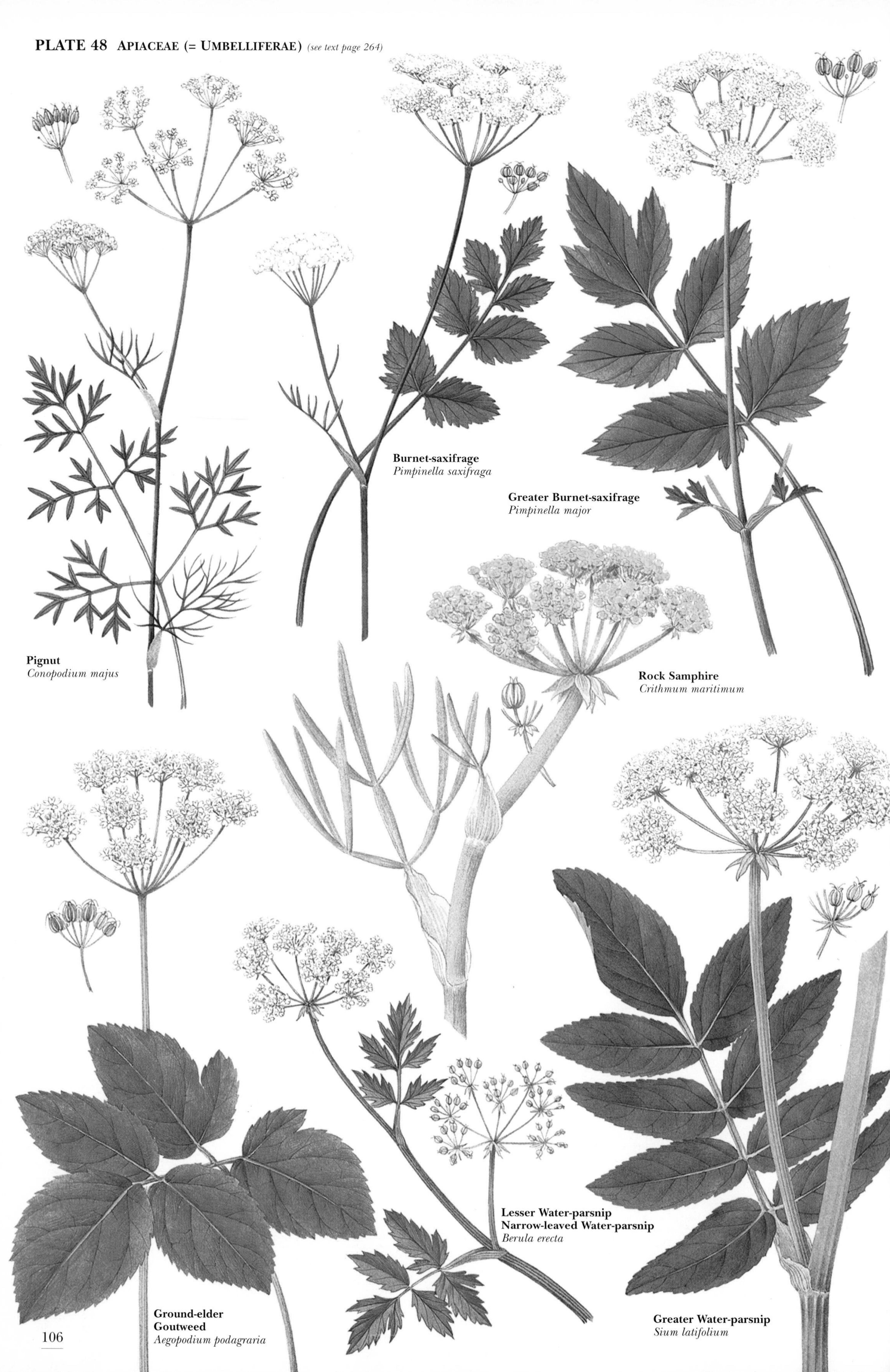
Pignut
Conopodium majus
Burnet-saxifrage
Pimpinella saxifraga
Greater Burnet-saxifrage
Pimpinella major
Rock Samphire
Crithmum maritimum
Ground-elder
Goutweed
Aegopodium podagraria
Lesser Water-parsnip
Narrow-leaved Water-parsnip
Berula erecta
Greater Water-parsnip
Sium latifolium

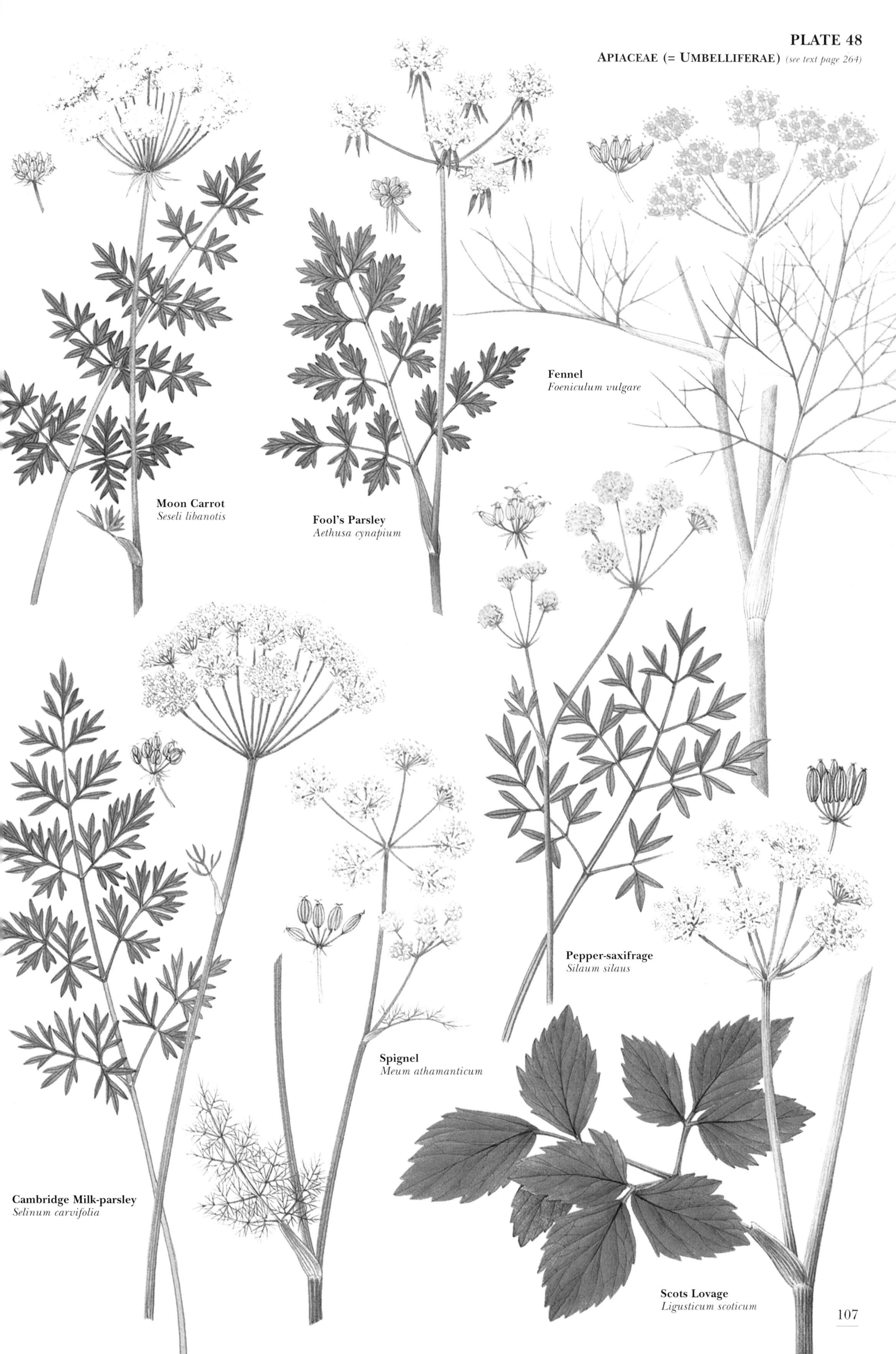
Moon Carrot
Seseli libanotis
Fool's Parsley
Aethusa cynapium
Fennel
Foeniculum vulgare
Pepper-saxifrage
Silaum silaus
Cambridge Milk-parsley
Selinum carvifolia
Spignel
Meum athamanticum
Scots Lovage
Ligusticum scoticum

PLATE 49
APIACEAE (= UMBELLIFERAE) (see text page 265)
Giant Hogweed
Heracleum mantegazzianum
Hog's Fennel
Peucedanum officinale
Milk-parsley
Peucedanum palustre
Hogweed
Heracleum sphondylium
Wild Carrot
Daucus carota
Hartwort
Tordylium maximum
Wild Angelica
Angelica sylvestris

(see text page 265)

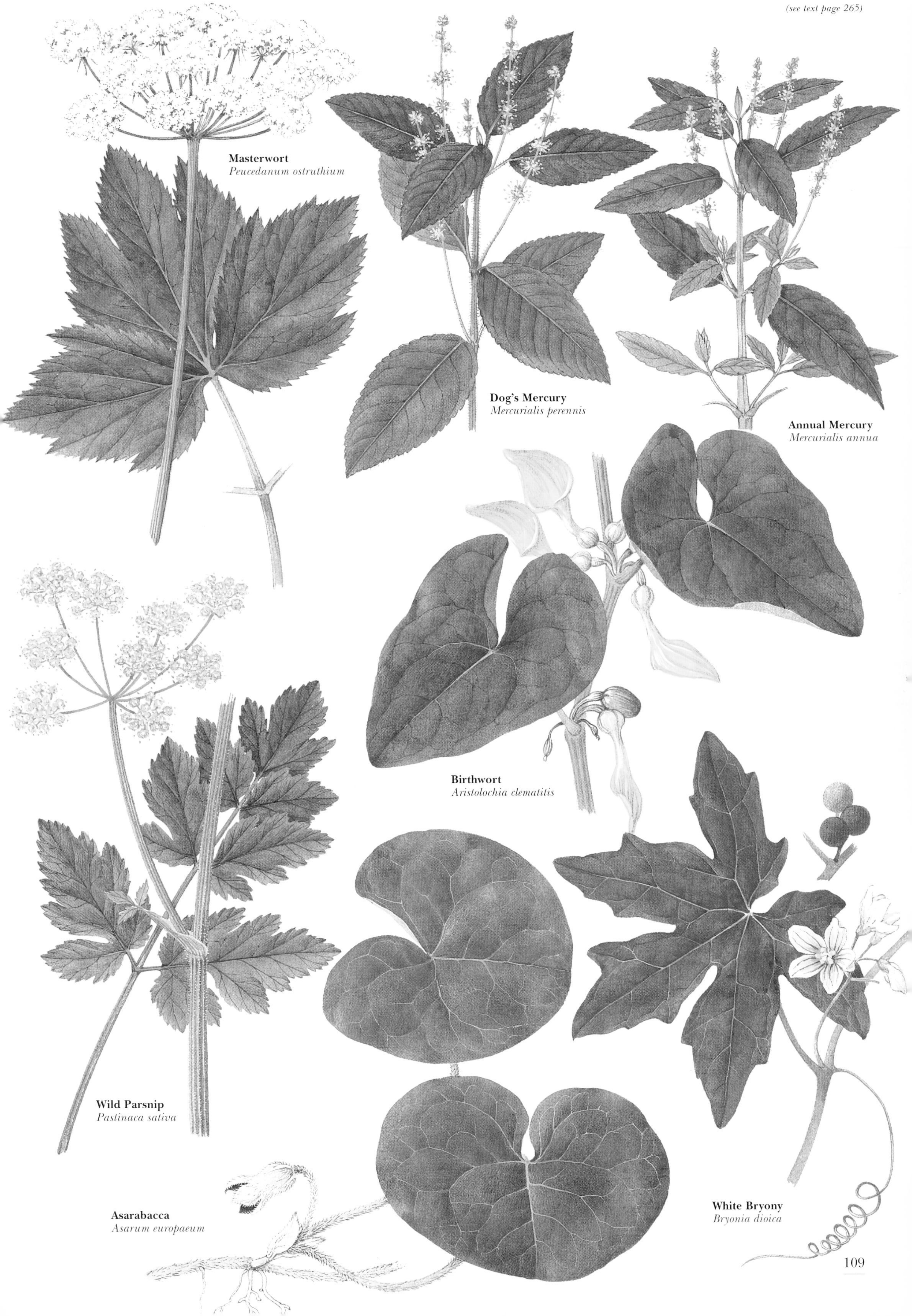

Masterwort
Peucedanum ostruthium

Dog's Mercury
Mercurialis perennis

Annual Mercury
Mercurialis annua

Birthwort
Aristolochia clematitis

Wild Parsnip
Pastinaca sativa

Asarabacca
Asarum europaeum

White Bryony
Bryonia dioica

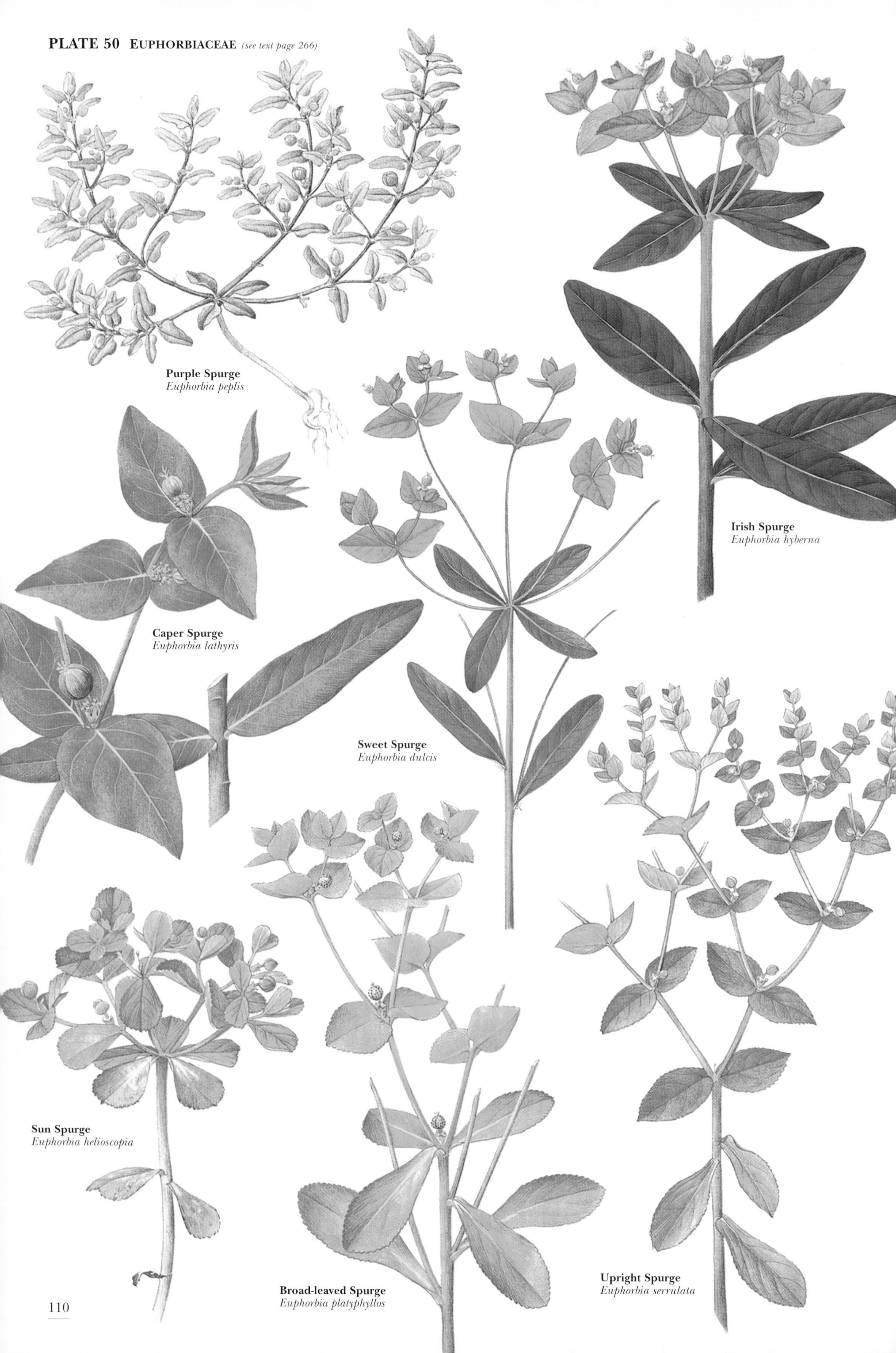
Purple Spurge
Euphorbia peplis
Irish Spurge
Euphorbia hyberna
Caper Spurge
Euphorbia lathyris
Sweet Spurge
Euphorbia dulcis
Sun Spurge
Euphorbia helioscopia
Broad-leaved Spurge
Euphorbia platyphyllos
Upright Spurge
Euphorbia serrulata

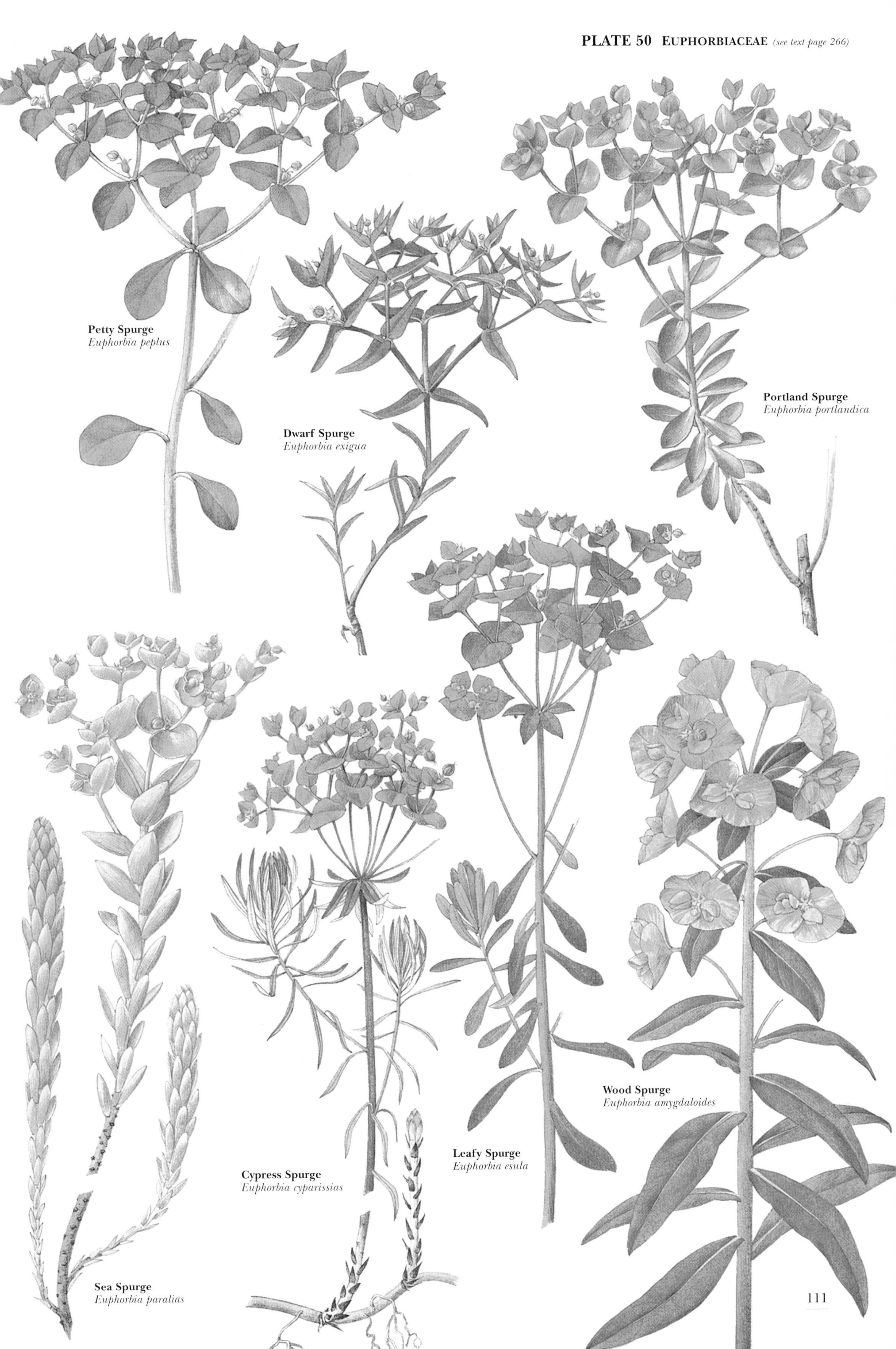
Petty Spurge
Euphorbia peplus
Dwarf Spurge
Euphorbia exigua
Portland Spurge
Euphorbia portlandica
Sea Spurge
Euphorbia paralias
Cypress Spurge
Euphorbia cyparissias
Leafy Spurge
Euphorbia esula
Wood Spurge
Euphorbia amygdaloides

PLATE 51

POLYGONACEAE *(see text page 267)*

 (see text page 267)

PLATE 52
POLYGONACEAE *(see text page 268)*

 (see text page 268)

Mountain Sorrel
Oxyria digyna
Sheep's Sorrel
Rumex acetosella
Common Sorrel
Rumex acetosa
French Sorrel
Rumex scutatus
Water Dock
Rumex hydrolapathum
Monk's-rhubarb
Rumex pseudoalpinus
Scottish Dock
Rumex aquaticus

Patience Dock
Rumex patientia
Greek Dock
Rumex cristatus
Curled Dock
Rumex crispus
Northern Dock
Rumex longifolius
Broad-leaved Dock
Rumex obtusifolius

 (see text page 269)

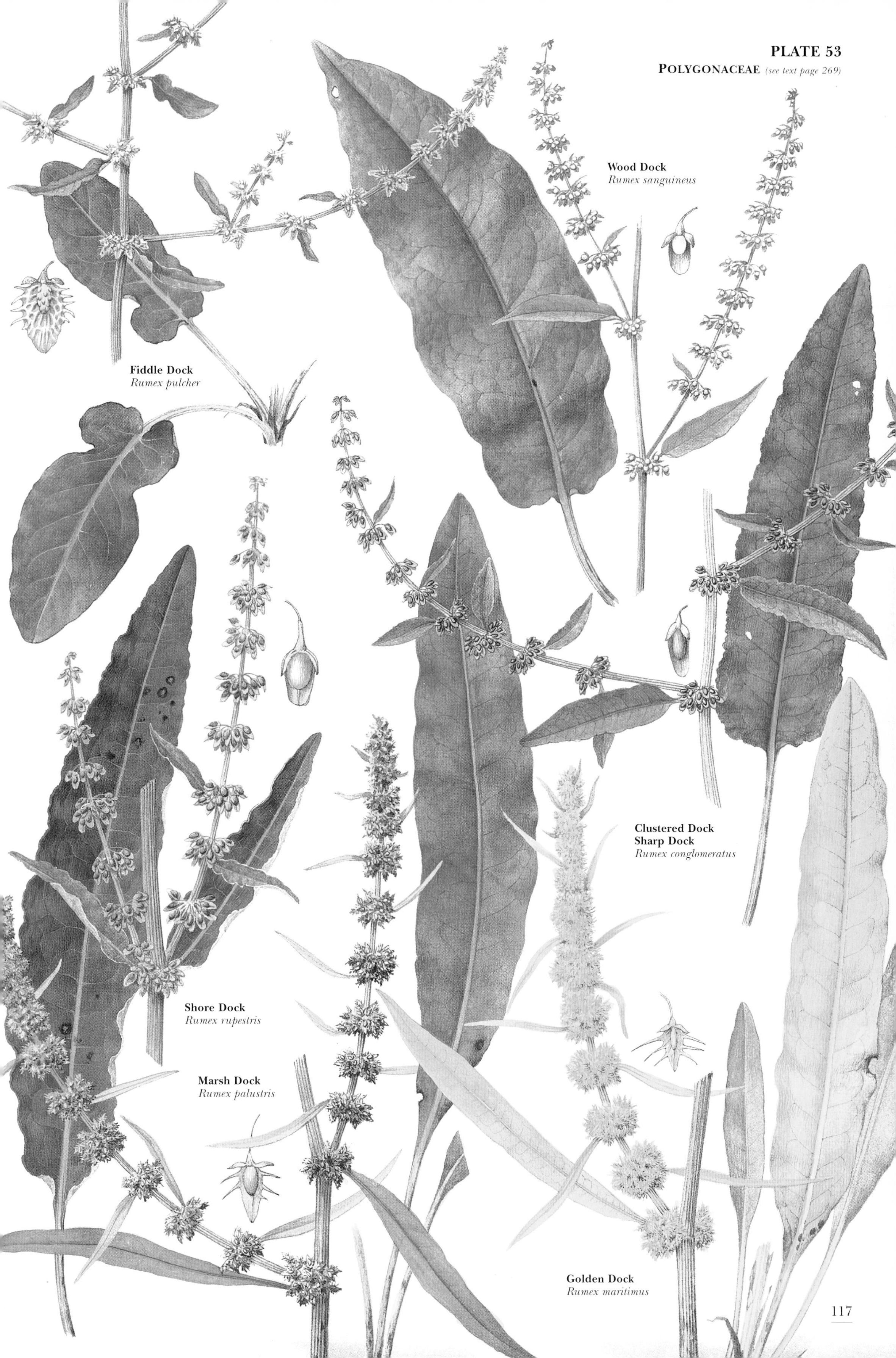
Wood Dock
Rumex sanguineus
Fiddle Dock
Rumex pulcher
Clustered Dock
Sharp Dock
Rumex conglomeratus
Shore Dock
Rumex rupestris
Marsh Dock
Rumex palustris
Golden Dock
Rumex maritimus

PLATE 54

URTICACEAE • CANNABACEAE • MYRICACEAE *(see text page 270)*

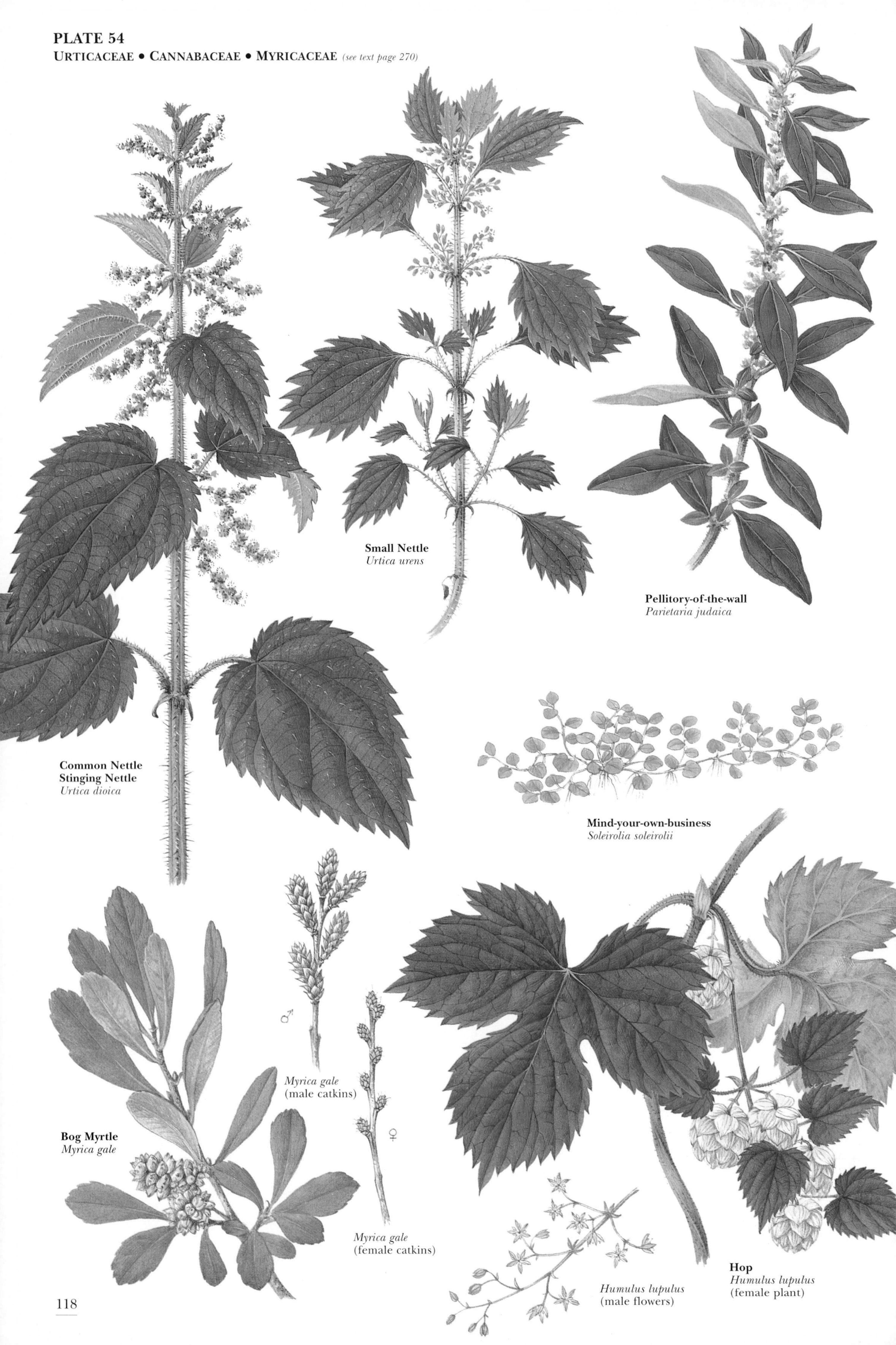

Small Nettle
Urtica urens

Pellitory-of-the-wall
Parietaria judaica

Common Nettle
Stinging Nettle
Urtica dioica

Mind-your-own-business
Soleirolia soleirolii

Myrica gale
(male catkins)

Bog Myrtle
Myrica gale

Myrica gale
(female catkins)

Hop
Humulus lupulus
(female plant)

Humulus lupulus
(male flowers)

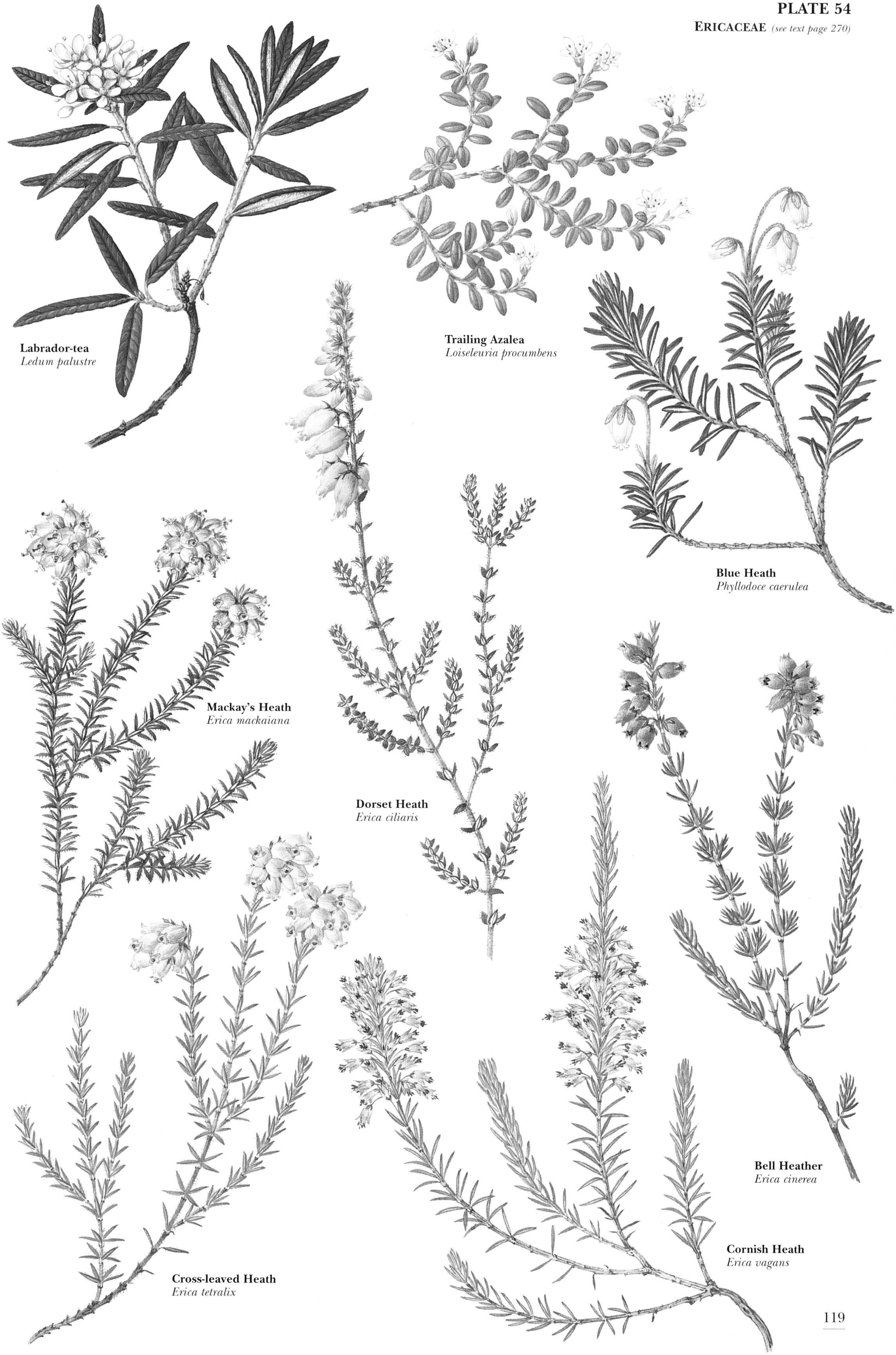

Labrador-tea
Ledum palustre

Trailing Azalea
Loiseleuria procumbens

Blue Heath
Phyllodoce caerulea

Mackay's Heath
Erica mackaiana

Dorset Heath
Erica ciliaris

Bell Heather
Erica cinerea

Cornish Heath
Erica vagans

Cross-leaved Heath
Erica tetralix

PLATE 55
ERICACEAE *(see text page 271)*

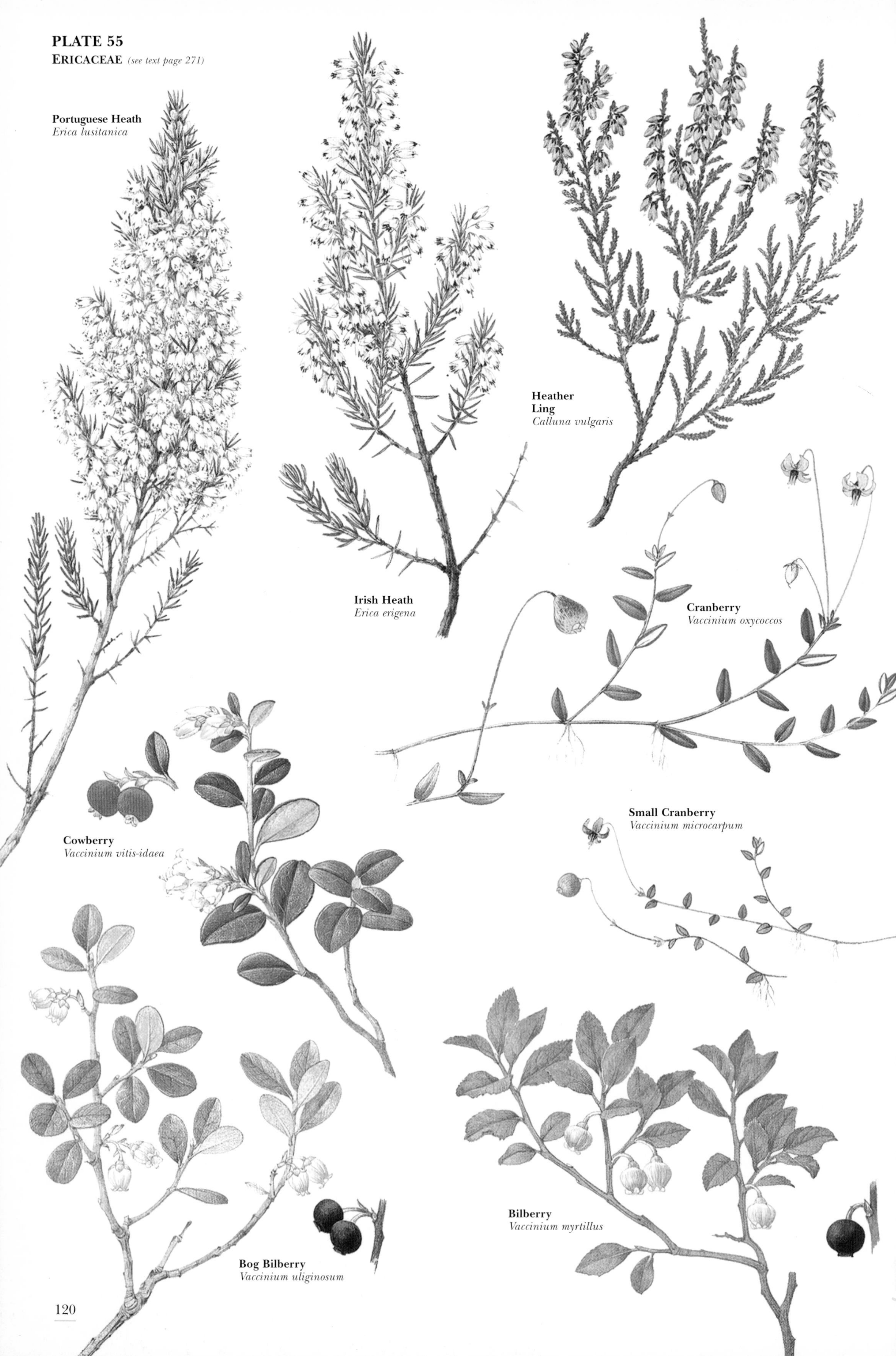

 (see text page 271)

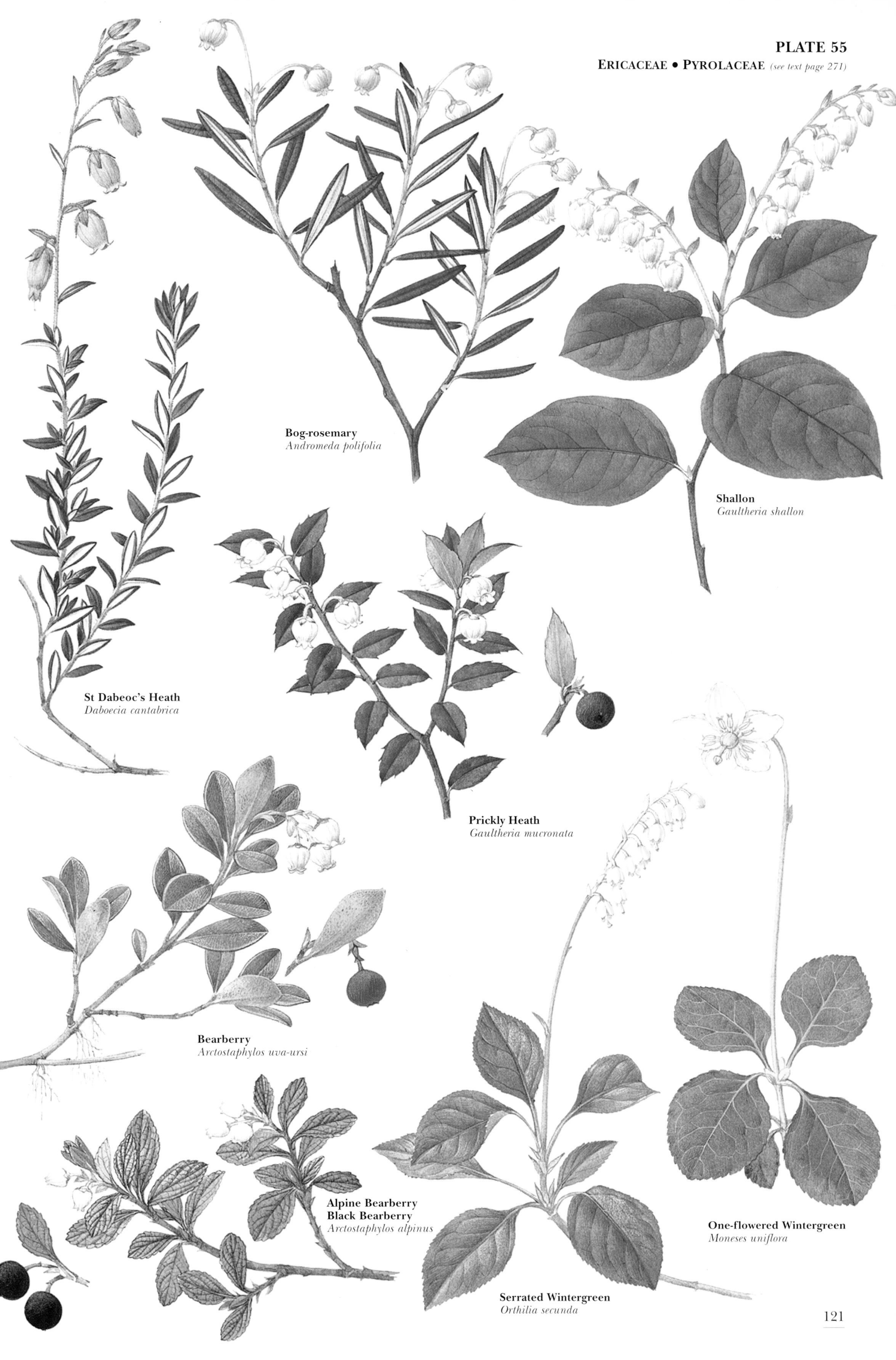
Bog-rosemary
Andromeda polifolia
Shallon
Gaultheria shallon
St Dabeoc's Heath
Daboecia cantabrica
Prickly Heath
Gaultheria mucronata
Bearberry
Arctostaphylos uva-ursi
Alpine Bearberry
Black Bearberry
Arctostaphylos alpinus
One-flowered Wintergreen
Moneses uniflora
Serrated Wintergreen
Orthilia secunda

PLATE 56

PYROLACEAE • MONOTROPACEAE • EMPETRACEAE DIAPENSIACEAE • PLUMBAGINACEAE *(see text page 272)*

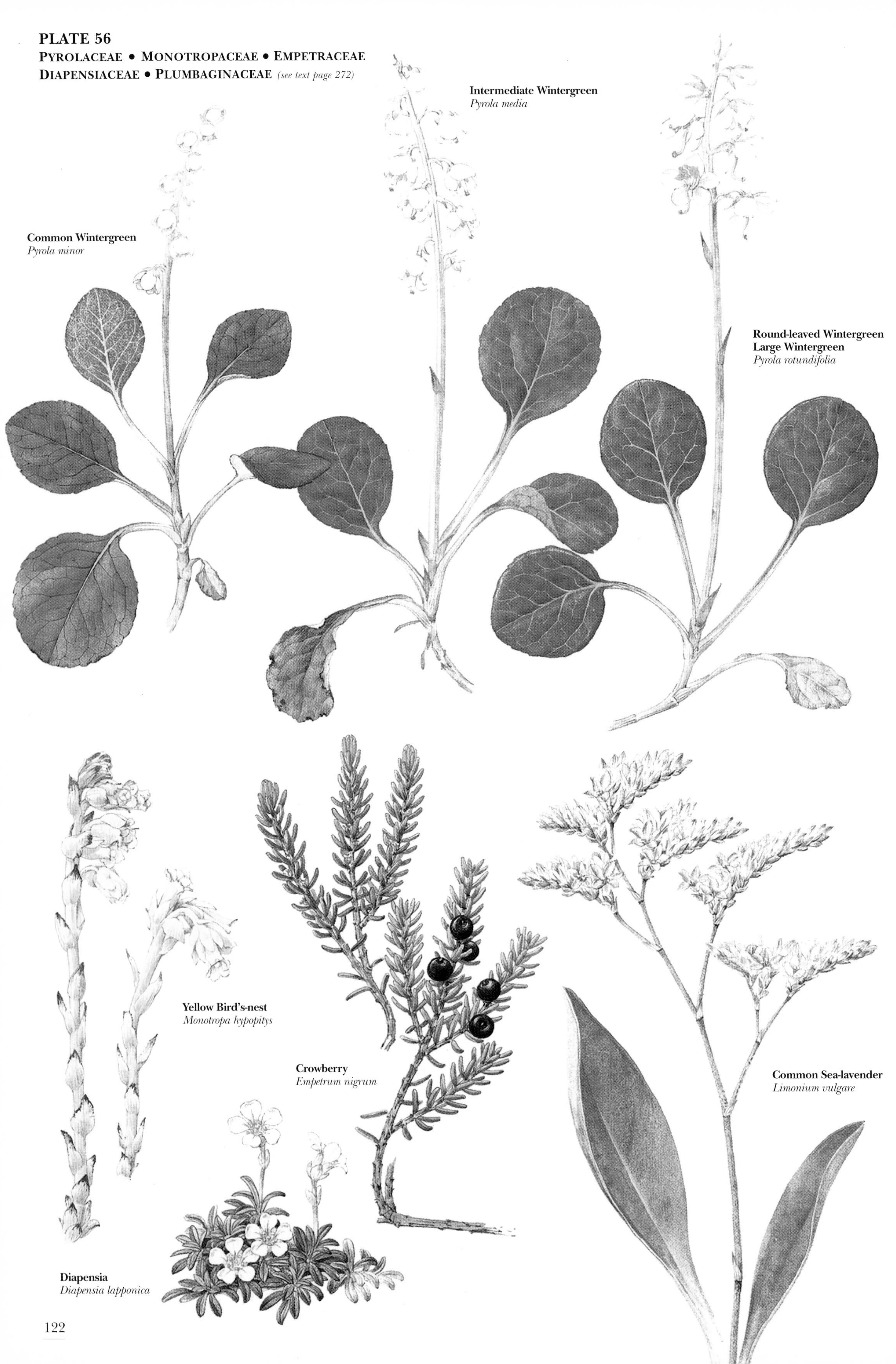

Intermediate Wintergreen
Pyrola media

Common Wintergreen
Pyrola minor

Round-leaved Wintergreen
Large Wintergreen
Pyrola rotundifolia

Yellow Bird's-nest
Monotropa hypopitys

Crowberry
Empetrum nigrum

Common Sea-lavender
Limonium vulgare

Diapensia
Diapensia lapponica

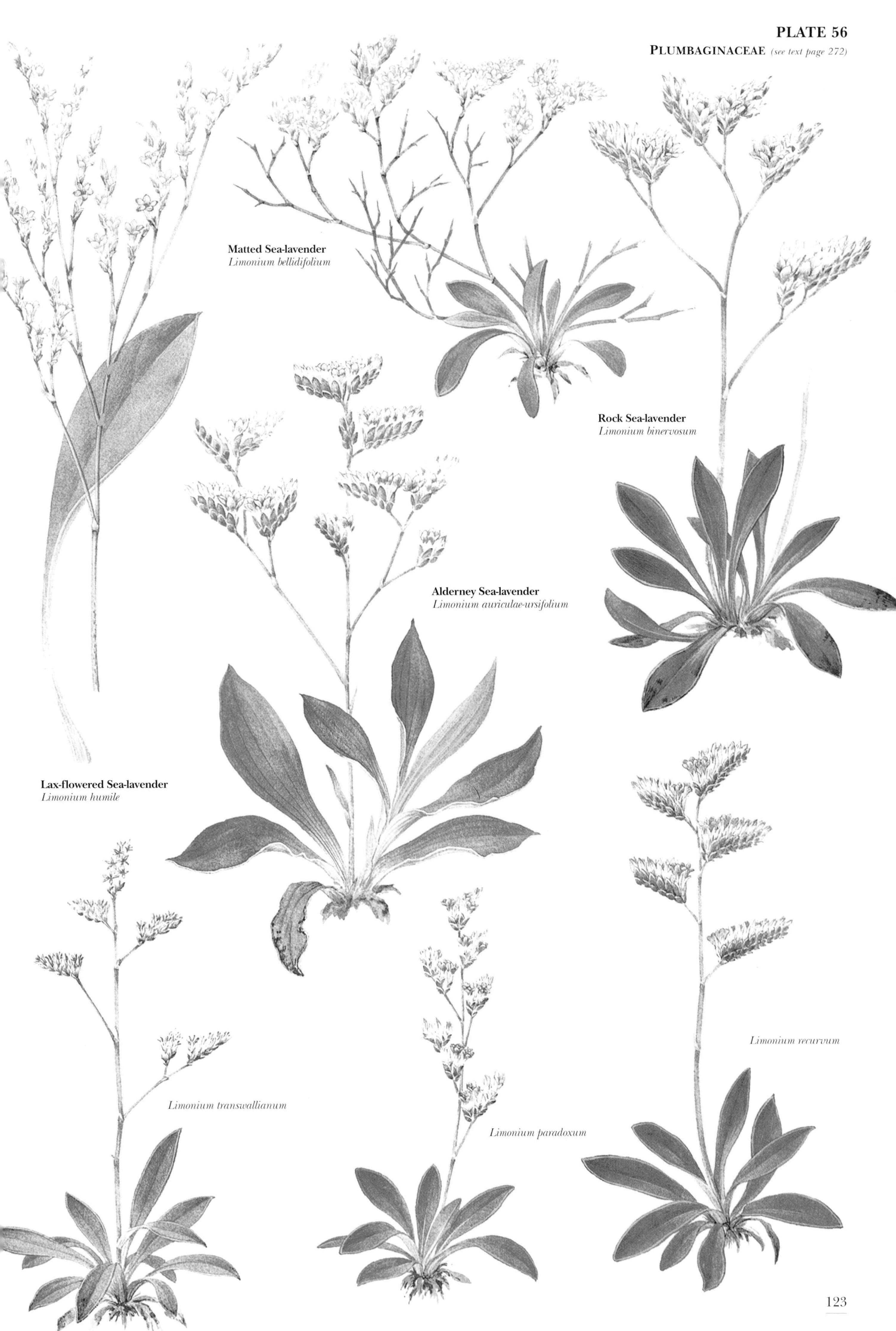
Matted Sea-lavender
Limonium bellidifolium
Rock Sea-lavender
Limonium binervosum
Alderney Sea-lavender
Limonium auriculae-ursifolium
Lax-flowered Sea-lavender
Limonium humile
Limonium recurvum
Limonium transwallianum
Limonium paradoxum

PLATE 57

PLUMBAGINACEAE • PRIMULACEAE *(see text page 273)*

Thrift
Sea Pink
Armeria maritima

Jersey Thrift
Armeria arenaria

Primrose
Primula vulgaris

Cowslip
Primula veris

Scottish Primrose
Primula scotica

Oxlip
Primula elatior

Bird's-eye Primrose
Primula farinosa

Yellow Pimpernel
Lysimachia nemorum

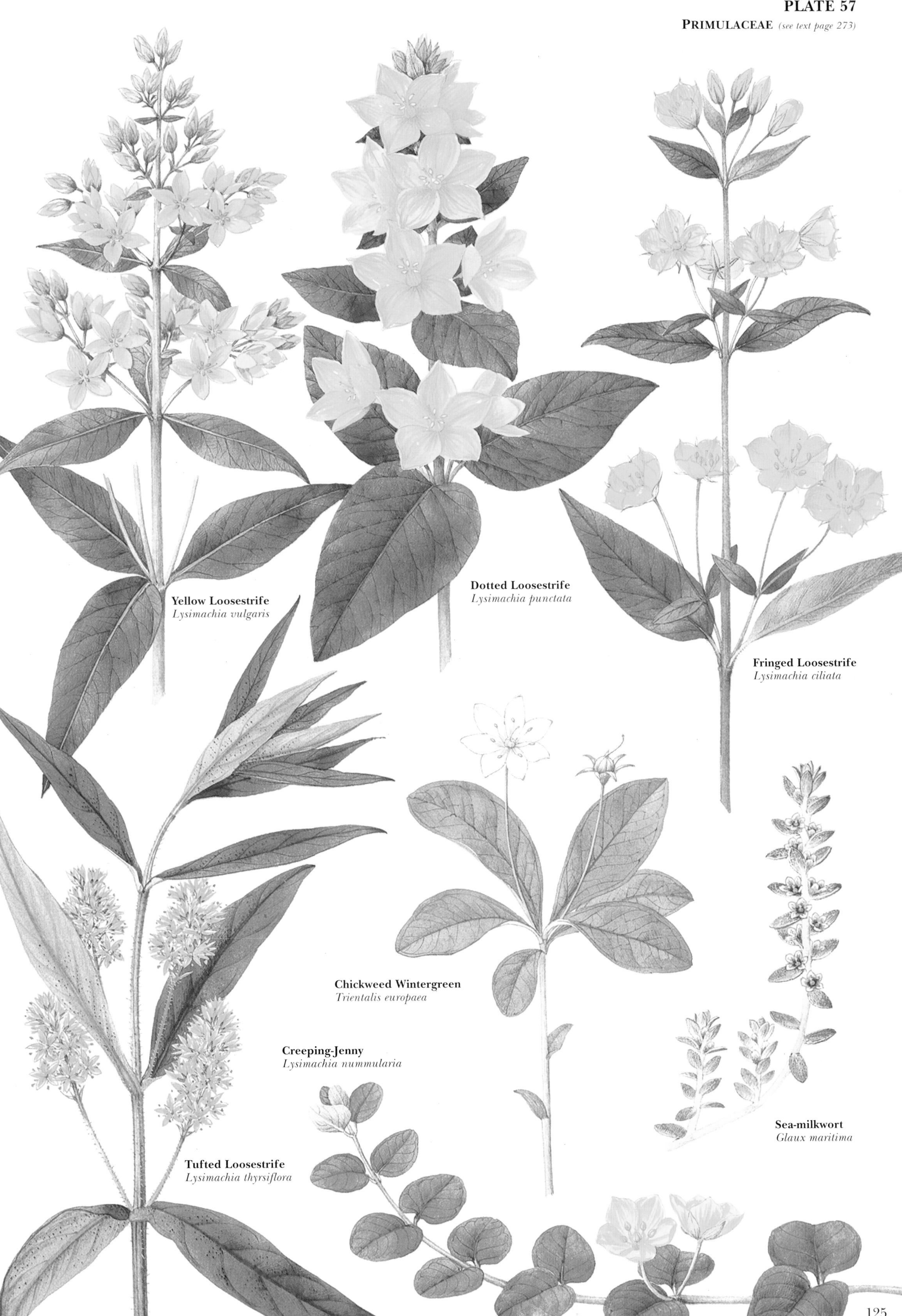
Yellow Loosestrife
Lysimachia vulgaris
Dotted Loosestrife
Lysimachia punctata
Fringed Loosestrife
Lysimachia ciliata
Chickweed Wintergreen
Trientalis europaea
Creeping-Jenny
Lysimachia nummularia
Sea-milkwort
Glaux maritima
Tufted Loosestrife
Lysimachia thyrsiflora

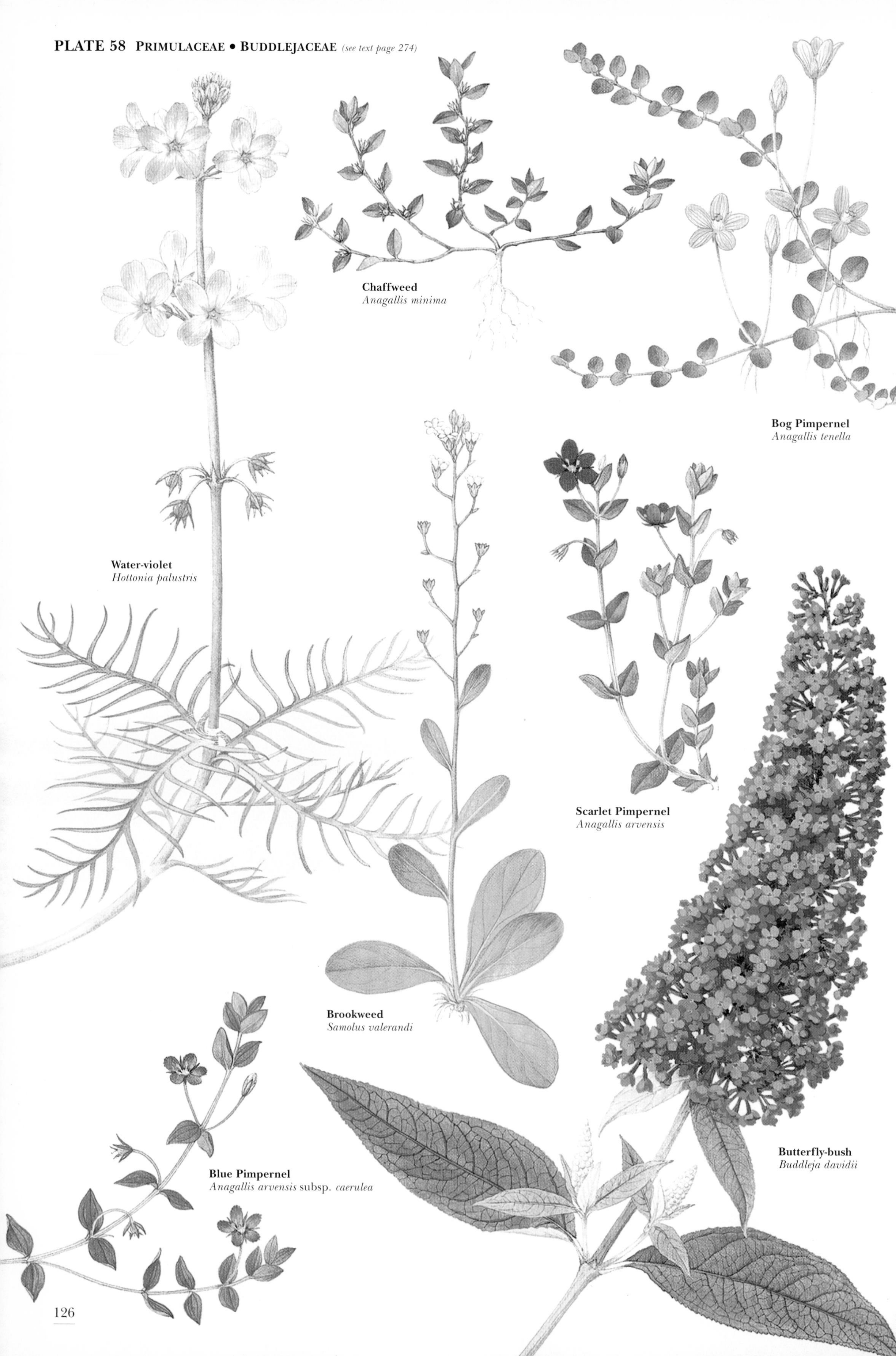
Chaffweed
Anagallis minima
Bog Pimpernel
Anagallis tenella
Water-violet
Hottonia palustris
Scarlet Pimpernel
Anagallis arvensis
Brookweed
Samolus valerandi
Butterfly-bush
Buddleja davidii
Blue Pimpernel
Anagallis arvensis subsp. *caerulea*

OLEACEAE • APOCYNACEAE • GENTIANACEAE (see text page 274)

Lilac
Syringa vulgaris

Garden Privet
Ligustrum ovalifolium

Wild Privet
Ligustrum vulgare

Lesser Periwinkle
Vinca minor

Guernsey Centaury
Exaculum pusillum

Greater Periwinkle
Vinca major

Yellow Centaury
Cicendia filiformis

PLATE 59
GENTIANACEAE *(see text page 275)*

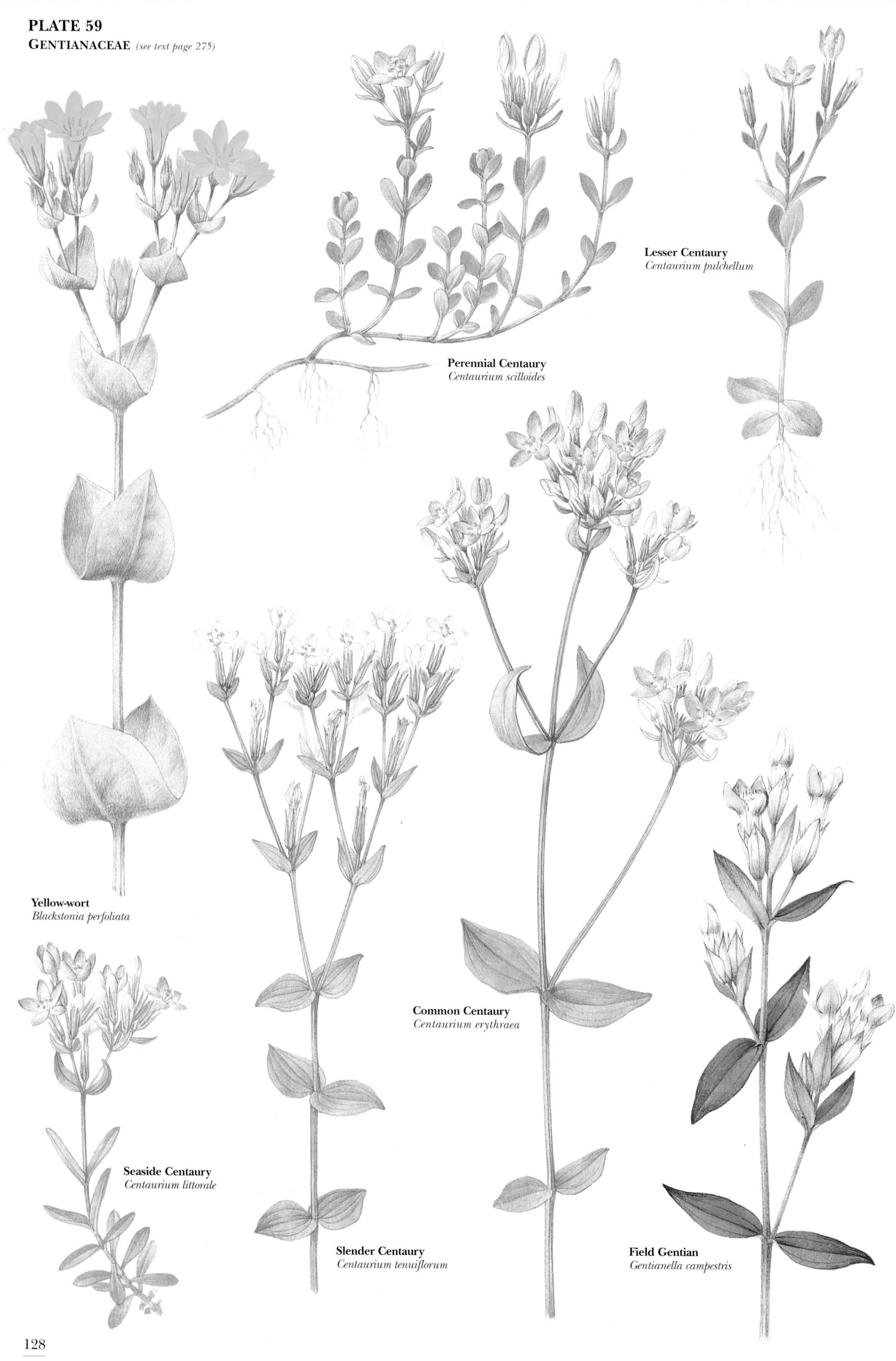

PLATE 59

GENTIANACEAE *(see text page 275)*

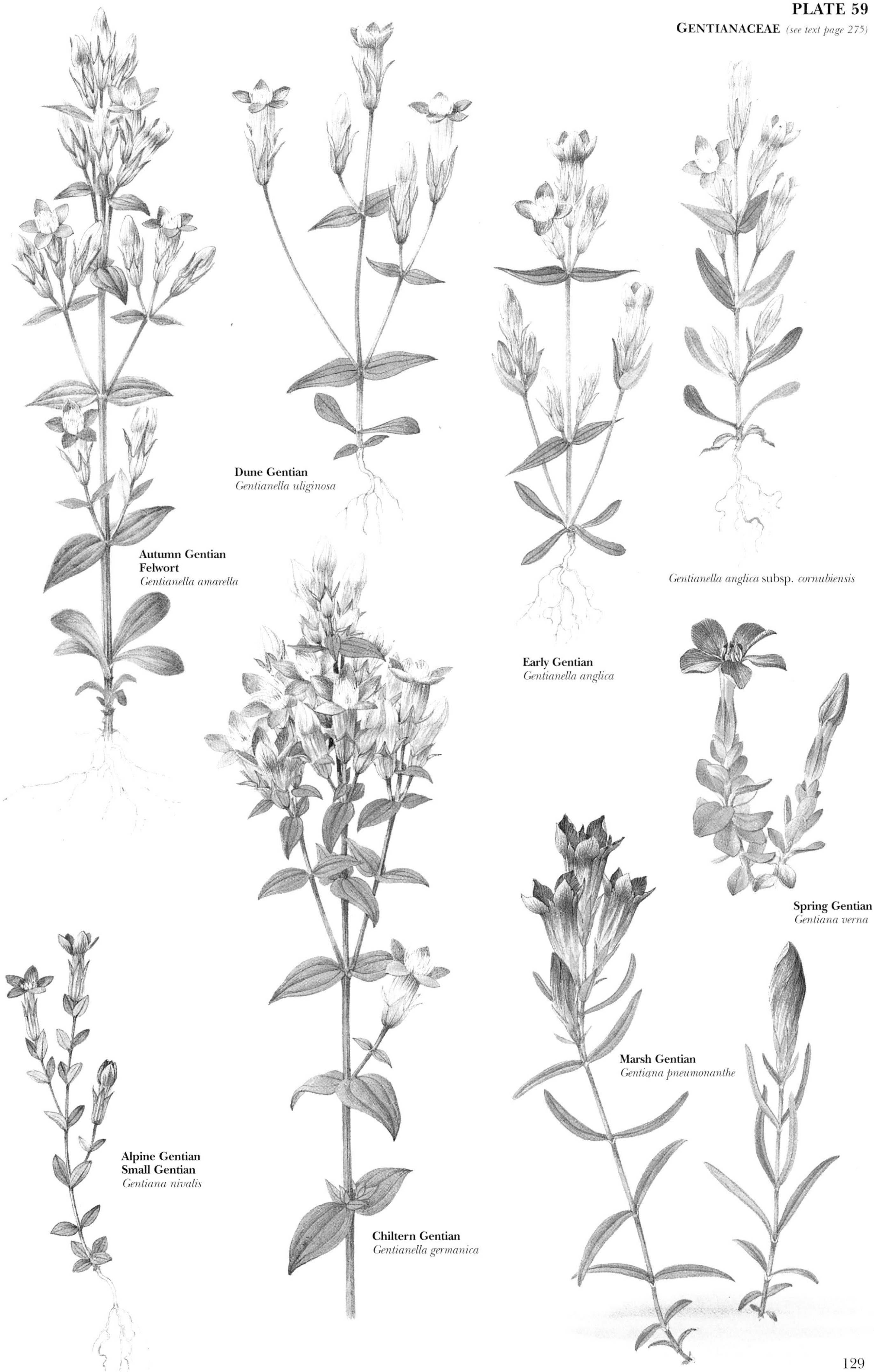

Dune Gentian
Gentianella uliginosa
Autumn Gentian
Felwort
Gentianella amarella
Early Gentian
Gentianella anglica
Gentianella anglica subsp. cornubiensis
Spring Gentian
Gentiana verna
Marsh Gentian
Gentiana pneumonanthe
Alpine Gentian
Small Gentian
Gentiana nivalis
Chiltern Gentian
Gentianella germanica

PLATE 60
MENYANTHACEAE • POLEMONIACEAE • BORAGINACEAE *(see text page 276)*

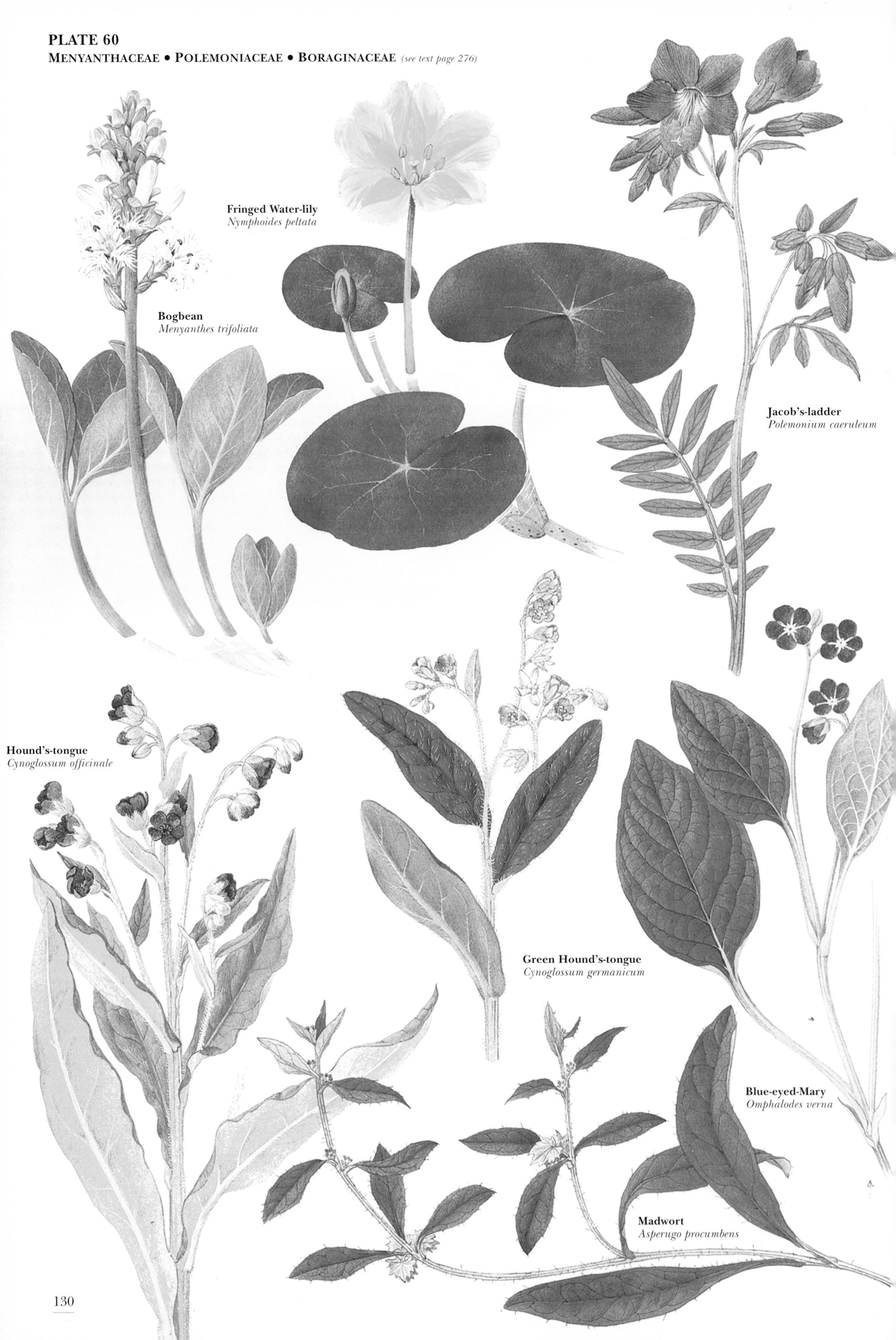

Fringed Water-lily
Nymphoides peltata

Bogbean
Menyanthes trifoliata

Jacob's-ladder
Polemonium caeruleum

Hound's-tongue
Cynoglossum officinale

Green Hound's-tongue
Cynoglossum germanicum

Blue-eyed-Mary
Omphalodes verna

Madwort
Asperugo procumbens

Common Comfrey
Symphytum officinale
Russian Comfrey
Blue Comfrey
Symphytum × uplandicum
Rough Comfrey
Symphytum asperum
White Comfrey
Symphytum orientale
Borage
Borago officinalis
Tuberous Comfrey
Symphytum tuberosum

Narrow-leaved Lungwort
Pulmonaria longifolia

Green Alkanet
Pentaglottis sempervirens

Bugloss
Anchusa arvensis

Creeping Forget-me-not
Myosotis secunda

Water Forget-me-not
Myosotis scorpioides

Lungwort
Pulmonaria officinalis

Pale Forget-me-not
Myosotis stolonifera

Tufted Forget-me-not
Myosotis laxa

Jersey Forget-me-not
Myosotis sicula

Alpine Forget-me-not
Myosotis alpestris

Field Forget-me-not
Common Forget-me-not
Myosotis arvensis

Wood Forget-me-not
Myosotis sylvatica

Early Forget-me-not
Myosotis ramosissima

Changing Forget-me-not
Yellow and blue Forget-me-not
Myosotis discolor

PLATE 62

BORAGINACEAE *(see text page 278)*

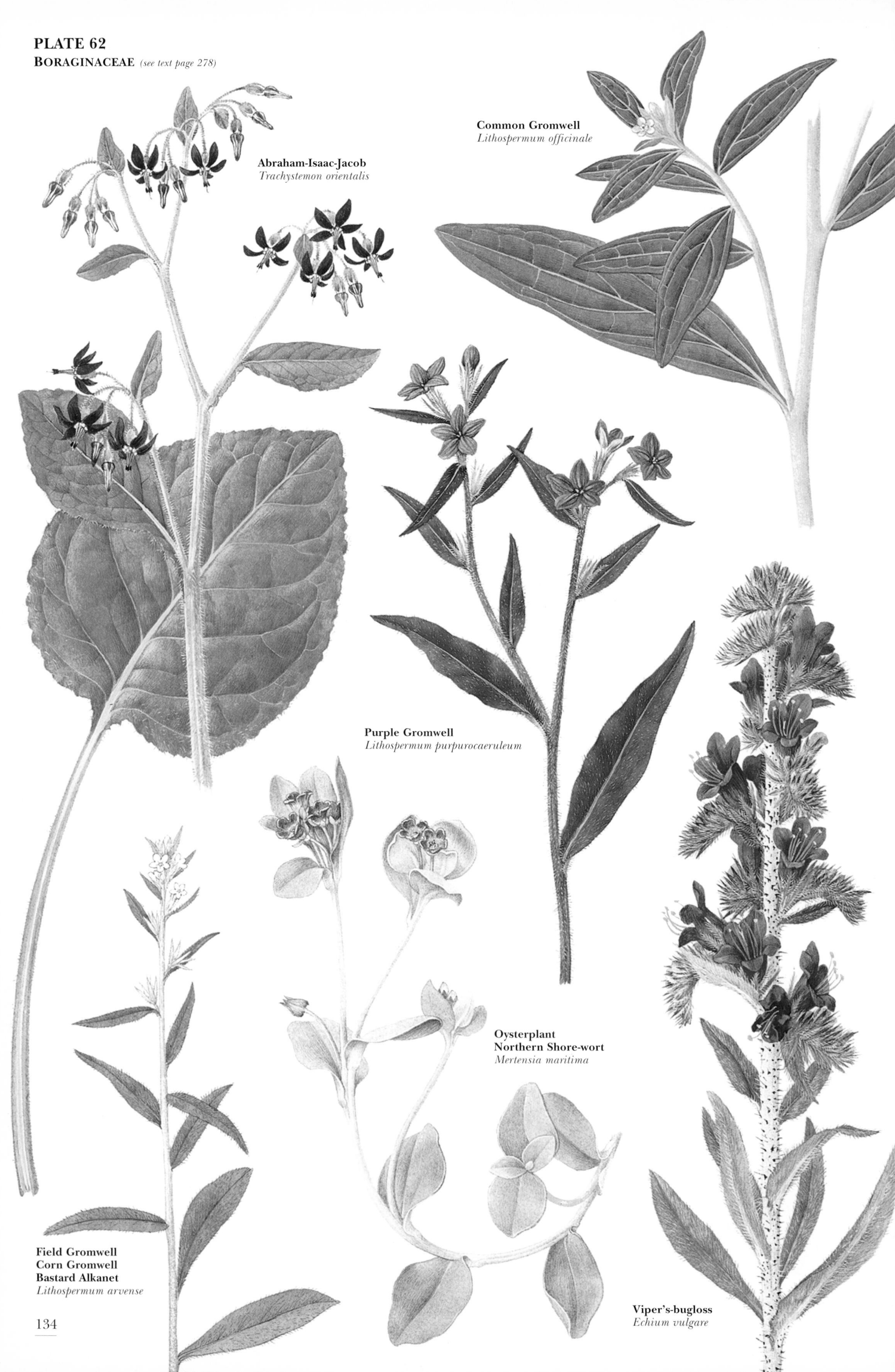

 (see text page 278)

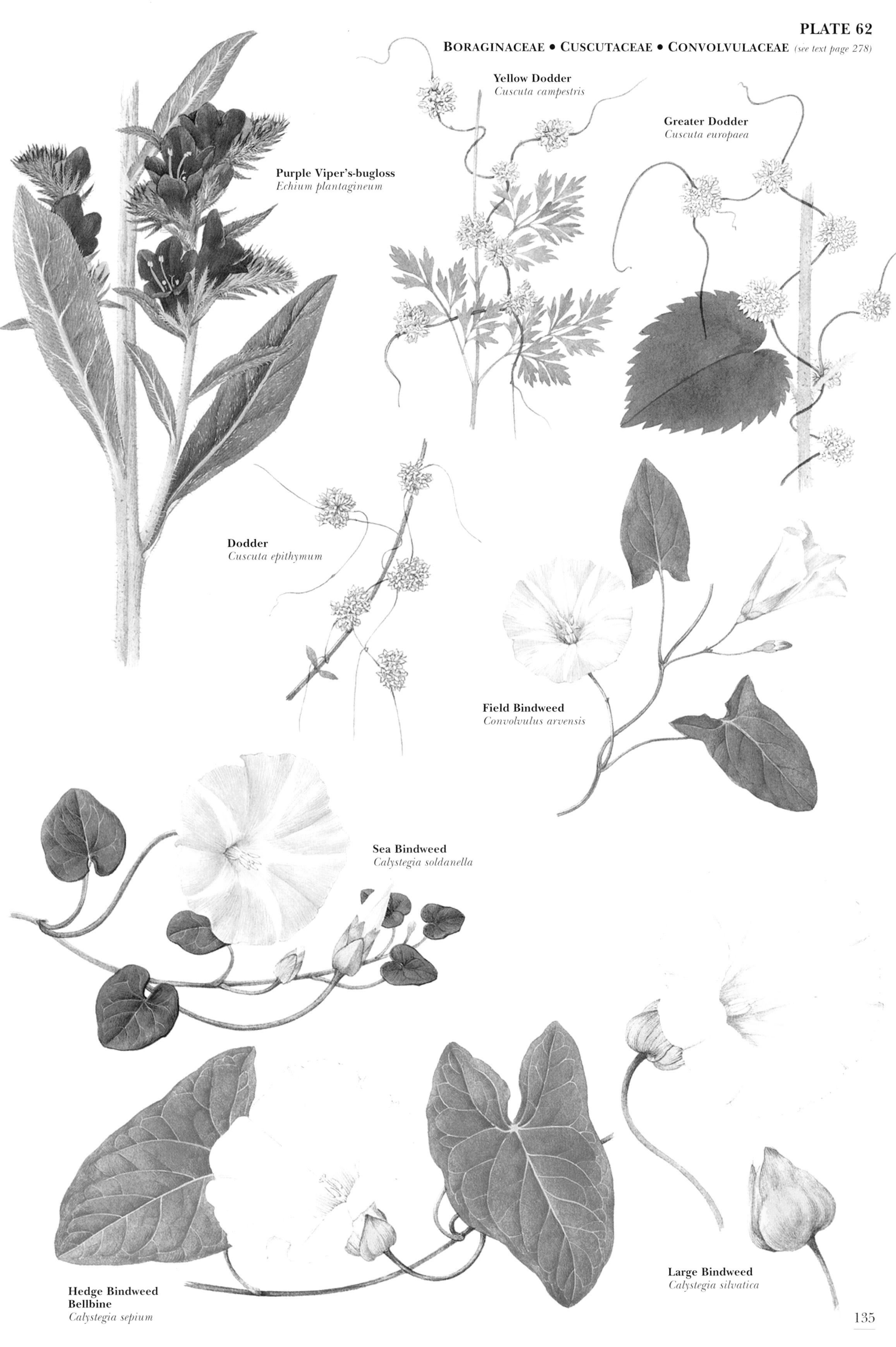
Yellow Dodder
Cuscuta campestris
Greater Dodder
Cuscuta europaea
Purple Viper's-bugloss
Echium plantagineum
Dodder
Cuscuta epithymum
Field Bindweed
Convolvulus arvensis
Sea Bindweed
Calystegia soldanella
Large Bindweed
Calystegia silvatica
Hedge Bindweed
Bellbine
Calystegia sepium

PLATE 63
SOLANACEAE *(see text page 279)*

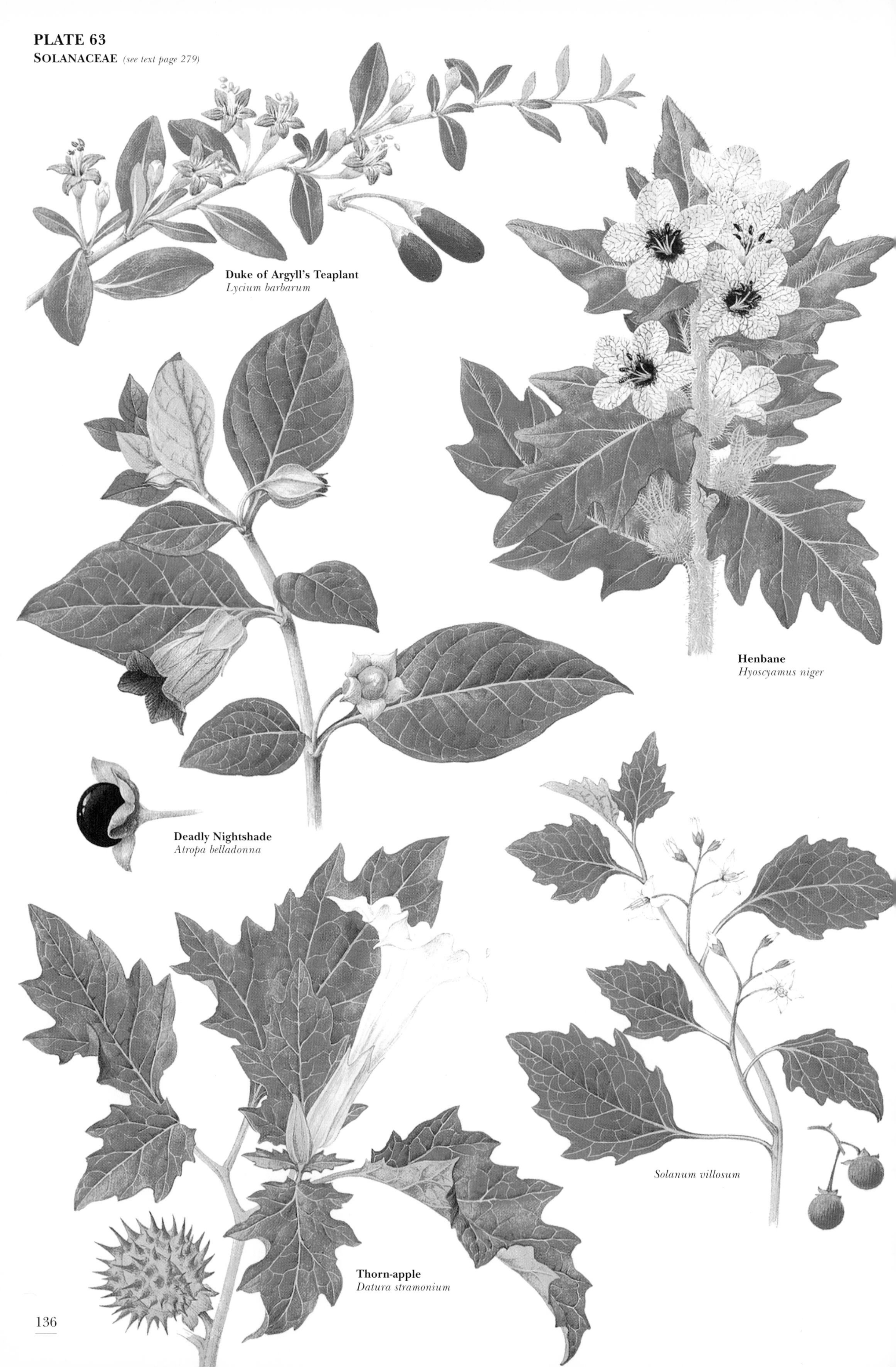

Duke of Argyll's Teaplant
Lycium barbarum

Henbane
Hyoscyamus niger

Deadly Nightshade
Atropa belladonna

Solanum villosum

Thorn-apple
Datura stramonium

Green Nightshade
Solanum sarachoides

Bittersweet
Woody Nightshade
Solanum dulcamara

Black Nightshade
Solanum nigrum

Small Nightshade
Solanum triflorum

Cock's-eggs
Salpichroa origanifolia

Snapdragon
Antirrhinum majus

Mudwort
Limosella aquatica

Lesser Snapdragon
Weasel's Snout
Misopates orontium

Welsh Mudwort
Limosella australis

Hoary Mullein
Verbascum pulverulentum
White Mullein
Verbascum lychnitis
Moth Mullein
Verbascum blattaria
Great Mullein
Aaron's Rod
Verbascum thapsus
Twiggy Mullein
Verbascum virgatum
Dark Mullein
Verbascum nigrum

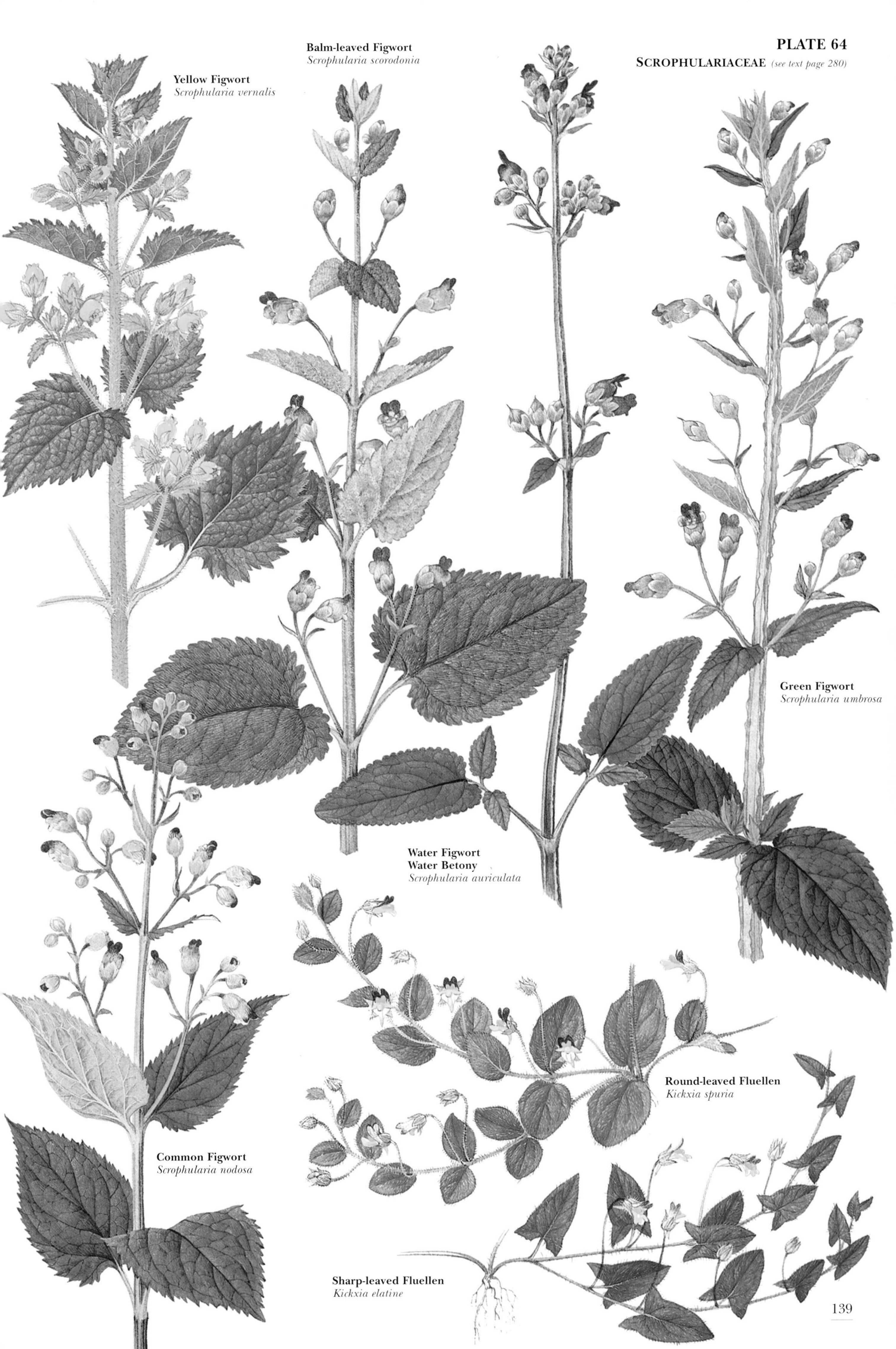
Yellow Figwort
Scrophularia vernalis
Balm-leaved Figwort
Scrophularia scorodonia
Green Figwort
Scrophularia umbrosa
Water Figwort
Water Betony
Scrophularia auriculata
Common Figwort
Scrophularia nodosa
Round-leaved Fluellen
Kickxia spuria
Sharp-leaved Fluellen
Kickxia elatine

PLATE 65

SCROPHULARIACEAE *(see text page 281)*

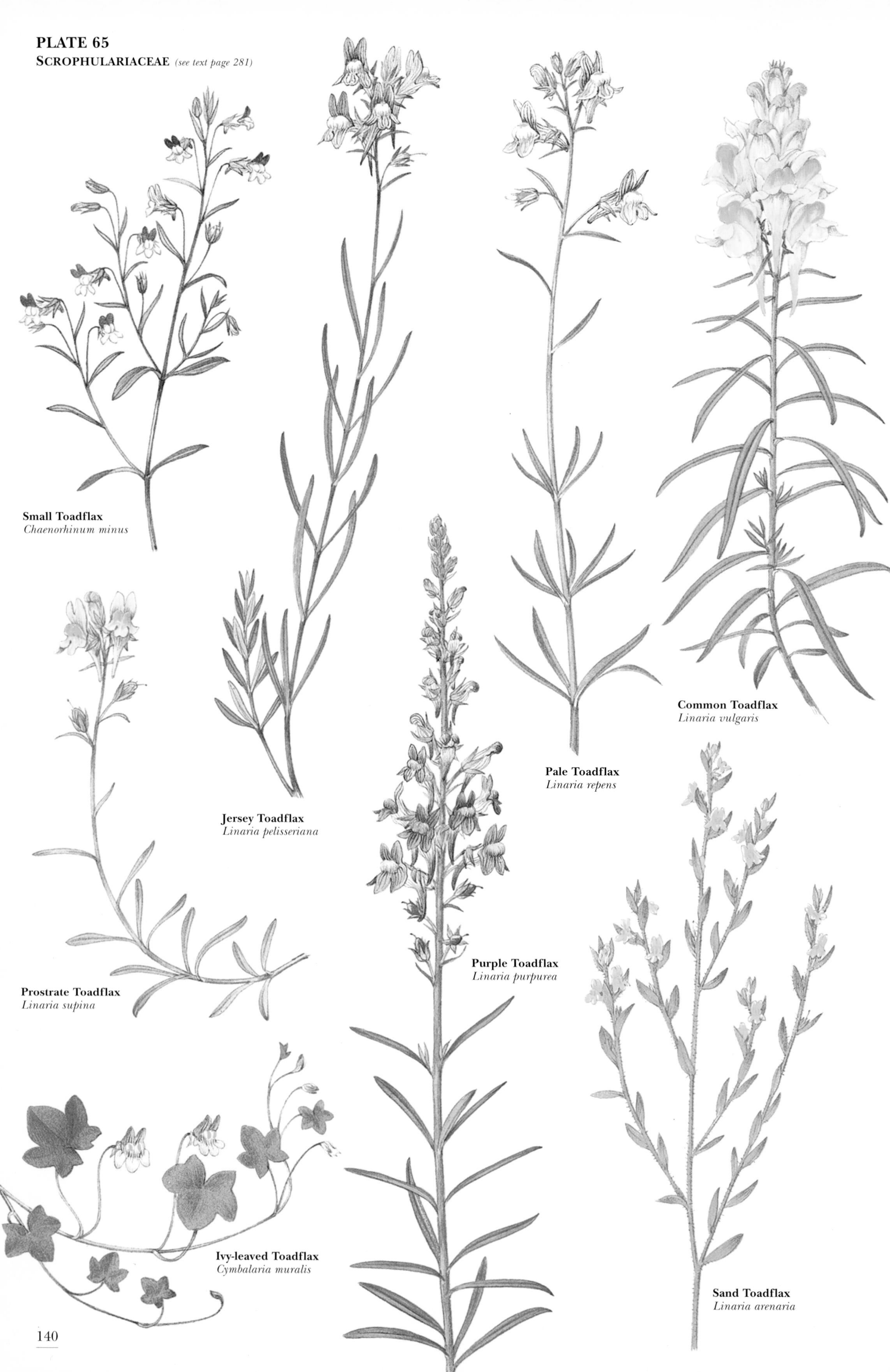

Small Toadflax
Chaenorhinum minus

Jersey Toadflax
Linaria pelisseriana

Pale Toadflax
Linaria repens

Common Toadflax
Linaria vulgaris

Prostrate Toadflax
Linaria supina

Purple Toadflax
Linaria purpurea

Ivy-leaved Toadflax
Cymbalaria muralis

Sand Toadflax
Linaria arenaria

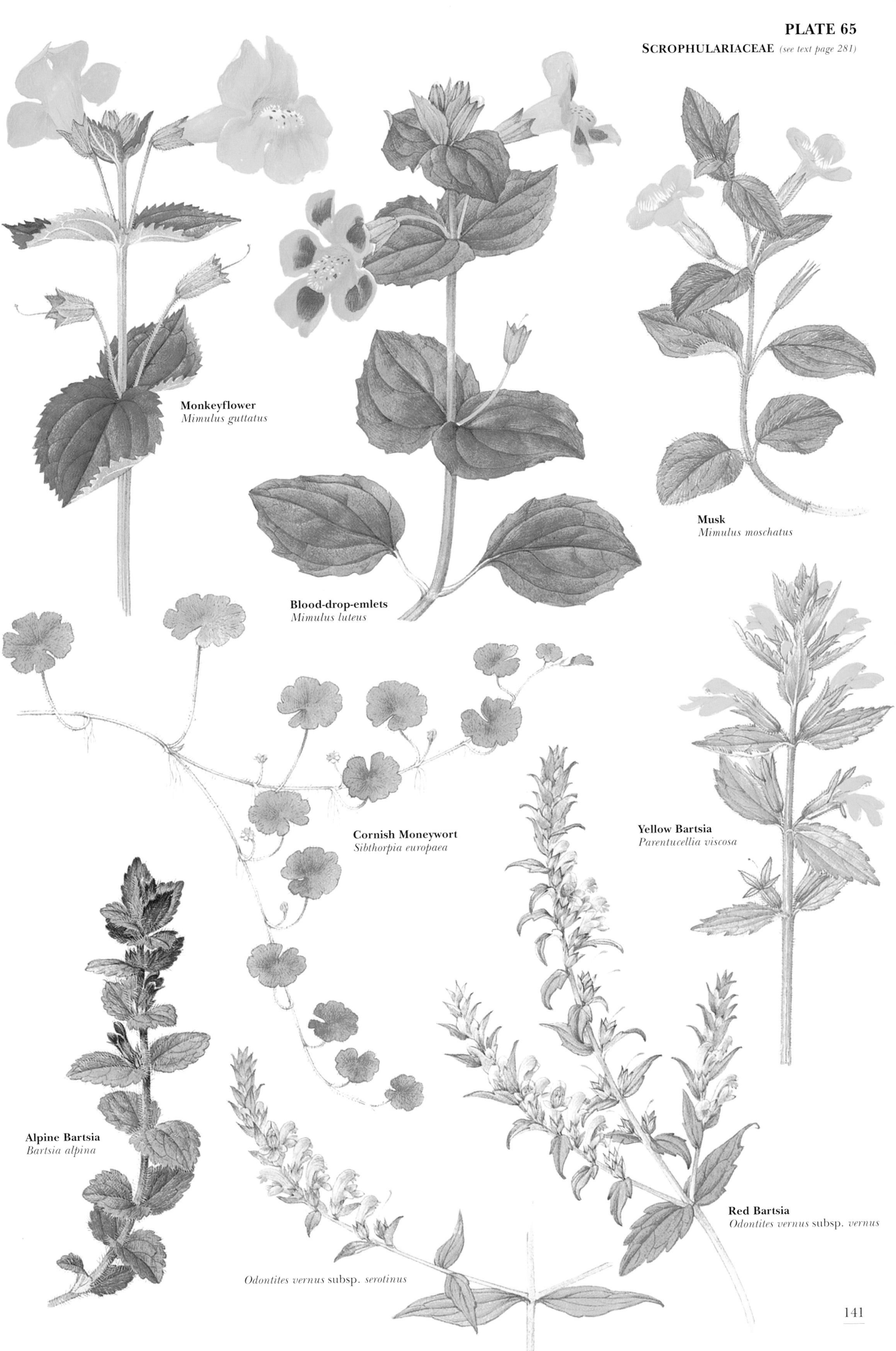
Monkeyflower
Mimulus guttatus
Blood-drop-emlets
Mimulus luteus
Musk
Mimulus moschatus
Cornish Moneywort
Sibthorpia europaea
Yellow Bartsia
Parentucellia viscosa
Alpine Bartsia
Bartsia alpina
Red Bartsia
Odontites vernus subsp. vernus
Odontites vernus subsp. serotinus

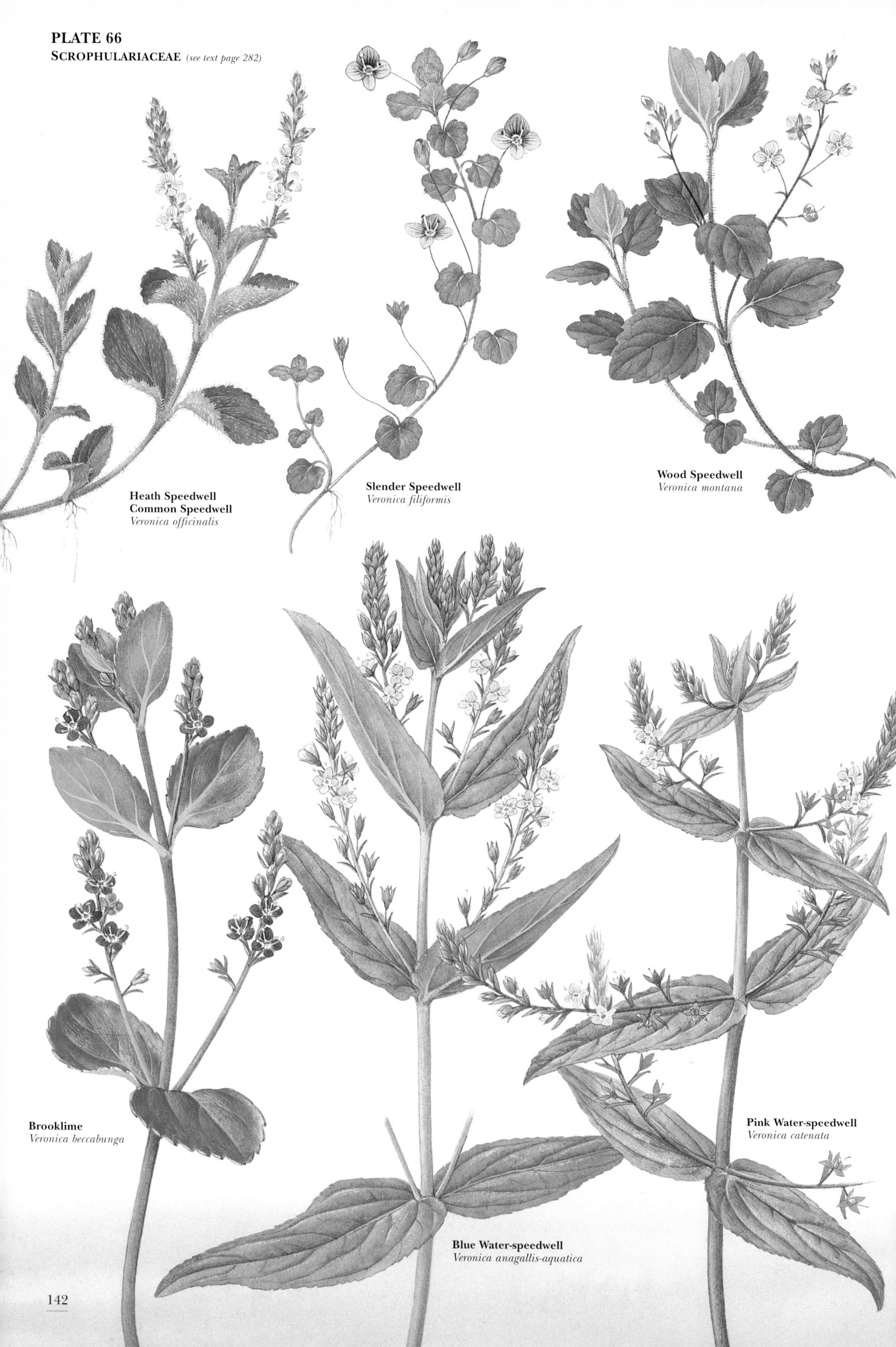
PLATE 66
SCROPHULARIACEAE (see text page 282)
Heath Speedwell
Common Speedwell
Veronica officinalis
Slender Speedwell
Veronica filiformis
Wood Speedwell
Veronica montana
Brooklime
Veronica beccabunga
Pink Water-speedwell
Veronica catenata
Blue Water-speedwell
Veronica anagallis-aquatica

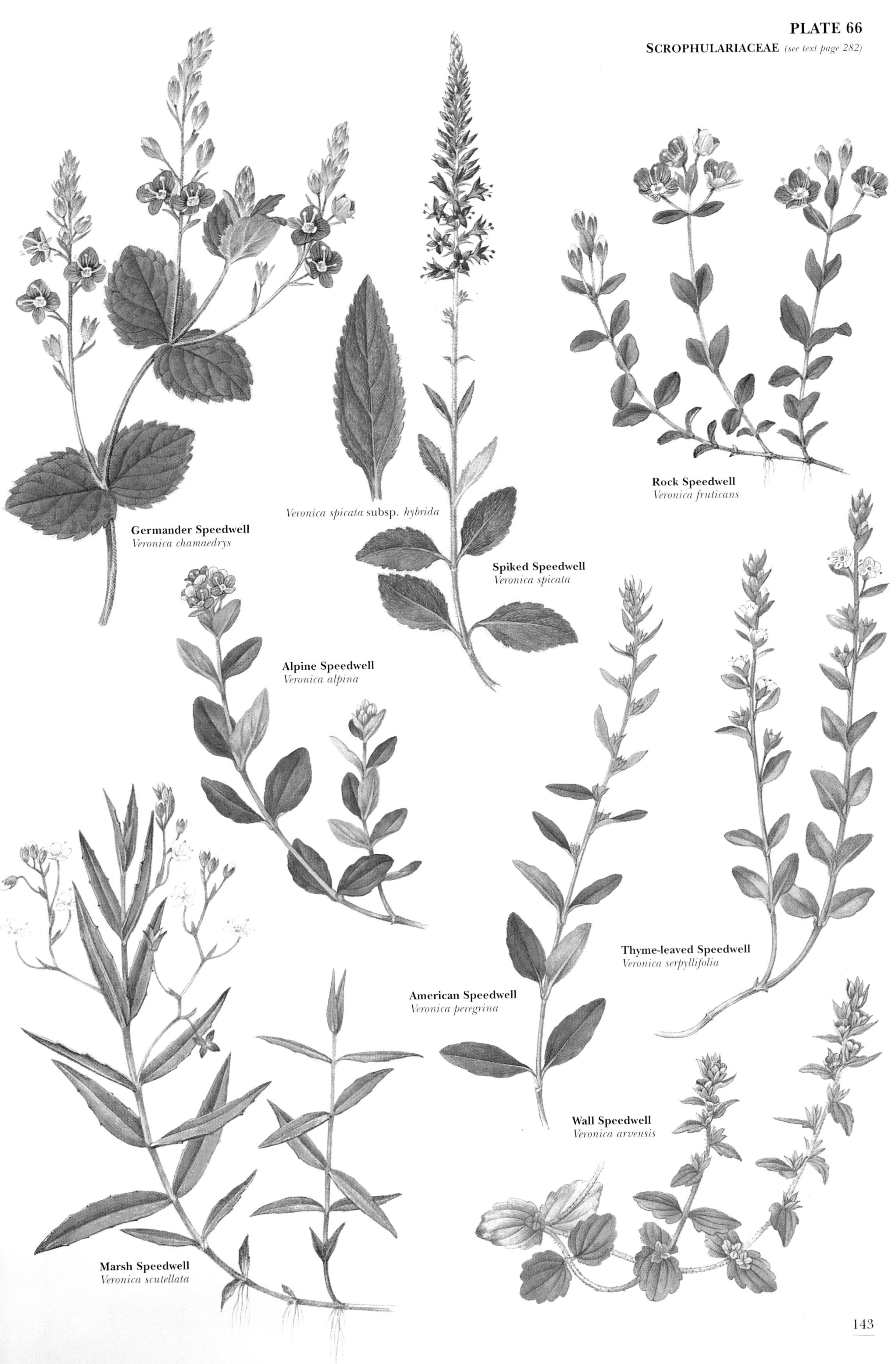
Germander Speedwell
Veronica chamaedrys
Veronica spicata subsp. *hybrida*
Rock Speedwell
Veronica fruticans
Spiked Speedwell
Veronica spicata
Alpine Speedwell
Veronica alpina
Thyme-leaved Speedwell
Veronica serpyllifolia
American Speedwell
Veronica peregrina
Wall Speedwell
Veronica arvensis
Marsh Speedwell
Veronica scutellata

PLATE 67

SCROPHULARIACEAE *(see text page 283)*

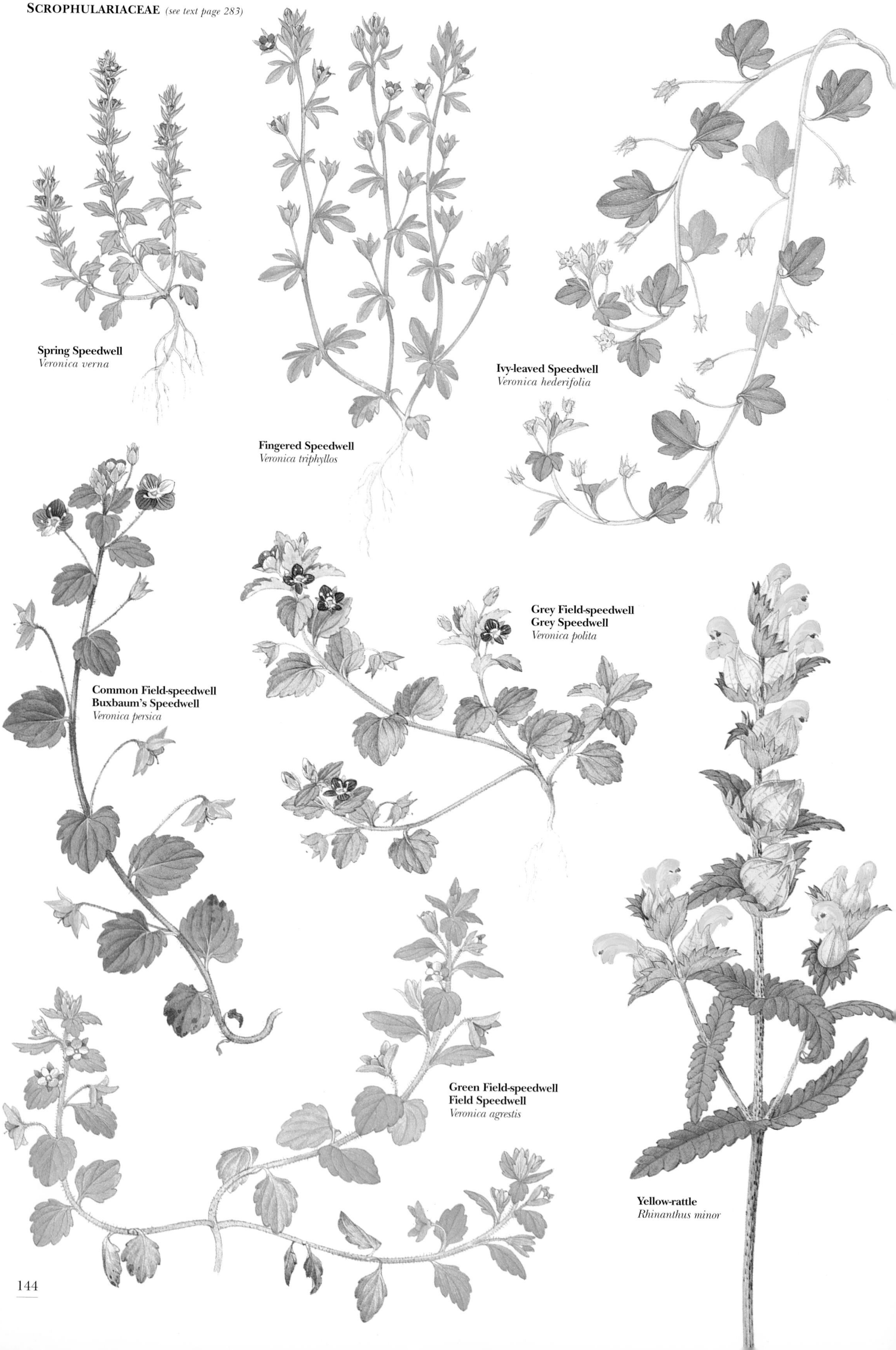

Spring Speedwell
Veronica verna

Fingered Speedwell
Veronica triphyllos

Ivy-leaved Speedwell
Veronica hederifolia

Common Field-speedwell
Buxbaum's Speedwell
Veronica persica

Grey Field-speedwell
Grey Speedwell
Veronica polita

Green Field-speedwell
Field Speedwell
Veronica agrestis

Yellow-rattle
Rhinanthus minor

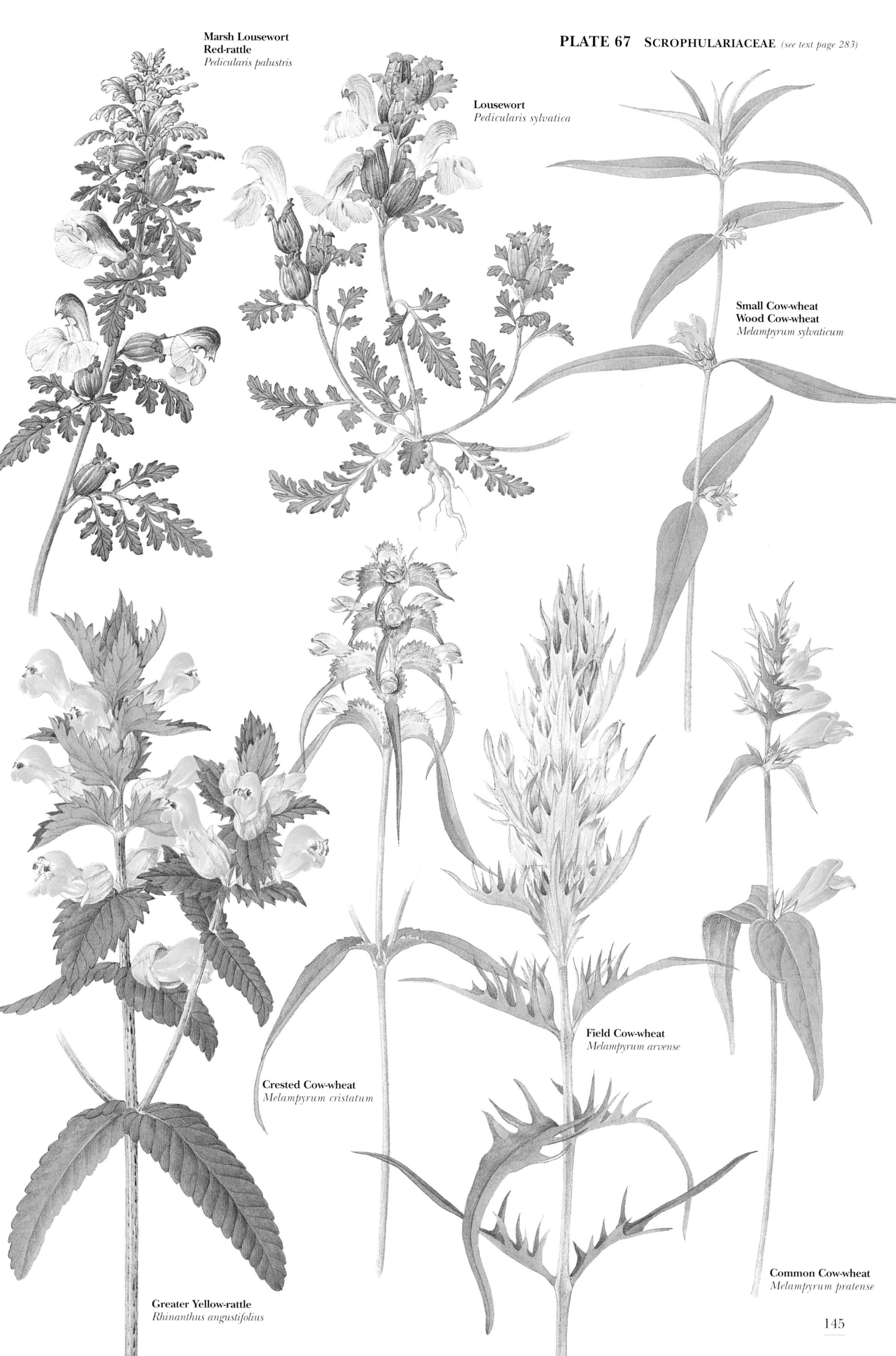
Marsh Lousewort
Red-rattle
Pedicularis palustris
Lousewort
Pedicularis sylvatica
Small Cow-wheat
Wood Cow-wheat
Melampyrum sylvaticum
Field Cow-wheat
Melampyrum arvense
Crested Cow-wheat
Melampyrum cristatum
Common Cow-wheat
Melampyrum pratense
Greater Yellow-rattle
Rhinanthus angustifolius

PLATE 68
SCROPHULARIACEAE *(see text page 284)*

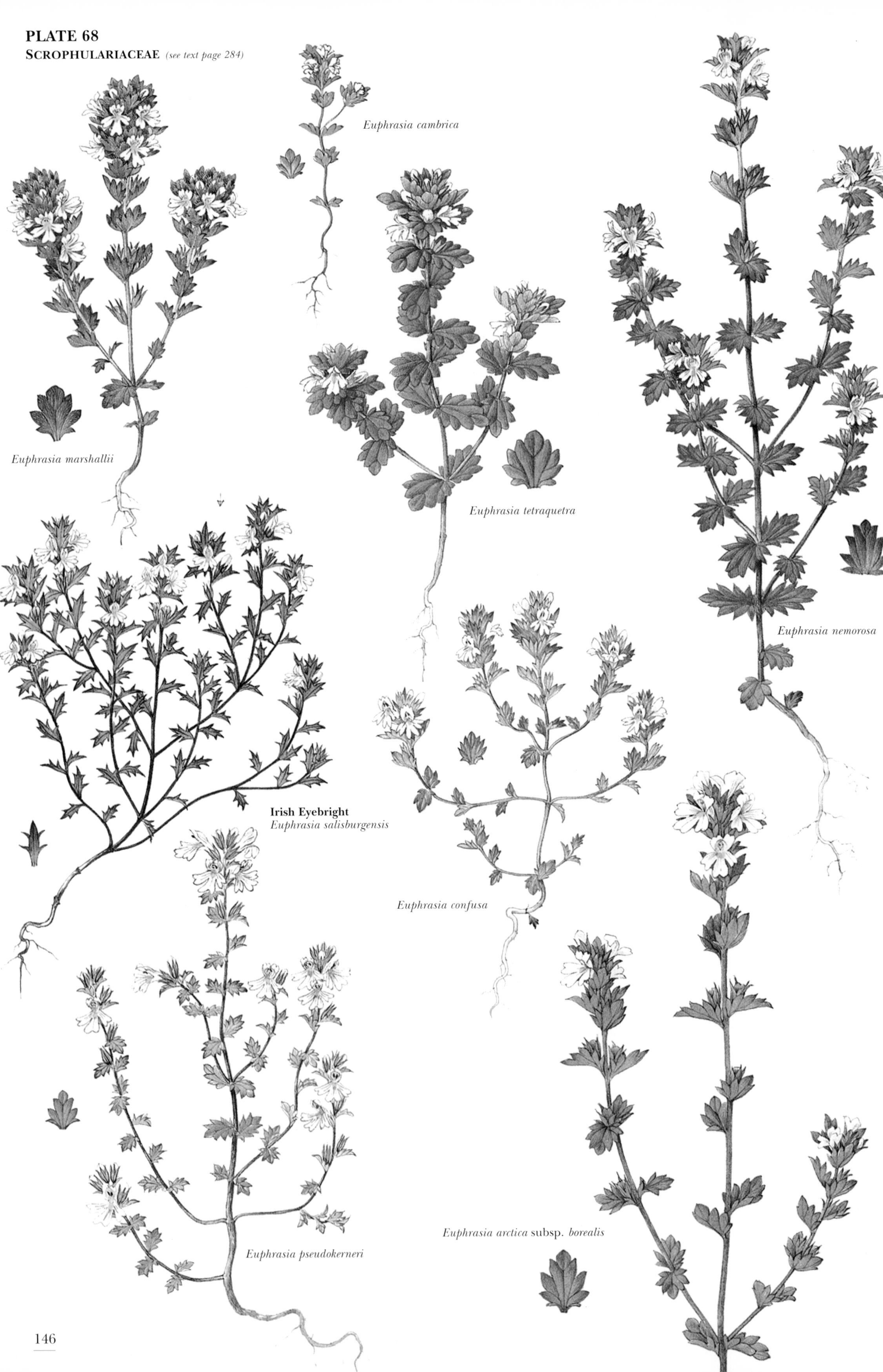

PLATE 68

SCROPHULARIACEAE *(see text page 284)*

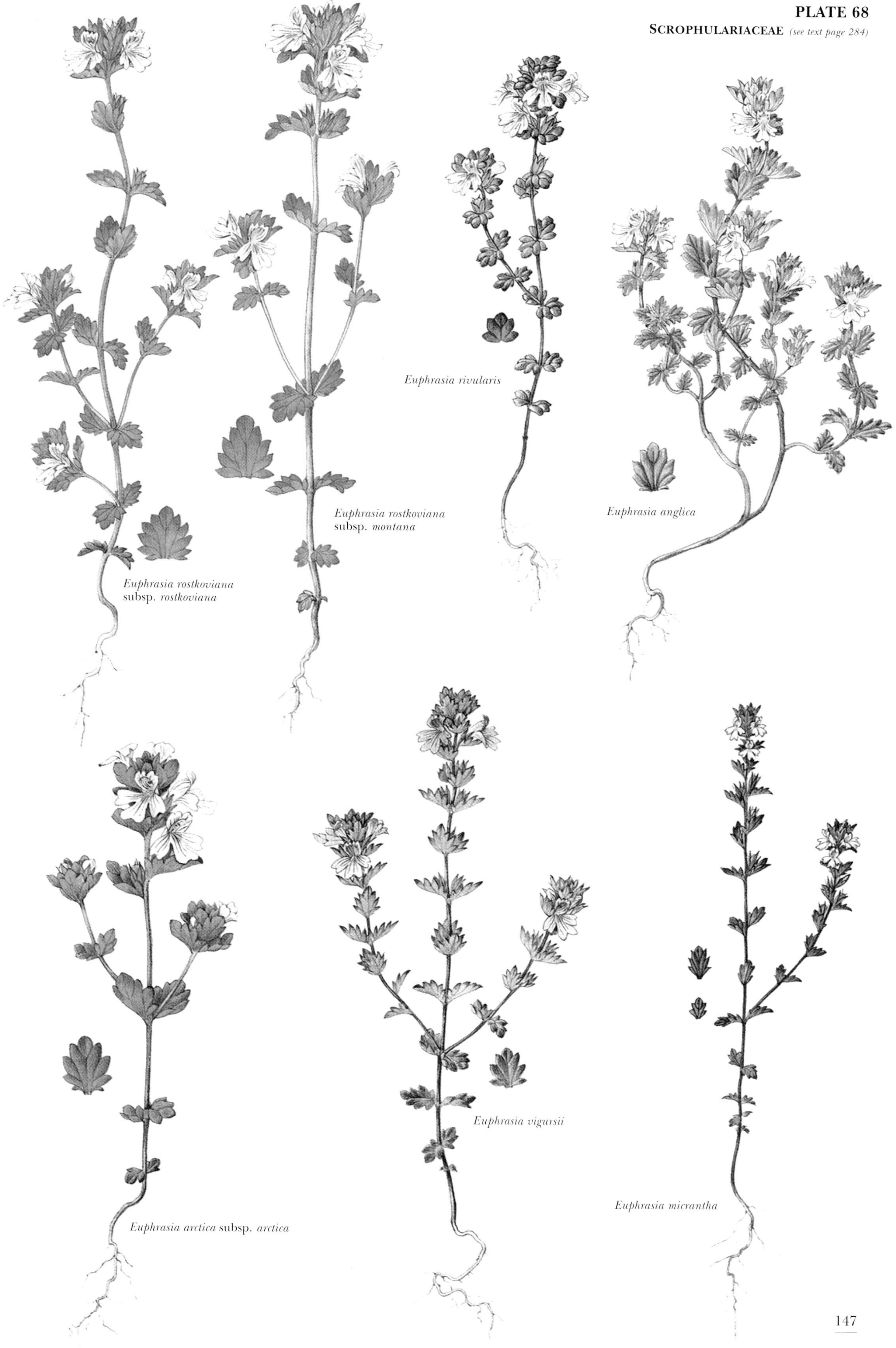
Euphrasia rostkoviana subsp. *rostkoviana*
Euphrasia rostkoviana subsp. *montana*
Euphrasia rivularis
Euphrasia anglica
Euphrasia arctica subsp. *arctica*
Euphrasia vigursii
Euphrasia micrantha

PLATE 69
SCROPHULARIACEAE *(see text page 285)*

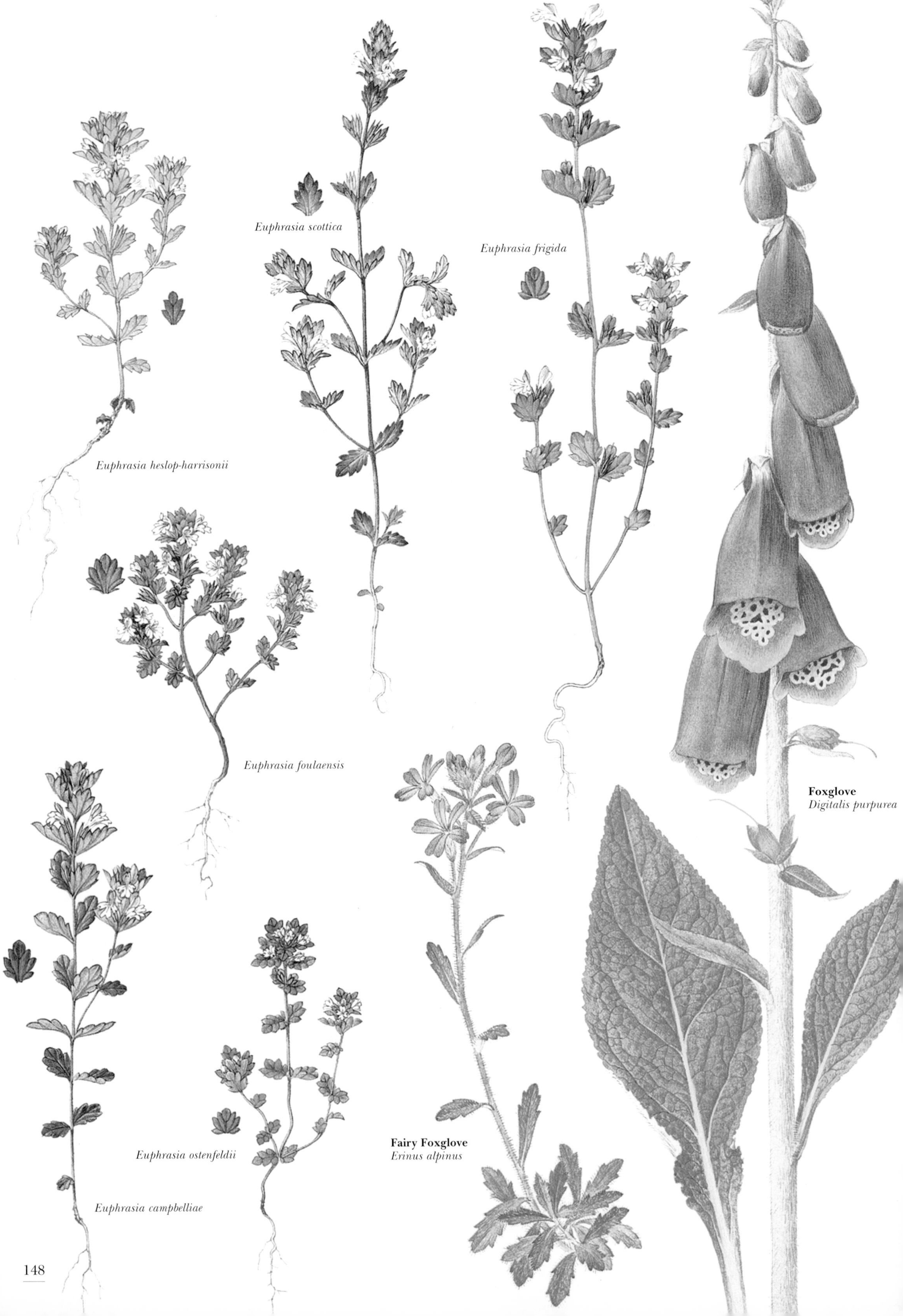

Euphrasia heslop-harrisonii

Euphrasia scottica

Euphrasia frigida

Foxglove
Digitalis purpurea

Euphrasia foulaensis

Euphrasia campbelliae

Euphrasia ostenfeldii

Fairy Foxglove
Erinus alpinus

 (see text page 285)

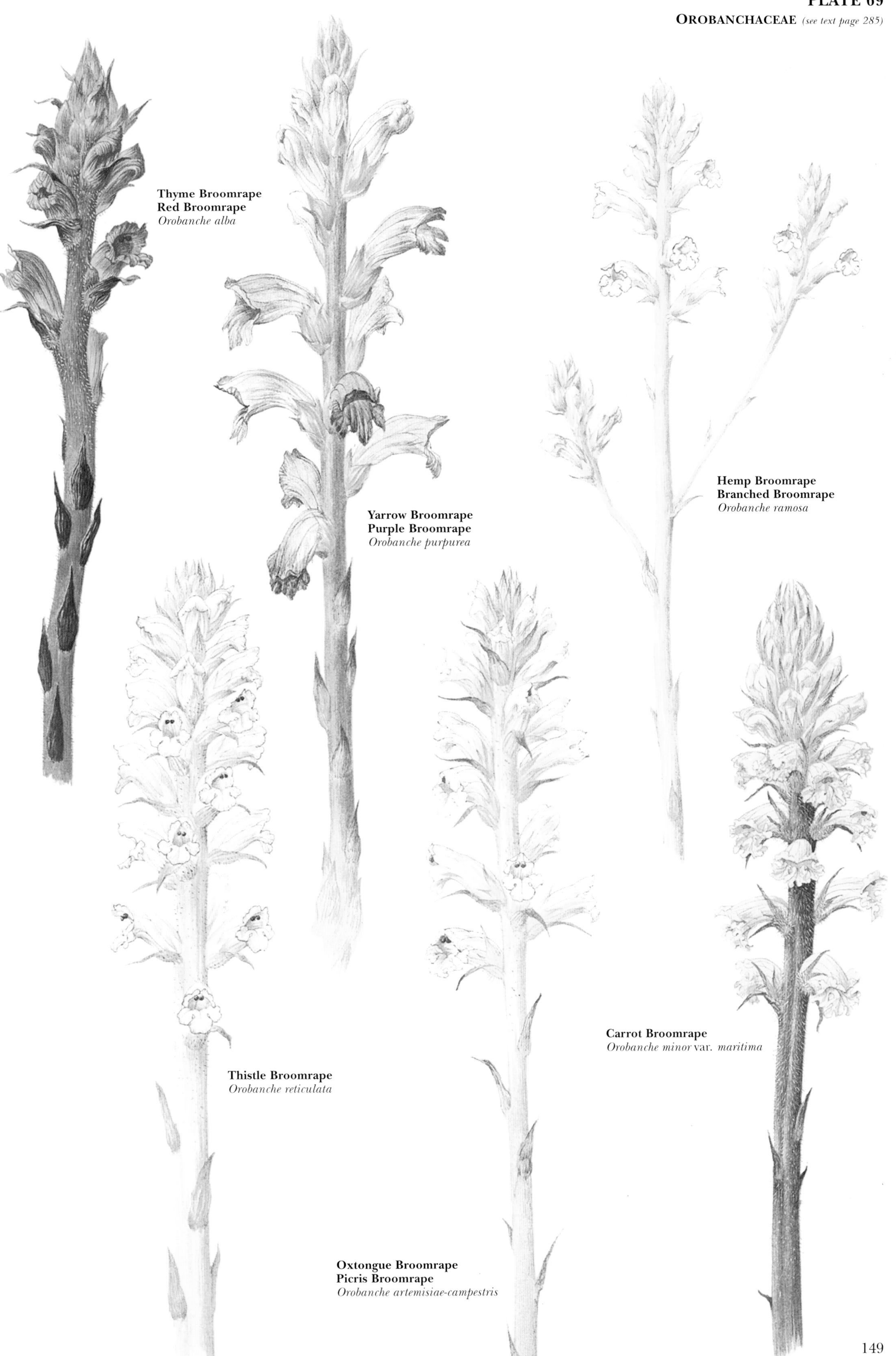
Thyme Broomrape
Red Broomrape
Orobanche alba
Yarrow Broomrape
Purple Broomrape
Orobanche purpurea
Hemp Broomrape
Branched Broomrape
Orobanche ramosa
Thistle Broomrape
Orobanche reticulata
Oxtongue Broomrape
Picris Broomrape
Orobanche artemisiae-campestris
Carrot Broomrape
Orobanche minor var. *maritima*

PLATE 70

OROBANCHACEAE *(see text page 286)*

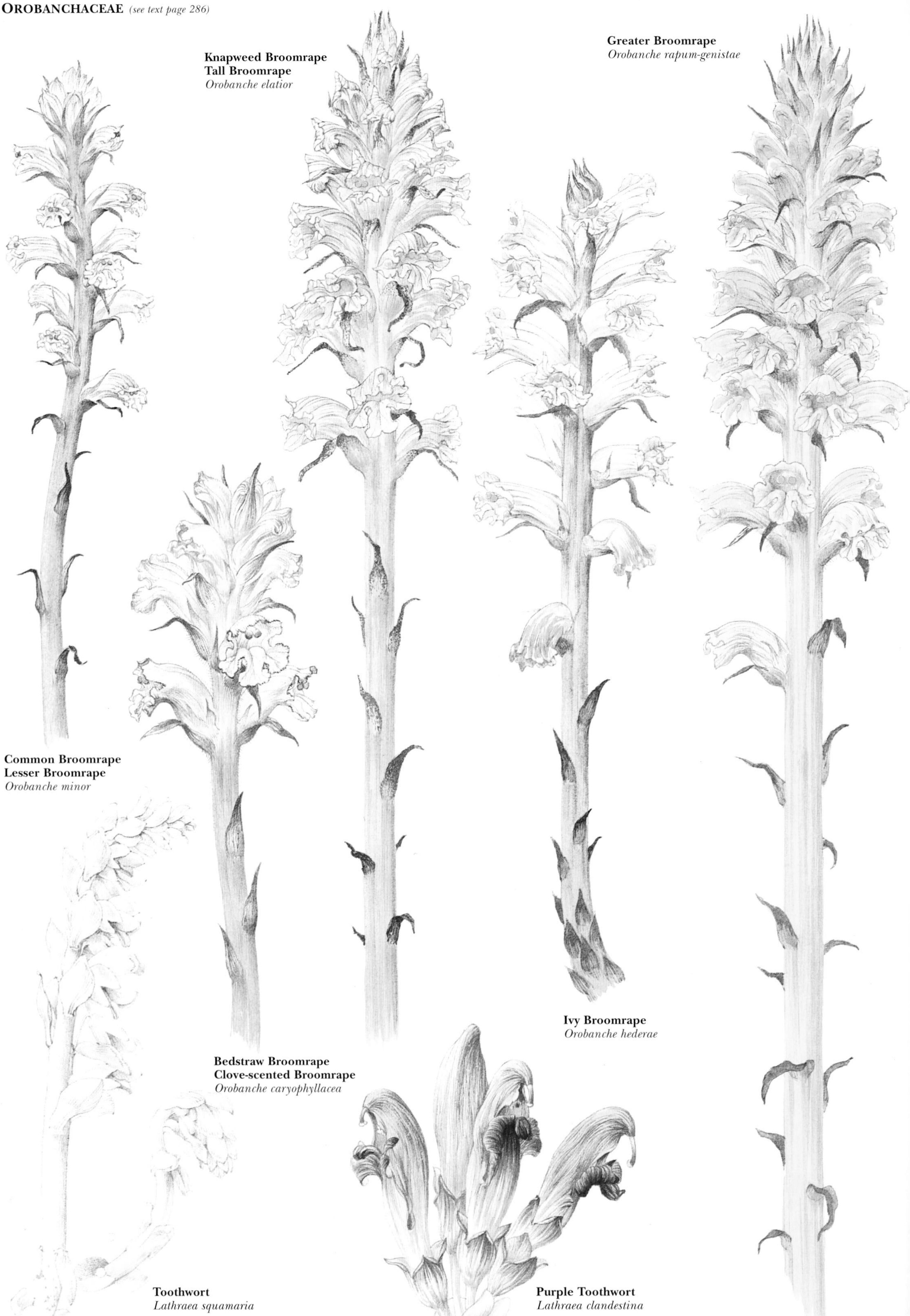

Knapweed Broomrape
Tall Broomrape
Orobanche elatior

Greater Broomrape
Orobanche rapum-genistae

Common Broomrape
Lesser Broomrape
Orobanche minor

Ivy Broomrape
Orobanche hederae

Bedstraw Broomrape
Clove-scented Broomrape
Orobanche caryophyllacea

Toothwort
Lathraea squamaria

Purple Toothwort
Lathraea clandestina

Pale Butterwort
Pinguicula lusitanica
Large-flowered Butterwort
Pinguicula grandiflora
Common Butterwort
Pinguicula vulgaris
Lesser Bladderwort
Utricularia minor
Greater Bladderwort
Utricularia vulgaris
Utricularia australis
Intermediate Bladderwort
Utricularia intermedia

PLATE 71

ACANTHACEAE • VERBENACEAE • LAMIACEAE (= LABIATAE) *(see text page 287)*

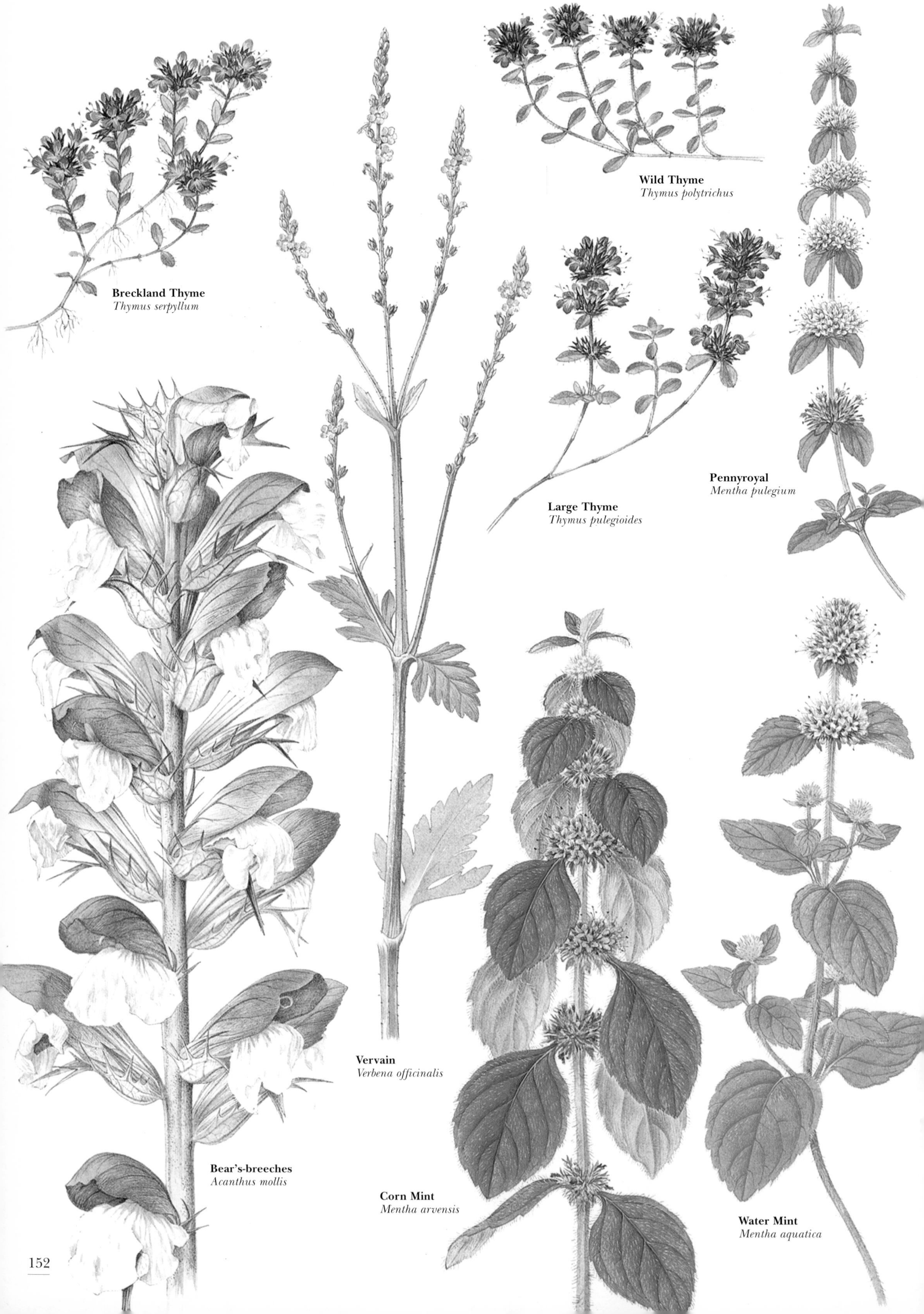

Breckland Thyme
Thymus serpyllum

Wild Thyme
Thymus polytrichus

Large Thyme
Thymus pulegioides

Pennyroyal
Mentha pulegium

Vervain
Verbena officinalis

Bear's-breeches
Acanthus mollis

Corn Mint
Mentha arvensis

Water Mint
Mentha aquatica

 (see text page 287)

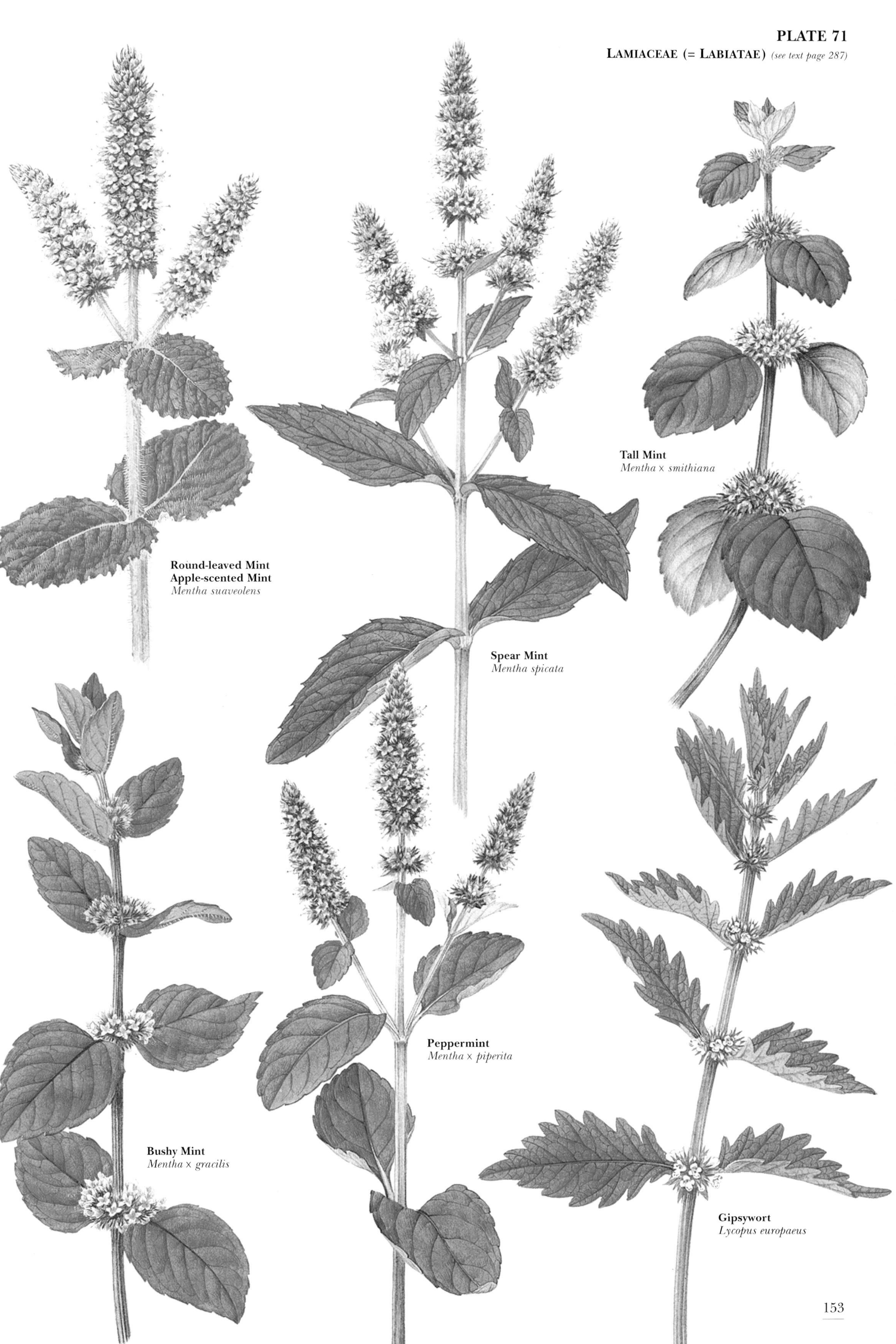

Round-leaved Mint
Apple-scented Mint
Mentha suaveolens

Spear Mint
Mentha spicata

Tall Mint
Mentha × smithiana

Bushy Mint
Mentha × gracilis

Peppermint
Mentha × piperita

Gipsywort
Lycopus europaeus

PLATE 72
LAMIACEAE (= LABIATAE) *(see text page 288)*

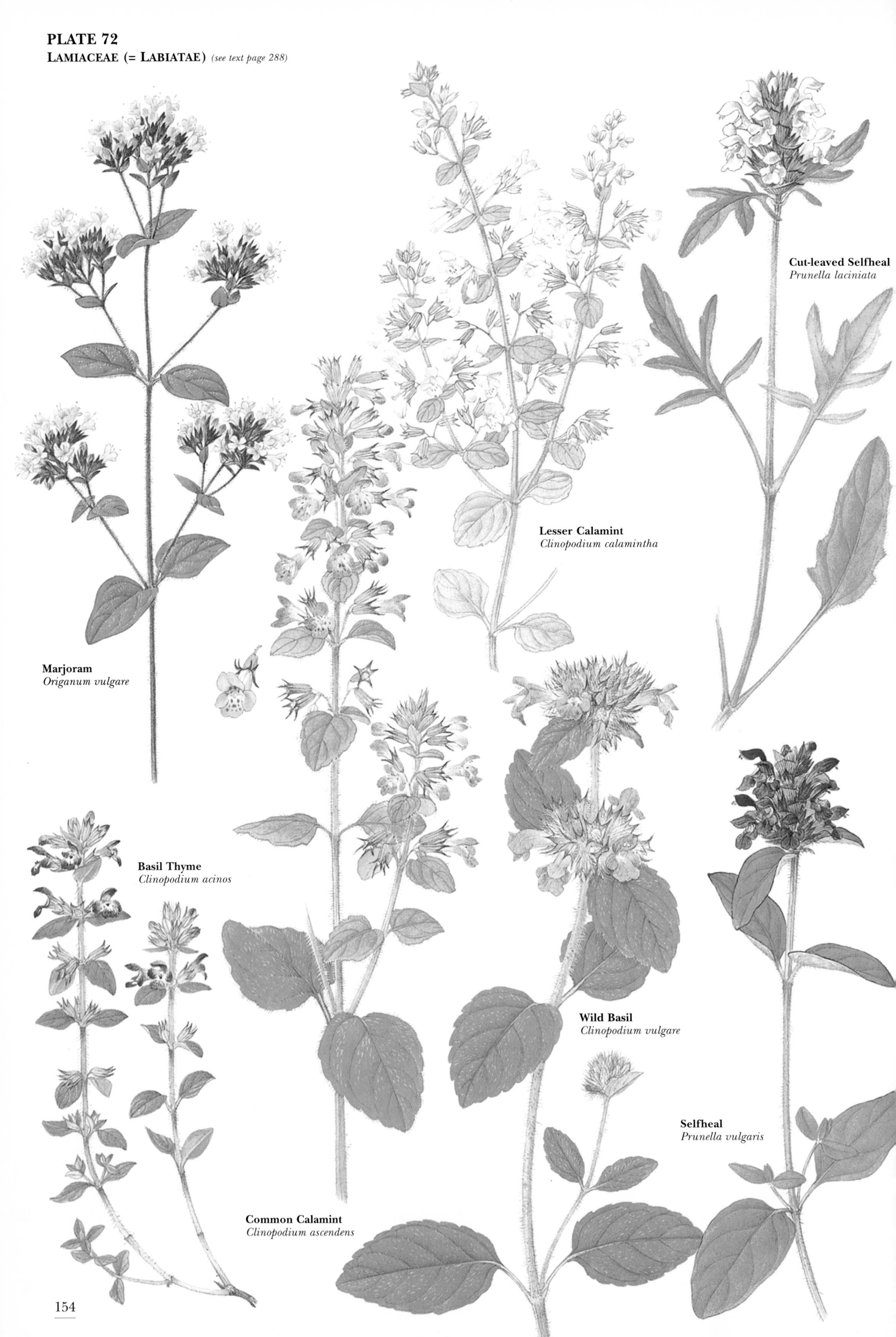

Marjoram
Origanum vulgare

Lesser Calamint
Clinopodium calamintha

Cut-leaved Selfheal
Prunella laciniata

Basil Thyme
Clinopodium acinos

Common Calamint
Clinopodium ascendens

Wild Basil
Clinopodium vulgare

Selfheal
Prunella vulgaris

Meadow Clary
Salvia pratensis
Motherwort
Leonurus cardiaca
Bastard Balm
Melittis melissophyllum
Yellow Archangel
Lamiastrum galeobdolon
Black Horehound
Ballota nigra
Wild Clary
Salvia verbenaca

PLATE 73

LAMIACEAE (= LABIATAE) *(see text page 289)*

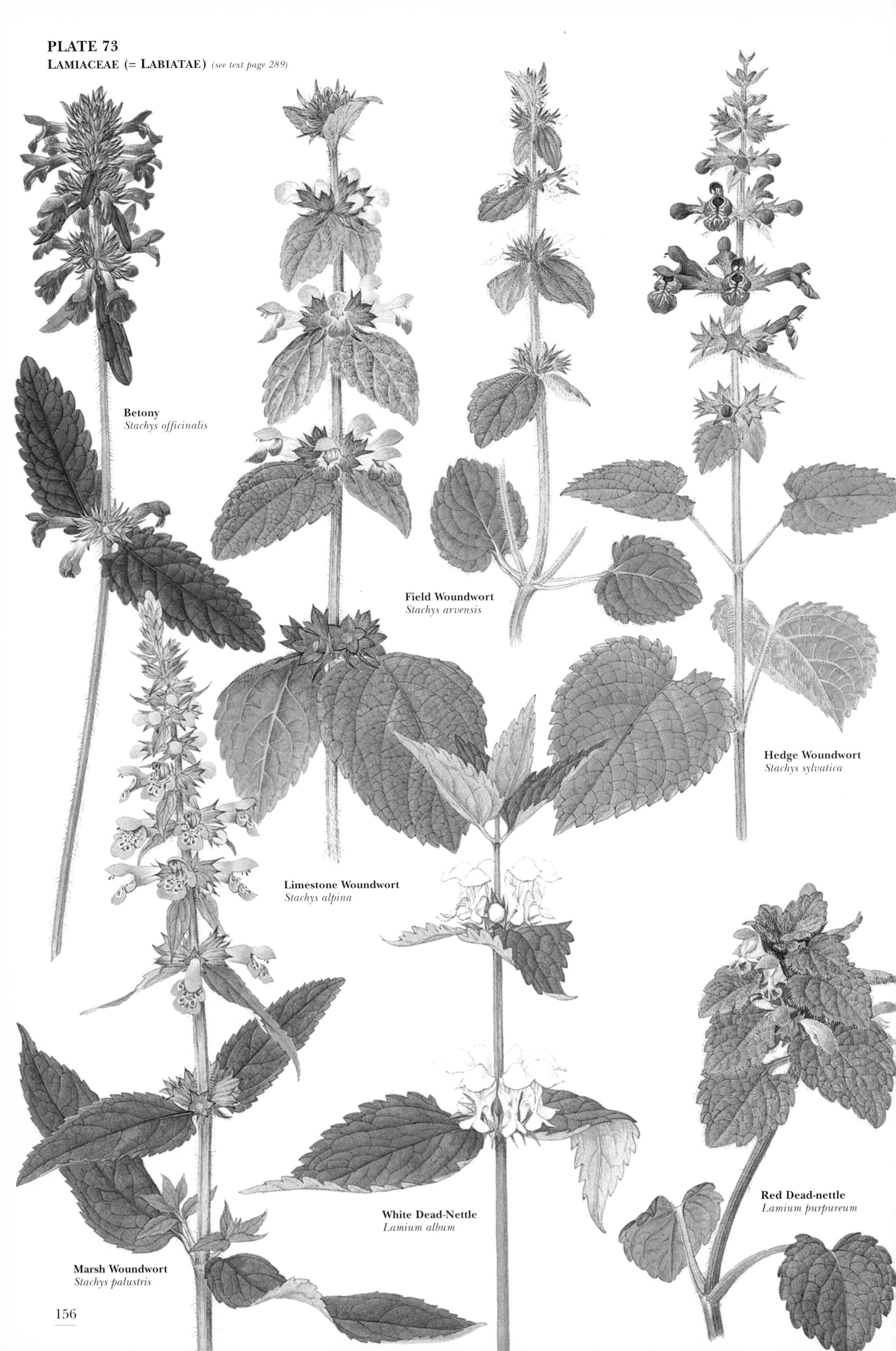

Betony
Stachys officinalis

Limestone Woundwort
Stachys alpina

Field Woundwort
Stachys arvensis

Hedge Woundwort
Stachys sylvatica

Marsh Woundwort
Stachys palustris

White Dead-Nettle
Lamium album

Red Dead-nettle
Lamium purpureum

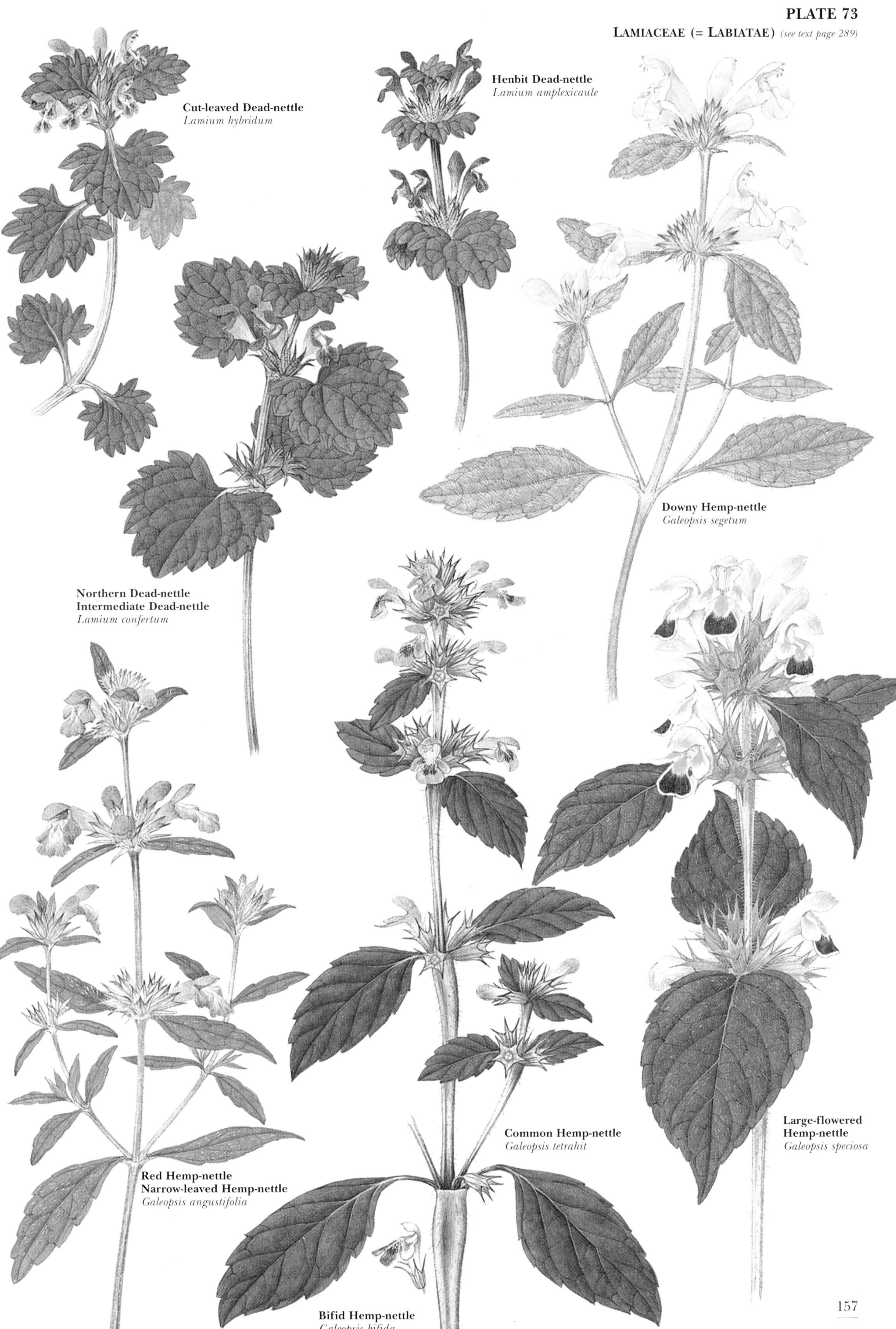
Cut-leaved Dead-nettle
Lamium hybridum
Henbit Dead-nettle
Lamium amplexicaule
Downy Hemp-nettle
Galeopsis segetum
Northern Dead-nettle
Intermediate Dead-nettle
Lamium confertum
Common Hemp-nettle
Galeopsis tetrahit
Large-flowered
Hemp-nettle
Galeopsis speciosa
Red Hemp-nettle
Narrow-leaved Hemp-nettle
Galeopsis angustifolia
Bifid Hemp-nettle
Galeopsis bifida

PLATE 74

LAMIACEAE (= LABIATAE) *(see text page 290)*

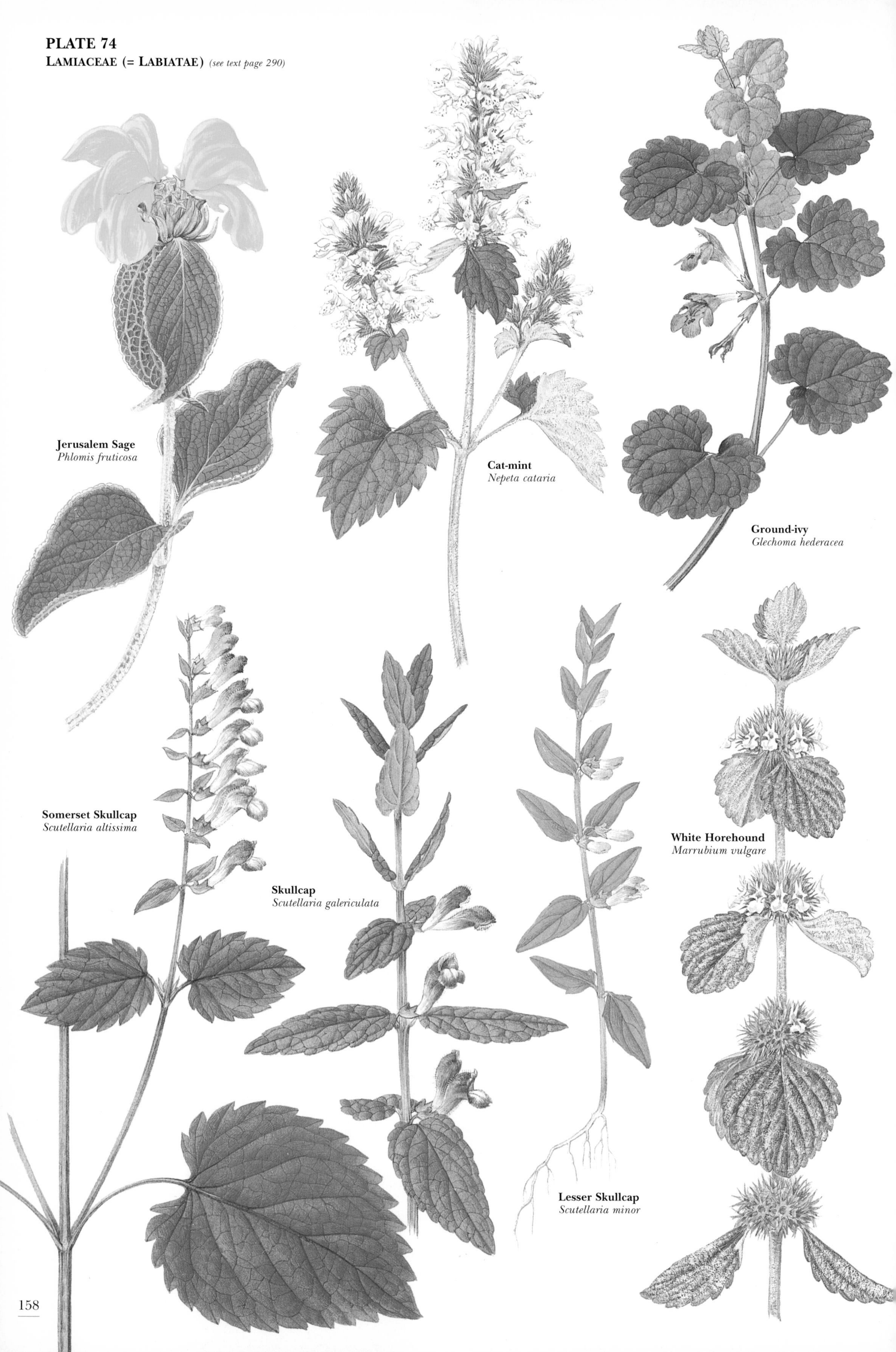

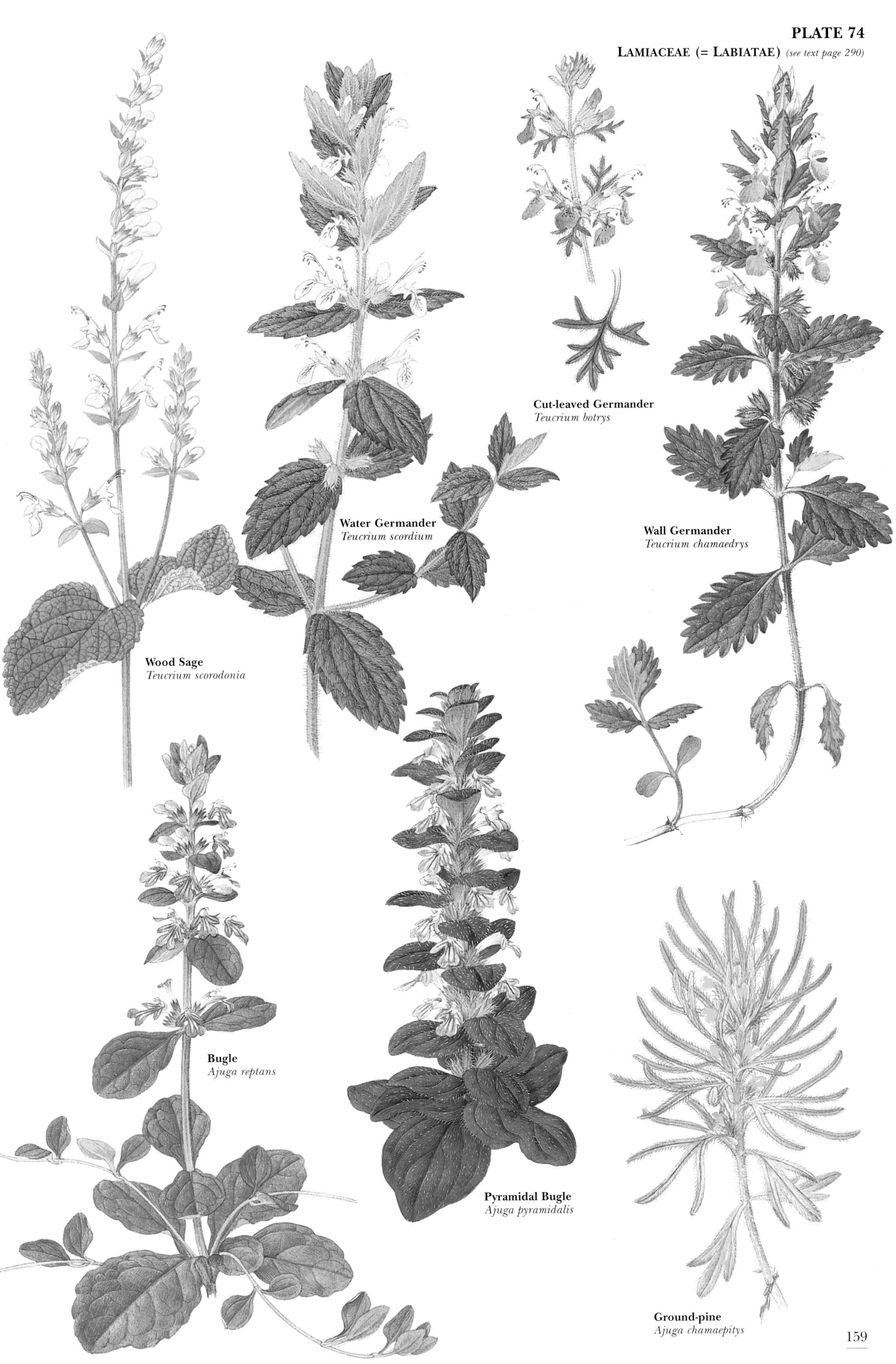
Wood Sage
Teucrium scorodonia
Water Germander
Teucrium scordium
Cut-leaved Germander
Teucrium botrys
Wall Germander
Teucrium chamaedrys
Bugle
Ajuga reptans
Pyramidal Bugle
Ajuga pyramidalis
Ground-pine
Ajuga chamaepitys

 (see text page 291)

Ribwort Plantain
Plantago lanceolata
Hoary Plantain
Plantago media
Sea Plantain
Plantago maritima
Shore-weed
Littorella uniflora
Buck's-horn Plantain
Plantago coronopus
Ivy-leaved Bellflower
Wahlenbergia hederacea
Greater Plantain
Plantago major

Giant Bellflower
Large Campanula
Campanula latifolia

Spiked Rampion
Phyteuma spicatum

Nettle-leaved Bellflower
Bats-in-the-Belfry
Campanula trachelium

Clustered Bellflower
Campanula glomerata

Creeping Bellflower
Creeping Campanula
Campanula rapunculoides

Peach-leaved Bellflower
Campanula persicifolia

Round-headed Rampion
Phyteuma orbiculare

PLATE 76

CAMPANULACEAE *(see text page 292)*

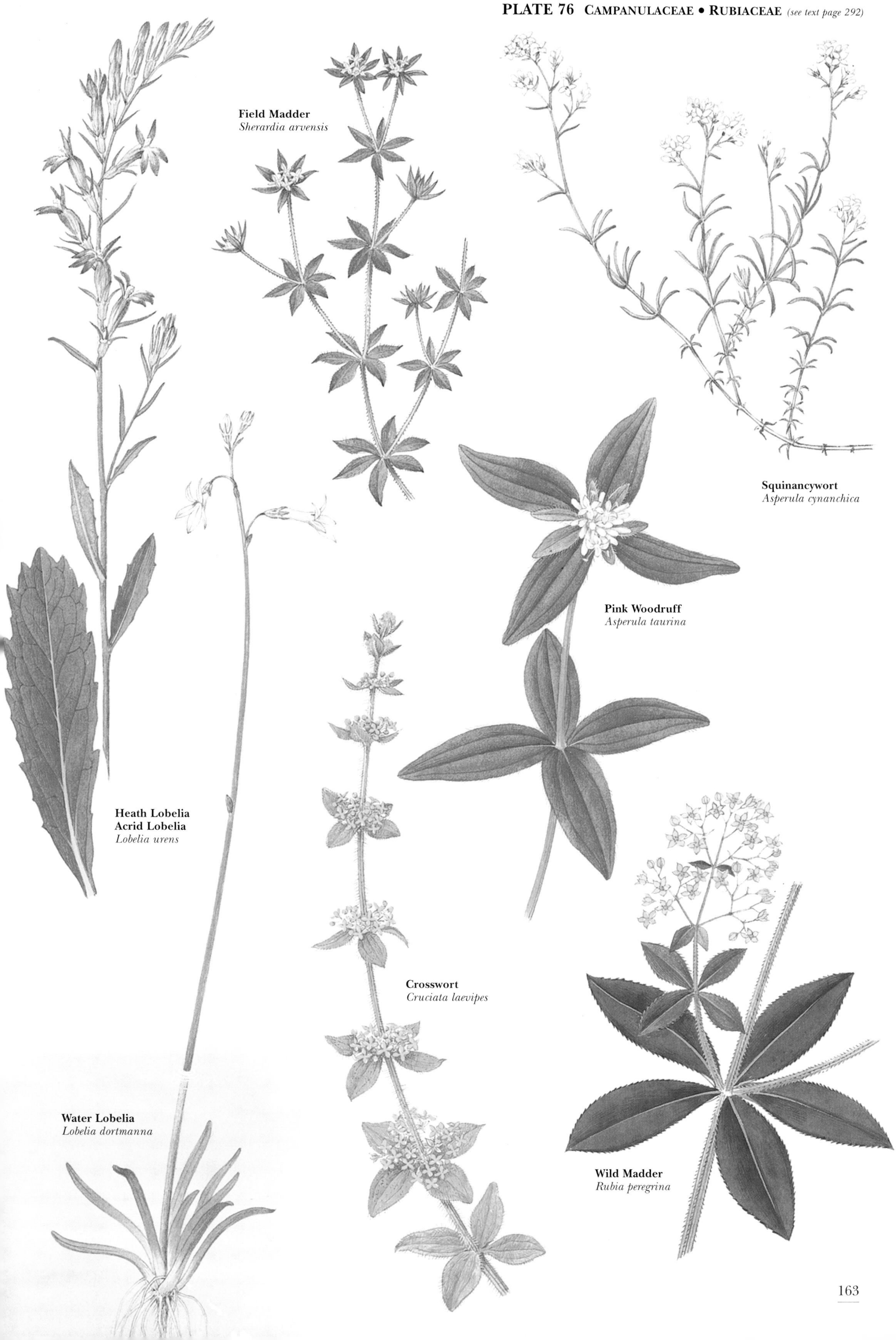

 (see text page 292)

Field Madder
Sherardia arvensis

Squinancywort
Asperula cynanchica

Pink Woodruff
Asperula taurina

Heath Lobelia
Acrid Lobelia
Lobelia urens

Crosswort
Cruciata laevipes

Water Lobelia
Lobelia dortmanna

Wild Madder
Rubia peregrina

PLATE 77

RUBIACEAE *(see text page 293)*

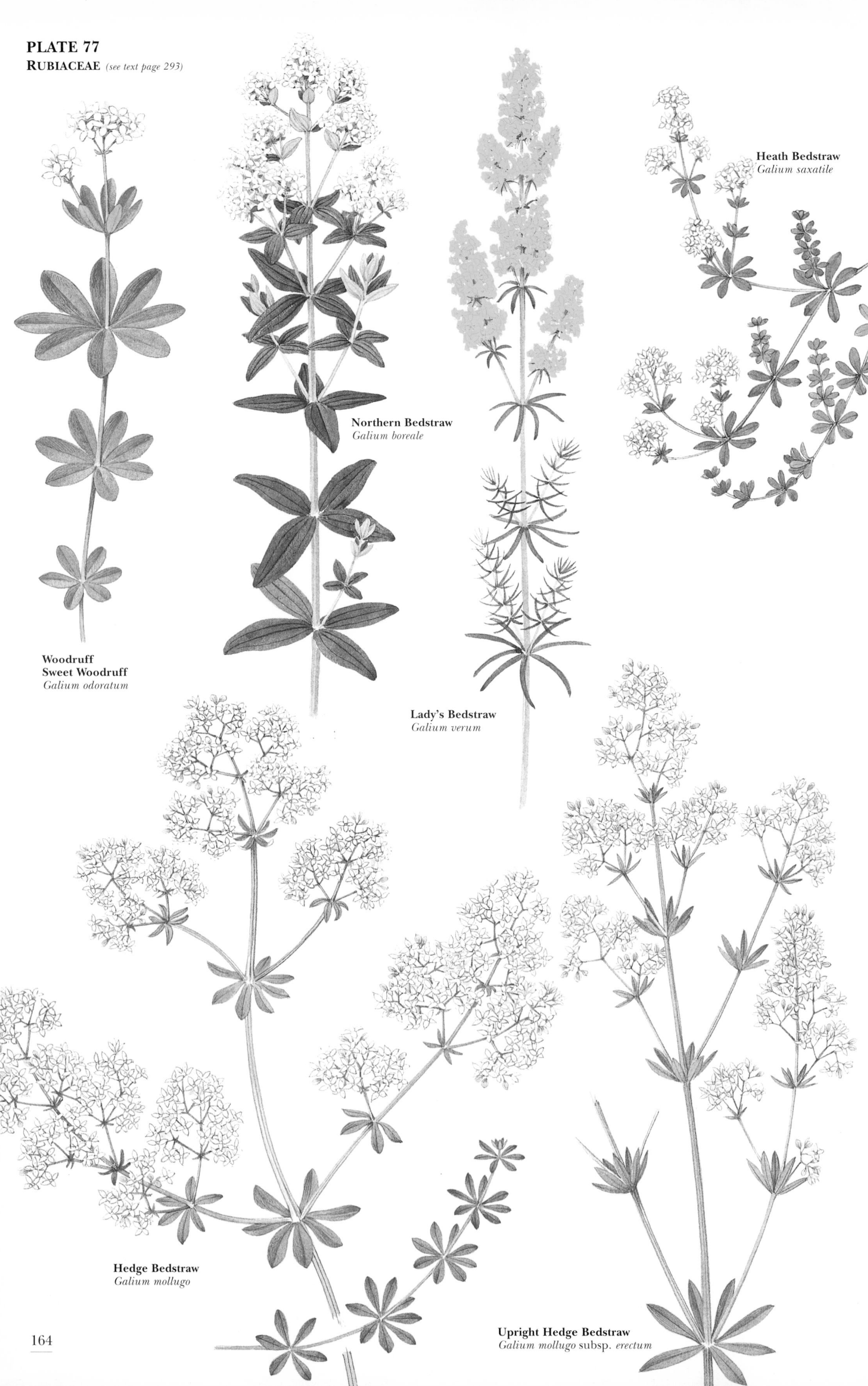

Galium fleurotii
Slender Bedstraw
Galium pumilum
Limestone Bedstraw
Galium sterneri
Common Marsh-bedstraw
Galium palustre subsp. *palustre*
Slender Marsh-bedstraw
Galium constrictum
Corn Cleavers
Rough Corn Bedstraw
Galium tricornutum
Fen Bedstraw
Galium uliginosum
Great Marsh-bedstraw
Galium palustre subsp. *elongatum*

PLATE 78

RUBIACEAE • CAPRIFOLIACEAE *(see text page 294)*

Wall Bedstraw
Galium parisiense

False Cleavers
Galium spurium

Cleavers
Goosegrass
Galium aparine

Wayfaring-tree
Viburnum lantana

Elder
Sambucus nigra

Dwarf Elder
Danewort
Sambucus ebulus

Guelder-rose
Viburnum opulus

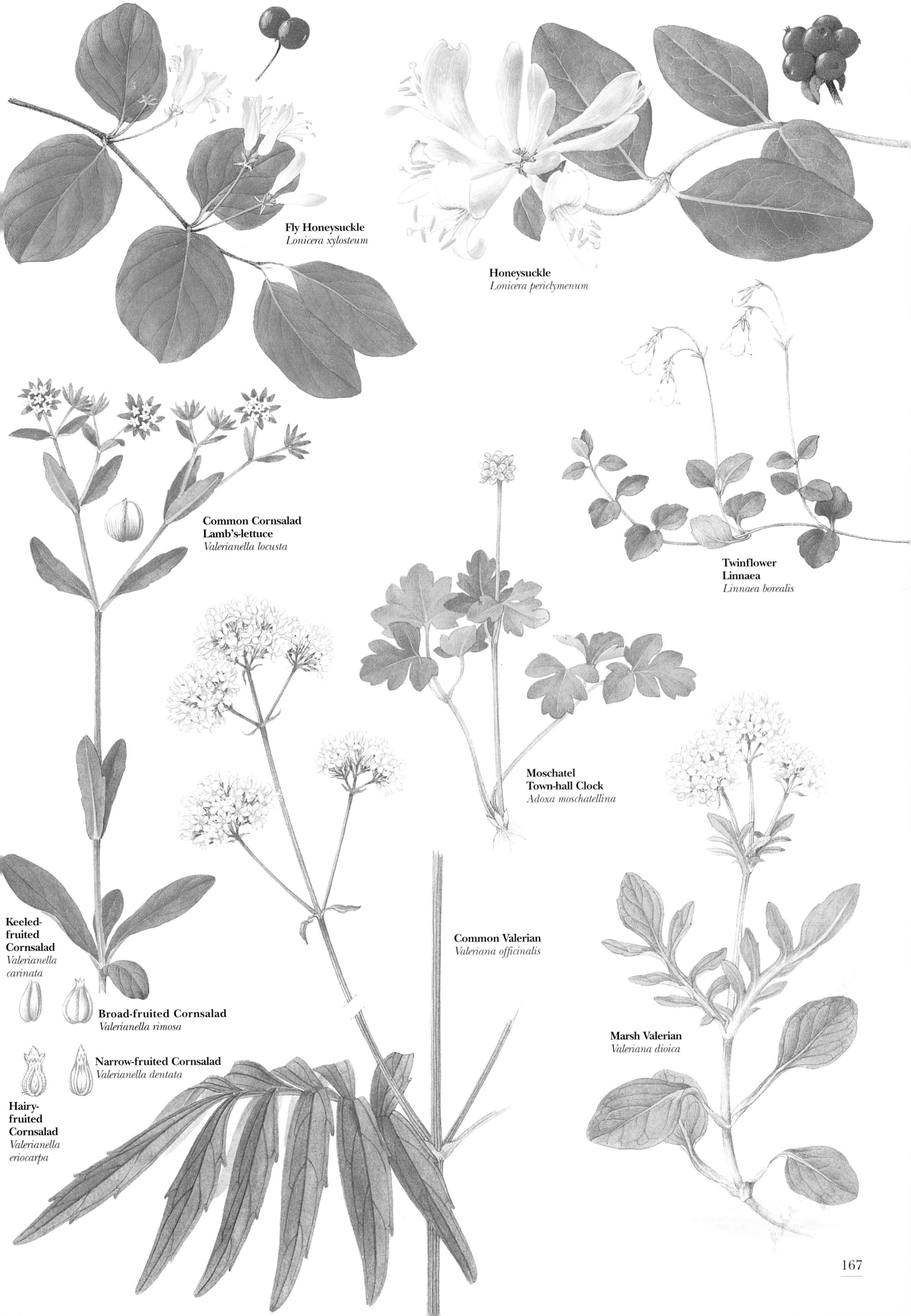

 (see text page 294)

Fly Honeysuckle
Lonicera xylosteum

Honeysuckle
Lonicera periclymenum

Common Cornsalad
Lamb's-lettuce
Valerianella locusta

Twinflower
Linnaea
Linnaea borealis

Moschatel
Town-hall Clock
Adoxa moschatellina

Keeled-fruited Cornsalad
Valerianella carinata

Common Valerian
Valeriana officinalis

Broad-fruited Cornsalad
Valerianella rimosa

Marsh Valerian
Valeriana dioica

Narrow-fruited Cornsalad
Valerianella dentata

Hairy-fruited Cornsalad
Valerianella eriocarpa

PLATE 79

VALERIANACEAE • DIPSACACEAE *(see text page 295)*

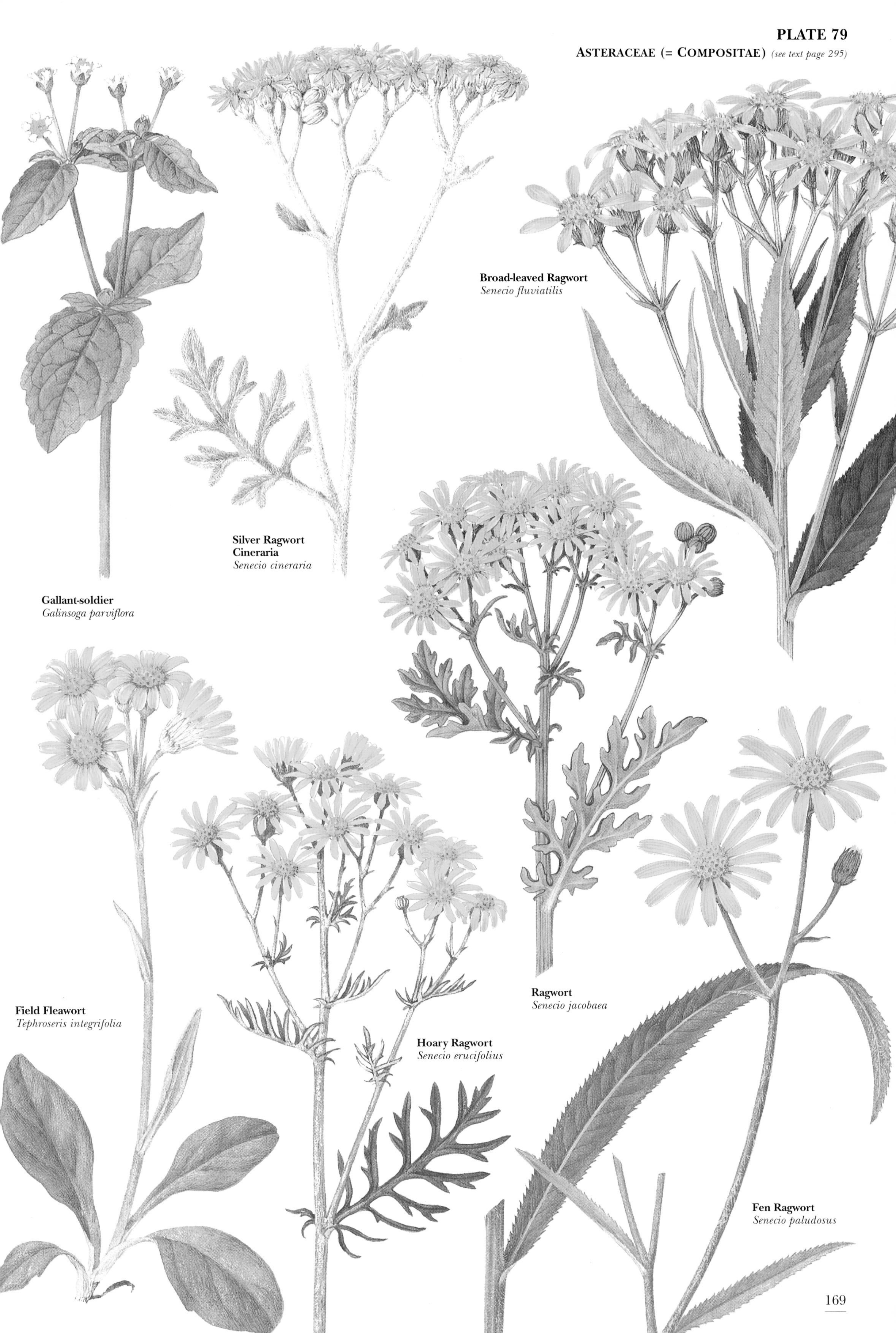
Broad-leaved Ragwort
Senecio fluviatilis
Silver Ragwort
Cineraria
Senecio cineraria
Gallant-soldier
Galinsoga parviflora
Ragwort
Senecio jacobaea
Field Fleawort
Tephroseris integrifolia
Hoary Ragwort
Senecio erucifolius
Fen Ragwort
Senecio paludosus

PLATE 80

ASTERACEAE (= COMPOSITAE) *(see text page 296)*

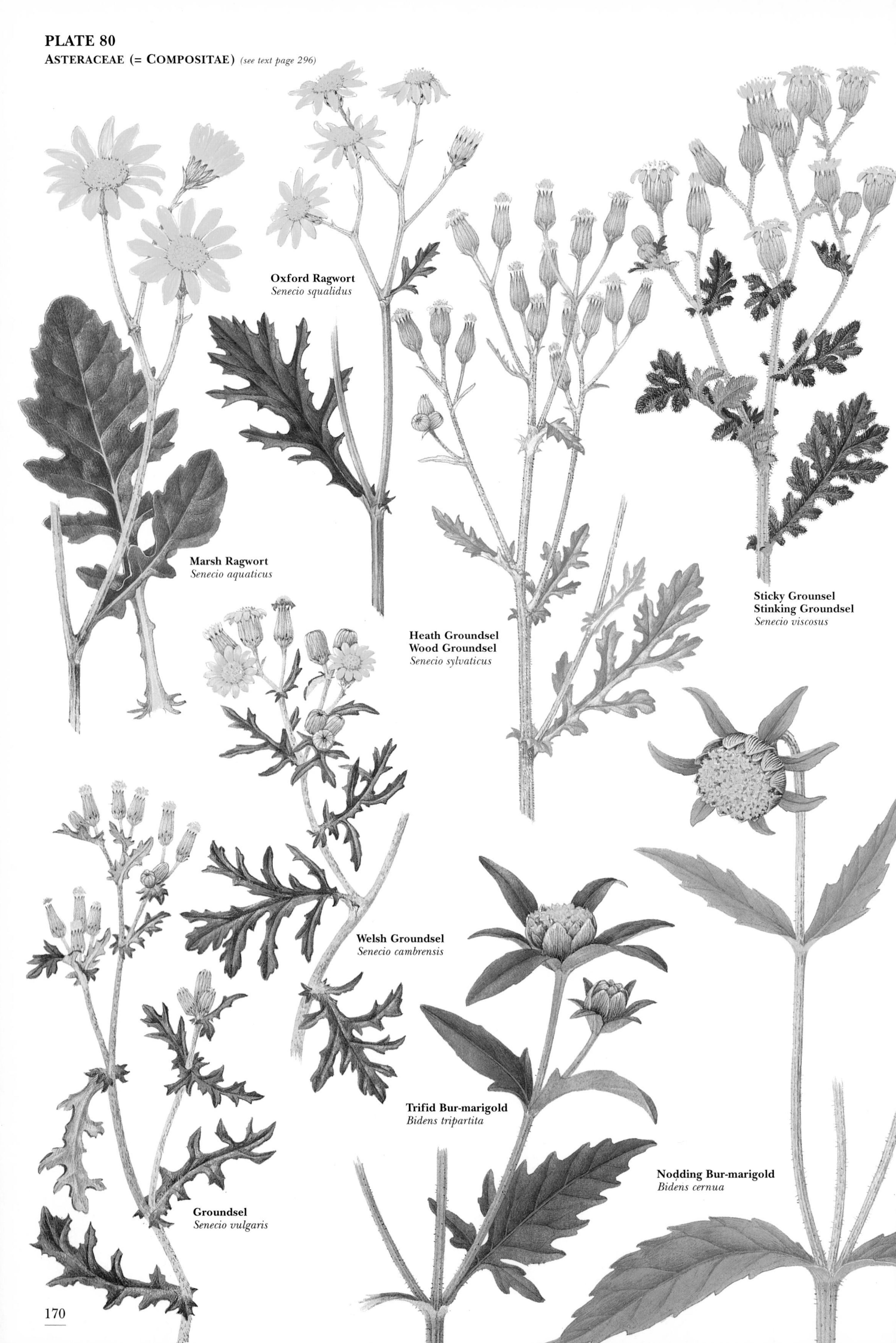

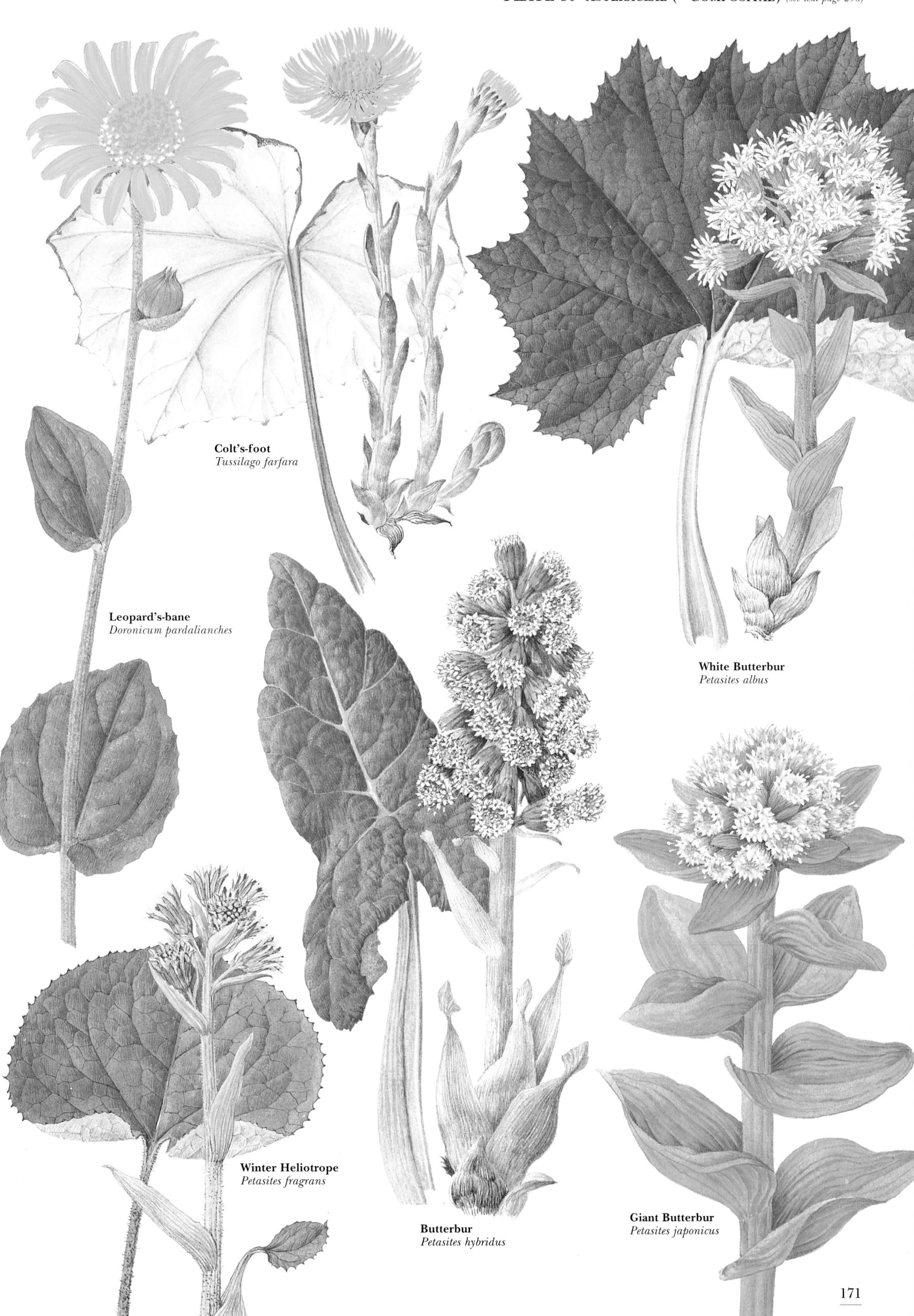

Colt's-foot
Tussilago farfara

Leopard's-bane
Doronicum pardalianches

White Butterbur
Petasites albus

Winter Heliotrope
Petasites fragrans

Butterbur
Petasites hybridus

Giant Butterbur
Petasites japonicus

PLATE 81

ASTERACEAE (= COMPOSITAE) *(see text page 297)*

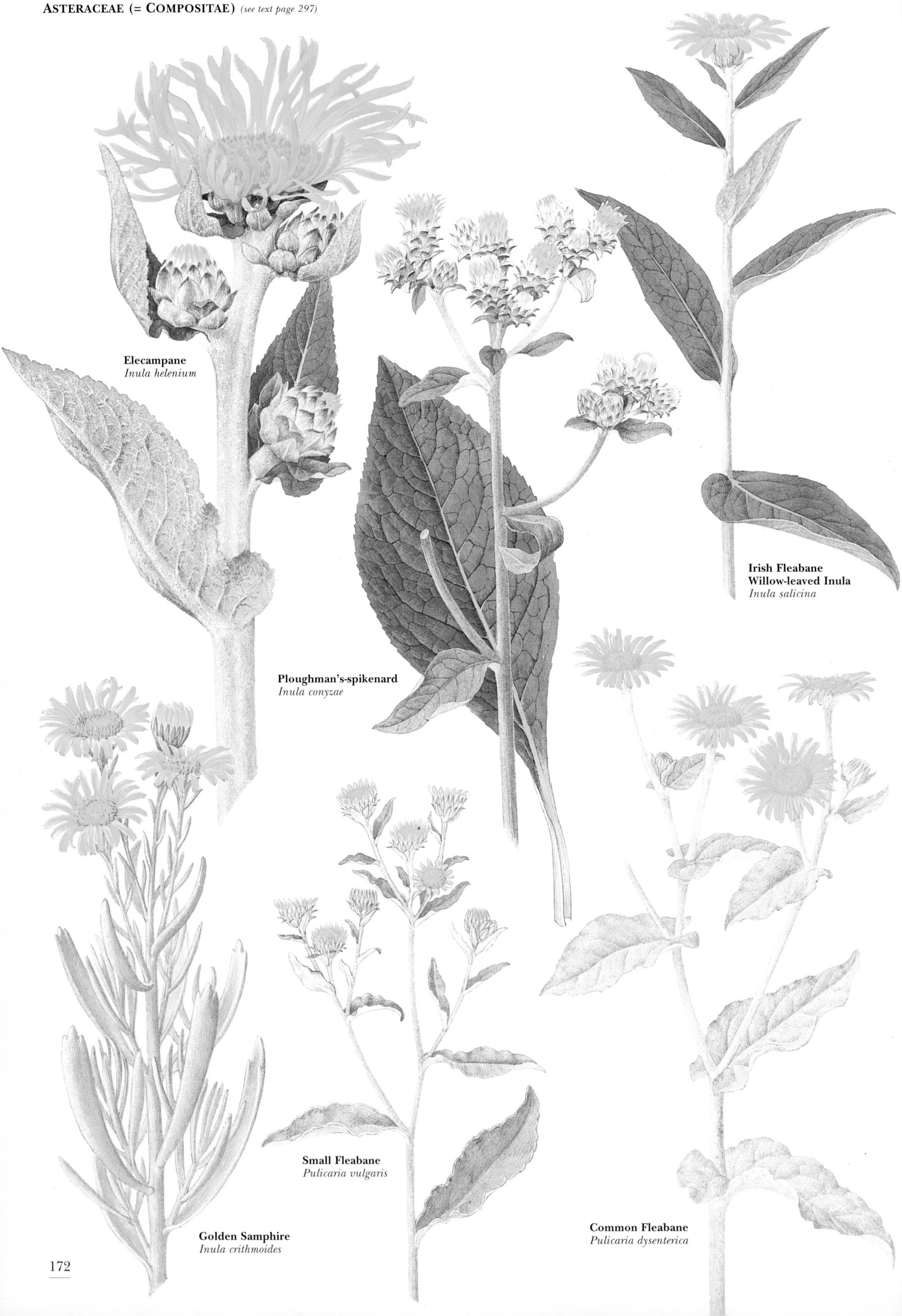

Elecampane
Inula helenium

Irish Fleabane
Willow-leaved Inula
Inula salicina

Ploughman's-spikenard
Inula conyzae

Small Fleabane
Pulicaria vulgaris

Golden Samphire
Inula crithmoides

Common Fleabane
Pulicaria dysenterica

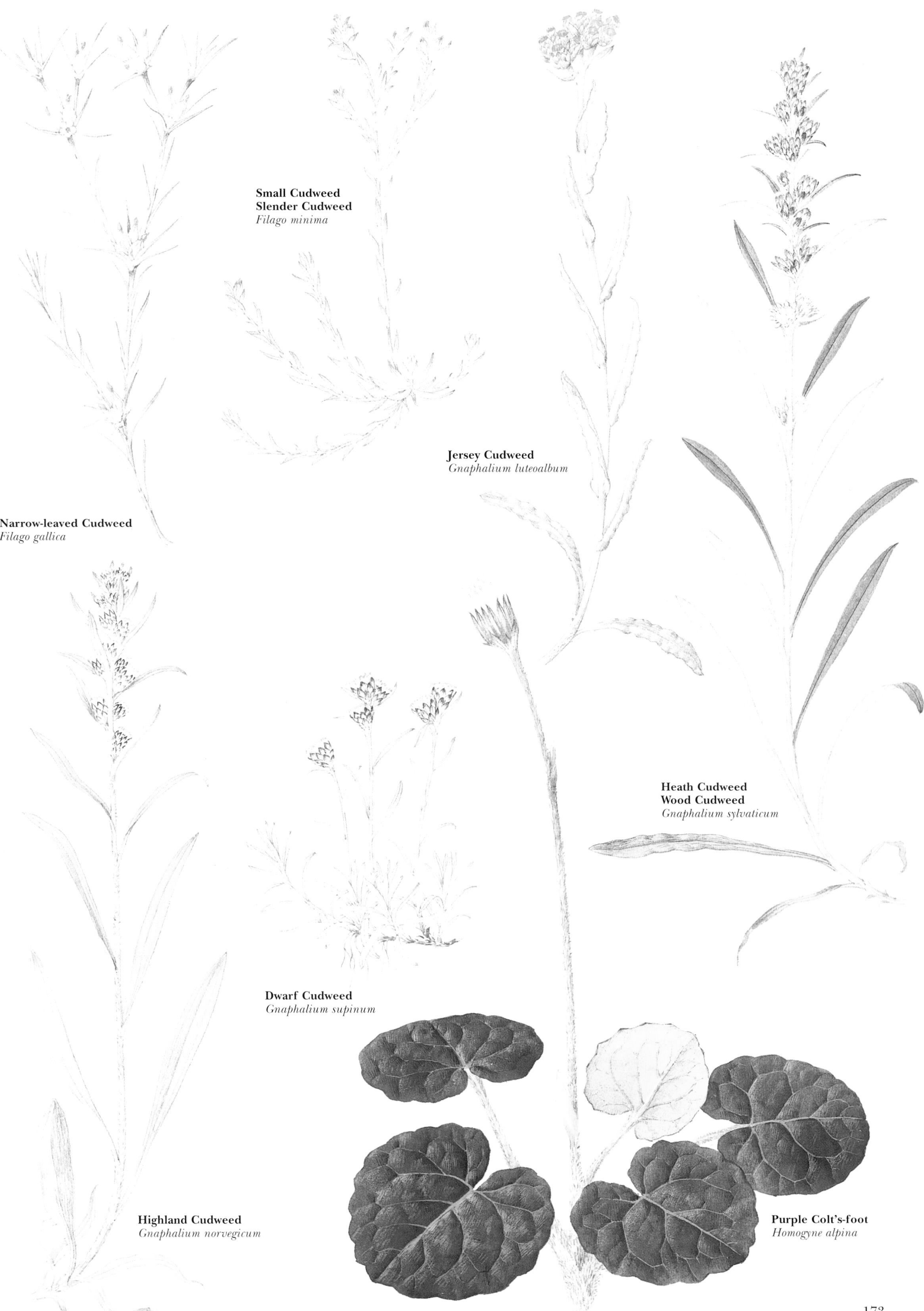
Small Cudweed
Slender Cudweed
Filago minima
Jersey Cudweed
Gnaphalium luteoalbum
Narrow-leaved Cudweed
Filago gallica
Heath Cudweed
Wood Cudweed
Gnaphalium sylvaticum
Dwarf Cudweed
Gnaphalium supinum
Highland Cudweed
Gnaphalium norvegicum
Purple Colt's-foot
Homogyne alpina

PLATE 82

Asteraceae (= Compositae) *(see text page 298)*

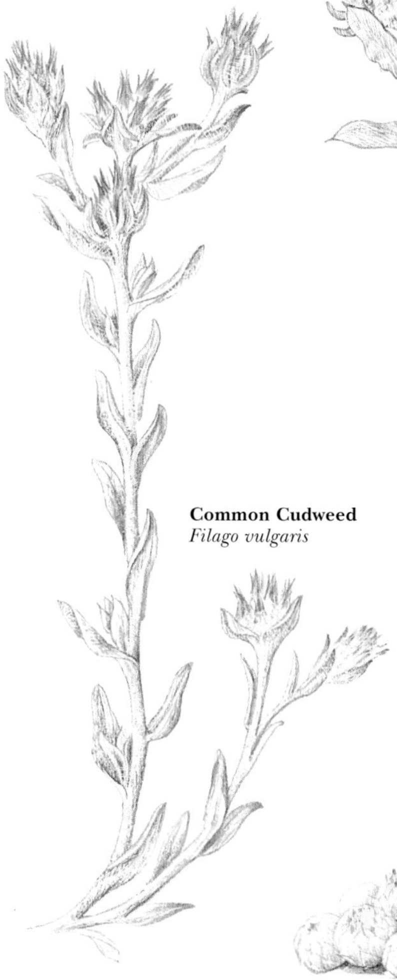

Common Cudweed
Filago vulgaris

Red-tipped Cudweed
Filago lutescens

Marsh Cudweed
Gnaphalium uliginosum

Broad-leaved Cudweed
Spathulate Cudweed
Filago pyramidata

Mountain Everlasting
Cat's-foot
Antennaria dioica

Pearly Everlasting
Anaphalis margaritacea

Michaelmas-daisy
Aster novae-angliae

Michaelmas-daisy
Aster × salignus

Aster puniceus

Michaelmas-daisy
Aster novi-belgii

Sea Aster
Aster tripolium

Goldilocks Aster
Aster linosyris

PLATE 83

ASTERACEAE (= COMPOSITAE) *(see text page 299)*

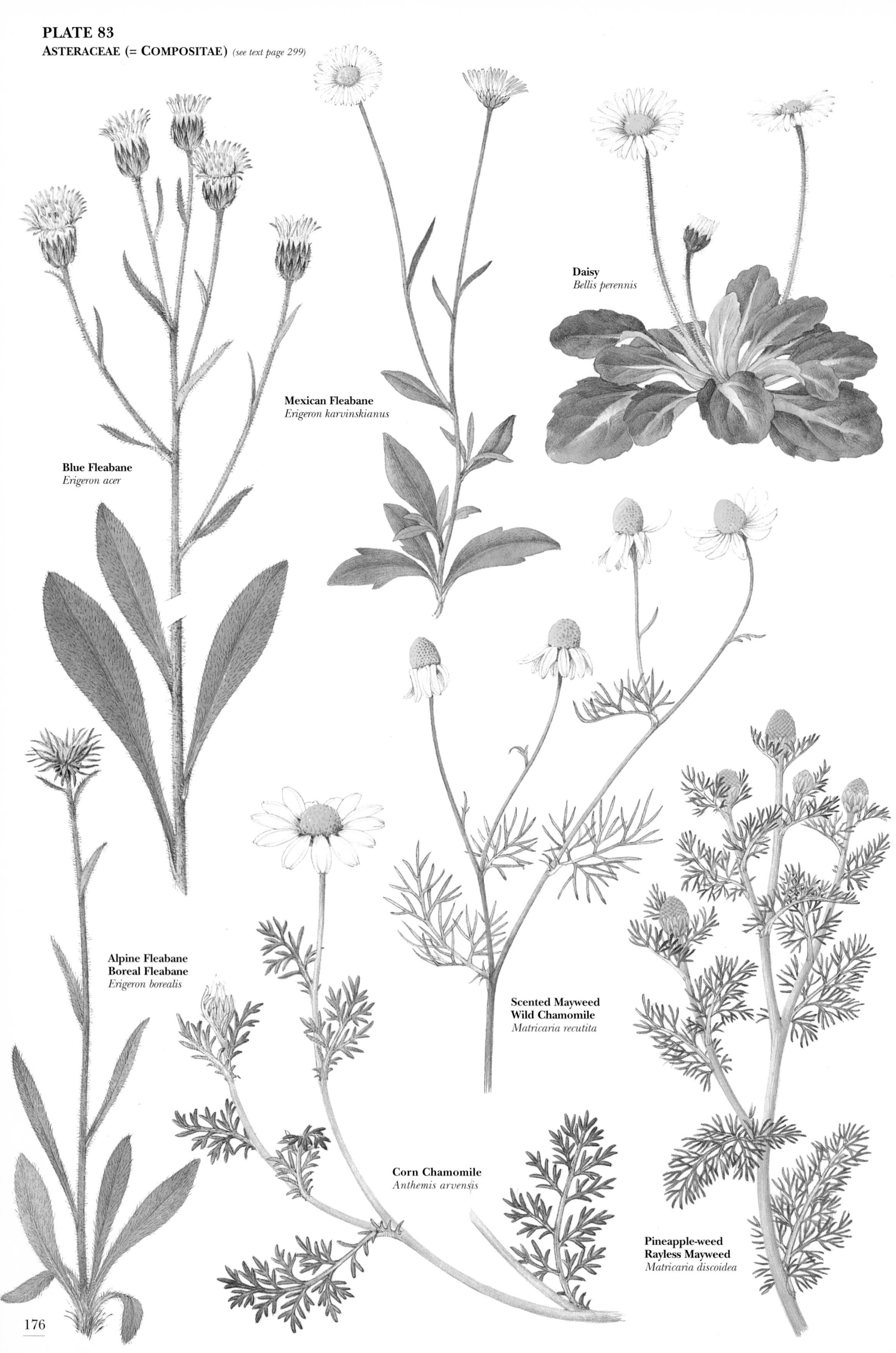

PLATE 83 Asteraceae (= Compositae) (see text page 299)

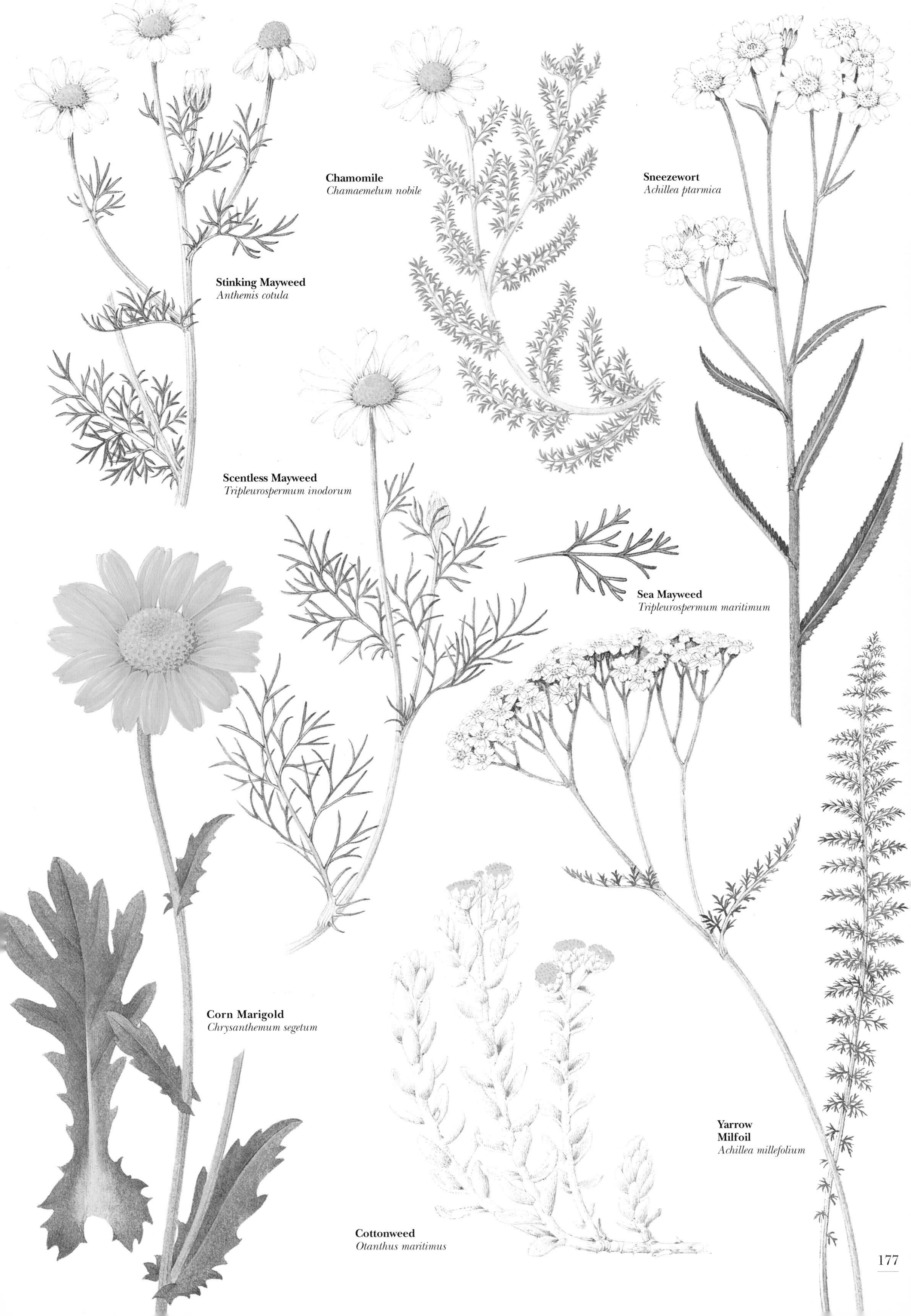
Stinking Mayweed
Anthemis cotula
Chamomile
Chamaemelum nobile
Sneezewort
Achillea ptarmica
Scentless Mayweed
Tripleurospermum inodorum
Sea Mayweed
Tripleurospermum maritimum
Corn Marigold
Chrysanthemum segetum
Yarrow
Milfoil
Achillea millefolium
Cottonweed
Otanthus maritimus

PLATE 84
ASTERACEAE (= COMPOSITAE) *(see text page 300)*

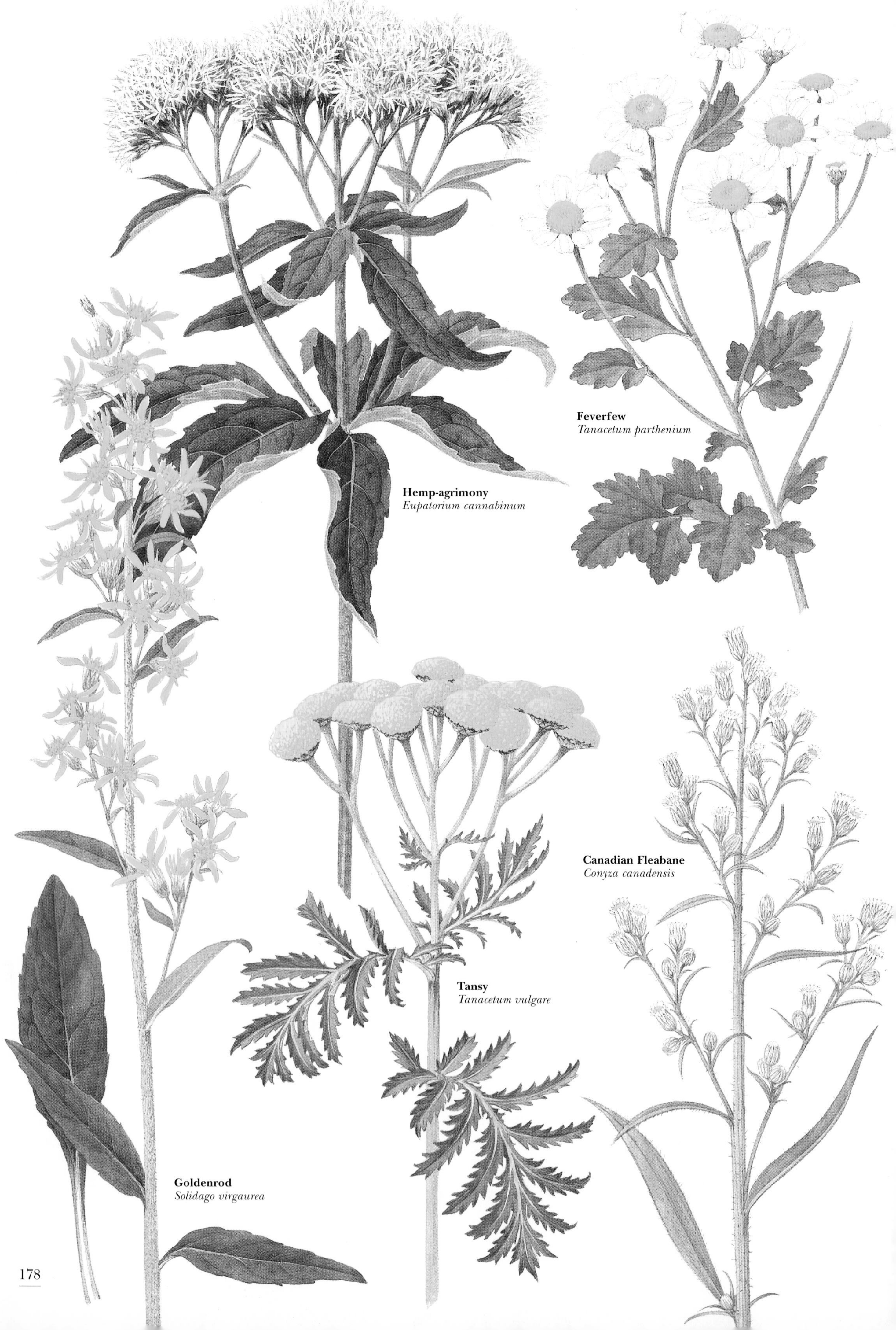

Hemp-agrimony
Eupatorium cannabinum

Feverfew
Tanacetum parthenium

Canadian Fleabane
Conyza canadensis

Tansy
Tanacetum vulgare

Goldenrod
Solidago virgaurea

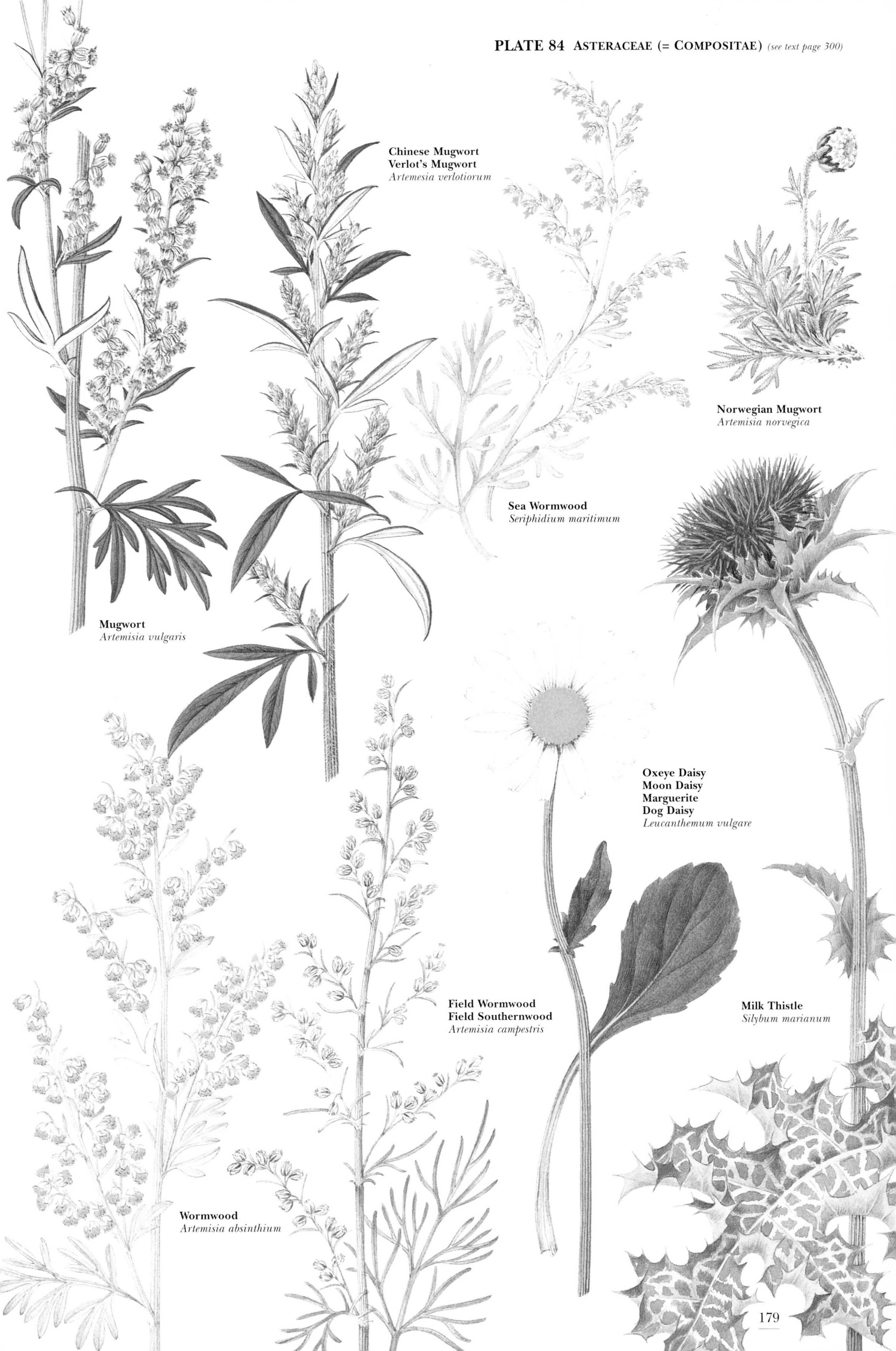
Chinese Mugwort
Verlot's Mugwort
Artemesia verlotiorum
Norwegian Mugwort
Artemisia norvegica
Sea Wormwood
Seriphidium maritimum
Mugwort
Artemisia vulgaris
Oxeye Daisy
Moon Daisy
Marguerite
Dog Daisy
Leucanthemum vulgare
Field Wormwood
Field Southernwood
Artemisia campestris
Milk Thistle
Silybum marianum
Wormwood
Artemisia absinthium

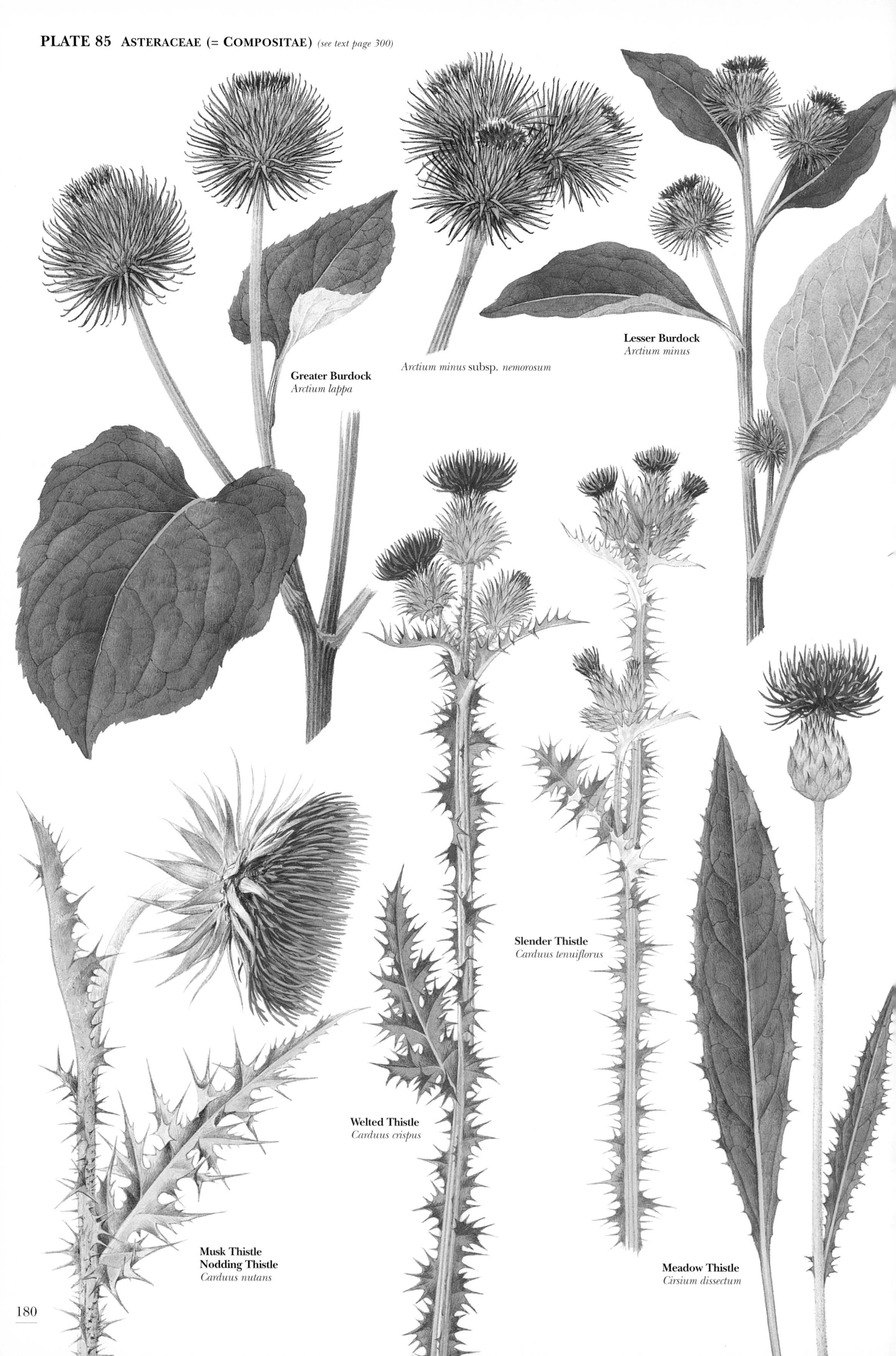
Greater Burdock
Arctium lappa
Arctium minus subsp. *nemorosum*
Lesser Burdock
Arctium minus
Slender Thistle
Carduus tenuiflorus
Welted Thistle
Carduus crispus
Musk Thistle
Nodding Thistle
Carduus nutans
Meadow Thistle
Cirsium dissectum

Marsh Thistle
Cirsium palustre
Woolly Thistle
Cirsium eriophorum
Creeping Thistle
Field Thistle
Cirsium arvense
Spear Thistle
Cirsium vulgare
Dwarf Thistle
Stemless Thistle
Cirsium acaule
Melancholy Thistle
Cirsium heterophyllum
Tuberous Thistle
Cirsium tuberosum

PLATE 86

ASTERACEAE (= COMPOSITAE) *(see text page 302)*

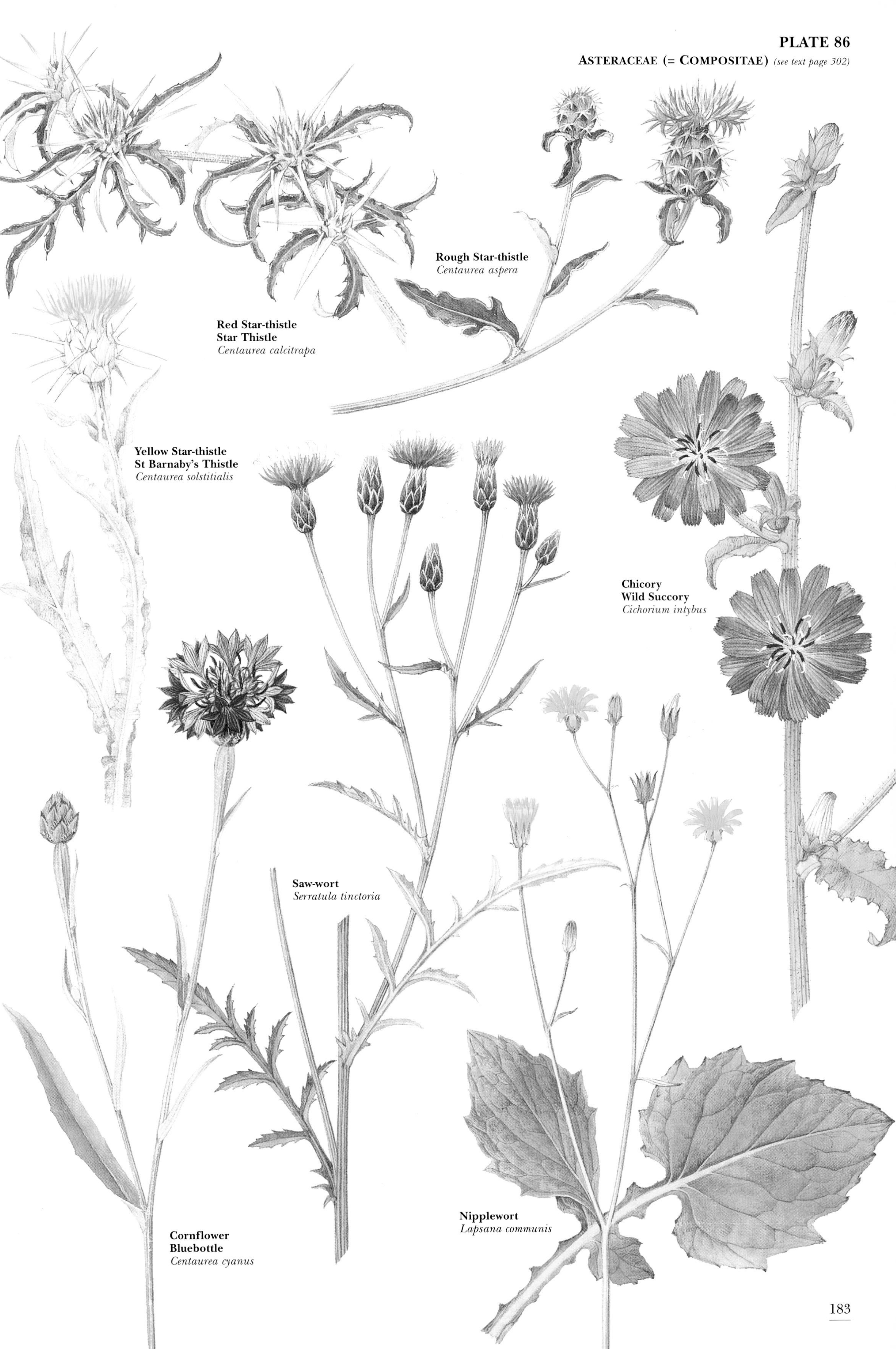
Rough Star-thistle
Centaurea aspera
Red Star-thistle
Star Thistle
Centaurea calcitrapa
Yellow Star-thistle
St Barnaby's Thistle
Centaurea solstitialis
Chicory
Wild Succory
Cichorium intybus
Saw-wort
Serratula tinctoria
Nipplewort
Lapsana communis
Cornflower
Bluebottle
Centaurea cyanus

PLATE 87
ASTERACEAE (= COMPOSITAE) *(see text page 303)*

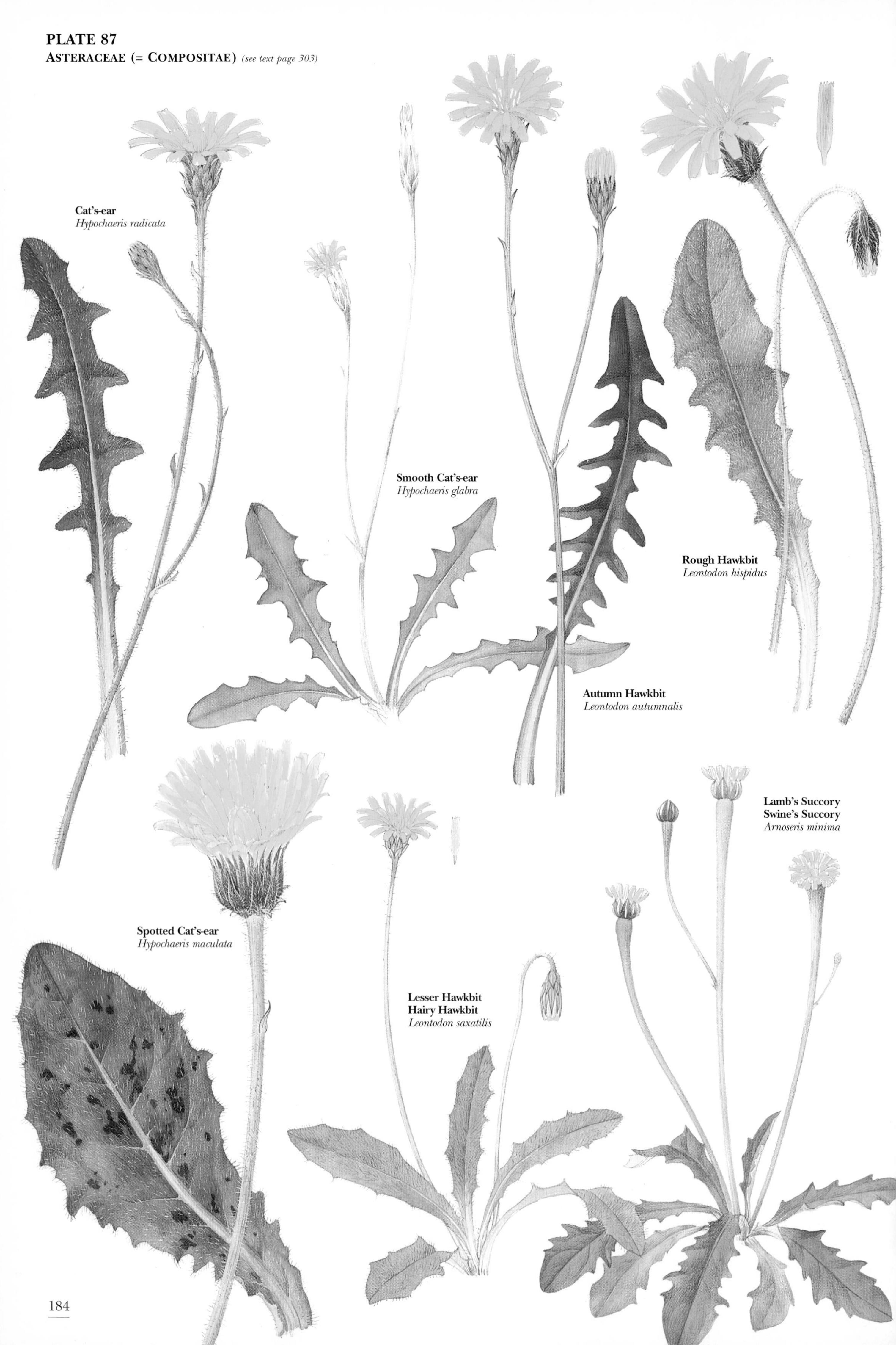

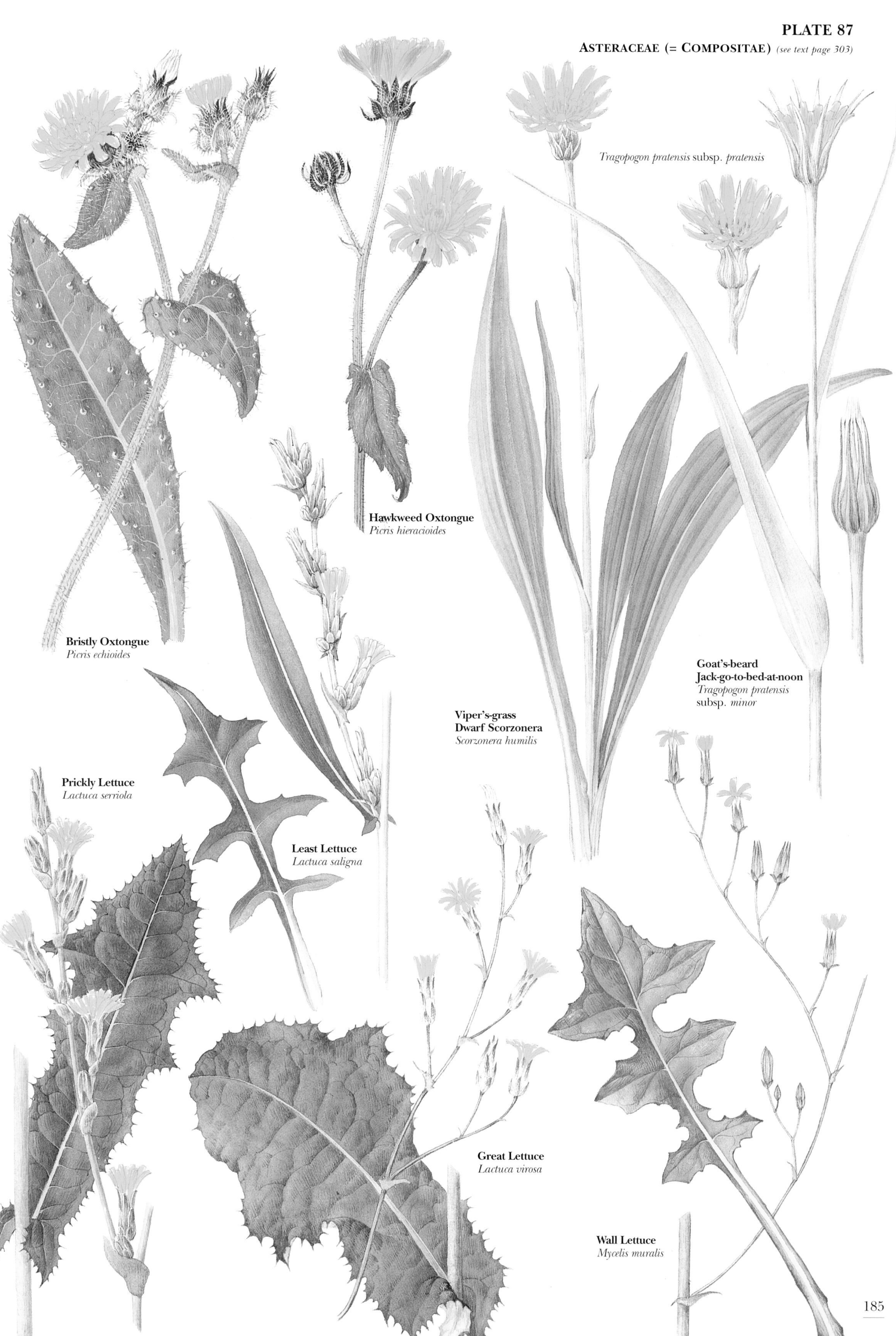
Tragopogon pratensis subsp. *pratensis*
Hawkweed Oxtongue
Picris hieracioides
Bristly Oxtongue
Picris echioides
Goat's-beard
Jack-go-to-bed-at-noon
Tragopogon pratensis
subsp. *minor*
Viper's-grass
Dwarf Scorzonera
Scorzonera humilis
Prickly Lettuce
Lactuca serriola
Least Lettuce
Lactuca saligna
Great Lettuce
Lactuca virosa
Wall Lettuce
Mycelis muralis

Smooth Sow-thistle
Milk-thistle
Sonchus oleraceus
Prickly Sow-thistle
Spiny Milk-thistle
Sonchus asper
Marsh Sow-thistle
Sonchus palustris
Perennial Sow-thistle
Field Milk-thistle
Sonchus arvensis
Bristly Hawk's-beard
Crepis setosa
Stinking Hawk's-beard
Crepis foetida
Alpine Sow-thistle
Blue Sow-thistle
Cicerbita alpina

Beaked Hawk's-beard
Crepis vesicaria

Northern Hawk's-beard
Soft Hawk's-beard
Crepis mollis

Rough Hawk's-beard
Crepis biennis

Marsh Hawk's-beard
Crepis paludosa

Smooth Hawk's-beard
Crepis capillaris

Narrow-leaved Marsh Dandelion
Taraxacum (section *Palustria*)

Dandelion
Taraxacum
(section *Ruderalia*)

PLATE 89

ASTERACEAE (= COMPOSITAE) *(see text page 305)*

Lesser Dandelion
Taraxacum (section *Erythrosperma*)

Mouse-ear Hawkweed
Pilosella officinarum

Taraxacum (section *Spectabilia*)

Hieracium holosericeum
(section *Alpina*)

Hieracium anglicum (section *Cerinthoidea*)

Hieracium dewarii
(section *Alpestria*)

Hieracium lingulatum
(section *Subalpina*)

Hieracium britannicum
(section *Oreadea*)
Hieracium acuminatum (section *Vulgata*)
Hieracium decolor
(section *Oreadea*)
Hieracium vulgatum
(section *Vulgata*)
Hieracium orcadense
(section *Vulgata*)
Hieracium caledonicum
(section *Oreadea*)

 (see text page 306)

Hieracium prenanthoides
(section *Prenanthoidea*)

Hieracium sabaudum
(section *Sabauda*)

Narrow-leaved Water-plantain
Alisma lanceolatum

Hieracium trichocaulon
(section *Tridentata*)

Hieracium latobrigorum
(section *Foliosa*)

Hieracium umbellatum
(section *Umbellata*)

Lesser Water-plantain
Baldellia ranunculoides

 (see text page 306)

Frogbit
Hydrocharis morsus-ranae

Flowering-rush
Butomus umbellatus

Ribbon-leaved Water-plantain
Alisma gramineum

Water-plantain
Alisma plantago-aquatica

Arrowhead
Sagittaria sagittifolia

Floating Water-plantain
Luronium natans

Starfruit
Thrumwort
Damasonium alisma

PLATE 91

HYDROCHARITACEAE • SCHEUCHZERIACEAE • JUNCAGINACEAE *(see text page 307)*

(see text page 307)

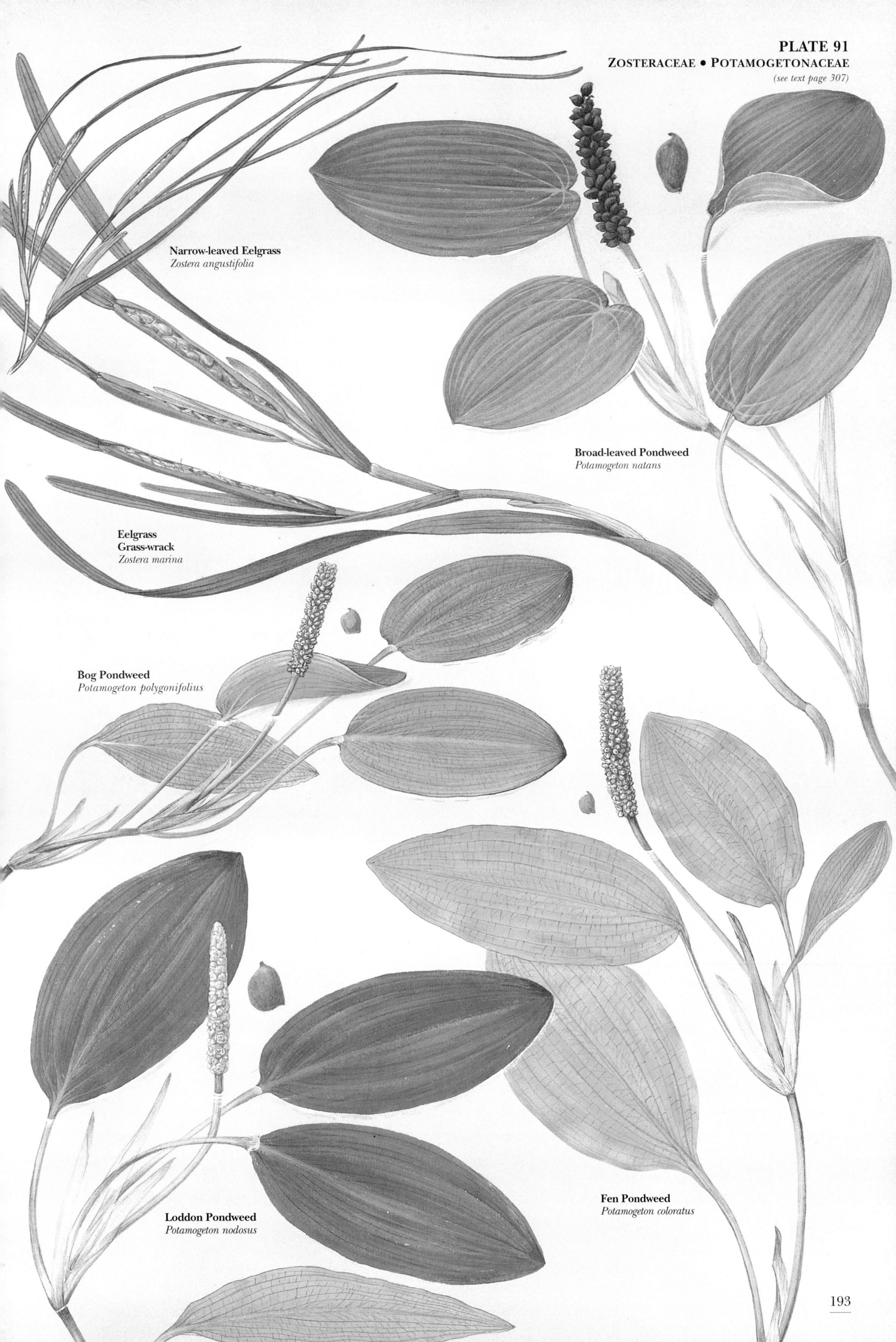
Narrow-leaved Eelgrass
Zostera angustifolia
Broad-leaved Pondweed
Potamogeton natans
Eelgrass
Grass-wrack
Zostera marina
Bog Pondweed
Potamogeton polygonifolius
Fen Pondweed
Potamogeton coloratus
Loddon Pondweed
Potamogeton nodosus

PLATE 92
POTAMOGETONACEAE (see text page 308)
Shining Pondweed
Potamogeton lucens
Various-leaved Pondweed
Potamogeton gramineus
Red Pondweed
Potamogeton alpinus
Long-stalked Pondweed
Potamogeton praelongus
Perfoliate Pondweed
Potamogeton perfoliatus
American Pondweed
Leafy Pondweed
Potamogeton epihydrus

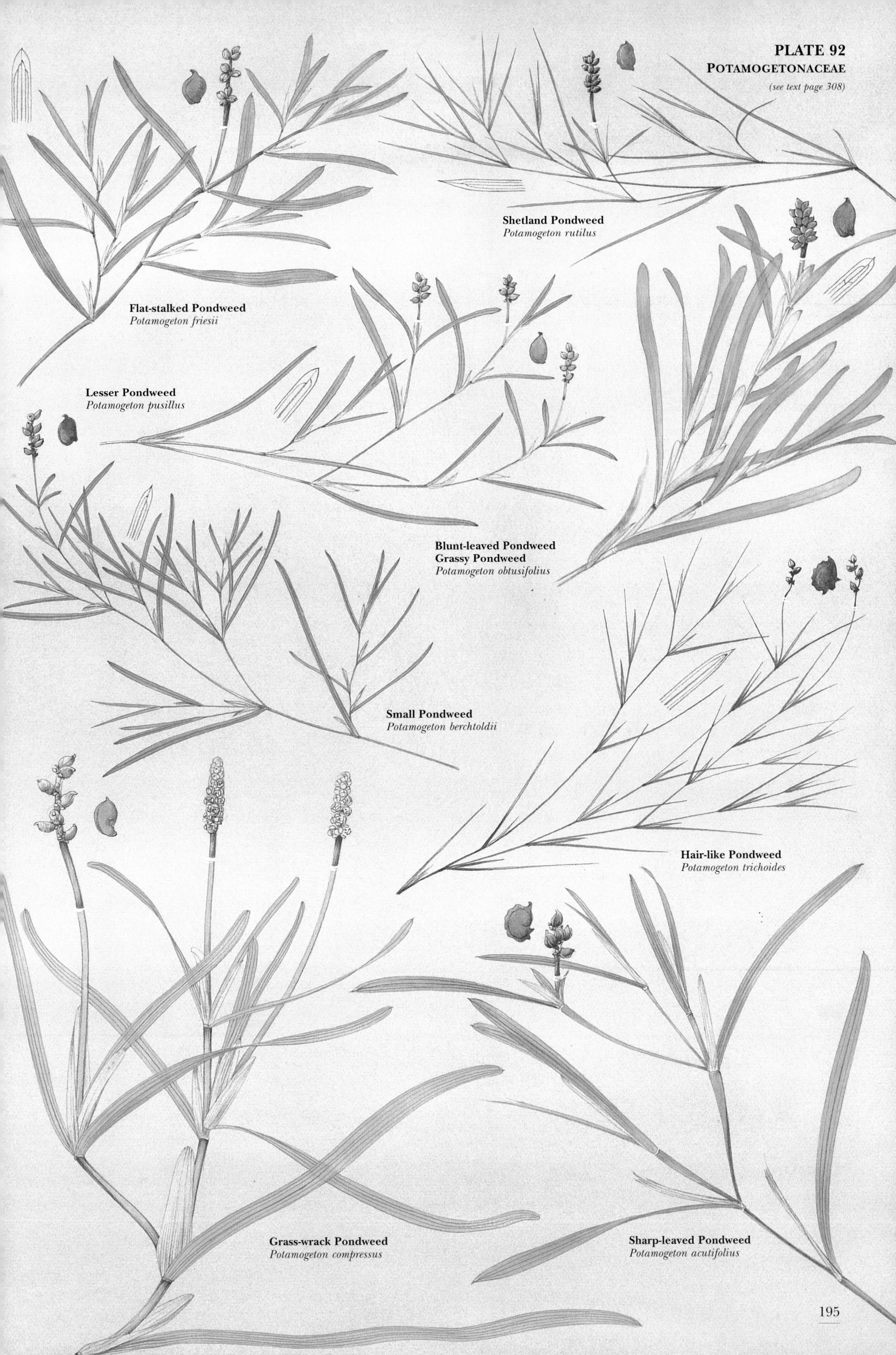
PLATE 92
POTAMOGETONACEAE
(see text page 308)
Shetland Pondweed
Potamogeton rutilus
Flat-stalked Pondweed
Potamogeton friesii
Lesser Pondweed
Potamogeton pusillus
Blunt-leaved Pondweed
Grassy Pondweed
Potamogeton obtusifolius
Small Pondweed
Potamogeton berchtoldii
Hair-like Pondweed
Potamogeton trichoides
Grass-wrack Pondweed
Potamogeton compressus
Sharp-leaved Pondweed
Potamogeton acutifolius

PLATE 93

POTAMOGETONACEAE • RUPPIACEAE *(see text page 309)*

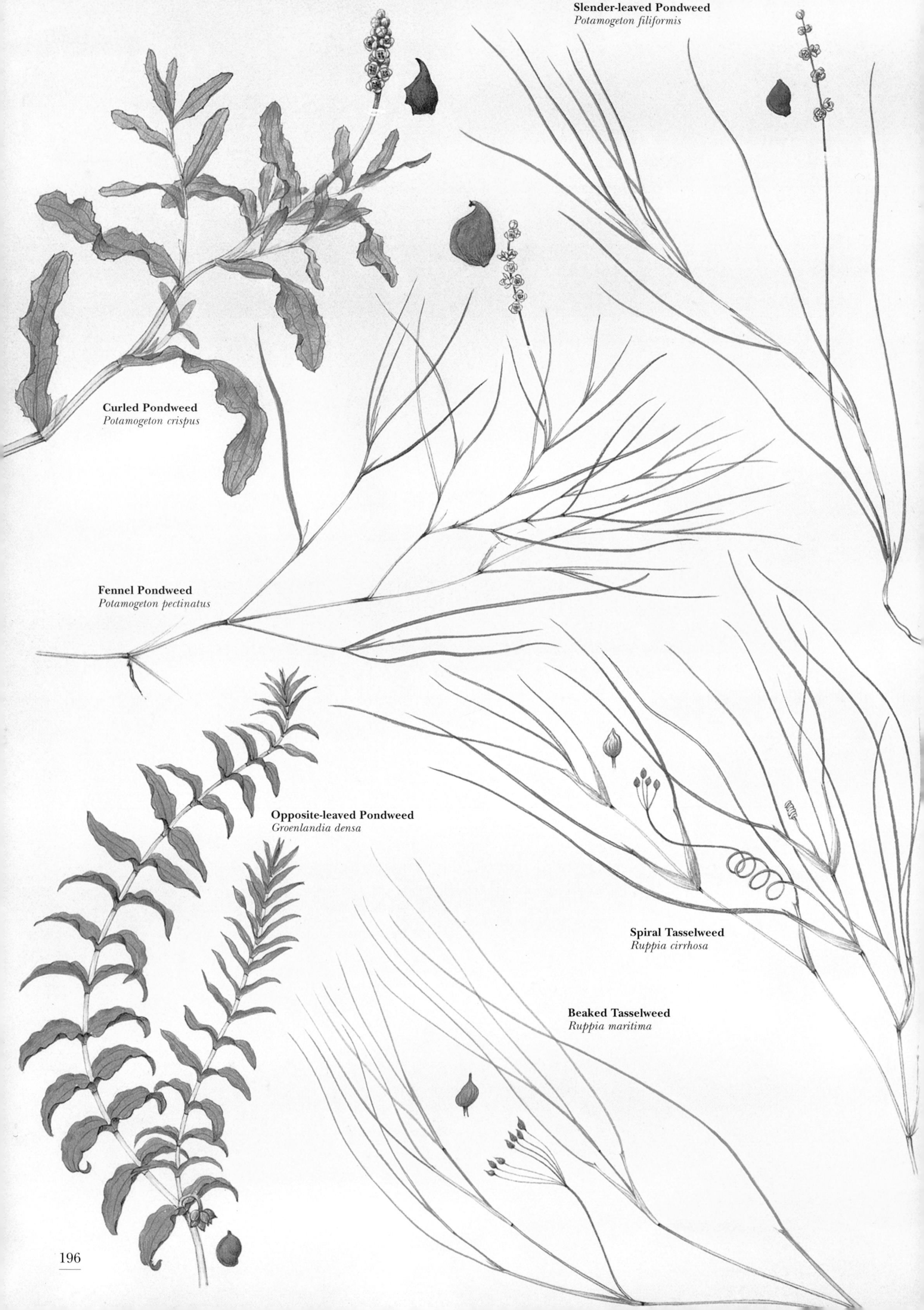

Slender-leaved Pondweed
Potamogeton filiformis

Curled Pondweed
Potamogeton crispus

Fennel Pondweed
Potamogeton pectinatus

Opposite-leaved Pondweed
Groenlandia densa

Spiral Tasselweed
Ruppia cirrhosa

Beaked Tasselweed
Ruppia maritima

 (see text page 309)

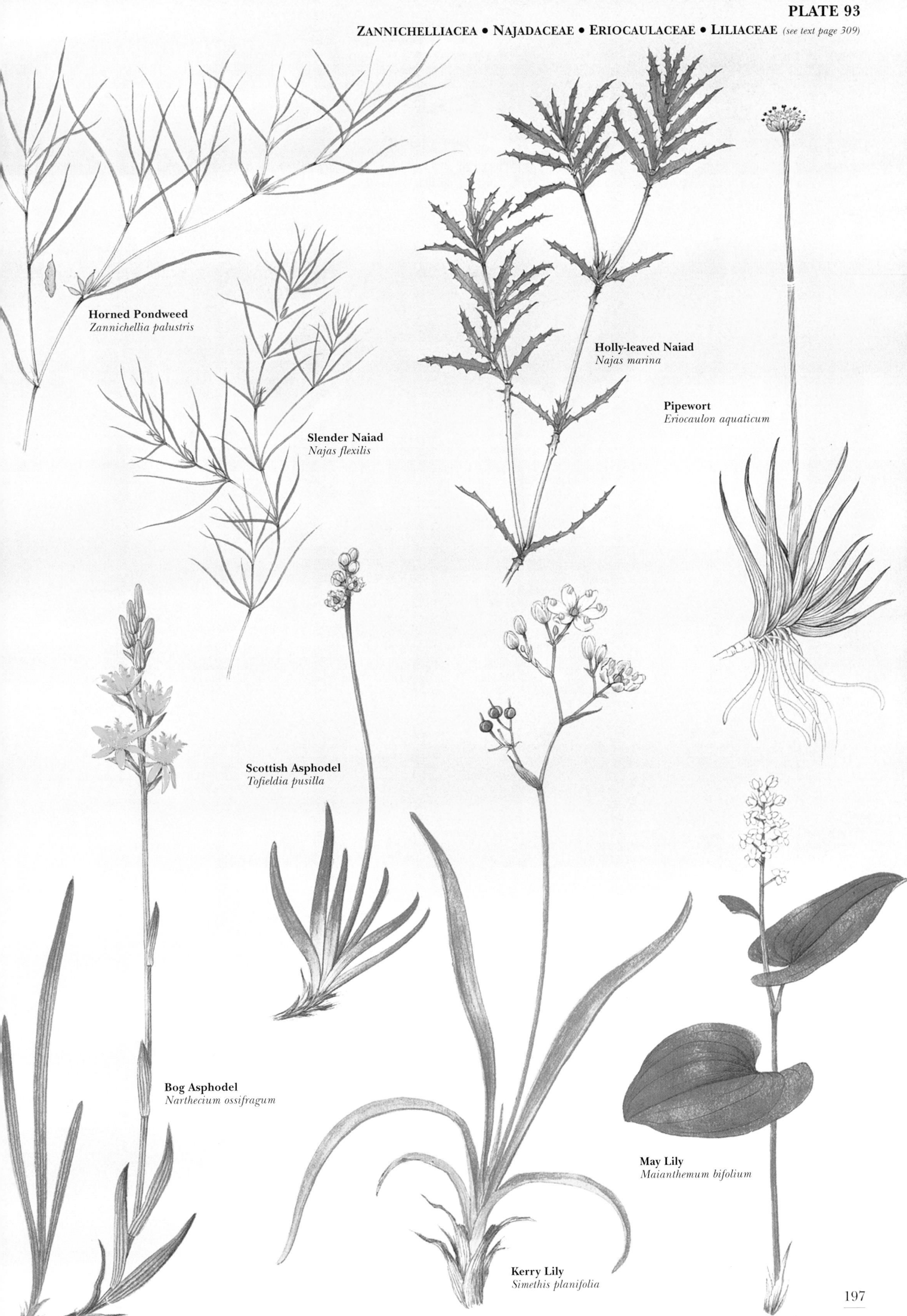

Horned Pondweed
Zannichellia palustris

Slender Naiad
Najas flexilis

Holly-leaved Naiad
Najas marina

Pipewort
Eriocaulon aquaticum

Scottish Asphodel
Tofieldia pusilla

Bog Asphodel
Narthecium ossifragum

May Lily
Maianthemum bifolium

Kerry Lily
Simethis planifolia

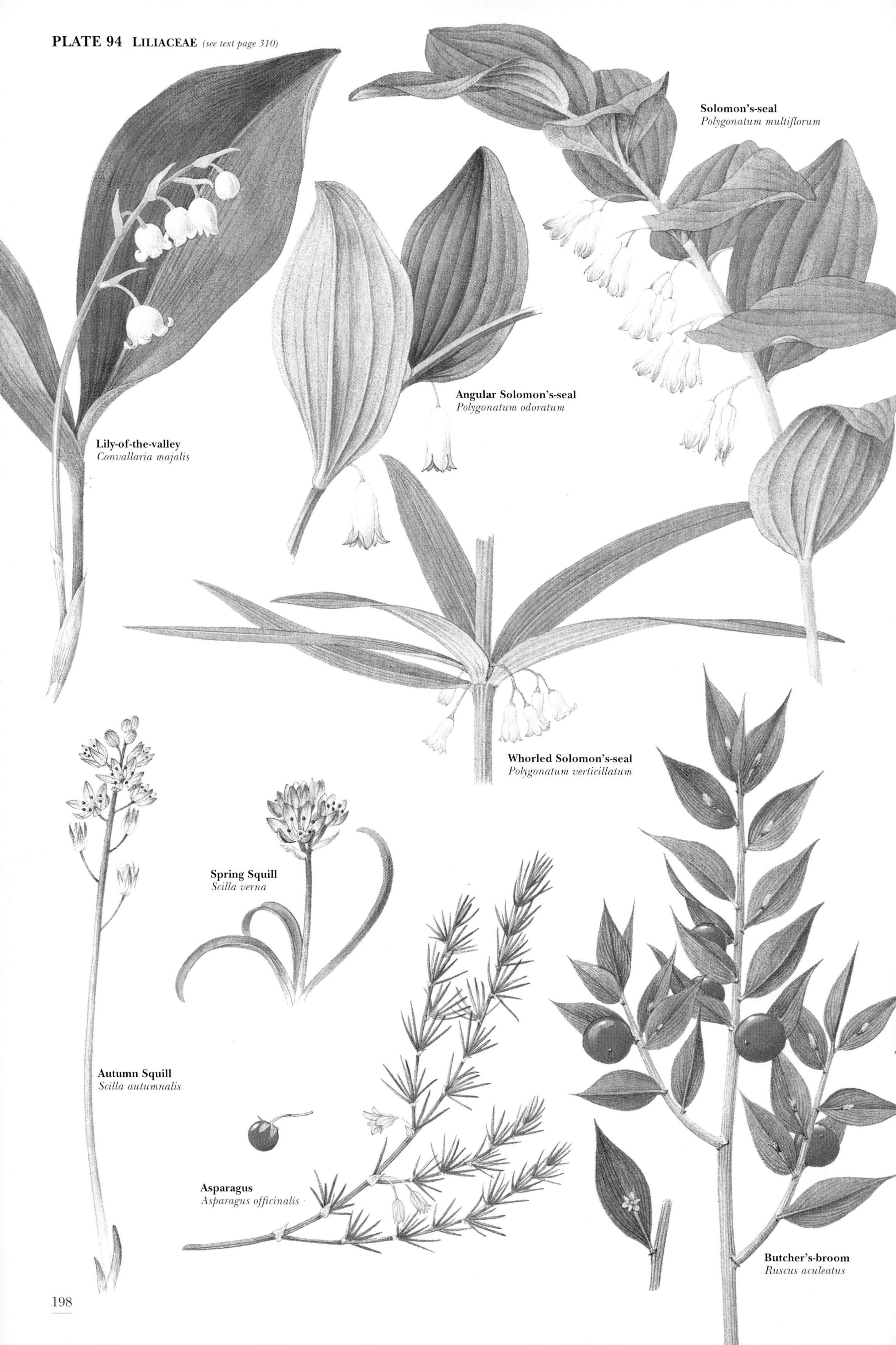
Solomon's-seal
Polygonatum multiflorum
Angular Solomon's-seal
Polygonatum odoratum
Lily-of-the-valley
Convallaria majalis
Whorled Solomon's-seal
Polygonatum verticillatum
Spring Squill
Scilla verna
Autumn Squill
Scilla autumnalis
Asparagus
Asparagus officinalis
Butcher's-broom
Ruscus aculeatus

PLATE 94

LILIACEAE *(see text page 310)*

PLATE 95
LILIACEAE *(see text page 310)*

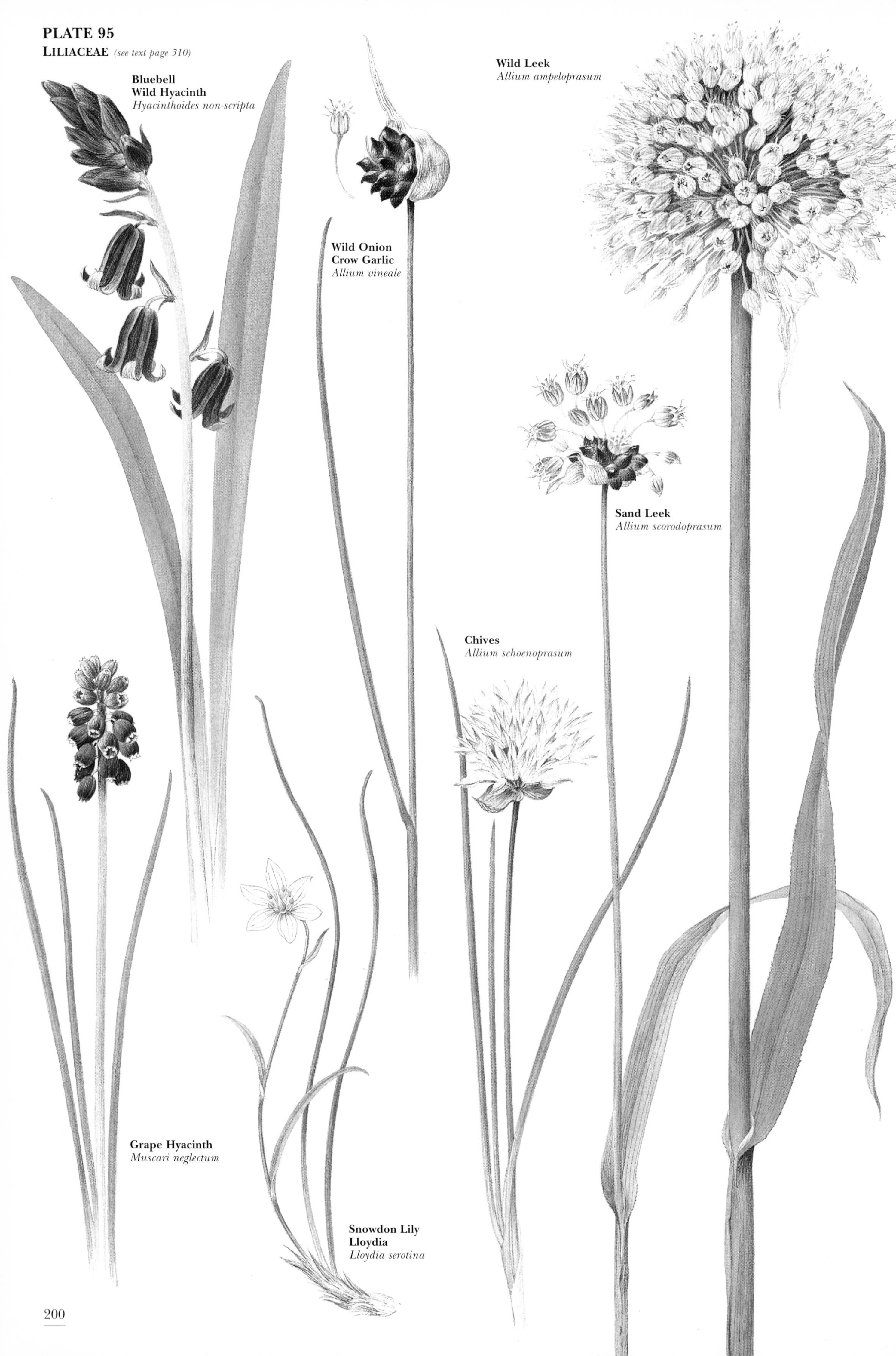

PLATE 95

LILIACEAE *(see text page 310)*

PLATE 96

LILIACEAE *(see text page 311)*

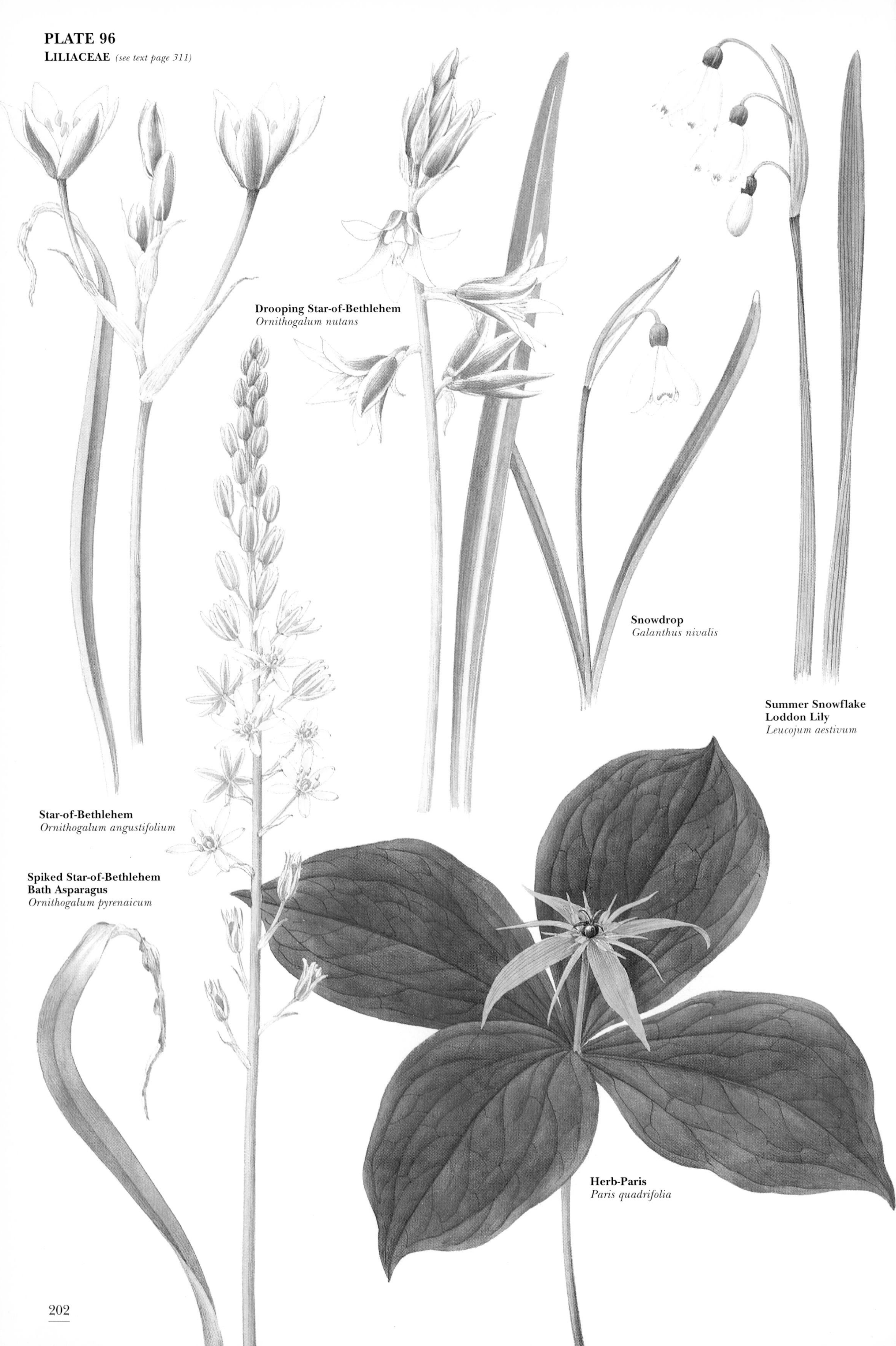

Drooping Star-of-Bethlehem
Ornithogalum nutans

Snowdrop
Galanthus nivalis

Summer Snowflake
Loddon Lily
Leucojum aestivum

Star-of-Bethlehem
Ornithogalum angustifolium

Spiked Star-of-Bethlehem
Bath Asparagus
Ornithogalum pyrenaicum

Herb-Paris
Paris quadrifolia

 (see text page 311)

Spanish Daffodil
Narcissus pseudonarcissus
subsp. *major*
Wild Daffodil
Lent Lily
Narcissus pseudonarcissus
subsp. *pseudonarcissus*
Tenby Daffodil
Narcissus pseudonarcissus
subsp. *obvallaris*
Primrose-peerless
Narcissus × *medioluteus*
Pheasant's-eye
Narcissus poeticus
subsp. *poeticus*
Spring Crocus
Purple Crocus
Crocus vernus
Autumn Crocus
Crocus nudiflorus
Blue-eyed-grass
Sisyrinchium bermudiana

PLATE 97

IRIDACEAE *(see text page 312)*

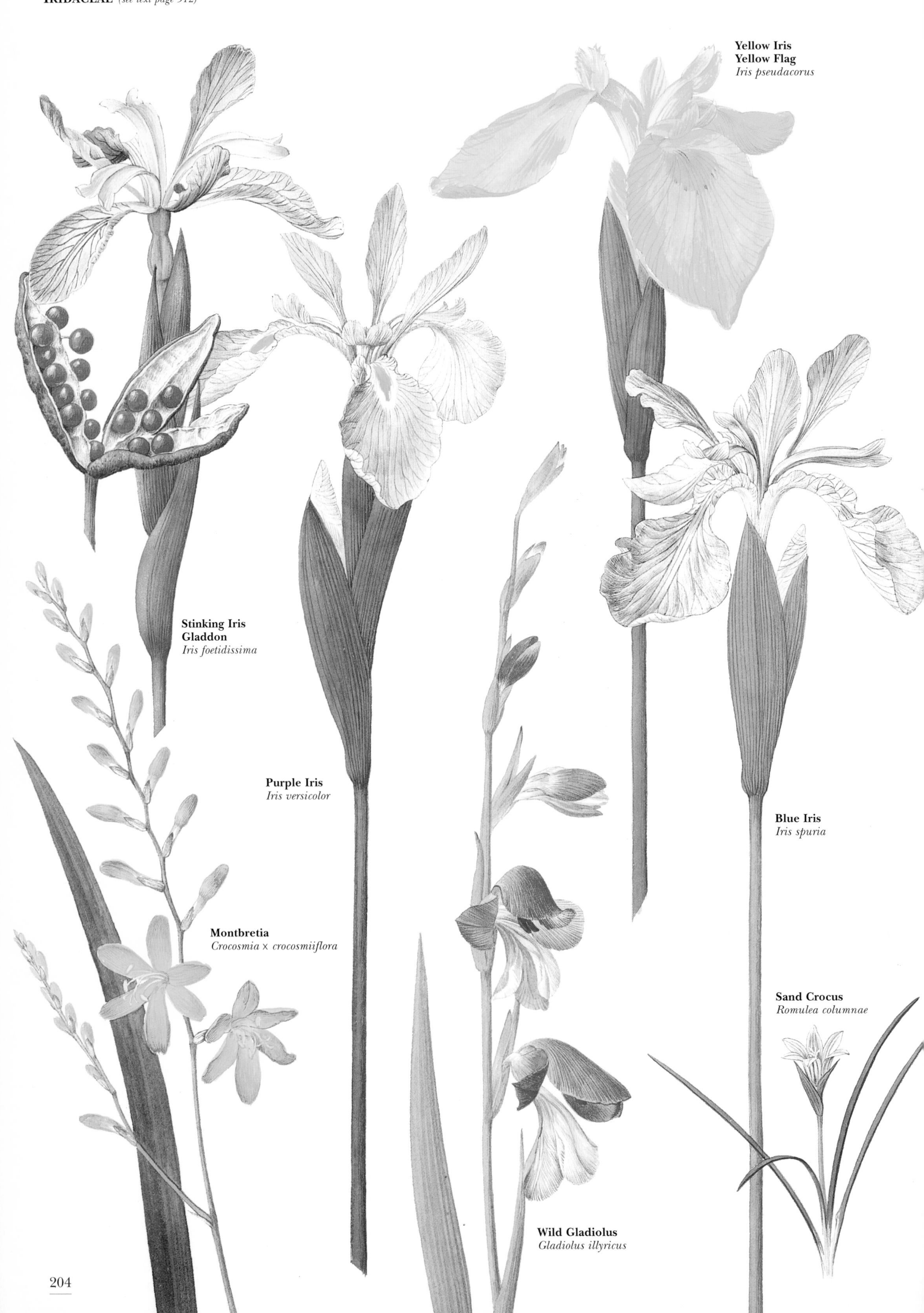

 (see text page 312)

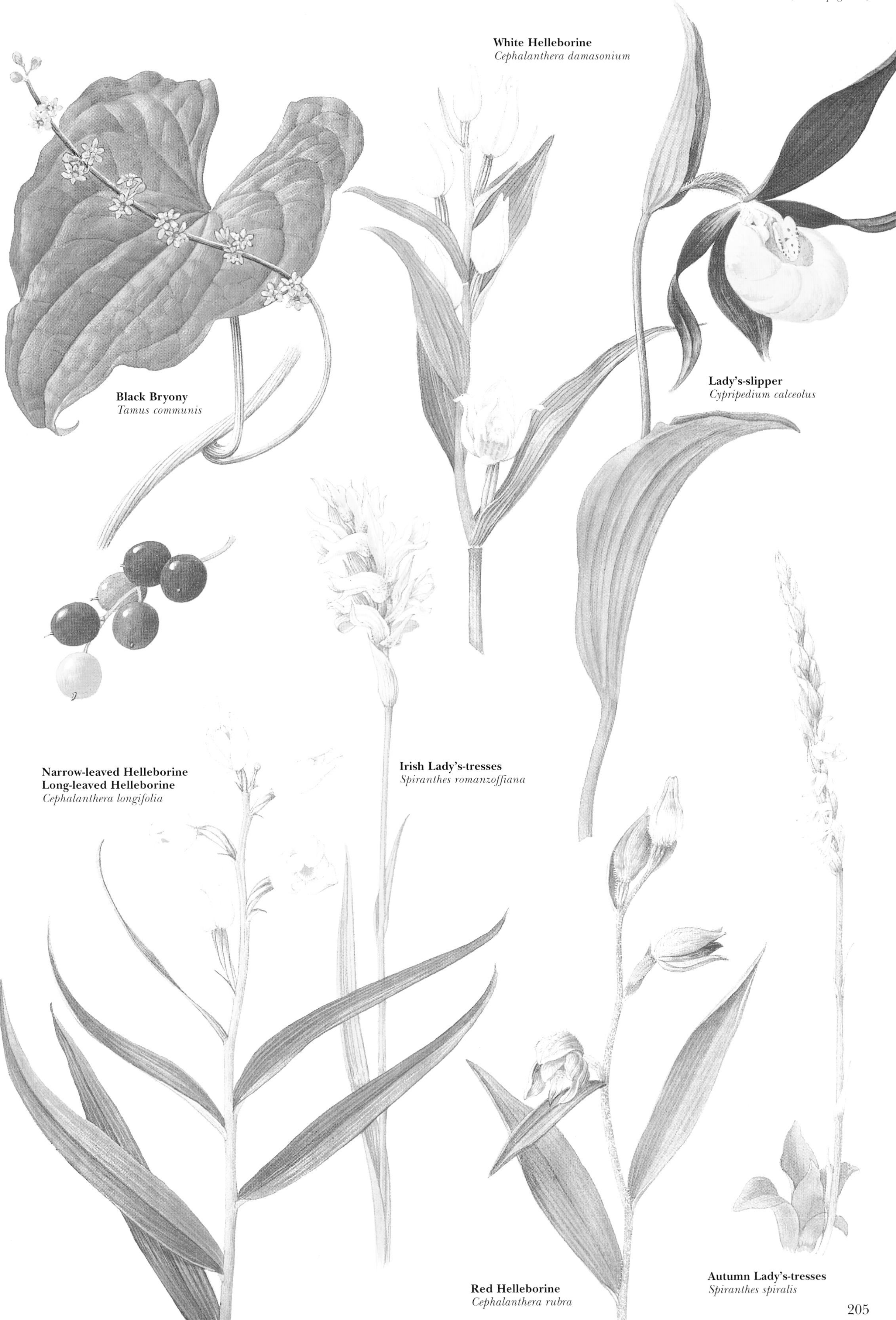
White Helleborine
Cephalanthera damasonium
Black Bryony
Tamus communis
Lady's-slipper
Cypripedium calceolus
Narrow-leaved Helleborine
Long-leaved Helleborine
Cephalanthera longifolia
Irish Lady's-tresses
Spiranthes romanzoffiana
Red Helleborine
Cephalanthera rubra
Autumn Lady's-tresses
Spiranthes spiralis

PLATE 98

ORCHIDACEAE *(see text page 313)*

Marsh Helleborine
Epipactis palustris

Broad-leaved Helleborine
Epipatis helleborine

Violet Helleborine
Epipactis purpurata

Green-flowered Helleborine
Epipactis phyllanthes

Dark-red Helleborine
Epipactis atrorubens

Narrow-lipped Helleborine
Epipactis leptochila var. *leptochila*

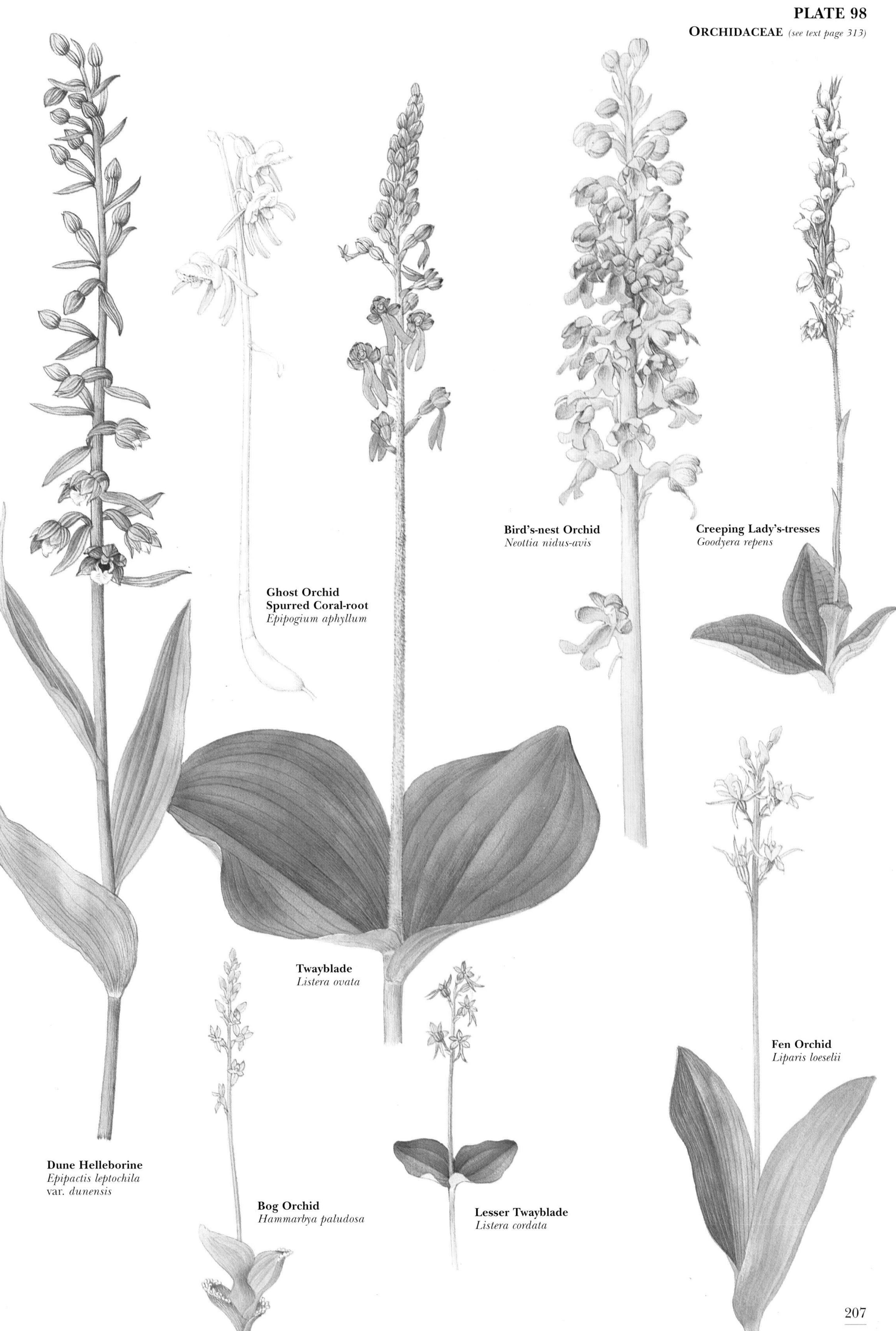
Dune Helleborine
Epipactis leptochila
var. *dunensis*
Ghost Orchid
Spurred Coral-root
Epipogium aphyllum
Twayblade
Listera ovata
Bird's-nest Orchid
Neottia nidus-avis
Creeping Lady's-tresses
Goodyera repens
Bog Orchid
Hammarbya paludosa
Lesser Twayblade
Listera cordata
Fen Orchid
Liparis loeselii

PLATE 99

ORCHIDACEAE *(see text page 314)*

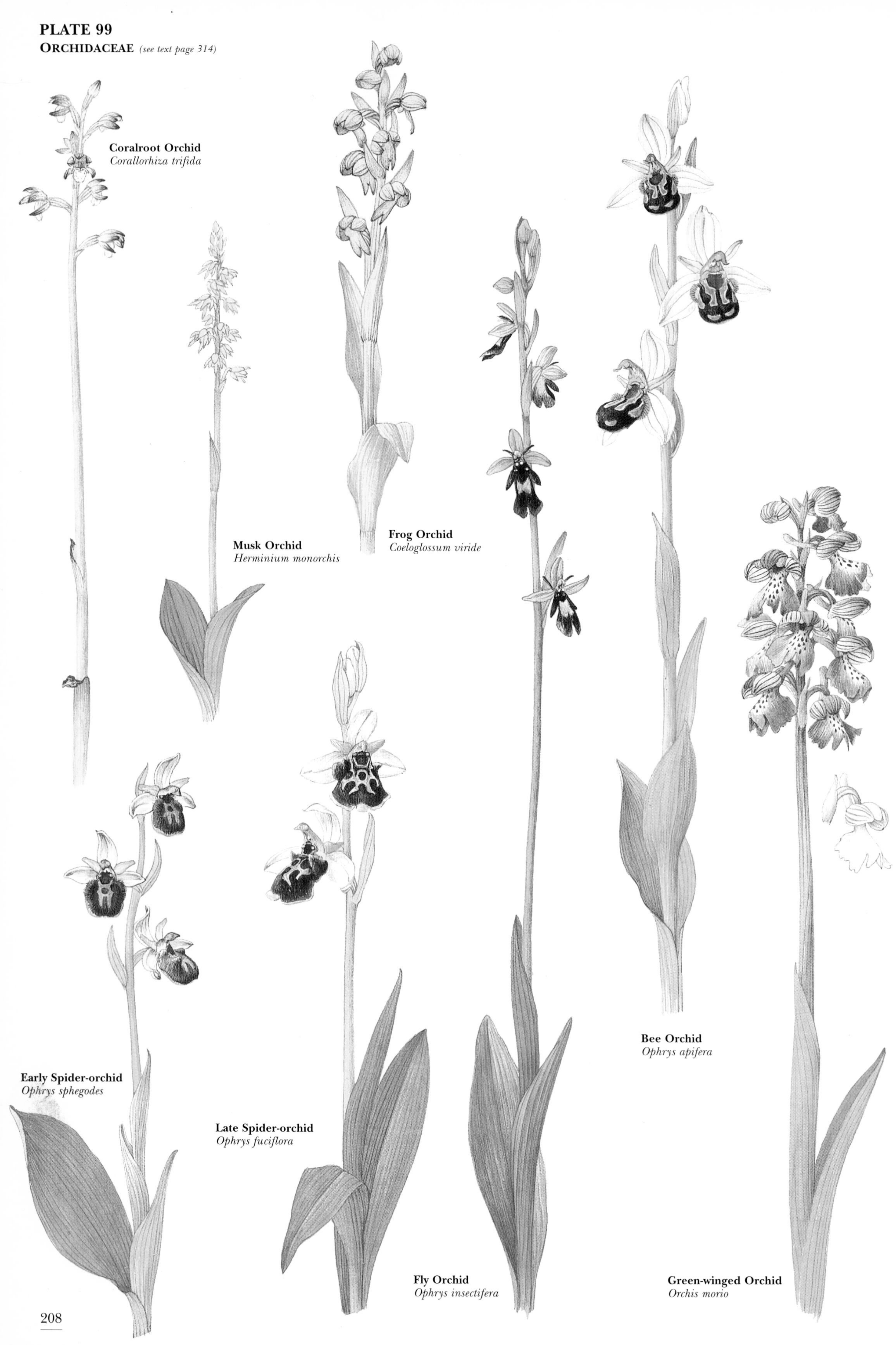

Burnt Orchid
Orchis ustulata

Monkey Orchid
Orchis simia

Early Purple Orchid
Orchis mascula

Military Orchid
Soldier Orchid
Orchis militaris

Lady Orchid
Orchis purpurea

Loose-flowered Orchid
Jersey Orchid
Orchis laxiflora

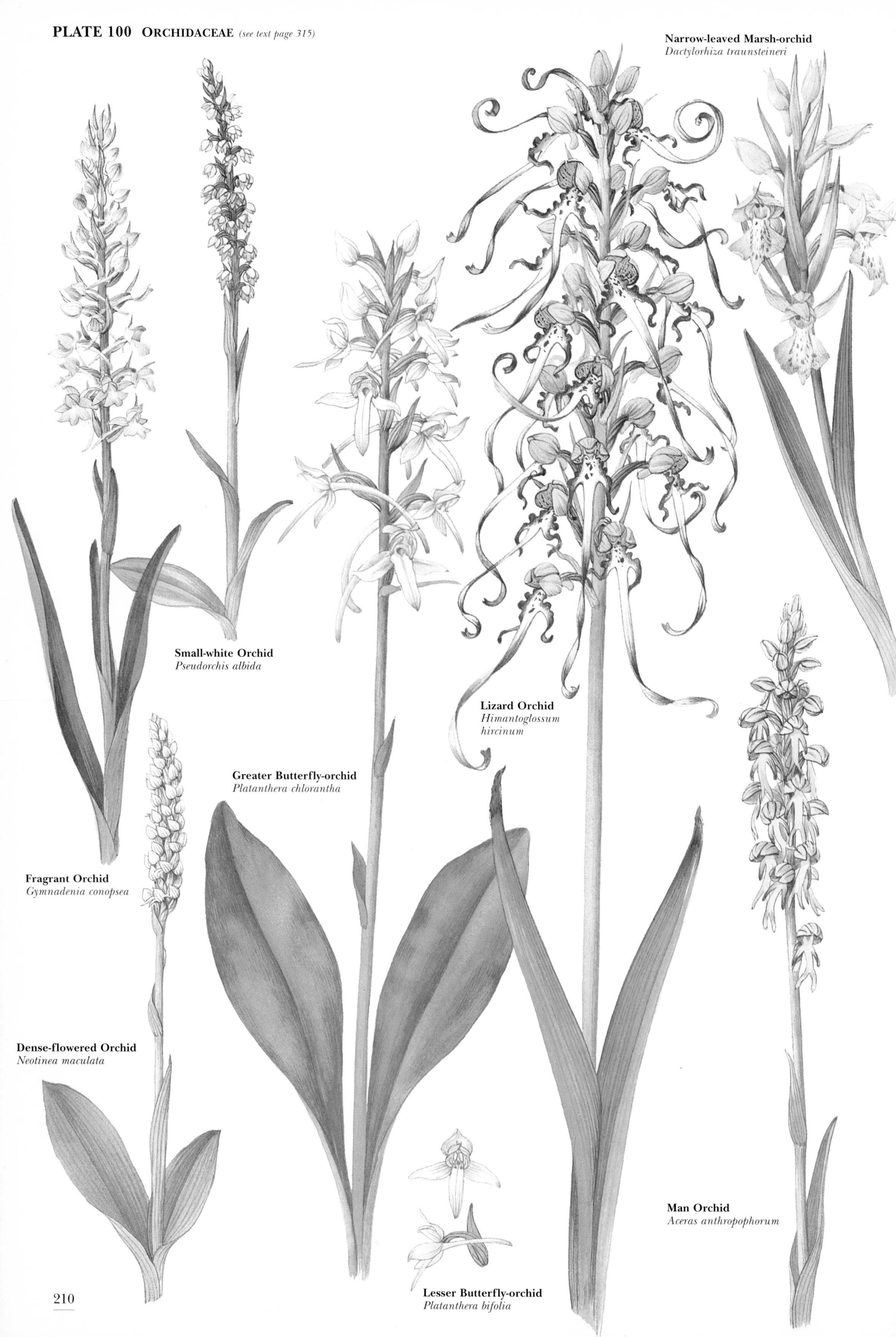
Narrow-leaved Marsh-orchid
Dactylorhiza traunsteineri
Small-white Orchid
Pseudorchis albida
Lizard Orchid
Himantoglossum
hircinum
Greater Butterfly-orchid
Platanthera chlorantha
Fragrant Orchid
Gymnadenia conopsea
Dense-flowered Orchid
Neotinea maculata
Man Orchid
Aceras anthropophorum
Lesser Butterfly-orchid
Platanthera bifolia

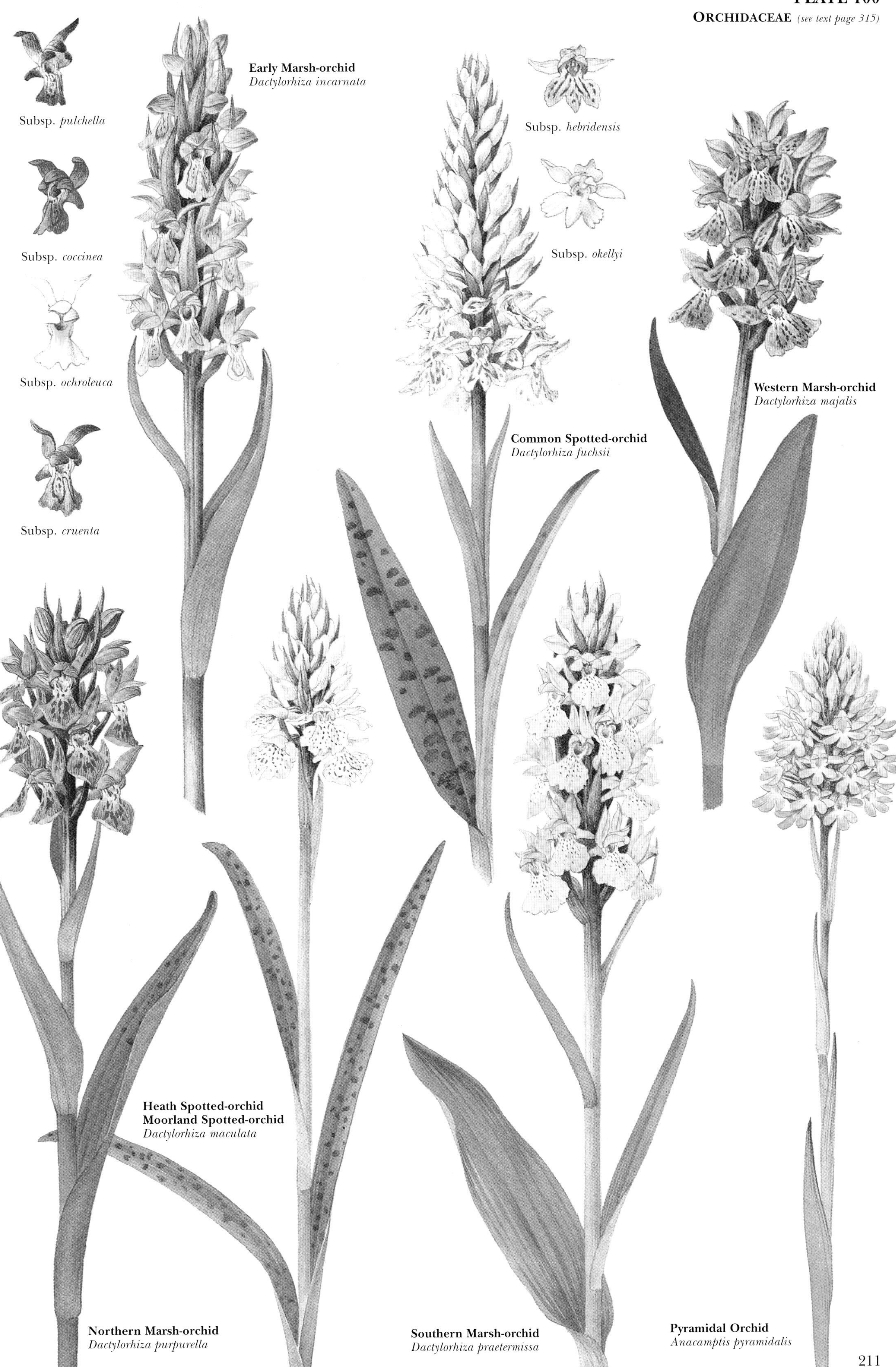
Early Marsh-orchid
Dactylorhiza incarnata
Subsp. *pulchella*
Subsp. *coccinea*
Subsp. *ochroleuca*
Subsp. *cruenta*
Subsp. *hebridensis*
Subsp. *okellyi*
Common Spotted-orchid
Dactylorhiza fuchsii
Western Marsh-orchid
Dactylorhiza majalis
Heath Spotted-orchid
Moorland Spotted-orchid
Dactylorhiza maculata
Northern Marsh-orchid
Dactylorhiza purpurella
Southern Marsh-orchid
Dactylorhiza praetermissa
Pyramidal Orchid
Anacamptis pyramidalis

PLATE 101
ARACEAE • LEMNACEAE *(see text page 317)*

 (see text page 317)

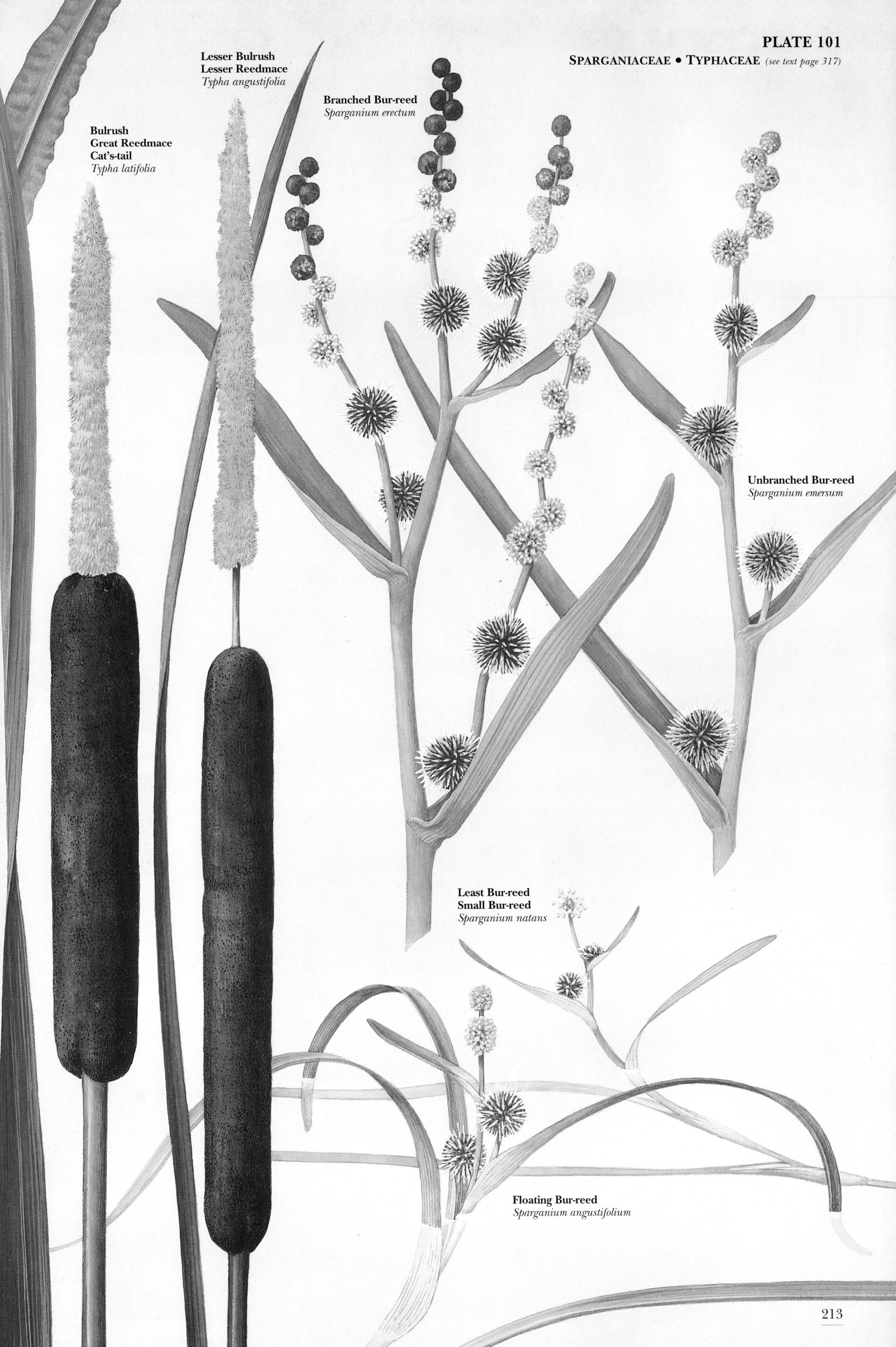
Lesser Bulrush
Lesser Reedmace
Typha angustifolia
Bulrush
Great Reedmace
Cat's-tail
Typha latifolia
Branched Bur-reed
Sparganium erectum
Unbranched Bur-reed
Sparganium emersum
Least Bur-reed
Small Bur-reed
Sparganium natans
Floating Bur-reed
Sparganium angustifolium

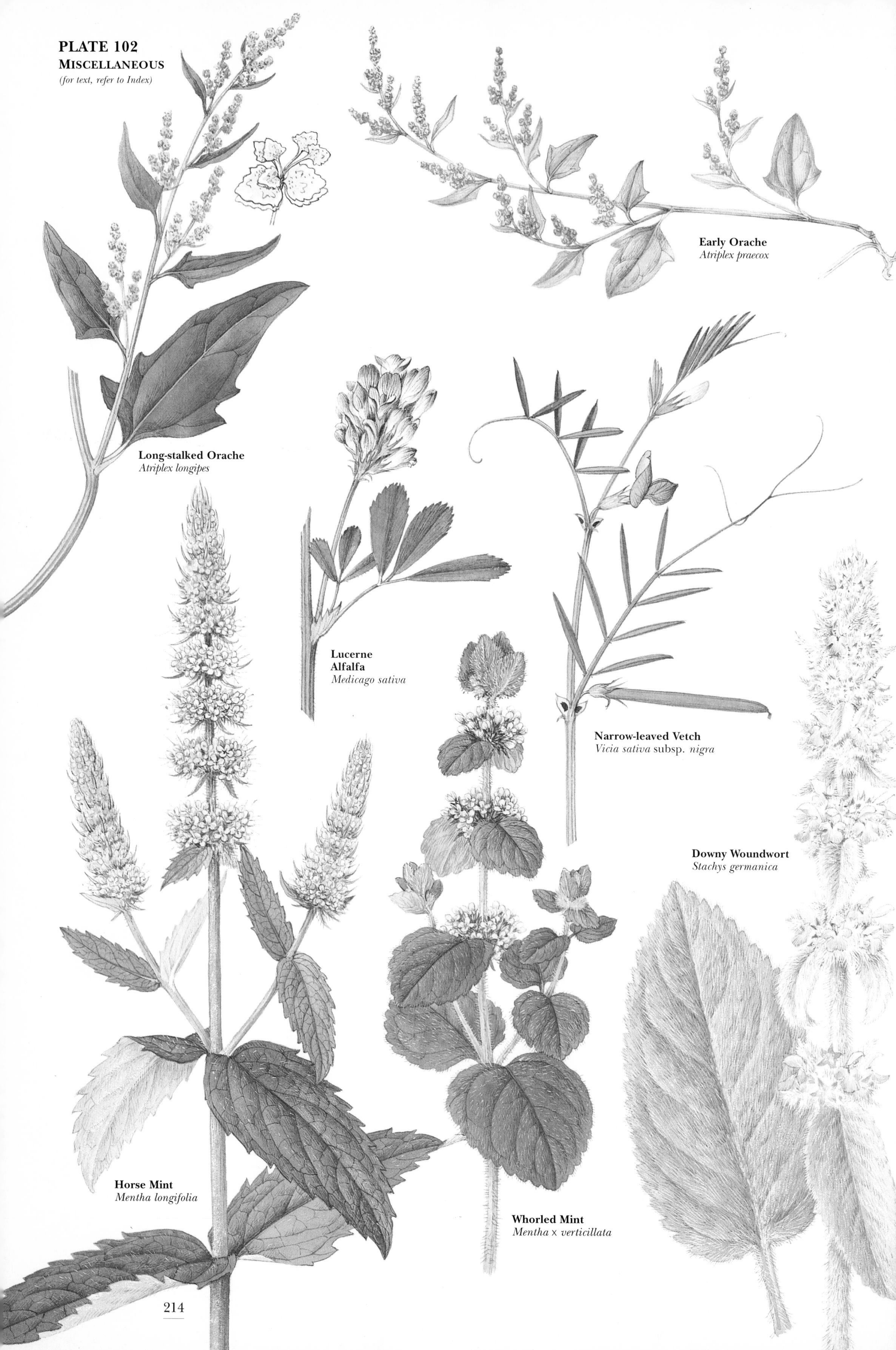
PLATE 102
MISCELLANEOUS
(for text, refer to Index)
Early Orache
Atriplex praecox
Long-stalked Orache
Atriplex longipes
Lucerne
Alfalfa
Medicago sativa
Narrow-leaved Vetch
Vicia sativa subsp. nigra
Downy Woundwort
Stachys germanica
Horse Mint
Mentha longifolia
Whorled Mint
Mentha x verticillata

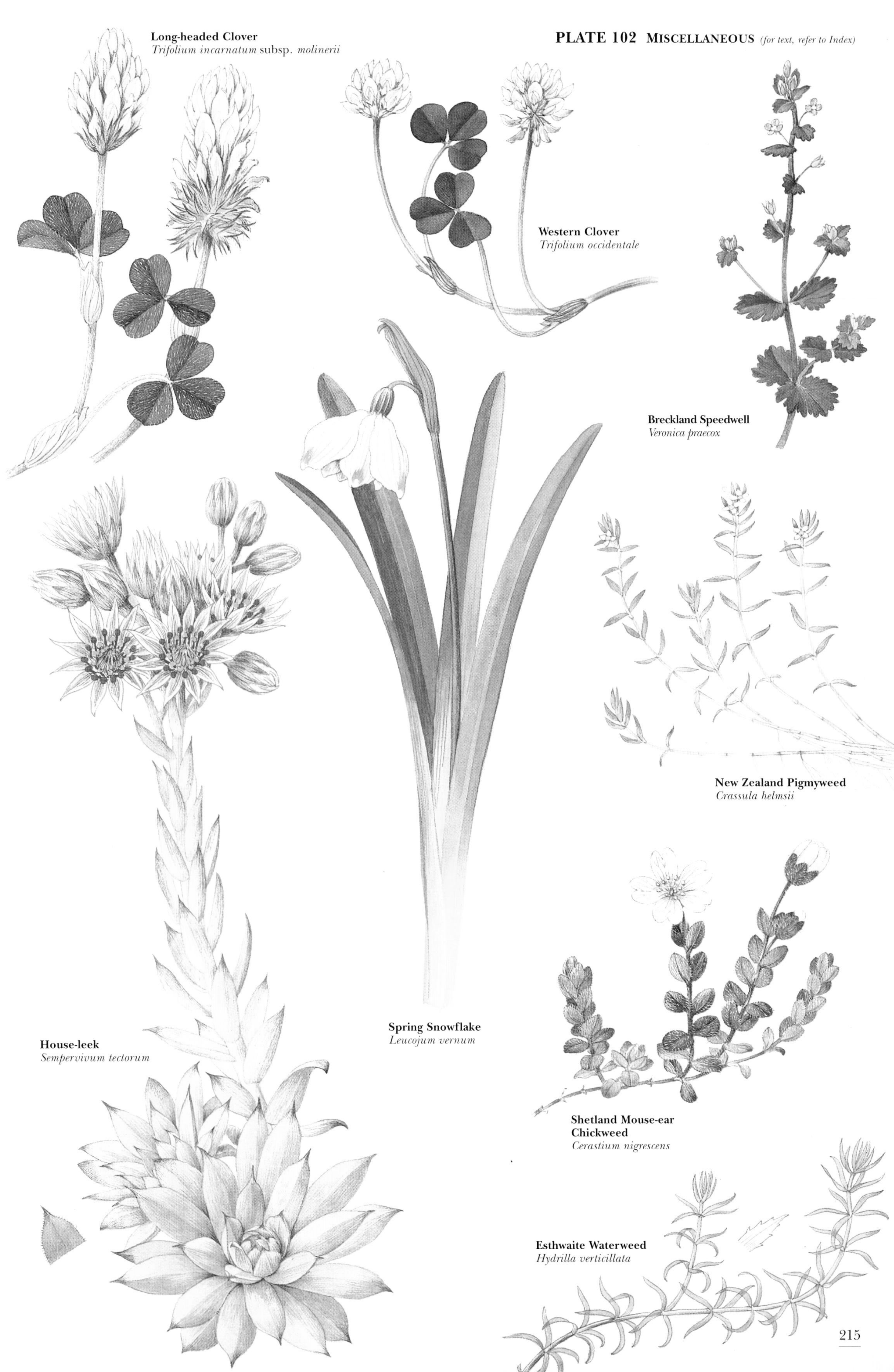
Long-headed Clover
Trifolium incarnatum subsp. *molinerii*
Western Clover
Trifolium occidentale
Breckland Speedwell
Veronica praecox
New Zealand Pigmyweed
Crassula helmsii
Spring Snowflake
Leucojum vernum
House-leek
Sempervivum tectorum
Shetland Mouse-ear Chickweed
Cerastium nigrescens
Esthwaite Waterweed
Hydrilla verticillata

Symbols, Abbreviations and Conventions used in the text

subsp. (plural: subspp.) subspecies

var. variety

x preceding a specific name indicates that the plant is a hybrid

* after the Latin name indicates that the species is included in the *British Red Data Book* (see Introduction)

(*) indicates a species occurring in the British Isles outside the United Kingdom that would otherwise qualify for inclusion in the *British Red Data Book*

** indicates that the species is specially protected under the Wildlife and Countryside Act 1981

❁ Notes indicated with this symbol are intended to supplement the illustrations and to draw attention to important points as an aid to identification. They are not complete descriptions of the plants and are not intended to perform the function of the formal keys to be found in the standard floras, which should always be consulted in cases of difficulty.

Names The Latin names follow those used in the *New Flora of the British Isles* (see Introduction). The first English name given is that recommended in *English Names of Wild Flowers*. Other names in widespread use follow (see Introduction).

Plate 102 The texts to the plants illustrated on Plate 102 are included in their family groupings and can be found by using the Index.

RANUNCULACEAE

The three common species of BUTTERCUP each have hairy leaves. *R. bulbosus* has reflexed sepals and a swollen, corm-like base to the stem. *R. acris* and *R. repens* both have spreading sepals. *R. repens* has creeping runners and stalked leaflets, while *R. acris* has no runners and unstalked leaflets.

Ranunculus acris L.

MEADOW BUTTERCUP

An abundant plant throughout the British Isles, characteristic of damp meadows and pastures, particularly those that are grazed or regularly cropped for hay. Like most other buttercups the foliage is poisonous to stock due to the presence of protoanemonin in the sap, but animals usually avoid the plant because of the acrid taste of the leaves. The peak flowering period is slightly later than that of the bulbous buttercup. The stigmas ripen before the stamens, and pollination is effected by a variety of short-tongued insects attracted by the nectaries at the base of the petals.

Ranunculus repens L.

CREEPING BUTTERCUP

Abundant throughout the British Isles, particularly on heavy wet soils, especially grassland on clays. It is most characteristic of damp grassland, marshes and fens, clearings and paths in woodland and as an arable weed. It avoids the most acid soils and well-drained grasslands and occurs more commonly in woodland than either *R. bulbosus* or *R. acris*, and is tolerant of trampling.

Ranunculus bulbosus L.

BULBOUS BUTTERCUP

Occurs throughout the British Isles, abundant in the south and east but becomes scarcer in the north and west and is absent from Shetland. It is characteristic of drier and better-drained soils than either of the two other common species. It is particularly abundant in chalk and limestone grassland but is not a strict calcicole. It also occurs in calcareous dune turf. Its abundance in pastures is increased by grazing, but it is unable to compete with tall hay-meadow vegetation and is intolerant of trampling. The earliest of the common buttercups to flower, it is pollinated particularly by honey-bees.

❁ *R. sardous* **is similar to *R. bulbosus* but is more hairy and lacks the swollen base to the stem.**

Ranunculus sardous Crantz

HAIRY BUTTERCUP

An annual herb of grazed pastures on damp, often alluvial soils, it was once scattered throughout lowland Britain but is now more or less confined to places close to the sea, especially in East Anglia and the south-east, and is absent from Ireland. It sometimes appears as a casual weed of waste land. It flowers from midsummer through to October and is pollinated by a variety of flies and small bees.

Ranunculus paludosus L.

JERSEY BUTTERCUP

As its English name suggests, this perennial buttercup is confined in the British Isles to Jersey, where it was first recorded from near St Aubyns on 13 May 1872. It occurs in situations that are seasonally waterlogged in winter but dry out in summer. It flowers during May, after which it soon dies down.
❁ *R. paludosus* **has root tubers, hairy leaves, and rather large, glossy flowers.**

Ranunculus arvensis L.

CORN BUTTERCUP
CORN CROWFOOT

An annual weed of cereal crops, especially on calcareous and clay soils, it is more or less confined to the country south and east of a line from the Humber to the Severn, being rare in Scotland, Wales and the south-west and absent from Ireland. Like many cornfield weeds, the corn crowfoot has decreased dramatically as a result of stubble burning and since the introduction of the selective herbicides MCPA and 2-4-D. It flowers in June and July and is probably pollinated by small flies.

❁ *R. arvensis* **and** *R. parviflorus* **both have fruits that are covered by spines or hooked hairs.**
R. parviflorus **is a spreading plant with characteristic yellow-green leaves and small flowers, less than 6 mm in diameter.** *R. arvensis* **is erect, with flowers 5-12 mm in diameter.**

Ranunculus parviflorus L.

SMALL-FLOWERED BUTTERCUP

A scarce and rapidly decreasing inconspicuous annual, occurring in dry, sandy, exposed habitats such as roadsides, grassy banks, track sides and occasionally as a garden weed. It is most frequent in the south-west, usually in places close to the sea, and is common as a bulb-field weed in the Isles of Scilly; it is absent from Scotland. It flowers from April onwards.

Ranunculus auricomus L.

GOLDILOCKS BUTTERCUP

A widespread perennial herb of deciduous woodland, more frequent in the lowlands and decreasing northwards and westwards. It sometimes occurs in great abundance and is more frequent on the heavier and more fertile soils, avoiding both very acid and very dry sites.
❁ *R. auricomus* **has almost hairless leaves and a variable number of petals from 0-5.**

Ranunculus lingua L.

GREATER SPEARWORT

A local perennial species growing in shallow water of fens, marshes and pond margins, often on calcium-rich organic or mineral soils. It is scattered throughout Britain but very rare in Scotland. Frequently planted in water gardens and around ornamental ponds and lakes, it occasionally escapes from cultivation. It flowers from June to September and is probably pollinated by small flies.

❁ *R. lingua* **is a robust plant growing to a height of 90 cm and with flowers more than 2 cm in diameter.** *R. flammula* **is prostrate or ascending with flowers less than 2 cm in diameter.**

Ranunculus flammula L.

LESSER SPEARWORT

A perennial, common in wet places throughout the British Isles, it occurs in marshes, fens, woodland flushes, wet woodland rides, stream sides and pond margins, but avoids acid bogs. Subsp. *scoticus* is restricted to lake shores in Argyll and the Inner Hebrides and subsp. *minimus* to exposed places near the sea in north Scotland, Orkney, Shetland and the Outer Hebrides. It flowers from May to September and is pollinated by a variety of small flies and bees.

Ranunculus reptans L.

CREEPING SPEARWORT

A very rare perennial of a few lake margins in the Lake District and Scotland such as Ullswater and Loch Leven. However, the British populations all show intermediate characters with *R. flammula* and a high degree of pollen sterility. As a result they are now all regarded as hybrids, and no persistent populations of pure *R. reptans* are known. It flowers from June to August.
❁ *R. reptans* **is characterised by the fine, arching prostrate stems that root at each node, and the solitary flowers.**

Ranunculus ophioglossifolius Vill**

ADDER'S-TONGUE SPEARWORT
SNAKE-TONGUE CROWFOOT

A very rare annual of marshes, now occurring only in two sites in Gloucestershire. One of these, at Badgeworth, was acquired in 1933 by the Society for the Promotion of Nature Reserves (now the Royal Society for Nature Conservation) and is now cared for by the Gloucestershire Trust for Nature Conservation.

Careful management is required to provide the right conditions for autumn germination and to prevent the plants from being overwhelmed by vigorous growth of flote-grass, *Glyceria fluitans*. It flowers in June and July.

❁ *R. ophioglossifolius* **differs from the other entire-leaved species in its broad, cordate basal leaves.**

Ranunculus sceleratus L.

CELERY-LEAVED BUTTERCUP
CELERY-LEAVED CROWFOOT

Widely distributed throughout lowland Britain, but in the south-west, Wales, northern England, Scotland and Ireland it is scarce or local and has a predominantly coastal distribution. It is a plant of the muddy margins of ponds, ditches and dykes, wet meadows and marshes on fertile, mineral-rich, often alluvial soils. It is tolerant of brackish conditions. An overwintering annual, it flowers from May to September and is probably pollinated chiefly by small flies.
❁ *R. sceleratus* **has glossy, hairless leaves and small flowers with an elongated receptacle.**

Ranunculus ficaria L.

LESSER CELANDINE

A perennial species represented by two subspecies: a diploid subsp. *ficaria* and tetraploid subsp. *bulbilifer*. Both occur throughout the British Isles, but subsp. *bulbilifer* is more common in the east. It is a characteristic plant of deciduous woodland, hedgerows, road verges, stream sides and damp pastures on seasonally wet or flooded soils. Subsp. *ficaria* occurs in both open and shaded conditions but subsp. *bulbilifer* is more usually found in shade or in disturbed ground. It flowers from March to May.
❁ **Subsp.** *ficaria* **has broad overlapping petals and no axillary leaf bulbils. Subsp.** *bulbilifer* **has narrow non-overlapping petals and small bulbils in the axils of the leaves.**

RANUNCULACEAE *(see illustrations page 14)*

The WATER-CROWFOOTS are not always easy to identify, and for certain identification the keys and descriptions in *Excursion Flora of the British Isles, New Flora of the British Isles, British Water Plants* **or** *A Guide to Identification of Batrachian Ranunculus Species in Britain* **should be consulted. Some species have both floating and submerged leaves; others have only entire floating or divided submerged leaves. Details of the fruits and nectaries are also important.**

Ranunculus hederaceus L.

IVY-LEAVED CROWFOOT

Scattered throughout the British Isles, but becoming less frequent in northern Scotland, it is a plant of still or slow-moving shallow water such as ditches and small streams. It often grows in temporary pools and frequently occurs on bare disturbed mud, and behaves as an annual or perennial, flowering from April through to September.

❁ *R. hederaceus* **and** *R. omiophyllus* **have entire leaves only. In** *R. hederaceus* **the lobes of the leaf are broadest at the base and the petals are small and more or less the same length as the sepals. The leaf lobes of** *R. omiophyllus* **are narrowest at the base and the petals are at least twice as long as the sepals.**

Ranunculus omiophyllus Ten. (*R. lenormandii* Schultz)

ROUND-LEAVED CROWFOOT

A plant of small, shallow, slow-moving streams and ditches and pools on acid non-calcareous soils, it nearly always occurs in open situations and often where there has been some disturbance. It behaves either as an annual or a biennial, flowering from April to August. It is frequent in western Britain and southern Ireland but absent from much of Scotland. In the south it is more or less confined to the sandstones of the Weald and the heaths of Dorset and the New Forest.

❁ *R. peltatus, R. aquatilis, R. penicillatus* **subsp.** *penicillatus, R. baudotii* **and** *R. tripartitus* **have both entire and divided leaves.**

Ranunculus aquatilis L.

COMMON WATER-CROWFOOT

The commonest and most widespread of the British water-crowfoots but becoming rare and scattered in northern Scotland, it occurs in both running and still, usually fairly shallow, nutrient-rich waters such as ponds, drainage dykes and small streams. It occurs on hard rocks more commonly than *R. peltatus.* Although normally perennial, it can behave as an annual when growing in habitats that are only temporarily wet. It flowers during late spring and midsummer.

❁ *R. aquatilis* **has more sharply toothed leaves than** *R. peltatus,* **the flowers are smaller and the fruit stalk is shorter than the stalk of its paired leaf.**

Ranunculus peltatus Schrank

POND WATER-CROWFOOT

A frequent plant throughout the British Isles but becoming less common in the west, it occurs in a wide range of shallow habitats from small pools and drainage dykes to small lakes and fast streams, preferring fairly nutrient-rich water. Like *R. aquatilis, R. peltatus* is normally perennial but can occur in habitats that are only temporarily wet, when it usually behaves like an annual. Unlike *R. aquatilis,* it is more frequent on soft rocks. It flowers from late spring through to late summer.

❁ *R. peltatus* **differs from** *R. aquatilis* **in its larger flowers, less sharply toothed leaves and the fruit stalk being longer than the stalk of its paired leaf. It differs from** *R. penicillatus* **in the divided submerged leaves being rather stiff and shorter than the internodes.**

Ranunculus penicillatus (Dumort.) Bab.

STREAM WATER-CROWFOOT

Occurs throughout the British Isles south of Scotland, but is more frequent in central and southern England and in Wales. The longer-leaved forms of the subsp. *penicillatus* prefer fairly nutrient-rich streams on the harder rocks of the Pennines and western Britain. The subsp. *pseudofluitans* is a characteristic, often dominant, plant of the shallow, clear waters of lowland chalk streams. It flowers during midsummer.

❁ *R. penicillatus* **subsp.** *penicillatus* **is very similar to** *R. peltatus,* **from which it can be distinguished by the more flaccid divided leaves, which are longer than the internodes.** *R. penicillatus* **subsp.** *pseudofluitans* **is most easily confused with** *R. fluitans,* **from which it differs in having a hairy receptacle and shorter leaves (up to 25 cm long).**

Ranunculus baudotii Godr.

BRACKISH WATER-CROWFOOT

A coastal species which is of local occurrence in southern and eastern England and also in Orkney, but rare elsewhere, and declining especially in the west and south-west. It grows in shallow, nutrient-rich brackish water pools, ditches and dykes, chiefly on fine alluvial soils. It often occurs in temporary disturbed habitats and can behave either as an annual or a perennial. It flowers from May to September.

❁ *R. tripartitus* **and** *R. baudotii* **both have three-lobed floating leaves. The submerged leaves of** *R. baudotii* **are a characteristic yellow-green and the tips of the sepals are blue. The flowers are larger than** *R. tripartitus* **(petals 25 mm long).**

Ranunculus tripartitus DC.

THREE-LOBED CROWFOOT

A rare and rapidly declining species that was formerly widespread in the extreme south-west and scattered throughout the rest of southern England south of the Thames; it is now almost confined to south-west Wales and western Cornwall. It is usually to be found in small pools, ponds and ditches, often of a temporary nature, on acid or non-calcareous soils; it occurs either as an annual or a perennial and flowers in the spring and early summer.
❁ *R. tripartitus* **can occur without divided leaves, in which case the deeply three-lobed entire leaves will separate it from** *R. hederaceus* **and** *R. omiophyllus.*

❁ *R. fluitans, R. trichophyllus, R. circinatus* **and** *R. pencillatus* **subsp.** *pseudofluitans* **all lack floating leaves.**

Ranunculus fluitans Lam.

RIVER WATER-CROWFOOT

Scattered throughout Britain from the Clyde southwards, but very rare in Ireland, Wales and the south-west. In the lowlands it is typically a plant of medium- to fast-flowing rivers and streams with a hard, rock bottom. It occurs in depths of up to 1 m, or deeper in highland rivers, preferring rather nutrient-deficient or calcium-rich water. It is a perennial species flowering from June to August.
❁ *R. fluitans* **is only likely to be confused with** *R. penicillatus* **subsp.** *pseudofluitans,* **from which it differs in the much longer leaves (up to 50 cm) and in the glabrous receptacle and fruits.**

Ranunculus circinatus Sibth.

FAN-LEAVED WATER-CROWFOOT

Primarily a plant of the Midlands, eastern and southern Britain, it is very rare in Scotland and declining in Ireland. It prefers still or slow-moving water such as ponds, drainage dykes, canals and slow streams where the water is fairly rich in nutrients and the bottom soft or silty. In such situations it may be locally common. A perennial species, it flowers from mid to late summer.
❁ *R. circinatus* **is distinguished from all other water-crowfoots by the absence of floating leaves and the submerged leaves being all in one plane.**

Ranunculus trichophyllus Chaix

THREAD-LEAVED WATER-CROWFOOT

This species is locally frequent in eastern and southern England, and is scattered throughout the rest of the British Isles, including Ireland. It has a very wide habitat range occurring in still and moderately fast-moving waters from ponds to shallow streams, drainage dykes and canals and also in temporary wet habitats. It prefers fairly shallow water but is not particular about the nature of the bottom. It can behave either as an annual or a perennial and flowers from spring until midsummer.
❁ *R. trichophyllus* **has small flowers, with petals less than 5 mm long and more or less the same length as the sepals.**

Anemone nemorosa L.

WOOD ANEMONE

Wood anemone occurs throughout the British Isles, being absent only from Orkney and Shetland and from the wholly unwooded area of the East Anglian fens. It occurs in a wide range of different kinds of woodlands but is most abundant in ancient woodland that is regularly coppiced, on acid or waterlogged soils. It comes into leaf and flower in the early spring, the leaves soon withering, so that on less acid and better-drained soils it is unable to compete with more evergreen herbs like dog's mercury. In East Anglia it is strongly associated with ancient woodlands, but is able to survive woodland clearing in hedgerows and also occasionally in acid grassland. The flowers produce no nectar, but pollination is effected by bees, bumble-bees and a large variety of flies.

Anemone ranunculoides L.

YELLOW ANEMONE

Alien. Native over almost the whole of Europe except the north-west and becoming very rare in the Mediterranean, it extends from Scandinavia south to Spain, Italy and Yugoslavia and eastwards into Russia. It is a woodland plant that has become naturalised in a few scattered places in England.

Anemone apennina L.

BLUE ANEMONE

Alien. A native of south-east Europe, it occurs from Italy to Greece, including Corsica and Sicily. It is frequently planted for naturalising in orchards and wild gardens, whence it occasionally escapes and may become naturalised in the wild for a short time.

Consolida ajacis (L.) Schur *(C. ambigua, Delphinium ambiguum, D. ajacis)*

LARKSPUR

Alien. A native of the Mediterranean region but naturalised in many other parts of Europe, including at one time Cambridgeshire. It still occasionally appears as a rare casual of cornfields and disturbed ground on light sandy soils in several parts of the country. The basal petal is marked with a few dark lines resembling the letters AIA, hence the specific name *ajacis,* from the Greek word for Ajax once applied to this and some related species.

Pulsatilla vulgaris Miller
(Anemone pulsatilla)
PASQUE FLOWER
This beautiful flower has a remarkable restricted and distinctive distribution in Britain. It occurs only in the dry calcareous grasslands of the oolitic limestone of the Cotswolds and the chalk of the Chilterns, East Anglia and Lincolnshire. It is one of the puzzles of British plant geography why it has never been recorded from the chalk south of the Thames although it is widespread on similar soils in northern France. In England it is almost confined to steep south- or south-west-facing slopes with shallow soils. It grows best in short grazed turf where competition from neighbouring species is not too intense. In ungrazed grassland it can persist for many years, but flowering may be severely restricted. Ploughing up of old downland turf has drastically reduced the localities of the plant so that it is now known in less than 30 sites. It flowers in April and May and its English name is derived from 'Pasch' (Easter).

Caltha palustris L.
MARSH-MARIGOLD KINGCUP
A perennial species distributed throughout the British Isles but absent from the Channel Islands. It is primarily a plant of wet meadows, marshes, fens, ditches and wet woodlands, growing well in partial shade. It occurs on mineral soils of varying fertility and acidity and also on calcareous fen peats, but is rare on acid peat. It is found in the marginal vegetation of ponds, lakes and streams and reaches 1,100 m in Scotland. It flowers from March through to midsummer and is visited by a variety of insects for both nectar and pollen.

Trollius europaeus L.
GLOBEFLOWER
A perennial species of northern Britain and Wales, in England extending as far south as Derbyshire. It also occurs in a few scattered localities in northern Ireland. It is a characteristic species of the luxuriant vegetation of wet meadows, alpine pastures, fens, fen carrs and damp woodlands. In Scotland it occurs up to 1,130 m. It flowers from June to August and is pollinated by a variety of small insects.

Helleborus foetidus L.
STINKING HELLEBORE
A rare plant of woodlands and scrub on shallow calcareous soils and scree. It occurs locally on the chalk of the North and South Downs, the oolitic limestone of the Cotswolds and Northamptonshire, the magnesian limestone of Yorkshire and the Carboniferous limestone of the Mendips, north Wales and Lancashire. In the south it is especially characteristic of beech and yew woods. It flowers from late January to early April, and the pendulous bell-shaped flowers are pollinated by early-flying honey-bees and bumble-bees.

❁ ***H. foetidus* differs from *H. viridis* in the absence of basal leaves, the unlobed upper leaves and the bell-shaped flowers.**

Helleborus viridis L.
GREEN HELLEBORE
A scarce species of damp calcareous woodlands and scrub. Although normally associated with limestone soils it also occurs on calcium-rich clays, such as the gault of south-east England. It occurs chiefly in southern England, it reaches as far north as the Lancashire Carboniferous limestone and the oolite and magnesian limestone of Yorkshire. It flowers during March and April and is pollinated by early-flying bees. The British plant is subsp. *occidentalis*.

Both species of hellebore are extensively grown in gardens and frequently occur as escapes from cultivation outside their normal distribution ranges. All parts of hellebore plants are extremely poisonous, the active principles being two glycosides, helleborin and helleborein. An infusion of *H. foetidus* used to be used as a dressing for lice.
❁ ***Helleborus viridis* differs from *H. foetidus* in having two basal leaves, lobed upper leaves and only one or two almost flat flowers on each flowering stem.**

Eranthis hyemalis (L.) Salisb.
WINTER ACONITE
Alien. A species endemic to Europe occurring from south-east France, through central Italy and Yugoslavia to Bulgaria. Frequently grown in gardens, it has become naturalised in parks and woodlands throughout Britain north to the Firth of Forth. It flowers from January to March and is pollinated by early flies and bees. The flowers are very temperature-sensitive and only open above 10°C.

Aconitum napellus L.
(includes *A. anglicum* Stapf.)
MONK'S-HOOD
A local plant of south-west England and south Wales and appearing as an occasional escape from cultivation elsewhere. It prefers damp woodland and shaded stream banks. Flowering occurs in May and June and the large helmet-shaped flowers are specifically adapted for pollination by bumble-bees. The 'helmet' protects two greatly enlarged nectaries and the pollen is deposited on the underside of the bee. Monk's-hood is one of the most poisonous of all British plants, containing the narcotic alkaloid aconitine, which acts by slowing the heart-rate.

Actaea spicata L.
BANEBERRY HERB CHRISTOPHER
A rare and local plant confined in Britain to the Carboniferous limestone of Yorkshire, Lancashire and Cumbria. Typically, it grows in the fissures or 'grikes' that separate the massive blocks of limestone or clints that make up the spectacular limestone pavements of northern England. It occurs in open pavement and also in ash-dominated limestone woodland up to an altitude of 500 m. The flowers, which are out in May and June, are visited by a variety of small pollen-feeding insects.

Clematis vitalba L.
TRAVELLER'S-JOY OLD MAN'S BEARD
A widespread plant of lowland Britain occurring south and east of a line from the Humber to the Severn and in north and south Wales. It is widely established elsewhere and in Ireland, where it is not native. Traveller's-joy is a common plant of scrub, hedgerows and wood margins on all types of calcareous soils. However, it is not confined to limestones, frequently occurring on calcium-rich clays. It can be a serious problem in young forestry plantations, climbing over and suppressing sapling trees. A perennial woody climber, it flowers in late summer and is visited by bees and hoverflies. 'Old Man's Beard' refers to the long, persistent feathery styles that deck the hedgerows in autumn.

Adonis annua L.
PHEASANT'S-EYE
Alien. Native in southern Europe from Spain to Turkey, including the Mediterranean islands and extending as far north as Switzerland. Pheasant's-eye has long been naturalised in a few scattered localities in southern England as an annual weed of arable land, mostly on chalk. It occasionally turns up as a casual elsewhere, often as a garden escape. Although usually appearing in cereal crops, it also occurs in temporary grass leys. It flowers during midsummer.

Myosurus minimus L.
MOUSETAIL
This inconspicuous little annual was once a widespread weed of damp arable soils in southern England. Like many ruderal species it has become drastically reduced in the present century due to changes in farming practice, so that now it is only of very local occurrence. It favours bare patches of ground such as appear around cattle troughs and the edges of paths as well as arable fields. The plant flowers in midsummer and probably is usually self-pollinated, although the nectar-secreting petals are attractive to small flies.

Aquilegia vulgaris L.
COLUMBINE
The columbine is native throughout Britain as far north as southern Scotland. It also grows wild in a few scattered localities in Ireland, and elsewhere it appears as an escape from cultivation. It is a local and decreasing species, usually occurring in damp woodland, marshes and fens, often on calcareous soils. It flowers during May and June and the nectar, which is secreted at the base of the long spur produced by each of the five petals, is collected by long-tongued bumble-bees.

Thalictrum alpinum L.
ALPINE MEADOW-RUE
A widely distributed plant in the eastern, central and western Highlands of Scotland, also occurring in Snowdonia, the Lake District and the northern Pennines. Although it has a preference for base-rich soils, it also occurs on more acid rocks, growing on rocky slopes, ledges and in mountain grassland to 1,200 m. In north-west Scotland it grows almost at sea level. A perennial species, it flowers during June and July and, unlike the other two species, is entirely wind-pollinated.
❁ ***T. alpinum* differs from the other two species of meadow-rue in its small size (less than 15 cm), unbranched inflorescence and absence of stem leaves.)**

Thalictrum flavum L.
COMMON MEADOW-RUE
A plant of wet meadows, marshes, fens and stream sides on base-rich or calcareous soils. It is widespread and sometimes common in eastern, central and southern England, but becoming rare in the west and north and absent from the extreme south-west and northern Scotland. It flowers during July and August and is pollinated by flies and bees; these are attracted by the yellow stamens as there are no petals, scent nor nectar. Some wind pollination may also occur.

❁ ***T. flavum* differs from *T. minus* in the dense inflorescence and erect stamens.**

Thalictrum minus L.
LESSER MEADOW-RUE
A most variable species appearing in a range of different habitats over most of Britain with the exception of much of the south. It occurs in dry chalk or limestone grassland from the East Anglian chalk to the Carboniferous limestone of the Pennines and Cumbria. It is a frequent constituent of sand dune vegetation, especially around the Scottish coast, and also appears in the marginal vegetation of lakes and streams, especially in the north and west. It flowers from mid to late summer and is usually wind-pollinated.

 (see illustrations page 18)

PAEONIACEAE

Paeonia mascula (L.) Miller
PEONY
The peony was first recorded from the island of Steep Holm in the Bristol Channel in 1803, where it grows in one or two places on the Carboniferous limestone cliffs. The present population is probably less than 20 plants, but they are now protected by the private Trust which owns the island. Since its first record there has been much speculation as to whether the species is truly native on the island; a small community of Austin Canons, the Brethren of St Michael, made the island their home for a short time in the 13th century and most people believe that it was they who originally introduced this southern European species as a medicinal plant.

BERBERIDACEAE

Epimedium alpinum L.
BARREN-WORT
Alien. A native of northern and central Italy, southern Austria, Yugoslavia and Albania, barren-wort has been cultivated in England since the end of the 16th century. Naturally a plant of shaded habitats on the lower slopes of mountains, it is occasionally found as a garden escape but is rarely able to establish itself.

Berberis vulgaris L.
BARBERRY
Barberry is native over most of continental Europe except for Scandinavia, and it becomes rare in the south. Its status in Britain is less certain. It was much planted in the Middle Ages both as an ornamental shrub and for its edible berries. Furthermore, its yellow bark suggested to medieval herbalists that it ought to be a remedy for jaundice. It occurs in hedges scattered throughout the British Isles and flowers in the late spring and early summer, the red berries ripening in September and October.

Mahonia aquifolium (Pursh) Nutt.
OREGON-GRAPE
Alien. An evergreen, winter-flowering shrub that was introduced into Britain in 1823 from western North America, where it occurs from British Columbia to North Carolina. It is shade-tolerant and frequently planted both as an ornamental shrub and for ground cover. It has become naturalised in many parts of Britain, particularly in central and eastern England.

NYMPHAEACEAE

Nymphaea alba L.
WHITE WATER-LILY
The white water-lily prefers still or very slow-moving nutrient-rich waters with a muddy bottom. It can be found in waters of all sizes from ponds to lakes and from drainage dykes to canals in depths up to about 3 m. Subsp. *alba* occurs in suitable habitats throughout the British Isles, but subsp. *occidentalis* is confined to the extreme north of Scotland and a few places in Ireland. The main flowering time is July and August and the flowers are pollinated by small beetles or, perhaps more usually, are self-pollinated.

Nuphar lutea (L.) Sm.
YELLOW WATER-LILY BRANDY-BOTTLE
The yellow water-lily occurs almost throughout the British Isles but is absent from the north of Scotland and the extreme south-west. It is most frequent in central and southern England, occurring in still or slow-moving nutrient-rich waters with a muddy bottom such as lowland rivers, canals, lakes and ponds. It will grow in depths up to 5 m and is more shade-tolerant than the white water-lily. In deep water it may lack floating leaves. The flowers, which appear from mid to late summer, are visited by a variety of small flies that are attracted by their alcoholic scent. This, together with the flask-shaped fruit, is responsible for the name 'brandy-bottle'.

❁ *N. lutea* **is much larger than** *N. pumila.* **The flowers are 4-6 cm in diameter and the top of the ovary does not have a wavy edge. The flowers of** *N. pumila* **are 1.5-4 cm in diameter and the top of the ovary has a wavy edge.**

Nuphar pumila (Timm) DC.
LEAST WATER-LILY
A rare plant of the lochs and lochans of the Scottish Highlands and the Shropshire meres. It occurs most often in acid, nutrient-deficient water in depths up to 2.5 m. It is a characteristic plant of open water mire communities around the edges of small pools as on Rannoch Moor in Perthshire. It flowers in late summer.

In some localities in northern England the hybrid between *N. lutea* and *N. pumila*, *N* × *spenneriana*, occurs in the absence of *N. pumila.*

CERATOPHYLLACEAE

Ceratophyllum demersum L.
RIGID HORNWORT
A frequent plant in suitable habitats throughout lowland England, but very rare elsewhere. It occurs in still or slow-moving nutrient-rich water with a muddy bottom and also in brackish drainage dykes near the coast. It is a rapid coloniser and can quickly choke quite large water bodies. The minute unisexual flowers are produced in late summer and are pollinated under water.

❁ *C. demersum* **differs from** *C. submersum* **in its more rigid habit and darker green colour. The leaves are twice forked.** *C. submersum* **is lighter green, more flaccid and the leaves are 3-4 times forked.**

Ceratophyllum submersum L.
SOFT HORNWORT
A rare species, now found mainly near the coasts of south-east England and in the south-west Midlands. It may be increasing. It occurs in still or very slow-moving, shallow, nutrient-rich habitats, such as canals, drainage dykes and ponds, with a muddy bottom. It flowers from July to September.

PAPAVERACEAE

The shape and size of the fruit is particularly important in the identification of the poppies. In all but *Papaver* **the fruit is a long pod-like capsule opening by means of valves.**

Meconopsis cambrica (L.) Vig.
WELSH POPPY
A local plant of south-west England (particularly north Devon), Wales and parts of Ireland. The Welsh poppy frequently appears as a garden escape, often becoming naturalised, especially in Scotland. It is primarily a plant of damp, hilly or rocky habitats, often under some shade, flowering from midsummer to September. It has an extremely restricted 'Atlantic' distribution in Europe, occurring elsewhere only in northern Spain, Portugal and western France.

Roemeria hybrida (L.) DC.
VIOLET HORNED-POPPY
Alien. A native of southern Europe from Portugal to south-west Russia, it now occurs in Britain only as a rare casual around ports, if at all. In the past it also occurred as a naturalised arable weed in East Anglia. An annual species, it flowers during May and June and is sometimes grown in gardens. The genus *Roemeria* is named in honour of Johann Roemer (1763-1819), Professor of Botany at Zürich.

Glaucium flavum Crantz
YELLOW HORNED-POPPY
A short-lived perennial maritime species occurring around the coasts as far north as the Wash on the east and the Solway on the west. It also occurs in Ireland and the Channel Islands. It is confined to open well-drained habitats such as sand dunes, shingle beaches, cliffs and waste ground, and has a distinct preference for basic rather than acid soils. It flowers from mid to late summer and is pollinated by a range of small bees and flies.

Glaucium corniculatum (L.) Rudolph
RED HORNED-POPPY
A native of the Mediterranean region, extending northwards to Hungary and eastwards to central and south-west Russia. An annual of waste ground and cultivated land, it most often occurs as a weed of lucerne fields, being introduced with seed imported from Eastern Europe. It flowers during midsummer. In Britain it now only appears as a casual, especially around ports, although in the past it has been reported as established at Portland Bill in Dorset and in Norfolk.

Chelidonium majus L.
GREATER CELANDINE
A perennial species occurring throughout the British Isles but becoming scarce in northern Scotland and scattered in Ireland. It has been cultivated at least since Anglo-Saxon times as a medicinal herb, the orange latex being used as a cure for warts and for various eye complaints. It is, however, extremely poisonous, the active principle consisting of four alkaloids: chelidonine, homochelidonine, sanguinarine and chelerythrine. Like many other plants with a similar history, it is a matter of some speculation whether the species is a true native. It is a frequent plant of hedgerows, hedge banks, walls and waysides, especially near buildings. It flowers throughout the summer and is pollinated by bees and flies.

 (see illustrations page 20)

Eschscholzia californica Cham.
CALIFORNIAN POPPY
Alien. A native of Oregon and California, it was first introduced to British gardens in 1790. It is now one of the most widely cultivated of hardy annuals, with a long flowering period and numerous differently-coloured cultivars from white to red in addition to the yellow and orange of the wild form. It frequently occurs as a garden escape. The genus *Eschscholzia* is named in honour of the naturalist Johann Frederick Eschscholz, 1793-1831.

Papaver rhoeas L.
COMMON POPPY
A spring or winter annual weed of arable land and disturbed ground such as quarries and road verges, it prefers light, well-drained soils on sands or chalk but avoids heavy clays. It is a lowland species, common in England but becoming scarce and local in Wales and Scotland, where it ascends to 300 m. It is more characteristic of cereals than root crops, but in some areas the use of selective herbicides has almost eliminated all poppy species from crops. Recently, fine displays have appeared on 'set-aside' fields. The main flowering period is June and July but extends into the early autumn. The large scarlet flowers are almost entirely self-sterile and pollination is effected by a range of social and solitary bees.
❁ **The capsule of *P. rhoeas* is almost globular and is glabrous.**

Papaver hybridum L.
ROUGH POPPY
A rare, spring-germinating annual of southern and eastern England. It is more or less confined to well-drained calcareous soils where it occurs as a weed of cereals and sugar beet, and on disturbed ground and waste places such as road verges. It flowers from May to August and is almost always self-pollinated while still in bud.
❁ **The capsule of *P. hybridum* is almost globular and is covered with spreading bristles. The petals are dark red and the anthers blue.**

Papaver argemone L.
PRICKLY POPPY
A spring-germinating annual weed of arable land and waste places. It is much less common than either *P. rhoeas* or *P. dubium*, and is most frequent in the south and east. It is particularly characteristic of dry, sandy soils, but is less often found on chalk and avoids heavy clays. It is commoner as a weed of barley than of wheat. Flowering commences earlier than any of the three previous species, and self-pollination often occurs while the flowers are still in bud.
❁ **The capsule of *P. argemone* is oblong and sparsely covered by stiff bristles. The petals are pale orange-red and do not overlap.**

Papaver dubium L.
LONG-HEADED POPPY
A summer annual weed of cereals and waste ground occurring in similar habitats to *P. rhoeas*, with which it often grows. Flowering occurs in June and July and pollination is effected primarily by bees and hoverflies, although the flowers are also self-fertile.
❁ **The capsule is oblong and glabrous. The petals are pale red.**

There are two subspecies. Subsp. *dubium* has colourless juice, and the bases of the petals overlap. It extends further north in Scotland than *P. rhoeas*, where it ascends to 450 m, and is commoner in Wales.

Subsp. *lecoqii* (**YELLOW-JUICED POPPY**) (*P. lecoqii*) is a spring-germinating annual weed of disturbed ground such as quarries and road verges. It is much rarer than *P. dubium* subsp. *dubium* and is much less frequently found in cereal crops. It is almost confined to the country south and east of a line from the Humber to the Severn. It flowers at the same time as *P. rhoeas* and subsp. *dubium* but is much more readily self-pollinated than the latter. *P. dubium* subsp. *lecoqii* was first recorded by Professor C.C. Babington from near Cambridge in 1860.

Papaver somniferum L.
OPIUM POPPY
Alien. Widely cultivated throughout Europe and eastern Asia since about the second millenium BC as an annual crop for the production of opium. Opium is the congealed latex obtained by making longitudinal incisions in the immature capsules immediately after petal-fall. It contains about 30 different alkaloids, of which the most important are morphine and codeine. Opium poppy occurs throughout the British Isles, either as a garden escape or as a relic of cultivation. The usual form is the subsp. *somniferum* and it flowers during July and August.

Papaver atlanticum (Ball) Coss.
ATLAS POPPY
Alien. A perennial poppy that is a native of Morocco. It was first introduced as a cultivated plant in 1890 and is now established in waste places in southern England. It may also be spread in seed put out for wild birds. It flowers from mid to late summer.

❁ **Both *P. atlanticum* and *P. lateritium* have lanceolate rosette leaves that distinguish them from other red-flowered species of *Papaver*. *P. atlanticum* has orange or orange-brown petals and a capsule that tapers evenly from apex to base. *P. lateritium* has red petals and the capsule is widest some distance below the apex.**

Papaver lateritium C. Koch
ARMENIAN POPPY
Alien. A perennial species originating in the mountains of Armenia in the southern USSR. It has been recorded in the past as established on garden walls and roadsides in several southern counties, such as Surrey, but almost certainly in error for *P. atlanticum*. It flowers during May.

FUMARIACEAE

The FUMITORIES are rather difficult to identify. The flowers should be examined while the plant is still fresh. Details of the lower petal, bracts and fruits are especially important.

❁ ***F. densiflora*, *F. officinalis*, *F. vaillantii* and *F. parviflora* all have small flowers (5-8 mm) with a paddle-shaped lower lip and narrow leaflets.**

Fumaria densiflora DC.
(*F. micrantha* Lag.)
DENSE-FLOWERED FUMITORY
A rare and declining species, at one time widely distributed on the chalk soils of south-east and eastern England but now confined to scattered localities within that area, north-east England and eastern Scotland. An arable weed of dry, well-drained, usually calcareous soils flowering from midsummer to late autumn.
❁ ***F. densiflora* has bracts that are longer than the flower stalks, sepals at least 2 mm long, and channelled leaflets.**

Fumaria officinalis L.
COMMON FUMITORY
An annual weed of arable soils distributed throughout the British Isles, common in the east but becoming scarcer in the west and in Ireland. It prefers light, well-drained conditions on either acid or calcareous soils. Like most of the fumitories, the common fumitory is little visited by insects and is probably almost always self-pollinated. It flowers continuously from early summer until late autumn.
❁ ***F. officinalis* has bracts that are shorter than the flower stalks, sepals at least 2 mm long, and unchannelled leaflets.**

Fumaria vaillantii Lois.
FEW-FLOWERED FUMITORY
A rare annual weed of arable soils, almost confined to the chalk of the North Downs, the Chilterns and East Anglia with a few scattered localities on the chalk and oolite further west. It flowers from June to September.
❁ ***F. vaillantii* has bracts shorter than the fruit stalks and pink flowers.**

Fumaria parviflora Lam.
FINE-LEAVED FUMITORY
An uncommon arable weed of chalk soils in eastern and south-east England. It is now almost confined to the North Downs, the Hampshire chalk, the Chilterns and the East Anglian chalk together with a few scattered localities in north-east Yorkshire. It flowers from June to September.
❁ ***F. parviflora* has bracts as long as or longer than the fruit stalks and white pink-tinged flowers.**

The remaining six species of *Fumaria* have broad, not narrow leaflets, larger flowers 9 mm or more long, and a lower lip that is not paddle-shaped.

Fumaria occidentalis Pugsley
WESTERN RAMPING-FUMITORY
A species endemic to the British Isles and confined to the Isles of Scilly and south-west Cornwall. It is an annual weed of arable fields and waste ground, especially on light sandy soils. On the Isles of Scilly it is particularly associated with bulb-fields and walls, where it is plentiful over a small area. On St Mary's it flowers from late spring through to the autumn.
❁ ***F. occidentalis* is a robust species with large flowers 12-14 mm long that start off-white, becoming pink. It differs from similar species in the broad, spreading margins of the lower petal.**

Fumaria capreolata L.
WHITE RAMPING-FUMITORY
A local plant that is scattered throughout the British Isles but with a markedly coastal distribution. It is more frequent in Wales and the south-west than elsewhere and it also occurs in Ireland. It is an annual weed of waste ground, arable soils and hedge banks, with a flowering period from May to September. The British plant is subsp. *babingtonii*.
❁ ***F. capreolata* is distinguished by its red-tipped, cream-coloured flowers and rather dense inflorescence of about 20 flowers.**

Fumaria purpurea Pugsley
PURPLE RAMPING-FUMITORY
A scarce species endemic to the British Isles, found mainly in Cornwall and Lancashire and with scattered localities in Scotland, Ireland and the rest of England. A plant of hedge banks and waste ground, flowering from July to October.
❁ ***F. purpurea* differs from other large-flowered species, except for the white-flowered *F. capreolata*, in the long inflorescence stalk, the same length as or longer than the inflorescence itself.**

Fumaria reuteri Boiss.**
(F. martinii)
MARTIN'S RAMPING-FUMITORY
Formerly occurred as a very rare annual weed of arable land in Sussex, Surrey, Somerset, Devon, Cornwall and Guernsey. The only recent records are from the Isle of Wight and Cornwall.
❁ **Both *F. reuteri* and *F. bastardii* have lower petals with spreading margins. The smooth fruit and untoothed sepals of *F. martinii* separate it from *F. bastardii,* which has a rough fruit and toothed sepals. The flowers of *F. martinii* are a little larger (11-13 mm) than those of *F. bastardii* (9-11 mm).**

Fumaria bastardii Boreau
TALL RAMPING-FUMITORY
A widespread species in western Britain and Ireland but scarce or absent over large areas of Scotland and southern and eastern England. It occurs on waste ground and as a weed of cultivation, flowering from April to October.

Fumaria muralis Sond. ex Koch
COMMON RAMPING-FUMITORY
A very variable species, the commonest form in Britain being the subsp. *boraei* which occurs on waste ground, hedge banks, walls and as an arable weed throughout the British Isles, being most frequent in the south and west. The subsp. *muralis* is very rare and may be an introduction. *F. muralis* subsp. *neglecta* was described by Pugsley in 1912 and is endemic to Britain, occurring only in a few fields in Cornwall.
❁ ***F. muralis* is similar to *F. reuteri* and *F. bastardii,* but has fewer flowers to each inflorescence and the lower petal has erect rather than spreading margins.**

Ceratocapnos claviculata (L.) Liden
(*Corydalis claviculata*)
CLIMBING CORYDALIS WHITE CLIMBING FUMITORY
An annual species distributed throughout the British Isles, but absent from Ireland. It is typically a plant of acid woodlands and shaded rocky hillsides, being particularly characteristic of the oak woods of the Lake District, Wales, Exmoor and Dartmoor. In eastern England, where it is uncommon, it is often associated with ancient woodland although it also occurs in open heathy situations and on calcareous peat. It flowers from June to September and is visited by bees but may be self-pollinated.

Pseudofumaria lutea (L.) Borkh.
(*Corydalis lutea*)
YELLOW CORYDALIS YELLOW FUMITORY
Alien; confined as a native species to the southern foothills of the central and eastern Alps, occurring in Italy, Switzerland and Yugoslavia. In its natural habitat it is a plant of shaded limestone rocks and scree. It has long been cultivated as a cottage garden plant and frequently occurs as an escape throughout the whole country, growing on the mortar of old walls and buildings. It flowers throughout the summer.

Corydalis solida (L.) Sw.
BIRD-IN-A-BUSH
Alien. It is native throughout almost all of Europe except for the extreme north and west, and becomes rare in the Mediterranean region. It is sometimes grown in gardens and escapes, becoming naturalised in a few places. It flowers in the spring and is pollinated by bumble-bees.
❁ ***C. solida* can be distinguished from the fumitories by its uniformly coloured petals without darker tips.**

BRASSICACEAE (= CRUCIFERAE)

The Brassicaceae is a notoriously difficult family to become acquainted with. This is partly due to the fact that a large number of the species are either weeds or casuals, and partly because reliable identification is often dependent upon the characters of the fruits. The fruit is usually a capsule which opens from below by means of two valves and is either long and pod-like, a *siliqua*, or short (less than three times as long as broad), a *silicula.* In cases of doubt the keys in *New Flora of the British Isles* , *Excursion Flora of the British Isles* or *Crucifers of Great Britain and Ireland* should always be consulted.

❁ **The fruit of *Erucastrum* is beaked and has keeled valves each with a *single* vein so that it is square in section. *E. nasturtiifolium* has stem leaves that clasp the stem, an inflorescence without bracts and bright yellow flowers. The base of the stem leaves of *E. gallicum* do not clasp the stem, the inflorescence has bracts, and the flowers are pale yellow.**

Erucastrum nasturtiifolium (Poir.) O.E. Schulz
Alien. A native of south-west Europe from Spain and Portugal north to France, southern Germany and Switzerland. Introduced to much of the rest of Europe, in Britain it occured only as a rare casual around ports. A biennial or short-lived perennial, it flowers from mid to late summer and is pollinated by flies and bees.

Erucastrum gallicum (Willd.) O.E. Schulz
HAIRY ROCKET
Alien. Native and endemic in central and south-west Europe from Hungary and Czechoslovakia to Spain. In Britain it frequently occurs as a casual and has established itself in a number of places in the past near ports or on waste ground. It is an annual or biennial species, flowering from early to late summer.

❁ **The fruit of *Coincya* is beaked, each valve has three veins and the sepals are erect.**

Coincya monensis (L.) Greuter & Burdet
(*Rhynchosinapis monensis*)
ISLE OF MAN CABBAGE
C. monensis subsp. *monensis* is confined to the British Isles, where it occurs in a number of localities on the west coast. It grows in sandy habitats near the sea from Lancashire north to Ayrshire and the Isles or Arran as well as on the Isle of Man itself. It also occurs in one or two localities on the Welsh coast. A biennial, it flowers from June to August.
❁ **Subsp. *monensis* differs from subsp. *recurvata* in being hairless.**

Subsp. *recurvata* (*Rhynchosinapis cheiranthos*) (**Wallflower Cabbage**) is an alien, a native of central and south-west Europe from Spain and Portugal to north-west Germany. It occurs as a casual of waste places, but is now more or less confined to south Wales. The flowers, which are attractive to butterflies, are out in June and August.
❁ **Subsp. *recurvata* has hairs on the lower part of the stem and the sepals are as long as or longer than the flower stalks.**

Coincya wrightii (O. Schulz) Stace**
(*Rhynchosinapis wrightii*)
LUNDY CABBAGE
A species endemic to the British Isles, being found only on the slate and granite cliffs of the east side of Lundy Island in the Bristol Channel. A short-lived perennial, it flowers from June to August and is attractive to small beetles of the genus *Meligethes,* but is also self-fertile. The species is under some threat from grazing animals and from tourist pressure.
❁ ***C. wrightii* has a densely hairy stem and the sepals are shorter than the flower stalks.**

***Brassica* is distinguished from other yellow-flowered, long-fruited (more than three times as long as broad) crucifers by the rounded valves of the fruits, each of which have a single vein, and by the seeds being arranged in a single row in each cell.**

❁ ***B. oleracea, B. napus* and *B. rapa* are similar in having unstalked clasping stem leaves. *B. oleracea* is distinguished by having all the leaves glabrous and the flower buds overtopping the open flowers.**

Brassica oleracea L.

WILD CABBAGE

Probably alien. Current opinion favours the view that the wild cabbage was originally introduced to Britain as a crop either by the Romans or the Saxons. In Britain it is confined to steep maritime cliffs, usually of chalk or limestone; some populations, like those on the cliffs of Dover (from where it was reported as growing wild as long ago as 1551), Lulworth, St Alban's Head and the Great Orme, consist of several thousand plants. In all it occurs in about 30 localities around the coast, mostly in the south and west and often associated with sea bird colonies. A perennial, it flowers throughout the summer. The cabbage was certainly cultivated around the Mediterranean, whence the wild populations originate, by both the Greeks and the Romans. The numerous cultivated races have given rise to cauliflower, broccoli, kale, kohl-rabi and Brussels sprouts.

Brassica napus L.

RAPE

Introduced and now common as an escape from cultivation. The original home of this plant is lost in history, but it probably arose as a result of hybridisation between *B. oleracea* and *B. rapa*. Rape or coleseed, the subsp. *oleifera* now widely cultivated for its oil-rich seeds, frequently occurs as an arable weed or along the banks of streams and ditches. Swede is the subsp. *rapifera*. It flowers from May to August and is pollinated by bees.
❁ **All the leaves of *B. napus* are grey-green and the lowest bristly. The buds are at the same level as or slightly overtop the open flowers, which are pale yellow.**

Brassica rapa L.

WILD TURNIP

Alien. The wild turnip was probably originally introduced into Britain. An annual or biennial, it now occurs throughout the British Isles as a weed of waste ground and cultivation or along the bank of streams or ditches. The cultivated turnip with the white, fleshy tuberous root belongs to the subsp. *rapa*, while the wild plants belong to the subsp. *campestris*. It flowers from May to August and is pollinated by a variety of bees and hoverflies.

❁ **The leaves of *B. rapa* are grass-green and the lowest bristly. The flower buds are overtopped by the bright yellow open flowers.**

Brassica fruticulosa Cirillo
Alien. A native of the western Mediterranean, occurring in Spain, southern France, Italy, Sardinia and Sicily. An annual to perennial species, flowering in midsummer, it is now a very rare casual in Britain, usually around ports.
❁ ***B. fruticulosa* grows to about 30 cm and all the leaves are stalked. The fruit stalk continues for 1-3 mm above the scar left by the sepals.**

Brassica nigra (L.) Koch

BLACK MUSTARD

Native. It occurs throughout the British Isles, but becomes scarce in northern England and absent from northern Scotland, and is rare in Ireland. In Wales and south-west England it is primarily a plant of maritime cliffs, while elsewhere it occurs inland along ditches and streams and as a ruderal species of waysides and waste ground. It has long been cultivated for its seeds, which are the source of black mustard, and its exact status and original home remain obscure. An annual species, it flowers in midsummer and pollination is probably effected by small flies.
❁ ***B. nigra* is a tall robust plant growing to a height of 1 m or more. The base of the plant is very bristly, all the leaves are stalked and the fruits are held close to the stem. The fruit stalk is not continued above the scar left by the sepals.**

❁ ***Sinapis* is distinguished from other yellow-flowered long-fruited (at least three times as long as broad) crucifers by a combination of spreading sepals and beaked fruits with rounded valves each with several distinct veins. The fruits are not held close to the stem. *Coincya* (Plate 6) is similar but has erect sepals.**

Sinapis arvensis L.

CHARLOCK
WILD MUSTARD

Probably native; now introduced into almost all temperate parts of the world. It occurs throughout the British Isles with the exception of parts of north-west Scotland, and is an abundant annual arable weed, less frequently occurring on roadsides and waste ground. It has a distinct preference for calcareous soils and clays and is least abundant on light sandy ground. It is intolerant of shading. It is easily controlled by selective herbicides, especially the phenoxyacetic acids. It flowers during midsummer and is pollinated by various bees and flies.
❁ ***S. arvensis* is distinguished from *S. alba* by the toothed, not deeply lobed, upper stem leaves.**

Sinapis alba L.

WHITE MUSTARD

Alien. An annual species, native to the Mediterranean region but now introduced into many parts of the world.

S. alba subsp. *alba* is extensively cultivated as a green fodder crop and for the seeds which, when ground, produce mustard. In Britain it occurs commonly as a weed of arable land, especially on calcareous soils. It occurs throughout the British Isles, being frequent in the south and east but rare or local in the north and west. It flowers from June to August and is pollinated by flies and bees.

S. alba subsp. *dissecta* occurs on the Continent as a weed of flax fields and sometimes turns up in Britain as a casual of waste or arable land.
❁ ***S. alba* is distinguished from *S. arvensis* by the deeply lobed stem leaves. Subsp. *dissecta* is separated from subsp. *alba* by being almost glabrous with more deeply divided leaves, the terminal lobe being no longer than the laterals.**

❁ ***Diplotaxia* is distinguished from other yellow- or white-flowered, long-fruited (more than three times as long as broad) crucifers by a combination of the slightly flattened, beaked fruits with a single vein to each valve and the seeds arranged in TWO ROWS in each cell.**

Diplotaxis muralis (L.) DC.

ANNUAL WALL-ROCKET
WALL MUSTARD

Alien; a native of central, southern and eastern Europe from Spain to Greece and north to Poland. It occurs as an annual or short-lived perennial and in lowland Britain is well-established on chalk and limestone cliffs, quarry faces and walls and also as a weed of arable and waste places, especially on calcareous soils. It is rare in the north and west. It flowers from midsummer to the autumn and is pollinated by bees and flies.

❁ ***D. muralis* is distinguished from *D. tenuifolia* by being sparsely hairy with leaves with short lobes. *D. tenuifolia* is quite glabrous with grey-green leaves with long lobes and, unlike *D. muralis,* the fruit stalk continues above the scar left by the sepals.**

Diplotaxis tenuifolia (L.) DC.

PERENNIAL WALL-ROCKET

Alien. Probably native throughout most of central, southern and western Europe from Spain to Poland and Romania but introduced into Britain. It is frequent in south-east England, where it grows on wasteland and old walls, but occurs only as a casual elsewhere north to the Firth of Forth. It is absent from Ireland. A perennial species, it flowers throughout the summer.

Diplotaxis erucoides (L.) DC.

WHITE ROCKET

Alien; a native of south-west Europe from Spain to Italy with a single outlier in the Danube delta. In parts of the Continent it is a troublesome weed, but in Britain it occurs only sporadically in southern England as a casual of waste places or as a weed of disturbed ground. An annual species, it flowers from May to September.

Eruca vesicaria (L.) Cav. subsp. *sativa*
(*E. sativa* Mill.)

GARDEN ROCKET

Alien; a native of south-east Europe and the Mediterranean region. It is an annual species that has long been cultivated as a salad vegetable so that its original distribution has become obscured. In Britain it occasionally appears as a casual of waste ground and waysides.
❁ ***Eruca* differs from similar-looking pale-yellow-flowered, long-fruited crucifers (the fruit more than three times as long as broad) in the deeply two-lobed, rather than disc- or knob-shaped, stigma.**

Crambe maritima L.

SEA-KALE

Occurs all around the British coast as far north as the Clyde but is commonest on the south and south-east coasts and the coast of Cumbria, where suitable habitats are most frequent. It is a plant of undisturbed shingle beaches, growing best where there is some buried seaweed humus. It will grow with varying admixtures of sand and occasionally occurs on sand dunes. Flowering is from June to August and pollination is effected by bees, flies and beetles. The large fruits are dispersed by wind and by the sea, in which they can float for several days without loss of viability. The young shoots used to be blanched and collected as a vegetable. The species is increasing in parts of Britain, perhaps because the shoots are no longer collected. In other areas it continues to decline due to the pressure of tourism on its shingle habitats.
❁ ***Crambe* cannot be mistaken for any other species. It is a large, robust, cabbage-like plant with large (up to 30 cm), long-stalked, grey-green glabrous leaves.**

Hirschfeldia incana (L.) Lagr.-Fossat

HOARY MUSTARD

Alien; a native of southern Europe and the Near East, where it is a common annual weed. It has become established in sandy places on Jersey and Alderney and occasionally turns up as a casual in southern England. It flowers from June to September and is pollinated by bees.
❁ ***Hirschfeldia* is distinguished from all other species by a combination of the dense covering of grey or white hairs and the erect fruits held close to the stem.**

BRASSICACEAE (= CRUCIFERAE) *(see illustrations page 26)*

***Raphanus* is distinguished from other long-fruited (more than three times as long as broad) crucifers by the fruits being clearly constricted between the seeds and not opening from below upwards by means of two valves.**

Raphanus raphanistrum L. subsp. *raphanistrum*

WILD RADISH

Probably not native in Britain but distributed throughout the rest of Europe and introduced to most temperate parts of the world. It occurs as a common and persistent weed of arable land throughout the British Isles, the white-flowered form being rare in the north. It is most abundant on clay or sandy soils, avoiding most calcareous habitats. It flowers from May to September.

Raphanus raphanistrum subsp. *maritimus* (*R. maritimus*)

SEA RADISH

A maritime species occuring in open habitats, rough grassland, on cliffs and the drift line on rock, sand and stabilised shingle along the south and west coasts of Britain. It is rare in the east. It flowers from June to August and the fruits are dispersed by sea water, in which they will float for several days without loss of viability.
❁ **Subsp. *maritimus* can be distinguished from subsp. *raphanistrum* by the more numerous contiguous lobes to the lower leaves and the fruit with a shorter beak and not breaking easily into segments.**

Raphanus sativus L.

GARDEN RADISH

Alien; a cultivated plant of unknown origin and occurring nowhere in the wild, occasionally appearing as an escape from gardens. It flowers from June to August.
❁ **The swollen root (the radish) of *R. sativus* is absent in the wild species, and the fruit is a quite different shape.**

❁ **The fruit of *Rapistrum*, consisting of two distinct segments, is quite characteristic.**

Rapistrum perenne (L.) All.

STEPPE CABBAGE

Alien. Native to the steppes of central and eastern Europe, it occurs as far west as Germany. In Britain it usually appears as a casual but sometimes turns up as a weed of arable or waste land. A biennial or perennial, it flowers in midsummer.

❁ **The upper part of the fruit of *R. perenne* narrows into a conical beak, while the upper part of the fruit of *R. rugosum* terminates in the persistent style.**

Rapistrum rugosum (L.) Bergeret

BASTARD CABBAGE

Alien. A native of southern Europe and the Mediterranean from Portugal to Turkey. In Britain it is established as an annual weed of arable and waste land in parts of the Midlands and the south-east. Elsewhere it frequently appears as a casual. It flowers from May to September.

Cakile maritima Scop.

SEA ROCKET

An annual maritime plant occurring all around the coasts of the British Isles. It is a characteristic species of the strand line on sandy shores, often growing in association with *Salsola kali*. It is also associated with the earlier stages of sand dune succession, being one of the few species to colonise young embryo dunes dominated by *Elymus juncea*. It flowers from June to August, is pollinated by bees and flies and the fruits are dispersed by the sea.
❁ **A combination of the habitat and the succulent, blue-green, deeply lobed leaves of *Cakile* distinguishes it from all other violet-flowered, short-fruited crucifers.**

❁ **The blue-green untoothed leaves, pale flowers and keeled fruits, square in section, distinguish *Conringia* from other long-fruited crucifers.**

Conringia orientalis (L.) Dumort.

HARE'S-EAR MUSTARD

Alien; a native of southern and eastern Europe. In Britain it appears as a casual chiefly on clay and calcareous soils, where it grows on arable and waste ground and on cliffs near the sea. An annual, it flowers in midsummer.

❁ ***C. orientalis* grows to 50 cm, has yellow-white flowers and a four-angled fruit. *C. austriaca* is a larger plant, growing to a height of 1 m, has lemon-yellow flowers and an eight-angled fruit.**

Conringia austriaca (Jacq.) Sweet

Alien. A native of south-east Europe extending westwards to Austria and Italy, Asia Minor and the Caucasus. In Britain it occurs as a rare casual of waste ground and arable land and of cliffs near the sea. An annual species, it flowers from May to June.

❁ **The prostrate habit, finely divided leaves and inflorescences arising opposite the leaves distinguish *Coronopus* from other crucifers.**

Coronopus squamatus (Forsk.) Aschers.

SWINE-CRESS

Native. An abundant annual species, widespread south of a line from the Humber to the Severn. Elsewhere it has a distinctly coastal distribution, reaching Inverness on the east and the Clyde in the west. It is a common plant of trampled habitats such as pathways, gateways and around cattle troughs, and also of arable and waste ground. It avoids well-drained acid soils, preferring neutral or alkaline loams. It flowers from mid to late summer and is usually self-pollinated.

❁ ***C. squamatus* has six fertile stamens and the fruit is longer than its stalk, while *C. didymus* has two (or four) fertile stamens and fruit shorter than the stalk.**

Coronopus didymus (L.) Sm.

LESSER SWINE-CRESS

Alien, probably originating in South America. It is now widespread as an annual weed of cultivated and waste ground throughout southern England, south Wales and southern Ireland and is an infrequent casual elsewhere. It flowers during the late summer and is self-pollinated.

Lepidium draba (L.) Desv.

HOARY CRESS
HOARY PEPPERWORT

Alien; probably native in southern Europe and west Asia. It was first recorded at Ramsgate in East Kent in 1829, although it may have appeared a few years earlier near Swansea. It now occurs throughout the British Isles with its main area of distribution south and east of a line from the Humber to the Severn. It is still scarce in Scotland and Ireland. It is a common weed of disturbed ground along roadsides, ditch banks, field margins, hedgerows and waste ground on neutral to alkaline loamy soils. A serious perennial weed of arable crops, it can be adequately controlled by the selective herbicides MCPA and 2-4-D. It flowers during May and June and is largely self-pollinated. The seeds have been used as a substitute for pepper.
❁ ***L. draba* is distinguished by the toothed and clasping stem leaves, the dense flat-topped inflorescence of small white flowers, and small flattened triangular fruits. It grows up to 65 cm.**

Isatis tinctoria L.*

WOAD

Alien. Probably originated as a native of eastern Europe, but was spread throughout the Continent during prehistoric times. It was known to the Greeks and Romans as a medicinal plant, but by the early middle ages its cultivation for the production of the blue dye indigotine had become a major industry. The dye itself was produced by a complicated process of crushing, drying and fermenting the leaves. At the beginning of the century it was still widespread as a relic of cultivation, but now only persists in two localities, one in Surrey and the other on a river cliff of the Severn in Gloucestershire. It flowers during July and August.
❁ **Woad is a tall plant growing to a height of 120 cm, and the characteristic pendulous fruits distinguish it from all other crucifers.**

❁ **The two short and two long petals of *Iberis* distinguish it from all other crucifers except *Teesdalia*, which has no stem leaves.**

Iberis amara L.

WILD CANDYTUFT

A rare or local plant confined in Britain to the chalk of the Chilterns north eastwards into Cambridgeshire and to one site on the North Downs in Surrey. It occurs on dry, bare calcareous hillsides in the open, in clearings in beech wood or on chalk scrub. It is often associated with the disturbed ground around rabbit warrens or the borders of arable fields. An annual, it flowers in the late summer.

Iberis umbellata L.

GARDEN CANDYTUFT

Alien. A native of the central and eastern Mediterranean, widely cultivated in Britain as a garden annual since the 16th century and occasionally occurring as an escape from cultivation. In the wild it is a plant of open scrub on rocky calcareous or serpentine hillsides. It flowers during the spring and summer.

***Lepidium* resembles *Thlaspi* with its leafy stems, small white flowers and short, flattened fruits. However, each cell of the fruit of *Lepidium* contains only one seed, whereas those of *Thlaspi* contain two or more. Accurate identification depends largely on characteristics of the fruit and the stem leaves.**

Lepidium sativum L.
GARDEN CRESS
An alien species of uncertain origins, but probably a native of Egypt and western Asia. It is now cultivated as a salad plant throughout the world, and in Britain it occasionally appears as a garden escape. An annual flowering in midsummer, it is pollinated by small insects.
❁ **The fruit of *L. sativum* is longer than its stalk and the stem leaves do not clasp the stem. It grows to about 30 cm.**

Lepidium campestre (L.) R. Br.
FIELD PEPPERWORT
An annual or biennial plant occurring throughout the British Isles except for north-west Scotland; rare in Ireland and most frequent in south-east England. A ruderal species of dry soils, it occurs in open habitats on wasteland, roadsides, walls and banks and also as a weed of gardens, pasture and arable land. It flowers from May to August.
❁ **The fruit of *L. campestre* is longer than its stalk and covered by small white vesicles, and the style does not extend beyond the notch of the fruit. The stem leaves clasp the stem and it grows to about 50 cm.**

Lepidium heterophyllum Benth.
SMITH'S PEPPERWORT
SMITH'S CRESS
Distributed throughout the British Isles but most frequent in the south and west, and absent from north-west Ireland. A perennial species of dry soils, it occurs in open habitats on waysides and banks and as an arable weed. It flowers from May to August.
❁ ***L. heterophyllum* is similar to *L. campestre*, but the fruit is glabrous with a hairy stalk and the style projects beyond the notch in the fruit. It is branched and grows to about 40 cm.**

Lepidium hirtum (L.) Sm.
Alien; a native of the central Mediterranean region from Spain to Greece. It is a perennial species, rarely appearing in Britain as a casual. It is usually treated as a form of *L. heterophyllum.*
❁ ***L. hirtum* is similar to *L. heterophyllum*, but both the fruit and the fruit stalk are hairy.**

Lepidium perfoliatum L.
PERFOLIATE PEPPERWORT
Alien; a native of east and south-east Europe and western Asia and widely introduced throughout temperate latitudes in the northern hemisphere. In Britain it appears as a rare casual near docks and also in grass-seed mixtures. An annual or biennial species, it flowers in early summer.
❁ ***L. perfoliatum* is distinguished by the broad clasping stem leaves which are quite different to the finely divided basal leaves.**

Lepidium ruderale L.
NARROW-LEAVED PEPPERWORT
Occurs throughout England but its distribution is concentrated around the east coast, being particularly characteristic of the area around the Essex marshes and the Thames estuary and formerly abundant on rubbish tips around London. An annual or biennial species, growing in waste places, on sea walls and in dry, open habitats at the top end of salt marshes, it flowers in midsummer and is self-pollinated.
❁ ***L. ruderale* is a much-branched plant with an unpleasant smell, growing to about 25 cm. The fruits are small (less than 2.5 mm wide), shorter than their stalks and with the style not projecting beyond the terminal notch.**

Lepidium latifolium L.
DITTANDER
A coastal species occurring locally around the east and south coast from Norfolk to west Sussex; elsewhere it is introduced and locally abundant in waste places, mainly on railway ballast. Concentrated around the Essex and north Kent marshes, it occurs in the tall, rough vegetation at the top end of salt marshes and in damp, sandy soil. A perennial species, it flowers in midsummer. It was formerly grown in gardens and used in sauces before the use of pepper became widespread.
❁ ***L. latifolium* is a tall (up to more than 1 m) distinctive plant, quite unlike any of the other species. The sepals have a broad, white margin and the petals are up to twice as long as the sepals.**

Lepidium graminifolium L.
TALL PEPPERWORT
Alien. A native of central, south-east and southern Europe from Portugal to Turkey and the Near East, it occurs as a casual in Britain and occasionally persists for a short time, especially around docks. A perennial species, flowering during midsummer.
❁ ***L. graminifolium* is distinguished from similar-looking species by the fruit, which is shorter than its stalk and lacks a notch at its tip. The sepals have a narrow white border towards the tip.**

❁ ***L. virginicum, L. densiflorum* and *L. neglectum* all have fruits that are shorter than their stalks and with a distinct notch in the tip.**
***L. virginicum* differs from both *L. densiflorum* and *L. neglectum* in having petals that are longer than the sepals.**

Lepidium virginicum L.
LEAST PEPPERWORT
Alien. A native of North America but introduced into many parts of the world, and occasionally occurring as a casual in Britain. An annual or biennial, it flowers during midsummer.

Lepidium densiflorum Schrad.
Alien. A native of North America but introduced into many parts of the world, and occasionally occurring as a rare casual in Britain. An annual or biennial, it flowers during midsummer.

❁ **Both *L. densiflorum* and *L. neglectum* have petals that are either shorter than the sepals or absent. *L. densiflorum* differs from *L. neglectum* in the toothed rather than entire upper stem leaves.**

Lepidium neglectum Thell.
LEAST PEPPERWORT
Alien; a native of North America and introduced into many parts of the world. An early summer-flowering annual that occasionally appears as a casual, it is now usually regarded as a form of *L. densiflorum.*
Recent work suggests that *L. densiflorum* and *L. neglectum* are indistinguishable from *L. virginicum* and that all three should be regarded as the same species.

Teesdalia nudicaulis (L.) R. Br.
SHEPHERD'S CRESS
An early-flowering overwintering annual of open or disturbed habitats on acid sandy or gravelly soils. It occurs throughout the British Isles but is scarce in Scotland and absent from Ireland, except for a few isolated localities in the north-east. It is particularly characteristic of areas such as the Breckland of East Anglia and the heaths of north-west Surrey. It also occurs in coastal sand and shingle, especially in the south-east.
The record of the southern European *Teesdalia coronopifolia* (Bergeret) Thell. from the island of Eigg in the Inner Hebrides was an error.

❁ ***Capsella* is distinguished from similar species by the leafy stems and heart- or purse-shaped fruits.**

Capsella bursa-pastoris (L.) Medik.
SHEPHERD'S-PURSE
An abundant annual weed throughout the British Isles, growing as a ruderal of gardens, arable fields, verges, gateways and open habitats and disturbed ground everywhere. Like many successful weeds it flowers throughout the year from January to December and is normally self-pollinated, although the flowers do produce some nectar.

Capsella rubella Reut.
PINK SHEPHERD'S-PURSE
Alien and a native of southern Europe. It has been recorded from Surrey, Sussex and Buckinghamshire, presumably as a casual, although it does extend as far north as northern France on the Continent.
❁ ***C. rubella* differs from *C. bursa-pastoris* in its shorter (2mm) petals, usually pink-tinged.**

PLATE 10
BRASSICACEAE (= CRUCIFERAE)
(see illustrations page 30)

***Thlaspi* is rather similar to *Lepidium* (Plate 9), with leafy stems and short, rounded, flattened fruits which are distinctly winged, but there are two or more seeds in each cell of the fruit instead of one.**

Thlaspi arvense L.
FIELD PENNY-CRESS
Native. Occurs throughout the British Isles, abundant and widespread south and east of a line from the Humber to the Severn but scattered in the north and west. An annual weed of gardens, arable fields, wasteland and disturbed ground on fertile soils, it flowers during midsummer and is pollinated by small insects or self-pollinated.
❁ ***T. arvense* is distinguished from the other three species by the almost circular fruits, which are more than 1 cm in diameter.**

Thlaspi caerulescens J.S. & C. Presl (*T. alpestre*)
ALPINE PENNY-CRESS
Native. An alpine or sub-alpine species that has its main area of distribution in the British Isles in the Carboniferous limestone of the north Pennines, also occurring on the same rock in Derbyshire and the Mendips. It occurs as a rare alpine in Scotland, including the island of Rhum, and in Snowdonia. It grows in open habitats, screes and rock faces and is one of the species able to tolerate soils rich in minerals such as zinc and lead. A biennial or perennial, it flowers from April to August.
❁ **The persistent style in *T. caerulescens* is as long as or longer than the notch in the tip of the fruit, and this distinguishes it from both *T. alliaceum* and *T. perfoliatum.***

BRASSICACEAE (= CRUCIFERAE) *(see illustrations page 30)*

Thlaspi perfoliatum L.**

PERFOLIATE PENNY-CRESS

Native. A rare plant now confined to less than a dozen localities on the oolitic limestone of Wiltshire, Oxfordshire and Gloucestershire. An overwintering annual, it occurs on limestone spoil, bare ground, walls and railway banks. It also occurs as a casual in a few other places in southern England.

❁ ***T. perfoliatum* is a smaller plant than *T. alliaceum*, growing to about 20 cm; the stem is smooth and quite without hairs. The stem leaves are blue-green with blunt tips to the auricles.**

***T. alliaceum* grows to about 50 cm and, in contrast to *T. perfoliatum*, the stem is grooved and the lower part is hairy. The stem leaves are green with pointed tips to the auricles; the plant smells of garlic when crushed.**

Thlaspi alliaceum L.

GARLIC PENNY-CRESS

Alien. A native of central and south-eastern Europe, it was first recorded in Britain from near Hothfield in Kent in 1923. An early-flowering annual, it is still established as a weed of arable fields in the area but has only rarely been recorded from elsewhere. The plant has a strong smell of garlic.

Cochlearia officinalis L.
(*C. alpina, C. scotica, C. islandica*)

COMMON SCURVYGRASS

Native. A maritime species occurring all around the British coast except for much of the south and south-east. The coastal populations are characteristic of the upper parts of salt marshes, brackish marshes and grassy cliffs, banks and sea walls. It flowers from May to August and is pollinated by a variety of small flies and beetles. Scurvygrass is rich in ascorbic acid (vitamin C), and was widely cultivated and used as a prevention and cure for scurvy right up until the early years of the last century.

❁ **The *C. officinalis* group differs from *C. anglica* and *C. danica* in the rounded or cordate basal leaves and usually sessile or clasping stem leaves. It comprises a confusing array of coastal and inland alpine or sub-alpine species. Some are virtually indistinguishable on external appearance but have different chromosome numbers. Coastal forms usually have succulent leaves and rounded fruits, while inland forms normally have thinner leaves and fruits that taper at each end. Five species are generally recognised in the British Isles, three coastal and two inland: the coastal plants are *C. officinalis*, *C. anglica* and *C. danica*, and the inland *C. pyrenaica* and *C. micacea*. A sixth species, *C. atlantica*, has recently been recognised.**
❁ ***C. officinalis* differs from the other maritime species in the larger basal leaves (up to 5 cm wide), cordate stem leaves and white flowers.**

Cochlearia scotica Druce

SCOTTISH SCURVYGRASS

Native and endemic to the British Isles; it is a local maritime plant of north-west Scotland, northern and western Ireland and the Isle of Man. A biennial or perennial, it flowers from June to August.
❁ ***C. scotica* is a smaller plant than *C. officinalis*, and is now usually treated as a form of it, with smaller basal leaves (up to 1.5 cm wide) which are rarely cordate, and pink or lilac-coloured flowers.**

Cochlearia atlantica Pobed.
Very similar to *C. scotica*, but with white petals and all the stem leaves clasping. It has only recently been recognised and so far has been recorded from the Outer Hebrides, Mull and Arran. (Not illustrated.)

Cochlearia anglica L.

ENGLISH SCURVYGRASS LONG-LEAVED SCURVYGRASS

A coastal species occurring all around the British Isles, but very rare and local in Scotland and absent from Orkney and Shetland. It is especially characteristic of the salt marshes of the east and south coasts, where it grows on the upper levels of muddy shores and tidal estuaries. It also occurs in brackish marshes and, less commonly, on sandy or shingle foreshore. A biennial or perennial, it flowers from April to July and is visited by small wasps and flies.

❁ ***C. anglica* differs from both *C. danica* and the *C. officinalis* group in the tapering base of the leafblade.**

Cochlearia danica L.

DANISH SCURVYGRASS

A coastal species occurring all around the British Isles, but most frequent in the west and south-west. It is locally common on cliffs, banks and walls, the upper parts of sandy and rocky shores and in the older parts of shingle beaches. Inland, it is now often abundant on the salted verges of motorways. An overwintering annual, it flowers from January to midsummer. It is visited by various small insects and is automatically self-pollinated.

❁ **The two sub-alpine or alpine species, *C. pyrenaica* and *C. micacea*, are almost impossible to distinguish from their external appearance. *C. pyrenaica* is a diploid species with a chromosome number of 2n = 12, while *C. micacea* appears to be a tetraploid with a chromosome number of 2n = 26. Inland forms of *C. officinalis* were formerly distinguished as *C. alpina*.**

Cochlearia micacea E. Marshall

MOUNTAIN SCURVYGRASS

A rare alpine species, apparently occurring at altitudes above 800 m on a few mountains in Perthshire, Angus, Ross and Forfar. *C. micacea* may be endemic to Scotland but its true distribution still has to be discovered. It occurs in damp habitats, appearing to prefer calcareous rocks, although it is occasionally found on more acid soils. A biennial or perennial, it flowers during midsummer.

Cochlearia pyrenaica DC.

PYRENEAN SCURVYGRASS

A local species, so far only identified with certainty in Britain from the Carboniferous limestone of northern England, where it occurs in highly calcareous habitats between 150 m and 750 m. At higher altitudes it appears to be replaced by alpine forms of *C. officinalis*. It has been recorded from wet cliffs, stream sides and mine spoilheaps. A biennial or perennial, it flowers during midsummer and is pollinated by flies and beetles. (Not illustrated.)

Neslia paniculata (L.) Desv.

BALL MUSTARD

Alien. A native of central, southern and eastern Europe and the Near East, widely introduced into northern Europe. In Britain it is a common casual of wasteland, especially near ports, and of arable land. An annual species flowering from midsummer, it is automatically self-pollinated.
❁ **The small globose fruits distinguish *Neslia* from similar-looking species.**

Bunias erucago L.

SOUTHERN WARTY-CABBAGE

Alien; native in southern Europe from Portugal to Turkey and north to Switzerland. It was formerly a casual of waste ground in Britain, especially around ports. An annual or biennial, it flowers throughout the summer and is either self-pollinated or pollinated by bees. The roots and shoots are used as a salad vegetable in parts of south-east Europe.

❁ **The fruits of *B. erucago* and *B. orientalis* distinguish them from other yellow-flowered crucifers and from each other.**

Bunias orientalis L.

WARTY CABBAGE

Alien; a native of western Asia and eastern Europe as far west as Hungary. Widely introduced into central and western Europe, it was first recorded in Britain towards the end of the last century. The seed probably first arrived with imported grain and it now frequently occurs as a ruderal of waste ground, rubbish tips and roadsides, especially around London and the Thames valley. In addition, it has become established in several places on the chalk of the North Downs. A biennial or perennial, it flowers from May to August and is self-pollinated or visited by various small insects. It has been widely cultivated as a fodder crop or salad plant in parts of eastern Europe.

Subularia aquatica L.

AWLWORT

Native. Awlwort grows submerged in the shallow margins of the clear soft water pools and lakes of north-west Wales, the Lake District, northern and western Scotland and western Ireland, to an altitude of 610 m. It prefers a fine, gravelly bottom and is usually found growing with *Littorella uniflora*, *Lobelia dortmanna* and the quillwort, *Isoetes lacustris*. A small annual plant, it flowers from June to September. The submerged flowers usually remain closed and are self-pollinated, although some flowers may open fully under water. Emergent and terrestrial flowers open fully and are insect-pollinated.
❁ ***Subularia* is the only aquatic crucifer with awl-shaped leaves and tiny white flowers.**

Hornungia petraea (L.) Reichb.

HUTCHINSIA

Native. A rare plant of the Carboniferous limestone in Yorkshire, Derbyshire, north and south Wales and the Mendips. It also occurs on calcareous dune sand in south and west Wales. *Hornungia* is exclusively a species of shallow, skeletal soils rich in free calcium carbonate and a pH in excess of 6.8. In Britain it grows on well-drained slopes of a south or south-west aspect subject to summer drought. An overwintering annual, it flowers from March to May and is automatically self-pollinated. It was first recorded from Britain by John Ray in 1690 from St Vincent's Rock, near Bristol.
❁ **Its small size (2-14 cm), pinnate leaves, small flowers and small flattened fruits distinguish *Hornungia* from other white-flowered, short-fruited crucifers.**

Alyssum alyssoides (L.) L.**

SMALL ALISON

Alien; a native of western Asia and the whole of Europe except for the north and north-west. It was once widely distributed in scattered localities throughout southern and eastern England and in eastern Scotland, but is now known from fewer than 10 locations. It is an annual or biennial ruderal of grassland or arable land, chiefly on sandy soils such as the Breckland of East Anglia. The few remaining British populations vary in size from year to year depending on the agricultural management. It flowers during May and June.
❁ **The whole plant is covered by a grey down of star-shaped hairs, which together with the leafy stem and flattened circular fruits distinguish *Alyssum* from other yellow-flowered crucifers.**

Lunaria annua L.
HONESTY

Alien. A native and endemic to south-east Europe and possibly Italy, it is a spring-flowering biennial introduced into Britain as a garden plant late in the 16th century and now commonly grown particularly for the persistent silvery-white septa of the fruits, which are used in flower arrangements. It often occurs as an escape from cultivation and is attractive to butterflies and longer-tongued bees, or is automatically self-pollinated.

Lunaria rediviva L.
Alien. A native of damp woodland throughout most of Europe from Portugal to Russia, but absent from the extreme north, north-west and south. It occurs in Britain as a rare garden escape and is a perennial species flowering from May to August.
❁ ***L. rediviva*** **is distinguished from *L. annua* by the stalked, not sessile, upper leaves and the shape of the fruit.**

Berteroa incana (L.) DC.
HOARY ALISON

Alien. A native of central and eastern Europe and western Asia, extending north to Denmark and south to Italy. It is an annual or perennial weed of waste places and cultivated ground on light or sandy soils. The seed has been imported as an impurity in clover seed. It flowers from mid to late summer.
❁ ***Berteroa*** **is distinguished from other white-flowered and short-fruited (less than three times as long as wide) crucifers by the leafy stems and deeply notched petals.**

❁ ***Erophila*** **is distinguished from other white-flowered and short-fruited (less than three times as long as wide) crucifers by the leafless stems and deeply notched petals.**

Erophila verna (L.) DC.
E. verna var. *verna*
COMMON WHITLOWGRASS

Widely distributed throughout the British Isles, but perhaps less frequent in the west and in Ireland and absent from Shetland. Whitlowgrass is a common plant of open sandy habitats, coastal and inland sand dunes, bare areas in sandy heaths, walls and dry rocks. An annual, it flowers from March to June and is normally self-pollinated, only rarely being visited by insects.

E. verna var. *praecox* (Steven) Diklic
A local plant with the same general distribution as var. *verna* but rare in the north and west, where it is almost confined to coastal dunes. Further south it is more local, with an apparent preference for more calcareous soils.
❁ **It differs from var. *verna* in having up to 40 ovules in the fruits, instead of 40 to 60.**

Lobularia maritima (L.) Desv.
SWEET ALISON

Alien; a native of sandy and rocky habitats all the way around the Mediterranean coast. It is an annual or perennial species commonly grown as an edging plant in British gardens, occasionally escaping and becoming established from the south-west north to Scotland. It flowers from May to September.
❁ **The whole plant is grey-green and covered by dense appressed hairs which, together with the simple, untoothed leaves, entire petals and round or oval, flattened fruits, distinguish *Lobularia* from other white-flowered crucifers.**

Armoracia rusticana Gaertn., Meyer & Scherb.
HORSE-RADISH

Alien. Horse-radish probably originated as a native plant in southern Russia and the eastern Ukraine and was introduced and cultivated as a culinary plant throughout Europe during the Middle Ages. It was well known to the 16th century English herbalists such as Turner and Gerard. Horse-radish sauce, the traditional accompaniment to roast beef, is prepared by mixing the freshly grated root with soured cream. The plant occurs commonly throughout England as a ruderal of wasteland, roadsides, railway embankments, fields and stream sides, but is rare in Scotland, west Wales and Ireland. A perennial, it flowers in early summer and is visited by a variety of small insects.
❁ **Horse-radish is unlikely to be confused with any other species. A large, robust plant, it grows to a height of about 125 cm and the large, dark-green, wavy-edged basal leaves grow to a length of 60 cm.**

❁ ***Draba*** **has simple, entire or toothed leaves, small flowers and small flattened, oval, unwinged fruits.**

Draba aizoides L.*
YELLOW WHITLOWGRASS

Confined in Britain to the Carboniferous limestone cliffs of the south coast of the Gower Peninsula in south-west Glamorgan, where it occurs over a distance of about 16 km. It was first discovered by John Lucas in 1795. It grows in crevices on dry, open, sunny cliffs and rock faces and has also spread to old walls in the vicinity. Flowering occurs from late February to April. The flowers are attractive to a range of bees and flies, but self-pollination occurs if insect pollination fails.

Draba norvegica Gunn.
ROCK WHITLOWGRASS

A rare alpine species which has the centre of its distribution in the high mica-schist mountains of the central Highlands of Scotland, especially the Ben Lawers range and the rest of the Breadalbanes, where it reaches an altitude of 1,200 m. It also occurs in a few isolated localities in the Cairngorms, where more base-rich rocks appear, and on Ben Hope. A perennial species, it flowers during July and August.
❁ ***D. norvegica*** **is distinguished from the other white-flowered species by the leafless stems.**

Draba incana L.
HOARY WHITLOWGRASS

A local alpine species of limestone rocks and screes and calcareous dunes in the north. In England it is confined to the Carboniferous limestone of the Pennines, Lake District and north Wales. In Scotland it is particularly characteristic of the mica-schist mountains of the Central Highlands, where it reaches 1,080 m, but it also occurs on limestone mountains further north. On the north coast, the Outer Hebrides and the Shetlands it grows on shelly dune sands. A biennial or perennial, it flowers during June and July and is self-pollinated.

❁ ***D. muralis*** **differs from *D. incana* in the broader, clasping stem leaves and straight fruits.**

Draba muralis L.
WALL WHITLOWGRASS

As a native, it is a rare plant of the Carboniferous limestone of the Pennines of Derbyshire, Staffordshire and Yorkshire, of the Lake District and a few isolated localities in the West Country. It grows on shallow, well-drained rocky soils in sheltered, sunny locations with a western or southern aspect. In Britain it does not occur above 490 m. An overwintering annual, it flowers during April and May and is automatically self-pollinated. As an adventive, it is widely distributed in Britain as a garden weed, having spread from nurseries.

❁ ***Barbarea*** **differs from other yellow-flowered crucifers with long fruits (more than three times as long as wide) in the deeply-lobed, glabrous, dark-green leaves and square-sectioned fruits with distinct midribs and one row of seeds in each cell.**

Barbarea vulgaris R. Br.
WINTER-CRESS
YELLOW ROCKET

Distributed throughout the British Isles, but rare in west Wales and north-west Scotland. A frequent plant of the damp fertile soils of stream banks, roadsides, ditches and hedgerows. A biennial or perennial, it flowers throughout the summer and is pollinated by short-tongued bees, honey-bees, bumble-bees, flies, beetles and small moths. In dull weather the flowers are self-pollinated.
❁ ***B. vulgaris*** **is distinguished by the broad, rounded terminal lobes of the basal leaves, almost unlobed stem leaves and hairless flower buds.**

Barbarea stricta Andrz.
SMALL-FLOWERED WINTER-CRESS

Of doubtful status in Britain, but native in central, eastern and northern Europe. A rare plant of waste places and stream banks, scattered throughout England north of the Thames and in eastern Wales. A biennial species, it flowers from May to August.
❁ ***B. stricta*** **is similar to *B. vulgaris* but differs in the shorter (2mm) style on the fruit and in having hairy flower buds.**

Barbarea intermedia Boreau
MEDIUM-FLOWERED WINTER-CRESS

Alien; a native of south and central Europe from southern Germany to northern Portugal and southern Yugoslavia. It is established throughout the British Isles as an occasional ruderal of arable fields, stream banks and waysides. A biennial, it flowers from May to August.
❁ ***B. intermedia*** **differs from both *B. vulgaris* and *B. stricta* in its more deeply lobed stem leaves and from *B. verna* in having basal leaves with three to five pairs of leaflets and straight fruits 1-3 cm long.**

Barbarea verna (Mill.) Asch.
AMERICAN WINTER-CRESS
LAND-CRESS

Alien; native to south-west Europe from Portugal to Italy. In Britain it is widespread in damp, cultivated and waste ground north to the Scottish border, but most frequent in the south and south-west. It is widely cultivated as a salad vegetable and used as an alternative to water-cress. A biennial species, it flowers from May to July.
❁ ***B. verna*** **is similar to *B. intermedia* but the basal leaves have 6-10 pairs of lateral lobes and the fruits are curved and 3-6 cm long.**

❁ *Cardamine* **is distinguished by the long (more than three times as long as broad) flattened fruits, the ternate or pinnate leaves and white or lilac-coloured flowers.**

Cardamine bulbifera (L.) Crantz
(*Dentaria bulbifera* L.)

CORAL-ROOT CORALWORT

Coralroot is strangely confined in Britain to two quite separate areas of southern England, the Chilterns and the Weald of Kent and Sussex. In the Chilterns it grows, as on the Continent, in beechwoods on the chalk. In the Weald it is most characteristic of the damp loamy soils along the banks of woodland streams on sandstones and clays, where it often grows with ramsons and bluebells. It rarely sets seed in this country and reproduction is effected by the small brown bulbils which develop in the axils of the upper leaves. A perennial species, it flowers during May.
❁ *C. bulbifera* **is easily distinguished by the ternate leaves and the bulbils.**

❁ *C. amara, C. pratensis* **and** *C. palustris* **all have large, spreading petals (about three times as long as the sepals).**

Cardamine amara L.

LARGE BITTER-CRESS

Distributed throughout most of the British Isles, but absent south-west of a line from the Dee to the Isle of Wight, from the north-west of Scotland and from most of Ireland. It is a locally abundant plant of woodland flushes, stream sides, marshes, fens and spring lines. It appears to require conditions with moving ground water, is shade-tolerant, often growing abundantly in alder woodland, and will grow in soils rich in iron. A perennial species, it flowers from April to June.

❁ *C. amara* **has almost white flowers and violet anthers. The terminal leaflet of the basal leaves is not so much longer than the laterals as it is in** *C. pratensis.*

Cardamine pratensis L.

CUCKOOFLOWER LADY'S-SMOCK

Occurs throughout the British Isles. A common and widespread plant of damp meadows, pastures, marshes, roadsides, hedgerows, woodland flushes and along streams, ascending to over 1,000 m in Scotland. A familiar spring-flowering perennial, it is the foodplant of the caterpillar of the orange-tip and green-veined white butterflies. The flowers are visited by long-tongued hoverflies and bee-flies. Like many widespread and attractive wild flowers, it has acquired much folklore and over 50 local country names.
❁ **The flowers of** *C. pratensis* **are usually lilac and it has** *yellow* **anthers. The terminal leaflet of the basal leaves is usually much longer than the laterals.**

Cardamine palustris (Wimmer & Grab.) Peterm.
Separated from *C. pratensis* by Continental botanists on both cytological and morphological grounds, in Britain it has not proved possible to separate the two species as the morphological variation of *C. pratensis* in this country spans that of both species. On the Continent *C. palustris* is separated from *C. pratensis* by the more numerous stem leaves (usually more than five) and by the broader, stalked leaflets.

❁ *C. impatiens, C. flexuosa* **and** *C. hirsuta* **have small, white petals that are scarcely longer than the sepals.** *C. impatiens* **can be distinguished from** *C. flexuosa* **and** *C. hirsuta* **by the narrow leaflets of the stem leaves which clasp the stem.**

Cardamine impatiens L.

NARROW-LEAVED BITTER-CRESS

A local plant of rocks and scree of limestone woodlands such as beech and ash woods of the Carboniferous limestone of the Wye Valley, the Avon Gorge, Derbyshire, Yorkshire and Cumbria. In the south-east it is a rare plant of woods overlying calcareous sands such as the Bargate Beds in Surrey and the Kentish ragstone. An annual or biennial, it flowers from May to August.

Cardamine flexuosa With.

WAVY BITTER-CRESS WOOD BITTER-CRESS

A common plant of woodland stream sides, where it often grows on the silt deposited by the previous winter's floods, and damp shaded conditions such as the sides of ditches and paths that are inundated in winter. It occurs throughout the British Isles, reaching an altitude of 1,190 m in Scotland, but is absent from Shetland. It is normally perennial, but can also behave as an annual. It flowers from April to September.

❁ *C. flexuosa* **is distinguished from** *C. hirsuta* **by having six, nor four, stamens.**

Cardamine hirsuta L.

HAIRY BITTER-CRESS

Common throughout the British Isles. A short-lived annual, successful as a garden weed and abundant on bare ground and walls. It is also frequent on rocks and scree, especially limestone. It flowers from spring to late summer and is automatically self-pollinated. In still air the seeds can be projected up to 0.75 m from the plant by an explosive mechanism of the pod. The seeds germinate early in the year, enabling the plant to complete its life cycle before being killed by summer drought.

❁ *Rorippa* **is distinguished by the simple to pinnate leaves, white or yellow flowers, and fruits with numerous seeds in one or two rows in each loculus.**

Rorippa nasturtium-aquaticum (L.) Hayek
(*Nasturtium officinale*)

WATER-CRESS

An abundant plant throughout Britain but rare in central and northern Scotland and at high altitudes. Water-cress is a plant of shallow, clear, unpolluted streams, spring heads, dykes and small pools on moderately fertile soils in unshaded conditions. A perennial, or rarely an annual, species flowering from early summer into early autumn and pollinated by various small bees and flies. Commercial cultivation of water-cress began in this country in Kent around 1808.
❁ **The leaves of** *N. officinale* **remain green in the autumn and the seeds are arranged in two rows in each cell.**

Rorippa microphylla (Boenn.) Hyland.
(*Nasturtium microphyllum*)

ONE-ROWED WATER-CRESS NARROW-FRUITED WATER-CRESS

Occurs throughout the British Isles in similar habitats to *R. nasturtium-aquaticum*, but is commoner in northern England and Scotland, and flowers about two weeks later.

The hybrid *R. nasturtium-aquaticum* x *R. microphylla* (*R.* x *sterilis*) frequently occurs, but is also commoner in the north. All three are grown in commercial water-cress beds.
❁ *R. microphylla* **is very similar to** *R. nasturtium-aquaticum*, **except that the stems and leaves usually turn purplish in the autumn, and the fruits are more slender and curved with the seeds usually in a single row in each cell.**

Rorippa amphibia (L.) Besser

GREAT YELLOW-CRESS

Distributed throughout England south of the Humber, but absent from Wales and the south-west and scattered throughout Ireland. A plant of the margins of shallow ponds, ditches, drainage dykes and slow streams on fertile soils, it is a perennial species flowering in midsummer and pollinated by bees or self-pollinated.

❁ *R. amphibia* **can be distinguished from** *R. austriaca,* **the only other species with simple, toothed leaves, by the stem leaves not clasping the stem and larger (6 mm diameter) flowers.**

R. austriaca **is distinguished from** *R. amphibia* **by the clasping stem leaves and smaller (3-4 mm diameter) flowers.**

Rorippa austriaca (Crantz) Besser

AUSTRIAN YELLOW-CRESS

Alien. A native of western Asia and central and eastern Europe as far west as Germany and Austria. In Britain it is established as a rare plant of ditches and river and railways bank in Surrey, Middle-sex, Berkshire, Oxfordshire, Gloucestershire, Monmouthshire, Glamorgan, Leicestershire, Nottinghamshire and Lancashire. A perennial species flowering from June to August.

Rorippa sylvestris (L.) Besser

CREEPING YELLOW-CRESS

Distributed throughout the British Isles but rare or absent from much of Scotland. A plant of wet ground at the margins of pools, dykes and streams and where water stands only in winter. It is often found growing with *R. palustris, Ranunculus sceleratus* and *Chenopodium rubrum.* It also occurs as a garden weed on wet soils. A perennial species, it flowers in midsummer and is pollinated by flies and small bees.
❁ *R. sylvestris* **has larger flowers (petals about twice as long as sepals) and longer fruits (8-18 mm) than the other species with divided leaves.**

Rorippa prostrata (J.P. Bergeret) Schinz & Thell.
Alien. It occurs throughout much of central and eastern Europe and more locally in the west and south. Its taxonomic status is disputed; it is more or less intermediate between *R. amphibia* and *R. sylvestris* and is probably of hybrid origin, but is generally regarded as a separate species on the Continent. Plants referable to *R. prostrata* have been recorded from Britain but their status is uncertain.

Rorippa islandica (Oeder) Borbas

NORTHERN YELLOW-CRESS

So far recorded from about half a dozen localities only from coastal sites in Scotland, western Ireland and the Isle of Man. It grows on bare ground subject to winter flooding, and its habitat outside the British Isles, in Iceland, Greenland and the islands off the north-west coast of Norway, appears to be the margins of small lakes and temporary pools or along damp paths. It has been suggested that it reached northern Britain by seed carried by migrating geese. (Not illustrated.)
❁ **In** *R. palustris* **the fruit is less than twice as long as its stalk and the sepals are 1.6 mm or more long. The fruit of** *R. islandica* **is 2-3 times as long as its stalk and the sepals are less than 1.6 mm long.**

Rorippa palustris (L.) Besser

MARSH YELLOW-CRESS

Distributed throughout the British Isles but rare or absent over much of Scotland and uncommon in Wales and the south-west. It is a plant of seasonally wet habitats, especially bare mud where water stands in the winter. It often appears in abundance on the exposed mud of reservoirs during periods of summer draw-down, frequently in association with *R. sylvestris* and *Chenopodium rubrum.* An annual or biennial species, it flowers from mid to late summer and is usually self-pollinated.
❁ **The petals of** *R. palustris* **are about as long as, not longer, than the sepals, and it has shorter fruits (up to 8 mm) than** *R. sylvestris.*

Aubrieta deltoidea (L.) DC.
AUBRETIA
Alien. A native of southern Greece, Crete and Sicily. An alpine species of rocks and scree, it is widely cultivated on rock gardens and walls and occasionally escapes. A perennial, it flowers during April and May. The genus is named in honour of the French botanical artist Claude Aubriet (1688-1743).

❁ ***Arabis* is distinguished from other white-flowered crucifers by having flattened, elongated fruits (at least three times as long as wide) and simple or lobed, but not pinnate, leaves.**

Arabis alpina L.**
ALPINE ROCK-CRESS
Very rare. Confined in Britain to two small colonies on the Cuillin Mountains in Skye at about 820 m where it grows on wet rock ledges. It was first discovered in 1887 by H.C. Hart and has never been found in any other place in Britain. It is a perennial, self-pollinating species, flowering from June to August.

❁ ***A. alpina* and *A. caucasica* both form mats and have large flowers, more than 6 mm in diameter. *A. alpina* has leaves with 3-6 teeth on each side and flowers up to 10 mm in diameter, while *A. caucasica* has flowers of about 15 mm in diameter and leaves with 2-3 teeth on each side.**

Arabis caucasica Willd.
GARDEN ARABIS
Alien. A native of the mountains of Iran, the Near East and the Eastern Mediterranean. It is frequently grown in rock gardens and on walls, sometimes escaping and becoming naturalised. A perennial, it flowers from March to May. It seems to have been introduced to British gardens in 1798.

Arabis brownii Jord.
FRINGED ROCK-CRESS
Confined and endemic to the west coast of Ireland, it occurs in sand dunes and other sandy habitats in scattered localities along the coast from Kerry north to Donegal. It is a biennial and flowers in July and August. It is now regarded as a form of *A. hirsuta*.

❁ ***A. brownii* is distinguished from *A.hirsuta* and *A. scabra* by the glabrous stems and leaves with hairs only on the margins.**

Arabis scabra All.
BRISTOL ROCK-CRESS
Very rare. Confined in Britain to the Carboniferous limestone of the Avon Gorge near Bristol, where it was first recorded from St Vincent's Rocks by John Ray in 1686. It grows on south-facing rocky slopes in small crevices, on loose rubble or in the shallow limestone spoil. A perennial, flowering in the early spring, it is probably self-pollinated.
❁ ***A. scabra* has larger flowers than *A. hirsuta* (5-6 mm in diameter) and fewer flowers (3-6) in each inflorescence.**

Arabis hirsuta (L.) Scop.
HAIRY ROCK-CRESS
A local species scattered throughout the British Isles, it is a plant of dry chalk and limestone slopes, the short turf of calcareous grassland and dry banks and limestone rocks and walls. It also grows in calcareous dunes around the coast. A biennial or perennial, it flowers from June to August.
❁ ***A. hirsuta* has a hairy stem and hairy leaves and the flowers are smaller than *A. scabra* (3-4 mm in diameter) in a many-flowered inflorescence.**

Arabis glabra (L.) Bernh.
(*Turritis glabra* L.)
TOWER MUSTARD
A local species scattered throughout central, southern and eastern England where it was formerly most frequent, especially in the Breckland of East Anglia. It is a plant of dry heaths, banks, roadsides and waste places, but is now becoming increasingly scarce. An overwintering annual or biennial, it flowers in midsummer and is usually self-pollinated.
❁ **The glabrous, clasping stem leaves and the yellowish or greenish petals are distinctive.**

Arabis turrita L.
TOWER CRESS
Alien; a native of Algeria, Asia Minor and central and southern Europe from Spain to Greece and southern Russia and north to Germany. In Britain it is now known only from the walls of St John's College, Cambridge, where it is thoroughly naturalised. It is a biennial or perennial, flowering from May to August, and is probably self-pollinated.
❁ **The distinctive fruits and pale yellow flowers distinguish *A. turrita* from other crucifers.**

Arabis petraea (L.) Lam.
NORTHERN ROCK-CRESS
A local alpine species occurring principally on the volcanic hills of the western Highlands and islands of Scotland, the Cairngorms and Snowdonia. In Ireland it is confined to the Galtee and Glenade Mountains. A plant of rocks or scree, it prefers basic soils and ranges from near sea level to over 1,220 m. There appear to be two forms of the plant in Britain: one with small white flowers and a compact habit and the other with larger, pale mauve flowers and a straggling habit. A perennial, it flowers from June to August and is usually self-pollinated.
❁ **The basal leaves of *A. petraea* have long stalks and the flowers are pale lilac.**

Matthiola incana (L.) R. Br.*
HOARY STOCK
Doubtfully native in Britain, it occurs all around the south and south-west coasts of Europe. A rare plant of sea cliffs in southern England, it is possibly native in a few inaccessible places on the chalk cliffs of Sussex and the Isle of Wight. It occurs in other localities scattered around the south coast, including the Channel Islands, from where it was first recorded in 1578. An annual or perennial, flowering during midsummer, it is widely cultivated as a garden plant and occasionally escapes to become naturalised. The flowers are attractive to butterflies.

❁ ***M. sinuata* differs from *M. incana* in its lobed leaves, paler flowers and in not having a woody stem.**

Matthiola sinuata (L.) R. Br.*
SEA STOCK
A rare plant of sea cliffs and sand dunes, now known only from north Devon, Glamorgan and the Channel Islands. It was formerly more widespread, occurring in Pembrokeshire, Merioneth, Caernarvonshire, Anglesey and Ireland, but had disappeared from all of those by the beginning of the century. A biennial, it flowers from June to August.

❁ **The habitat should be sufficient to distinguish *Hesperis* from *Matthiola*, but the two can be reliably separated by the swellings on the back of each of the stigma lobes in *Matthiola* that are absent in *Hesperis*.**

Hesperis matronalis L.
DAME'S-VIOLET
Alien; a native of western and central Asia and central and southern Europe. It was cultivated since the Middle Ages as a garden plant and frequently occurring throughout Britain as a garden escape and naturalised in hedgerows, hedge banks, roadsides and verges, nearly always near habitations. A biennial or perennial, it flowers in midsummer and is pollinated by a variety of insects, including butterflies and moths.

Erysimum cheiri (L.) Crantz
(*Cheiranthus cheiri*)
WALLFLOWER
Alien. The origins of the cultivation of the wallflower as a garden plant are lost in the mists of history. It is a native of Greece and the islands of the Aegean but is naturalised on walls, cliffs and rocks throughout central, western and southern Europe, including the whole of Britain. It becomes less common northwards and is absent from the north of Scotland. Although normally grown as a biennial, it is a perennial species flowering from April to June.

❁ ***E. cheiranthoides* can be distinguished from the perennial *E. cheiri* by its much smaller flowers (6 mm diameter, rather than 2.5 cm diameter).**

Erysimum cheiranthoides L.
TREACLE MUSTARD
Doubtfully native but widespread in lowland England, especially the eastern counties, and rare in the south-west and Wales, Scotland and Ireland. An annual weed of gardens, arable fields, road verges and waste ground, it prefers light sandy soils. It flowers from June to August and is self-pollinated. It has been known in Britain since the 16th century and probably originated as a garden escape.

BRASSICACEAE (= CRUCIFERAE) *(see illustrations page 38)*

Alliaria petiolata (M. Bieb.) Cavara & Grande

GARLIC MUSTARD JACK-BY-THE HEDGE

Distributed throughout the British Isles but scarce or absent over large areas of northern and western Scotland and Ireland. A common plant of hedgerows, wood margins, roadsides and a weed of shaded places, it is also a plant of the ground flora of deciduous woodland on calcareous or base-rich soils. It is a food plant of the caterpillars of the orange-tip and green-veined white butterflies. A spring-flowering biennial, it is visited by a variety of small insects but is also self-pollinated. The crushed leaves have a strong small of garlic.

❁ ***Sisymbrium* differs from similar-looking yellow-flowered crucifers with long fruits (more than three times as long as broad) in having unbeaked fruits with each valve having a distinct midrib and two slightly fainter lateral veins.**

Sisymbrium officinale (L.) Scop.

HEDGE MUSTARD

Distributed throughout the British Isles, but scarce or absent from large parts of central and north-west Scotland. It is a common plant of hedgerows, roadsides, verges, banks, waste places and, less often, as a weed or arable land. An overwintering annual, it flowers during midsummer and is self-pollinated.

❁ ***S. officinale* is distinguished by the erect fruits held close to the stem.**

❁ ***S. irio, S. loeselii, S.volgense* and *S. austriacum* are all rather similar.**

Sisymbrium irio L.*

LONDON-ROCKET

Alien. A native of southern Europe from Portugal to Bulgaria but widely distributed as an introduction in other parts of the Continent. The name 'London-rocket' refers to the fact that the plant became abundant in the ruins following the Great Fire of London in 1666. It is now a rare plant of waste land and roadsides and only persists in three or four places in London. An overwintering annual, it flowers from June to August.

❁ ***S.irio* has paler flowers than *S. loeselii* which are overtopped by the young fruits.**

Sisymbrium volgense M. Bieb. ex E. Fourn.

RUSSIAN MUSTARD

Alien; native only in south-east Russia in the lower reaches of the rivers Volga and Don. First recorded in Britain from Bristol in 1896, it is perennial and occurs as a rare casual around docks and flour mills, probably being introduced with Russian grain.

❁ **The upper leaves of *S. volgense* are almost unlobed, which distinguishes it from *S. irio* and *S. loeselii*.**

Sisymbrium austriacum Jacq.

Alien; a native of central to south-west Europe from Austria and Czechoslovakia to Spain and Portugal. There appear to be no recent records of *S. austriacum* in Britain, and some of the old records of its occurrence as a casual may be errors. It is biennial to perennial.

❁ ***S. austriacum* can be distinguished by the longer, persistent style (about 1-2 mm) at the tip of the fruit.**

Sisymbrium loeselii L.

FALSE LONDON-ROCKET

Alien. Native in western Asia and central and eastern Europe west to Germany and Italy, it is a fairly frequent casual of waste ground that occasionally becomes established. It is an overwintering annual.

❁ ***S. loeselii* has brighter-coloured flowers than *S. irio*, which overtop the young fruits.**

Sisymbrium orientale L.

EASTERN ROCKET

Alien; a native of north Africa, the Near East and southern Europe from Portugal to Bulgaria and Turkey, it is widely established on waste ground throughout England, especially in the south-west. It was especially abundant on London bomb sites following the Second World War. In the north, the west and in Ireland it only occurs as a rare casual. An overwintering annual, it flowers from June to August.

❁ ***S. orientale* can be separated from similar species by the longer fruits (more than 5 cm), which are hairy when young.**

Sisybrium altissimum L.

TALL ROCKET

Alien; a native of the Near East and central and southern Europe west to Switzerland. First recorded in Britain from Liverpool in 1872, it is now established in waste places throughout England, especially in the south-east. In the rest of the British Isles it occurs as a rare casual. An overwintering annual, it flowers in midsummer.

❁ ***S.altissimum* is distinguished by the combination of the sessile upper stem leaves with very narrow lobes and pale flowers.**

Sisymbrium strictissimum L.

PERENNIAL ROCKET

Alien. Native and endemic to central and eastern Europe from France and Italy east to Russia and Bulgaria, it has established itself as a weed of waste places in a few parts of the country. It is a perennial and flowers from June to August.

❁ **The simple leaves distinguish *S. strictissimum* from all other species.**

❁ ***Arabidopsis* looks superficially similar to *Capsella* and grows in similar kinds of places, but can easily be distinguished by the fruits. It differs from *Arabis* in the fruits being more or less square in section, rather than flattened.**

Arabidopsis thaliana (L.) Heynh.

THALE CRESS COMMON WALL CRESS

Distributed throughout the British Isles, but becoming scarcer in the west and in Ireland. An occasionally abundant weed of arable land and gardens on dry acid stony soils, it is also common on dry hedge banks, walls and waste places. It is a short-lived annual that can produce seed within four weeks of germination. There are also numerous physiological races with different flowering and germination requirements. Flowering usually occurs in the spring and autumn.

❁ ***Camelina* is characterised by the pear-shaped fruits and almost untoothed leaves.**

Camelina sativa (L.) Crantz

GOLD-OF-PLEASURE

Alien. Its geographical origins are obscure, but they are probably centred in south-east Europe and western Asia. It has been introduced over almost the whole of Europe both as a weed of flax and as a crop cultivated for its oil-yielding seeds. Archaeological evidence indicates that it has been cultivated in eastern Europe since Neolithic times. With improvements in agriculture, it is now becoming scarce in Britain. An overwintering annual, it flowers during midsummer and is either pollinated by bees or self-pollinated.

❁ **The fruits of *C. sativa* are yellowish, about 1½ times as long as broad and have prominent midribs.**

Camelina microcarpa Andrz. ex DC.

LESSER GOLD-OF-PLEASURE

Alien. A native of north Africa, western Asia and central and southern Europe, it is a rare weed of lucerne fields, probably being introduced with seed imported from eastern Europe, and occasionally appears as a weed of other arable crops. It is an overwintering annual.

❁ ***C. microcarpa* is a densely hairy and a characteristic grey-green colour. The fruits are rounded at the apex.**

Camelina alyssum (Mill.) Thell.

Alien. A native of central and southern Europe and introduced as a weed of flax fields, it occasionally appears as a casual in waste places and is an annual.

❁ **The fruits of *C. alyssum* are very rounded and truncate or notched at the apex.**

Descurainia sophia (L.) Webb ex Prantl

FLIXWEED

Probably native. Flixweed was once widely distributed throughout England but is now more or less restricted to parts of East Anglia, where it is still common and widespread, as on the sandy soils of the Breck where it grows as a weed of arable land, road verges and waste ground. It also occurs scattered up the eastern side of Britain as far north as the Moray Firth. An annual, flowering from June to August, it is self-pollinated.

❁ **The grey-green, hairy, much-divided leaves separate *Descurainia* from other yellow-flowered crucifers with elongated fruits.**

RESEDACEAE

Reseda lutea L.
WILD MIGNONETTE
Widely distributed in southern and eastern Britain, but rare or scattered in the west and north of the Firth of Forth. It almost always occurs on chalk or limestone, but is absent from most of the older limestones of the north and west. It is normally a plant of disturbed ground, path sides, field edges and road verges and of bare patches in closed downland turf, such as around rabbit warrens. Biennial to perennial, it flowers from mid to late summer and is pollinated by small bees or self-pollinated.

Reseda luteola L.
WELD
DYER'S ROCKET
Distributed throughout most of Britain, but becoming scarcer northwards, being rare or absent from western and northern Scotland except along the southern shore of the Moray Firth. It is more widespread in the west than *R. lutea*. *R. luteola* is a plant of disturbed and waste ground on calcareous soils such as field margins, roadsides, path sides and abandoned quarries. It also occurs in coastal habitats such as calcareous dunes, particularly in the west. Used since Neolithic times for the production of a yellow dye, weld was formerly grown as a crop in east Kent, Essex and Yorkshire.

❁ **Both *R. lutea* and *R. luteola* have yellow flowers. *R. luteola* is a much more robust plant than *R. lutea*, growing to 150 cm, and is distinguished by the entire leaves with wavy margins. *R. lutea* grows to about 70 cm and the leaves are divided into narrow lobes.**

Reseda alba L.
WHITE MIGNONETTE
UPRIGHT MIGNONETTE
Alien; native in western Asia and southern Europe north to Germany and east to Yugoslavia. In Britain it occurs as a casual of waste land and old walls, especially near ports and in south-west England. Occasionally grown in gardens since the end of the 16th century. An annual or perennial, it flowers in midsummer.

❁ **Both *R. alba* and *R. phyteuma* have white flowers. *R. phyteuma* grows to about 30 cm and has the lower stem leaves entire. *R. alba* is a taller plant growing to 70 cm and all the leaves are deeply lobed.**

Reseda phyteuma L.
CORN MIGNONETTE
Alien. Native in north Africa, western Asia and southern Europe north to central France. Probably introduced with lucerne seeds imported from southern Europe, it is a rare casual in several places in southern England. An annual or biennial, it flowers in midsummer.

VIOLACEAE

Viola odorata L.
SWEET VIOLET
Widespread throughout England but scarce in Scotland, Wales and Ireland. It is a plant of woodland margins, plantations, scrub and shady hedge banks on calcareous or neutral soils. It flowers from early February to April and sometimes again in the autumn. Sweet violets are commonly grown in gardens and have been used since earliest times for their perfume, and Oil of Violets was made from the petals.

❁ **In both *V. odorata* and *V. hirta* all the leaves and the flowers arise from the base of the plant. *V. odorata* differs from *V. hirta* in the long creeping stolons (runners) and its sweet smell. *V. hirta* has no smell.**

Viola hirta L.
HAIRY VIOLET
Distributed throughout England, but scarce in the north and south-west and rare or absent over most of Wales, Scotland and Ireland. It is virtually confined to calcareous soils overlying chalk or limestone and is a plant of open woodland, woodland margins, scrub and grasslands. It flowers during March and April.

V. hirta subsp. *calcarea* is confined to the short, closely-grazed turf of calcareous grasslands and flowers slightly earlier than subsp. *hirta*, which is more characteristic of shaded habitats. However, the two subspecies are connected by a series of intermediates.

Viola rupestris Schmidt**
TEESDALE VIOLET
Very rare. Confined to open, mossy sheep-grazed turf or bare ground on the sugar limestone of Upper Teesdale in Yorkshire and Durham, and is one of the famous 'Teesdale rarities'. It also grows in one place in Cumbria. In all it is now known from only 11 localities in Britain. A perennial, it flowers during May.
❁ ***V. rupestris* differs from all the other violets in which leaves and flowers arise from the stems in having hairy leaf stalks and capsules.**

Viola riviniana Reichb.
COMMON DOG-VIOLET
Occurs throughout the British Isles. A common plant of hedge banks, deciduous woodland, grass heaths, chalk downs, old pasture and mountain grassland ascending to 1,020 m. It grows on both acid and calcareous soils but avoids wet conditions. It flowers from April to June and occasionally again at the end of summer.

Subsp. *riviniana* grows in woodland and hedge banks, while subsp. *minor* is a plant of grassy heaths and mountain grassland.

❁ **The main stem of both *V. riviniana* and *V. reichenbachiana* produces a rosette of leaves. *V. riviniana* differs from *V. reichenbachiana* in having larger lobes at the base of the sepals and a spur that is paler than the petals. The sepal lobes of *V. reichenbachiana* are very small and the spur is darker than the petals.**

Viola reichenbachiana Jord. ex Bor.
EARLY DOG-VIOLET
PALE WOOD-VIOLET
Occurs throughout England, becoming scarce in the west and in Ireland and very rare or absent in Scotland. Locally abundant in hedge banks and deciduous woodland, it is less often found in unshaded habitats than *V. riviniana* and avoids the more acid soils and wet conditions. It flowers during March and April, two to three weeks earlier than *V. riviniana*, with which it often grows.

❁ ***V. canina* differs from both *V. lactea* and *V. persicifolia* in the darker flowers, broader leaves and stipules which are usually no more than one-third as long as the leaf stalk. Subsp. *montana* differs from subsp. *canina* in the longer stipules and narrower leaves.**

Viola canina L.
HEATH DOG-VIOLET
HEATH VIOLET
Scattered throughout the British Isles in suitable habitats, it is a local plant of grassy heaths, sandy commons, coastal dunes and fens, ascending to 370 m. The subsp. *montana* is known from only a few fens in Cambridgeshire and Huntingdonshire. It flowers in May and June, but slightly later than *V. riviniana*.

Viola lactea Sm.
PALE DOG-VIOLET
PALE HEATH-VIOLET
A rare and declining species more or less confined to the acid heaths of southern and south-west England, where it grows in short fescue-bent turf. In many localities it hybridises freely with *V. riviniana* and the offspring appear to be suppressing the *V. lactea* parent by vigorous vegetative spread. It flowers during May and June, slightly later than *V. canina*. *V. lactea* is closely related to *V. canina*, with which it will also hybridise. However, they seldom meet in the field as they occur in slightly different habitats, *V. lactea* apparently growing in more nutrient-deficient, organic soils than *V. canina*.

❁ **Both *V. lactea* and *V. persicifolia* have very pale (sometimes almost white) flowers. The leaves of *V. persicifolia* are broadest at the base and are usually cordate, while the leaves of *V. lactea* are broadest about one-third of the way up and taper at the base.**

Viola persicifolia Schreb.**
(*V. stagnina* Kit.)
FEN VIOLET
Very rare. It was once widely distributed in the fens of East Anglia, but as a result of drainage and reclamation it now persists in three sites in Cambridgeshire, Huntingdonshire and Yorkshire. The Huntingdonshire site is carefully managed to maintain the disturbed conditions, such as fresh peat cuttings, on which its survival depends. It also occurs in a few localities in Ireland where it grows in wet grassy hollows overlying limestone. A perennial, it flowers in May and June.

Viola palustris L.
MARSH VIOLET
A widespread plant of upland, northern and western Britain but local and restricted by suitable habitats in the south and south-east. It is a plant of acid bogs, marshes, wet woods and woodland flushes, often growing within a matrix of *Sphagnum* moss. It flowers from April to July.
The common form is *V. palustris* subsp. *palustris*, the subsp. *juressii* occurring mostly in western Britain. The two subspecies are connected by intermediates.
❁ ***V. palustris* differs from the other violets in having a creeping underground stem (rhizome) from which the very broad, rounded leaves and the flowers arise individually. Subsp. *juressii* is distinguished from subsp. *palustris* by the more pointed leaves and hair leaf stalks.**

Viola cornuta L.
HORNED PANSY
Alien. A native of the Pyrenees and often grown in gardens and sometimes escaping and becoming naturalised. It flowers during June and July.
❁ ***V. cornuta* is distinguished from the native species of pansy by the large flowers and very long spur.**

The PANSIES *V. lutea, V. arvensis, V. tricolor, V. cornuta* and *V. kitaibeliana* are most easily distinguished from the violets by their deeply lobed, leaf-like stipules.

Viola lutea Huds.
MOUNTAIN PANSY
A plant of the hills of Scotland, Wales and northern England. In Ireland it is very rare. Although its distribution in England is closely associated with the Carboniferous limestone, it is not a strict calcicole. It prefers the short turf of fescue/bent grasslands where surface leaching has decalcified the soil or where thin glacial drift overlies the underlying limestone; elsewhere it occurs on similar base-rich but calcium-deficient soils. In Scotland it ascends to 1,070 m. A perennial, it flowers from April to August.
❁ ***V. lutea* differs from the other pansies by its larger flowers (2-3-5 cm from the tips of upper to lower petals) and longer spur (more than twice as long as the sepal appendages). The flowers are most often yellow, but can also be violet or a mixture of the two.**

Viola tricolor L.
WILD PANSY
Widely distributed throughout the British Isles, but not as frequent as *V. arvensis* in the south-east. It flowers from spring to autumn and is pollinated by bees.

V. tricolor subsp. *tricolor* is an annual weed or arable land, rough grassland and, less often, waste ground on acid or neutral soils. Unlike *V. arvensis,* it avoids calcareous soils.

V. tricolor subsp. *curtisii* is a perennial plant of coastal sand dunes and rough grassland along the south-west and west coasts, the east coast of Scotland and the Irish coast. It also occurs inland on the sandy soil of the Breck of Norfolk and Suffolk.
❁ ***V. tricolor* differs from *V. lutea* in the smaller flowers (1.5-2.5 cm from the tips of the upper to lower petals) and shorter spur (up to twice as long with the sepal appendages). The spur of subsp. *tricolor* is a little longer than the sepal appendages; the spur of subsp *curtisii* is about twice as long as the sepal appendages.**

Viola arvensis Murr.
FIELD PANSY
Occurs throughout the British Isles but is scarce or local in west and north-west Scotland and in Ireland. It is a common annual weed of arable fields and, less often, waste ground on calcareous or neutral soils. It flowers from spring to autumn and is pollinated by a variety of insects or, more usually, self-pollinated.
❁ ***V. arvensis* differs from *V. tricolor* in the cream-coloured flowers and petals shorter than the sepals.**

Viola kitaibeliana Schultes*
DWARF PANSY
Very rare and confined in Britain to the Channel Islands and the Isles of Scilly, where it was first discovered in 1873. It is a plant of disturbed ground on sand dunes, such as rabbit warrens and around sand diggings. It will also grow in fairly close dune turf and as a weed of sandy arable fields. An annual species, the usual flowering period is March and April, occasionally extending into June.
❁ ***V. kitaibeliana* is distinguished by its small size (flowers about 0.5 cm), and the whole plant is covered by a down of greyish hairs.**

POLYGALACEAE

Polygala vulgaris L.
COMMON MILKWORT
Widely distributed throughout the whole of the British Isles. It is a plant of the short turf of chalk and limestone grassland, heaths, commons and sand dunes, avoiding the most acid soils. Like most milkworts, it produces blue-, pink- and white-flowered forms. A perennial, it flowers from May to September.

❁ ***P. vulgaris* and *P. serpyllifolia* are very similar. The lower leaves of *P. serpyllifolia* are opposite and the flowers are 4.5-6 mm; all leaves of *P. vulgaris* are alternate and the flowers are 4-7 mm.**

Polygala serpyllifolia Hose
HEATH MILKWORT
Widely distributed over the whole of the British Isles and abundant in the north and west but becoming scarce in parts of the Midlands and East Anglia. It is a plant of heaths, moors, mountain sides and acid grasslands on calcium-deficient soils. It is a perennial producing blue-, pink- and white-flowered forms and flowering from May to August.

❁ ***P. calcarea* and *P. amarella* differ from *P. vulgaris* and *P. serpyllifolia* in the lower leaves being larger than the upper and forming a loose rosette. The flowers of *P. calcarea* are larger (6-7 mm) than those of *P. amarella* (about 4 mm) and the rosette of *P. amarella* is at the base of the stem and above the base in *P. calcarea.***

Polygala calcarea F. Schultz
CHALK MILKWORT
A local plant almost confined to the short grazed turf of the chalk downs of southern and south-east England. It occurs all along the North Downs of Kent and Surrey, the eastern end of the South Downs in Sussex and westwards to Salisbury Plain and the Vale of Pewsey and south to the Purbeck Hills of Dorset. It also appears further north in the limestone grasslands of Northamptonshire and Leicestershire. A perennial, it flowers during May and June.

Polygala amarella Crantz*
(*P. amara, P. austriaca*)
DWARF MILKWORT
A rare species, confined in Britain to two quite separate geographical areas, one in northern England and the other in the extreme south-east. The first is in wet limestone grassland in the Craven area of the northern Pennines and in Teesdale. In the south-east it is confined to open chalk grassland on the North Downs in Kent. Some authorities treat the two as different species, separating the Kent population as *P. austriaca.* A perennial, it flowers from June to August.

CLUSIACEAE (= HYPERICACEAE)

Hypericum androsaemum L.
TUTSAN
Widely distributed throughout western and southern Britain and Ireland but rare and scattered elsewhere. It is a plant of damp, deciduous woodland, usually on a base-rich soil but avoiding the most acid conditions. In the south-west it is a characteristic plant of the high banks of Devon and Cornish hedges, while in northern England it grows in the grikes (crevices) of limestone pavement. The name 'Tutsan' is derived from the Norman-French *toute-saine,* 'all-heal'. A shrubby perennial, it flowers from June to August.

❁ ***H. androsaemum* is distinguished from *H. inodorum* by the sepals being as long as the petals and the style shorter than the stamens. The sepals of *H. inodorum* are distinctly shorter than the petals and the styles longer than the stamens.**

Hypericum x *inodorum* Miller
(*H. elatum* Ait.)
TALL TUTSAN
Alien. A hybrid between *H. androsaemum* and *H. hircinum,* it was introduced to British gardens in 1762 and is now widely cultivated and naturalised in mild areas in a few scattered localities in England, Wales and Ireland. A shrubby perennial, it flowers from July to October.

Hypericum hircinum L.
STINKING TUTSAN
Alien; a native of western Asia and the central and eastern Mediterranean. First introduced in 1640, it is often planted in woodland and has become naturalised in a few localities in England, Wales and Ireland. A shrubby perennial, it flowers from May to August. The plant smells strongly of goats, hence both its English and specific names (Latin *hircus,* a he-goat).
❁ ***H. hircinum* differs from *H. androsaemum* and *H. inodorum* in its square stems and stamens longer than the petals.**

Hypericum calycinum L.
ROSE-OF-SHARON
Alien. A native of Turkey and south-east Bulgaria, first introduced into Britain in 1676 and now widely planted and naturalised throughout Britain in parks and on roadsides and railway embankments. A shrubby perennial, it is shade-tolerant and flowers from June to September.
❁ ***H. calycinum* differs from the other shrubby species in its unbranched stems, long rhizomes and five, not three, styles.**

Hypericum perforatum L.
PERFORATE ST JOHN'S-WORT COMMON ST JOHN'S-WORT
Distributed throughout the British Isles, but rare north of the Solway Firth, it is a common and characteristic plant of rough grassland, meadows, road verges, hedge banks and open woodlands on neutral and calcareous soils. A perennial species, it flowers from mid to late summer. The flowers are without nectar and are apomictic. St John's-wort was much involved in medieval folklore, being one of the herbs of St John the Baptist.
❁ ***H. perforatum* is distinguished from similar-looking species by the glabrous stem with two ridges, but not square in section and the leaves dotted with numerous small translucent glands. It grows to about 80 cm.**

Hypericum maculatum Crantz
IMPERFORATE ST JOHN'S-WORT
Unevenly distributed throughout the British Isles, being most frequent in the west Midlands, central Wales, southern Ireland and the Weald of south-east England. It is a plant of damp wood margins, hedge banks and roadsides on clay and sandy soil. A perennial, it flowers from June to August.

H. maculatum subsp. *maculatum* is a rare plant in Britain, apparently being more or less confined to parts of central and western Scotland.

H. maculatum subsp. *obtusiusculum* is the widespread plant in the British Isles.
❁ ***H. maculatum* grows to about 60 cm and has a square stem, but is distinguished from *H. tetrapterum* by the longer petals (twice as long or more than the sepals) and from *H. undulatum* by the tapering, not clasping, leaves without undulate margins. Subsp. *maculatum* is rather sparsely branched, the inflorescence branches making an angle of about 30° with the stem, and the leaves lack pellucid glands. Subsp. *obtusiusculum* is a more robust, branched plant, the inflorescence branches making an angle of about 50° with the stem, and the leaves often possess pellucid glands.**

 (see illustrations page 44)

Hypericum undulatum Schousb. ex Willd.

WAVY ST JOHN'S-WORT

Very local. A declining species, found only in Devon and Cornwall and a few localities in west Wales. It grows in small boggy and marshy patches along stream sides on acid soils. A perennial, it flowers during the late summer.

❁ ***H. undulatum* is distinguished from other square-stemmed species by the almost clasping stem leaves with undulate margins and numerous glandular dots. It grows to about 60 cm.**

Hypericum tetrapterum Fr.

SQUARE-STALKED ST JOHN'S-WORT

Widely distributed throughout the whole of the British Isles except for northern Scotland and the Outer Hebrides. A frequent plant of damp grassland habitats, it occurs in meadows, woodland clearings and sides, road verges and the margins of ponds, rivers and streams. A perennial, it flowers from June to September.

❁ ***H. tetrapterum* has square stems, but is distinguished from *H. undulatum* and *H. maculatum* by the shorter petals (about as long as the sepals). It grows up to about 60 cm.**

Hypericum linariifolium Vahl*

FLAX-LEAVED ST JOHN'S-WORT

Very rare. Now confined to about five places in south Devon, one in Caernarvonshire and to the Channel Islands. It grows on steep, rocky, warm, south-west-facing slopes on thin, acid soils among sparse moss and lichen-dominated vegetation. A perennial species, it flowers during June and July and is either insect- or self-pollinated. It was first recorded from Jersey in 1837.

❁ ***H. linariifolium* is distinguished by the unridged stems and narrow leaves with revolute margins. It grows to between 20 and 60 cm.**

Hypericum pulchrum L.

SLENDER ST JOHN'S-WORT

Widely distributed throughout the whole of the British Isles except for parts of the east Midlands and East Anglia. It grows in grassy heaths, commons, rough grassland and woodland clearings and rides on acid, well-drained soils. A perennial, it flowers from June to August.

❁ ***H. pulchrum* grows to about 50 cm and is recognised by the smooth unbridged stems and cordate bases to the leaves which almost meet across the stem. The petals are at least twice as long as the sepals.**

Hypericum hirsutum L.

HAIRY ST JOHN'S-WORT

Distributed throughout most of England but absent from the south-west. It is scarce in Wales, Ireland and south-east Scotland and absent from northern Scotland. It is a plant of rough grassland, scrub and woodland clearings on chalk, limestone or calcareous glacial drift and other neutral base-rich soils. It avoids dry, well-drained conditions. A perennial, it flowers during July and August.

❁ ***H. hirsutum* is easily distinguished from similar species by its hairy stems and leaves. It grows to over 75 cm.**

Hypericum humifusum L.

TRAILING ST JOHN'S-WORT

Distributed throughout the British Isles, but most frequent in the south and west and absent from the extreme north of Scotland, Orkney and Shetland. It is a plant of heaths, moors and woodlands, paths and clearings on acid soils, growing in short turf with patches of bare ground. A perennial, it flowers from mid to late summer.

❁ ***H. humifusum* is recognised by its slender prostrate stems, small flowers (c. 10 mm diameter) and petals just longer than the sepals.**

Hypericum montanum L.

PALE ST JOHN'S-WORT MOUNTAIN ST JOHN'S-WORT

A plant of chalk and limestone scattered throughout England and Wales including the North Downs of Kent and Surrey, the Chilterns, south Devon, the Mendips, north Wales, the magnesian limestone of Yorkshire and the Carboniferous limestone of the north-west. It is a local and declining plant of woodlands, scrub and hedge banks on calcareous soils, especially with a thin overlay of sand or gravel. A perennial, it flowers in midsummer.

❁ ***H. montanum* grows to about 75 cm and has stiff unbranched, unridged stems. It differs from *H. perforatum* in the denser inflorescence and sepals fringed by stalked black glands. The leaves lack translucent dots.**

Hypericum elodes L.

MARSH ST JOHN'S-WORT

A rather limited distribution in Britain, being widely found in western Ireland, Wales, south-west England and on the heaths of Dorset, the New Forest, north-west Surrey and the Weald. In Scotland it is restricted to the extreme west, and only occurs in a few scattered localities in eastern England. It is a plant of the margins of acid pools, ponds, streams and flushes on heaths and bogs, often forming almost pure carpets of semi-floating vegetation. A perennial, it flowers from mid to late summer.

❁ ***H. elodes* is easily recognised by its soft, densely hairy stems and rounded hairy leaves.**

Hypericum canadense L.

IRISH ST JOHN'S-WORT

Confined in Europe to two areas in Western Ireland and to one locality in Holland. It was first discovered growing near Lough Mark in Co. Mayo in 1954 and in 1968 it turned up in west Cork. It grows in wet, acid, peaty grassland, flushes and stream sides, always with moving ground water usually grazed by sheep or cattle. Several suggestions have been made as to how this North American species reached western Europe, as it is most unlikely to have been accidentally or deliberately introduced. An annual or perennial, it flowers in late summer.

❁ ***H. canadense* is distinguished by its small size (10-20 cm tall), square stems and small widely-separated, golden-yellow petals.**

CISTACEAE

Cistus incanus L.

Alien. A native of south-east Europe and the Mediterranean region west to the Balearic Islands. It is occasionally naturalised in mild parts of the country as a garden escape. A small shrub, it flowers in midsummer.

Tuberaria guttata (L.) Fourr.*

SPOTTED ROCK-ROSE ANNUAL ROCK-ROSe

Very local and rare. Confined in Britain to Anglesey, the Lleyn peninsula in Caernarvonshire, to five localities in western Ireland and to Alderney and Jersey in the Channel Islands. It grows on bare patches among the heather and gorse of exposed maritime heath and rocky moorland near the sea on thin humus-rich soil overlying hard, acid rocks. An annual species, it flowers from May to August, and if insect pollination fails is self-pollinated.

T. guttata subsp. *guttata* occurs on Jersey and Alderney; *T. guttata* subsp. *breweri* is confined and endemic to the Welsh and Irish localities of the species, but may not be worthy of recognition.

Helianthemum nummularium (L.) Miller (*H. chamaecistus* Miller)

COMMON ROCK-ROSE

Distributed throughout the British Isles, but absent from the extreme south-west and from north-west Scotland. In Ireland it is known only from one locality in Donegal. It is a plant of short, grazed chalk or limestone grassland, especially where the turf is broken as on terraced slopes. It also grows at the edge of scrub and on cliffs, rocks and screes ascending to 640 m. In the northern part of its range, as in the eastern Highlands of Scotland, it grows in dry, acid, fescue/bent grassland. A shrubby perennial, flowering from June to September, it is pollinated by bees and various other insects or, if this fails, is self-pollinated.

Helianthemum apenninum (L.) Miller*

WHITE ROCK-ROSE

A rare plant, confined in Britain to the Carboniferous limestone around Brean Down in north Somerset and the Devonian limestone around Berry Head and Torbay in south Devon. It is locally abundant in dry calcareous grassland and on rocks and cliff edges on south- or west-facing slopes. A shrubby perennial, the usual flowering period is from May to July.

Helianthemum canum (L.) Baumg.

HOARY ROCK-ROSE

A very local plant in Britain confined to the Carboniferous limestone of the Gower Peninsula in Glamorgan, north Wales, the head of Morecambe Bay, Teesdale and the Burren district of County Clare and Galway in western Ireland. It grows in the thin, dry, open turf of steep limestone slopes, rocks and cliffs with a south or west aspect. A shrubby perennial, it is pollinated by bees and flowers from May to July.

H. canum subsp. *canum* has the distribution of the species, but is absent from Teesdale. *H. canum* subsp. *levigatum** is confined and endemic to shallow skeletal soils on the 'sugar limestone', a highly metamorphosed form of Carboniferous limestone, near the summit of Cronkley Fell in Upper Teesdale.

❁ **As well as its smaller flowers (up to 15 mm diameter), *H. canum* differs from *H. nummularium* in the absence of stipules. Subsp. *levigatum* has darker, smaller leaves (c. 6 mm) than subsp. *canum* that are glabrous above and 1-3 flowered inflorescences. Subsp. *canum* has leaves 6-12 mm long that are hairy above and 3-6 flowered inflorescences.**

 (see illustrations page 46)

TAMARICACEAE

Tamarix gallica L.
(includes *T. anglica* Webb)
TAMARISK
Alien. A native of the Canaries, north Africa and south-west Europe east to Italy and north to Finisterre. A shrub resistant to salt spray, it is often planted in coastal areas, particularly on sandy soils, and is frequently naturalised in southern England around the coast from Norfolk to south Wales. It grows to 1-3 m.

FRANKENIACEAE

Frankenia laevis L.
SEA-HEATH
A species of the western Mediterranean and south-west Europe, reaching the northern limits of its distribution in England, it is a local plant of coastal habitats in southern and eastern England from Gibraltar Point in Lincolnshire to the Isle of Wight. It has recently been found in Anglesey but may have been introduced. It grows on sand or sandy mud at the upper levels of salt marshes, on stable shingle and at the edges of dune slacks. A prostrate perennial, it flowers from June to September and is pollinated by hoverflies. The seeds are probably dispersed in sea water.

ELATINACEAE

Elatine hexandra (Lapierre) DC.
SIX-STAMENED WATERWORT
A local and declining species of the shallow margins of ponds and small lakes on moderately fertile soils, where it grows either submerged or on bare mud. Once most frequent in Surrey and Sussex, it now occurs scattered in eight English counties, four Welsh, four Scottish and in 11 localities in Ireland. An annual species, it flowers from July to September.

❁ *E. hexandra* **has stalked flowers, three petals and six stamens.** *E. hydropiper* **has sessile flowers, four petals and eight stamens.**

Elatine hydropiper L.*
EIGHT-STAMENED WATERWORT
A rare species, now only in one site in England (Worcestershire) but increasing in the central lowlands of Scotland and also found in north Wales and Anglesey. In Ireland there are records from Armagh, Down and Antrim, the most recent being from Lough Neagh. It is an annual species of ponds, small lakes and canals and was formerly known from other scattered localities in England. Changes in water level seem to be the main reason for its decline. It flowers during July and August.

CARYOPHYLLACEAE

Dianthus armeria L.
DEPTFORD PINK
A rare and local, rapidly declining species of southern England and one or two localities in Wales. It is a plant of dry, well-drained grassland, hedge banks and roadsides on light, sandy or, more rarely, chalk soils. An annual or biennial, it flowers during July and August and is self-pollinated.

Dianthus plumarius L.
PINK
Alien. A native of and endemic to the mountains of east central Europe from the Italian Alps to the Tatra. It has long been a favourite garden plant, and a large number of hybrids and cultivars have been produced. In the wild it is calcicolous and occasionally becomes naturalised on old walls and chalk banks. A perennial, it flowers from June to August.

❁ *D. plumarius* **differs from** *D. deltoides* **and** *D. gratianoplitanus* **in the frilled edges to the petals.**

Dianthus deltoides L.
MAIDEN PINK
Scattered throughout England and Wales, but absent from the south-west, western and northern Scotland and from Ireland. It is a local plant of rough grassland, meadows, grassy banks and hill pastures on dry, well-drained calcareous or acid soils. A perennial, it flowers from June to September and is pollinated by butterflies and moths.
❁ *D. deltoides* **differs from** *D. gratianopolitanus* **in the lower part of the stems being downy and in the pale spots and dark bars at the base of the petals. The stems of** *D. gratianopolitanus* **are entirely glabrous.**

Dianthus gratianopolitanus Vill.**
CHEDDAR PINK
Very rare; confined to the Carboniferous limestone cliffs of the Cheddar Gorge in north Somerset. In its more accessible stations it has declined markedly since the 1950s due to over-collecting and is now protected by law. The nearest Continental population is in the Belgian Ardennes. A perennial, it flowers during midsummer and is pollinated by butterflies and day-flying moths.

Lychnis flos-cuculi L.
RAGGED-ROBIN
Widely distributed throughout the British Isles, it is a common plant of wet meadows, marshes, fens and wet woodlands on mineral or peaty soils, ascending to 610 m in Scotland. It avoids very acid conditions. A perennial, it flowers during late spring and early summer and is pollinated by a variety of butterflies and long-tongued bees and flies.

Lychnis alpina L.**
ALPINE CATCHFLY
Very rare. Confined in Britain to only two localities: one in the Lake District, where a small population is restricted to two inaccessible gullies, and the other to the Clova area of Angus in the central Highlands of Scotland, where it was first discovered by George Don at the end of the 18th century. It is a plant of serpentine and other rocks rich in heavy metals like copper, nickel and zinc. In the past it has suffered severely from the depredations of gardeners and collectors. A perennial, it flowers during June and July and is pollinated by butterflies or other long-tongued insects or self-pollinated.
❁ *L. alpina* **is usually less than 15 cm and the stems are glabrous.**

Lychnis viscaria L.**
STICKY CATCHFLY GERMAN CATCHFLY
Very rare. A plant of cliffs, rocks and rock debris on acid soils of igneous origin, ascending to 425 m in Scotland. In Wales it occurs in Radnorshire and Montgomeryshire, and in Scotland it is scattered among six counties: Kirkcudbrightshire, Selkirkshire, Roxburghshire, Midlothian, Stirlingshire and Perthshire. A perennial flowering from June to August, it is pollinated by butterflies and long-tongued bees.
❁ *L. viscaria* **grows to about 60 cm, is densely tufted, and the stems are covered by sticky glands beneath the nodes.**

Cucubalus baccifer L.
BERRY CATCHFLY
Alien. A native of central and southern Europe and central Asia east to Japan which occasionally becomes naturalised in Britain. The black, berry-like fruits, which are unusual in the Caryophyllaceae, are attractive to birds. A perennial species, it flowers during the late summer.
❁ *Cucubalus* **is distinguished from white-flowered** *Silene* **(Plate 19) by its scrambling habit and black, berry-like fruit.**

Saponaria officinalis L.
SOAPWORT BOUNCING BETT
Native throughout Europe southwards from Belgium and north Germany, but only doubtfully native in Britain. It has long been cultivated as a garden plant and the leaves were indeed used to produce a lather. It is a frequent plant of hedge banks, roadsides, stream banks and damp shady habitats, usually near habitations, throughout the British Isles, but it is rare in Scotland. The double-flowered garden form is frequently met. A perennial, it flowers from July to September and is pollinated by moths.
❁ *Saponaria* **is distinguished from** *Silene* **by having two, not three or five, styles.**

Agrostemma githago L.*
CORNCOCKLE
Alien. A native of the Mediterranean, corncockle was a common and serious cornfield weed up until the end of the last century. Its dramatic decline was accelerated by the introduction of cleaner seed corn in the 1920s and its fate was finally sealed with the appearance of selective herbicides in the 1950s. In recent years it has only been reported from Norfolk, Cambridgeshire and Morayshire. An annual, flowering from June to August, it is pollinated by butterflies or self-pollinated.
❁ *Agrostemma* **is distinguished by its long, fine calyx teeth that are longer than the petals.**

Silene dioica (L.) Clairv.
RED CAMPION
Widely distributed throughout the British Isles but rather scarce in East Anglia and scarce on local in Ireland and parts of northern Scotland. It is a plant of deciduous woodlands, woodland clearings and margins and hedgerows and hedge banks on fertile, base-rich or calcareous soils. It is especially abundant in the west. It also occurs on cliff ledges and scree, reaching 1,070 m in Scotland, and it is a characteristic plant of bird cliffs. A dioecious perennial, it flowers during May and June and is pollinated by long-tongued flies and bees.

❁ ***S. vulgaris* and *S. uniflora* differ from *S. latifolia* in the strongly inflated calyces and three, not five, styles. *S. uniflora* is usually easily distinguished from *S. vulgaris* by its mat-forming habit and numerous prostrate non-flowering shoots. In addition *S. uniflora* has two small scales at the base of the petals and the capsule is hardly contracted at the mouth.**

Silene vulgaris (Moench) Garcke
BLADDER CAMPION
Distributed throughout the British Isles, but rare or absent from large parts of northern and western Scotland. It is a plant of arable fields, permanent grassland, hedge banks, roadsides and disturbed ground on dry, calcareous or base-rich soils. A perennial, flowering from June to August, the fragrant flowers are pollinated by long-tongued bees and night-flying moths.

Silene vulgaris subsp. *macrocarpa* Turrill
Alien; a native of Cyprus that has long been established on Plymouth Hoe in south Devon.
❁ **In addition to the red petals, subsp. *macrocarpa* differs from *S. vulgaris* in the narrower leaves and the possession of stolons.**

Silene uniflora Roth
(*S. maritima* With.)
SEA CAMPION
A common and often abundant plant of sea cliffs, ledges, rocky ground and shingle beaches all around the coasts of the British Isles. Inland, it occasionally occurs as an alpine plant of cliff ledges, stream sides and lake margins up to 970 m in Scotland.

Silene latifolia Poir.
(*S. alba* (Mill.) Krause)
WHITE CAMPION
Distributed throughout the British Isles north to Shetland, but much less frequent in the west and only scarce or local in Ireland and parts of northern Scotland. It is a weed of arable and waste places and roadsides on dry, especially calcareous, soils. Because of their habitat differences, *S. latifolia* and *S. dioica* do not normally grow together, but when they do fertile hybrids with pink flowers frequently result. *S. alba* is an annual or short-lived dioecious perennial flowering from May to September.

❁ ***S. noctiflora* differs from *S. latifolia* in the covering of sticky glandular hairs on the upper part of the plant, three, not five, styles, and the petals which are yellowish below and pinkish above and rolled inwards during the day.**

Silene noctiflora L.
NIGHT-FLOWERING CATCHFLY
A local plant scattered throughout England south of a line from the Tees to the Severn but rare west of Dorset. It is an annual weed of arable fields, usually on sandy soils. Along with many other arable weeds, it has become much scarcer in recent years. It flowers from July to September and its decline is probably attributable to the development of stubble-burning followed by early ploughing. The heavily scented flowers open at night and are pollinated by moths.

Silene conica L.
SAND CATCHFLY
STRIATED CATCHFLY
A local species of stabilised sand dunes in a few localities on the east and south-east coasts and in the Channel Islands, and of the Breckland of East Anglia. Inland it grows in open, calcareous-sandy grassland, roadsides, trackways and abandoned arable, nearly always where there has been some man-made disturbance. An annual species, it flowers from June to August.

Silene gallica L.
SMALL-FLOWERED CATCHFLY
A local and declining species, scattered throughout East Anglia, southern England and south Wales. It occurs in sandy arable fields and waste places, is a winter annual and flowers from June to October. The var. *quinquevulnera* is native in the Channel Islands and has been cultivated as an ornamental annual, and sometimes appears as a casual.
❁ ***S. gallica* is distinguished by the short-stalked flowers, alternating along the inflorescence, and petals with only a shallow notch.**

Silene acaulis (L.) Jacq.
MOSS CAMPION
An arctic-alpine species that is distributed throughout the Highlands of Scotland from Stirling northwards. In Wales it grows in Snowdonia and on Cader Idris, and also occurs in a few scattered localities in the Lake District. In Ireland it is confined to Sligo and Donegal. It grows in rock crevices, small ledges, scree and mountain-top detritus to 1,310 m in Scotland. It has a distinct preference for base-rich habitats and is especially frost- and wind-resistant. It flowers during July and August and is pollinated by moths and a variety of other insects.

Silene otites (L.) Wibel*
SPANISH CATCHFLY
A widespread grassland species of central, southern and eastern Europe and western Asia, reaching the north-west limits of its distribution in the Breckland heaths of East Anglia to which it is confined in Britain. It grows in open areas in short turf on shallow, calcareous soils and on short grass verges. It is dependent on patches of bare soil, such as rabbit scratches and human disturbance, for seed germination. A perennial, it flowers from June to August.

Silene nutans L.
NOTTINGHAM CATCHFLY
A rare and local species of calcareous and shingle habitats scattered throughout Great Britain but absent from Ireland. It is a plant of open habitats, growing in the short, broken turf of chalk and limestone grassland and field borders, on inland and coastal cliff tops and ledges and on stabilised coast shingle. A perennial, the flowers open at night and the petals curl up during the day. Pollinated by moths and bees, it flowers from June to August. It was first recorded from the walls of Nottingham Castle by John Ray in 1696, hence its English name. It is a variable species that has been divided into two varieties in Britain, but these are no longer considered worthy of recognition.

❁ ***S. nutans* differs from *S. italica* in the short non-flowering shoots and horizontal or drooping flowers.**

Silene italica (L.) Pers.*
ITALIAN CATCHFLY
Alien; native throughout central and southern Europe and has become established in less than half a dozen places in England and Scotland, primarily on the sides of quarries. It has persisted in one quarry in Kent for over 100 years. A perennial, it flowers during June and July and the flowers open in the evening.

Petrorhagia nanteuilii (Burnat) Ball & Heywood**
CHILDING PINK
Very rare. A native of the Canary Islands, Morocco and western Europe north to Britain. It is confined to two adjacent localities on the coast in West Sussex and to Jersey, and grows on shingle and sandy places close to the sea. An annual species, it flowers in June and July and is visited by butterflies.

❁ *Cerastium, Stellaria* **(Plate 21) and** *Myosoton* **all have deeply notched petals.** *Stellaria* **differs from the other two (except for** *Cerastium cerastoides*) **in having three styles. Both** *Myosoton* **and** *Cerastium* **have five styles, and** *Myosoton* **differs from** *Cerastium* **in having the petals divided almost to the base and in the cordate base to the leaves.**

Cerastium cerastoides (L.) Britton
STARWORT MOUSE-EAR
A local alpine species of the Cairngorms, the Ben Nevis range and a few scattered localities north to Sutherland, it is a plant of siliceous acid rocks on scree or grassy slopes at high altitudes. A perennial, it flowers during July and August and is visited by flies and self-pollinated.
❁ *C. cerastoides* **differs from other species in usually having three, rather than five, styles.**

Cerastium arvense L.
FIELD MOUSE-EAR
Distributed throughout the British Isles north to Orkney, but rare or absent from south-west England, most of Wales and western Scotland and rare in Ireland. It is a local plant of dry, well-drained permanent grassland, hedge banks and road verges on calcareous or slightly acid sandy soils. A perennial, it flowers throughout the summer and is pollinated by bees and flies.
❁ *C. arvense* **differs from the other large-flowered species in the narrow and almost hairless leaves.**

Cerastium alpinum L.
ALPINE MOUSE-EAR
An arctic-alpine species that is local but widespread on the granites and mica schists of the central and eastern Highlands of Scotland and extending northwards to Sutherland. It also occurs in a few localities at high altitudes in Snowdonia and the Lake District. A plant of alpine rock ledges, it ascends to 1,210 m on Ben Lawers. It is perennial and flowers from June to August.
❁ *C. alpinum* **is distinguished by the dense covering of** *long,* **soft white hairs.**

❁ *C. arcticum* **has shorter, stiffer, less dense hairs than** *C. alpinum* **and narrower leaves.**

Cerastium arcticum Lange
ARCTIC MOUSE-EAR
An arctic species, occurring in Snowdonia and scattered localities in the eastern, central and western Highlands of Scotland. It is a local plant of rock ledges on acid or calcareous rocks at high altitudes, and reaches 1,070 m in Scotland. A perennial, it flowers from June to August.

Cerastium nigrescens (H. Watson) Edmonston ex H. Watson
SHETLAND MOUSE-EAR CHICKWEED
An endemic subspecies confined to an area of serpentine debris at about 15 m on the island of Uist in Shetland. (Illustrated on Plate 102.)
❁ *C. nigrescens* **differs in its purple colour and almost circular leaves.**

Cerastium fontanum Baumg.
(*C. holosteoides* Fr., *C. fontanum* subsp. *glabrescens* (Meyer) Salman et al.)
COMMON MOUSE-EAR
Occurs throughout the whole of the British Isles. It is a common plant of arable and cultivated soils, permanent grassland, roadside verges, waysides, stabilised sand dunes and shingle, especially on well-drained calcareous and neutral soils. Alpine forms reach 1,220 m in Scotland. A perennial species, flowering from early spring to late autumn, it is pollinated by flies or self-pollinated.
❁ *C. fontanum* **differs from the rare large-flowered alpine species in its smaller flowers (12-25 mm diameter) and pale tips and borders to the bracteoles.**

Cerastium glomeratum Thuill.
STICKY MOUSE-EAR
Distributed throughout the British Isles. It is a common weed of arable soils, pathways, roadsides and waste places on light sandy soils and of walls, banks and sand dunes. An annual, flowering from April to September, it is self-pollinated.
❁ **The combination of the yellowish-green leaves, glandular stem and flowers in compact clusters distinguishes** *C. glomeratum* **from the other smaller-flowered species.**

❁ *C. pumilum, C. semidecandrum* **and** *C. diffusum* **are small plants, sticky with dense glandular hairs. The bracts of** *C. diffusum* **are wholly green, while at least the upper bracts of** *C. pumilum* **and** *C. semidecandrum* **have colourless tips and edges.**

Cerastium pumilum Curtis
DWARF MOUSE-EAR CURTIS' MOUSE-EAR
A rare and local species of calcareous soils in southern England north to Leicestershire and southern Lincolnshire. It grows in short, open calcareous grassland and chalk and limestone quarries. An overwintering annual, it flowers during the spring and is self-pollinated.
❁ *C. pumilum* **is usually rather reddish and the petals are notched to about one-quarter of their length and are as long as the sepals, while those of** *C. semidecandrum* **are slightly notched and about two-thirds the length of the sepals.**

Cerastium semidecandrum L.
LITTLE MOUSE-EAR
Scattered throughout the British Isles, most frequent in East Anglia and the south-east and rare in Scotland and Ireland, where it is almost wholly coastal. It is a frequent plant of short open, broken turf, stabilised sand dunes, walls and waste ground on dry, sandy or calcareous soils. An annual species, it flowers in April and May and is self-pollinated.

Cerastium diffusum Pers.
(*C. atrovirens* Bab.)
SEA MOUSE-EAR DARK-GREEN MOUSE-EAR
Occurs all around the coasts of the British Isles in open sandy or gravelly habitats close to the sea. It is a frequent plant of stabilised sand dunes. Inland it is often recorded growing on railway ballast, and occasionally on waste ground or rough grassland. An annual flowering from May to July, it is self-pollinated. The British plant is *C. diffusum* subsp. *diffusum.*

Cerastium brachypetalum Pers.*
GREY MOUSE-EAR
Discovered growing on a railway cutting between Sharnbrook and Irchester in Bedfordshire in 1946, and since discovered in Northamptonshire and Kent. It occurs throughout central Europe extending to France and Belgium, so it could well be native. An annual, it flowers in May. (Not illustrated.)

Myosoton aquaticum (L.) Moench
WATER CHICKWEED
Widely distributed throughout lowland England south of a line from the Tees to the Mersey, but rare in Wales and the south-west and absent from Scotland and Ireland. It grows in marshes, wet meadows, riverbanks, pond and stream sides, ditches and clearings in wet woodlands on fertile or base-rich soils. A perennial, it flowers in July and August and is pollinated by flies and small bees.

Moenchia erecta (L.) Gaertn., Mey. & Scherb.
UPRIGHT CHICKWEED
A local species, widely distributed throughout southern England and Wales. It is a plant of sandy heaths and woodland paths, rough open grassland, banks and maritime cliffs on acid, well-drained soils and sand dunes. An annual, it flowers in May and June. The flowers remain closed in dull weather and are then self-pollinated. It has suffered a significant decline since the beginning of the century, presumably due to habitat loss.
❁ *Moenchia* **is distinguished from the chickweeds by the narrow blue-green leaves and un-notched sepals. The four styles are opposite the sepals.**

Honckenya peploides (L.) Ehrh.
SEA SANDWORT
A maritime species occurring all round the coasts of the British Isles. It is a common plant of sand and sandy shingle, colonising the youngest sand dunes, where it grows with the sand couch grass, *Elymus juncea.* It is able to withstand burial by accreting sand and is tolerant of periodic immersion in salt water. A perennial species, it flowers throughout the summer. The flowers are hermaphrodite or dioecious and the former are normally self-pollinated.
❁ *Honkenya* **is unlikely to be confused with any other plant, with its broad, succulent, yellow-green leaves and greenish flowers.**

Corrigiola litoralis L.**
STRAPWORT
Confined in Britain to the shores of Slapton Ley in south Devon, where it grows in a narrow zone on the bare shaly gravel just above the summer water-level. It fluctuates enormously in abundance from year to year, apparently in relation to the water-level in the Ley, and is usually to be found growing with *Littorella uniflora* and *Potentilla anserina.* An annual, it flowers during July and August.
❁ *Corrigiola* **is the only member of the family with alternate leaves.**

Illecebrum verticillatum L.
CORAL-NECKLACE ILLECEBRUM
A rare plant confined to a few localities only in Cornwall and the New Forest in Hampshire. *Illecebrum* is a small, spreading annual plant of damp sandy habitats. It flowers in late summer and is self-pollinated.
❁ **The prostrate habit with dense clusters of flowers in the axils of the rounded leaves distinguishes** *Illecebrum* **from other members of the family.**

The STITCHWORTS, *Stellaria*, differ from *Myosoton* and the chickweeds, *Cerastium* (except for *C. cerastoides*), in having three rather than five styles. *S. nemorum*, *S. neglecta*, *S. media* and *S. pallida* all have ovate leaves, at least some of which are stalked. *S. holostea*, *S. graminea*, *S. alsine* and S. *palustris* have narrow, sessile leaves.

Stellaria nemorum L.

WOOD STITCHWORT

A local plant of upland Britain, occurring in northern England, Wales, central and southern Scotland but absent from Ireland. It grows in damp deciduous woodland and by stream sides, usually on base-rich soils, up to an altitude of 915 m in Scotland. A perennial, it flowers during the early summer and is pollinated by a variety of flies and beetles.

There are two subspecies in Britain: subsp. *nemorum* occurs throughout the range of the species, while subsp. *montana* is confined to Wales.

❁ ***S. nemorum* differs from the other broad-leaved species in having petals that are twice as long as the sepals. Subsp. *montana* differs from subsp. *nemorum* in the bracts decreasing rapidly in size and in the characters of the seeds.**

Stellaria media (L.) Vill.

COMMON CHICKWEED

Common throughout the British Isles, it is an abundant and persistent weed of arable crops and gardens, wasteland, roadsides, farmyards and rubbish tips. It prefers weakly acid to alkaline, well-aerated, moist, fertile soils that are subject to frequent disturbance. It is particularly luxuriant when growing around the breeding colonies of sea birds and seals and also occurs along the drift line of coastal shingle beaches and on the shingle banks of inland rivers. A serious weed of agricultural crops, it increases with fertiliser treatment and is resistant to a number of commonly-used selective herbicides, such as MCPA, 2-4-D and MCPB, but can be controlled by a variety of chemicals including Dinoseb, Mecoprop and Linuson. It is also a host to a number of important diseases of cultivated crops. Like many successful weeds, it is a short-lived annual that flowers throughout the year and is self-pollinated.

❁ ***S. media* is a rather variable plant, but differs from *S. neglecta* in being a much smaller plant with 3-8, rather than 10, stamens with red anthers.**

Stellaria neglecta Weihe

GREATER CHICKWEED

A local species, scattered throughout England and Wales but commoner in the west. It is very rare in Scotland and Ireland and absent from Orkney, Shetland and the Channel Isles. A plant of wet woodlands, shady stream sides, hedgerows and wood margins, it flowers from April to July and behaves as an annual or a short-lived perennial.

Stellaria pallida (Dumort.) Piré

LESSER CHICKWEED

Scattered throughout the British Isles but very rare in Scotland and Ireland and most frequent in eastern and south-east England. It is a plant of stabilised coastal sand dunes and of light, sandy soils inland. It occurs as a ruderal of waste places, road verges, arable, heath grassland and in the rides and clearings of pine plantations. An annual, it flowers from March to May and is self-pollinated.

❁ ***S. pallida* is similar to *S. media* but is much more slender, lacks petals and the flowers have 1-3 stamens with violet anthers.**

Stellaria uliginosa Murray

BOG STITCHWORT

Widely distributed throughout the whole of the British Isles. It is a plant of grassy stream sides, woodland flushes, wet woodland rides, marshes and spring lines on acid soils to 1,005 m in Scotland. A perennial, it flowers from May to June and is probably pollinated by small flies.

❁ ***S. alsine* has a characteristic blue-green colour and is distinguished from other narrow-leaved stitchworts by having petals shorter than the sepals.**

❁ ***S. holostea* differs from *S. graminea* and *S. palustris* in having bracts that are wholly green, from *S. graminea* by the larger flowers and from *S. palustris* by the green, not blue-green, leaves.**

Stellaria holostea L.

GREATER STITCHWORT

Widely distributed throughout the whole of the British Isles, but absent from Orkney, Shetland and the Outer Hebrides and less frequent in north-west Scotland and western Ireland. It is a common plant of hedgerows, open woodland,woodland clearings, wood margins and roadsides on well-drained, mildly acid to base-rich soils throughout most of its range. A perennial, it flowers from April to June and is pollinated by a variety of beetles, butterflies, moths, flies and bees. If insect pollination fails, it is self-pollinated. The name 'stitchwort' goes back to at least the 13th century and, as the name implies, the plant was used to cure stitches and sharp pains. It was much involved in folklore and has acquired almost a hundred local vernacular names.

Stellaria palustris Retz.

MARSH STITCHWORT

A local and declining species with a scattered distribution throughout the British Isles but absent from northern Scotland and extinct in the south-west. It has suffered much from habitat destruction but is still widespread in the Norfolk Broads and parts of south-east Yorkshire. It is a plant of open marshes, fens and dyke margins on base-rich or calcareous soils. A perennial, it flowers during midsummer and is probably pollinated by small flies.

❁ ***S. palustris* has blue-green leaves and larger flowers (12-18 mm diameter) than *S. graminea*.**

Stellaria graminea L.

LESSER STITCHWORT

Occurs throughout the whole of the British Isles; a common plant of rough grassland, permanent pasture, grassy commons, woodland rides and clearings, roadsides and hedge banks on acid, usually well-drained soils. A perennial, it flowers from May to August. It is pollinated chiefly by flies and the flowers are either hermaphrodite or male-sterile.

❁ ***S. graminea* has smaller flowers (5-10 mm diameter) than either *S. palustris* or *S. holostea*; the leaves are green and the bracts have long, fine points.**

❁ ***Minuartia* has similar flowers to *Moehringia*, usually with 3 styles, but capsule opens by 3, not 6-8, teeth.**

Minuartia sedoides (L.) Hiern (*Cherleria sedoides* L.)

CYPHEL
MOSSY CYPHEL

A local alpine species characteristic of the central and western Highlands of Scotland and the Inner Hebrides. It grows on rocky slopes, on bare open stony ground and in species-rich flushed grassland on base-rich soils to an altitude of 1,190 m. It flowers from June to August and is probably pollinated by small flies. It is one of the few British alpine species that is not also found in the Arctic.

❁ ***M. sedoides* is a small tufted alpine plant with small greenish flowers.**

Minuartia hybrida (Vill.) Schischk.

FINE-LEAVED SANDWORT

A local and declining species, scattered throughout England and Ireland but rare in the south-west and Wales and absent from Scotland. It is a plant of dry, well-drained sandy and calcareous soils and is most frequent in the Breckland of East Anglia. It grows on disturbed gound on the edges of arable fields, in abandoned arable, on road verges, railways, waste ground and old walls. An annual, it flowers during May and June.

❁ ***M. hybrida* differs from *M. rubella*, *M. verna* and *M. stricta* in the lack of sterile shoots and the erect stems.**

Minuartia rubella (Wahlenb.) Hiern*

MOUNTAIN SANDWORT
ALPINE SANDWORT

A rare arctic species, confined in Britain to rock ledges and rock detritus near the summits of a few of the mica-schist mountains of the central Highlands of Scotland and still possibly occurring in Inverness and Sutherland. Extinct in Shetland. A perennial species, it flowers from June to August.

❁ ***M. rubella* differs from both *M. verna* and *M. stricta* in its smaller leaves (4-8 mm) and smaller petals which are shorter than the sepals.**

Minuartia verna (L.) Hiern

SPRING SANDWORT

A local species that is widespread on the Carboniferous limestone of Derbyshire, the north Pennines, Cumbria, north Wales and western Ireland. It also occurs in the Mendips on the Lizard Peninsula in Cornwall and on a few Scottish mountains. It grows in open rocky habitats, on rock debris and scree and on the spoil heaps of old lead mines. Plants from the serpentine of the Lizard are morphologically distinct and have been separated as subsp. *gerardii*. A cushion-forming perennial, it flowers throughout the summer.

❁ ***M. verna* differs from *M. stricta* in its distinctly three-veined leaves and glandular-hairy flower stalks.**

Minuartia stricta (Sw.) Hiern**

TEESDALE SANDWORT
BOG SANDWORT

Very rare. An arctic-alpine species that is confined in Britain to two areas of calcareous flush on the sugar limestone of Widdybank Fell in Upper Teesdale at an altitude of 460-500 m. Its nearest localities are the French Jura and the mountains of southern Norway. A perennial species, it flowers during June and July.

❁ ***M. stricta* is a smaller, more slender plant than *M. verna*. The leaves have a single indistinct vein and the flower stalks are glabrous.**

❁ ***Moehringia* differs from *Stellaria* in the un-notched petals and from other similar-looking species in the ovate leaves with three distinct veins on the underside and flowers with 2-3 styles.**

Moehringia trinervia (L.) Clairv.

THREE-NERVED SANDWORT

Distributed throughout the British Isles but scarce and local in northern Scotland and Ireland and absent from Orkney and Shetland. It is an annual herb of deciduous woodland on weakly acid to neutral, fertile, well-drained soils. In some parts of the country it is more characteristic of ancient than secondary woodland. It flowers during May and June and, although visited by a variety of small insects, it is usually self-pollinated.

PLATE 22

CARYOPHYLLACEAE *(contd)*

(see illustrations page 54)

❁ **The PEARLWORTS differ from other members of the Caryophyllaceae in the combination of small, often tufted habit, the linear leaves and small flowers with white, unnotched petals or no petals, and 4-5 styles that alternate with the sepals.**

Sagina nodosa (L.) Fenzl

KNOTTED PEARLWORT

A local species, scattered throughout the whole of the British Isles, it is primarily a plant of short, wet turf on sandy or peaty, calcareous or neutral soils,

continued on next page

 (see illustrations page 54)

up to an altitude of 640 m. It is a characteristic species of such habitats as wet dune slacks, the broken turf of wet calcareous flushes of the northern Pennines and of the margins of the Breckland meres of East Anglia. A late-summer-flowering perennial, it is visited by a variety of small insects but is usually self-pollinated.
❁ *S. nodosa* **differs from the other species with obvious petals that are twice as long as the sepals.**

❁ *S. subulata* **differs from** *S. intermedia, S. saginoides* **and** *S.* x *normaniana* **in having the flower stalks and sepals with glandular hairs and more obviously pointed leaves.**

Sagina subulata (Sw.) C. Presl
HEATH PEARLWORT AWL-LEAVED PEARLWORT
A local species scattered throughout Scotland and western and southern Britain east to Dorset, the New Forest and Surrey. Absent from most of the rest of the country and in Ireland confined to a few scattered coastal localities in the north and west. It is a plant of sandy heaths and rocky or gravelly soils in moist, open conditions. A perennial, it flowers during midsummer and is self-pollinated.

Sagina nivalis (Lindbl.) Fries*
(*S. intermedia* Fenzl)
SNOW PEARLWORT LESSER ALPINE PEARLWORT
Very rare. A circum-polar arctic species apparently confined in Britain to four localities only in the mountains of Scotland, it grows on fine scree and broken rocky ground at high altitudes, up to 1,213 m, in the Ben Lawers area of Perthshire and in Aberdeenshire. It flowers from June to August and is self-pollinated.
❁ **A small perennial growing to 3 cm,** *S. nivalis* **is smaller than both** *S. saginoides* **and** *S.* x *normaniana* **with leaves 3-6 mm long and a dull greenish-yellow capsule.**

Sagina saginoides (L.) Karsten
ALPINE PEARLWORT
A rare arctic-alpine species confined in Britain to high altitudes in the central and eastern Highlands of Scotland and a few localities in the western Highlands and on Skye. It grows on broken rocky ground, wet rock ledges and in gullies on wet gravel slides to 1,213 m on Ben Lawers. A perennial, it flowers from June to August and is visited by small flies. On dull days the flowers remain closed and are self-pollinated.
❁ **A perennial growing to more than 3 cm,** *S. saginoides* **has leaves up to 20 mm, ascending non-rooting branches and 10 stamens.**

Sagina x *normaniana* Lagerh.*
SCOTTISH PEARLWORT
The hybrid between *S. procumbens* and *S. saginoides* and in most respects intermediate between the two; some botanists have regarded it as a distinct species. It grows in the same kind of places as *S. saginoides* but does not reach such high altitudes and flowers a little later. It is also much rarer than *S. saginoides*, only seven populations being known with certainty in Perthshire, Angus and Inverness-shire.
❁ *S.* x *normaniana* **has basal leaves up to 30 mm, prostrate rooting branches and usually less than 10 stamens. The seeds are rarely fertile.**

❁ *S. procumbens, S. maritima* **and** *S. apetala* **have four sepals and either minute petals or no petals. All the other species have five sepals and five fairly conspicuous petals.**

Sagina procumbens L.
PROCUMBENT PEARLWORT
Distributed throughout the whole of the British Isles, it is an abundant plant of paths, banks, wall-tops, lawns, grass verges and waste ground, usually in damp and shady places, ascending to 1,160 m. A perennial, it flowers from May to September and is self-pollinated.
❁ *S. procumbens* **differs from both** *S. maritima* **and** *S. apetala* **in having long, spreading branches rooting at the nodes that arise from the non-flowering central rosette.**

Sagina apetala Ard.
ANNUAL PEARLWORT COMMON PEARLWORT
Consists of *S. apetala* subsp. *erecta* F. Herman and *S. apetala* subsp. *apetala* (=*S. ciliata* Fr.). Occurs throughout the whole of the British Isles, but is rare or local in northern Scotland and absent from Orkney and Shetland. It is a common plant of walls, paths, verges, bare ground in grass heaths and waste places on well-drained, sandy or gravelly soils. An annual, it flowers from May to August and is pollinated either by small insects or is self-pollinated.
❁ *S. apetala* **subsp.** *apetala* **has acute sepals that remain erect in fruit. Subsp.** *erecta* **has blunter sepals that spread in fruit.**

❁ **The main stem of both** *S. apetala* **and** *S. maritima* **flowers, and the branches do not root.** *S. maritima* **has blunt or minutely pointed leaves;** *S. apetala* **has leaves that end in a fine point.**

Sagina maritima Don
SEA PEARLWORT
A local plant, growing on the bare soil of dune slacks, cliff tops and on open rocky and shingly ground all around the coasts of the British Isles. An alpine form occurs as a rare plant of the Scottish mountains, reaching 1,300 m in the eastern Highlands. A self-pollinated annual, it flowers from May to September.
❁ *Arenaria* **differs from other members of the Caryophyllaceae with small white flowers in the combination of small ovate leaves, unnotched petals and three styles.**

Arenaria serpyllifolia L.
THYME-LEAVED SANDWORT
Widely distributed throughout the British Isles but becoming scarce on the mainland of north-west Scotland, Orkney, Shetland and northern Ireland. It behaves either as an annual or a biennial, flowers from June to August and is usually self-pollinated. It is a common plant of bare ground in rough grassland, grass heath, field edges and walls on sandy or chalky, dry, well-drained soils.

❁ **Subsp.** *leptoclados* **and subsp.** *serpyllifolia* **both have petals shorter than the sepals. Subsp.** *serpyllifolia* **has flowers 5 mm or more in diameter and flask-shaped fruits with curved sides, while subsp.** *leptoclados* **has smaller flowers (5 mm or less in diameter) and narrowly conical fruits with straight sides.**

Arenaria serpyllifolia subsp. *leptoclados* (Reichb.) Nyman
SLENDER SANDWORT
Scattered throughout the British Isles but less common than subsp. *serpyllifolia* and rare in Scotland. It grows in similar places to subsp. *serpyllifolia* and the two sometimes occur together.

Arenaria balearica L.
MOSSY SANDWORT BALEARIC PEARLWORT
Alien. A native of the islands of the western Mediterranean – Corsica, Sardinia, the Balearic Islands and the Tyrrhenian Islands – it was introduced to Britain in 1787 and grown as a rockery plant and between paving stones of garden paths. It is scattered throughout the British Isles as an escape from cultivation. A perennial, it flowers from March to August.
❁ *A. balearica* **is distinguished by the thin, prostrate, fairly hairy stems and small oval and stalked leaves.**

Arenaria ciliata L. subsp. *hibernica** Ostenf. & Dahl.
FRINGED SANDWORT IRISH SANDWORT
Very rare; an endemic subspecies of an arctic-alpine plant that is confined to the Carboniferous limestone cliffs on the north side of the Ben Bulben range in Co. Sligo at an altitude of between 365 m and 600 m. A perennial, it flowers during June and July.
❁ *A. ciliata* **is distinguished from** *A. norvegica* **by the ciliate margins of the leaves and sepals and the larger flowers (12-16 mm diameter).**

❁ *A. norvegica* **has the leaves and sepals ciliate only towards the base, and smaller flowers (9-12 mm in diameter) than** *A. ciliata.*

Arenaria norvegica Gunn
(*A. norvegica* subsp. *norvegica***)
ARCTIC SANDWORT NORWEGIAN SANDWORT
A rare plant of calcareous or base-rich soil, rock debris and river shingle scattered in a few localities in the western Highlands of Scotland. At present it is known from Inverness-shire, Argyllshire, Rhum, the Durness limestone of Sutherland and from Serpentine in Shetland. It also occurs in a single locality in Co. Clare in Ireland. A perennial, it flowers from June to September.
❁ *A. norvegica* **subsp.** *norvegica* **is perennial with many non-flowering shoots, entirely glabrous sepals, and flowers 9-10 mm in diameter.**

Arenaria norvegica subsp. *anglica* Halliday**
ENGLISH SANDWORT
Very rare. It is an endemic subspecies that is confined to a single area of the Pennines in west Yorkshire where it grows in bare, damp depressions on limestone pavement and trackways. A winter annual or biennial, it flowers from June to September.
❁ *A. norvegica* **subsp.** *anglica* **is a winter-germinating annual or biennial with most shoots flowering, and the outer petals ciliate at the base and flowers 11-12 mm in diameter.**

Herniaria glabra L.*
SMOOTH RUPTUREWORT
A rare plant, now known from only 12 localities in Lincolnshire, Cambridgeshire and the Breckland of Norfolk and Suffolk. It grows on bare open ground on coarse sandy or gravelly soils that have become compacted by fluctuations in the water content. It is found on road verges, in compacted wheel-ruts, footpaths, on ditch and pond excavations and on chalk spoil on weakly acid to alkaline soils. It behaves either as an annual or a biennial, flowers during July and is self-pollinated or pollinated by a variety of small insects. The rather unusual English name refers to the fact that medieval herbalists used the plant to cure ruptures (Latin: hernia).

❁ *H. glabra* **differs from** *H. ciliolata* **in being an annual or biennial non-woody prostrate plant with the fruits noticeably longer than the sepals.**

Herniaria ciliolata Meld.*
FRINGED RUPTUREWORT CILIATE RUPTUREWORT
Very rare. Found only in cliff grassland and sandy turf on the Lizard Peninsula in Cornwall and Guernsey and Jersey in the Channel Islands. On the Lizard it is abundant in cliff-top grassland on shallow soils over a large area and is colonising coastal footpaths. It also grows on nearby walls. It flowers during July and August and is either insect- or self-pollinated.
❁ *H. ciliolata* **is a prostrate perennial woody evergreen which differs from** *H. glabra* **in the fruits being no longer than the sepals.**

❁ ***Spergularia* and *Spergula* differ from similar-looking members of the family in possessing leaves with stipules.**

Spergula arvensis L.
CORN SPURREY
Widely distributed throughout the British Isles; a common annual weed of arable land and less often of other open habitats such as roadsides and the sea shore. It is characteristic of light acid sandy soils, hardly ever occurring where the pH exceeds 5.5. Its altitudinal limit coincides with the limit of arable farming at about 460 m in England. Flowering is from June to September, the flowers only opening for 3-5 hours a day from noon onwards. Most flowers are self-pollinated while closed, although flies and bees are attracted by the unpleasant smell of the open flowers. It is a persistent and troublesome weed that is only partly controlled by the phenoxyacetic acid herbicides; both liming and the application of DNC are more effective.
❁ ***Spergula* differs from *Spergularia* in having five stigmas rather than three.**

Spergularia rubra (L.) J. & C. Presl
SAND SPURREY
Distributed throughout the British Isles, but rare in western Scotland, Orkney, the Outer Hebrides and Ireland and absent from Shetland. It is an annual or biennial species of dry, sandy or gravelly habitats on acid soils such as open or broken ground on heathlands, commons, cliff tops and coastal dunes. It flowers from mid to late summer and is either pollinated by small flies or self-pollinated.
❁ **The flowers of *S. rubra* are larger (3-5 mm in diameter) than *S. bocconii* and the flower stalks are longer than the sepals.**

Spergularia bocconii (Scheele) Graebn*
GREEK SEA-SPURREY
Very rare. A plant of the Mediterranean and south-west Europe that is now confined in Britain to two localities in Cornwall and to Jersey and Guernsey in the Channel Islands. In the past it also occurred in Devon and on St Mary's in the Isles of Scilly. It grows in open or broken ground in dry sandy, gravelly or rocky places, tracksides and waste ground near the sea. An annual or biennial, it is in flower from May to September.
❁ **The branches of the inflorescence elongate characteristically in *S. bocconii*, the flowers are smaller (2 mm in diameter) than *S. rubra*, and the flower stalks are shorter than the sepals.**

Spergularia rupicola Lebel ex Le Jolis
ROCK SEA-SPURREY
A local species of the west coast of Britain extending from North Uist south to Cornwall and east to the Isle of Wight. It occurs all round the Irish coast, but is decreasing, especially in the west. It grows in short turf and broken ground and on rocks, cliffs, scree and walls close to the sea. A perennial species, it flowers from June to September.
❁ ***S. rupicola* differs from all other species in the whole plant being densely glandular and hairy.**

Spergularia media (L.) C. Presl
GREATER SEA-SPURREY
A perennial species of salt marshes on sandy and muddy shores all around the coasts of the British Isles. It most often occurs as a frequent constituent of the mid-zone general salt marsh community. In recent years it has turned up on roadside verges in north-east England which have been contaminated with de-icing salt. Pollination is probably effected by small flies, and separate female and hermaphrodite plants sometimes occur. It flowers from June to September.
❁ ***S. media* can be distinguished from all other species by the conspicuously winged seeds. It also has paler and larger flowers than *S. marina*, the other salt marsh species.**

Spergularia marina (L.) Griseb.
LESSER SEA-SPURREY
An annual species occurring all around the coasts of the British Isles, but less frequent than *S. media* on the east coast of Scotland. *S. marina* is found on the drier parts of salt marshes on sandy and muddy shores and on saline soils inland, as in Cheshire and Worcestershire. In recent years it has been reported from salt-contaminated roadside verges in both north-east England and Kent. It is usually self-pollinated and flowers from June to August.
❁ ***S. marina* differs from *S. media* in the smaller, darker flowers and unwinged seeds and from *S. rubra* and *S. bocconii* in having bright yellow-green, rather blunt, fleshy leaves.**

❁ **The leaves in whorls of four, much-branched inflorescence and small flowers distinguish *Polycarpon* from all other species.**

Polycarpon tetraphyllum (L.) L.
FOUR-LEAVED ALLSEED
A rare plant of south-west Britain and confined to Devon, Cornwall, the Isles of Scilly and the Channel Islands. In the Scilly Isles it is common on sand dunes, in bulb fields and on roadside walls but it seems to have achieved its present abundance only since the 1930s. In the Channel Islands, where it is also common, it has been dubbed the 'Guernsey chickweed'. It is an efficient coloniser of bare ground in sandy and waste places. An annual, it flowers during June and July and is self-pollinated.

Plants from Jersey and Guernsey with the leaves paired and shorter inflorescences can be distinguished as var. *diphyllum* DC.

❁ **The flowers of *Scleranthus* have five sepals and no petals. The paired leaves are joined across the stem and the inflorescences are in dense terminal and axillary clusters.**

Scleranthus annuus L.
ANNUAL KNAWEL
Distributed throughout the British Isles, frequent in the south but scarce in the north-west and in Ireland. Absent from Orkney, Shetland, the extreme north of Scotland and the Outer Hebrides. It is a plant of open and disturbed ground of grassy heaths, arable and waste places on dry, sandy, lime-free soils. An annual or biennial, it is usually self-pollinated and flowers from June to August.

❁ ***S. annuus* differs from *S. perennis* in its annual habit, glabrous calyx tube and finely pointed sepals with narrow pale margins.**

Scleranthus perennis L.**
PERENNIAL KNAWEL
Very rare. A perennial species, flowering from June to August and either pollinated by small flies or self-pollinated, it is divided into seven subspecies in Europe, two of which occur in Britain.

S. perennis subsp. *perennis*
Confined to a single locality in Wales, where it grows in pockets of dry shallow soil overlying doleritic rock on east- and south-facing cliffs at Stanner Rocks in Radnorshire. The status of the population is very precarious, in some years being reduced to a single plant.

S. perennis subsp. *prostratus* P.D. Sell
An endemic subspecies, once known from almost a dozen sites in the Breckland of East Anglia but now restricted to three localities in the parish of Eriswell in Suffolk. It grows in broken turf or on bare ground on trackways, abandoned arable and fallow on dry, acid, sandy soils.

PORTULACACEAE

❁ **The two sepals characteristic of the Portulacaceae will distinguish *Montia* from all members of the Caryophyllaceae. Non-flowering plants can look similar to *Lythrum* (Plate 42) or to some species of *Callitriche* (Plate 42).**

Montia fontana L.
BLINKS
Widespread and common throughout most of the British Isles, but rather less frequent in the Midlands, eastern England and central Ireland. It is a plant of springs, flushes, stream sides, wet rocks, marshes, and damp meadows and trackways, usually on acid, calcium-deficient soils and ascending to 1,035 m in Scotland. An annual or short-lived perennial, it flowers from May to October. The tiny flowers remain closed in dull weather. *M. fontana* is a very variable species and four subspecies are usually recognised, separable only on characters of the seed coat. Descriptions of the four subspecies can be found in both *New Flora of the British Isles* and *Excursion Flora of the British Isles.*

M. fontana subsp. *fontana* is the commonest form in northern England and Scotland. It occurs in very wet habitats and often grows submerged.

M. fontana subsp. *variabilis* Walters is most frequent in Wales and northern England.

M. fontana subsp. *amporitana* Sennen is widespread in Wales, southern and south-west England. *M. fontana* subsp. minor Hayw. (subsp. *chondrosperma* (Fenzl) Walters) occurs throughout the British Isles, but is the common subspecies of southern England. It will grow in drier conditions that the previous three, often in moist sandy places.

❁ **Species of *Claytonia* differ from *Montia* in possessing only one pair of stem leaves.**

Claytonia perfoliata Donn ex Willd. (*Montia perfoliata* (Donn ex Willd.) Howell)
SPRINGBEAUTY
Alien. A native of the Pacific coast of North America from Alaska to Mexico and also Cuba. Introduced about 1749, and now established in many parts of the British Isles, but scarce in the north and west and in Ireland. It occurs in light sandy soils on disturbed ground, stabilised coastal dunes and wasteland, sometimes in abundance. An annual, it flowers from May to July. It has sometimes been grown as a salad vegetable.

Claytonia sibirica L. (*Montia sibirica* (L.) Howell)
PINK PURSLANE
Alien. A native of the Pacific coast of North America from Alaska south to California and of eastern Siberia. Introduced in about 1768, it is now naturalised in damp woodland and along shaded stream banks on sandy soils in many parts of northern and western Britain, although it is scarce in north-west Scotland and absent from Ireland. An annual or short-lived perennial, it flowers from April to July and is pollinated by flies and other small insects.

AIZOACEAE

Carpobrotus edulis (L.) N.E. Br.
HOTTENTOT-FIG
Alien. A succulent perennial and native of South Africa that has become completely naturalised on coastal cliffs, walls, banks and sand dunes in Devon, Cornwall, the Isles of Scilly and the Channel Islands. It can reproduce vegetatively from small fragments and will spread rapidly in a short time, although it is severely damaged by frosts. It was planted with marram grass, *Ammophila*

continued on next page

arenaria, to stabilise sand dunes in the Isles of Scilly in the middle of the last century. It flowers from May to July. Several other members of the Aizoaceae have become naturalised in south-west Britain, especially in the Isles of Scilly where they have escaped from the large collection in the gardens of Tresco Abbey.

CHENOPODIACEAE

Beta vulgaris subsp. *maritima* (L.) Arcang.

SEA BEET

Distributed all around the coast of the British Isles north to the Solway and the Firth of Forth, with a few isolated localities further north. Sea beet is a characteristic plant of the drift line of shingle beaches. It also grows in the drier parts of salt marshes, on grassy sea walls, sand dunes and cliff tops and further inland can be found along the banks of brackish drainage dykes. Beet can behave as an annual, biennial or perennial. It flowers from July to September and is wind-pollinated.

PLATE 24

CHENOPODIACEAE *(cont.)*
(see illustrations page 58)

❁ ***Atriplex*** **is similar to** ***Chenopodium*** **(Plate 25), but the flowers are unisexual and the female flowers are enclosed in a pair of more or less triangular bracteoles.**

Atriplex laciniata L.

FROSTED ORACHE

A local species scattered around the whole of the British coastline. It grows on both sandy shores and shores of fine shingle, usually in a distinct zone at about high water mark, often as part of the drift line and frequently in association with *Salsola kali*. An annual species, it flowers during August and September.
❁ *A. laciniata* **is easily recognised by its silvery or frosted appearance, often with reddish stems.**

Atriplex littoralis L.

GRASS-LEAVED ORACHE
SHORE ORACHE

A rather local coastal species, frequent on the east coast north to the Moray Firth, less common on the south coast except around Southampton Water and scattered up the west coast north to Morecambe Bay. Very rare in Ireland. It grows in the upper parts of salt marshes, usually on muddy soils, in rough grassland close to the sea and along sea walls. An annual species, it flowers during July and August.
❁ *A. littoralis* **is distinguished from other species by the very narrow entire or toothed leaves.**

Atriplex patula L.

COMMON ORACHE

Common throughout the whole of the British Isles except for north-west Scotland and parts of northern Ireland. An annual weed of cultivated soils, gardens, arable and open ground close to the sea, avoiding the more acid soils. It flowers from July to September and the seeds have been shown to remain viable for up to 30 years.

❁ *A. patula* **is similar to** *A. prostrata* **but differs in the shape of the leaves, which are rather mealy on both surfaces. The base of the leaf blade tapers into the stalk.**

❁ *A. glabriuscula, A. prostrata, A praecox* **and** *A. longipes* **are all similar, closely related, rather variable and often interfertile species. Reliable identification is often difficult. Keys and descriptions can be found in** *Excursion Flora of the British Isles* **and in** *Watsonia 11.*

Atriplex glabriuscula Edmonst.

BABINGTON'S ORACHE

Distributed around the whole of the British coast. It is a common plant of shingle and sandy shores, except where disturbed by heavy recreational use. On shingle beaches it is often the earliest coloniser with *Lathyrus japonicus*, successfully establishing on the previous winter's storm crest. An annual species, it flowers from July to September.
❁ *A. glabriuscula* **is distinguished from the other three species by the spongy, inflated bracteoles, the edges of which are joined from the base to the middle, and prostrate habit.**

❁ *A. longipes, A. prostrata* **and** *A. praecox* **have thin bracteoles that are joined only at the base.**

Atriplex prostrata DC.
(*A. hastata* L.)

SPEAR-LEAVED ORACHE

A common plant in Britain, both inland and around the coast, south of a line from the Humber to the Mersey. North of this and in Ireland it has a markedly maritime distribution. Inland it occurs as a weed of recently disturbed soils, cultivated land, gardens, arable and roadsides. Near the sea it grows in brackish marshes, along brackish dykes, the upper levels of salt marshes and on sand and shingle above high water mark. An annual, it flowers from July to September.
❁ *A. prostrata* **is a prostrate or erect plant growing up to 1 m with triangular, usually non-mealy leaves and unstalked bracteoles.**

Atriplex praecox Hülpthers*

EARLY ORACHE

An annual species that was first recorded from Britain in 1975. It is a coastal species which grows in meadows of short vegetation and on exposed shingle beaches just above the high water mark. Most records have come from north-west Scotland and Shetland, on shingle and sand of the sheltered shores of Scottish sea-lochs. (Illustrated on Plate 102.)
❁ *A. praecox* **is a small, often spreading and reddish plant growing up to 10 cm tall, with diamond-shaped leaves and unstalked bracteoles.**

Atriplex longipes Drejer*

LONG-STALKED ORACHE

Only confirmed as a British plant in 1977. It is an annual of coastal tall, brackish marsh vegetation dominated by species like *Scirpus maritimus* and *Phragmites australis.* It has now been identified with certainty from scattered sites around the coast of the British Isles north to the Forth-Clyde valley. (Illustrated on Plate 102.)
❁ *A. longipes* **is distinguished from** *A. prostrata* **and** *A. praecox* **by its erect habit, growing to 80 cm, with at least some of the bracteoles having distinct stalks, at least 5 mm long.**

❁ *A. portulacoides* **and** *A. pedunculata* **were formerly separated as the genus** *Halimione. A. portulacoides* **is a shrubby grey-leaved perennial, common on salt marshes.** *A. pedunculata* **differs from all other species of** *Atriplex* **in its bracteoles, which have a small apical lobe and two much larger laterals.**

Atriplex portulacoides L.
(*Halimione portulacoides* (L.) Aellen)

SEA-PURSLANE

Occurs all around the British coast south of a line from the Tweed to the Solway Firth and also along the east coast of Ireland. A low evergreen shrub, it characteristically forms a conspicuous zone along the upper levels of coastal and estuarine marshes immediately above the 'general salt marsh community' and also as a fringe along the tops of the banks of salt marsh creeks and pools. It seems to require the combination of good drainage and nutrients derived from the silt trapped among its branches. It is know locally as 'crab grass', from the habit of shore crabs seeking cover beneath its branches. It is in flower from July to September.

Atriplex pedunculata L.**
(*Halimione pedunculata* L.)

PEDUNCULATE SEA-PURSLANE

An annual species of muddy salt marshes that formerly occurred in a few localities along the east coast from Kent to Lincolnshire. First recorded in 1650, it was until recently believed extinct in Britain, but was re-found in 1987.

Sarcocornia perennis (Miller) A.J. Scott
(*Salicornia perennis* Miller)

PERENNIAL GLASSWORT

Found in coastal salt marshes of south and south-east England from the Wash to the Exe, and especially from Suffolk to north Kent and around Southampton Water. There are also isolated localities in north Wales and (formerly) north-east England. It usually grows in the middle levels of the marsh as a constituent of the 'general salt marsh community' on shores where there is an admixture of gravel and mud. A perennial, it flowers during August and September.

❁ *S. perennis* **is the only perennial** *Salicornia*-**like species in Britain. The creeping stems are woody and rooting and the plant develops a characteristic orange colour.**

❁ **The annual species of** *Salicornia* **are rather difficult to identify and there is still some confusion about the identity of several British populations. The fleshy part of the segments of which the plant is composed are the leaves which develop in opposite pairs and fuse across the stem. The small, fleshy flowers are produced in groups of one or three in the axils of the leaves. Identification is usually not possible until the autumn, when most species develop characteristic pigments.**

Salicornia L.

GLASSWORT
MARSH SAMPHIRE

The annual species of *Salicornia* are all plants of coastal and estuarine salt marshes. Many show great variation in habit, branching and colour depending on habitat and season, and the group has always posed serious problems for the taxonomist. On many parts of the coast populations exist that do not obviously belong to any of the species so far described, and much work still remains to be done on both the taxonomy and the ecology of the group. In accordance with the convention adopted in the rest of the book, our treatment follows that of the *New Flora of the British Isles.* The notes on the natural history of the various species are based on Ball and Tutin, 1959.

The name 'glasswort' stems from the use of the ashes of the plant by the 16th century glass-makers. The plant can also be used as a pickle, like rock samphire, *Crithmum maritimum*, and this has give rise to the alternative English name.

Salicornia pusilla J. Woods

A rather local species occurring along the coasts of Norfolk and Essex and from Kent to Dorset and also in south Wales and southern Ireland. It is usually to be found growing in the drier upper levels of salt marshes, often close to sea walls, and also along the drift line. An annual, it flowers during August and September.
❁ *S. pusilla* **is recognised by its short, stubby branches and from all other species by the flowers occurring singly instead of in groups of three.**

❁ *S. europaea* **and** *S. ramosissima* **have convex flowering segments and the two lateral flowers are smaller than the central one.**

Salicornia europaea L.

A rather local species occurring in coastal salt marshes along the south and west coasts of England and possibly also in Ireland. It normally grows on open sandy mud fairly low down on the shore. An annual, it flowers during August.

continued on next page

Salicornia ramosissima Woods
A widespread and common plant of salt marshes in eastern and southern England, south Wales and south and east Ireland. It is a very variable species both in habit and colour, being erect or prostrate and varying from dark green through yellow-green to dark purple. It can be found growing in the upper levels of the marsh, often just below the sea wall, along the drift line, as a constituent of the 'general salt marsh community' in salt pans and along the sides of creeks. A prostrate form grows on firm, muddy shingle. An annual, it flowers during August and September.

❁ ***S. ramosissima*** **is very variable in habit, branching and colour. It can be distinguished from *S. europaea* in the distinct colourless border to the upper edges of the leaves, but the two may not in fact be distinct. The upper edges of the leaves of *S. europaea* have an indistinct border.**

❁ ***S. nitens, S. fragilis*** **and *S. dolichostachya* have cylindrical fertile segments and the lateral flowers are about as large as the middle one.**

Salicornia nitens Ball & Tutin
A species of salt marshes in scattered localities along the coasts of eastern and southern England and southern Ireland. It grows on bare mud and in salt pans in the upper parts of the marsh. An annual, it flowers during September.

❁ ***S. nitens*** **differs from *S. fragilis* and *S. dolichostachya* in the narrower lower fertile segments of the terminal spike and the orange or brownish-purple colour of the mature plant. *S. fragilis* and *S. dolichostachya* usually lack any purplish pigment when mature.**

Salicornia fragilis Ball & Tutin
Known from most coasts of Britain and Ireland where suitable marshes occur. It is a coloniser of the bare mud at the lower levels of the marsh and the sides of salt-marsh creeks. An annual, it flowers during August and September.

Salicornia dolichostachya Moss
Recorded from almost all around the coasts of the British Isles, except western and northern Scotland. It is a common plant of gently sloping intertidal flats of mud or muddy sand on sheltered coasts and estuaries. An annual, it flowers from July to August.

❁ ***S. dolichostachya*** **differs from *S. fragilis* in the long, tapering terminal spikes consisting of between 12 and 30 fertile segments and often prostrate habit. The terminal spikes of *S. fragilis* are more uniformly cylindrical and consist of up to 15 fertile segments.**

PLATE 25

CHENOPODIACEAE

(see illustrations page 60)

Chenopodium L.
The GOOSEFOOTS are not an easy group to identify and many resemble some species of *Atriplex* (Plate 24), from which they can be distinguished by the hermaphrodite flowers and the absence of the two vertical bracteoles that enclose the fruit of *Atriplex*. In some cases certain identification relies on the sculpturing of the seedcoat, and details of these are illustrated in *Flora of the British Isles* and *New Flora of the British Isles*.

Chenopodium bonus-henricus L.

GOOD-KING-HENRY

There is some doubt as to the status of this plant in Britain. It is usually assumed to be an alien, although it appears to be native over most of Europe except for the extreme east and parts of the south. It was grown from early times as a green vegetable and is now widely distributed throughout Britain, presumably as a relic of cultivation, but is less frequent in Wales and the south-west and rare in Scotland and Ireland. It is particularly associated with organically enriched habitats such as farmyards, manure heaps, rich pasture and hedge banks and along old walls near buildings. A perennial species, it flowers from May to July.

The original name 'Good Henry' served to distinguish it from the poisonous 'Bad Henry', *Mercurialis perennis*, or dog's mercury. Medieval English herbalists later interpolated 'King'.
❁ ***C. bonus-henricus*** **is distinguished by the triangular, spear-shaped leaves and long-exserted stigmas.**

Chenopodium hybridum L.

MAPLE-LEAVED GOOSEFOOT
SOWBANE

Scattered throughout England south of a line from the Humber to the Severn and absent from the south-west. It is a rare annual plant of waste ground, arable soils, farmyards and manure heaps, and flowers from August to October.
❁ ***C. hybridum*** **is distinguished from other species by the cordate base to the leaves. It grows up to 1 m.**

Chenopodium polyspermum L.

MANY-SEEDED GOOSEFOOT
ALLSEED

Widely distributed throughout lowland England south of a line from the Humber to the Severn. North and west of this it is very rare and possibly not native. It is a common weed of arable crops, cultivated soil and waste ground on both heavy and lighter soils. An annual species, it flowers during the late summer.
❁ ***C. polyspermum*** **is distinguished by the almost untoothed, ovate leaves and strongly four-angled stems.**

Chenopodium glaucum L.

OAK-LEAVED GOOSEFOOT
GLAUCOUS GOOSEFOOT

Status in Britain is uncertain, but probably a native. It is a local plant scattered throughout the British Isles, but absent from Ireland and the north of Scotland, and is found on waste ground, gardens, refuse tips and arable on rich fertile soils. It occasionally occurs on the sea shore. It has been suggested that the seeds are distributed in horse manure. An annual, it flowers from mid to late summer.
❁ ***C. glaucum*** **is distinguished by the usually prostrate habit and narrow leaves, which are distinctly mealy and glaucous beneath and green above.**

Chenopodium capitatum (L.) Asch.

STRAWBERRY-BLITE

Alien; a plant of uncertain origins Occurs as a casual in scattered localities throughout most of Europe. In Britain it appears to be naturalised in fields in north Wales and in Northern Ireland. Elsewhere it turns up as a rare casual of rubbish tips. An annual, it flowers during July and August.
❁ ***C. capitatum*** **has narrowly triangular leaves but is distinguished by the inflorescence, which consists of a spike of dense, sessile, round heads of flowers, which turns red at fruiting.**

Chenopodium rubrum L.

RED GOOSEFOOT

Widespread and frequent in suitable habitats throughout lowland Britain. It is rare and almost wholly coastal in distribution in the south-west, Wales, northern England, Scotland and Ireland and is commonly found as a weed of arable land on rich fertile soils, in farmyards and on manure heaps. It is also a characteristic plant of the seasonally exposed nutrient-enriched muds of dried-up ponds and reservoirs, where it typically grows with *Rorippa palustris* and *R. sylvestris*. On the coast it occurs in brackish marshes, dune slacks and on the landward side of sand dunes. An annual, it flowers from May to September and pollination is probably effected by a mixture of wind-, insect- and self-pollination.
❁ ***C. rubrum*** **is nearly always reddish in colour with coarsely and irregularly toothed leaves and prostrate or erect in habit.**

Chenopodium chenopodioides (L.) Aellen
(*C. botryodes* Sm.)

SALTMARSH GOOSEFOOT

A very local species, restricted to the east and south-east coasts from the Wash to Hampshire, with the centre of its distribution around the salt marshes of Essex and north Kent. It typically grows on mud or muddy shingle and along the margins of brackish ditches and salt marsh creeks close to the sea. An annual, it flowers from July to September.

❁ ***C. chenopodioides*** **is very similar to small coastal forms of *C. rubrum*. It has weakly toothed leaves that are always reddish beneath. The only certain distinction is in the form of the perianth of the lateral flowers. Those of *C. rubrum* are free to at least the middle and have no ridge on the back; those of *C. chenopodioides* are joined almost to the tip, and the narrow part of each has a distinct ridge on the back, most easily seen when young.**

Chenopodium vulvaria L.**

STINKING GOOSEFOOT

Once widespread in southern and eastern England but now rare and rapidly declining, still persisting in a few coastal localities in Kent, Sussex and Devon as well as in Jersey and Guernsey. Elsewhere it occurs inland in a few places on rubbish tips and waste places. Characteristically it grows on waste ground near the sea, at the landward edge of salt marshes and shingle beaches and on the strand line. The plant contains trimethylamine, which gives it an unpleasant smell of rotting fish and hence its English name. An annual, it flowers from July to September.
❁ **Apart from its unpleasant smell, *C. vulvaria* is distinguished by its prostrate and ascending habit, mealy inflorescence, stalks and flowers, and triangular, almost untoothed leaves.**

Chenopodium murale L.

NETTLE-LEAVED GOOSEFOOT

Scattered throughout England and Wales and occurring only as a casual in northern England, Scotland and Ireland. May only be truly native along the east and south coasts where it occurs on dunes, disturbed ground and waste places on light soils. Inland it occasionally turns up in fields, cultivated land and on rubbish tips. An annual, it flowers from July to October.
❁ ***C. murale*** **is distinguished by the broadly triangular, sharply and coarsely toothed leaves, and slightly mealy inflorescence that is leafy almost to the tip. The sculpturing on the seedcoat should be examined to confirm identification.**

Chenopodium opulifolium Schrad. ex Koch & Ziz

GREY GOOSEFOOT

Alien. Native in southern, eastern and central Europe and widespread in temperate regions of the Old World. It is an annual species which occasionally turns up as a casual of waste places in southern England. It flowers from August to October.
❁ ***C. opulifolium*** **is distinguished by the broad leaves, often broader than long, that are distinctly bluish-green and mealy beneath, and the mealy inflorescence. The sculpturing on the seed-coat is distinctive.**

continued on next page

Chenopodium urbicum L.
UPRIGHT GOOSEFOOT
Once widely distributed throughout England, but now rare and declining. In Scotland and Wales it has been recorded less than half a dozen times in recent years and is absent from Ireland. An annual plant of rich arable soils, manure heaps, farmyards and waste ground, it flowers during August and September.
❁ ***C. urbicum* has five perianth segments and five stamens instead of 2-4 perianth segments and 2-3 stamens, and the seeds are black rather than red-brown.**

Chenopodium ficifolium Sm.
FIG-LEAVED GOOSEFOOT
A local species, scattered throughout England but most frequent in the south and east, particularly the Fenlands, and absent from the south-west, Scotland, Wales and Ireland. It is an annual weed of arable soils on rich, fertile clays and loams and also around manure heaps and farmyards. It flowers from July to September.
❁ ***C. ficifolium* can usually be distinguished from *C. album* by the characteristically-shaped leaves, with the long, almost parallel-sided terminal lobe and distinctive sculpturing on the seed-coat.**

Chenopodium album L.
FAT-HEN
Occurs throughout the whole of the British Isles, becoming less frequent in western and northern Scotland. It is an abundant annual weed of arable crops, waste ground, gardens, manure heaps and roadsides. It grows best on rich, fertile clays and loams and is less common on calcareous soils and peat. It is a particularly troublesome weed of root crops and barley but is easily controlled with MCPA or 2-4-D. It has been widely cultivated since early times. The seeds, which were ground to a flour, have been recovered from Bronze Age deposits in Britain, and it was commonly grown as a green vegetable until the introduction of spinach from south-west Asia. The plant was also used to produce a red dye. It flowers from July to October and is probably pollinated partly by wind and partly by insects.
❁ ***C. album* is a very variable species, usually deep green and mealy and often with reddish stems.**

Chenopodium suecicum J. Murr
SWEDISH GOOSEFOOT
Alien; a native of northern and eastern Europe and Asia. A rare casual of rubbish tips and waste ground. It is an annual species closely related to *C. album*, and flowers in late summer.
❁ ***C. suecicum* can only be distinguished from *C. album* with certainty by examining the sculpturing on the seed coat. It is usually a bright bluish-green, with more rhomboid stem leaves than *C. album*, and never develops reddish pigment in the stem.**

PLATE 26
CHENOPODIACEAE • MALVACEAE • LINACEAE
(see illustrations page 62)

Suaeda maritima (L.) Dumort.
ANNUAL SEA-BLITE
A common plant of sandy and muddy salt marshes all around the British coast. It is a very variable species and many of the different forms have been named. It occurs as a primary colonist among *Salicornia* on the bare mud at the lower end of salt marshes and on the muddy banks of drainage creeks, as part of the general salt marsh vegetation, on muddy shingle and in saline dune slacks, but nearly always below the high water mark of spring tides. An annual, it flowers during July and August.
❁ ***S. maritima* and *S. vera* are quite distinct. *S. maritima* is an annual growing to about 30 cm, while *S. vera* is a small shrub growing to more than 1 m.**

Suaeda vera Gmelin
(*S. fruticosa* auct.)
SHRUBBY SEA-BLITE
A small Mediterranean shrub with a very local and restricted distribution around the British shore. It occurs along the north Norfolk coast and the coasts of Suffolk and Essex. There are also isolated localities around the Wash, in Kent and on Chesil Beach in Dorset. It is occasionally planted elsewhere. It typically grows in a distinct zone or zones along the drift line of shingle beaches, at the landward end of salt marshes or at the foot of sand dunes. The seeds are distributed by the tide and germinate in the organic debris of the drift. Once established, it is able to continue growing through accreting shingle. At the top end of salt marshes the bases of the plants are often covered by a growth of the red algae *Bostrychia scorpioides* and *Catenella repens*. It flowers from July to October.

Salsola kali L.
PRICKLY SALT-WORT
A local species, scattered all around the coasts of the British Isles, except for Orkney and Shetland. It is a plant of the drift line of sandy shores, typically growing along the seaward edge of developing sand dunes, often with *Cakile maritima* and *Atriplex laciniata*. An annual, it flowers from July to September.
❁ ***S. kali* is distinguished from other family members by the spiny tips to the succulent leaves.**

MALVACEAE

❁ ***Althaea* is distinguished from both *Malva* and *Lavatera* by having an outer calyx (epicalyx) of 6-9 lobes rather than three.**

Althaea hirsuta L.*
ROUGH MARSH-MALLOW
HISPID MALLOW
Very rare as a native and now known from only two localities in Kent, and in north Somerset. It is a rare but widespread casual throughout England and Wales. It probably originated as a weed of lucerne fields and now occurs in scrub and along field borders and wood margins. An annual or biennial, it flowers in midsummer.

❁ ***A. hirsuta* is distinguished from *A. officinalis* by its smaller size (up to 60 cm in height) and hispid stem. *A. officinalis* is taller (up to 120 cm in height) and has soft, velvety stems and leaves.**

Althaea officinalis L.
MARSH-MALLOW
A local coastal species scattered from the Wash southwards, along the south coast west to Dorset, the Somerset Levels, Severn Estuary, south Wales and south-west Ireland. It grows in the upper parts of salt marshes, in brackish marshes and along the banks of brackish drainage ditches and stream sides and occasionally inland as a casual along stream banks. A perennial, it is pollinated by bees or self-pollinated and flowers in August and September. Marsh-mallows were originally made from mucilage obtained from the roots and the plant was used medicinally to prepare a soothing ointment.

❁ ***Lavatera* is distinguished from *Malva* by having the lobes of outer calyx (epicalyx) joined at the base, whereas they are free in *Malva*.**

Lavatera arborea L.
TREE-MALLOW
A tree-like biennial which will grow to a height of about 3 m. A Mediterranean species, it grows around the south-west coasts of Britain from Dorset to north Wales, Anglesey and the Isle of Man and scattered along the south-west coast of Ireland. Elsewhere, it occurs as an introduction along the rest of the south coast and north to Lincolnshire. It grows on cliffs, rocks and stony waste ground close to the sea and flowers from July to August.
❁ ***L. arborea* is a much larger plant than *L. cretica*, with a stem that is woody at the base and softly hairy above, and the outer calyx (epicalyx) enlarges in fruit.**

Lavatera cretica L.*
SMALLER TREE-MALLOW
A Mediterranean species, very rare in Britain, occurring only in the Isles of Scilly and on Jersey and Guernsey in the Channel Islands. It has been recorded from west Cornwall, but not since the beginning of the century. It is a plant of disturbed ground such as old quarries, roadsides and waste ground. In the Isles of Scilly it is locally common in hedge banks on Tresco, St Agnes and St Mary's. An annual or biennial, it flowers from April to July.
❁ ***L. cretica* grows up to 150 cm, the stem is covered by stiff hairs and the outer calyx does not enlarge in fruit.**

❁ ***Malva* differs from *Lavatera* in the lobes of the outer calyx (epicalyx) being free to the base.**

Malva moschata L.
MUSK MALLOW
Widespread throughout the British Isles but becoming scarce in west Wales, northern England, Scotland and Ireland and absent from Orkney and Shetland. It is a plant of roadsides, hedge banks, pastures and field borders on dry fertile soils. A perennial, it flowers from July to August and is most attractive to bees and other insects. The musk-like smell only becomes obvious if the flowers are taken indoors.

Malva sylvestris L.
COMMON MALLOW
Occurs throughout the British Isles, but is scarce north of the Solway where it is more or less confined to the east coast. It is absent from Orkney, Shetland and the Hebrides. In lowland Britain it is a common plant of roadsides, banks and waste ground, usually on dry, well-drained soils. Many of its local names refer to the cheese-like shape of the disc of nutlets. A perennial, it flowers from June to September and is usually pollinated by bees.
❁ ***M. sylvestris* differs from both *M. neglecta* and *M. pusilla* in the larger flowers (up to 4 cm in diameter), with the petals more than three times as long as the sepals.**

Malva pusilla Sm.
SMALL MALLOW
Alien. A native of northern and central Europe. It occurs as a casual of waste ground, rubbish heaps, cultivated land and coastal habitats throughout most of Britain, occasionally becoming established. An annual, it flowers from June to September and is self-pollinated.

Malva neglecta Wallr.
DWARF MALLOW
Widespread east of a line from the Tees to Dorset but rare and scattered elsewhere and usually coastal. It is absent from Orkney, Shetland and the Hebrides. It occurs on dry soils in waste places, on grassy banks and roadsides and on the foreshore drift line. An annual, it flowers from June to September and is usually self-pollinated.
❁ ***M. neglecta* differs from *M. pusilla* in the larger flowers (up to 2.5 cm in diameter) with petals up to twice as long as the sepals. The flowers of *M. pusilla* are only about 0.5 cm in diameter, and the petals are about as long as the sepals.**

LINACEAE

Linum perenne L. subsp. *anglicum* (Mill.) Ockendon
(*L. anglicum* Mill.)
PERENNIAL FLAX
This beautiful plant is a rare and decreasing species of permanent calcareous grassland in eastern England. It occurs in a few scattered localities on the chalk and oolite of north Essex, Cambridgeshire, Leicestershire,

continued on next page

Yorkshire and Durham, with an outlier on the Carboniferous limestone in Cumbria. It is perennial, it flowers during June and July.

❁ *L. perenne* **subsp.** *anglicum* **has darker blue flowers than** *L. bienne* **and the inner sepals are obtuse and without glandular hairs. All the sepals of** *L. bienne* **are acute and the inner are edged with glandular hairs.**

Linum bienne Mill.

PALE FLAX

A plant of coastal areas of southern Britain from the Thames estuary to Pembrokeshire, with isolated localities in north Wales, Anglesey and the Isle of Man. It is widespread in south-east Ireland but rare in the south-west. It grows in dry, well-drained permanent pasture on neutral or calcareous soils, usually near the sea. An annual, it flowers from May to September.

Linum catharticum L.

FAIRY FLAX
PURGING FLAX

Widespread and common throughout the whole of the British Isles to an altitude of 850 m. It is particularly characteristic of grazed calcareous grassland but also occurs on limestone cliffs and rock ledges and on calcareous coastal dunes. It is found less often on grassy heaths and moorland, when it may indicate some local calcium enrichment or a raised pH. An annual, it flowers from June to September and is pollinated by small insects or self-pollinated. As its English name suggests, it was used by medieval herbalists as a powerful purgative.
❁ **A small species, growing to about 15 cm.**

PLATE 27

LINACEAE • GERANIACEAE

(see illustrations page 64)

Radiola linoides Roth

ALLSEED

A local and declining species, scattered throughout the British Isles. It grows on bare patches of damp sandy or peaty soil on heaths, short open grassland and woodland rides. It is most frequent on the Wealden sands, in the New Forest, Dorset and parts of the south-west. An annual, it is self-pollinated and flowers during July and August.
❁ *Radiola* **is a tiny annual growing to about 8 cm with four sepals and four petals, each hardly 1 mm long. Superficially it resembles** *Anagallis minima* **(Plate 58), with which it sometimes grows, but it is usually more branched and** *A. minima* **has five, not four, petals and alternate leaves.**

GERANIACEAE

Erodium maritimum (L.) L'Hérit

SEA STORK'S-BILL

A rather local species, distributed around the coasts from Sussex to the Scillies and northwards to the Solway Firth. It also occurs scattered along the east and south coasts of Ireland and inland in Worcestershire and Stafford. It is a plant of mature dunes, short maritime grassland, cliff tops, walls and open habitats, usually close to the sea. An annual, it flowers from May to September.

Erodium moschatum (L.) L'Hérit

MUSK STORK'S-BILL

A local maritime species scattered around the west coast from south Devon to Cumbria and in Ireland from Co. Down south and west to Kerry. It is probably most abundant in the Isles of Scilly. Inland there are numerous scattered localities in England and Wales, but they are all almost certainly introductions. It is a plant of waste places, roadsides and cultivated land. It was once cultivated as a pot and medicinal herb and for the rather doubtful musk-like scent of the leaves. An annual, it flowers from May to July.

❁ *E. moschatum* **differs from** *E. cicutarium* **in the less deeply divided leaflets.** *E. cicutarium* **has no 'musk-like' scent.**

Erodium cicutarium (L.) L'Hérit

COMMON STORK'S-BILL

Distributed throughout the whole of the British Isles, but almost wholly coastal in Ireland. It occurs on heaths, commons, short grassland and arable on dry, sandy soils and on coastal and inland sand dunes. An annual, it flowers from mid to late summer and is pollinated by various small insects or self-pollinated. There are three subspecies in Britain.

❁ *E. cicutarium* **subsp.** *cicutarium* **is the common inland plant but is also frequent around the coast.** *E. cicutarium* **subsp.** *dunense* **Andreas is a dwarf coastal form.** *E. lebelii* **can be distinguished by its smaller flowers (usually less than 10 mm across) and fewer flowers on each peduncle (2-4, not 3-7).**

Erodium lebelii Jordan (*E. cicutarium* subsp. *bipinnatum* (Willd.) Tourlet; *E. glutinosum* Dum.)

STICKY STORK'S-BILL

A plant of sand dunes and sandy places, scattered all along the south coast and up the west coast as far north as the Solway. Very rare on the south coast of Ireland. (Not illustrated.)

Geranium pratense L.

MEADOW CRANE'S-BILL

Widespread throughout most of Britain but absent from northern Scotland and south-west England and in Ireland found only in Antrim and Londonderry. It also occurs as an introduction outside its natural range. It grows along roadsides and hedge banks and in meadows and permanent pastures on base-rich or calcareous soils to an altitude of about 550 m. A perennial, it is pollinated by bees, and flowers from June to September.

Geranium sylvaticum L.

WOOD CRANE'S-BILL

Widely distributed and often common in northern Britain, south to Yorkshire, but rare in the extreme north of Scotland and in Ireland and absent from the Outer Hebrides, Orkney and Shetland. It is a plant of damp woodlands, hedge banks, permanent pastures, meadows and mountain rock ledges, usually on base-rich or calcareous soils, to an altitude of about 1,000 m. A perennial, it flowers during June and July and is pollinated by a variety of small insects, including parasitic wasps. The flowers possess the distinction of being those which first attracted the attention of the 18th century German theologian, Christian Konrad Sprengel, who laid the foundations of the study of insect pollination.

Geranium versicolor L.

PENCILLED CRANE'S-BILL

Alien. A native of southern Italy and Sicily, Yugoslavia and the Caucasus. Introduced into the British Isles in the 17th century, it has become naturalised in hedgerows and shaded habitats in a number of places in southern England and south Wales and occasionally in Ireland. It is especially frequent on the high earth banks of Devon and Cornish hedges. A perennial, it flowers from May to September.

Geranium phaeum L.

DUSKY CRANE'S-BILL

Alien. A native of central Europe as far south as the Pyrenees and central Italy and east to the western former Soviet Union. It is widely grown in gardens and frequently occurs as an escape from cultivation in hedge banks and shaded habitats throughout the British Isles, but is rare in Scotland and Ireland. A perennial, it flowers during May and June and is pollinated chiefly by bees.

Geranium sanguineum L.

BLOODY CRANE'S-BILL

Scattered throughout much of northern and western Britain, but absent from the south and east. It occurs in two main habitats. Inland it is a plant of limestone rocks, woodland, scree and grassland to about 370 m, especially of the Carboniferous limestone of north Wales, Gower, Cumbria and the Burren in Co. Clare in Ireland. On the coast it grows in fixed calcareous dunes as far north as Caithness. A perennial, it flowers during July and August.
❁ *G. sanguineum* **is distinguished from other large-flowered species by the solitary crimson flowers.**

Geranium pyrenaicum Burm. f.

HEDGEROW CRANE'S-BILL
MOUNTAIN CRANE'S-BILL

There is some debate as to whether *G. pyrenaicum* is truly native in Britain. It was first recorded in 1762 and is now frequent over the whole of southern and eastern England. It becomes rarer northwards and westwards, extending as far as the Moray Firth, and is scattered in Ireland. It is a plant of hedgerows, field margins and waste ground on dry, well-drained soils. A perennial, it flowers from June to August.
❁ *G. pyrenaicum* **has larger and brighter pink-purple flowers than both** *G. molle* **and** *G. pusillum* **(Plate 28), with petals 8-10 mm long.**

Geranium columbinum L.

LONG-STALKED CRANE'S-BILL

A rather local species, most frequent in southern England and becoming increasingly rare northwards as far as the Moray Firth. Scattered throughout Ireland, but absent from the Scottish islands. It occurs in open grassland, scrub and occasionally as an arable weed, chiefly on dry calcareous or base-rich soils. An annual, it flowers during midsummer.
❁ **The long flower stalks, up to 2 cm, are a characteristic of** *G. columbinum* **and distinguish it from other small-flowered species with deeply divided leaves.**

Geranium dissectum L.

CUT-LEAVED CRANE'S-BILL

Widespread and common throughout the whole of the British Isles, but becoming scarce in central and northern Scotland. It is a plant of waste ground, cultivated soils, roadsides, hedge banks and grassland, especially on fertile soils. An annual, it flowers from May to August and is self-pollinated.
❁ **The leaves of** *G. dissectum* **are divided nearly to the base, which distinguishes it from both** *G. molle* **and** *G. pusillum*.

Geranium rotundifolium L

ROUND-LEAVED CRANE'S-BILL

A local plant of southern Britain as far north as Northamptonshire, south Wales and southern Ireland. It is most frequent in the south-west and the Channel Islands. It is usually found in dry hedge banks and on walls on both sandy and calcareous soils. It occasionally appears as a weed of arable land. An annual, it flowers during midsummer and is normally self-pollinated.
❁ *G. rotundifolium* **can be distinguished from similar species by the rounded, not notched, tips to the petals and the relatively shallowly-lobed leaves.**

continued on next page

Geranium molle L.
DOVE'S-FOOT CRANE'S-BILL

Widely distributed and common throughout the whole of the British Isles, but becoming scarcer in parts of northern and central Scotland. It is a plant of dry grassland, lawns, cultivated ground, sand dunes and waste places on both calcareous and sandy soils. It often occurs as a weed of arable crops. A winter-germinating annual, it flowers from April through to September and is probably most often self-pollinated.
❁ ***G. molle* is very similar to *G. pusillum* (Plate 28) but has longer hairs on the stem, the fruits are glabrous, and all 10 stamens have fertile anthers.**

PLATE 28
GERANIACEAE • OXALIDACEAE • BALSAMINACEAE
(see illustrations page 66)

Geranium pusillum L.
SMALL-FLOWERED CRANE'S-BILL

Widespread in lowland England, but thinly scattered and usually coastal elsewhere. It extends as far north as the Moray Firth but is rare in western Scotland, Wales and Ireland. It is a plant of short grassland, waste places and cultivated ground on dry, well-drained soils. A winter annual, it flowers from June to September and is usually self-pollinated.
❁ ***G. pusillum* differs from *G. molle* (Plate 27) in the shorter hairs on the stem, hairy fruits and in five of the 10 stamens lacking anthers.**

Geranium lucidum L.
SHINING CRANE'S-BILL

Widespread throughout the British Isles but most abundant in upland areas of England and Wales and in western Ireland. Elsewhere it is rather thinly distributed and is absent from northern Scotland, the Hebrides, Orkney and Shetland. It grows on shaded rocks, walls and hedge banks and occasionally as a garden weed, reaching an altitude of 760 m. It is most characteristic of basic or calcium-rich conditions, but is not confined to soils derived from limestones. An annual, it flowers from May to August.
❁ **The distinctive glossy texture to the relatively shallowly-lobed leaves distinguishes *G. lucidum* from other small-flowered species.**

Geranium robertianum L.
HERB-ROBERT

Widespread and common throughout the whole of the British Isles except for the Outer Hebrides, Orkney and Shetland, where it is rare. Usually biennial, it flowers from May to September. It features prominently in local folklore as it was probably the plant of the house goblin Robin Goodfellow. Geoffrey Grigson lists no less than 111 different regional vernacular names. There are three subspecies in Britain.

G. robertianum subsp *robertianum* is the common inland form.

G. robertianum subsp *maritimum* Bab. (H.G. Baker) is a prostrate biennial, characteristic of shingle beaches. It also occurs rarely on cliffs and walls close to the sea.
❁ ***G. robertianum* subsp. *maritimum* has smaller flowers than subsp. *robertianum* and has usually hairless, not hairy, fruits. (Not illustrated.)**

G. robertianum subsp. *celticum* Ostenfeld is a rare endemic annual with large pale flowers and hairy fruits.

❁ ***G. robertianum* is distinguished from *G. purpureum* by the larger flowers (petals 9 mm long or more) and orange or purple anthers. *G. purpureum* has small flowers (petals 9 mm or less) and yellow anthers.**

Geranium purpureum Vill.*
LITTLE-ROBIN

G. purpureum subsp. *purpureum*
Very rare and local. The only recent records are from Cornwall, Dorset, Hampshire, Gloucestershire, Cork, Jersey and Guernsey. It is a plant of open rocky habitats and hedge banks, usually close to the sea, on fertile, calcium-rich soils. It formerly occurred in Sussex, Somerset, Devon, Carmarthen and Waterford. An annual or biennial, it flowers from May to September.

G. purpureum subsp. *forsteri* (Wilmott) H.G. Baker
A rare endemic confined to stabilised shingle beaches in Hampshire, the Isle of Wight and West Sussex. The taxonomic status of this subspecies is in some doubt and it may possibly have arisen as a result of initial hybridisation between subsp. *purpureum* and prostrate forms of *Geranium robertianum*.
❁ **It is a procumbent plant, with a habit similar to *G. robertianum* subsp. *maritimum*.**

OXALIDACEAE

Oxalis acetosella L.
WOOD-SORREL

Widespread and common throughout almost the whole of the British Isles, but rather infrequent in the least wooded areas of eastern England. It prefers well-drained, humus-rich woodland soils and is very shade-tolerant. In East Anglia and parts of the east Midlands it is strongly associated with ancient woodlands. In limestone areas of upland Britain it grows in the grikes of limestone pavement and ascends to 1,220 m among shaded rocks. In heavily wooded areas it is frequent in hedge banks and will also grow as an epiphyte. A spring-flowering perennial, it characteristically produces a crop of closed, self-pollinating flowers later in the summer. The plant has been cultivated in the past and the leaves used in a green sauce.

Oxalis stricta L.
(*O. europaea* Jord.)
UPRIGHT YELLOW-SORREL

Alien. A native of North America from Nova Scotia south to Texas but naturalised in most temperate parts of the world. In Britain it occurs chiefly as a garden weed, occasionally appearing as a casual on other cultivated soils. It is most frequent on sandy soils in the south-east, becoming rare in the west, south-west and Scotland. A perennial that often behaves as an annual, it flowers from June to September and is probably self-pollinated.

Oxalis corniculata L.
PROCUMBENT YELLOW-SORREL

Alien. It has been grown in gardens since the Middle Ages, and was first recorded as established in the wild before the end of the 16th century. It occurs as a garden weed over much of England and Wales but is most frequent in the south-west and the Channel Islands, and is rare in Scotland and Ireland.

Oxalis exilis Cunn.
(*O. corniculata* var. *microphylla* Hook. f.)
LEAST YELLOW-SORREL

Alien. A native of the mountains of New Zealand and Tasmania.
❁ ***O. corniculata* differs from other yellow-flowered species in its slender creeping stems, rooting at the nodes, and alternate leaves. *O. exilis* is smaller and the flowers are solitary.**

Oxalis articulata Savigny
PINK-SORREL

Alien and a native of east temperate South America from south Brazil southwards. It is the commonest pink *Oxalis* in cultivation. It is frequently found naturalised in the south-west on waste ground, roadsides and on seashores where it sometimes becomes established, and unlike other alien *Oxalis* species it will grow among native vegetation. A perennial, it flowers from May to October.
❁ **The leaves and flowers arise from the tip of a stout rhizome, which distinguishes *O. articulata* from both *O. latifolia* and *O. debilis*.**

Oxalis latifolia Kunth
GARDEN PINK-SORREL

Alien. A native of the West Indies and central and equatorial South America, where it grows in hillside meadows. It was formerly cultivated as a garden plant, but is now a troublesome weed in old gardens and greenhouses in the south-west and Jersey. A perennial, it flowers from May to September.
❁ ***O. latifolia* and *O. debilis* can be distinguished by the shape of their leaves, and those of *O. latifolia* are glabrous while those of *O. debilis* are hairy.**

Oxalis debilis Kunth
(*O. corymbosa* DC.)
LARGE-FLOWERED PINK-SORREL

Alien and native in most of South America. It was formerly widely cultivated as a garden plant and now occurs naturalised as a relic of cultivation. It most often appears as a weed of garden paths and cultivated ground and is especially common in gardens in the south and west of London. Elsewhere, it occasionally turns up in market gardens and nurseries. A perennial, it can spread rapidly by vegetative propagation. It flowers from July to September.

Oxalis pes-caprae L.
BERMUDA-BUTTERCUP

Alien and a native of South Africa. It was originally cultivated as a greenhouse plant in Britain, as it is not frost-hardy. In the Isles of Scilly it is a frequent bulb-field weed, possibly originating as an escape from the gardens of Tresco Abbey. It has also been reported from south Devon, Jersey and Guernsey. A perennial, it flowers from March to June.
❁ ***O. pes-caprae* differs from other yellow-flowered species in having all the leaves arising from the base of the plant and the presence of basal bulbils.**

Oxalis incarnata L.
PALE PINK-SORREL

Alien and a native of South Africa, where it grows in shaded habitats. A popular plant in cottage gardens, it has become naturalised in hedge banks and stone walls in Devon and Cornwall but rarely appears as an escape from cultivation elsewhere. A perennial, it flowers during late spring and midsummer.
❁ ***O. incarnata* differs from other pink-flowered species in the leafy stem and solitary flowers.**

BALSAMINACEAE

Impatiens noli-tangere L.
TOUCH-ME-NOT

Very local and only native in the Lake District, Yorkshire and north Wales. Elsewhere it occurs probably only as a casual in scattered localities in Sussex, Surrey, Kent, Dorset, Hampshire, Northamptonshire, Norfolk and Kintyre. It is a plant of riverbanks, wet woodlands and woodland stream sides. An annual, it flowers from July to September and is pollinated by bees. In addition it produces cleistogamous (closed and self-pollinated) flowers. The English names alludes to the method of seed dispersal of all the balsams; the seeds are forcibly ejected from the ripe capsules 'at a touch'.

Impatiens capensis Meerb.
ORANGE BALSAM

Alien. A native of eastern North America from Newfoundland south to Florida and west to Nebraska. First recorded from the River Wey in Surrey in 1822, it

continued on next page

rapidly spread to Hertfordshire and Middlesex by way of the Grand Junction Canal. It is now completely naturalised along canals and riverbanks in many parts of central, southern and eastern England and south Wales. An annual, it flowers from June to August and in addition regularly produces cleistogamous (closed and self-pollinated) flowers.

PLATE 29

BALSAMINACEAE • FABACEAE

(see illustrations page 68)

Impatiens parviflora DC.

SMALL BALSAM

Alien. A native of Siberia and Turkistan, where it grows along stream sides and in moist, shaded habitats. It is completely naturalised over much of Europe and was first recorded in Britain from Cheshire in 1848 and from Battersea, Surrey (now south London) in 1851. In Britain it is exclusively lowland, being most frequent in the south-east, but extending as far north as the Moray Firth. It is absent from the south-west and from Ireland. It occurs in woodland, parks, shelter belts and along shaded river and stream banks on fertile loam soils. A spring-germinating annual, it flowers from July to November and is pollinated principally by hoverflies or is self-pollinated.

Impatiens glandulifera Royle

INDIAN BALSAM
POLICEMAN'S HELMET

Alien. This handsome species is a native of the Himalayas and was first introduced as a garden plant in about 1839. It is now widespread throughout the British Isles, forming tall, dense monocultures along riverbanks and in damp waste places, especially in parts of northern and western England and Wales. An annual, it flowers from July to October and is pollinated by bumble-bees.

FABACEAE (= LEGUMINOSAE)

Lupinus nootkatensis Donn ex Sims

NOOTKA LUPIN

Alien; a native of the area around Nootka Sound in British Columbia. It was introduced into British gardens around 1794 and is now naturalised on river shingle in several parts of Scotland and Orkney. A perennial, it flowers from May to July.

Lupinus arboreus Sims

TREE LUPIN

Alien; a native of California and introduced to British gardens around 1794. It is now thoroughly naturalised in waste places on well-drained soils especially around the south and east coasts, where it will grow on stabilised shingle and sand. It is frequent in the Channel Islands. A medium-sized shrub, it flowers from June to September.

Genista anglica L.

PETTY WHIN
NEEDLE FURZE

Widespread throughout Britain in suitable habitats, but absent from Ireland, the Hebrides, Orkney and Shetland. It is characteristic of dry or damp heathlands and moorland and is common on the lowland heaths of Dorset, the New Forest and the Weald. It is also frequent in eastern Scotland, but elsewhere it is local and declining due to habitat loss. A low spiny shrub, it flowers during May and June and is pollinated by bees.

❁ ***G. anglica* is distinguished from both *G. tinctoria* and *G. pilosa* by the spiny stem.**

Genista tinctoria L.

DYER'S GREENWEED

Distributed throughout the British Isles as far north as Berwickshire; it is absent from Ireland and scarce in south-west England. It is a plant of grassy commons, rough pastures, old meadows and roadside verges, often on heavy, badly-drained land. It avoids both the more acid and shallow calcium-rich soils. A dwarf shrub, it flowers from July to September and is pollinated by bees. Prostrate forms occur along the coasts of Devon, Cornwall and Pembrokeshire. Those with broad leaves and glabrous pods are often placed as subsp. *littoralis* (Corb.) Rothm.

❁ ***G. pilosa* is distinguished from *G. tinctoria* by the densely hairy leaves and hairy flowers. *G. tinctoria* has sparse hairs along the leaf margins only.**

Genista pilosa L.*

HAIRY GREENWEED

Very rare. Now confined to the north coast of Cornwall and the Lizard Peninsula, where it is still relatively abundant, to St David's Head in Pembrokeshire and to Cader Idris in Merionethshire. Until very recently it was also known from Ashdown Forest in Sussex, but now seems to have been lost due to a combination of heath fires and disturbance. A prostrate shrub, it grows on cliffs and sandy or gravelly heaths usually on acid, mineral-deficient soils. On the Lizard it occurs on soils derived from the serpentine. It flowers during May and June and is pollinated by bees.

❁ **The medicks differ from the clovers (*Trifolium*) in having coiled or sickle-shaped, rather than straight, pods. (Both *M. minima* and *M. polymorpha* have spiny fruits, but those of *M. minima* are also hairy, while they are hairless in *M. polymorpha*.)**

Medicago minima (L.) L.

BUR MEDICK
SMALL MEDICK

Very local. Confined to the south-east coast from south Norfolk to East Sussex and to the Breckland heaths of south-west Norfolk and north-west Suffolk. It is a plant of dry, open habitats on coarse calcareous soils but will also tolerate a slight degree of acidity. It grows on heath tracks, disturbed areas on banks, road verges and arable fields and mature coastal sand dunes. A biennial, it flowers from May to July.

Medicago arabica (L.) Huds.

SPOTTED MEDICK

Distribution is concentrated south and east of a line from the Wash to the Severn. North of this it is confined to a few scattered localities in England and north Wales. In addition it has a distinctly maritime distribution, growing in grassy habitats and waste ground on dry, well-drained soils. A spring-germinating annual, it flowers from April to August and is pollinated by bees.

❁ ***M. arabica* is easily distinguished by the black spots on the leaflets.**

Medicago polymorpha L.

TOOTHED MEDICK
HAIRY MEDICK

A local coastal species occurring all along the south coast, north to north Norfolk in the east and to north Devon in the west. It is widespread and local as a casual inland to south Scotland. It grows in open habitats on sandy or grassy ground close to the sea. An autumn and spring-germinating annual, it flowers from May to August and is usually self-pollinated.

Medicago lupulina L.

BLACK MEDICK

Common and widespread throughout England and Wales. In the north it becomes mostly coastal in distribution; it is scarce in Northern Ireland and absent from Scotland. It is a plant of short permanent grassland on well-drained soils up to an altitude of 370 m. It is a characteristic component of limestone turf and avoids the more acid conditions. It is frequent on mown roadsides verges, lawns and grassy paths in the open. An annual or short-lived perennial, it flowers from April to August and is usually self-pollinated.

❁ ***M. lupulina* differs from the other species in the many-flowered heads and black, spineless fruits. The leaves can be distinguished from those of similar-looking clovers by the presence of a tooth in the apical notch of the leaflets, which is absent in the clovers.**

Medicago sativa subsp. *falcata* (L.) Arcang.
(*M. falcata* L.)

SICKLE MEDICK

Very local in Britain, being confined to Norfolk, Suffolk and Cambridgeshire and within that area mainly to the Breckland and a few coastal sites. It is widely introduced elsewhere in England. It grows in a variety of open or closed grasslands on slightly acid or calcareous coarse soils. It is sensitive to both grazing and mowing and typically occurs on grass banks and the backs of roadside verges. A perennial, it flowers during June and July and is pollinated by bees.

Medicago sativa L. subsp. *sativa*

LUCERNE
ALFALFA

Alien; probably a native of the Mediterranean and western Asia. It has been cultivated as a fodder crop since about 1650 and frequently occurs naturalised on roadsides, waste ground and field borders, but is scarce in the north and west and in Ireland. An autumn-germinating perennial, it flowers during June and July and is pollinated by bees. (Illustrated on Plate 102.)

❁ **Lucerne can be distinguished from other purple-flowered legumes by its trifoliate leaves.**

Anthyllis vulneraria L.

KIDNEY VETCH

Widely distributed throughout the whole of the British Isles. It is a characteristic component of the shallow, dry rendzina soils of chalk and limestone grassland. It also occurs in dry coastal grassland, rock ledges, cliff tops and maritime heath. A perennial, it flowers from June to September.

A. vulneraria is a highly polymorphic species, *Flora Europaea* describing 24 distinct subspecies, five of which have been recorded from Britain. The commonest is subsp. *vulneraria*. Subsp. *corbierei* (Salmon & Travis) Cullen is endemic to the coasts of Anglesey, Cornwall and in the Channel Islands, subsp. *lapponica* (Hyland) Jalas occurs in Scotland and subsp. *polyphylla* (DC) Nyman is probably an introduction. The fifth, subsp. *carpatica* (Pant.) Nyman (*ssp. vulgaris* (Koch) Corbière) is a casual European form scattered throughout England and Wales. A detailed account of their distribution can be found in Perring and Sell (1968) 'Critical Supplement to the Atlas of the British Flora'.

❁ ***Anthyllis* is distinguished by the pinnate leaves without tendrils and in the paired heads of flowers. The calyx is white, woolly and inflated.**

Galega officinalis L.

GOAT'S-RUE

Alien. A native of southern and eastern Europe and western Asia, it was widely grown for fodder and as a garden plant. It was introduced to Britain about 1568 and occasionally naturalised on waste ground. A perennial, it flowers during June and July.

❁ ***Galega* is a taller plant (up to 150 cm) than *Onobrychis* (Plate 34) and has green stipules, while those of *Onobrychis* are scarious.**

❁ *Ulex europaeus* **is a much larger, more robust plant than either** *U. minor* **or** *U. gallii,* **growing to a height of over 2 m. Small specimens can be distinguished from large plants of the other two species by the deeply furrowed main spines and the spreading, not appressed, hairs on the calyx.**

Ulex europaeus L.
GORSE
FURZE
Widespread, and in many areas abundant, throughout the whole of the British Isles. It is common and sometimes locally abundant on heaths, commons, rough land and sea cliffs on dry, well-drained acid mineral soils. Although generally regarded as a calcifuge, it is sometimes found growing on calcareous soils, especially in maritime areas. It is especially abundant in parts of Wales and the south-west. A densely spiny shrub, it flowers from December to June and is pollinated primarily by bees.

Ulex gallii Planch.
WESTERN GORSE
WESTERN FURZE
In contrast to *U. minor, U. gallii* is more or less confined to the west of the British Isles, extending as far north as Kirkcudbrightshire and east as far as a line from the Humber to the Severn. It also occurs in one or two scattered maritime areas of East Anglia. In Ireland it is abundant in the south and south-west. It occurs on heathland grassy hillsides, maritime heaths, cliff tops and stabilised coastal shingle. Usually a more robust shrub than *U. minor,* it flowers at the same time of year from July to October.

❁ *U. minor* **and** *U. gallii* **rarely grow taller than 1 m.** *U. gallii* **has more the appearance of a small** *U. europaeus* **but can be separated from** *U. minor* **by its larger flowers, with the standard exceeding the calyx by at least 2.5 mm, and longer pods (c. 10 mm). The standard of** *U. minor* **exceeds the calyx by less than 2 mm and the pod is 7 mm long.**

Ulex minor Roth
DWARF GORSE
DWARF FURZE
Has a peculiarly restricted geographical distribution in Britain, being virtually confined to south-east England west to Dorset and north to Berkshire. It also occurs in scattered localities in Norfolk and Nottinghamshire. It is a plant of dry to damp, acid sandy heaths, often growing in association with the grass *Molinia caerulea* and *Erica tetralix.* A dwarf shrub, it flowers from July to October during the period when *U. europaeus* is not flowering.

❁ **Broom is distinguished from gorse by the absence of spines and from the spineless species of** *Genista* **(Plate 29) by the angled, not smooth, twigs.**

Cytisus scoparius (L.) Link (*Sarothamnus scoparius* (L.) Wimmer)
BROOM
Distributed throughout the British Isles, except for Orkney and Shetland. It is a frequent plant of grassy heaths, commons, rough grassland, open woodland, roadside verges and waste ground on dry, acid well-drained soils. Two prostrate maritime forms occur in the British Isles. Subsp. *maritima* (Rouy) Ulbr. occurs on the Lizard peninsula and in Jersey, Guernsey, Cork and Dublin. The other (unnamed) occurs on Dungeness in Kent and the coast of Pembrokeshire. It flowers in May and June and is pollinated primarily by bumble-bees.

Ononis repens L.
COMMON RESTHARROW
Distributed throughout most of the British Isles, north to the Clyde in the west and the Moray Firth in the east. In the west it has a predominately maritime distribution and in Ireland is more or less restricted to the south-east. It grows in rough grassland, tracksides and roadside verges on dry, well-drained calcareous or basic-sandy soils. A perennial, it flowers from June to September.

❁ *Ononis repens* **and** *O. spinosa* **are both dwarf shrubs, growing to about 80 cm.** *O. spinosa* **differs from** *O. repens* **in the spiny stems.**

Ononis spinosa L.
SPINY RESTHARROW
More or less restricted in Britain to the area south and east of a line from the Humber to the Severn and absent from the south-west. There are some scattered, mostly maritime localities, in north Wales and on the west coast as far north as the Solway. It is a plant of rough grassland, permanent pasture and scrub margins on dry, well-drained, especially calcareous soils. A perennial, it flowers from June to September.

Ononis reclinata L.**
SMALL RESTHARROW
Very rare. Restricted in Britain to about half a dozen maritime localities. It occurs on the Carboniferous limestone in south Pembrokeshire and Glamorgan, on the Devonian limestone in south Devon and on Alderney and Guernsey. An annual of 4-15 cm, it flowers during June and July.

❁ **The CLOVERS are a relatively large group but identification is not difficult. As well as flower colour, the habit, hairiness, position of flower heads, stipules and number of flowers in the heads are important characters. The clovers are distinguished from the medicks by their straight pods.**

Trifolium ornithopodioides L.
FENUGREEK
BIRD'S-FOOT CLOVER
A local coastal species of southern Britain, extending as far north as Anglesey in the west and the Wash in the east and rare on the east and south coasts of Ireland. It grows in short turf and cliffs on dry, sandy or gravelly soils usually close to the sea. An annual, it flowers from May to September.

❁ *T. ornithopodioides* **is distinguished by the few-flowered heads and is only likely to be confused with** *T. subterraneum,* **from which it can be separated by the glabrous, not hairy, stems and leaves.**

Trifolium micranthum Viv.
SLENDER TREFOIL
Frequent in eastern and south-east England and scattered and local throughout the rest of Britain north to the Solway. It is coastal in eastern and southern Ireland. It grows in short open grassland, garden lawns, grass tracks, road verges and waste ground on well-drained sandy or gravelly soils. A small spring annual, it flowers during midsummer.

❁ **The flowers of** *T. micranthum* **are 2-3 mm long in heads of 2-6 flowers, and the terminal leaflet is sessile.**

Trifolium dubium Sibth.
LESSER TREFOIL
SUCKLING CLOVER
Distributed throughout the British Isles except for parts of the Scottish Highlands, it is common in most kinds of short open grassland: roadside verges, lawns, grass tracks, chalk grassland, grass heaths, commons and occasionally arable land, usually on well-drained soils. A small, spring-germinating annual, it flowers from May to October. This is the Irish 'shamrock' worn as a protection against evil.

❁ *T. dubium* **is similar to** *T. campestre* **with a distinctly stalked terminal leaflet, but the heads are fewer-flowered (10-15) and the standard petal becomes folded over the pod after flowering, not broad and pleated.**

Trifolium campestre Schreb.
HOP TREFOIL
Widely distributed throughout the British Isles, but becoming scarce in northern Scotland and absent from Orkney and Shetland. It is rather local in Ireland. It is a plant of roadside verges, short rough grassland, sand dunes, tracks, waste ground, and grass heaths on dry well-drained soils. An autumn- and spring-germinating annual, it flowers from June to September.

❁ **The terminal leaflet of** *T. campestre* **is stalked, the heads are many-flowered and the broad standard petal becomes distinctly pleated as the flowers fade.**

Trifolium aureum Poll.
LARGE TREFOIL
Alien; native in most of central and eastern Europe, absent from the extreme north, west and the Mediterranean. It occurs as an infrequent casual throughout the British Isles in fields, scrub, wood margins and waste places. A spring- and autumn-germinating annual, it flowers during July and August.

❁ *T. aureum* **has larger flowers (6-7 mm) than the other three species; as in** *T. campestre* **the standard is not folded over the pod, but the stipules are linear rather than broad.**

Trifolium hybridum L.
ALSIKE CLOVER
Alien. It has been cultivated since the 18th century as a forage plant and its true native European distributions is now obscured: probably central, eastern and southern Europe. It is naturalised throughout the British Isles in meadows, pastures, and on roadside verges and is less frequent in the north and west. A perennial, it flowers from June to September.

❁ *T. hybridum* **is superficially similar to** *T. repens* **but lacks the creeping rooting stems. The long-stalked axillary and terminal heads and untoothed stipules distinguish it from other species.**

Trifolium repens L.
WHITE CLOVER
DUTCH CLOVER
Abundant throughout the whole of the British Isles. It is a very polymorphic species, with numerous physiological races which enable it to grow in a wide range of habitats. The most commonly cultivated clover for fodder, it appears in meadows, pastures, limestone grassland, lawns and grass tracks on a wide range of soils, but is most successful on fertile loams. A perennial, it flowers from June to September.

❁ *T. repens, T. occidentale* **and** *T. fragiferum* **are distinguished from other clovers by their creeping stems, rooting at the nodes. Apart from the pinkish flowers,** *T. fragiferum* **differs from** *T. repens* **and** *T. occidentale* **in the characteristically swollen calyx after flowering.** *T. occidentale* **differs from** *T. repens* **in its smaller size, thicker, darker green, more rounded leaflets without white markings or translucent veins, and usually pink-striped stipules.**

Trifolium occidentale D.E. Coombe
WESTERN CLOVER
Confined in Britain to west Cornwall, the Isles of Scilly, south Wales and south-east Ireland, and to Jersey and Guernsey. It is also widespread on the rocky coasts of Brittany and the Cotentin peninsula in north-west France. It was described as a new species in 1961, closely related to but morphologically, genetically and ecologically distinct from *T. repens.* It grows in short cliff-top vegetation overlying shallow serpentine, hornblende schist or granite soils close to the sea and fully exposed to wind and salt spray. On Guernsey and in the Scillies it also grows on stable coastal dunes. A perennial, it flowers earlier than *T. repens,* from April to July. (Illustrated on Plate 102.)

Trifolium fragiferum L.

STRAWBERRY CLOVER

A local species of lowland Britain, widespread south and east of a line from the Humber to the Severn. In the south-west, Wales, the north-west and southern Ireland it is exclusively coastal, extending as far north as the Solway. It is a plant of short rough grassland, grassy commons and grazed pasture, usually on heavy clay soils. In coastal grassland it is tolerant of brackish conditions. A perennial, it flowers from July to September.

❁ ***T. fragiferum* has creeping, rooting stems similar to *T. repens* (Plate 30), but is characterised by the soft swollen fruiting heads, caused by the inflated calyces, that give it its English name.**

❁ ***T. glomeratum, T. suffocatum, T. bocconii, T. striatum* and *T. scabrum* all have sessile heads. *T. glomeratum* and *T. suffocatum* are both hairless; the other three species are hairy.**

The pink petals of *T. glomeratum* are longer than the sepals; the white petals of *T. suffocatum* are shorter than the sepals.

Trifolium glomeratum L.

CLUSTERED CLOVER

A local and declining coastal species extending from Suffolk to east Kent to north and south Devon, the Scillies and the Channel Islands, but now absent from the Cornish mainland. It grows in the short grass turf of sand dunes, cultivated ground, wall tops, pathsides and old quarries on sandy or gravelly soils close to the sea. An annual, it flowers from June to August.

Trifolium suffocatum L.

SUFFOCATED CLOVER

A local and declining coastal species extending southwards from Spurn Head to east Kent to Cornwall, the Scillies and the Channel Islands. It is a plant of dune turf, cliff grassland, tracksides and sandy or gravelly ground close to the sea. It also occurs inland on sandy soils in three localities in the Breckland of Suffolk. An annual, it flowers early from March to May.

Trifolium bocconii Savi*

TWIN-HEADED CLOVER
TWIN-FLOWERED CLOVER

Very rare. It is confined to five coastal localities near the Lizard in Cornwall and to Jersey, where it grows in grassy places close to the sea. An annual, it flowers during May and June.

❁ **The heads of *T. bocconii* are in pairs and the leaves are hairless above. The leaves of *T. scabrum* are hairy on both surfaces and the calyx teeth are characteristically stiff and spreading.**

Trifolium scabrum L.

ROUGH CLOVER
ROUGH TREFOIL

A local species, scattered around the coasts as far north as Angus in the east and north Wales and the Isle of Man in the west. It is also found on the east coast of Ireland. Inland in Britain it is more or less confined to the Breckland of East Anglia. It grows in the open turf of fixed dunes, on the sides of tracks and on banks on calcareous or slightly acid sand and fine gravel. An annual, it flowers from May to July.

Trifolium arvense L.

HARE'S-FOOT CLOVER

Scattered throughout the British Isles north to the Moray Firth; it is commonest in the south-east from Norfolk to Dorset and elsewhere largely coastal. It is a plant of sand dunes, field borders, road verges, grassy heaths, forest rides and waste ground on dry, sandy, well-drained soils. An annual, it flowers from June to September.

Trifolium strictum L.*

UPRIGHT CLOVER

Very rare; now known from only six localities in Cornwall and from one in Jersey. In Cornwall it is locally common in short open grassland around the Lizard. It appears to do best in places that receive some degree of disturbance such as grazing, burning or trampling. An annual, it flowers from May to July.

❁ ***T. strictum* can be distinguished from similar-looking species by the long stalks to the heads, which are both axillary and terminal.**

Trifolium striatum L.

KNOTTED CLOVER
SOFT TREFOIL

A local species, widely scattered throughout most of the British Isles north to Kincardineshire and on the east coast of Ireland. North of the Humber and in the south-west it is mostly coastal. It is a plant of short open dune turf, heath grassland and grassy banks on warm, dry, sandy well-drained soils. An annual, it flowers from May to July.

❁ **The pink flowers of *T. striatum* distinguish it from the white-flowered *T. scabrum* and *T. bocconii.***

***T. incarnatum* L. is divided into two subspecies.**

Trifolium incarnatum subsp. *incarnatum*

CRIMSON CLOVER

Alien. A native of southern Europe and the Mediterranean, formerly extensively cultivated as a forage crop in the south from the middle of the 19th century. It is now naturalised in many places in southern England. An annual, it flowers from May to September.

❁ ***T. incarnatum* subsp. *incarnatum* is only likely to be confused with *T. medium* and *T. pratense*, which have either glabrous or sparsely hairy calyces.**

Trifolium incarnatum subsp. *molinerii* (Balb.) Syme*

LONG-HEADED CLOVER

Very rare and confined to Jersey and to seven localities near the Lizard in Cornwall, where it grows in short cliff-top grassland exposed to salt spray. An annual, it flowers during May and June. (Illustrated on Plate 102.)

❁ ***T. incarnatum* subsp. *molinerii* is distinguished from subsp. *incarnatum* by its cream-coloured flowers, and from *T. ochroleucon* and *T. squamosum* by its densely hairy calyx.**

❁ ***T. incarnatum* has flower-heads at the ends of the stems and the calyx tube is densely covered by long brown hairs.**

Trifolium squamosum L.

SEA CLOVER

A rare and declining local species with an area of distribution around the coasts of Essex and north Kent, but extending as far north as Lincolnshire and along the south coast and west to south Wales. It grows in short open turf close to the sea, at the top end of estuarine salt marshes and along the banks of brackish drainage dykes. An annual, it flowers during June and July.

❁ ***T. squamosum* has heads of small flowers at the ends of the stems, with a pair of leaves just beneath.**

Trifolium subterraneum L.

SUBTERRANEAN CLOVER

A local species of southern and eastern England from Lincolnshire southwards and extending along the coasts of south-west England and south Wales. It grows on cliff tops, walls, roadsides and pastures on dry sandy or gravelly soils, usually close to the sea. The pods become buried in the ground by the stiff tips of the teeth of the fruiting calyx – hence the English name. An annual, it flowers during May and June.

❁ ***T. subterraneum* is distinguished by its hairy stems and leaves, and few-flowered heads.**

Trifolium pratense L.

RED CLOVER

Widely distributed throughout the whole of the British Isles. A common plant of pastures, meadows, rough grassland, roadside verges and cultivated ground on calcareous to weakly acid soils. A very variable species; several varieties are commonly cultivated as forage crops and have become naturalised. A perennial, it flowers from May to September.

❁ ***T. pratense* and *T. medium* both have the flower heads at the ends of the branches. In *T. pratense* the free part of the stipules of the stem leaves narrows abruptly to a brown bristle; in *T. medium* the point is not abrupt and is green.**

Trifolium medium L.

ZIGZAG CLOVER

Widespread throughout the whole of the British Isles, but rare in central and northern Scotland, in parts of East Anglia and in Ireland. It is a local species of meadows, pastures and grassy roadsides, usually on fertile soils. A perennial, it flowers from June to September.

Trifolium ochroleucon Huds.

SULPHUR CLOVER

A local species, restricted to the counties of Norfolk, Suffolk, Cambridgeshire, Lincolnshire, Huntingdonshire, Northamptonshire, Bedfordshire, Hertfordshire and Essex. It grows in pastures and on grass tracks and grassy roadside verges on the heavy clay loams and boulder clays of eastern England. A perennial, it flowers during June and July.

Melilotus altissimus Thuill.
TALL MELILOT
Alien. Native throughout almost the whole of mainland Europe, but rare in the east. It is well established in Britain, being widespread south and east of a line from the Tyne to the Severn, but rare elsewhere and in eastern Ireland. It occurs on roadsides, waste ground, wood margins and coastal habitats. A biennial or short-lived perennial, it flowers from June to August. The crushed leaves of all the melilots smell strongly of new-mown hay.

❁ ***M. altissimus* differs from *M. officinalis* in the black pods, which are hairy when young. The pods of *M. officinalis* are brown and glabrous when young.**

Melilotus officinalis (L.) Lam.
RIBBED MELILOT
COMMON MELILOT
Alien; native over much of central and eastern Europe. It is well established over a large part of Britain south and east of a line from the Tyne to the Severn, rare in the south-west and a casual elsewhere. In many places it may have originated as a relic of cultivation or as seed with imported clover seed. It occurs as a weed of cultivated ground, in waste places, on roadsides and in coastal habitats, often on heavy soils. A biennial, it flowers from July to September.

Melilotus indicus (L.) All.
SMALL MELILOT
Alien; native in the Mediterranean and south-west Europe from Portugal eastwards. It is widely introduced and established in many parts of the world and now almost cosmopolitan. Probably introduced into this country with imported clover seed, it occurs naturalised in scattered localities from the Moray Firth southwards, on cultivated land, roadsides and waste places. An annual, it flowers from June to October and is usually self-pollinated.
❁ ***M. indicus* differs from both *M. altissimus* and *M. officinalis* in the small flowers (2-3 mm) and small pods (2-3 mm) and paler yellow flowers.**

Melilotus albus Medik.
WHITE MELILOT
Alien; native throughout almost the whole of mainland Europe, but only doubtfully so in the north. It is naturalised in Britain north to the Firth of Forth, but commonest in the south-east. It was formerly grown as a forage crop and now appears as a weed of arable soils, waste ground and roadsides, often as a relic of cultivation. A spring-germinating annual or biennial, it flowers from July to September.

❁ **The leaves consisting of five leaflets are characteristic of the BIRD'S-FOOT-TREFOILS.**

Lotus glaber Miller
(*L. tenuis* Waldst. & Kit.)
NARROW-LEAVED BIRD'S-FOOT-TREFOIL
SLENDER BIRD'S-FOOT-TREFOIL
A local species of lowland Britain, more or less confined to an area south and east of a line from the Humber to the Severn, with a few outlying localities in coastal areas of Cumbria. It is a plant of short, dry, permanent grassland, often close to the sea, where it grows in rough brackish grassland at the landward edge of salt marshes and on stabilised shingle. Inland it occurs chiefly on calcareous soils, such as chalk and boulder clay. A perennial, it flowers from June to August.
❁ ***L. glaber* is distinguished by the characteristic narrow leaflets.**

Lotus pedunculatus Cav.
(*L. uliginosus* Schk.)
GREATER BIRD'S-FOOT-TREFOIL
Distributed throughout the British Isles except for the north and north-west of Scotland and parts of central Ireland. It is a plant of damp pastures and meadows, wet ditches, woodland paths and clearings and pond and river banks on neutral to weakly acid soils. A perennial, it flowers from June to August.

❁ ***L. pedunculatus* is distinguished from *L. corniculatus* by its larger size, hairiness and hollow stems.**

Lotus corniculatus L.
COMMON BIRD'S-FOOT-TREFOIL
Widespread throughout the whole of the British Isles. It is a common species of the short turf of chalk and limestone grassland, grassy cliffs, heath grassland, roadside verges, meadows and pasture, usually in dry well-drained places, but occurring on both acid and calcium-rich soils. A perennial, it flowers from June to September and is usually pollinated by bumble-bees. It is a very variable species that was formerly widely used as a forage crop.

Lotus subbiflorus Lag.
(*L. hispidus*)
HAIRY BIRD'S-FOOT-TREFOIL
A species of south-west Europe, confined in Britain to coastal areas of Hampshire, Dorset, Devon, Cornwall, Pembrokeshire and the Isles of Scilly and the Channel Islands. It grows on walls, cliff tops, stabilised sand dunes, grassy places and cultivated fields on dry sandy soils close to the sea. An annual, it flowers during July and August.

❁ ***L. subbiflorus* and *L. angustissimus* are both small, very hairy species. The pod of *L. angustissimus* is more than three times as long as the calyx and the inflorescence stalks are usually shorter than the leaves. The pod of *L. subbiflorus* is three times as long as the calyx or less, and the inflorescence stalks are always longer than the leaves.**

Lotus angustissimus L.
SLENDER BIRD'S-FOOT-TREFOIL
Rare. It is confined in Britain to about 16 coastal localities in east Kent, Hampshire, north and south Devon, Cornwall and the Channel Islands, where it grows in dry grassy places close to the sea. An annual, it flowers during July and August.

Astragalus danicus Retz.
PURPLE MILK-VETCH
A very distinct distribution in Britain, being almost confined to the eastern side of the country from the Thames northwards. It occurs in two main habitats. It is locally abundant in the short, species-rich calcareous turf of the East Anglian chalk and the Yorkshire Wolds, the oolite of Northamptonshire, Lincolnshire and Leicestershire and the Magnesian limestone in Yorkshire. It also occurs on the Cotswolds and the Wiltshire chalk. From the Tees northwards to the Dornoch Firth, it is a plant of coastal sand dunes. In western Ireland there is an isolated locality in the Arran Islands. A perennial, it flowers from May to July.

❁ ***A. danicus* is distinguished from *A. alpinus* by the erect flowers and from *Oxytropis halleri* by the blunt tip to the lower petal.**

Astragalus alpinus L.*
ALPINE MILK-VETCH
Very rare. Confined to four known colonies in Perthshire, Angus and Aberdeenshire, where it grows on grassy mountain slopes overlying shallow basic soils or on bare cliffs of mica-schist or limestone, at altitudes between 880 m and 1,140 m. A perennial, it flowers during July.
❁ ***A. alpinus* is distinguished from *A. danicus* by the horizontal or deflexed flowers and from *Oxytropis halleri* by the blunt tip to the lower petal.**

Astragalus glycyphyllos L.
WILD LIQUORICE
A local species, with a scattered distribution north to Angus in the east. Absent from Ireland and most of Wales and the south-west. It grows on roadsides and in rough grassy places on the edge of scrub and woodland on dry calcareous soils. A perennial, it flowers during July and August.
❁ ***A. glycyphyllos* is unlikely to be confused with any other species. It is a large plant growing to almost 1 m and, unlike *Oxytropis campestris*, is completely hairless.**

Oxytropis campestris (L.) DC.*
YELLOW OXYTROPIS
Very rare. An arctic-alpine species, confined in Britain to about half a dozen localities in Perthshire, Angus and Kintyre. It grows on rock ledge and scree on basic mica-schist or limestone rocks up to an altitude of about 880 m. All the existing populations are flourishing and one is expanding. A perennial, it flowers during June and July.

Oxytropis halleri Bunge*
PURPLE OXYTROPIS
Very rare. One of the few British alpine, as opposed to arctic-alpine, species. It occurs in about 21 populations in Perthshire, Argyllshire, Ross-shire and Sutherland. In Scotland it is coastal in all but the Perthshire site, growing on dry grassy cliffs, rocks and banks close to the sea. The populations vary in size from a few plants to several thousand, and in some sites it is heavily grazed. A perennial, it flowers during June and July.
❁ ***O. halleri* is distinguished from *Astragalus* by having a pointed tip to the lower petal (keel).**

Tetragonolobus maritimus (L.) Roth*
DRAGON'S-TEETH
Alien. A native of central and southern Europe, north to southern Sweden and east to the Ukraine. In Britain it occurs as a rare naturalised alien in less than 10 localities in Kent, Essex, Buckinghamshire and Gloucestershire and occasionally turns up as a casual elsewhere. It occurs on waste ground and in rough permanent places on dry calcareous soils.
❁ **The large (25-30 mm) solitary yellow flowers and trifoliate leaves distinguish *Tetragonolobus*.**

❁ ***Vicia* and *Lathyrus* (Plate 34) both have pinnate leaves which lack a terminal leaflet, this usually being replaced by tendrils or a short point. *Lathyrus* differs from *Vicia* in the winged or angled stems and in usually having fewer leaflets.**

***V. hirsuta*, *V. tetrasperma* and *V. parviflora* are superficially rather similar. *V. hirsuta* is distinguished from the other three species by the hairy pods.**

Vicia hirsuta (L.) S.F. Gray
HAIRY TARE
Distributed throughout the British Isles, but rare in western and northern Scotland, north-west England and in much of Wales and Ireland. It occurs in rough grassland, pastures, open scrub and roadside verges, usually on dry, mildly acid to calcareous soils. It was once a troublesome arable weed. An annual, it flowers from May to August.

❁ ***V. tetrasperma* is distinguished from *V. parviflora* by having four-seeded pods, while the pods of *V. parviflora* have 5-8 seeds.**

Vicia tetrasperma (L.) Schreb
SMOOTH TARE
A plant of southern Britain, widely distributed south and east of a line from the Humber to south Wales and occurring as a rare casual in Ireland and Scotland. It is a frequent plant of rough grassland, old pastures, open scrub and waysides on mildly acid to calcareous or basic, often moist soils. It also occurs as an arable weed. An annual, it flowers from May to August.

Vicia parviflora Cav.
(*V. tenuissima* auct.)
SLENDER TARE
A very local and apparently declining species of southern England with the centre of its distribution in the area of Essex, Cambridgeshire, Bedfordshire and Huntingdonshire. It is a plant of rough grassland, hedge banks, roadsides and tracksides on dry, mildly acid to neutral soils. An annual, it flowers from June to August.

Vicia cracca L.
TUFTED VETCH
Generally distributed throughout the whole of the British Isles, but scarce in the Scottish Highlands. It is a common plant of rough grassland and old pastures, roadsides, hedge banks, scrub and woodland edges on mildly acid to neutral or calcareous soils on a range of soil textures from clay to stabilised coastal shingle. A perennial, it flowers from June to August.
❁ ***V. cracca* differs from *V. sylvatica* in the purple-blue flowers and from *V. orobus* in the possession of tendrils.**

Vicia orobus DC.
WOOD BITTER-VETCH
A local and decreasing species of western Britain from Cornwall and Somerset to Sutherland, but most frequent in central and north-west Wales. In northern Scotland it is almost wholly coastal. It is a plant of rocky woodlands, cliffs and shaded rocks on mildly acid to calcareous soils. A perennial, it flowers from June to September.
❁ ***V. orobus* differs from *V. cracca* and *V. sylvatica* in the absence of tendrils.**

Vicia sylvatica L.
WOOD VETCH
Very local, but scattered throughout the British Isles. In Ireland it is rare and found mostly around the north coast. It is absent from East Anglia and most of the south-east, except for east Kent. It is an attractive plant of rocky woodland, scrub and wood margins and shaded maritime or inland cliffs. A small, few-flowered, densely leafy form is found on shingle beaches. A perennial, it flowers from June to August.

Vicia lutea L.
YELLOW-VETCH
A rare and local maritime species scattered around the coast as far north as Angus in the west and Wigtownshire in the east. It grows in open, well-drained habitats close to the sea, such as stabilised shingle grassland, rough grassland at the back edge of salt marshes, at the foot of mature sand dunes and on cliff tops and cliff ledges. It also occurs as an occasional casual inland in southern England. An annual, it flowers from June to August.
❁ ***V. lutea* is the only yellow-flowered vetch. The leaves of *Lathyrus pratensis* (Plate 34) have only one pair of leaflets.**

Vicia sativa L.
V. sativa subsp. *sativa*
COMMON VETCH
Alien; native throughout most of Europe except for the north and north-west. It has been widely cultivated as a fodder crop in the past and is frequently naturalised in pastures, meadows, road verges, grassy hedge banks and on arable soils as a relic of cultivation. An annual, it flowers from May to September. The smaller plant, most commonly found in grassy places, is subsp. *segetalis* (Thuill.) Gaudin.

Vicia sativa subsp. *nigra* (L.) Ehrh.
(*V. sativa* subsp. *angustifolia* (L.) Gaud.)
NARROW-LEAVED VETCH
Widely distributed throughout the British Isles, commonest in the south and becoming scarce in central and northern Scotland and in Ireland. It is absent from Orkney, Shetland and the Hebrides. A frequent plant of road verges, hedge banks, waste ground, grass tracks and pastures on dry, well-drained, mildly acid to calcareous soils. An annual, it flowers from May to September. (Illustrated on Plate 102.)
❁ **The pods of *V. sativa* subsp. *sativa* are constricted between the seeds, while those of subsp. *nigra* and subsp. *segetalis* are not constricted. Subsp. *sativa* has broader leaflets than subsp. *nigra*.; subsp. *nigra* has narrow upper leaves, while those of subsp. *segetalis* are as wide as the lower.**

***V. sativa* differs from *V. sepium* in the narrower leaflets and solitary or paired flowers.**

Vicia sepium L.
BUSH VETCH
Widely distributed throughout the British Isles but rather scarce in the East Anglian fenland and in parts of the Scottish Highlands. It is a common plant of hedge banks, woodland clearings and tracksides, rough grassland, scrub and grassy woodland edges on mildly acid to neutral or calcareous soils. A perennial, it flowers throughout the summer from May to August and is pollinated by bumble-bees.

Vicia lathyroides L.
SPRING VETCH
A local species of the eastern side of the British Isles from Hampshire north to the east coast of Scotland and of the west coast from south Wales to Kintyre. It also occurs on the east coast of Ireland. It is a plant of open ground on road verges, commons, heath grassland, waste places and arable on dry sandy and gravelly well-drained soils. An annual, it flowers during May and June.
❁ ***V. lathyroides* differs from other small-flowered species in having only 2-5 pairs of leaflets and in the almost sessile flowers.**

Vicia bithynica (L.) L.
BITHYNIAN VETCH
A rare, local and declining species with scattered localities in Cornwall, Devon, Dorset, Somerset, Kent, Essex, Glamorgan, Breconshire, Gloucerstershire, Nottinghamshire, north-east Yorkshire, Wigtownshire and Guernsey. It grows on waste ground, field borders, hedge banks and bushy cliffs, usually close to the sea. A perennial, it flowers during May and June.
❁ ***V. bithynica* differs from both *V. sepium* and *V. sativa* in the large (1 cm or more) toothed stipules and white wings to the flowers.**

❁ ***Ornithopus* differs from *Vicia* in the terminal leaflet and from *Hippocrepis* in the fewer-flowered inflorescences and rounded segments to the fruits.**

Ornithopus perpusillus L.
BIRD'S-FOOT
Widely distributed in suitable habitats in England and Wales but very rare in Scotland and Ireland. It is a tiny prostrate annual growing in open patches in the short turf of grass heaths, commons, dunes, lawns, trackways, road verges, waste ground and arable on dry, acid sandy or gravelly soils. It flowers from May to August and is self-pollinated.

❁ ***O. perpusillus* is hairy with whitish flowers; *O. pinnatus* is glabrous with yellow flowers.**

Ornithopus pinnatus (Mill.) Druce(*)
ORANGE BIRD'S-FOOT
Very rare and now found only in the Scilly Isles, where it is frequent on seven of the islands, and on Guernsey, Alderney and Sark in the Channel Islands, where it was first discovered on Guernsey by Babington in August 1837. It grows in short open heath turf, on sandy tracks and among grazed heather on shallow granite or sandy soils. An annual, it flowers from April to October.

❁ *Securigera* **has flowers in umbels, which distinguishes it from other pink-flowered species with pinnate leaves with a terminal leaflet.**

Securigera varia (L.) Lassen
(*Coronilla varia* L.)
CROWN VETCH
Alien. A native of central and southern Europe from Spain to central Russia; it was formerly cultivated as a fodder crop and sometimes grown in gardens as a rockery plant. It is naturalised in scattered localities throughout Great Britain north to Aberdeenshire, but is more frequent in the south. A perennial, it flowers during June.

Onobrychis viciifolia Scop.
SAINFOIN
Doubtfully native; widely distributed in suitable habitats in England north to Yorkshire, but absent from Scotland, Ireland and most of Wales. It is a strict calcicole growing in permanent chalk and limestone grassland and on roadside verges and cuttings on the chalk of the North and South Downs, Hampshire, Wiltshire, Dorset, the Chilterns and East Anglia north to the Yorkshire Dales and on the oolite from the Cotswolds to Lincolnshire. Its native distribution is obscure in Europe due to the fact that formerly it was widely grown as a fodder crop and in many places it occurs as a relic of cultivation. A perennial, it flowers from June to August. The English name is borrowed from the French and means literally 'wholesome hay'.

❁ *Onobrychis* **differs from** *Galega* **(Plate 29) in the thin, papery, pale brown (rather than green) stipules.**

❁ *Hippocrepis* **differs from** *Lotus* **(Plate 32) in the pinnate leaves, from** *Anthyllis* **(Plate 29) in the normal, not woolly and inflated, calyx and from** *Ornithopus* **(Plate 33) in the larger flowers and horseshoe-shaped segments to the pods.**

Hippocrepis comosa L.
HORSESHOE VETCH
Restricted in Britain to calcareous soils extending as far north as Cronkley Fell in Yorkshire. A strict calcicole, it grows in short dry chalk and limestone turf and on sunny slopes from the North and South Downs, Dorset, Hampshire, Wiltshire, the Chilterns and East Anglia to the Yorkshire Wolds. It also occurs in the Cotswolds and on the oolite of Northamptonshire and Lincolnshire. There are also scattered localities in grassland and cliff ledges on the Devonian limestone of south Devon, the Carboniferous limestone of north Somerset, north and south Wales, Derbyshire, the Yorkshire Pennines and Cumbria. A perennial, it flowers from May to July and is pollinated chiefly by bumble-bees. The leaves are the food plant of the larvae of the Adonis blue, *Lysandra bellargus*, and chalkhill blue, *L. coridon*, butterflies.

❁ *Lathyrus* **differs from** *Vicia* **(Plate 33) in the angled or winged stem and in the leaves usually having fewer leaflets.**

Lathyrus aphaca L.
YELLOW VETCHLING
A plant of central and southern Europe; only doubtfully native in Britain, where it is a local and declining species of southern England from Suffolk and Cambridgeshire west to Somerset and south Devon. It grows in short dry grassland and at the edge of scrub, usually on calcareous soils, but also on well-drained sands and gravels. An annual, it is in flower from June to August.
❁ *L. aphaca* **is distinguished by the large stipules and absence of leaflets.**

Lathyrus nissolia L.
GRASS VETCHLING
Widely distributed in south-east England from Suffolk to Bedfordshire and Huntingdonshire and south to Hampshire. Elsewhere, it is scattered north to Lincolnshire and west to south Wales and south Devon. It is a plant of rough grassland, grassy roadside verges, hedge banks and woodland edges on mildly acid to neutral, often heavy soils. An autumn germinating annual, it flowers from May to July.
❁ *L. nissolia* **is distinguished from all other legumes by the grass-like leaves.**

❁ **The leaves of** *L. hirsutus, L. sylvestris* **and** *L. tuberosus* **all have one pair of leaflets. The stem of** *L. tuberosus* **is square in section; the stems of the other two are distinctly winged.**

Lathyrus sylvestris L.
NARROW-LEAVED EVERLASTING-PEA
A local plant, scattered throughout the southern half of Britain as far north as north Wales but with some isolated coastal localities further north. It is absent from Ireland. In the west it has a distinctly maritime distribution. It is a plant of wood margins, thickets, banks and hedgerows. A perennial, it flowers from June to August.

❁ *L. sylvestris* **differs from** *L. hirsutus* **in the larger flowers (15-17 mm) and glabrous pod. The flowers of** *L. hirsutus* **are 10-12 mm long and the pods are densely hairy.**

Lathyrus hirsutus L.
HAIRY VETCHLING
Alien; a native of most of central and southern Europe. It occurs as a casual, and more rarely naturalised, in a number of localities north to the Firth of Forth. A plant of fields, grassy woodlands and waste places, it is a perennial and flowers from May to July.

Lathyrus tuberosus L.
TUBEROUS PEA EARTH-NUT PEA
Alien; a native of most of Europe except for the north and the extreme south. Widely cultivated in gardens up to the end of the 19th century, it is now naturalised in a number of scattered localities north to the Firth of Forth but is absent from Ireland. It occurs in hedgerows, rough scrub and as a weed of cereal crops on neutral or calcium-rich soils. Well known in the parish of Fyfield in Essex since about 1800, it is sometimes known by the alternative name of Fyfield pea. A perennial, it flowers during July.

Lathyrus pratensis L.
MEADOW VETCHLING
Widespread and common throughout the whole of the British Isles except for parts of northern Scotland. It is a plant of rough grassland, pastures, hedge banks, roadside verges and rough ground close to the sea on weakly acid, neutral or calcareous soils. A perennial, it is in flower from May to August.

Lathyrus palustris L.
MARSH PEA
Rare and declining. It is now more or less confined in Britain to the fens of the Norfolk Broads, with a few additional localities in suitable habitats in Suffolk, Cambridgeshire, Nottinghamshire, Yorkshire and Somerset, together with about five sites in Ireland. It typically grows among tall herbaceous vegetation on wet, calcium-rich fen peats. A perennial, it flowers from May to July.

❁ *L. palustris* **and** *L. japonicus* **both have leaves with several pairs of leaflets. The stem of** *L. japonicus* **is angled and that of** *L. palustris* **winged, but the habit and habitats of the two species are so different that they can never be confused.**

Lathyrus japonicus Willd.
SEA PEA
A local species, distributed around the east and south coasts of the British Isles in Suffolk, east Kent, east Sussex, Hampshire, Dorset and south Devon. It is a primary coloniser of shingle beaches, often forming extensive pure patches. It also occurs less commonly on fixed dunes or dune-covered shingle ridges. A perennial, the main flowering period is from May to July and it is pollinated by bumble-bees. The seeds are dispersed by the sea and can remain floating and viable for up to five years.

Lathyrus linifolius (Reichard) Baessler
(*L. montanus* Bernh.)
BITTER VETCH
Distributed throughout the British Isles, but absent from most of the Midlands and almost the whole of East Anglia. Rare in central Ireland. *L. linifolius* is a calcifuge, occurring in hill grassland, rocky woodlands, scrub, wood borders, hedge banks and roadside verges on acid, usually well-drained soils. A perennial, it flowers from April to July. The plant possesses tuberous rhizomes which were once collected for food, and in parts of Scotland were even used for flavouring whisky.

❁ *L. linifolius* **and** *L. niger* **differ from other species of** *Lathyrus* **in the absence of tendrils, the leaves ending in a short point. The stem of** *L. linifolius* **is winged and the inflorescence stalk is glabrous; the stem of** *L. niger* **is angled and the inflorescence stalk hairy.**

Lathyrus niger (L.) Bernh.
BLACK PEA
Native over most of Europe except for the north-east and the extreme south. It may once have been native in a few rocky woodlands in mountain valleys in Scotland but now occurs only as a naturalised garden escape. A perennial, it flowers during June and July.

ROSACEAE

Spiraea salicifolia L.
BRIDEWORT WILLOW SPIRAEA
Alien. A native of central and eastern Europe from Austria eastwards. Frequently planted in hedgerows and as an ornamental garden shrub, it is naturalised in scattered localities throughout the British Isles. It flowers from June to September.

Filipendula vulgaris Moench
DROPWORT
A plant of dry calcareous grassland, extending as far north as the Yorkshire Wolds. It is widespread and frequent on the chalk and oolitic limestones of England and also occurs on the Devonian limestone of south Devon and on the Carboniferous limestone of west and north Wales, Derbyshire, Yorkshire, Cumbria and Co. Clare in Ireland. On the east coast it extends in scattered localities as far north as Angus. It also grows on other well-drained base-rich soils such as the serpentine of the Lizard peninsula in Cornwall. In Yorkshire it reaches an altitude of 370 m. A perennial, it flowers from May to August.

❁ *F. vulgaris* **differs from** *F. ulmaria* **in its smaller size (up to 60 cm tall) and differently shaped leaves.**

Filipendula ulmaria (L.) Maxim.
MEADOWSWEET
Widespread throughout the whole of the British Isles. It is a common plant of marshes, fens, wet woods, streams, river and lake margins, damp ditches and wet alpine meadows and rock ledges on mildly acid to neutral or calcareous soils to an altitude of 915 m. It is absent from acid peats. A perennial growing to over 1 m, it flowers from June to September. The flowers have a heavy, sweet scent that is attractive to flies.

Rubus chamaemorus L.
CLOUDBERRY
A widespread plant of upland Britain growing on hummocks and well-drained areas of acidic blanket peat, usually where heather *Calluna vulgaris* and cotton-grass *Eriophorum vaginatum* predominate. It is common in suitable areas throughout the Pennines, the Cheviots and the Scottish Highlands where it reaches an altitude of 1,140 m. It is rare in the Lake District and confined to the Berwyn Mountains in Wales. In Ireland it occurs in a single locality in Co. Tyrone. Male and female flowers occur on separate plants and flowering is from June to August; pollination is effected mainly by small flies. The fruit is greatly prized in Scandinavia.
❁ *R. chamaemorus* **differs from other** *Rubus* **species in its simple leaves and single terminal flowers.**

Rubus saxatilis L.
STONE BRAMBLE
A widespread but declining species in hilly parts of the British Isles. It grows in open, damp, rocky woodland and among shaded rocks and scree, usually on calcareous or base-rich soils. A local plant in suitable places from the Derbyshire limestone northwards, scattered in Wales and south to north Devon and more or less restricted in Ireland to the limestones of Co. Clare, Co. Galway and Co. Limerick. It flowers from June to August and is pollinated by a variety of bees and flies or is self-pollinated.
❁ *R. saxatilis* **grows to 40 cm and differs from other** *Rubus* **species, with compound leaves in its herbaceous, non-woody habit.**

Rubus idaeus L.
RASPBERRY
Generally distributed throughout the whole of the British Isles but absent from Orkney and Shetland. Raspberry is a frequent plant of open woodlands, wood margins, heaths and commons on moist, usually sandy soils, and is more frequent in hilly areas and in the north. The woody stems are biennial and flowering is from June to August. Pollination is effected by various insects or the plant is self-pollinated. The original English name was 'hindberry' (berries eaten by hinds); the origin of 'raspberry' is obscure but probably French.
❁ *R. idaeus* **is distinguished by its pinnate leaves, which are white beneath, and red berries.**

Rubus caesius L.
DEWBERRY
A widespread plant throughout the British Isles, north to the Firth of Forth but more frequent on the east and rather local in Wales, the south-west and Ireland. Dewberry grows in rough, dry grassland and scrub on neutral or calcareous soils and is often common in fen carr and calcareous coastal dune slacks. It flowers from June to September.

❁ *R. caesius* **differs from** *R. fruticosus* **in its unridged stems covered by a whitish bloom, and the fruits also covered by a 'bloom'.**

Rubus fruticosus L. (*sensu lato*)
BRAMBLE
BLACKBERRY
An aggregate name for a large number of separate species that are taxonomically very difficult. There are probably about 2,000 different species of bramble in Europe and more than 300 in the British Isles. Most reproduce apomictically; that is, they produce fertile seed without prior sexual fusion, although pollination is necessary for fruit development. No attempt is made here to treat the different segregate species.
Brambles are common throughout the whole of the British Isles, except for parts of the Scottish Highlands and northern Scotland, occurring in woodland, scrub, commons, heaths, hedgerows and on cliffs. Flowering extends from May to September and the flowers are pollinated by a wide variety of insects.

Sibbaldia procumbens L.
SIBBALDIA
A widespread but local species occurring throughout most of the Scottish Highlands. It is typically a plant of areas of prolonged snow cover growing in rock crevices, on ledges, in mountain grassland and among summit detritus to an altitude of 1,350 m on a wide range of different soils. A perennial, it flowers from June to August and is pollinated by a variety of bees, flies and ants.
❁ *Sibbaldia* **differs from** *Potentilla* **(Plate 36) in the three teeth at the tips of the leaflets and small petals.**

Geum urbanum L.
WOOD AVENS
Generally distributed throughout the whole of the British Isles except for parts of central and northern Scotland. It is common in woodlands, scrub, hedgerows, roadsides and shaded habitats or calcareous soils. A perennial, it flowers from June to August and is usually self-pollinated.

Geum rivale L.
WATER AVENS
Distributed throughout the British Isles, but much more common in the north and local in most of southern Britain and in Ireland. It is often common in wet meadows, marshes, fens, damp woodlands and hedge banks, stream sides, mountain pastures and wet rock ledges to an altitude of 975 m. It prefers shaded conditions on fertile, base-rich or calcareous soils. A perennial, it is in flower from May to September and is pollinated by bumble-bees or self-pollinated.

Dryas octopetala L.
MOUNTAIN AVENS
An arctic-alpine species with a very local distribution in upland Britain. A strict calcicole, it grows on rock ledges, cliffs and steep slopes to 1,050 m in the Cairngorms. It is locally common on the mica-schist outcrops of the central Highlands of Scotland and on the Durness limestone in Sutherland. It also grows at sea level on coastal dunes on the north coast of Scotland and on the Carboniferous limestone of the Burren in Co. Clare in Ireland. In England and Wales it is very rare, being restricted to a few sites in the Pennines, including Teesdale, and in the Lake District and to two localities in Snowdonia. A dwarf shrub, it flowers from April to July, depending on the habitat, and is pollinated primarily by flies.

Fragaria vesca L.
WILD STRAWBERRY
A widespread plant throughout the British Isles, but becoming less frequent in northern Scotland. Wild strawberry is a common plant of woodlands, scrub, hedge banks and rough grassland, most often on well-drained, calcareous or base-rich soils and reaching an altitude of about 730 m. A perennial, it flowers from April to July and is pollinated by a wide variety of insects, including beetles. The cultivated 'Alpine Strawberry' is a variety of *F. vesca.*
❁ *F. vesca* **can always be distinguished from** *Potentilla sterilis* **(Plate 36) by the terminal tooth of the leaflets being as long as or longer than its two neighbours. In** *P. sterilis* **the tooth is shorter than its neighbours and the leaves are a bluish-green.**

Aremonia agrimonioides (L.) DC.
BASTARD AGRIMONY
Alien. A native of mountain woodland in southern central and eastern Europe from Germany and Italy eastwards, and naturalised in a few woods in central Scotland. A perennial, it flowers during June and July.

Acaena novae-zelandiae Kirk
PIRRI-PIRRI-BUR
Alien; a native of New Zealand and eastern Australia. Possibly introduced in about 1796 as a garden plant or, more likely, accidentally with wool. Completely naturalised in several places in the British Isles, especially on coastal sand dunes where it can spread rapidly and is tolerant of trampling and sand-compaction. On the Holy Island dunes in Northumberland the hooked burrs on the fruiting heads so clog the feathers of ground-nesting birds that they die of starvation. A serious weed in the southern hemisphere, it may well become a problem in some areas. It is a perennial and flowers during June and July.
❁ *Acaena* **is distinguished from** *Sanguisorba* **(Plate 39) by its prostrate habit and spiny fruits.**

ROSACEAE *(see illustrations page 82)*

Potentilla fruticosa L.*

SHRUBBY CINQUEFOIL

A rare plant of open habitats on river and lake margins and rock ledges, on calcium-rich soils confined to three areas in Britain. In Upper Teesdale it grows along both banks of the Tees in places where it is liable to periodic flooding, at altitudes between 260 m and 420 m. It occurs in two localities in the Lake District on rock ledges in Wasdale and Ennerdale. In western Ireland it grows in a zone around the banks of the turloughs (temporary winter lakes) on the Carboniferous limestone of the Burren in Co. Clare, Ireland. It exhibits a wide degree of variation throughout the extent of its geographical range; this has given rise to numerous cultivated varieties that are commonly grown as ornamental shrubs. The plant is dioecious in Britain and flowers during June and July.
❁ ***P. fruticosa*** **is a small deciduous shrub, growing to about 1 m.**

Potentilla palustris (L.) Scop.

MARSH CINQUEFOIL

Widespread in northern and upland Britain and in the area of the Norfolk Broads and the heaths of Dorset and the New Forest; local and scattered elsewhere. It is a common plant of fens, marshes, flushed bogs, wet heath and the margins of upland pools to an altitude of 920 m. A perennial, it flowers from May to July and is pollinated by a wide variety of insects.

Potentilla rupestris L.**

ROCK CINQUEFOIL

Very rare. Known in only three localities, two in Wales and one in Scotland. All three are on basic rock. The Radnorshire population is secure, but the Montgomeryshire site is threatened by quarrying. The cliff population in east Sutherland is flourishing and spread over quite a large area. In the past *P. rupestris* has suffered at the hands of collectors and gardeners. A perennial, it flowers during May and June and is usually self-pollinated.

Potentilla anserina L.

SILVERWEED

Widespread and common throughout the whole of the British Isles except for parts of northern Scotland. It is an abundant plant of roadsides, farm tracks, field gateways, waste ground, disturbed pastures and old abandoned arable on fertile soils. It is tolerant of trampling and soil compaction and also occurs on compacted sand dune soils. A perennial, it flowers from June to August and is pollinated by various insects or self-pollinated.

Potentilla sterilis (L.) Garcke

BARREN STRAWBERRY

Common throughout most of the British Isles except for parts of northern Scotland, and absent from the Outer Hebrides, Orkney and Shetland. It grows on hedge banks, walls, road verges and in scrub and woodland rides and clearings, usually on dry well-drained sandy or calcareous soils. A perennial, it flowers from February to May and is pollinated by various insects or self-pollinated.
❁ **The leaves of *P. sterilis* differs from those of *Fragaria* (Plate 35) in that they are blue-green and the terminal teeth of the leaflets are shorter than their neighbours.**

Potentilla argentea L.

HOARY CINQUEFOIL

A local species, occurring mostly in eastern and south-east England but extending as far north as the Firth of Tay. Absent from most of Wales and the south-west and from the whole of Ireland. It is a plant of short open turf on roadside verges, trackways, abandoned arable and coastal habitats on dry, well-drained sandy soils. A perennial, it flowers from June to September.
❁ ***P. argentea*** **is distinguished by the undersides of the leaves being covered by a dense felt of silky white hairs.**

Potentilla norvegica L.

TERNATE-LEAVED CINQUEFOIL

Alien. A native of northern, central and eastern Europe naturalised on waste ground and roadsides in a number of widely scattered localities, north to Moray. It is absent from Ireland. An annual or short-lived perennial, it flowers from June to September.

Potentilla neumanniana Reichb.
(*P. tabernaemontani* Aschers.)

SPRING CINQUEFOIL

A very local species of warm, dry calcareous grassland and rock outcrops with a southerly aspect, scattered from the chalk of Wiltshire and the Carboniferous limestone of the Mendips north to the Dalradian limestone of Banffshire. It is absent from Ireland. A perennial, it flowers from April to June.

❁ ***P. neumanniana*** **is much more hairy than *P. erecta*, with the flowers in distinct inflorescences. It differs from *P. crantzii* in forming spreading mats, with the inflorescences not much longer than the leaves, and in the narrow stipules. *P. crantzii* never forms mats; the inflorescences stand up well above the leaves; and the stipules are ovate.**

Potentilla crantzii (Crantz) G. Beck

ALPINE CINQUEFOIL

An arctic-alpine species of very local occurrence in Britain, growing on rock ledges and crevices and occasionally in mountain grassland, on calcareous or base-rich rock from 120 m to 1,020 m. It occurs on the Carboniferous limestone of Cumbria and Craven and Teesdale in the Pennines, and is widespread on the mica-schist mountains of the central Highlands of Scotland. Further north it occurs on the Durness limestone of Ross and Sutherland. There is a single locality in north Wales and it is absent from Ireland. A perennial, it flowers during June and July.

❁ ***P. erecta, P. anglica*** **and *P. reptans* all have solitary flowers, while *P. crantzii* and *P. neumanniana* both have inflorescences consisting of several flowers.**

Potentilla erecta (L.) Raüsche

TORMENTIL

A common plant throughout the whole of the British Isles. It is found on grass heaths, commons and woodland rides and clearings in bogs and fens and on grassy moorland and mountain grassland to an altitude of 1,070 m, usually on acid soils and avoiding heavy fertile clays and calcareous grassland. A perennial, it is in flower from June to September.

❁ ***P. erecta*** **has ternate leaves (the stem leaves sessile), non-rooting stems and flowers about 10 mm in diameter with four petals. *P. reptans* has long-stalked stem leaves with five leaflets and flowers 18-25 mm in diameter with five petals. The stems are prostrate and rooting.**

Potentilla reptans L.

CREEPING CINQUEFOIL

Common throughout the British Isles north to the Clyde and the Firth of Forth, but rare further north and absent from Orkney and Shetland. It is a frequent plant of road verges, trackways, hedge banks and waste ground, usually on fertile, mildly acid to neutral or calcareous soils, reaching an altitude of 430 m. It is a perennial and flowers from June to September.

Potentilla anglica Laich.

TRAILING TORMENTIL

Widespread but local throughout the British Isles, but rare in Scotland and absent from the extreme north and most frequent in the west and south-east. It grows in the grassland of woodland margins, clearings, hedge banks, verges, field borders and grass heaths on well-drained, mildly acid soils. It is less tolerant of montane conditions than *P. erecta*, reaching about 410 m. A perennial, it flowers from June to September.

❁ **Care is needed in identifying *P. anglica*, which is more or less intermediate between *P. erecta* and *P. reptans*. It is easily confused with hybrids between those two species, which are, however, usually sterile. The leaves have three or five leaflets, the stem leaves have stalks 1-2 cm long and the flowers are 15-18 mm in diameter with four or five petals.**

Agrimonia eupatoria L.

AGRIMONY

Occurs throughout the British Isles, is common in the south but becomes scarce northwards and is absent from northern Scotland, Orkney and Shetland. It is found in rough grassland, field borders, scrub, hedge banks, roadsides and woodland clearings on mildly acid to neutral and calcareous, usually well-drained soils to an altitude of about 490 m. A perennial, it flowers from June to August and is pollinated by a variety of small insects or self-pollinated.

❁ ***A. procera*** **differs from *A. eupatoria* in the more robust habit, the leaves, which are abundantly glandular beneath, and the fruit, grooved only in the lower three-quarters and with the basal spines deflexed. *A. eupatoria* has no glands on the leaves and the fruits are grooved with spreading basal spines.**

Agrimonia procera Wallr.
(*A. odorata* auct.)

FRAGRANT AGRIMONY

A local plant occurring throughout Britain as far north as the Moray Firth. Commonest in the south and south-east, it gets progressively rarer northwards and is absent from the Hebrides, Orkney and Shetland. It is a plant of rough grassland, scrub, roadside verges and hedge banks, especially on mildly acid to neutral clays but usually avoiding dry calcareous soils. A perennial, it flowers from June to August.

Alchemilla
LADY'S-MANTLE
Nearly all British species of *Alchemilla* reproduce apomictically; that is, viable seed is produced without fertilisation, as the pollen is nearly always defective. As a result, with the exception of *A. alpina*, the lady's mantles are all very difficult to identify and the keys and descriptions in *New Flora of the British Isles* or *Excursion Flora of the British Isles* should always be consulted. The following account is based on the work of Dr M. Bradshaw and Dr S.M. Walters.

❁ **The four commonest and most widespread plants are** *A. glabra, A. xanthochlora, A. filicaulis* **subsp.** *filicaulis* **and** *A. filicaulis* **subsp** *vestita*.

Alchemilla glabra Neyg.
This is the commonest species of *Alchemilla* in the mountains of Wales, northern England, Scotland and Northern Ireland. It is, however, the least frequent of the three common species in southern Britain. It grows in meadows, pastures, roadside verges, open woodland and on rock ledges to an altitude of 1,250 m.
❁ *A. glabra* **has scattered appressed hairs on the stems and petioles or is almost wholly glabrous.**

Alchemilla xanthochlora Rothm.
Abundant in northern Britain but absent from the extreme north of Scotland, Orkney, Shetland, the Outer Hebrides and southern Ireland. One of the three commonest species of *Alchemilla* in Britain, it also occurs as a local and scattered species of southern Britain, especially in the south-west. It grows in herb-rich meadows, pastures and roadside verges at low altitudes.

❁ *A. xanthochlora* **and** *A. filicaulis* **have densely pubescent stems and petioles with spreading hairs. The leaves of** *A. xanthochlora* **are glabrous above and those of** *A. filicaulis* **are pubescent above, at least in the folds.**

Alchemilla filicaulis Buser
A. filicaulis and *A. vestita* were previously regarded as separate species, but intermediates exist between them. Accordingly, they are both now treated as subspecies of *A. filicaulis*.

A. filicaulis subsp. *filicaulis*
A plant of mountain grassland but absent from meadow communities, widespread in Scotland above 450 m and reaching to 900 m. It is rare in England, occurring in Derbyshire, Craven and Teesdale in the Pennines and in Cumbria. It also occurs in north Wales and in one locality, on Ben Bulben, in western Ireland.

❁ *A. filicaulis* **subsp.** *filicaulis* **has almost glabrous inflorescence branches and upper internodes, and the leaves are only hairy in the folds above and on the veins beneath.** *A. filicaulis* **subsp.** *vestita* **has pubescent inflorescence branches and upper internodes, and the leaves are more hairy all over on both surfaces.**

A. filicaulis subsp. *vestita* (Buser) M.E. Bradshaw
The most widespread *Alchemilla* in Britain and the commonest in lowland England. It is, however, absent from Orkney and Shetland, where it is replaced by subsp. *filicaulis*.

Alchemilla alpina L.
ALPINE LADY'S-MANTLE
A widespread plant of the central, eastern and western Highlands of Scotland and the Lake District. In Ireland it is confined to isolated localities in Co. Kerry and Co. Wicklow. It is a locally common plant of mountain grassland, scree, rock ledges and summit detritus to an altitude of more than 1,220 m but descending almost to sea level in parts of the west coast of Scotland. A perennial, it flowers from June to August.

Alchemilla conjuncta Bab.
SILVER LADY'S-MANTLE
This grows apparently wild in two places in Scotland; it is well established among rocks by streams in Glen Clova in Angus and in Glen Lennox on the Isle of Arran. A native of the Jura and western Alps, it was once regarded as native in Scotland but is now thought to have been introduced. Often grown in gardens, it is known as an escape in several places in England and Scotland. It is a perennial and flowers during June and July.

Alchemilla glaucescens Wallr.*
A Continental species, confined in Britain to about a dozen localities on limestone grassland on the Carboniferous limestone of Craven in the north Pennines, to a few sites on the Durness limestone in Ross and Sutherland and an isolated locality in Leitrim in western Ireland.

Alchemilla subcrenata Buser*
A very rare northern-montane species, first reported in Britain growing in Teesdale in 1951. Altogether it is now known from about five localities in the dale, in some of which it is quite frequent. Found in pastures and herb-rich meadows and occasionally on roadside verges.

Alchemilla minima S.M. Walters*
Very rare and the only species of *Alchemilla* endemic to Britain. It grows in closely-grazed fescue/bent grassland on or just below the Carboniferous limestone of the Ingleborough district of the north Pennines in Yorkshire. It occurs at altitudes between 210 m and 610 m on mildly acid to calcareous, moist, dark peaty loams. First described as a new British plant by Dr S.M. Walters in 1949.

Alchemilla monticola Opiz*
A northern-montane species in Europe, confined in Britain to Teesdale in Durham and Yorkshire, particularly around Middleton-in-Teesdale, where it grows in hay meadows, herb-rich pastures and along roadside verges. Its distribution extends north-eastwards into the catchment of the River Wear.

Alchemilla acutiloba Opiz*
A northern-montane species that was not identified as British until 1946. It is confined to parts of Upper Teesdale and Weardale in Durham, where it grows along roadside and railway verges. In Weardale it is also a common plant of hay meadows.

Alchemilla glomerulans Buser
An arctic-alpine species more or less confined in Britain to upper Teesdale in the northern Pennines and to the Cairngorms and the central and western Highlands of Scotland. In Teesdale it grows on limestone outcrops by the side of small streams, in herb-rich meadows and along roadside verges. In Scotland it is usually found as a rock-ledge plant above 610 m.

Alchemilla wichurae (Buser) Stefansson
A sub-arctic species, occurring in five main areas of upland Britain on damp, base-rich or calcareous soils. In Wharfedale and the Craven district of the Yorkshire Pennines it grows on rocky outcrops and in damp pastures, herb-rich meadows and open oak woodland between 300 m and 460 m. It grows in similar habitats in Upper Teesdale and on mountain ledges in the Lake District. In the Central Highlands of Scotland it is found in the tall herb-rich vegetation of wet, calcareous rock ledges between 305 m and 915 m and in closed mat-grass (*Nardus*) grassland at 840 m. Lastly, in the north-west Highlands it grows in the open calcareous grassland of the Durness limestone.

Alchemilla gracilis Opiz*
Very rare. *A. gracilis* was first discovered in Britain as recently as 1976, but its identity was not established until 1978. It grows in three small populations in base-rich grassland in Northumberland. On the Continent it has a northern-montane distribution.

Aphanes arvensis L.
PARSLEY-PIERT
Widely distributed throughout the British Isles but apparently scarce in parts of western and northern Scotland. It is a plant of bare ground and open patches in grass heaths, commons and on roadsides, waste places and arable on dry, well-drained soils. It occurs in both acid and calcareous habitats, but is intolerant of competition from more vigorous species. An annual, it flowers from April to October.

❁ **The stipule teeth of** *A. arvensis* **are triangular; those of** *A. inexspectata* **are oblong.**

Aphanes inexspectata Lippert
(*A. microcarpa* auct.)
SLENDER PARSLEY-PIERT
Widely distributed throughout the whole of the British Isles. It grows in similar kinds of habitats to *A. arvensis* but is more or less restricted to acid soils, occurring in open grassland on sandy heathland and commons and along woodland paths and trackways. It is less restricted to well-drained conditions than *A. arvensis* and, of the two, seems to be the least frequent as an arable weed. An annual, it flowers from April to October.

Rosa canina agg.

Dog Rose

The dog roses are a very variable group that have been the subject of several different taxonomic treatments. Volume 2 of *Flora Europaea* recognises 10 species in Britain, but we follow the more conventional treatment of recent British Floras, which admit three variable species, *R. canina* L., *R. obtusifolia* Desv. and *R. caesia* Sm. A detailed illustrated account of the British roses can be found in *Roses of Great Britain and Ireland* (G.G. Graham & A.L. Primavesi, 1993).

The dog roses are all plants of hedgerows, scrub, thickets and woodland margins, and the aggregate occurs throughout the whole of the British Isles, reaching an altitude of 550 m. By far the commonest, and indeed the most abundant British rose, is *R. canina* L. itself. It occurs throughout the British Isles but is rare in Scotland. *R. obtusifolia* is commonest in the south and extends no further north than Northumberland and Cheshire. *R. caesia* is the commonest rose in central and northern Scotland, where it replaces *R. canina*, but is very rare in southern England.

❁ **The *R. canina* aggregate differs from the *R. rubiginosa* group in the absence of a dense covering of apple-scented glands and from the *R. tomentosa* group by the more hooked prickles and glabrous or sparsely hairy leaves.**

***R. canina* itself has pink or white flowers, glabrous leaflets and reflexed sepals that fall before the fruit ripens. *R. obtusifolia* has more rounded leaflets that are pubescent and sparsely glandular beneath, white flowers, and reflexed sepals that fall before the fruit is ripe. *R. caesia* has smaller prickles than either *R. canina* or *R. obtusifolia* and sepals that become erect after flowering and persist till the fruits ripen.**

Rosa tomentosa Sm.

Downy Rose

Widespread throughout England, Wales and Ireland but becoming scarce in Scotland and absent from the extreme north. It is a rather local species of hedgerows, scrub, wood margins, thickets and railway cuttings on both acid and calcareous soils. It flowers during June and July.

❁ **The *R. tomentosa* group consists of *R. tomentosa* itself, *R. sherardii* and *R. mollis*. It is distinguished from the *R. canina* group by the dull, usually densely hairy leaves and less strongly hooked prickles.**

❁ ***R. tomentosa* and *R. sherardii* both have arching or flexuous stems and slightly curved prickles. *R. sherardii* is more or less intermediate between *R. tomentosa* and *R. mollis* but can be distinguished from *R. tomentosa* by the blue-green leaves and shorter sepals.**

Rosa sherardii Davies

Primarily a plant of northern England and Scotland, being very rare in southern England and also in Ireland. It occurs in hedgerows, scrub and open woodland and flowers during June and July.

Rosa mollis Sm.
(*R. villosa* auct.)

A plant of northern Britain, common in Scotland but extending as far south as Derbyshire and south Wales. It occurs in hedgerows, on the edges of woods and in scrub on both acid and calcareous soils, reaching an altitude of 610 m. It flowers during June and July.

❁ ***R. mollis* is most easily distinguished by the deep flower colour, but also differs from both *R. tomentosa* and *R. sherardii* in the erect, not arching, stems and the straight prickles.**

Rose rubiginosa L.

Sweet Briar

Widespread in lowland Britain south and east of a line from the Wash to Dorset and scattered throughout the rest of the country, decreasing northwards and absent from Orkney and Shetland. It is primarily a plant of scrub on calcareous soils, and is locally common on the downlands of southern England and an early invader of ungrazed chalk grassland. Unlike many other species of rose, it is uncommon in hedgerows but does appear in a range of coastal habitats including stabilised shingle. It flowers during June and July.

❁ **The *R. rubiginosa* group differs from both the *R. canina* and *R. tomentosa* groups in the densely glandular leaves that produce a characteristic apple smell when crushed.**

***R. rubiginosa* has erect stems, rounded bases to the leaflets, long hairs on the styles and glandular flower stalks.**

Rosa micrantha Borrer ex Sm.

Widespread in England and Wales but rare in Scotland, and in Ireland confined to the south-west. It is locally frequent in hedgerows, scrub and wood margins on calcareous soils but is less confined to them than *R. rubiginosa*, as it also occurs in heaths and pastures on both sands and clays. It flowers during June and July.

❁ ***R. micrantha* is similar to *R. rubiginosa* but has arching stems and glabrous styles.**

Rosa agrestis Savi

Very rare. It is a species of scrub, thickets and woodland edges on calcareous soils in a few scattered localities throughout England and central Ireland. It flowers during June and July.

❁ *R. agrestis* has white to pale pink flowers, rhomboidal leaf-bases, arching stems and almost glabrous styles.

Plants named as *Rosa elliptica* Tausch are probably the same as *R. agrestis* or hybrids with it.

Rosa arvensis Huds.

Field Rose

Widely distributed throughout England and Wales but becoming scarcer in the north, in parts of west Wales and also in the East Anglian Fens. It is absent from Scotland except where introduced but present throughout Ireland, where it is commonest in the south-east. It is found in hedgerows, scrub and wood margins, always scrambling among other shrub species, and seeming to prefer heavy textured soils. It flowers during June and July, slightly later than *R. canina*. *R. arvensis* is probably one of the parents of *R.* x *alba*, the White Rose of York.

❁ ***R. arvensis* has white flowers and is distinguished from other roses by the styles being united into a column that is as long as the stamens.**

Rosa pimpinellifolia L.

Burnet Rose

Occurs throughout Britain except for the Shetlands. Its most characteristic habitats are stabilised coastal sand dunes and dune slacks and sandy heathlands close to the sea. Inland it is more calcicole, growing to an altitude of 520 m on limestone pavement in northern England and also occurring in rough chalk grassland in the south. It flowers from May to July.

❁ ***R. pimpinellifolia* forms a densely bristly and pricky low-spreading shrub. The creamy-white flowers are borne singly, the sepals are untoothed, and the hips are purplish-black.**

Rosa stylosa Desv.

A species of southern Britain, extending as far north as Leicester and north Wales and in Ireland rare and more or less confined to the south-east. It is a local species occurring in hedgerows, thickets and scrub, often on heavy soils. It flowers during June and July.

❁ ***R. stylosa* has white or pale pink flowers with glandular hairs on the stalks. The styles are united into a column that is shorter than the stamens and the disc is conical and prominent.**

Rosa sempervirens L.

Alien and a native of south-west Europe and the Mediterranean east to Turkey. It was formerly naturalised in Worcestershire.

❁ ***R. sempervirens* is distinguished from native species by its evergreen habit.**

 (see illustrations page 88)

❁ *Sanguisorba* **differs from** *Acaena* **(Plate 35) in its erect, not prostrate, habit and non-spiny fruiting heads.**

Sanguisorba officinalis L.
GREAT BURNET
A widespread plant of northern and central England from Cumbria and Northumberland south to Wiltshire and Cambridge. Also in central Wales and local in parts of south-west England; rare elsewhere and in Ireland. It grows in wet meadows, pastures, marshes and damp roadsides to an altitude of 460 m. A perennial, it flowers from June to September and is pollinated by a wide variety of insects.

❁ *S. officinalis* **is larger than** *S. minor*, **growing to 1 m; it has dark red sepals and four stamens to each flower.**

Sanguisorba minor Scop. subsp. *minor*
(*Poterium sanguisorba* L.)
SALAD BURNET
A widespread species throughout England and parts of Wales but rare and local in southern Scotland and Ireland and absent from northern Scotland and the isles. It is strongly calcicolous, being locally abundant in dry chalk and limestone grasslands to an altitude of 500 m. Male, female and hermaphrodite flowers are borne on the same inflorescence and the flowers are wind-pollinated. A perennial, it flowers from May to August.

Sanguisorba minor subsp. *muricata* (Gremli) Briq.
(*Poterium polygamum* Waldst & Kit.)
FODDER BURNET
Alien. A native of southern Europe but formerly widely cultivated as a fodder crop and now completely naturalised in pastures, field borders and roadsides in a number of scattered localities throughout England. A perennial, it flowers from June to August and is wind-pollinated.
❁ *S. minor* **differs from** *S. officinalis* **in the smaller size, green sepals and numerous stamens to each flower.**

Subsp. *minor* **grows to 15-40 cm and has few or no stem leaves; subsp.** *muricata* **is larger and more robust (30-80 cm) with several stem-leaves.**

Cotoneaster integerrimus Medik.**
WILD COTONEASTER
Very rare. It is restricted to a single population of less than half a dozen plants on Carboniferous limestone rocks on Great Orme's Head in north Wales. By the beginning of the century the plant had been reduced to virtual extinction by over-collecting and grazing by sheep and goats. A low deciduous shrub, it flowers from April to June and is pollinated by wasps or self-pollinated.

Cotoneaster simonsii Baker
HIMALAYAN COTONEASTER
Alien and a native of the Khasi Hills in Assam. Introduced in 1865 and widely cultivated as an ornamental shrub, it has become naturalised in many places in England, Wales, Scotland and southern Ireland. A half-evergreen shrub, it is in flower from February to April.

Cotoneaster integrifolius (Roxb.) Klotz
(*C. microphyllus* auct.)
SMALL-LEAVED COTONEASTER
Alien. A native of the Himalayas and south-west China, introduced to Britain as an ornamental shrub in 1824. It is naturalised in numerous localities throughout the British Isles, most often on limestone cliffs and rock faces, frequently near the sea. A small evergreen shrub, it flowers during May and June.

CRASSULACEAE

Sedum telephium L.
ORPINE
LIVELONG
Distributed throughout the British Isles but absent from Ireland except as an introduction. It is most frequent in the south and west and is rare in the north and west of Scotland. It is to be found in hedge banks, lane sides, woodland clearings and scrub, often on light sandy soils, to an altitude of 460 m. A perennial, it is pollinated by bees and flies and flowers from July to October.

Sedum dasyphyllum L.
THICK-LEAVED STONECROP
Alien. Native in southern and central Europe from Spain to Greece and north to southern Germany. It is naturalised in a few localities scattered throughout England, Wales and Ireland but chiefly in the south-west, where it usually occurs on old walls or limestone rocks. A perennial, it flowers during June and July and is pollinated by small flies and bees.
❁ *S. dasyphyllum* **is distinguished from** *S. anglicum* **and** *S. album* **by its opposite and pubescent leaves.**

Sedum anglicum Huds.
ENGLISH STONECROP
Has a strongly oceanic distribution in Britain, being widespread in the south-west, Wales, north-west England, the whole of western Scotland and southern and western Ireland. Elsewhere it is chiefly coastal. It grows in rocky woodland to an altitude of 1,070 m, usually on acid soils. Around the coast it is a plant of mature sand dunes and shingle beaches. A perennial, it flowers from June to September.

❁ *S. album* **is distinguished from** *S. anglicum* **by its longer (more than 6 mm) green leaves and inflorescence with several branches.** *S. anglicum* **has shorter (less than 6 mm) blue-green leaves and two main branches to the inflorescence.**

Sedum album L.
WHITE STONECROP
Occurs throughout the British Isles but its status is doubtful. A native throughout most of the rest of Europe, it is almost certainly an introduction in Ireland. In the rest of Britain it may only be truly native in south Devon, the Mendips and the Malverns. Characteristically, it is a plant of rocks and old walls. A perennial, it flowers from June to August.

Sedum acre L.
BITING STONECROP
WALL-PEPPER
Widely distributed throughout the whole of the British Isles except for parts of north-west Scotland and Shetland. It is a frequent plant of coastal and inland sand dunes, mature shingle beaches, maritime rocks and heaths, walls and dry open grassland on sandy or calcareous soils. A perennial, it flowers during midsummer.

❁ *S. acre* **and** *S. sexangulare* **have small (7 mm or less) blunt leaves.** *S. forsteranum* **and** *S. reflexum* **have longer (more than 7 mm) pointed leaves.**

S. acre **is distinguished from** *S. sexangulare* **by its oval, overlapping leaves and by its acrid taste. The leaves of** *S. sexangulare* **are linear and spreading.**

Sedum sexangulare L.
TASTELESS STONECROP
INSIPID STONECROP
Alien; endemic to central Europe from France to Greece and north to Finland. It is naturalised on old walls in a few localities in England and Wales, probably originating as a garden escape. A perennial, it flowers during July and August.

Sedum forsterianum Sm.
ROCK STONECROP
A local species of western and south-west Britain occurring in Devon, Somerset, Dorset, Shropshire and Wales. It grows on rocks, scree and rocky hillsides and in open rocky woodland to an altitude of 365 m. It is often cultivated as a rockery plant and occurs as an infrequent escape throughout England and Ireland. A perennial, it flowers during June and July.

❁ *S. forsterianum* **differs from** *S. rupestre* **in its flat leaves, forming a tight head at the top of the non-flowering shoots. The leaves of** *S. rupestre* **are cylindrical and the non-flowering shoots are equally leafy throughout their length.**

Sedum rupestre L.
REFLEXED STONECROP
Alien; endemic in Europe from Norway to Sicily and France to the western Ukraine. It is widely cultivated as a rockery plant and is established on old walls and on rocks in a number of localities throughout Britain, mostly in the south but scattered as far north as the Firth of Forth. It is rare in Ireland. A perennial, it flowers from June to August. The leaves were formerly used as a spring salad.

Sedum villosum L.
HAIRY STONECROP
A local alpine species of northern England and central and southern Scotland. It grows in wet mountain pastures, stream sides and on rocky or stony ground, often on calcareous or base-rich soils, to an altitude of 1,100 m. A perennial, it flowers during June and July.
❁ *S. villosum* **is distinguished by its pink flowers and alternate, glandular leaves.**

Umbilicus rupestris (Salisb.) Dandy
NAVELWORT PENNYWORT
Widespread in south-west England, Wales, north-west England and western Scotland as far north as Mull and the whole of Ireland. It is a common plant of rock crevices, cliffs, walls and dry, sandy hedge banks, usually on acid soils, reaching an altitude of about 550 m. A perennial, it flowers from June to September and is probably self-pollinated, although thrips are sometimes found in the flowers.

Crassula tillaea Lester-Garl.
MOSSY STONECROP
A plant with a very local distribution, being almost confined to Norfolk and Suffolk but also occurring in Hampshire, Dorset and the Channel Islands. It grows on bare sandy or gravelly ground where the surface has been compacted and is often associated with paths, tracks and car parks. The compaction increases the water-holding properties of the soil which seem to be necessary to ensure autumn germination. A tiny annual, it flowers during June and July and is self-pollinated.
❁ ***C. tillaea* is distinguished by its reddish colour, prostrate habit and small, fleshy, crowded leaves.**

Crassula helmsii (T. Kirk) Cockayne
NEW ZEALAND PIGMYWEED
Alien and a native of Australia and South Island, New Zealand. *C. helmsii* first seems to have been recorded from Essex in 1956, probably having originated from nursery-grown stock. Since then it has turned up in an increasing number of localities from Sussex to Argyll. It grows in the shallow water at the edges of ponds and dykes, usually on fertile soils. A perennial, it frequently forms extensive carpets and flowers freely from June to August. (Illustrated on Plate 102.)

❁ ***C. helmsii* can be distinguished from *C. aquatica* by its perennial habit and stalked flowers.**

Crassula aquatica (L.) Schönl.*
PIGMYWEED
Very rare. It was first recorded growing on the margin of a muddy pool in Yorkshire in 1921 but it had disappeared by 1945. It was always doubtful whether the plant was truly native, but in 1969 it was discovered in a completely new locality in Inverness-shire, where it appears to have been established for some time. (Not illustrated.)

Sedum rosea (L.) Scop
(*Rhodiola rosea* L.)
ROSEROOT
Widespread in the Scottish Highlands, especially in the west, and occurring as far south as Snowdonia and the Pembrokeshire coast. In Ireland it is more or less confined to the west coast. It is a plant of mountain rock ledges and crevices, often but not exclusively on base-rich soils and reaching an altitude of 1,175 m. It is also a common plant of sea cliffs in both western Scotland and Ireland. The English name refers to the smell of the plant, which resembles that of the damask rose.

Sempervivum tectorum L.
HOUSE-LEEK
An alien species of uncertain geographical origins, *Sempervivum* has been grown on old walls, rockeries and roofs for centuries. However, it hardly ever becomes truly naturalised in the wild. A perennial, it flowers during June and July and is pollinated by a variety of small insects. (Illustrated on Plate 102.)

SAXIFRAGACEAE

Chrysosplenium oppositifolium L.
OPPOSITE-LEAVED GOLDEN-SAXIFRAGE
Widely distributed throughout the British Isles, but scarce in parts of East Anglia and absent from Shetland. It is a frequent plant of woodland flushes and stream sides, shaded springs and wet rocks, usually on acid or calcium-deficient soils. It extends from the lowlands to over 1,035 m. It flowers from April to July and is either pollinated by small insects, such as spring-tails and small flies, or self-pollinated.

Chrysosplenium alternifolium L.
ALTERNATE-LEAVED GOLDEN-SAXIFRAGE
A local species scattered throughout most of the British Isles, but absent from Orkney, Shetland and Ireland. It occurs in similar kinds of habitats to *C. oppositifolium*, with which it sometimes grows, but is more restricted by the chemical nature of the water. It frequently grows on calcareous sandstones and also on the harder limestones, and always where there is significant ground-water movement. It flowers from April to July.
❁ ***C. alternifolium* differs from *C. oppositifolium* in its alternate leaves.**

Saxifraga hirculus L.**
MARSH SAXIFRAGE YELLOW MARSH-SAXIFRAGE
Very rare. It is now confined to about 20 localities in Britain, chiefly in Yorkshire and Cumbria but also in Midlothian, Aberdeenshire, Banffshire and Inverness-shire in Scotland and in Co. Mayo and Co. Antrim in Ireland. It grows in the wet, base-rich hollows of damp mountain grassland and moorland and bogs. In recent years it has disappeared from several localities due to land drainage. A perennial, it flowers during August and is pollinated by small flies.
❁ ***S. hirculus* differs from *S. aizoides* (Plate 41) in its long-stalked basal leaves, red hairs on the stems, and usually solitary flowers.**

Saxifraga nivalis L.
ALPINE SAXIFRAGE
A rare and local plant of the mountains of the central and western Highlands of Scotland, Snowdonia and the Lake District. In Ireland it is confined to the Ben Bulben range of Co. Sligo. It grows on damp, shaded rock ledges, often on base-rich soils, between 360 m and 1,310 m. A perennial, it flowers during July and August.
❁ ***S. nivalis* differs from similar-looking species in its erect or spreading, not reflexed, sepals.**

❁ ***S. stellaris* differs from *S. hirsuta, S. umbrosa* and *S. spathularis* by its sessile leaves and from *S. nivalis* in its reflexed sepals.**

Saxifraga stellaris L.
STARRY SAXIFRAGE
Widespread in the mountains of Snowdonia, the Lake District, the northern Pennines and the southern uplands, and the central, eastern and western Highlands of Scotland and in most of the mountains of Ireland. It grows on wet rock ledges, by streams, springs and on wet stony ground to over 1,340 m. A perennial, it is in flower from June to August and is pollinated chiefly by flies.

Saxifraga umbrosa L.
PYRENEAN SAXIFRAGE
Alien and an endemic of the western and central Pyrenees. It is established at Haseldon Gill in Yorkshire, from where it has been known since 1792. A perennial, it flowers during June and July and is pollinated by a variety of small insects.
❁ ***S. umbrosa* has blunt teeth to the leaves and the terminal tooth is shorter than its neighbours.**

Saxifraga spathularis Brot.
ST PATRICK'S-CABBAGE
Confined to, but widespread in, mountain areas of western Ireland occurring in the counties of Kerry, Galway and Mayo with isolated localities in Tyrone, Cork, Waterford and Carlow. It grows among damp rocks and by streams in both woodland and exposed conditions, reaching 1,035 m. A perennial, it flowers from June to August.

❁ ***S. spathularis* differs from *S. umbrosa* in the teeth of the leaves being acute, and the terminal tooth as long as or longer than its two neighbours.**

❁ ***S. hirsuta* differs from *S. umbrosa* and *S. spathularis* in its hairy cordate leaves.**

Saxifraga hirsuta L.
KIDNEY SAXIFRAGE
Very local and virtually confined to upland areas of Co. Kerry in south-west Ireland. It occurs in similar habitats to *S. spathularis*, growing among damp shaded rocks and by streams, but avoiding the more open habitats, and reaching 915 m. A perennial, it is in flower from May to July.

Saxifraga tridactylites L.
RUE-LEAVED SAXIFRAGE
Widely distributed throughout England, Wales and Ireland, but very rare in Scotland. It is a plant of dry open habitats such as sand dunes, wall tops, heath grassland, waste ground, field margins and limestone rocks. An annual, it flowers from April to June and is self-pollinated.

Saxifraga granulata L.
MEADOW SAXIFRAGE
A local species throughout most of Britain, absent from much of northern and western Scotland and the south-west of England and very rare in Ireland. It is most frequent in parts of East Anglia. It is a plant of rough grassland, pastures and roadside verges on dry, well-drained neutral or calcareous soils, reaching an altitude of 460 m. A perennial, it flowers from April to June and is insect-pollinated.

Saxifraga cernua L.**
DROOPING SAXIFRAGE
One of the rarest of British wild plants, confined to three localities only at high altitudes in the mica-schist mountains of the central Highlands of Scotland in Argyllshire, Perthshire and Inverness-shire. It grows among basic rocks and in corries between 915 m and 1,220 m. Although protected by law, it is still threatened by collectors. It flowers during July but apparently never sets seed, reproducing vegetatively by means of axillary buds.
❁ ***S. cernua* differs from *S. rivularis* (Plate 41) in the red bulbils in the axils of the upper leaves and bracts, often replacing the flowers.**

Saxifraga rivularis L.*

HIGHLAND SAXIFRAGE
BROOK SAXIFRAGE

Very rare; known from only 17 scattered localities in the central, eastern and western Highlands of Scotland. In recent years it has been recorded from Perthshire, Aberdeenshire, Banffshire, Inverness-shire, Argyllshire and Ross-shire. It grows on wet, acid mountain rocks at altitudes between 915 m and 1,220 m. A perennial, it flowers during July and August and is probably pollinated by small flies.

❁ ***S. rivularis* differs from both *S. cernua* (Plate 40) and *S. granulata* (Plate 40) in the absence of bulbils in the leaf axils, the branched inflorescence and smaller petals (3-5 mm).**

❁ ***S. hypnoides, S. cespitosa, S. hartii* and *S. rosacea* have a 'moss-like' habit, forming cushions with numerous small, leafy, non-flowering shoots.**

Saxifraga hypnoides L.

MOSSY SAXIFRAGE
DOVEDALE MOSS

Widespread but rather local in the uplands of northern England, Wales and Scotland. In Ireland it is most frequent in the mountains of Clare, although it does extend as far south as Waterford. It is most frequent on calcareous or base-rich soils, especially in England and Ireland. It extends as far south as Cheddar in Somerset, is scattered throughout Wales and is locally common on the limestones of northern England and throughout the Scottish Highlands. It grows by the sides of mountain streams, and on cliffs, screes and rocky slopes most often at altitudes between 200 m and 760 m, but in Scotland it is found from sea level to 1,215 m. A perennial, it flowers from May to July.

❁ ***S. hypnoides* differs from the other three species in the narrower (1 mm or less) and finely pointed lobes to the leaves and prostrate non-flowering shoots.**

Saxifraga cespitosa L.**

TUFTED SAXIFRAGE

Very rare; known in about 10 localities in three separate areas of upland Britain. It occurs in a single locality in Caernarvonshire, in the Cairngorms in Banffshire and Aberdeenshire and in the western Highlands in Inverness-shire and Ross-shire. It grows almost exclusively on inaccessible rock ledges at high altitudes between 920 m and 1,350 m. It has suffered from collecting but is now protected by law. A perennial, it flowers from May to July and is probably usually self-pollinated.

❁ **Both *S. cespitosa* and *S. rosacea* subsp. *hartii* have glandular hairs on the leaves. *S. cespitosa* usually has three blunt lobes to the leaves; *S. rosacea* subsp. *hartii* usually has five acute leaf lobes.**

Saxifraga rosacea Moench subsp. *rosacea* (*)

IRISH SAXIFRAGE

A rather rare plant of mountains and sea cliffs in southern and western Ireland where it occurs in Kerry, Clare, Galway, Mayo, Tipperary and Limerick. It grows on boulders and rocks in and alongside mountain streams on cliff ledges, steep but stable scree slopes and in rocky gullies, always where conditions are wet but well-drained, and sometimes close to the sea. It seems indifferent to rock type and soil pH but usually forms part of a discontinuous grassy or mossy sward at altitudes up to 1,070 m. A perennial, it flowers from June to August.

❁ ***S. rosacea* subsp. *rosacea* differs from *S. hypnoides* in the more tufted habit and distinctive pinkish colour of the stems and leaves. Subsp. *hartii* differs in having all the hairs on the leaves glandular.**

Saxifraga rosacea subsp. *hartii* (D.A. Webb) D.A. Webb (*)

A very rare endemic confined to Arranmore Island in Co. Donegal, where it was first discovered by Hart in 1880. It seems to grow exclusively on grassy sea cliffs and is in flower during May and June.

Saxifraga aizoides L.

YELLOW SAXIFRAGE
YELLOW MOUNTAIN-SAXIFRAGE

A widespread plant throughout the Scottish Highlands, also occurring in the Lake District, the northern Pennines and the mountains of Sligo, Leitrim, Donegal and Antrim. It is locally common among rocks and boulders alongside mountain streams and on wet gravelly or stony ground to an altitude of 1,175 m. A perennial, it flowers from June to September and is pollinated mainly by flies.

❁ ***S. aizoides* differs from *S. hirculus* (Plate 40) in the ascending habit, stemless leaves, spreading sepals, smaller petals (4-7 mm) and inflorescence of several flowers.**

Saxifraga oppositifolia L.

PURPLE SAXIFRAGE

Confined to the mountains of northern and western Britain, being found throughout the Highlands of Scotland, Orkney, Shetland and the Outer Hebrides, the Lake District and the north Yorkshire Pennines and in Snowdonia, on Cader Idris and in the Brecon Beacons. In Ireland it is found in a few scattered localities in the north and north-west. It is a plant of damp rocks, soil-covered mountain ledges and stony ground on steep slopes, always on calcareous or base-rich rocks. In Scotland it ranges from sea level to 1,213 m and is particularly resistant to exposure from both frost and wind. It is the earliest-flowering of British alpine plants, sometimes as early as February and continuing through to May and with an occasional second flowering period at the end of the summer. A perennial, it is either self- or insect-pollinated.

❁ ***S. oppositifolia* is the only British saxifrage with purple flowers and opposite leaves.**

Parnassia palustris L.

GRASS-OF-PARNASSUS

Widespread throughout most of northern England, Scotland and Ireland except for the south-west and also in East Anglia and Anglesey. It is a plant of marshes, fens, wet pastures, wet moorland and streamside flushes, often on base-rich soils, to an altitude of 790 m. It was previously more widespread in the English lowlands but has suffered from habitat loss and drainage. A perennial, it flowers from July to October and is pollinated by a variety of insects.

GROSSULARIACEAE

Ribes rubrum L.
(*R. sylvestre* (Lam.) Mert. & Koch)

RED CURRANT

Almost certainly not native in Britain, although it is widespread particularly in the south and east. It is absent from Ireland, Orkney, Shetland and the Outer Hebrides. It is a plant of wet woodlands, fen carr and shaded stream sides reaching an altitude of 460 m. A deciduous shrub of up to 2 m, it flowers during April and May.

❁ **The leaves of *R. rubrum* are almost glabrous beneath and the basal sinus of the leaf is narrow. The leaves of *R. spicatum* are usually hairy beneath and the base of the leaf is truncate.**

Ribes spicatum Robson

DOWNY CURRANT

A very local plant of limestone woodlands in northern England and Scotland, occurring in Yorkshire, Durham, Lancashire and Cumbria and in Scotland scattered north to Moray and reaching an altitude of 425 m. A deciduous shrub of up to 2 m in height, it flowers during April and May.

Ribes alpinum L.

MOUNTAIN CURRANT

A very local species almost confined to the Carboniferous limestone of northern England and north Wales. It is most frequent in the dales of Derbyshire and Staffordshire where it grows in rocky ash woodland on the sides of limestone cliffs. In north Wales it reaches an altitude of 380 m. Elsewhere it appears as an occasional escape from cultivation. A deciduous shrub of up to 3 m, it flowers during April and May and is pollinated by various flies and bees.

❁ ***R. alpinum* differs from both *R. rubrum* and *R. spicatum* in the erect inflorescence and long bracts which are longer than the pedicels.**

Ribes nigrum L.

BLACK CURRANT

A local plant distributed throughout the British Isles, but most frequent in the south-east. Black currant is cultivated throughout Europe so its native distribution in the west is obscure, but it may be native to Britain. It is to be found in wet woodlands, by shaded streams in fen carr and in hedgerows. A deciduous shrub of up to 2 m, it flowers during April and May and is often self-pollinated.

❁ ***R. nigrum* can be distinguished from the other species of currants when not in fruit by the characteristic smell of the crushed leaves.**

Ribes uva-crispa L.

GOOSEBERRY

Distributed throughout the British Isles, but absent from Orkney, Shetland and the Outer Hebridges and rare in north-west Scotland and introduced into Ireland. Gooseberry is very likely a true native in Britain, notwithstanding the fact that it frequently escapes from cultivation and becomes established. It is usually to be found in hedgerows, woodland and by shaded streamsides. A spiny deciduous shrub of up to 1 m, it flowers from March to May.

SARRACENIACEAE

Sarracenia purpurea L.

PITCHERPLANT

Alien and a native of eastern North America, it was first planted in bogs in central Ireland in 1906 and is now abundant in parts of Roscommon and West Meath. A perennial, insectivorous plant, it flowers during June. The 'pitchers' are modified lower leaves; insects fall into the liquid at the base of the 'pitcher' and drown.

PLATE 42
DROSERACEAE • LYTHRACEAE • THYMELAEACEAE • ELAEAGNACEAE • ONAGRACEAE
(see illustrations page 94)

DROSERACEAE

Drosera rotundifolia L.

ROUND-LEAVED SUNDEW

Occurs throughout the British Isles wherever suitable habitats occur. It grows on bare acid peat and among *Sphagnum* in bogs and on wet heaths and moors. It is often particularly abundant around the margins of bog pools. It is widespread and frequent in the north and west, but in the lowlands is more or less confined to East Anglia and to the heaths of the Weald, the New Forest and Dorset. A perennial insectivorous herb, it flowers from June to August, but the flowers only open in bright sunlight and occasionally never open and are self-pollinated. Insects are trapped by the sticky long-stalked glands around the margin of the leaf and digested by proteolytic enzymes

continued on next page

secreted by glands in the centre of the leaf. The glistening leaf glands attracted the attention of the medieval herbalists, for whom the plant possessed magical properties as it miraculously remained 'dew-covered' even in the hottest sun.

Drosera longifolia L.
(*D. anglica* Huds.)
GREAT SUNDEW
Widespread in western and north-west Scotland and in western Ireland, but of only scattered occurrence elsewhere as around the Solway, in parts of East Anglia, the Lake District and the heaths of Dorset and the New Forest. It grows in the wetter parts of acid *Sphagnum* bogs, often more or less floating around the margins of bog pools. A perennial, it flowers during July and August. The hybrid with *D. rotundifolia*, *D.* × *obovata* Mert. & Koch, occasionally occurs with the parents.

❁ *D. intermedia* **differs from** *D. longifolia* **in the lateral, not terminal, flower stem, arising from below the rosette, and which is not much longer than the leaves.**

Drosera intermedia Hayne
OBLONG-LEAVED SUNDEW
LONG-LEAVED SUNDEW
A local species, scattered throughout the British Isles in suitable habitats. The main centre of its distribution is in western Scotland south to the Lake District and in western Ireland. It is locally frequent on the heaths of the Central Weald, Surrey, the New Forest and Dorset but rare in Wales, the south-west and East Anglia. It generally grows in drier habitats than the two preceding species, often on patches of bare acid peat that become dry in summer. In Ireland it more usually grows among wet *Sphagnum*. A perennial, it flowers from June to August.

LYTHRACEAE

Lythrum salicaria L.
PURPLE-LOOSESTRIFE
Widespread throughout the whole of England, Wales and Ireland, but scarce in Scotland except for the west coast and absent from the extreme north, Orkney and Shetland. It is locally common along the banks of slow-moving rivers and canals, among the marginal vegetation of lakes and ponds, in reed swamp and the tall herb vegetation of fens and marshes. It avoids acid conditions and prefers the more fertile soils and will tolerate light shade. A perennial growing to over 1 m, it flowers from June to August. It is trimorphic; that is, there are three kinds of flowers with styles and stamens of three different lengths and pollen of three different sizes, with the longest stamens producing the largest pollen. Pollination is effected by various long-tongued insects.

Lythrum hyssopifolia L.**
GRASS-POLY
Very rare and erratic in its appearance. *L. hyssopifolia* was once widespread in south-east England, but the only recent records are from Sussex, Essex, Cambridgeshire, Bedfordshire, Huntingdonshire and Jersey, and of these it only appears regularly in Cambridgeshire and Jersey. An annual, it occurs on bare ground or in open vegetation in hollows that are flooded in winter. It flowers during June and July.
❁ *L. hyssopifolia* **grows to about 20 cm; the flowers are 5 mm in diameter.**

Lythrum portula (L.) D.A. Webb
(*Peplis portula* L.)
WATER-PURSLANE
Distributed throughout the British Isles but absent from the Shetlands and rare in northern and north-west Scotland. It is most abundant in southern and south-west England and western Ireland. *L. portula* is a plant of wet open communities and bare ground, the muddy margins of pools and temporarily wet habitats on acid or calcium-deficient soils. An annual, it flowers from June to October.

L. portula is represented in Britain by two subspecies: subsp. *portula* and subsp. *longidentata* (Gay) P.D. Sell. The former occurs throughout the range of the species, while the latter has a more westerly and southern distribution.
❁ *L. portula* **is distinguished by its creeping habit, rooting at the nodes, and small flowers (1 mm diameter), with six sepals and six petals. It is unlikely to be confused with any other plant except perhaps terrestrial forms of** *Callitriche* **(Plate 44),** *Montia* **(Plate 23) or** *Ludwigia* **(Plate 43).**

THYMELAEACEAE

Daphne mezereum L.
MEZEREON
Very rare and now confined to a few scattered localities in England from Sussex to Yorkshire. It is a plant of woodland on chalk or limestone and was formerly much more widespread, having been heavily collected for garden cultivation. It occasionally appears as an escape from cultivation, not always on calcareous soils. A deciduous shrub of up to 1.5 m, it flowers from February to April before the leaves appear and is pollinated by early-flying Lepidoptera and bumble-bees or is self-pollinated.

Daphne laureola L.
SPURGE-LAUREL
Widespread in England, but rare in Wales and the south-west and absent from Scotland and Ireland except for the occasional introduction. *D. laureola* is a local plant of woods, chiefly on dry calcareous, or at least base-rich, soils. An evergreen shrub of up to 1 m, it flowers from February to April and is pollinated by early-flying Lepidoptera and bumble-bees.

ELAEAGNACEAE

Hippophaë rhamnoides L.
SEA-BUCKTHORN
Occurs all round the coasts of Britain, but is only native on the south and east coast from Sussex to East Lothian. In Britain it is a plant of fixed coastal sand dunes and has been widely planted for coastal protection, sand stabilisation and shelter belts. In some areas its rapid spread is eliminating other elements of the sand dune flora. It also occurs occasionally on coastal cliffs. Sea buckthorn scrub supports a high density of nesting birds and the orange berries are an important autumn bird food. *Hippophaë* is dioecious, with separate male and female plants. The roots develop nodules as a result of infection by certain micro-organisms and these have been shown to fix atmospheric nitrogen. A thorny, deciduous shrub of up to 3 m, it flowers during March and April and is wind-pollinated.

ONAGRACEAE

Oenothera biennis L.
COMMON EVENING-PRIMROSE
Alien and a native of Europe. It was introduced during the 19th century and is now established, but apparently decreasing, throughout southern England as far as the Humber with new scattered localities only further north. It is absent from Ireland. It occurs on waste ground, roadsides, railway banks and sand dunes. A spring-germinating biennial, it flowers from June to September.

❁ **The petals of** *O. biennis* **and** *O. cambrica* **are less than 30 mm long.** *O. cambrica* **has red-based hairs on the stems, and the petals are up to 16 mm long. The stems of** *O. biennis* **lack red-based hairs and the petals are 20-30 mm long.**

Oenothera cambrica Rost.
SMALL-FLOWERED EVENING-PRIMROSE
First described as a new species in 1977, *O. cambrica* was previously often erroneously recorded as *O. parviflora* L. It is frequent along the cost of south Wales and also on sand dunes in north Somerset and north Devon. It has also been recorded from Gloucestershire, Jersey, Cornwall, Hampshire, Kent, Surrey, Oxfordshire, Caernarvonshire, Denbigh, Yorkshire and Edinburgh. A biennial, it flowers during late summer, and probably originated in North America.

Oenothera glazioviana C. Martins
(*O. erythrosepala* Borbas)
LARGE-FLOWERED EVENING-PRIMROSE
Alien; a native of North America. It is established throughout England and Wales as far north as Yorkshire, but is absent from Scotland and Ireland. Our commonest species of evening primrose, it grows on roadside banks and verges, railway embankments, sand dunes and waste places. It is a biennial, and flowers from June to September.
❁ *O. glazioviana* **is distinguished from** *O. biennis* **and** *O. cambrica* **by its larger flowers (petals more than 30 mm long).**

Oenothera parviflora L.
A native of eastern North America and a rare alien in Britain, having only been recorded from Glamorgan early in the century. Other records for *O. parviflora* are usually *O. cambrica.* (Not illustrated.)

Circaea lutetiana L.
ENCHANTER'S-NIGHTSHADE
Widespread throughout the whole of the British Isles as far north as central Scotland; very rare in northern Scotland and absent from Orkney, Shetland and the Outer Hebrides. *C. lutetiana* is a common plant of woodlands and coppice on moist, base-rich or calcareous soils to an altitude of 370 m. It is very shade-tolerant, retaining its leaves throughout the summer. It also occurs as a weed of shaded gardens. A perennial, it flowers from June to August and is probably pollinated by small flies.

❁ *C. alpina* **differs from** *C. lutetiana* **in the smaller flowers (petals up to 1.5 mm), which form a cluster at the top of the inflorescence when open. The flowers of** *C. lutetiana* **are distributed along the inflorescence and the petals are 2-4 mm long. The hybrid,** *C.* × *intermedia*, **is intermediate between the parents but the fruits rarely ripen.**

Circaea alpina L.
ALPINE ENCHANTER'S-NIGHTSHADE
Very rare. It is only at all frequent in the Lake District and on the Isle of Arran, with additional scattered localities in Wales, Durham and a single locality on the Scottish mainland in Wester Ross. *C. alpina* is a plant of shaded rocks, stream banks, scree and waterfalls in mountain and upland woodlands. A perennial, it flowers during July and August and is probably pollinated by small flies.

The sterile hybrid between *C. alpina* and *C. lutetiana*, *C.* × *intermedia* Ehrh., has a much more extensive distribution in upland Britain, being widespread in western Scotland and also occurring in Ireland. This would suggest that *C. alpina* was more widespread in earlier post-glacial times and has since contracted its range.

Ludwigia palustris (L.) Elliott*

HAMPSHIRE PURSLANE

Very rare and confined to about 12 localities in the New Forest in Hampshire and to a single locality in Epping Forest in Essex, it grows in shallow pools and streams on acid soils and is often abundant in some of its remaining localities. It formerly occurred in Sussex and in Jersey, where it was last recorded in 1926. An annual or perennial, it flowers during June and is self-pollinated.

❁ **The prostrate habit, deep purplish-red stems and leaves and small flowers without petals prevent confusion of *Ludwigia* with any other species, except perhaps with *Lythrum portula* (Plate 42).**

Many of the WILLOWHERBS, *Epilobium*, look superficially similar and they can give rise to problems of identification, partly because hybrids between several of the species are frequent. If particular attention is paid to the distribution and type of hairs, the shape of the stigma (four-lobed or clubbed) and the leaf base, few difficulties should arise, except in the case of hybrids.

Epilobium hirsutum L.

GREAT WILLOWHERB CODLINS AND CREAM

Widely distributed throughout England, Wales and Ireland but in Scotland more or less restricted to the east coast as far north as Caithness. Rare or absent from the rest of Scotland, Orkney, Shetland and the Western Isles. *E. hirsutum* is a plant of river, stream, lake and pond sides, wet ditches, fens and marshes on fertile, base-rich or calcareous soils. In suitable habitats it is often abundant, forming dense stands. It is intolerant of shading and reaches an altitude of 370 m. A tall perennial, it flowers during July and August and is pollinated by bees and flies.

❁ ***E. hirsutum* and *E. parviflorum* are distinguished from similar-looking species by the dense clothing of spreading hairs on the stems and the four-lobed stigma. *E. hirsutum* is a larger plant than *E. parviflorum*; the petals are deep pink and more than 1 cm long. The petals of *E. parviflorum* are pale pink and less than 1 cm long.**

Epilobium parviflorum Schreb.

HOARY WILLOWHERB SMALL-FLOWERED HAIRY WILLOWHERB

Distributed throughout the British Isles but scarce and local in northern England and Scotland and absent from Shetland. A frequent plant of waste ground on damp soils, stream banks, fens and marshes, reaching an altitude of 370 m. It is perennial, flowering during July and August, and is either pollinated by bees or self-pollinated.

Epilobium montanum L.

BROAD-LEAVED WILLOWHERB

Widespread and abundant throughout the whole of the British Isles. It occurs in woodland, waste ground, walls, hedge banks, ditches and as a garden weed, usually on neutral, base-rich or calcareous soils up to an altitude of 790 m. A perennial, it flowers from June to August and is insect- or self-pollinated.

❁ ***E. montanum* and *E. lanceolatum* differ from other similar species that lack spreading hairs on the stem by the four-lobed, not clubbed, stigmas. *E. montanum* has broader, short, stalked leaves that are all opposite. The leaves of *E. lanceolatum* are narrower and distinctly stalked, and the upper are alternate.**

Epilobium lanceolatum Sebast. & Mauri

SPEAR-LEAVED WILLOWHERB

A plant of southern England and south Wales that has spread significantly in the last 50 years. It was first recorded in 1843, and until 1930 was only known from the area south of the Thames and the Severn estuary but has now been recorded as far north as west Norfolk and also from Ireland. It grows on walls, roadsides, railway banks, waste ground and in dry quarries and gardens. A perennial, it flowers from July to September and is self-pollinated.

Epilobium palustre L.

MARSH WILLOWHERB

Widely distributed throughout the British Isles, but less frequent in parts of the English Midlands. It is a plant of fens, marshes, valley bogs and wet flushes on mildly acid, more often mineral than peat soils. It will tolerate a degree of shading and is often found in acid woodland flushes. It reaches an altitude of 760 m. A perennial, it flowers during July and August.

❁ ***E. palustre* is distinguished by its unridged stems, narrow bluish-green leaves, slender underground stolons and club-shaped stigmas.**

❁ ***E. ciliatum*, *E. obscurum* and *E. tetragonum* have raised lines or ridges running down the stems from the leaf bases and club-shaped stigmas.**

Epilobium ciliatum Rafin.
(*E. adenocaulon* Hausskn.)

AMERICAN WILLOWHERB

Alien and a native of North America. It was first recorded in Britain from near Leicester in 1891, but did not attract much attention until it was recorded from Surrey in 1932. Since that time it has spread dramatically throughout lowland England, with records from Wales, the south-west and as far north as Angus. In many places it is now a common plant of waste ground, walls, banks, roadsides, gardens, stream sides and damp woodland. A perennial, it flowers from June to August and is self-pollinated.

❁ ***E. ciliatum* is distinguished by the upper part of the stem having numerous spreading, glistening, glandular hairs.**

Epilobium obscurum Schreb.

SHORT-FRUITED WILLOWHERB

Distributed throughout the British Isles but absent from Shetland. It is a frequent plant of moist woodlands, stream sides, ditches and marshes on mildly acid to neutral, mineral soils. A perennial, it flowers during July and August and is self-pollinated.

❁ ***E. obscurum* differs from *E. ciliatum* in the absence of glandular hairs on the stem (although they may be present on the calyx tube) and from *E. tetragonum* in the less prominent stem ridges and shorter capsule (4-6 cm).**

❁ ***E. tetragonum* differs from *E. obscurum* in the square stem, total absence of glandular hairs and longer capsule (7-10 cm).**

Epilobium tetragonum L.

SQUARE-STALKED WILLOWHERB

A lowland species of England and Wales extending as far north as Yorkshire and virtually absent from Scotland and Ireland. It occurs in hedge banks, roadsides, ditch and stream sides, damp woodland clearings and waste and cultivated ground on damp soil. A perennial, it flowers during July and August and is self-pollinated.

E. tetragonum is represented in Britain by two subspecies; subsp. *tetragonum* and subsp. *lamyi* (F. Schultz) Léveillé. The former is widespread, while subsp. *lamyi* is more or less confined to eastern and south-east England.

Epilobium roseum Schreb.

PALE WILLOWHERB SMALL-FLOWERED WILLOWHERB

A local species, scattered throughout the English and Welsh lowlands but rare in Scotland and Ireland and absent from Orkney, Shetland and the Western Isles. It is a plant of waste ground on damp soils, gardens and moist woodland, copses and hedgerows. A perennial, it flowers during July and August.

❁ ***E. roseum* is distinguished by its club-shaped stigma, distinctly stalked leaves and very pale flowers.**

Epilobium anagallidifolium Lam.

ALPINE WILLOWHERB

Widespread in the Scottish Highlands and with isolated localities in north-west Yorkshire, Durham and Cumbria. It is typically a plant of mossy mountain stream sides, springs and flushes on either acid or base-rich soils, usually at moderate altitudes, although it reaches 1,220 m in the Cairngorms. A small perennial herb, it flowers during July and August and is self-pollinated.

❁ ***E. anagallidifolium* and *E. alsinifolium* are both small species with prostrate as well as erect stems. *E. anagallidifolium* has very slender stems, yellow-green leaves and above-ground stolons, and the flowers are up to 5 mm in diameter. *E. alsinifolium* has thicker stems, broader, blue-green leaves and underground stolons, and the flowers are 8 mm or more in diameter.**

Epilobium alsinifolium Vill.

CHICKWEED WILLOWHERB

Widespread in the Scottish Highlands and also in the Lake District and the northern Pennines and with a single locality in Ireland on the Ben Bulben range in Leitrim. Like *E. anagallidifolium*, *E. alsinifolium* is a plant of mossy mountain flushes, springs and stream sides but more usually on base-rich soils, from 125 m to 1,100 m. A small perennial herb, it flowers during July and August and is self-pollinated.

Epilobium brunnescens (Cockayne) Raven & Engelhorn
(*E. nerteroides* auct.)

NEW ZEALAND WILLOWHERB

Alien and a native of New Zealand. Probably introduced as a rock garden plant and also with other cultivated New Zealand plants. The first record appears to be for 1904 in Edinburgh. It is now widespread at high altitudes in the wetter parts of British Isles where it is rapidly spreading in well-drained habitats on grits, shales, gravel and shingle derived from a range of parent rocks. It has also been found on damp walls, in quarries, gravel pits and on ballast heaps. Outside the north and west it is restricted to a few isolated occurrences in the south-east. A prostrate perennial, it flowers during June and July and is self-pollinated.

❁ ***E. brunnescens* is readily recognised by the wholly prostrate stems and almost circular leaves.**

Chamerion angustifolium (L.) J. Holub
(*Chamaenerion angustifolium* L.)

ROSEBAY WILLOWHERB

Widespread and common throughout Great Britain but becoming less common and local in north-west Scotland and scarce in Ireland. It frequently forms dense stands in such recently disturbed conditions as fire sites, felled woodlands, derelict buildings and waste ground on a variety of soils from dune sands to organic peats, but grows best on the more fertile soils. It tolerates a wide range of soil acidity but avoids waterlogged sites. A tall perennial, it flowers from June to September and is pollinated by bees and moths.

❁ ***Chamerion* grows to over 1 m and is distinguished from *Epilobium* by the spirally arranged leaves.**

HALORAGACEAE

❁ *Myriophyllum*, WATER-MILFOIL, is superficially rather similar to *Ceratophyllum* (Plate 4), but the pinnate leaves and terminal spike-like inflorescence are quite different.

Myriophyllum verticillatum L.
WHORLED WATER-MILFOIL
Scattered throughout lowland Britain and Ireland but absent from Scotland, Wales and the south-west. It is a rapidly declining species of ponds, canals and dykes growing in depths of up to 1 m. It prefers fertile, base-rich, unpolluted waters and is tolerant of slightly brackish conditions. A perennial, it flowers during July and August and is wind-pollinated. It overwinters by means of detachable vegetative buds, 'turions', which are produced in the autumn and sink to the bottom to develop in the following spring.

❁ *M. verticillatum* differs from both *M. alterniflorum* and *M. spicatum* in the leaves being five in a whorl.

Myriophyllum spicatum L.
SPIKED WATER-MILFOIL
Distributed throughout the British Isles but most frequent in the English lowlands. It is found in both still and running water including ponds, lakes, ditches and streams. It grows in up to 2 m of water, preferring clear, calcium-rich conditions. A perennial, it flowers during June and July and is wind-pollinated.

❁ Both *M. alterniflorum* and *M. spicatum* have their leaves in whorls of four. *M. alterniflorum* has 6-18 segments to the leaf and a short drooping spike: *M. spicatum* has leaves of 13-35 segments and an erect spike.

Myriophyllum alterniflorum DC.
ALTERNATE WATER-MILFOIL
Widely distributed in upland areas of the British Isles to altitudes of 720 m, local and decreasing in the lowlands. It is found in lakes, ponds, streams and dykes in depths of up to 2 m in acid, nutrient-deficient or peaty waters. A perennial, it flowers from May to August and is wind-pollinated.

Myriophyllum aquaticum (Vell. Conc.) Verde.
PARROT'S-FEATHER
A native of South America, it is now rapidly establishing itself across southern Britain from aquarists' throw-outs.
❁ The leaves are five in a whorl, but it differs from *M. verticillatum* in the densely glandular emergent leaves. (Not illustrated.)

HIPPURIDACEAE

❁ *Hippuris* is distinguished from both *Ceratophyllum* (Plate 4) and *Myriophyllum* by the entire leaves arranged in whorls of eight or more.

Hippuris vulgaris L.
MARE'S-TAIL
Distributed throughout the British Isles, but less frequent in western Scotland, Wales and the south-west. It is found in the shallow, nutrient-rich waters of lowland lakes, ponds, slow-moving streams and dykes. It is most frequent in calcium-rich waters and ascends to 550 m in Scotland. It occasionally grows on bare mud. A perennial, it flowers during June and July and is wind-pollinated.

VISCACEAE (= LORANTHACEAE)

Viscum album L.
MISTLETOE
Mistletoe is found throughout most of England and Wales as far north as the Humber. It is rare in the south-west and western Wales and absent from Scotland and Ireland. It is particularly characteristic of the counties around the Severn: Hereford, Gloucestershire and Worcestershire. A woody evergreen, it is parasitic on a wide variety of deciduous trees, but rarely on evergreens. Its most common host is apple and, contrary to legend, it is only rarely found on oak – no doubt heightening its significance in druidic ritual. The flowers are unisexual and the plant is normally dioecious, with male and female flowers on separate plants. It flowers from February to March and the familiar berries ripen in November and December. Pagan European folklore invested mistletoe with a wealth of magical properties, many of which became incorporated into Christian traditions.

SANTALACEAE

Thesium humifusum DC.
BASTARD-TOADFLAX
Confined to calcareous soils in southern England, found on the chalk of the North and South Downs, Hampshire, Dorset and Salisbury Plain. A rare and decreasing species of the Gloucestershire Cotswolds, it reaches as far north as the East Anglian chalk and south Lincolnshire. It grows in short fescue-bent-dominated turf on dry, thin calcareous soils, usually on south- or west-facing slopes. *Thesium* is a partial parasite on the roots of other chalk herbs. A perennial, it flowers from June to August.
❁ *Thesium* is only likely to be confused with some members of the Caryophyllaceae; it differs in the alternate leaves and single perianth whorl.

ARALIACEAE

Hedera helix L.
IVY
Ivy is an abundant plant throughout the British Isles, except for parts of the Scottish Highlands. An evergreen, woody climber, it attaches itself to trees, walls and rocks by means of 'adhesive' roots. It is found in woods, hedgerows, cliffs and gardens on all but the most waterlogged and most acid soils. It is very shade-tolerant and reaches altitudes of about 610 m. It flowers in the late autumn from September to November and is pollinated by flies and wasps. The plant known as the 'Irish Ivy', *Hedera helix* subsp. *hibernica*, may turn out to be a separate species. It is neither confined to nor especially frequent in Ireland.

CALLITRICHACEAE

Callitriche
WATER STARWORT
The water starworts are a difficult group to identify, and all except *C. hermaphroditica* and *C. truncata* can produce terrestrial, mud-inhabiting forms. Many can behave either as annuals or perennials, depending upon local conditions, and the distribution and ecology of most British species is still incompletely known.
❁ Reliable identification is only possible with the aid of the fruits, vegetative characters alone rarely being sufficient to name the plants with certainty. Detailed keys for the identification of the British species can be found in *New Flora of the British Isles* **and in** *British Water Plants.*

Callitriche hermaphroditica L.
AUTUMNAL WATER-STARWORT
A local species of northern Britain extending as far south as Worcestershire and ascending to 380 m. it grows in depths of up to 1 m in ponds, lakes, streams and canals where the water is moderately fertile. It flowers from May to September.
❁ *C. hermaphroditica* always grows entirely submerged, with no floating leaves; the leaves are yellow-green, translucent, up to 2 cm long and taper gradually from the base to the deeply-notched tip.

Callitriche truncata Guss.
SHORT-LEAVED WATER-STARWORT
A very local species confined to a few localities in Devon, Somerset, Kent, Essex, Nottinghamshire, Leicestershire and Lincolnshire. It occurs in pools and ditches on fertile soils. It flowers from May to September and is water-pollinated.
❁ *C. truncata* always grows entirely submerged with no floating leaves. It differs from *C. hermaphroditica* in the shorter (up to 1 cm) parallel-sided leaves, which are a characteristic translucent deep blue-green colour.

Callitriche stagnalis Scop.
COMMON WATER-STARWORT
Widespread throughout the whole of the British Isles, found in both still and fast-moving clear, fertile, often calcium-rich waters, to an altitude of 915 m. It grows in depths of up to 1 m in pools and in woodland rides. An annual or perennial, it flowers from May to September and is wind-pollinated.

❁ *C. stagnalis* and *C. platycarpa* both differ from *C. obtusangula* in having winged fruits. *C. stagnalis* also differs from *C. obtusangula* in the rounded, not angular, floating leaves and smaller stamens (c. 2 mm) and styles (2-3 mm), and from *C. platycarpa* in the paler green leaves and submerged leaves that are not parallel-sided.

Callitriche platycarpa Kütz.
VARIOUS-LEAVED WATER-STARWORT
LONG-STYLED WATER-STARWORT
A local species of lowland Britain, but its distribution is not fully known. It grows in both still and flowing, usually shallow, base-rich water, including small pools, dykes, streams and ditches. A perennial, it flowers from April to October and is wind-pollinated.
❁ *C. platycarpa* differs from *C. stagnalis* in the darker green leaves, narrower floating leaves, almost parallel-sided submerged leaves, and narrower wing to the fruit.

Callitriche obtusangula Le Gall
BLUNT-FRUITED WATER-STARWORT
Widely distributed in lowland Britain but apparently absent form Scotland. It occurs in ponds, ditches, dykes and streams in depths up to 1 m where the water is clear, fertile or calcium-rich. It will also tolerate mildly brackish conditions. It flowers from May to September and is wind-pollinated.
❁ *C. obtusangula* differs from *C. stagnalis* and *C. platycarpa* in the angular rhomboidal floating leaves and round, unwinged fruit, which is about 1.5 mm wide. The stamens are 5 mm or more and the styles 4-7 mm.

Callitriche palustris L.
Only once definitely recorded as British (in 1877), but has a wide distribution in Europe and may well occur. It grows in shallow, still water. (Not illustrated.)
❁ *C. palustris* is similar to *C. stagnalis* and *C. platycarpa,* from which it differs in only the upper part of the fruit being winged.

continued on next page

Callitriche hamulata Kütz. ex Koch (*C. intermedia* Hoffm.)
INTERMEDIATE WATER-STARWORT
Widespread throughout the British Isles and frequent in the south-east. It is found in cool, clear, acid, nutrient-poor ponds, lakes and streams on hard rocks, ascending to 990 m in Scotland. A perennial, it flowers from April to September and is water-pollinated.
❁ **The submerged leaves of *C. hamulata* are narrow with an abruptly expanded spanner-shaped tip. The flowers are submerged and the fruits are almost round, black, narrowly winged and 1.3-1.4 mm wide.**

❁ ***C. brutia* is similar to *C. hamulata*, from which it differs in the asymmetric leaf-tips and smaller fruits (1-14 mm) which in terrestrial forms is distinctly stalked.**

Callitriche brutia Petagna (*C. intermedia* ssp. *pedunculata* (DC.) Clapham)
PEDUNCULATE WATER-STARWORT
A local and decreasing species with a scattered distribution in Britain. It is found in the shallow water of still or slow-moving lakes, pools, ditches, dykes and streams. (Not illustrated.)

Hydrocotyle vulgaris L.
MARSH PENNYWORT
(Described in text for Plate 45.)

PLATE 45
CORNACEAE • APIACEAE (= UMBELLIFERAE)
(see illustrations page 100)

CORNACEAE

Cornus sanguinea L. (*Thelycrania sanguinea* (L.) Fourr.)
DOGWOOD
Dogwood has a markedly southern distribution in Britain, occurring as far north as Yorkshire but absent from most of Wales and the south-west. In Ireland it is known from only a few isolated localities. A common plant of scrub, woodland and hedgerows on calcareous or base-rich soils, it is frequently the dominant constituent of chalk downland scrub in areas of abandoned arable. A deciduous shrub of up to 4 m, it flowers during June and July and is pollinated by various insects.

Cornus suecica L. (*Chamaepericlymenum suecicum* (L.) Aschers & Graebn.)
DWARF CORNEL
A frequent plant of the Scottish Highlands but very rare and local in England, occurring only in isolated localities in Lancashire, Yorkshire and Northumberland. It is absent from Wales and Ireland. It grows among bilberry, heather and mosses on mountain moorland on moist, acid soils to an altitude of 915 m. It will also grow in light shade. A perennial herb growing to about 20 cm, it flowers during July and August.

APIACEAE (= UMBELLIFERAE)

The **UMBELLIFERS** are a large and notoriously confusing family of plants. Hairiness, the shape and lobing of the leaves, whether the stem is hollow, and the number of bracts and bracteoles are particularly important in identification. Detailed keys and descriptions of the British species can be found in *New Flora of the British Isles* or *Umbellifers of the British Isles*.

Hydrocotyle vulgaris L.
MARSH PENNYWORT
Widely distributed throughout the British Isles. It is a frequent plant of bogs, fens, marshes and ponds and stream margins on neutral to acid soils to an altitude of 380 m. It is tolerant of light shade and is a characteristic plant of acid woodland flushes. A perennial, it flowers from June to August and is self-pollinated. (Illustrated on Plate 44.)

Sanicula europaea L.
SANICLE
Distributed throughout the British Isles, but rare in northern and eastern Scotland and rather sparse in Ireland. It is typically a plant of deciduous woodlands on calcareous and base-rich soils and is a characteristic species of the ground flora of beech and ash woodland on chalk and limestone and of oak woodlands on fertile loams. It is very shade-tolerant. A perennial, it flowers from May to August and is pollinated by various small insects or is self-pollinated.

Astrantia major L.
ASTRANTIA
Alien and a native of southern and central Europe east to the Caucasus. *Astrantia* is naturalised in a few localities in northern and western Britain in meadows, woodland clearings and wood margins. A perennial, it flowers from May to July and is pollinated principally by beetles.

❁ ***Astrantia* differs from *Sanicula* in the large bracts forming an involucre around the umbels.**

❁ ***Eryngium* is the only genus of spiny-leaved umbellifers. *E. maritimum* is glaucous with broad bracts. *E. campestre* is green with linear bracts.**

Eryngium maritimum L.
SEA-HOLLY
Distributed all around the coast of Britain as far north as Flamborough Head on the east and Barra on the west. It occurs all around the Irish coast and is typically a plant of coastal sand dunes, growing from just above the high water mark of spring tides. Less often, it is to be found growing on fine shingle. A perennial, it flowers from June to September.

Eryngium campestre L.**
FIELD ERYNGO
Very rare. It was formerly native or long-established in a number of localities in southern England, but is now confined to a few localities in Cornwall, Devon, Hampshire, Kent and Guernsey. It grows in dry, rough grassland usually near the coast and flowers during July and August.

Chaerophyllum temulum L. (*C. temulentum* L.)
ROUGH CHERVIL
Widely distributed throughout England and Wales but in Scotland more or less confined to the east as far north as the Moray Firth. Very local and scattered in Ireland. It is a plant of roadsides, hedge banks and rough grassland usually on dry, well-drained neutral or calcareous soils. A biennial, it flowers during June and July after *Anthriscus sylvestris* and usually before *Torilis japonica*.
❁ ***C. temulum* is a hairy plant and differs from *Anthriscus* in the solid, purple-spotted stems. The fruits are about 5 mm long.**

Chaerophyllum aureum L.
GOLDEN CHERVIL
Alien and a native of central and eastern Europe and Persia. It is naturalised in meadows and rough grassland in a few places in southern Scotland, such as near Callander, and in southern England. A perennial, it flowers during June and July.

❁ ***C. aureum* is rather similar to *Anthriscus sylvestris* but has a solid, slightly purple-spotted stem. It differs from *C. temulum* in the yellow-green leaves and longer fruits (about 12 mm).**

❁ ***Anthriscus* is hairy at least on the leaves, and differs from similar-looking umbellifers, except for *Myrrhis* (Plate 46), in the hollow stems. It differs from *Myrrhis* in not being aromatic.**

Anthriscus sylvestris (L.) Hoffm.
COW PARSLEY
Widely distributed and common throughout the whole of the British Isles except for parts of northern and north-west Scotland. It is almost exclusively a plant of hedgerows, roadsides and wood borders and is the commonest early-flowering umbellifer throughout most of Britain. An annual to perennial, it flowers from April to June and is pollinated by a wide variety of short-tongued insects.
❁ ***A. sylvestris* differs from *Torilis japonica* in having hollow stems and from *A. caucalis* in the hairy stems.**

Anthriscus caucalis M. Bieb.
BUR CHERVIL
BUR PARSLEY
Frequent in parts of East Anglia and Bedfordshire but local and scattered elsewhere and almost absent from Western Scotland, Orkney, Shetland and the Western Isles. It grows in hedge banks, rough grassland and waste ground on dry, well-drained soils and in sandy ground near the sea. An annual, it flowers during May and June. The British plant is var. *caucalis*.
❁ ***A. caucalis* differs from *A. sylvestris* in having glabrous, not pubescent, stems.**

Scandix pecten-veneris L.
SHEPHERD'S-NEEDLE
Until quite recently, widespread and rather common in eastern and southern England as far west as Wiltshire. It is a weed of arable land, especially on dry calcareous soils, but modern herbicides and stubble-burning have now reduced it to the status of a rather rare and local plant. An annual, it flowers from April to July.
❁ ***Scandix* is distinguished by the characteristic fruits that give it its Latin and vernacular names.**

❁ ***Torilis* has solid, unspotted stems with short, appressed downward-pointing hairs. *T. japonica* has 5-12 rayed umbels and several bracts. *T. arvensis* has 3-5 rayed umbels and 0-1 bracts.**

Torilis japonica (Houtt.) DC.
UPRIGHT HEDGE-PARSLEY
Distributed throughout the British Isles except for parts of northern and western Scotland and south-west Ireland. It is a common plant of hedgerows, roadsides, wood borders and rough grassland, especially on light dry soils. An autumn- and spring-germinating annual, it is the most frequent wayside umbellifer to flower in July and August, following *Chaerophyllum temulentum*.

Torilis arvensis(Hudson) Link
SPREADING HEDGE-PARSLEY
A local and decreasing species; a rare casual south and east of a line from the Humber to the Severn. It is a weed of arable fields on dry, often calcareous, soils. It may have been introduced to Britain with imported seed. An autumn- and spring-germinating annual, it flowers from July to September.

Torilis nodosa (L.) Gaertner
KNOTTED HEDGE-PARSLEY
A local species of eastern and southern England with scattered localities north to southern Scotland and in Ireland. It grows around the margins of arable fields, on road sides, banks and in open patches in rough grassland on dry, well-drained soils. An annual, it flowers May to July.
❁ ***T. nodosa* is distinguished from both *T. japonica* and *T. arvensis* by the sessile umbels.**

APIACEAE (= UMBELLIFERAE) *(see illustrations page 102)*

Myrrhis odorata (L.) Scop.
SWEET CICELY
Alien and a native of the Pyrenees, Alps, Apennines and the mountains of the western side of the Balkan Peninsula. It is thoroughly established in Britain from Montgomeryshire and Staffordshire northwards, but is rare or absent from much of western and north-west Scotland, and in Ireland is of scattered occurrence in the north only. It is a common plant of roadsides, hedge banks, wood borders and of grassy places near buildings. A perennial, it flowers during May and June. It was once commonly cultivated as a pot-herb for flavouring.
❁ ***M. odorata* is distinguished from similar-looking hollow-stemmed umbellifers by the strong, characteristic, aniseed-like scent of the whole plant. It is a tall plant growing to 1 m.**

Smyrnium olusatrum L.
ALEXANDERS
Alien. In the British Isles it generally grows within 20 km of the coast, being a frequent plant as far north as north Wales and north Norfolk, the Isle of Man and the east coast of Ireland. Elsewhere and inland it is an infrequent local species and is absent from northern and western Scotland. It is thoroughly established on roadsides, hedgerows, cliffs and rough grassland. A biennial, it flowers from April to June. It was once commonly cultivated as a pot-herb, the young stems tasting rather like celery.
❁ ***Smyrnium* is a large, robust, glabrous plant growing to 150 cm with dark, shiny green leaves. *Pastinaca* (Plate 49) also has yellow flowers, but the plant is hairy.**

❁ ***Bupleurum* is distinguished from other umbellifers by its entire leaves. *B. rotundifolium* differs from *B. subovatum* in the broader leaves and 5-10 rays to the umbels. *B. subovatum* has 2/3-rayed umbels.**

Bupleurum rotundifolium L.*
THOROW-WAX
Alien and a native of most of central and southern Europe; now very rare and probably extinct. At the beginning of the century it was still a frequent plant of lowland Britain south and east of a line from the Severn to the Tees. A cornfield weed of light, well-drained, both mildly acid and calcareous soils, it is one of the many species that suffered from the advent of cleaner seed corn in the 1920s and more recently of selective herbicides. Since 1960 it has only been recorded from Devon, Wiltshire, Norfolk and Scotland. Many of the more recent records have turned out to be of *B. subovatum*. An annual, it flowers during June and July.

Bupleurum subovatum Link ex Spreng.
(*B. lancifolium* auct.)
FALSE THOROW-WAX
Alien and a native of southern Europe from Portugal to Turkey and of central Asia and north-west Africa. It appears as an ever-increasing casual of gardens and waste ground throughout Britain, being introduced in wild bird food and chicken feed. An annual, it flowers from June to October. It is frequently mistaken for *B. rotundifolium.*

Bupleurum baldense Turra**
SMALL HARE'S-EAR
Very rare and now confined in England to the area around Beachy Head in Sussex and Berry Head in south Devon. It is also still found on Jersey, Guernsey and Alderney. It grows in the dry, open, broken turf of cliff tops and sand dunes close to the sea. A tiny annual, it flowers during June and July.
❁ ***B. baldense* is seldom more than a few centimetres tall, with ovate bracteoles.**

Bupleurum tenuissimum L.
SLENDER HARE'S-EAR
A local plant of the coasts of southern and eastern Britain as far north as the Tees on the east and the north shore of the Bristol Channel on the west. It is a plant of the rough grassland found at the upper levels of salt marshes and behind shingle ridges on usually dry but saline soils. An annual, it flowers from July to September.
❁ ***B. tenuissimum* is a wiry annual, growing to about 50 cm, with awl-shaped bracteoles.**

Bupleurum falcatum L.**
SICKLE-LEAVED HARE'S-EAR
Very rare and confined to a single site in Essex. It was first discovered in Essex in 1831, growing along several miles of roadside between Ongar and Chelmsford. The last remaining population was destroyed by hedgerow clearing and ditch cleaning in 1962, but seed from this site was collected and has now established a population on a nature reserve of the Essex Naturalists' Trust. A perennial, it flowers from July to October.

Physospermum cornubiense (L.) DC.*
BLADDERSEED
A very local species, confined to east Cornwall and south Devon and to a single locality in Buckinghamshire, where it is probably not native. It is found in scrub, open woodland, hedge banks and cornfields and in some of its localities it can be quite abundant. A perennial, it flowers during July and August.
❁ ***Physospermum* is distinguished by the ribbed glabrous stem, long stalked leaves with stalked segments, and umbels with long rays and bracts and bracteoles. It grows to 30-75 cm.**

Conium maculatum L.
HEMLOCK
Distributed throughout the British Isles and often abundant in the south, but becoming increasingly coastal northwards and in Wales. Scattered and rather local in Ireland, it is a plant of damp waste ground, river, stream and canal banks, sea walls and roadsides, usually on fertile, heavy soils. Hemlock is well known as the poison administered to Socrates. All parts of the plant are highly toxic due to the presence of several polyacetylenes, the most important of which is coniine. It acts by paralysing the respiratory nerves so that the victim dies of suffocation. A biennial, it flowers during June and July.
❁ **A tall, robust plant growing up to 2 m, *Conium* is easily recognised by the glabrous, purple-spotted stems and its unpleasant smell.**

Apium graveolens L.
WILD CELERY
Occurs in coastal areas all round Britain as far north as Northumberland on the east and the Solway on the west. Inland it is a scarce and local plant of England south of the Wash, and in Ireland it is an infrequent species of coastal areas only. It is a plant of river, stream, ditch and dyke sides on fertile, base-rich, often brackish soils. A biennial, it flowers from June to August. Cultivated celery is the var. *dulce* (Miller) DC. and celeriac the var. *rapaceum* (Miller) DC.
❁ ***A. graveolens* smells strongly of celery and differs from *A. nodiflorum* in the heavily grooved stems, shape of the leaflets of the basal leaves and the absence of bracteoles.**

Apium nodiflorum (L.) Lag.
FOOL'S WATER-CRESS
Widely distributed throughout England, Wales and Ireland, but getting scarcer northwards and very rare in Scotland and the Outer Hebrides and absent from Orkney and Shetland. It is an abundant and often dominant plant of shallow, nutrient-rich or calcareous dykes, ditches, streams and ponds on fine-textured soils. A perennial, it flowers during July and August.
❁ ***A. nodiflorum* is easily confused with *Berula erecta* (Plate 48), from which it can be distinguished by the absence of bracts and the absence of a septum across the base of the leaf stalk.**

❁ ***A. repens* is distinguished from *A. nodiflorum* by the creeping stem, rooting at the nodes, and the long peduncles, longer than the rays.**

Apium repens (Jacq.) Lag.**
CREEPING MARSHWORT
Very rare and known from only a few localities in Oxfordshire. It is found in old wet meadows, dykes, ditches and shallow ponds. An apparent hybrid with *A. nodiflorum* occurs in a few scattered localities in eastern England and Scotland. A perennial, it flowers during July.

Apium inundatum (L.) Reichb. f.
LESSER MARSHWORT
A local and decreasing plant scattered throughout the British Isles and rare on the Scottish mainland. It grows in the still or slow-moving water of acid or nutrient-poor pools, ponds, lakes, ditches and streams, in shallow sheltered conditions. A submerged or floating perennial, it flowers from June to August.
❁ ***A. inundatum* is distinguished by the finely divided, submerged leaves.**

Petroselinum crispum (Miller) A.W. Hill
GARDEN PARSLEY
The geographical origins of parsley have become obscured by centuries of cultivation and by becoming naturalised in the wild. It is probably a native of south-east Europe. It occurs scattered throughout England, Wales and Ireland as an escape from cultivation in waste places and on rocks and walls, but is very rare in Scotland. A biennial, it flowers from June to August.
❁ ***P. crispum* has a glabrous solid stem. The yellowish flowers will distinguish it from similar species.**

Petroselinum segetum (L.) Koch*
CORN PARSLEY
CORN CARAWAY
A local and decreasing plant of lowland Britain occurring south and east of a line from the Humber to the Severn and in Pembrokeshire, most frequent around the Thames estuary. It grows in brackish grassland, arable fields, river banks, hedgerows and roadsides on fertile or calcareous soils. An annual or biennial, it flowers during August and September.
❁ ***P. segetum* is easily confused with *Sison amomum* (Plate 47). The bracts of *P. segetum* are at least half as long as the shortest rays, while those of *Sison* are shorter. The best way of distinguishing the two is probably by the unpleasant petrol-like smell of *Sison*.**

Sison amomum L.
STONE PARSLEY
Restricted in Britain to the area south and east of a line from the Humber to the Severn and to the coast of north Wales. It is locally frequent in hedgerows and on grassy banks and roadside verges, often on heavy soils. The crushed leaves have an unpleasant smell, resembling that of petrol. A biennial, it flowers from July to September.
❁ ***Sison* is very similar to *Petroselinum segetum* (Plate 46). The bracts are usually less than half as long as the shortest rays, but the best way of distinguishing it is by the smell of the crushed leaves.**

Trinia glauca (L.) Dumort.*
HONEWORT
Very rare and confined to 10 localities on the Devonian limestone in south Devon and on Carboniferous limestone in Gloucestershire and Somerset. It grows in short, dry, limestone grassland, and in some of its localities it is reasonably abundant. A short (up to 20 cm) biennial or perennial, it flowers during May and June and is dioecious, with male and female flowers on separate plants.
❁ **The deeply grooved stem, branched from the base, and the dead remains of the old leaf stalks attached to the base of the plant are characteristic of *Trinia*.**

Cicuta virosa L.
COWBANE
Very local and more or less restricted to the Norfolk Broads, the Shropshire and Cheshire meres, southern Scotland north to Angus, Ulster and the north of the Republic of Ireland and with single localities in Staffordshire and West Sussex. *Cicuta* grows in the shallow water of marshes, pond margins, ditches and drainage dykes. It is also slightly shade-tolerant and can be found growing in open carr woodland. A perennial, it flowers during July and August. Cowbane is extremely poisonous due to a resinous substance, cicutoxin, which occurs in the yellow juice of the roots and in the stems.
❁ ***Cicuta* is a tall, robust plant growing to more than 1 m and is only likely to be confused with *Sium latifolium* (Plate 48), which has simply pinnate leaves.**

Falcaria vulgaris Bernh.
LONGLEAF
Alien and a native of central and southern Europe and western Asia. It occasionally turns up as a casual in East Anglia, south-east England and the Channel Islands. An annual, biennial or perennial, it flowers from July to September.
❁ ***Falcaria* grows to 30-50 cm and the leaves are quite distinctive.**

Carum carvi L.
CARAWAY
Alien and a native of northern and central Europe, temperate Asia and Morocco, it occurs throughout the British Isles north to Shetland as a naturalised but decreasing plant of waste places. A biennial, it flowers during June and July. It is widely cultivated as a pot-herb. The dried fruits are used for flavouring and commercially to flavour the liqueur kümmel.
❁ ***C. carvi* is glabrous, bracts and bracteoles are few or absent, and the basal leaves are finely segmented and persistent.**

Carum verticillatum (L.) Koch
WHORLED CARAWAY
A local plant of western Scotland north to Argyll, the Isle of Man, Wales, Devon and Cornwall, northern and south-west Ireland and isolated localities in Dorset, Surrey and Aberdeen. It is found in wet meadows, marshes and by streams on acid soils. A perennial, it flowers during July and August.
❁ **No other British umbellifer has leaves similar to *C. verticillatum*.**

Bunium bulbocastanum L.*
GREAT PIGNUT
Very local and confined to the chalk of Hertfordshire, Bedfordshire, Buckinghamshire and Cambridgeshire. It grows in dry, rough, calcareous grassland, on grassy banks and arable in about 30 separate localities. A perennial, it flowers during June and July. The distribution of the species in Britain is something of a puzzle; it occurs frequently on the chalk in northern France, so its absence from the chalk south of the Thames is rather surprising.
❁ ***Bunium* is rather similar to *Conopodium* (Plate 48), the stem leaves soon withering, but the stem is solid after flowering.**

❁ **The *Oenanthes* are all glabrous aquatic or marsh plants, with many bracteoles.**

❁ ***O. lachenalii, O. pimpinelloides* and *O. silaifolia* are all rather similar, growing to a height of about 80 cm. *O. silaifolia* differs in the lack of bracts and in the linear lobes of the lower leaves.**

Oenanthe lachenalii C. Gmelin
PARSLEY WATER-DROPWORT
Scattered throughout the British Isles north to the Clyde and North Uist, but in Scotland, Ireland, Wales and the south-west it is almost exclusively coastal. It is found in marshes, wet meadows and fens on fine-textured, fertile, often brackish soils. A perennial, it is in flower from June to September.

❁ **Both *O. lachenalii* and *O. pimpinelloides* have bracts. In *O. pimpinelloides* the rays and pedicel become thickened in fruit and the umbels flat-topped. The styles are about as long as the fruit (3.5 mm.**
The umbels of *O. lachenalii* are not flat-topped in fruit and the styles are as long as the fruit (2.5-3.5 mm), or shorter.

Oenanthe pimpinelloides L.
CORKY-FRUITED WATER-DROPWORT
A local species more or less confined to the counties of Devon, Dorset, Somerset and Hampshire with isolated localities in Cornwall, Gloucestershire, Sussex, Surrey and Kent. It is primarily a plant of old damp meadows and other damp grassy habitats on fertile soils, but has recently colonised new road banks. A perennial, it flowers during June and July.

Oenanthe silaifolia M. Bieb.
NARROW-LEAVED WATER-DROPWORT
A rare and decreasing species scattered throughout an area south and east of a line from the Humber to the Severn as far west as Worcestershire. It is a plant of old wet meadows on rich fertile soils bordering rivers. A perennial, it flowers in May and June.

Oenanthe fistulosa L.
TUBULAR WATER-DROPWORT
Widely distributed throughout England but rarer in the south-west, Wales and Scotland and rather scattered in Ireland. It is a rather local plant of the shallow water and the margins of drainage dykes, ditches, ponds and canals on fine-textured, usually fertile soils. A perennial, it flowers from July to September.
❁ ***O. fistulosa* grows to about 50 cm and is distinguished from other species by the long, hollow petioles that are longer than the pinnate part of the leaves.**

Oenanthe crocata L.
HEMLOCK WATER-DROPWORT
Widely distributed throughout southern and western Britain and in northern and southern Ireland but scarce in the English Midlands, eastern Britain, northern Scotland and central Ireland. It is a frequent plant of wet ditches, stream, river and lake margins and wet woodlands, usually on acid soils. A perennial, it flowers during June and July. The plant is extremely toxic, containing a convulsant poison, oenanthetoxin. All parts of the plant, especially the tubers, are dangerous.

❁ ***O. crocata* is a robust plant growing to over 1 m. It differs from other species in the broad lobes to the upper leaves combined with the presence of bracts.**

Oenanthe fluviatilis (Bab) Coleman
RIVER WATER-DROPWORT
A local species, scattered throughout lowland England south and east of a line from the Wash to the Severn, but absent from the south-west and rare in Ireland. It is a plant of ponds and slow-flowing rivers and streams on fertile calcareous soils where the water is clear, growing in depths of up to 1 m. A perennial, it flowers from July to September.

❁ ***O. aquatica* and *O. fluviatilis* are similar. The fruits of *O. aquatica* are 3-4.5 mm, and if submerged leaves are present they have very fine segments. The fruits of *O. fluviatilis* are 5-6 mm and segments of the submerged leaves are narrowly wedge-shaped.**

Oenanthe aquatica (L.) Poir.
FINE-LEAVED WATER-DROPWORT
Distributed throughout England as far west as the Somerset Levels, but absent from most of Wales and from Scotland except for the extreme south-east and scattered throughout central Ireland. It is found in the shallow water of ponds and slow-moving ditches and dykes on fine-textured, fertile soils. It frequently grows on wet ground, or in situations that dry out during the summer. An annual or biennial, it flowers from June to September.

APIACEAE (= UMBELLIFERAE) *(see illustrations page 106)*

Conopodium majus (Gouan) Loret

PIGNUT

Distributed throughout the whole of the British Isles, but scarce in the fens of East Anglia, the Outer Hebrides and central Ireland. It is a plant of open woodlands, rough grassland, grass heaths, commons and hedge banks on well-drained, mildly acid soils. The stems arise from a rounded subterranean tuber which is edible raw or cooked and is described as having a pleasant nutty flavour. A perennial, it flowers during May and June.

❁ *Conopodium* **grows to about 50 cm, is glabrous and the basal leaves soon wither. It is very similar to** *Bunium* **(Plate 47) but the stems are hollow after flowering, not solid.**

❁ **All or most of the leaves of** *Pimpinella* **are pinnate and the plants lack both bracts and bracteoles.** *P. saxifraga* **grows to about 75 cm, the stem has very small, soft hairs and is slightly ridged, and the lower stem leaves are usually twice pinnate.** *P. major* **is larger (up to more than 1 m tall), has glabrous prominently ridged stems, and all the leaves are simply pinnate.**

Pimpinella saxifraga L.

BURNET-SAXIFRAGE

Widely distributed over most of the British Isles but rare in northern and western Scotland and in northern Ireland, and absent from the Outer Hebrides, Orkney, Shetland and the Channel Islands. It is a plant of dry, rough grassland or grazed swards, hedge banks, grassy roadsides and rocky ground on calcareous or base-rich soils. A perennial, it flowers during July and August.

Pimpinella major (L.) Huds.

GREATER BURNET-SAXIFRAGE

A local plant of central and eastern England with its main distribution concentrated in a belt from north-west Yorkshire south to Kent, extending as far west as Staffordshire and Bedfordshire but more or less absent from East Anglia. It also occurs in south Devon and Co. Limerick. Elsewhere it has a scattered distribution and is absent from Scotland. It is a plant of rough grassland, wood borders, hedge banks and grassy roadsides, usually on dry calcareous or base-rich soils. A perennial, it flowers from June to August.

Aegopodium podagraria L.

GROUND-ELDER GOUTWEED

Probably not native to Britain, although it has long been naturalised as an escape from cultivation over almost the whole of the British Isles except for parts of the north-west Scottish mainland. It is native to most of Europe and temperate Asia as a woodland plant. In Britain it occurs in hedgerows, along the margins of woods, roadsides and near buildings, and is a particularly resistant and troublesome garden weed. It was formerly grown as a pot-herb. A perennial, it flowers from May to July.

❁ *Aegopodium* **is unlikely to be confused with any other umbellifer; the long, creeping rhizomes, ternate leaves and absence of both bracts and bracteoles are distinctive. It grows to about 80 cm.**

Sium latifolium L.

GREATER WATER-PARSNIP

A local and rapidly declining species of lowland England and a few places in central Ireland, now more or less confined to Lincolnshire, the East Anglian Fens, the Norfolk Broads, the coastal levels of Kent and Sussex and the Somerset Levels. It was previously widespread along the Thames valley. It grows along the edges of dykes, ditches and drains in fens and alluvial levels where the water is shallow and calcareous or base-rich. A perennial, it flowers during July and August.

❁ *S. latifolium* **is a tall robust plant growing up to 2 m, the only other umbellifer of similar stature in the same kind of habitat being** *Cicuta virosa* **(Plate 47). In addition, it differs from** *Apium* **(Plate 46) in the presence of bracts and from** *Berula* **in having 20 or more rays to the umbel.**

Berula erecta (Huds.) Colville

LESSER WATER-PARSNIP NARROW-LEAVED WATER-PARSNIP

A frequent plant of lowland England and central Ireland, but scarce in the south-west, Wales and northern England. Very rare in Scotland and absent from the north. It grows around the margins of ponds, ditches, dykes canals, slow-moving rivers and fens and marshes on fertile, alkaline soils. A perennial, it flowers from July to September.

❁ *B. erecta* **is easily confused with** *Apium nodiflorum* **(Plate 46), from which it is distinguished by the more bluish-green leaves which have a distinct 'joint' towards the base of the stalk and the 4-7 bracts. The umbel consists of up to 14 rays.**

Crithmum maritimum L.

ROCK SAMPHIRE

Distributed around the south and west coasts of Britain as far north as Suffolk on the east and Wigtownshire on the west, with isolated localities farther north on Islay and in Ayrshire. It occurs all around the coast of Ireland. Primarily a plant of maritime rocks and cliffs, it is less often found on shingle and sand dunes. It was formerly extensively collected and used as a pickle, and large amounts were exported from the Isle of Man to Covent Garden market. A succulent perennial, it flowers from June to August.

❁ **The yellow flowers and succulent blue-green leaves and stems make** *Crithmum* **quite distinct.**

Seseli libanotis (L.) Koch*

MOON CARROT

Very rare. Restricted to six localities in East Sussex, Bedfordshire and Cambridgeshire and to a single locality in Hertfordshire, where there is but one plant. It grows in rough grassland and open scrub on the chalk hills of the South Downs and the East Anglian Heights. A biennial or perennial, it flowers during July and August.

❁ *Seseli* **grows to about 50 cm, the stem is solid and the base of the plant is covered with the dead remains of old leaf bases. It has both bracts and bracteoles.**

Aethusa cynapium L.

FOOL'S PARSLEY

Widely distributed and frequent throughout England, but becoming scarcer northwards, rare in Scotland and absent from Shetland and the Western Isles. It is local and scattered in Ireland. It occurs as a weed of waste ground, arable fields, farmyards and gardens. The plant is very poisonous, containing the polyacetylenes coniine and cynopine. However, these disappear on drying, so that hay containing *Aethusa* is harmless to animals. An annual, it flowers from June to September.

❁ *Aethusa* **is distinguished by the 3-4 conspicuous downward-pointing bracteoles on the outside of each partial umbel and the absence of bracts.**

Foeniculum vulgare Miller

FENNEL

Fennel is only doubtfully native in Britain as it has long been cultivated for its leaves, which are used as a flavouring. It is a widespread plant of coastal areas in England, Wales and the Isle of Man, but is of more local occurrence inland and is rare in Scotland and Ireland. It is to be found on cliffs, waste ground, rough grassland and roadsides, especially close to the sea. A perennial, it flowers from July to October. The British plant is subsp. *vulgare*, and the plant grown as a vegetable with enlarged overlapping leaf-bases is var. *azoricum* (Miller) Mell.

❁ *Foeniculum* **is a tall robust plant growing to 2.5 m and is unlikely to be confused with any other yellow-flowered umbellifer. The fine leaf segments and characteristic smell are distinctive.**

Silaum silaus (L.) Schinz & Thell.

PEPPER-SAXIFRAGE

Distributed throughout an area south and east of a line from the Tees to the Exe and with some scattered localities in north-west England, and absent from Ireland. It is a plant of rough grassland, grassy commons, old meadows, roadsides and hedge banks, usually on clay soils. A perennial, it flowers from June to August.

❁ *Silaum* **is distinguished from other pale-yellow-flowered umbellifers by the narrow leaf lobes with finely toothed margins.**

Meum athamanticum Jacq.

SPIGNEL

A local species more or less confined to southern and central Scotland from Kirkcudbrightshire north-east as far as south Aberdeenshire. There are isolated localities further north, and also in Northumberland and Cumbria. It is a plant of rough grassland in mountainous districts. A perennial, it flowers during June and July. The roots were used as a spice and also dried and chewed.

❁ *Meum* **grows to about 60 cm and is most easily distinguished by the narrow leaf segments and by the base of the stem being surrounded by the fibrous remains of the old leaves.**

Selinum carvifolia (L.) L.**

CAMBRIDGE MILK-PARSLEY

Very rare and now restricted to only three localities in Cambridgeshire, in some of which it is reasonably abundant. It formerly also occurred in Nottinghamshire and Lincolnshire. It is a plant of wet meadows and the rich herbaceous vegetation of calcareous fens. A perennial, it flowers from July to October.

❁ *Selinum* **and** *Peucedanum palustre* **(Plate 49) are superficially rather similar. Both are glabrous and have narrow untoothed lobes to the lower leaves and grow to about 1 m, and occur in similar habitats.** *Selinum* **has solid stems, a sharp point to the tip of the leaf lobes and less than four bracts or none.** *P. palustre* **has hollow stems, no distinct sharp tip to the leaf-lobes, and at least four bracts.**

Ligusticum scoticum L.

SCOTS LOVAGE

Occurs all around the Scottish coast as far south as Berwickshire on the east and Kirkcudbrightshire on the west, also around the north Irish coast from west Donegal to Co. Down, and with a single locality in Galway. It is a local plant of maritime cliffs and rocks by the sea. A perennial, it flowers during June and July. The leaves were formerly eaten as a vegetable as a protection against scurvy.

❁ *Ligusticum* **grows to about 90 cm, and the glabrous bright-green ternate leaves are distinctive. It has both bracts and bracteoles.**

 (see illustrations page 108)

Angelica sylvestris L.
WILD ANGELICA
Distributed throughout the whole of the British Isles. It is a common plant of wet meadows, marshes, fens, wet open woodlands, ditches, and stream, river and lake margins on mildly acid to calcareous soils. A perennial, it flowers from July to September.
❁ ***Angelica* is a tall, robust, sparsely hairy plant growing up to 2 m. The stems are hollow and the inflated sheathing petioles of the small upper stem leaves will distinguish it from similar species.**

Peucedanum officinale L.*
HOG'S FENNEL
Rare and local; confined to two small areas of the east coast of England in north Essex and north Kent, where about 15 populations are at present known. It grows in rough grassland and on clayey banks and grassy cliffs close to the sea. A perennial, it is in flower from July to September. The British plant is subsp. *officinale*.
❁ ***P. officinale* is a tall glabrous species growing to over 1 m. The 3-6-ternate leaves with long narrow lobes will distinguish it from other yellow-flowered species.**

Peucedanum palustre (L.) Moench
MILK-PARSLEY
A very local plant almost confined to the fenland of East Anglia and the Norfolk Broads, where it is quite common. Elsewhere there are scattered localities in south-west Yorkshire, north Lincolnshire, Somerset and East Sussex. It is a constituent of the rich herbaceous vegetation of wet calcareous fens and marshes. A biennial, it is in flower from July to September. The leaves are the food plant of the larvae of the swallowtail butterfly.
❁ ***P. palustre* is superficially similar to *Selinum carvifolia* (Plate 48). Both grow to about 1 m and occur in similar habitats. *P. palustre* has hollow, not solid, stems, and at least four bracts.**

Peucedanum ostruthium (L.) Koch
MASTERWORT
Alien and a native of the mountains of central and southern Europe from the Pyrenees to the Balkans. Masterwort was introduced by medieval herbalists to physic gardens and it is now naturalised by the side of streams, along river banks and in damp meadows in a number of scattered localities in northern England and Scotland. A perennial, it flowers during July and August.
❁ **The hollow, downy stems and 1-2-ternate leaves, which are downy beneath, distinguish *P. ostruthium*.**

Pastinaca sativa L.
WILD PARSNIP
Widespread in Britain south and east of a line from the Humber to the Severn. It is also a local coastal species further north in England, in south Wales and the south-west. It is rare in Ireland. Wild parsnip is a plant of rough grassland, roadside verges, hedge banks and grassy waste ground on dry, usually calcareous or base-rich soils. A biennial, it is in flower during July and August. There are two subspecies in Britain; subsp. *hortensis* is the cultivated plant, which may be found as an escape, while subsp. *sylvestris* (Miller) Rouy & Camus is the one most commonly encountered. *Pastinaca* can cause serious blisters if handled in bright sunlight.
❁ ***P. sativa* is the only yellow-flowered umbellifer with pinnate leaves that are pubescent.**

Heracleum sphondylium L.
HOGWEED
Generally distributed and common throughout the British Isles. It is a plant of hedgerows, roadside verges, woodland clearings and rough grassland. A biennial or perennial, it is the commonest flowering wayside umbellifer in late summer from June to September. There are two subspecies in Britain; subsp *sphonydylium* is the common and widespread plant, while subsp. *sibiricum* (L.) Simonkai appears to be confined to east Norfolk.
❁ ***H. sphondylium* is unlikely to be confused with any other umbellifer. It is a tall, robust, hairy species growing to 2 m, which together with the pinnate leaves and bracteoles is distinctive.**

Heracleum mantegazzianum Sommier & Levier
GIANT HOGWEED
Alien and a native of the Caucasus and south-west Asia. It was originally introduced as an ornamental garden plant and is now naturalised in a number of places throughout the British Isles, especially on waste ground and near rivers. A biennial or perennial, it flowers during June and July. Giant hogweed can cause serious skin blistering if handled in bright sunlight.
❁ ***H. mantegazzianum* is a huge plant, growing to 3.5 m and with stems up to 10 cm thick.**

Tordylium maximum L.
HARTWORT
Only doubtfully native, otherwise occuring in southern Europe, Asia Minor, the Caucasus and Persia. It is a local and rare species in Britain, being naturalised along the Thames with records from Essex, Middlesex, Oxfordshire and Buckinghamshire, where it grows in grassy places along hedge and river banks. An annual or biennial, it is in flower during June and July.
❁ ***Tordylium* is distinguished from other species with hairy pinnate leaves by the almost sessile flowers with calyx teeth almost as long as the petals.**

Daucus carota L.
WILD CARROT
Distributed throughout the British Isles but wholly coastal in the south-west, Wales, northern England, Scotland and northern Ireland, and absent from Orkney and Shetland. It is to be found on rough grassland, roadside verges, railway embankments and waste ground on well-drained calcareous or base-rich soils. A biennial, it flowers from June to August. Three subspecies occur in Britain; subsp. *carota* is the commonly encountered plant, subsp *gummifer* (Syme) Hook. f. is confined to the south-west coast of England, where it grows on sea cliffs and dunes, and subsp. *sativus* (Hoffm.) Arcangeli is the cultivated carrot.
❁ **The large branched bracts, umbels usually with a purple central flower and the spiny fruit distinguish *D. carota* from other umbellifers.**

Subsp. *carota* has dull, thin hairy leaves and the umbels contract and become concave in fruit. Subsp. *gummifer* has rather thick, almost hairless leaves that are glossy above, and the umbel does not contract in fruit. Subsp. *sativus* is distinguished by the fleshy tap-root (the carrot!).

CUCURBITACEAE

Bryonia dioica Jacq.
WHITE BRYONY
Widespread in lowland England south and east of a line from the Tees to Exe. It is a frequent plant of hedgerows, scrub, copse and woodland margins on well-drained calcareous or base-rich soils. A climbing perennial, the plant is dioecious with male and female flowers on separate plants. It flowers from May to September and is pollinated by bees and other insects. All parts of the plant are poisonous, especially the red berries and the massive root tubers. The toxin is a glycoside, bryonin, which acts as a drastic purgative. Apart from the cucumber, *B. dioica* is the only representative of the tropical 'gourd' family in Britain.

ARISTOLOCHIACEAE

Asarum europaeum L.
ASARABACCA
A rare and declining species occurring in a few scattered localities throughout England and Wales. A native of most of the European mainland, its status in Britain is uncertain. It was well known and widely cultivated by medieval herbalists and gardeners. A perennial evergreen herb, it grows in woods and hedgerows and flowers from May to August. It is pollinated by small flies or self-pollinated.

Aristolochia clematitis L.
BIRTHWORT
Alien. A native of central and southern Europe and Asia Minor, it has been cultivated in Britain for medicinal purposes since early times. As a naturalised escape from cultivation it is a rare and declining species in England and south Wales. The Greeks believed that the plant assisted conception, helped delivery and repelled the demons that were an ever-present danger at a birth. The flower bears a resemblance to the female reproductive organs. An evil-smelling herb, it flowers from June to September and is pollinated by small flies.

EUPHORBIACEAE

Mercurialis perennis L.
DOG'S MERCURY
Distributed throughout almost the whole of the British Isles but very rare in Ireland and northern Scotland and absent from Orkney, Shetland and the Outer Hebrides. It is a common plant of deciduous woodlands, old hedgerows, hillside scree and the grikes of limestone pavement on calcareous or base-rich soils to an altitude of 1,035 m in Scotland. It is tolerant of shade but very sensitive to waterlogging. It frequently dominates the ground vegetation, especially in ash and beech woods on chalk or limestone, where it forms extensive pure stands. The plant is dioecious, with separate male and female plants. It flowers from February to April and is wind-pollinated.

❁ *M. perennis* is distinguished from *M. annua* by being hairy, perennial and unbranched. *M. annua* is glabrous, annual and branched.

Mercurialis annua L.
ANNUAL MERCURY
More or less restricted to southern England, south of a line from the Wash to the Severn with scattered localities further north as far as southern Scotland, in south Wales, and south-east Ireland. It occurs most frequently as a garden weed and as a casual of waste ground, usually on light soils. An annual, it flowers from July to October, and is dioecious and wind-pollinated.

The SPURGES are awkward to identify unless the unusual flower and inflorescence structure is understood. The flowers are very small and have neither petals nor sepals. Several male flowers and a single female flower are grouped together within a perianth-like involucre, with four or five glands, which may be rounded or distinctly concave and shaped like the horns of a cow.

Euphorbia peplis L.
PURPLE SPURGE
Very rare and now probably extinct. Formerly occurred on Lundy Island in the Bristol Channel and Alderney and Guernsey in the Channel Islands; the last place where it was seen was Alderney. It grows on bare, fine shingle or coarse sand just above high water mark of spring tides, and even in Alderney it fluctuated in numbers quite dramatically from year to year depending upon the incidence of winter storms. A prostrate annual, it flowers from July to September.
❁ **The prostrate habit, purple stems and opposite, pale blue-green leaves of *E. peplis* distinguish it from other species.**

Euphorbia lathyris L.
CAPER SPURGE
Widely distributed in England and Wales as an occasional escape from cultivation and as a garden weed. It is sometimes thought to be native in a few woodlands in north Somerset, Gloucestershire, Wiltshire, Huntingdonshire and Northamptonshire, but it is probably only truly native in the central Mediterranean region. It was formerly cultivated for its fruits. A biennial, it flowers during June and July.
❁ ***E. lathyrus* is the only British species, except for *E. peplis*, with opposite leaves.**

Euphorbia villosa Waldst. & Kit. *
(*E. pilosa* L.)
HAIRY SPURGE
Extinct. First recorded from a wood near Bath in 1576, where it persisted until about 1924. Cessation of coppicing in about 1900 was responsible for its final extinction. (Not illustrated.)

Euphorbia hyberna L.
IRISH SPURGE
Confined to south-west Ireland, where it is locally common in Kerry, Co. Waterford and Limerick, and to isolated localities in north Cornwall, north Devon and Somerset. It occurs in damp woodlands, shaded stream banks and hedge banks on acid soils to an altitude of 550 m. A perennial, it is in flower from April to July. The British plant is subsp. *hyberna*.
❁ ***E. hyberna* grows to 60 cm, each plant with numerous stems. The leaves are 5-10 cm and the inflorescence bracts are yellowish green and almost cordate. The involucral glands are rounded. It is most likely to be confused with *E. dulcis*, which is a more slender plant, with smaller leaves (3-5 cm) and green truncate inflorescence bracts.**

Euphorbia dulcis L.
SWEET SPURGE
Alien and a native of central and southern Europe, south to Bulgaria and Yugoslavia. In Britain it occurs naturalised in shady places in a very few scattered localities in England, Wales and mainly in Scotland as far north as the Moray Firth. A perennial, it flowers from May to July.

❁ ***E. helioscopia*, *E. platyphyllos* and *E. serrulata* are annuals with single stems and rounded involucral glands. *E. helioscopia* differs from *E. platyphyllos* and *E. serrulata* in the broadly obtuse tips to the leaves and bracts which are tapered to the base. *E. serrulata* and *E. platyphyllos* have acute leaves that are cordate at the base. *E. serrulata* is a more slender plant than *E. platyphyllos*, from which it differs in the bracts on the inflorescence being similar in shape to those at the base of the inflorescence. Under a lens the warts on the capsule are cylindrical, while those on the capsule of *E. platyphyllos* are hemispherical.**

Euphorbia helioscopia L.
SUN SPURGE
Widely distributed throughout the British Isles but becoming increasingly scarce and more coastal in its distribution in Scotland. It is a frequent weed of arable crops, waste ground, roadsides and gardens to an altitude of 450 m and is most frequent on calcareous or base-rich soils. A summer annual, it flowers from May to October and, like several of the annual weed spurges, the seeds are dispersed by ants.

Euphorbia platyphyllos L.
BROAD-LEAVED SPURGE
An infrequent and local plant of southern England, occurring south and east of a line from the Humber to the Severn but absent from the south-west, but with a single locality in south Wales. It is an annual of waste ground and arable land, often on heavy soils, and it flowers from June to October.

Euphorbia serrulata Thuill.*
(*E. stricta* L.)
UPRIGHT SPURGE
Very rare and confined as a native plant to about 10 colonies in west Gloucestershire and Monmouthshire, where it grows in woodland clearings and areas of recent coppice on Carboniferous limestone. In most of these localities it is reasonably abundant, and occasionally turns up elsewhere as a casual. An annual, it flowers from June to September.

Euphorbia peplus L.
PETTY SPURGE
A common plant throughout England and Wales, but becoming scarce northwards and rare or absent in much of northern and western Scotland. Widely distributed in Ireland. It is an abundant weed of gardens, arable crops and disturbed ground on fertile soils to an altitude of 410 m. A spring and summer annual, it flowers from April to October.

❁ ***E. peplus* and *E. exigua* are both annuals with single stems and concave involucral glands. *E. peplus* has ovate to obovate petiolate leaves; those of *E. exigua* are linear and sessile.**

Euphorbia exigua L.
DWARF SPURGE
A plant of lowland Britain, more or less confined to the area south and east of a line from the Tees to the Severn. Elsewhere, it is scarce and local in the south-west, Wales, Ireland and southern Scotland. It is a frequent weed of arable crops on dry, base-rich or calcareous soils. A summer annual, it is in flower from June to October.

Euphorbia paralias L.
SEA SPURGE
Sea spurge occurs around the coasts of Britain as far north as Norfolk on the east and the Solway on the west. It grows all around the coast of Ireland except for parts of the west and north-west. It is a rather local species, but can be very abundant in suitable habitats. It is a plant of sandy shores and young sand dunes and is occasionally to be found on fine shingle. A perennial, it flowers from July to October.

❁ ***E. paralias* and *E. portlandica* both have narrowly ovate, rather succulent leaves, several stems and concave involucral glands. The leaves of *E. paralias* are broadest below the middle and the midrib is obscure; the leaves of *E. portlandica* are broadest above the middle and the midrib is distinct beneath.**

Euphorbia portlandica L.
PORTLAND SPURGE
A local plant of the west and south-west coasts of the British Isles, extending as far east as the Isle of Wight and as far north as Wigtownshire and with an isolated locality on Islay. In Ireland it extends from Donegal along the north-east and south coasts as far west as Kerry. *E. portlandica* is a plant of sandy shores, young sand dunes and sandy limestone cliffs. A biennial or short-lived perennial, it flowers from May to September.

Euphorbia cyparissias L.
CYPRESS SPURGE
Alien and a native of most of Europe except for the extreme north and extreme south. It occurs naturalised in scattered localities throughout Britain but is absent from Ireland and from most of Scotland except for the north coast. It appears as an apparent native in calcareous grassland and scrub and also as a casual of waste ground. A perennial, it flowers from May to August.

❁ ***E. cyparissias* and *E. esula* both have narrow leaves and concave involucral glands. The leaves of *E. cyparissias* are 2 mm broad or less; those of *E. esula* 4 mm broad or more.**

Euphorbia esula L.
LEAFY SPURGE
Alien, but a native of most of continental Europe; it is naturalised in a few places in Scotland and England in woods and by streams. The hybrid with *E. waldsteinii*, *E.* x *pseudovirgata* (Schur) Soó is naturalised in a number of places in England and Scotland on waste ground and rough grassland, particularly in central eastern England.

Euphorbia amygdaloides L.
WOOD SPURGE
A plant of southern England, occurring in most of the country as far north as the Wash; it is very rare in Wales but widespread in the south-west. It is characteristically a plant of clearings in deciduous woodland on mildly acid, damp soils and often appears in great abundance following coppicing, and in East Anglia is strongly associated with woodlands known to be ancient. A perennial, it flowers from March to May.
❁ ***E. amygdaloides* grows to 80 cm and is distinguished by the hairy stem and by the members of each pair of inflorescence bracts being joined at the base.**

POLYGONACEAE

❁ **The perianth segments of *Fallopia* are keeled or winged in fruit. *F. convolvulus* has shorter fruiting pedicels (1-3 mm) than *F. dumetorum* (3-8 mm) and a dull, not shiny, black nut.**

Fallopia dumetorum (L.) J. Holub (*Polygonum dumetorum* L.)

COPSE-BINDWEED

A rare annual of southern England, recently reported from Hampshire, Berkshire, Buckinghamshire, Kent, Surrey and Sussex. It appears erratically in scrub, wood borders, hedges and copses, often following coppicing. It prefers well-drained, often calcium-rich (but not necessarily chalk) soils, and flowers from July to September.

Fallopia convolvulus (L.) A. Löve (*Polygonum convolvulus* L.)

BLACK-BINDWEED

An autumn- or spring-germinating annual weed of arable land, gardens, rubbish tips, waste ground and roadsides. It is common throughout the British Isles except for the north and west of Scotland and the Scottish isles, where it is scarce. The seeds were eaten by prehistoric man and have been found in Bronze Age deposits from both England and Scotland, and it is one of the many plants where, in the past, the distinction between 'crop' and 'weed' was far from clear. It flowers from July to October.

Fallopia japonica (Houtt.) Ronse Decraene (*Polygonum cuspidatum* Sieb. & Zucc.; *Reynoutria japonica* Houtt.

JAPANESE KNOTWEED

Alien and a native of Japan, Taiwan and northern China, a tall perennial herb introduced to Britain from Japan in 1825. It was a popular garden plant with the Victorians and is now widely established throughout the British Isles, except for parts of Scotland and the north of England, growing along roadsides and railway banks, in waste places, rubbish tips and along river banks. Once established it can prove difficult to eliminate. It flowers from August to October.
❁ *R. japonica* **is a perennial which produces tall, annual stems up to more than 2 m and leaves up to 12 cm long.**

Fagopyrum esculentum Moench

BUCKWHEAT

Alien and probably a native of central Asia. Buckwheat was widely cultivated from the 16th to the 19th century, especially in the East Anglian fens and on light acid soils, for flour and for cattle and poultry feed. It occurs as a casual throughout England, on rubbish tips, field borders and waste ground as a relic of cultivation and near chicken runs. The fruit resembles beech mast in shape, hence its German name *Buchweize*, 'beech wheat', and the English 'buckwheat'. An annual, it flowers from July to September.
❁ *Fagopryrum* **grows to about 30 cm and differs from *Fallopia* in the outer perianth segments being neither keeled nor winged in fruit.**

Koenigia islandica L.*

ICELAND-PURSLANE

Very rare and confined in Britain to the islands of Skye and Mull, where it grows on bare stony ground and fine damp gravel at the foot of cliffs at an altitude of between 450 and 725 metres. It was not recognised as a British plant until 1950 when it was discovered in the Herbarium at Kew labelled as *Peplis portula*, having been collected on Skye in 1934. It is now known in several localities, in some of which it is locally abundant. A small annual, it is in flower from June to August.
❁ *Koenigia* is a tiny annual, no more than 5 cm tall, and with leaves only 3-5 mm long.

❁ *Polygonum aviculare, P. boreale, P. arenastrum* **and** *P. rurivagum,* **KNOTGRASS, are all closely related and are sometimes difficult to separate. As a group they differ from *P. oxyspermum* in the dull, not shiny, nut that is about as long as the perianth.**

Polygonum aviculare L.

KNOTGRASS

A common plant throughout the British Isles except for the extreme north of Scotland, Orkney and Shetland, where it is either very local or almost completely absent, being replaced by *P. boreale*. It is a weed of waste land, disturbed ground, roadsides, sea shores, gardens and arable. An annual, it flowers from July to November.
❁ *P. aviculare* **is a robust, erect, spreading species and the leaves on the main stem are 2-3 times as long as those on the flowering branches. The perianth segments are joined for less than one-quarter of their length.**

Polygonum boreale (Lange) Small

NORTHERN KNOTGRASS

Confined in Britain to Orkney and Shetland, where it is common, and to the extreme north of Scotland and the Outer Hebrides. In Orkney and Shetland it largely replaces *P. aviculare*. A northern species, it also occurs in Iceland, the Faroes, northern Scandinavia, Greenland and eastern Canada. An annual, it flowers from June to October.
❁ *P. boreale* **is similar to** *P. aviculare* **but is less branched, and the petioles are longer than the stipules.**

Polygonum arenastrum Boreau

EQUAL-LEAVED KNOTGRASS

Widespread and locally common throughout the British Isles. It is very resistant to trampling and thrives on the compacted and well-trodden sandy and gravelly soils of tracks, roadsides, footpaths, field gateways and waste ground, tolerating drier conditions than *P. aviculare*. An annual, it flowers from July to November.
❁ *P. arenastrum* **forms a dense mat and all the leaves are more or less the same size. The perianth segments are joined for at least one-third of their length.**

Polygonum rurivagum Jordan ex Boreau

CORNFIELD KNOTGRASS

A local and perhaps decreasing species scattered throughout southern and eastern England. It usually occurs as a weed of cereal crops on light, well-drained, usually calcareous soils. In common with many other species of arable weed, its decline is associated with the use of synthetic herbicides and cleaner seed. An annual, it flowers from August to November.
❁ *P. rurivagum* **differs from the other three species in the group in the narrower leaves (1-4 mm wide) and reddish perianth segments that are jointed at the base. The leaves of the main stem are 2-3 times as long as those on the flowering branches.**

Polygonum oxyspermum Meyer and Bunge subsp. *raii* (Bab.) Webb & Chater

RAY'S KNOTGRASS

A rare species, scattered around the south and west coasts of the British Isles north to Harris. It grows at the limits of extreme high water spring tides on sand, shingle or shell gravel, often in association with other drift-line species. Its appearance from year to year is very erratic, depending on the influences of winter storms. An annual, it flowers from June to September.
❁ *P. oxyspermum* **differs from the** *P. aviculare* **group in the shining nut that is longer than the perianth. The stipules are shorter than the internodes.**

Polygonum maritimum L.**

SEA KNOTGRASS

A very rare prostrate perennial growing just above high tide level on sand, fine shingle or shell-gravel beaches. A Mediterranean species that reaches the limits of its distribution in southern Britain, it is now known from Sussex, Hampshire, two localities in Cornwall and from the island of Herm in the Channel Islands. In 1973 it was also discovered in Waterford in southern Ireland. It tends to persist for a few years, then succumbs to exceptional tide conditions. It flowers from July to October.
❁ *P. maritimum* **differs from the other prostrate species with axillary flowers in its perennial habit, woody stem, leathery blue-green leaves with revolute margins and stipules almost as long as the internodes.**

❁ **Species of *Persicaria* differ from *Polygonum* in having inflorescences with more than 6 flowers, at least some of them terminal.**

Persicaria amplexicaulis (D. Don) Ronse Decraene

RED BISTORT

Alien and a native of the Himalayas. It is now established in several parts of Britain and especially in western Ireland. A perennial, it flowers from August to October.

Persicaria bistorta (L.) Samp. (*Polygonum bistorta* L.)

COMMON BISTORT

Distributed throughout Britain, but most frequent in north-west England. It is only doubtfully native in the south-east and was introduced into Ireland. It is a plant of wet meadows, alluvial pastures, damp roadsides and open alder carr on humus-rich, mildly acid soils. In the Lake District bistort is an essential ingredient on the Easter Ledger Pudding, eaten at Passiontide, and much local folklore surrounds the plant in northern England. A perennial, it flowers from June to August.
❁ *P. bistorta* **differs from all other species except for** *P. vivipara* **in the unbranched stems.**

Persicaria vivipara (L.) Ronse Decraene (*Polygonum viviparum* L.)

ALPINE BISTORT

A frequent plant of the mountains of Scotland and northern England, but rare in Wales and Ireland. It grows in alpine grassland and on scree and wet rocks to an altitude of 1,350 m. At lower altitudes it is often abundant in pastures. Reproduction is usually effected by purple bulbils which develop in the lower part of the inflorescence and which frequently begin to grow before being shed from the spike. Seed is rarely set in Britain. A perennial, it flowers from June to August. (Illustrated on Plate 52.)

Persicaria amphibia (L.) Gray (*Polygonum amphibium* L.)

AMPHIBIOUS BISTORT

Distributed throughout the British Isles, but becoming scarce in parts of central and northern Scotland. It occurs in two distinct forms: aquatic and terrestrial. The aquatic form grows floating in ponds, lakes, reservoirs, canals, dykes, streams and slow-flowing rivers in depths up to 2 m, usually in non-calcareous waters. The terrestrial form grows in damp places by the sides of reservoirs, lakes and ponds and also as a weed of arable land. A perennial, it flowers from July to September.
❁ *P. amphibia* **is distinguished by the rounded or cordate leaf bases and the stamens that are longer than the perianth.**

POLYGONACEAE *(see illustrations page 114)*

❁ *P. hydropiper, P. laxiflora* **and** *P. minor* **are similar with slender few-flowered inflorescences.**

Persicaria hydropiper (L.) Spach (*Polygonum hydropiper* L.)

WATER-PEPPER

Widely distributed and frequent throughout the British Isles except for parts of northern Scotland, it is characteristic of the marshy margins of ponds, lakes, rivers, streams, ditches and drainage dykes. It also grows in the shallow depressions of woodland rides where water stands in winter. It avoids acid peats, but has a slightly calcifuge tendency. An annual, it is in flower from July to September and is almost invariably self-pollinated. The leaves have a strong acrid taste which gives the plant its English name and also provides it with immunity from grazing animals.

❁ *P. hydropiper* **differs from** *P. laxiflora* **in the more nodding inflorescence, yellow glands on the perianth and shortly-toothed stipules.**

Persicaria laxiflora (Weihe) Opiz (*Polygonum mite* Schrank)

TASTELESS WATER-PEPPER

A rare and declining species that is scattered throughout the lowlands of England and Wales but is absent from Scotland. It is thought to have been introduced into Ireland. It grows in wet marshy meadows, and along the margins of ditches, dykes, rivers, ponds and lakes on rich fertile soils. An annual, it flowers from July to September.

Persicaria minor (Hudson) Opiz (*Polygonum minus* Hudson)

SMALL WATER-PEPPER

An uncommon species with a scattered distribution throughout England, Wales, Ireland and southern Scotland. Agricultural drainage is greatly reducing its former distribution, in common with many other species of similar habitat. It grows in similar places to *P. laxiflora*, being found in the marshy area around ponds, lakes, ditches and drainage dykes on rich fertile or gravelly soils. An annual, it flowers from July to October.
❁ *P. minor* **is smaller than either** *P. hydropiper* **or** *P. laxiflora* **with leaves less than 1 cm wide and pink flowers.**

Persicaria maculosa Gray (*Polygonum persicaria* L.)

REDSHANK

Widely distributed and common throughout the British Isles, it is a troublesome annual weed of arable land, gardens and cultivated land, generally to an altitude of 430 m. It is also found on waste ground, roadsides and railway banks and by the sides of ponds, rivers and streams. It is most abundant on heavy, non-calcareous soils but will also grow on black fen peat. It flowers from June to October and, although visited by a range of insects, it is probably most often self-pollinated.

Persicaria lapathifolia (L.) Gray (*Polygonum lapathifolium* L.)

PALE PERSICARIA

Common throughout most of Britain but scarce or scattered in parts of northern England, Scotland and Ireland. It is to be found in similar places to *P. maculosa*, with which it sometimes grows. A very variable species, it occurs as a weed of arable soils and waste ground and also by the sides of ponds and rivers, reaching an altitude of 365 m. An annual, it is in flower from June to August and is probably most often self-pollinated.
❁ *P. lapathifolia* **differs from** *P. maculosa* **in the presence of yellow glands on the inflorescence stalks. The colour of the flowers is not a reliable guide as pale forms of** *P. maculosa* **are not uncommon.**

Persicaria nodosa **Pers. is now regarded as a form of** *P. lapathifolia* **as, although extreme forms are very distinct, numerous intermediates exist.**

Persicaria wallichii Greuter & Burdet (*Polygonum polystachyum* Wall. ex Meissner)

HIMALAYAN KNOTWEED

Alien and a native of the Himalayas. It is a perennial species that has long been cultivated as a garden plant and has become thoroughly naturalised in a number of places, especially in north Devon and western Ireland. It spreads vegetatively from discarded rhizomes and flowers during August and September.
❁ *P. wallichii* **is a tall species with a rather woody base and differs from other species in the lanceolate and cordate leaves and branched inflorescence.**

Oxyria digyna (L.) Hill

MOUNTAIN SORREL

A locally common plant of the mountains of north Wales, the Lake District and the Scottish Highlands. In Ireland it is found in the mountains of Kerry and Donegal and in the Galtees. It grows among damp rocks by streams and on wet rock ledges to over 1,200 m. It is also carried downstream and occurs on river shingle at sea level. A perennial, it flowers during July and August.
❁ **The kidney-shaped leaves distinguish** *Oxyria* **from all other members of the family.**

The SORRELS, *Rumex acetosella, R. acetosa* **and** *R. scutatus,* **are distinguished from the docks only by their spear-shaped leaves and acid taste.**

Rumex acetosella L.

SHEEP'S SORREL

Common throughout the whole of the British Isles. It is a characteristic plant of grass heaths, commons and short grassland on acid, sandy, well-drained soils, often growing in association with common bent grass (*Agrostis capillaris*) and heath bedstraw (*Galium saxatile*). A perennial, it is dioecious, with separate male and female plants, and flowers from May to September.

Two subspecies occur. Subsp. *acetosella* has tepals that are easily rubbed off the fruit. It is probably more northern in distribution. Subsp. *pyrenaicus* has tepals tightly adherent to the ripe fruit so that they cannot easily be rubbed off.

❁ *R. acetosella* **is distinguished from** *R. acetosa* **by the spreading basal lobes of the leaves and grows to about 25 cm.**

Rumex acetosa L.

COMMON SORREL

Common throughout the whole of the British Isles. It is a characteristic plant of grassland on neutral to mildly acid soils, woodland rides and grassy clearings, roadside verges, river banks, stabilised coastal shingle and mountain ledges. A perennial, dioecious species with separate male and female plants, it flowers during May and June. Sorrel has long been used in salads and in sauces to accompany fish dishes.
❁ *R. acetosa* **grows to about 80 cm and differs from** *R. acetosella* **in the downward-pointing leaf lobes.**

Rumex scutatus L.

FRENCH SORREL

Alien and a native of central and southern Europe, western Asia and north Africa, where it grows as a plant of cliffs, screes and rocky roadsides. It was introduced into Britain as a perennial culinary herb for the cool, acid taste of the leaves, and is used in salads, soups and sauces. It is established in a number of places in England, Wales, Scotland and Ireland, but especially in parts of Yorkshire. It usually appears on old walls and flowers during June and July.
❁ *R. scutatus* **differs from** *R. acetosa* **in the leaves being more or less as broad as long and the upper leaves being stalked.**

The DOCKS are a difficult group to identify, and well-grown plants with ripe fruits are essential for accurate naming. Almost every conceivable hybrid combination has been reported, some of which are quite common. Detailed keys and descriptions can be found in *British Docks and Knotweeds.*

Rumex pseudoalpinus Hoefft (*Rumex alpinus* L.)

MONK'S-RHUBARB

Alien and a native of the mountains of central and southern Europe. It was originally introduced into northern Britain as a pot-herb and widely used for medicinal and veterinary purposes. It is still used in the Alps for curing sore places on cows' udders in alpine pastures. The large leaves were also used for wrapping butter. It is now established near farms and along streams and roadsides in upland areas from Staffordshire and Derbyshire northwards. It is most frequent in parts of eastern Scotland.
❁ *R. alpinus* **is distinguished by the leaf shape (leaves about as long as broad) and the fruit without tubercles.**

Rumex hydrolapathum Hudson

WATER DOCK

Widely distributed and frequent throughout England but less common in the south-west, Wales and Ireland, and rare in Scotland. It grows along the banks and margins of rivers, canals, streams, drainage dykes, ponds and lakes and in ditches and marshy ground, usually on fertile or base-rich fine-textured soils or fen peats in depths of up to 0.5 m. A perennial, it flowers from July to September and is sometimes planted for ornamental purposes. It is the foodplant of the Large Copper butterfly.
❁ *R. hydrolapathum* **is a tall, robust, distinctive plant growing to 2 m with leaves up to more than 1 m long. The inflorescence is dense and the perianth segments are without teeth.**

Rumex aquaticus L.*

SCOTTISH DOCK

A rare perennial, confined in Britain to about 20 localities around the south-east and west banks of Loch Lomond in Stirling and Dumbarton, where it grows at the margins of alder carr, on sand banks and by rivers, ditches and loch-sides. It hybridises freely with *R. obtusifolius* and flowers during July and August.
❁ *R. aquaticus* **is a tall robust plant growing up to 2 m. The fruits have no tubercle and it is distinguished from** *R. longifolius* **(Plate 53) by the more triangular leaves and slender fruit stalks, which have no joint at the base.**

Rumex longifolius DC.
NORTHERN DOCK
Found from Lancashire and Yorkshire northwards and common in parts of southern and eastern Scotland, it is less frequent on the west coast and is absent from Wales and Ireland. It is a plant of wet meadows and river, stream and lake sides, and it also occurs around farms and arable fields. A perennial, it flowers from June to August.
❁ *R. longifolius* **is a tall robust plant growing to about 120 cm. It is similar to** *R. aquaticus* **(Plate 52) in having fruits without tubercles, but differs in the long (up to 80 cm) narrow leaves with undulate and crisped margins and in the tepals, which are about as long as wide (not longer.)**

Rumex pulcher L.
FIDDLE DOCK
A plant of lowland Britain almost confined to the area south and east of a line from the Wash to the Severn. It is locally common in the south and south-west, especially near the coast. It is a plant of roadsides, grassy commons and the short turf of village greens, churchyards and waste ground on warm, dry, well-drained sandy or calcareous soils, most often where there has been some disturbance. A perennial, it flowers during June and July.

The native British plant is subsp. *pulcher*. Subspp. *anadontus* (Hausskn.) Rech. f. and *divaricatus* (L.) Murb. occasionally occur as rare adventives.
❁ *R. pulcher* **is distinguished by the characteristic 'waisted' leaves, rather short stem (up to about 40 cm), widely spreading tangled branches and toothed fruits.**

Rumex obtusifolius L.
BROAD-LEAVED DOCK
Distributed throughout the whole of the British Isles. It is a common plant of disturbed and trampled ground, waste places, hedge banks, cultivated soils, badly managed pastures, roadsides, and pond, lake, river and canal banks on both calcareous and non-calcareous soils. It grows best on fertile soils and is absent from acid peats but can be found growing in partial shade. Like *R. crispus* it is scheduled as an injurious weed under the Weeds Act, 1959. Young plants can usually be satisfactorily controlled with the phenoxyacetic acid herbicides, but established plants are more difficult to eliminate. A long-lived perennial, it flowers from June to October and is wind-pollinated.

The native British plant is var. *obtusifolius*. Var. *microcarpus* Dierb. (subsp. *sylvestris* (Wallr.) Rach.) and var. *transiens* (Simonkai) Kubat are naturalised in a few places in southern England.
❁ *R. obtusifolius* **has characteristic broad, cordate leaves, a dense inflorescence and fruits with long teeth on the perianth segments and one segment with a tubercle.**

Rumex palustris Sm.
MARSH DOCK
A local species of eastern and southern England almost confined to an area bounded by the Humber and the Thames and extending as far west as Somerset. It is a plant of the bare, muddy margins of ponds, lakes, reservoirs, clay pits, gravel pits and rivers that dry up in summer but are inundated in winter. A biennial or perennial, it flowers from June to August.

❁ *R. palustris* **and** *R. maritimus* **are very similar and almost impossible to separate except with ripe fruit. Both go yellowish when mature, have interrupted inflorescences and long, fine teeth on the fruits. Some of the fruiting perianth teeth of** *R. maritimus* **are longer than the fruit and the tubercle has an acute tip; the perianth teeth of** *R. palustris* **are shorter than the fruit and the tubercle is rounded at the tip.**

Rumex maritimus L.
GOLDEN DOCK
An uncommon and decreasing plant, scattered throughout England but with a few isolated localities only in Wales, Scotland and Ireland. In spite of its specific name, it has no particular preference for coastal habitats. It grows around the margins of pools, meres, clay pits and rivers and along ditches and in marshy fields, always in places where water stands until spring. It can behave as an annual, biennial or perennial, and flowers from July to September.

Rumex conglomeratus Murray
CLUSTERED DOCK
SHARP DOCK
Occurs throughout the British Isles but is local or absent from large parts of Wales, northern England and Scotland. A common plant of wet habitats or where water stands during the winter, it is found on pond, ditch, stream and river banks and in wet marshy meadows in both fresh and brackish conditions. A perennial, it flowers from July to October.

❁ *R. conglomeratus* **and** *R. sanguineus* **both have interrupted inflorescences and untoothed fruiting perianths with tubercles. They can be distinguished by the more acute branching of** *R. sanguineus*, **few-leaved inflorescence branches and single round tubercle on the perianth.** *R. conglomeratus* **has more spreading branches, leafy inflorescence branches and fruits with three oblong tubercles.**

Rumex sanguineus L.
WOOD DOCK
A common plant in southern England, Wales and Ireland but becoming rare in northern England and absent from Scotland north of the Clyde. It is the characteristic dock of woodland rides, pathsides and clearings, usually in the open on roadside verges and grassy waste ground. A perennial, it flowers during June and July.

The common wild plant is *R. sanguineus* var. *viridis* (Sibth) Koch. The type variety, *R. sanguineus* var. *sanguineus*, probably arose as a mutant and is known only in cultivation or as an escape.

Rumex rupestris Le Gall**
SHORE DOCK
Very rare and confined to only about 12 locations in Britain in the Isles of Scilly, Cornwall, Devon and Glamorgan and Guernsey, Jersey and Herm in the Channel Islands. It is known only from the west coast of Europe from northern Spain to south Wales. It grows in dune slacks, on sandy shores, on maritime cliffs or in places where water seeps from the foot of cliffs. A perennial, it is in flower during June and July.
❁ *R. rupestris* **has a characteristic blue-green colour, oblong leaves and grows to about 70 cm. The inflorescence is interrupted and the branching acute with only the lowest whorls with a leaf. The perianths are untoothed, with three prominent tubercles.**

Rumex patientia L.
PATIENCE DOCK
Alien and a native of eastern and south-eastern Europe and south-west Asia. *R. patientia* subsp. *orientalis* (Bernh.) Danser has long been established around docks, wharves, river banks and breweries in a number of localities in England, especially around London and Bristol. It was formerly cultivated as a vegetable. A tall perennial, it flowers during May and June.

❁ *R. patientia* **and** *R. cristatus* **are both tall, robust docks growing up to 2 m, with dense inflorescences. The broader leaves, without an undulate margin, distinguish them from the smaller** *R. crispus*. **The veins of the leaves of** *R. patientia* **make an angle of 40°-60° with the midrib, those of** *R. cristatus* **an angle of 60°-90°.**

Rumex cristatus DC.
GREEK DOCK
Alien and a native of southern Italy, Sicily, Greece and western Anatolia. It has become thoroughly established in waste places in the London area and around the Thames estuary, and in addition has been recorded from around Cardiff, Minehead and Reading. A tall perennial, it flowers during June and July.

Rumex crispus L.
CURLED DOCK
One of the most widely distributed plants in the world. It occurs throughout the British Isles, but is less common in the north of Scotland. It is a common plant of disturbed ground, waste places, cultivated soils, roadsides, hedge banks, pond, lake, river and canal banks and marshes on both calcareous and non-calcareous soils, but avoids the most acid conditions and shaded habitats. A distinct subspecies, subsp. *littoreus* (Hardy) Akeroyd, is common on shingle beaches and maritime dunes all around the coast. A serious agricultural pest, *R. crispus* is one of the five species scheduled as injurious weeds under the Weeds Act, 1959. A perennial, it flowers from June to October and is usually wind-pollinated.
❁ *R. crispus* **is a tall dock growing to about 1 m and is distinguished by the parallel-sided leaves with a characteristic crisped and wavy margin, dense inflorescence and almost untoothed, tubercled fruits.**

Rumex frutescens Thourars
ARGENTINE DOCK
Alien and a native of South America and the south Atlantic islands. It has been established in dune slacks in Braunton Burrows in north Devon since 1924 and on Kenfig Dunes in Glamorgan since 1934. It has also been reported as a temporary alien from a number of ports on the west coast of Britain, especially around the Bristol Channel. A creeping perennial, it is in flower during July and August. (Not illustrated.)

URTICACEAE

Urtica dioica L.

COMMON NETTLE
STINGING NETTLE

Ubiquitous throughout the British Isles and reaching to an altitude of 850 m in Scotland. It is a plant of woodlands, fens, ditches and river and stream sides and habitats associated with man, such as farms, gardens, rubbish tips, fire sites and abandoned buildings. It requires fertile soils and is especially characteristic of phosphorus-rich habitats. A dioecious perennial, it flowers from June to August and is wind-pollinated. Nettle fibres have been used for the making of cloth since the Bronze Age, and it was cultivated in Scandinavia and possibly in Scotland until the 18th century. The young leaves are also used in nettle soup and can be prepared and eaten like spinach.
❁ ***U. dioica*** **can be distinguished from** ***U. urens*** **by the cordate base to the lower leaves, which are longer than the petioles. The lower leaves of** ***U. urens*** **are not cordate and are shorter than their petioles.**

Urtica urens L.

SMALL NETTLE

Distributed throughout the British Isles; common in the east but more local in the west. It is a plant of gardens, arable and waste ground, on calcareous to mildly acid light, well-drained soils. An annual, it flowers from June to September.

Parietaria judaica L.
(*P. diffusa* Mert. & Koch)

PELLITORY-OF-THE-WALL

Widely distributed throughout England, Wales and Ireland, but rare in southern Scotland and absent from the north and west. It is a rather local plant which grows on old walls, in the crevices of rocks and in hedge banks on dry, well-drained soils. A perennial, it flowers from June until October.

Soleirolia soleirolii (Req.) Dandy
(*Helxine soleirolii* Req.)

MIND-YOUR-OWN-BUSINESS

Endemic to the islands of the western Mediterranean and commonly planted in rock gardens and cool greenhouses. It has become widely naturalised on damp walls and banks, especially in the south-west, but also scattered throughout the rest of lowland England north to the Wash and in south Wales. An evergreen mat-forming perennial, it flowers from May to October.

CANNABACEAE

Humulus lupulus L.

HOP

The native distribution of the hop extends over the whole of England and Wales north to the Solway, but becoming increasingly scarce north of the Humber. It has been introduced into both Scotland and Ireland, where it has become naturalised in widely scattered localities. It is a frequent plant of hedgerows, thickets and the woodland edge on loamy soils and fen peat. An herbaceous perennial climber, it flowers during July and August and is dioecious, with separate male and female plants.

Many records of wild hops are undoubted relics of cultivation. Hop-growing was introduced from Flanders early in the 16th century and is now confined to the counties of Kent, Sussex, Hampshire and Surrey and to Worcestershire and Herefordshire in the West Midlands. In the past it also extended to Essex, Suffolk and Nottinghamshire.

MYRICACEAE

Myrica gale L.

BOG MYRTLE

A distinctively northern and western distribution in the British Isles, being common in Scotland north and west of a line from the Clyde to Aberdeen, in Kirkcudbrightshire and Wigtownshire, the Lake District, north-west Wales, Cornwall and the west and north-west of Ireland. It is also frequent in the New Forest and the Dorset heaths. Elsewhere it occurs as a few scattered relic populations, as in the Norfolk Broads. It is an abundant and sometimes dominant plant of the wetter parts of acid bogs and fens, especially where there is moving ground water, to an altitude of 550 m. A dioecious shrub, it flowers during April and May and is wind-pollinated.

ERICACEAE

Ledum palustre L.*

LABRADOR-TEA

A rare escape from cultivation in bogs near Bridge of Allan in Perthshire, and sporadically in Surrey, Derbyshire, Lancashire, Yorkshire, Cumbria and Kirkcudbrightshire. It is an evergreen shrub of up to 1 m and flowers during June and July.

All British records are of subsp. *groenlandicum* (Oeder) Holten, a native of North America and west Greenland; the north European subsp. *palustre* has been recorded only in error.

❁ ***Ledum*** **differs from other members of the** ***Ericaceae*** **in the rusty-coloured hairs on the undersurface of the leaves and in the free petals.**

Loiseleuria procumbens (L.) Desv.

TRAILING AZALEA

Widespread in the Cairngorms and the central and western Highlands of Scotland at altitudes of more than 1,220 m, but down to 400 m on Orkney. It is a plant of bare stony ground and moorland on acid soils. An evergreen dwarf shrub, it flowers from May to July and is pollinated by small insects or self-pollinated.
❁ ***Loiseleuria*** **can be distinguished from other members of the family by its habit, opposite but not overlapping leaves, and the petals falling soon after flowering.**

Phyllodoce caerulea (L.) Bab.**

BLUE HEATH

Very rare and known from about three localities only in the Scottish Highlands, in Inverness-shire and on the Sow of Atholl in Perthshire, where it has been known for about 150 years growing in a single patch among other dwarf shrubs on acid rock at an altitude of about 740 m. It suffered from the depredations of collectors in the past but it is now protected by law. A dwarf evergreen shrub, it is in flower during June and July and is either insect- or self-pollinated.
❁ ***Phyllodoce*** **is only likely to be confused with** ***Andromeda*** **(Plate 53), from which it differs in the dense linear leaves and glandular pedicels and calyx.**

❁ ***Erica*** **differs from** ***Calluna*** **in the whorled, not opposite, leaves and the calyx, which is shorter than the corolla.** ***Daboecia*** **has alternate, not opposite or whorled, leaves.**

Erica vagans L.*

CORNISH HEATH

Confined to a small area of about 10 localities in west Cornwall in the neighbourhood of the Lizard and to a single locality in Fermanagh in Ireland. Around the Lizard, it is a major constituent of the mixed heath communities of the ultra-basic, magnesium-rich infertile soils of the serpentine growing in association with western gorse (*Ulex gallii*), black bog-rush (*Schoenus nigricans*) and moor-grass (*Molinia caerulea*). An evergreen dwarf shrub, it flowers in July and August. Forms of *E. vagans* are commonly cultivated and occasionally escape.

❁ **Both** ***E. vagans*** **and** ***E. erigena*** **(Plate 55) have stamens longer than the corolla.** ***E. vagans*** **grows to about 75 cm and the pedicels are longer than the flowers.** ***E. erigena*** **is a taller shrub, growing to about 2 m, and the pedicels are shorter than the flowers.**

❁ ***E. tetralix, E. ciliaris*** **and** ***E. mackaiana*** **have the leaves fringed with long, usually glandular hairs.** ***E. ciliaris*** **differs from** ***E. tetralix*** **and** ***E. mackaiana*** **in the elongated inflorescence.**

Erica tetralix L.

CROSS-LEAVED HEATH

Abundant in the north and west and on the heaths of southern England, and absent from most of the English Midlands. It is a common plant of acid bogs, wet heaths and moorland on waterlogged, poorly aerated peats to an altitude of about 760 m. It typically grows mixed with other ericaceous dwarf shrub species. An evergreen dwarf shrub, it flowers from July until September and is insect- or self-pollinated.

❁ **The flowers of** ***E. tetralix*** **and** ***E. mackaiana*** **are in terminal umbel-like heads. The leaves of** ***E. tetralix*** **are grey-green and hairy all over. The leaves of** ***E. mackaiana*** **are dark green and glabrous on the upper surface.**

Erica mackaiana Bab.*

MACKAY'S HEATH

Very rare and confined in the British Isles to blanket bog in west Donegal and west Galway. A dwarf evergreen shrub, it flowers during August and September, but seed is not set in Ireland.

Erica ciliaris L.*

DORSET HEATH

Very local and confined to heaths in Cornwall, Devon and Dorset and to a single small population in Galway in western Ireland. Over 40 localities are known, the majority of which are in Cornwall, and in some the plant is abundant. It is a plant of wet acid heaths, often with moor-grass, *Molinia caerulea*, *E. tetralix* and *Ulex gallii*. A dwarf evergreen shrub, it flowers from June to September.

Erica cinerea L.

BELL HEATHER

Abundant in the north and west and the heaths of southern England and absent from most of the English Midlands. It is a common plant of lowland sub-alpine heaths and open woodland and maritime heaths and on dry acid, well-drained mineral soils, most often growing in association with other ericaceous dwarf shrub species, and reaching an altitude of 930 m. It flowers from July to September and is either insect- or self- pollinated.
❁ ***E. cinerea*** **is distinguished by the dark green, glossy, glabrous leaves and short axillary shoots and purple flowers.**

Erica erigena R. Ross*
(*E. mediterranea sensu* auct)
IRISH HEATH
Very local and confined to West Mayo and to a single site in West Galway in western Ireland. It is locally abundant on the better-drained parts of acid peat bogs such as occur around the margins of lakes and streams. An evergreen shrub of up to 2 m, it flowers from March to May.
❁ ***E. erigena* is a medium-sized shrub growing to about 2 m. It is similar to *E. vagans* (Plate 54), which grows to about 75 cm, in that the stamens are longer than the corolla, but the pedicels are longer than the flowers. The pedicels of *E. erigena* are shorter than the flowers.**

Erica lusitanica Rudolphi
PORTUGUESE HEATH
Alien and a native of south-west Europe from southern Portugal to south-west France. It is occasionally cultivated and has become established in Dorset and on railway banks in Cornwall. An evergreen shrub of up to 2 m, it flowers from March to May.
❁ ***E. lusitanica* is a tall species growing to 1-2 m and is distinguished from other species by the glabrous leaves and white flowers when open.**

❁ ***Daboecia* differs from both *Erica* and *Calluna* in the leaves, which are alternate and white and felty beneath.**

Daboecia cantabrica (Huds.) K. Koch
ST DABEOC'S HEATH
Confined in the British Isles to West Galway and Mayo in western Ireland where it is common, it grows among *Ulex gallii* and *Calluna* in exposed heathland on thin, acid siliceous soils up to an altitude of 580 m. It appears unable to survive on either deep peat or limestone. A low evergreen straggling shrub, it flowers from July to September and is probably pollinated by bees and thrips. It is commonly grown in gardens and several colour varieties have been developed.

❁ ***Calluna* differs from *Erica* in the small opposite overlapping leaves and in the calyx being longer than, and the same colour as, the corolla. It usually grows to about 60 cm.**

Calluna vulgaris (L.) Hull
HEATHER
LING
Distributed throughout the whole of the British Isles except for the most intensively farmed clays and chalk soils of the lowlands. It is an abundant plant of heaths, moors, bogs and open birch, pine and oak woodland and mature leached sand dunes. It is characteristic of acid, nutrient-deficient mineral soils and peat to an altitude of 1,036 m. An evergreen dwarf shrub, it flowers from July to September and is pollinated by a wide variety of insects, particularly bees and thrips, and by wind.

❁ ***Vaccinium* differs from other ericaceous genera in the inferior ovary (the calyx and corolla are inserted above the ovary).**

Vaccinium oxycoccos L.
CRANBERRY
Widely distributed in Wales, northern England, central and southern Scotland and parts of Ireland; rare and local elsewhere. It is a plant of acid bogs and wet acid heaths and open boggy woodlands, usually creeping over a surface of *Sphagnum* moss. A prostrate evergreen plant with wiry stems, it flowers from June to August. The berries ripen in August to October.

❁ ***V. oxycoccos* and *V. microcarpum* have fine creeping stems and the petals are free almost to the base. *V. oxycoccus* has very shortly and softly hairy pedicels, and leaves that are parallel-sided for part of their length. The pedicels of *V. microcarpum* are glabrous, the leaves are more triangular and the flowers a darker pink.**

Vaccinium microcarpum (Rupr.) Schmalh.
SMALL CRANBERRY
A local species more or less confined to the eastern Highlands of Scotland from Perthshire to Inverness-shire. It grows in acid bogs characterised by an abundance of *Calluna*, the hare's-tail cotton-grass, *Eriophorum vaginatum* and *Sphagnum* moss at altitudes of up to 670 m. An evergreen, prostrate dwarf shrub, it flowers during July.

Vaccinium vitis-idaea L.
COWBERRY
A common plant throughout Scotland north of a line from the Clyde to Aberdeen. It occurs scattered throughout Wales, the Pennines and the uplands of northern England and southern Scotland, and is rather rare and local in Ireland. It is a plant of moors and open woodland on acid, nutrient-deficient soils to an altitude of 1,070 m. An evergreen dwarf shrub of up to 30 cm, it flowers from June to August and is pollinated by bees or self-pollinated.

❁ ***V. vitis-idaea* differs from *V. myrtillus* and *V. uliginosum* in the glossy, evergreen leaves.**

Vaccinium myrtillus L.
BILBERRY
Widely distributed throughout northern and western Britain and the heaths of southern England. It is a common, and sometimes dominant, plant on moors and heathland and in the field layer of oak, birch and pine woodlands on dry acid soils. It is tolerant of both shade and exposure and reaches altitudes of over 1,220 m in Scotland. A dwarf deciduous shrub of up to 60 cm, it flowers from April to June and is pollinated chiefly by bees or occasionally self-pollinated.

❁ **The leaves of *V. myrtillus* are finely toothed and bright green; the leaves of *V. uliginosum* are entire and blue-green.**

Vaccinium uliginosum L.
BOG BILBERRY
A local plant distributed throughout the eastern, central and western Highlands of Scotland with a few scattered localities south of the border in Cumbria and Northumberland. It reaches Orkney and Shetland but is absent from the Outer Hebrides. It is occasionally abundant on damp heather and bilberry moors on acid soils at altitudes of up to 1,070 m. A low deciduous shrub of up to 50 cm, it flowers during May and June and is pollinated by bees.
❁ ***Arctostaphylos* differs from *Vaccinium* in the superior ovary (petals and sepals inserted beneath the ovary). *A. uva-ursi* has evergreen, entire leaves; *A. alpinus* has deciduous, toothed leaves.**

Arctostaphylos uva-ursi (L.) Spreng.
BEARBERRY
Widespread and common in the Scottish Highlands north and west of a line from the Clyde to Aberdeen and including Orkney, Shetland and the Outer Hebrides. In England there are a few isolated localities in the Lake District and the Pennines south to Derbyshire, while in Ireland it is more or less confined to the north-west coast. Bearberry grows on exposed moorland on stony or thin peaty ground up to 915 m. A prostrate evergreen shrub, it flowers from May to July and is pollinated by bees or self-pollinated.

Arctostaphylos alpinus (L.) Spreng.
(*Arctous alpinus* (L.) Niedenzu)
ALPINE BEARBERRY
BLACK BEARBERRY
A local species confined to the mountains of northern and north-west Scotland extending as far south as Wester Ross and with isolated localities in Orkney and Shetland. It occurs at altitudes of up to 915 m in exposed mountain heathland on acid rock together with *Empetrum* and *Calluna* and also on peaty moorland with *Calluna* and the hare's-tail cotton-grass. A deciduous prostrate shrub, it flowers from May until August.

Andromeda polifolia L.
BOG-ROSEMARY
A local and decreasing species, scattered in west Wales, northern England and southern Scotland north to Ayrshire, with isolated localities north to Stirlingshire and distributed throughout central Ireland. It is a plant of the acid *Sphagnum* peats of raised and blanket bogs up to an altitude of 530 m. Rarely, it also occurs on wet heaths. A dwarf evergreen shrub of up to 30 cm, it flowers from May until September and is visited by bees, flies and butterflies, but capsules seldom develop.
❁ ***Andromeda* grows to about 30 cm and is unlikely to be confused with any other species except *Phyllodoce*, from which it differs in the broader, non-crowded leaves and glabrous calyx and pedicels.**

Gaultheria shallon Pursh
SHALLON
Alien and a native of western North America from California to Alaska. *G. shallon* was introduced to Britain in 1826 and has been commonly planted as game covert, and is now widely naturalised in open woodland on acid sands and peat in a number of places. A low shrub of up to 1.8 m, it flowers during May and June.

Gaultheria mucronata (L.) Hook. & Arn.
(*Pernettya mucronata* (L.f.) Gaudich. ex Spreng.)
PRICKLY HEATH
Alien and a native of Chile south to the Magellan region. It is commonly planted in gardens and occasionally appears as an escape on sandy, well-drained soils. Since its first introduction in 1828 a large number of cultivated varieties have been developed. An evergreen shrub of 1-2 m, it flowers during May and June.
❁ ***G. mucronata* is distinguished by the spiny leaves and white flowers.**

PYROLACEAE

Orthilia secunda (L.) House
SERRATED WINTERGREEN
Scattered throughout the Scottish Highlands from Stirlingshire northwards and with isolated localities in Dumfries, Cumbria, Brecon and Fermanagh. It is absent from Orkney, Shetland and the Outer Hebrides. It is a plant of montane woodland and damp rock ledges up to an altitude of 730 m. An evergreen perennial, it flowers during July and August and is insect- or self-pollinated.

Moneses uniflora (L.) A. Gray*
ONE-FLOWERED WINTERGREEN
A very rare, local and decreasing species, confined to the native pinewoods of Banffshire, Moray, Inverness-shire, Ross and Sutherland. An evergreen perennial herb, it flowers from June to August and is insect- or self-pollinated.

 (see illustrations page 122)

❁ ***P. rotundifolia*** **differs from *P. minor* and *P. intermedia* in the almost flat corolla and curved style. Subsp. *rotundifolia* has 1-2 scales on the flowering stem, the calyx lobes are acute and the style 6-10 mm long. Subsp. *maritima* has 2-5 scales on the flowering stem, the calyx lobes are obtuse and the style is 4-6 mm long.**

Pyrola rotundifolia L.
ROUND-LEAVED WINTERGREEN LARGE WINTERGREEN
A very scarce and local species scattered throughout the British Isles but completely absent from the south-west and the Outer Hebrides. An evergreen herb, it flowers from July to September and is insect- or self-pollinated.

In Britain, the species consists of two subspecies. Subsp. *rotundifolia* is most frequent in the Scottish Highlands where it occurs on damp mountain rock ledges, often on base-rich soils to an altitude of 760 m. It is also found in acid woodland, bogs and fens as in the Norfolk Broads. Subsp. *maritima* (Kenyon) E.F. Warburg is a rare plant of coastal calcareous dune-slacks in south Wales, Flintshire, Cumbria and Lancashire.

Pyrola minor L.
COMMON WINTERGREEN
A local and decreasing species scattered throughout the British Isles but absent from Orkney, Shetland, the Outer Hebrides, the south-west, East Anglia, most of Wales and rare in Ireland. In southern England it is a plant of woodlands, often on calcareous soils, but in northern England and Scotland it more frequently occurs on moorland and damp rock-ledges up to an altitude of 1,145 m. It is occasionally found on coastal dunes. An evergreen perennial, it flowers from June to August and is either insect- or self-pollinated.

❁ ***P. minor*** **and *P. intermedia* have bowl-shaped corollas and straight styles. The style of *P. minor* is 1-2 mm long and included in the corolla, that of *P. media* is 4-6 mm long and longer than the corolla.**

Pyrola media Swartz
INTERMEDIATE WINTERGREEN
A scarce and decreasing plant that is now only at all frequent in the eastern Highlands of Scotland, with a few scattered localities in the west. It has virtually disappeared from England and in Ireland it occurs only in the north, where it is also rare and decreasing. It is most characteristic of the Scottish pine woods but is also found on moorland up to an altitude of 550 m. An evergreen perennial, it flowers from June to August.

MONOTROPACEAE

❁ ***Monotropa*** **bears a superficial resemblance to *Lathraea* and *Orobanche*, from which it can be separated by its symmetrical flowers. The inside of the flower of subsp. *hypopitys* is hairy; that of subsp. *hypophegea* is glabrous.**

Monotropa hypopitys L.
YELLOW BIRD'S-NEST
A very local species of southern England, but with a few scattered localities further north. Very rare in Scotland, Ireland, Wales and the south-west. It is typically a plant of pine or beech woods on calcareous soils. It flowers from June until August and is insect-pollinated. The species is separated into subsp. *hypopitys* and subsp. *hypophegea* (Wallr.) Holmboe which are sometimes given specific rank. Subsp. *hypophegea* is also found on sand dunes on the west coast growing among creeping willow, *Salix repens* subsp. *argentea*.

EMPETRACEAE

Empetrum nigrum L.
CROWBERRY
Restricted to the north and west of Britain except for two isolated localities on the Norfolk coast. It is common on mountains and moorlands throughout Scotland, Wales, northern England, on high ground on Dartmoor and Exmoor and in northern and western Ireland. It grows from sea level to about 1,070 m, usually on dry acid peat in exposed conditions, but it is also found in open birch and pine woodland. A low evergreen shrub of up to 45 cm, it flowers during May and June and is wind-pollinated.

A very variable plant, it has been separated into two subspecies: subsp. *nigrum* is usually dioecious and is present throughout the range of the species. Subsp. *hermaphroditum* (Hagerup) Böcher is more or less confined in Britain to high altitudes in the mountains north and west of a line from the Clyde to Aberdeen and is absent from Ireland. The flowers are hermaphrodite.

❁ **Subsp. *nigrum* has red young stems, rooting along their length, and the leaves are 3-5 times as long as broad; the young stems of subsp. *hermaphroditum* are green, not rooting, and the leaves 2-4 times as long as broad.**

DIAPENSIACEAE

Diapensia lapponica L.**
DIAPENSIA
Known in Britain from two sites in west Inverness-shire. It was discovered in July 1951 by C.F. Tebbutt growing on an exposed rocky mountain crest at an altitude of about 760 m in an area covering less than 0.5 ha. A cushion-like dwarf of up to 5 cm, it flowers during May and June.

PLUMBAGINACEAE

Limonium vulgare Mill.
COMMON SEA-LAVENDER
Occurs around the coasts of the British Isles as far north as the Firth of Forth on the east and the north shore of the Solway on the west. It is absent from Ireland and from the extreme west of Pembrokeshire, where it is replaced by *L. humile*. It is abundant and frequently dominant in the intermediate zone of intertidal salt marshes on deep mud. A perennial, it flowers from late June until the beginning of October and is pollinated by various bees, flies and butterflies.

❁ ***L. vulgare*** **and *L. humile* can be distinguished from the other species of sea-lavenders by their long slender leaf stalks and the presence of five small teeth between the five main calyx teeth. *L. humile* differs from *L. vulgare* in the more diffuse inflorescence, which branches from below the middle. Hybrids between the two species are frequent.**

Limonium humile Mill.
LAX-FLOWERED SEA-LAVENDER
Distributed all round the coasts of England, Wales and Ireland, except for south-west England. In Scotland it is restricted to the coasts of Dumfries and Kirkcudbrightshire. It grows in similar habitats to *L. vulgare* but is never as abundant and has a narrower altitudinal range within the salt marsh. It also occurs on rocky sandy shores and in fine shingle along the drift line, especially in Ireland. A perennial, it flowers from late June until the beginning of October and is pollinated by various bees, flies and beetles.

Limonium bellidifolium (Gouan)Dum.*
MATTED SEA-LAVENDER
Very local, being confined to Britain to the coast of north Norfolk between Blakeney and Wolferton and to two small populations on the Lincolnshire side of the Wash. It characteristically grows in a more or less distinct zone along the sandy margins of the upper levels of salt marshes. A perennial, it flowers during July and August and is insect-pollinated.

❁ ***L. bellidifolium*** **is easily recognised by the numerous, richly-branched sterile shoots on the lower part of the inflorescence.**

Limonium auriculae-ursifolium (Pourret) Druce(*)
ALDERNEY SEA-LAVENDER
Very rare; found only on rocks by the sea in Alderney and Jersey. A perennial, it flowers from June to September and is insect-pollinated. It is also apomictic.

❁ ***L. auriculae-ursifolium*** **differs from the *L. binervosum* group in the broader, five-veined leaves. The leaf of *L. binervosum* is narrower and usually three-veined in the lower part.**

L. binervosum, *L. paradoxum*, *L. transwallianum* and *L. recurvum* are a confusing group of closely related species, most of which are probably apomictic. The true identity of some populations has still to be established. Recent research suggests that neither *L. transwallianum* nor *L. paradoxum* occurs in Ireland and that populations so named may represent previously undescribed species.

The spikes of *L. binervosum*, *L. transwallianum* and *L. recurvum* are more elongated than those of *L. paradoxum*.

Limonium binervosum (G.E. Sm.) C.E. Salmon
ROCK SEA-LAVENDER
A local species, distributed around the British coast as far north as the Humber on the east and Kirkcudbrightshire on the west and scattered and decreasing all around the coast of Ireland. It grows on dry maritime cliffs, rocks and consolidated shingle. A perennial, it flowers from July to September and is insect-pollinated.

❁ ***L. binervosum*** **is distinguished from *L. transwallianum* and *L. recurvum* by the individual spikelets being sufficiently separated to prevent overlap of the bracts of neighbouring spikelets.**

Limonium recurvum C.E. Salmon*
Very rare and confined to three sites: near Portland in Dorset, Cumbria and the Mull of Galloway, where it grows on maritime cliffs and rocks. The population is large and the plant is similar in appearance to *L. binervosum*, to which it is closely related. An apomictic perennial, endemic to the British Isles, it flowers from July to September.

❁ ***L. recurvum*** **has a three-veined leaf-stalk and the petals overlap. *L. transwallianum* has a one-veined leaf-stalk and the petals are separate.**

Limonium transwallianum (Pugsl.) Pugsl.*
Very rare and endemic. Now known only from two localities in Pembrokeshire and from the Burren and the Arran Isles in western Ireland. It is a plant of maritime cliffs, and flowers from July to September.

Limonium paradoxum Pugsl.*
Very rare and endemic to the British Isles, growing on igneous rocks near St David's Head in Pembrokeshire and possibly near Malin Head in East Donegal on the coast of Northern Ireland. An apomictic perennial, it flowers from July to September.

❁ **The individual flowers of *Limonium* are arranged in 1-5 flowered spikelets which are themselves clustered into spikes. *L. paradoxum* is distinguished by the inflorescence consisting of heads of spikes with only two spikelets.**

Armeria maritima (Mill.) Willd.
THRIFT
SEA PINK
Found all around the coasts of the British Isles where it is a common plant of the middle zone of muddy salt marshes, often growing with *Limonium vulgare*. It is tolerant of grazing and is sometimes found in the close-grazed turf of brackish meadows. It is also a characteristic and sometimes abundant plant of maritime rocks and cliffs. Inland it appears as an alpine in northern England and Scotland, especially in the west, where it grows on mountain rocks and cliffs to an altitude of 1,280 m. A perennial, it flowers from April to October but the main period is in June and July. It is insect-pollinated.

The common plant is subsp. *maritima*. Subsp. *elongata* (Hoffm.) Bonnier* is very rare and restricted in Britain to about three localities in old pasture on sandy soils near Ancaster in Lincolnshire.

❁ ***A. maritima* subsp. *elongata* differs from subsp. *maritima* in the longer (up to 50 cm) glabrous inflorescence stalks.**

Armeria arenaria (Pers.) Schult.
(*A. alliacea* auct.)
JERSEY THRIFT
Known in the British Isles only from Jersey in the Channel Islands, where it grows on stable coastal sand dunes. A perennial, it flowers from June to September and is insect-pollinated.

❁ ***A. arenaria* is a more robust plant than *A. maritima* and the leaves are broader with 3-5, not one, veins.**

PRIMULACEAE

Primula vulgaris Huds.
PRIMROSE
Distributed throughout the whole of the British Isles, although much less frequent in some areas than formerly due mainly to over-collecting. It is a characteristic plant of woodland clearings, coppice, hedge banks and, especially in the west, old grassland, particularly on heavy soils. A perennial, it flowers from January to May and is insect-pollinated. The familiar 'pin-eyed' and 'thrum-eyed' forms are an example of heterostyly. Pollination of a 'pin' flower by 'thrum' pollen results in a much higher degree of fertilisation than pollination by pollen from a flower of the same kind. The two different kinds of flowers have pollen of different sizes and surface sculpturing that are only compatible with stigmas of the opposite kind.

Primula veris L.
COWSLIP
Widely distributed throughout the British Isles north to the Solway. Further north it is also scarce in parts of Wales, the south-west and Ireland except for the central parts. It is absent from Shetland and the Outer Hebrides. Cowslips are plants of old meadows, pastures and grassland, hedgebanks, open scrub and woodland clearings usually on well-drained calcareous or base-rich soils, but in recent years it has often colonised the banks of motorways. A perennial, it flowers during April and May. Cowslip is the food plant of the larvae of the Duke of Burgundy fritillary, *Hamearis lucina*.

Primula elatior (L.) Hill
OXLIP
Very local and restricted in Britain to two small areas of eastern England comprising parts of Essex, Suffolk, Cambridgeshire and Huntingdonshire. Within this area it is abundant in almost every ancient coppice woodland on the poorly drained soils of the chalky boulder clay. Its distribution corresponds with areas in which the primrose is scarce. Where the two grow together in the same wood, the primrose tends to grow on the better-drained sandy areas; hybrids are frequent. A perennial, it flowers during April and May.

❁ ***P. elatior* can be distinguished from hybrids between *P. vulgaris* and *P. veris* by the small, paler flowers all nodding to the same side of the inflorescence and the absence of folds in the throat.**

Primula scotica Hook.*
SCOTTISH PRIMROSE
Endemic to the British Isles. Restricted to the north coast of Scotland in Sutherland and Caithness and to Orkney. It is locally abundant in coastal cliff pastures with poor drainage, wet dune-slacks and grass heaths on base-rich sands or boulder clay. A biennial or perennial, it flowers from May until June and again from mid-July to August and is probably self-pollinated. It was first recorded in 1819 as having been found by Mr Gibb of Inverness on Holborn Head near Thurso.

❁ ***P. scotica* differs from *P. farinosa* in the shorter stems (10 cm), absence of blunt teeth on the leaves, and darker flowers.**

Primula farinosa L.
BIRD'S-EYE PRIMROSE
Confined in Britain to an area of northern England comprising parts of Lancashire, Yorkshire, Co. Durham and Cumbria. It is often abundant in the damp grazed calcareous grassland and the drier parts of calcareous mires of the Carboniferous limestone. It is especially characteristic of the Craven district of north-west Yorkshire and of Upper Teesdale. A perennial, it flowers during May and June.

Lysimachia nemorum L.
YELLOW PIMPERNEL
Distributed throughout the British Isles, but rare or absent in parts of the East Midlands and absent from Shetland. It is a frequent plant of woodland flushes, damp woodland rides, the margins of woodland streams and damp hedge banks and ditch-sides on mildly acid soils. A perennial, it flowers from May to September.

❁ ***L. nemorum* differs from *L. nummularia* in the acute leaves and narrow sepals.**

Lysimachia nummularia L.
CREEPING-JENNY
Widespread throughout Britain north to the Clyde but rare north of the Humber, in north Wales and absent as a native plant in the south-west. It is rare over most of Ireland but local in the north. A plant of damp ditch-sides and hedgerows, damp shaded grassy habitats and the shaded margins of rivers and streams, it is a perennial and flowers from June to August.

Lysimachia punctata L.
DOTTED LOOSESTRIFE
Alien and a native of south-east Europe and Asia Minor. It is naturalised in a number of places throughout the British Isles by the sides of woodland streams and rivers and in marshy fields. A widely cultivated garden perennial, it flowers from June to September.

❁ ***L. punctata* differs from *L. ciliata* and *L. vulgaris* in the margins of the petals fringed with glandular hairs.**

Lysimachia ciliata L.
FRINGED LOOSESTRIFE
Alien and a native of North America. It occurs naturalised in a few scattered localities near buildings throughout England, Wales and Scotland. A perennial, it flowers in June and July.

❁ ***L. ciliata* differs from *L. vulgaris* in the longer pedicels (2-4 cm) and in the margins of the sepals being green, not orange.**

Lysimachia vulgaris L.
YELLOW LOOSESTRIFE
Scattered throughout most of the British Isles north to Aberdeen. It is a locally common plant of marshes, fens and river and lake margins on fertile, neutral or alkaline soils. A tall perennial, up to 150 m, it flowers during July and August.

Lysimachia thyrsiflora L.
(*Naumbergia thyrsiflora* (L.) Reichb.)
TUFTED LOOSESTRIFE
A rare and local plant now restricted in Britain to parts of east Yorkshire and to the Scottish lowlands, including Angus, Perth, Lanarkshire, Ayrshire and Renfrewshire. It grows in shallow water at the margins of still or slow-flowing lakes, ditches, canals and streams and in wet marshes. A perennial of up to 60 cm, it flowers during June and July.

❁ ***L. thyrsiflora* differs from the other species in the dense-flowered axillary inflorescences, small flowers and exserted stamens.**

Trientalis europaea L.
CHICKWEED WINTERGREEN
Widely distributed in Scotland north of the Clyde, but extending southwards as far as Derbyshire and with a few isolated localities in east Suffolk. It is a locally common plant of mossy pinewoods, reaching an altitude of 1,070 m. A short perennial of up to 25 cm, it flowers during June and July and is insect- pollinated.

Glaux maritima L.
SEA-MILKWORT
Distributed all around the coasts of the British Isles, it is a common plant of the drier parts of salt-marshes, brackish grassland and coastal rock crevices. It also occurs in saline habitats inland in Worcestershire and Staffordshire. A small perennial, it flowers from June to August and is either self-pollinated or pollinated by small flies.

❁ ***Glaux* is distinguished by the succulent stems and leaves, white to pink sepals and absence of petals.**

 (see illustrations page 126)

Hottonia palustris L.
WATER-VIOLET
A local species of lowland England with a few isolated localities in Wales and Ireland. Except for the Somerset Levels, it is most frequent in the east and south-east. It grows in shallow clear, unpolluted water in still or slow-moving ditches, dykes, pools and ponds on fertile soils. A floating perennial, it flowers during May and June and is insect-pollinated.

Anagallis minima (L.) E.H. Krause
CHAFFWEED
A local but widespread plant of southern England and coastal areas of Wales, Scotland and western Ireland, but rare and decreasing elsewhere. It is a plant of open or disturbed ground on damp sandy soils on heaths, commons and woodland rides and in the fine turf of damp dune-slacks by the sea. A small annual up to about 4 cm high, it flowers during June and July.
❁ ***A. minima* has much the stature of *Radiola linoides* (Plate 27), with which it often grows. It is less diffusely branched and has alternate leaves and tiny petals shorter than the sepals.**

Anagallis tenella (L.) L.
BOG PIMPERNEL
Distributed throughout the British Isles but much more frequent in the west and very scarce and decreasing in eastern Scotland and parts of the English lowlands. It is a plant of wet grassy habitats on acid soils, spring mires, bogs, the margins of acid pools and streams and wet woodland rides on sandy soils. A prostrate perennial, it flowers from June to August.

❁ ***A. tenella* differs from *A. arvensis* in the smooth creeping stems rooting at the nodes, rounded leaves and paler flowers.**

Anagallis arvensis subsp. *arvensis* L.
SCARLET PIMPERNEL
Widespread throughout the British Isles north to Orkney, but becoming increasingly scarce and coastal in its distribution from Co. Durham northwards and scattered throughout Ireland. It is a common and familiar weed of arable crops, gardens, pathsides, dunes and waste ground in a variety of conditions but showing a preference for lighter, well-drained soils. In warm, sunny weather the flowers open at about 8 a.m. and close at around 2 to 3 a.m. They also close in dull, cool weather. A procumbent winter annual, it flowers from June to August. The scarlet pimpernel produces a number of colour varieties including pink, lilac, blue-purple and white. The blue form is sometimes mistaken for the subsp. *caerulea*.
❁ **Subsp. *arvensis* has red or, more rarely, blue flowers with the petals densely fringed with glandular hairs.**

Anagallis arvensis subsp. *caerulea* Hartman
(*A. arvensis* subsp. *foemina* (Mill.) Schinz & Thell.)
BLUE PIMPERNEL
A local plant with a widely scattered distribution throughout the British Isles, but perhaps more frequent in the south and west. It has been frequently confused with the blue form of subsp. *arvensis* in the past so that its true distribution is unclear. Subsp. *foemina* is primarily a plant of arable fields and gardens. A summer annual, it is in flower from June to August.
❁ **Subsp. *foemina* has blue petals that are only sparsely fringed with glandular hairs.**

Samolus valerandi L.
BROOKWEED
Scattered around the coasts of the British Isles as far north as Skye and Lewis on the west and the Firth of Forth on the east. It also occurs inland in suitable habitats, especially in eastern England. It is a local plant of pond, pool, dyke and river margins and wet grassland on sandy, often brackish soils. A perennial, it flowers from June until August.

BUDDLEJACEAE

Buddleja davidii Franchet
BUTTERFLY-BUSH
Alien and a native of central and western China, introduced to British gardens about 1890. It was first recorded established in the wild in 1930 and is now thoroughly naturalised throughout southern England as well as in a number of scattered localities in Scotland, Wales and Ireland. It grows on railway and road embankments, waste ground and cliffs, often close to the sea. It was particularly abundant on London bomb sites after the Second World War. A shrub of up to 5 m, it flowers from June to October and is very attractive to butterflies. There are numerous cultivated varieties.

OLEACEAE

Ligustrum vulgare L.
WILD PRIVET
Distributed throughout the British Isles, but becoming scarcer in Wales and northern England and rare north of the Firth of Forth. It is probably only native as far north as Co. Durham and naturalised elsewhere. A common plant of scrub, old hedgerows and wood borders on base-rich or calcareous soils, it is particularly abundant on the chalk. A semi-evergreen shrub of up to 5 m, it flowers during June and July and is pollinated by a wide variety of insects.

❁ ***L. ovalifolium* differs from *L. vulgare* in the glabrous young twigs and broader leaves.**

Ligustrum ovalifolium Hassk.
GARDEN PRIVET
Alien and a native of Japan. It is one of the commonest garden shrubs and is widely used for hedging even in the middle of industrial areas. It was originally introduced around 1885 and occasionally becomes established in woodlands and hedgerows, usually near buildings. A semi-evergreen, it flowers during July. A form with yellow, green-centred leaves, cv. 'Aureum', is commonly cultivated.

Syringa vulgaris L.
LILAC
Alien and a native of the mountains of south-east Europe. Lilac has been cultivated in Britain since the 16th century and there is now a vast range of garden cultivars. It occasionally becomes naturalised in hedgerows and thickets close to gardens. A deciduous shrub or small tree of up to 7 m, it flowers during May and is pollinated by bees.

APOCYNACEAE

Vinca major L.
GREATER PERIWINKLE
Alien and a native of central and southern Europe and North Africa. It has long been cultivated in Britain and is now established as far north as the Moray Firth, but is very scarce and local north of a line from the Wash to the Severn. It is rare and scattered in Ireland. It occurs in hedgerows and copses, chiefly on fertile soils. A trailing shrub of up to 1 m, it flowers from April to June and is pollinated by long-tongued bumble-bees.

❁ ***V. major* differs from *V. minor* in the longer leaf-stalks, the sepals fringed with hairs and larger flowers (4-5 cm in diameter in *V. major*, 2.5-3 cm diameter in *V. minor*.**

Vinca minor L.
LESSER PERIWINKLE
Probably introduced to Britain, although it is widespread in Europe and western Asia. It is scattered throughout the British Isles as far north as the Moray Firth but is most common in the south; in Ireland it is rare. It is found in woodlands and hedgerows on fertile soils. It frequently occurs close to gardens, but on the other hand it also grows in ancient woodlands. A procumbent shrub of up to 60 cm, it flowers from March to May and is pollinated by bee-flies and bumble-bees.

GENTIANACEAE

Cicendia filiformis (L.) Delarbre
YELLOW CENTAURY
A very local and declining species of south-west Ireland, Caernarvonshire (Lleyn Peninsula), Pembrokeshire, Cornwall, Dorset, Hampshire (New Forest), the Sussex Weald, Jersey and Guernsey. It is a scarce plant of open, damp, sandy or peaty habitats, pond margins, woodland rides, hillsides, dune-slacks and cliffs, often close to the sea. A tiny annual, it flowers from June to October.

Exaculum pusillum (Lam.) Caruel (*)
GUERNSEY CENTAURY
Very rare. Known in the British Isles only from Guernsey in the Channel Islands, where it was first discovered by Captain J.C. Gosselin in 1850. Even in Guernsey it is exceedingly scarce and varies in abundance from year to year in the fine short turf of the damp dune-slacks where it grows. A tiny annual, it flowers from July to September.

❁ ***Exaculum* differs from small plants of *Centaurium* (Plate 59) in having four, not five, petals.**

Blackstonia perfoliata (L.) Huds.
YELLOW-WORT
Distributed throughout most of southern England, extending as far north as north-west Yorkshire on the Magnesian limestone inland and to Northumberland on the east coast. In Wales and the south-west it is almost wholly coastal, and is found in central Ireland and on the east coast. It is a locally frequent plant of dry, calcareous permanent grassland on shallow chalk and limestone soils, abandoned chalk quarries and of fixed calcareous coastal dunes. An annual, it flowers from June until October and is self-pollinated.
❁ ***Blackstonia* is easily recognised by the yellow flowers and stem leaves joined in pairs across the stem.**

❁ ***Centaurium* is distinguished from *Gentianella* and *Gentiana* by the pink, not purple or blue, flowers and from *Exaculum* (Plate 58) by the five, not four, petals.**

Centaurium scilloides (L.f.) Samp.* (*C. portense* (Brot.) Butcher)
PERENNIAL CENTAURY
Very rare and confined in Britain to a few localities in west Cornwall and Pembrokeshire. A perennial, it grows on grassy maritime cliffs and in dense turf. It occasionally occurs in lawns as an escape from cultivation. It flowers during July and August.
❁ ***C. scilloides* is distinguished by the numerous decumbent non-flowering stems and erect flowering stems.**

Centaurium pulchellum (Sw.) Druce
LESSER CENTAURY
A rather local species of southern England and extending as far north on the coast as the Tees on the east and Morecambe Bay in the west. Inland it is a plant of damp, open sandy habitats on acid soils such as woodland paths and bare patches in mossy heaths. It also grows in similar conditions in the short open turf of fixed coastal sand dunes. A slender annual, it flowers from June to September and is insect- or self-pollinated.

❁ ***C. pulchellum* and *C. tenuiflorum* both lack a basal rosette of leaves, and the individual flowers are stalked and not clustered together. *C. pulchellum* is 3-10 cm tall, has 3-5 pairs of stem leaves and more widely spreading branches. *C. tenuiflorum* is 10-30 cm tall, has 6-10 pairs of stem leaves, more erect branches and a rather denser inflorescence.**

Centaurium tenuiflorum (Hoffmans. & Link) Fritsch**
SLENDER CENTAURY
Very rare and possibly extinct. It grew in damp grassy places close to the sea in two places in Dorset and in one locality in the Isle of Wight. It was last seen in Dorset in 1960 and in the Isle of Wight in 1953. A slender spring-germinating annual, it flowers from July to September.

Centaurium erythraea Rafin. (includes *C. capitatum* (Willd.) Borbas)
COMMON CENTAURY
Widely distributed throughout the whole of England, Wales and Ireland. In Scotland it is almost wholly coastal and extends as far north as Lewis on the west. It is a locally frequent plant of permanent grassland, woodland borders, open scrub, road verges and dune grassland on dry, mildly acid to calcareous well-drained soils. An annual, it flowers from June to October and is insect- or self-pollinated.

❁ ***C. erythraea* and *C. littorale* both have a basal rosette of leaves. The lower stem leaves of *C. erythraea* are ovate and more than 5 mm broad, those of *C. littorale* narrow and 5 mm broad or less.**

Centaurium littorale (Turner ex Sm.) Gilmour
SEASIDE CENTAURY
A very local plant of the coasts of Wales, north-west England, Scotland and Northumberland with isolated localities in Hampshire (introduced) and Co. Londonderry. It grows on mature sand dunes and sandy places near the sea. An autumn-germinating annual, it flowers during July and August.

❁ ***Gentianella* differs from *Gentiana* in the absence of small lobes alternating with the large corolla lobes and in the presence of a white fringe at the top of the corolla tube or along the margins of the lobes.**

Gentianella campestris (L.) Börner
FIELD GENTIAN
A widespread plant in northern England and Scotland. In Wales and central and southern England it is very rare and decreasing. It is scattered throughout most of Ireland but is most frequent in the coastal areas of the north and west. It is a plant of pastures, hill grassland and dunes on acid to neutral soils, reaching an altitude of 790 m. An annual or biennial, it flowers from July to October and is pollinated by bees and Lepidoptera or self-pollinated.
❁ ***G. campestris* is distinguished by having two large and two small calyx lobes. The other four species have four or five calyx lobes of more or less equal size.**

Gentianella germanica (Willd.) Börner
CHILTERN GENTIAN
Very local and confined to the chalk of the Chilterns in Wiltshire, Berkshire, Oxfordshire, Buckinghamshire and Bedfordshire. It is a plant of rough chalk grassland and open scrub on shallow calcareous soils. It is frequent in similar habitats in north-east France and Belgium, and its absence from the chalk south of the Thames is surprising. A biennial, it flowers from August to October and is pollinated by bumble-bees.

❁ ***G. germanica* is distinguished from *G. amarella*, *G. uliginosa* and *G. anglica* by its larger flowers (25-30 mm long). The flowers of the other three species are 20 mm long or less.**

Gentianella amarella (L.) Börner
AUTUMN GENTIAN
FELWORT
Distributed throughout the British Isles but absent from large parts of Scotland, Wales, the south-west and north-east Ireland. It is a plant of short calcareous grassland on well-drained chalk and limestone soils and of calcareous dunes and dune-slacks. A biennial, it flowers during August and September and is pollinated by bumble-bees.

G. amarella is separated into four subspecies in the British Isles. Subsp. *amarella* occurs throughout the range of the species; subsp. *septentrionalis* (Druce) Pritchard is endemic to the British Isles and confined to dunes and limestone pastures in north-west Scotland, Lewis and Shetland; subsp. *druceana* Pritchard is also endemic and occurs in limestone pastures in Perth and Aberdeen and in coastal dune-slacks from Aberdeen to Sutherland and in Orkney; all Irish plants belong to the endemic subspecies *hibernica* Pritchard.

❁ ***G. amarella* is distinguished from *G. anglica* and *G. uliginosa* by the uppermost internode and flower-stalk together forming less than half the total height of the plant.**

Gentianella uliginosa (Willd.) Börner**
DUNE GENTIAN
Very rare and confined to about eight localities in dune-slacks in Glamorgan, Carmarthenshire and Pembrokeshire. An annual or biennial, it flowers from July to November.

❁ ***G. uliginosa* is distinguished from *G. anglica* by the spreading calyx lobes and ovate leaves. *G. anglica* differs from *G. uliginosa* in the erect sepals and narrower leaves. Subsp. *anglica* is branched from the base, and subsp. *cornubiensis* is branched from the middle.**

Gentianella anglica (Pugsl.) E.F. Warb.**
EARLY GENTIAN
Very local and endemic to the British Isles. It is confined to the chalk and limestone grassland of Sussex, Kent, Hampshire, Dorset, Wiltshire, Somerset, south Devon, Gloucestershire, Lincolnshire and west Norfolk. It grows in short, closely grazed turf on shallow calcareous soils. A biennial, it flowers from April to June.
The species is separated into two subspecies. Subsp. *anglica* occurs throughout the range of the species described above. Subsp. *cornubiensis* Pritchard is confined to two or three localities on maritime cliffs in north Cornwall.

Gentianella ciliata L. Borkh**
FRINGED GENTIAN
Very rare and confined to a single site in the Chilterns in Buckinghamshire, where it was discovered in 1982. The colony comprises an area of about 10 x 15 m on old sheep-grazed chalk grassland and is almost certainly the same locality as a report in 1875 that was considered to be an error. (Not illustrated).

❁ ***G. ciliata* differs from other species of *Gentianella* in its blue flowers and in the fringe of white hairs along the sides of the corolla-lobes.**

Gentiana pneumonanthe L.
MARSH GENTIAN
A local and declining species occurring in Dorset, Hampshire, East Sussex, Norfolk, Lincolnshire, Yorkshire, Cumbria, Cheshire and Anglesey. It is a plant of wet heaths, growing on thin acid peat usually in association with moor grass, *Molinia caerulea*; *Erica tetralix* and, in the south, *Ulex minor*. A perennial, it flowers from August to early October and is pollinated by bumble-bees. It is suffering from land reclamation and from the colonisation of open heath by birch and pine scrub.
❁ ***G. pneumonanthe* grows to between 10-40 cm and has linear leaves.**

Gentiana verna L.**
SPRING GENTIAN
Very rare and confined to Britain to two widely separated areas, one in Upper Teesdale in northern England and the other to the area around Galway Bay in western Ireland. In both areas it grows in open limestone grassland and calcareous flushes on Carboniferous limestone and calcareous glacial drift. In Teesdale it grows at altitudes between 400 m and 800 m on a metamorphosed limestone known as 'sugar limestone'. In western Ireland it occurs from 6 m on fixed calcareous dunes to about 300 m in the Burren. A perennial, it flowers from late April to May and is pollinated by bees.

❁ ***G. verna* grows to about 5 cm, has a distinct rosette of leaves, and the flowers are about 15 mm across. *G. nivalis* is more slender, grows to more than 10 cm and the flowers are up to 8 mm across.**

Gentiana nivalis L.**
ALPINE GENTIAN
SMALL GENTIAN
Very rare; known in about 10 localities only in the mica-schist mountains of the central Highlands of Scotland in Perthshire and Angus, on base-rich rocky slopes between 730 m and 1,050 m. It is almost the only annual species in the British alpine flora. It flowers from July to September and is self-pollinated. It has suffered a great deal in the past from the depredations of collectors, and in some places it is also suffering from grazing.

 (see illustrations page 130)

MENYANTHACEAE

Menyanthes trifoliata L.
BOGBEAN
Widely distributed throughout the British Isles but scarce in parts of the Midlands, and commonest in the north and west. It grows in the still, shallow water at the margins of acid or peaty pools, lakes, dykes and streams and in wet bogs and fens from sea level to 700 m. It is slightly shade-tolerant and prefers deep anaerobic organic muds. A perennial, it flowers from April to July and is pollinated by small insects. The flowers are of two kinds: short-and long-styled types with long and short filaments to the stamens respectively (heterostylous).

Nymphoides peltata Kuntze
FRINGED WATER-LILY
A local and decreasing species of eastern and southern England. It is usually thought to be native in the fenlands of Norfolk, Cambridgeshire, Huntingdonshire and Lincolnshire and in the Thames valley in Surrey, Middlesex, Berkshire and Oxfordshire. It is widely introduced and established elsewhere in lowland England. It occurs in fertile, still or slow-moving drains, dykes, canals, lakes and ponds in depths of up to 3 m. A floating perennial, it flowers during July and August and is pollinated by insects. The flowers are heterostylous (see *Menyanthes* above) and recent research has revealed that only the 'pin' form with long styles and short filaments occurs in the fens. This suggests that the species may also be an introduction there, and indeed everywhere in Britain, and is now reproducing vegetatively. It is native in most of central and southern Europe and northern and western Asia.
❁ ***Nymphoides*** **is likely to be confused only with** ***Nuphar***, **the yellow water-lilies, from which it is easily distinguished by the spreading petals with fringed margins and five stamens.**

POLEMONIACEAE

Polemonium caeruleum L.*
JACOB'S-LADDER
Rare, occurring only on the Carboniferous limestone of Derbyshire and Staffordshire in the southern Pennines and in Craven and Wharfedale in the Yorkshire Pennines. There is also an isolated locality in Northumberland on andesite. It is locally abundant on steep scree slopes with a northerly aspect growing with other tall herb species between 200 m and 630 m. It is tolerant of light shade and frequently grows in ash woodland. A perennial, it flowers during June and July and is pollinated by bumble-bees. *P. caeruleum* is frequently grown in gardens and occasionally escapes and becomes naturalised along river banks and on waste ground.

BORAGINACEAE

Asperugo procumbens L.
MADWORT
Alien and a native of most of Europe, western Asia and North Africa. It is usually no more than a rare casual of waste ground and arable fields on dry sandy soils, although it has occasionally become naturalised. A prostrate annual, it flowers from May to July and is self-pollinated.
❁ ***Asperugo*** **is distinguished by its prostrate habit, small (3 mm diameter) flowers and the deeply five-lobed calyx that enlarges after flowering to envelop the fruit.**

❁ ***Cynoglossum*** **is distinguished from similar members of the family by the fruits being covered by hooks and barbs and exposed by the spreading sepals.**

Cynoglossum officinale L.
HOUND'S-TONGUE
Widely distributed in Britain north to the Tees, but almost wholly coastal further north to the Moray Firth on the east and the Solway on the west and in Wales, the south-west and eastern Ireland. It is a rather local plant of wood margins, rough grassland and waste ground on dry well-drained soils on sands, chalk, limestone and gravel. It is particularly characteristic of stable coastal sand dunes. A biennial, it flowers from June to August. The plant smells distinctly of mice, and must be unpalatable to rabbits as it is often common around warrens.

❁ ***C. officinale*** **and** ***C. germanicum*** **are very similar.** ***C. officinale*** **has grey-green leaves that are silky with appressed hairs; the leaves of** ***C. germanicum*** **are green and roughly hairy beneath.**

Cynoglossum germanicum Jacq.**
GREEN HOUND'S-TONGUE
Very rare and decreasing. Now known from about 10 localities only on the North Downs in Surrey and Kent, the Chilterns in Buckinghamshire and the Cotswolds in Oxfordshire and Gloucestershire. It grows in woodlands and wood borders on dry calcareous soils on the chalk and oolitic limestone. A biennial of up to 90 cm, it flowers from May to July and is pollinated by bees or self-pollinated.

Omphalodes verna Moench
BLUE-EYED-MARY
Alien and a native of south-east Europe. It is frequently grown in gardens as a shade plant and occasionally becomes naturalised in woodland near gardens. A stoloniferous perennial, it flowers from February to May.
❁ ***Omphalodes*** **is distinguished from all other members of the family by all the leaves, including the upper stem leaves, being stalked.**

Borago officinalis L.
BORAGE
Alien and a native of central and southern Europe. Borage is commonly cultivated as a garden herb and the young leaves used to flavour salads and wine cups and the flowers as a garnish. It occasionally escapes and appears on waste ground near houses. An annual of up to 60 cm, it flowers from June to August.
❁ **Borage is most likely to be confused with** ***Trachystemon***. **Both have symmetrical flowers from projecting stamens, but the stamens of** ***Borago*** **are glabrous with long anthers (8-10 times as long as broad) and those of** ***Trachystemon*** **are hairy with shorter anthers (2-3 times as long as broad).**

❁ **The COMFREYS are distinguished by their nodding cylindrical flowers and short stamens that do not reach the mouth of the corolla.**

Symphytum tuberosum L.
TUBEROUS COMFREY
A local species distributed throughout England, Wales and Scotland, but absent from Orkney, Shetland, the Outer Hebrides and the Channel Islands and an escape from cultivation in Ireland. It is most frequent in Scotland, north to the Moray Firth on the east and north to the Clyde in the south-west. It is found in damp woods and hedgebanks. A perennial of up to 50 cm, it flowers during June and July.

❁ ***S. tuberosum*** **is distinguished from** ***S. orientale*** **and pale-flowered forms of** ***S. officinale*** **by its scarcely-branching habit and the middle stem-leaves, not the lowest, being the largest. As its name suggests it has a swollen tuberous rhizome, but the plant should not be dug up to establish its identity.**

Symphytum officinale L.
COMMON COMFREY
Distributed throughout most of the British Isles but scarce and possibly not native in northern and western Scotland and in Ireland. It is a locally frequent plant of fens, marshes, river, stream and canal banks and wet ditches on fertile, neutral or calcium-rich soils. A perennial of up to 120 cm, it flowers during May and June and is insect-pollinated. Comfrey is traditionally highly valued by herbalists and is credited with a number of rather dubious culinary virtues.

❁ ***S. officinale, S.*** **x** ***uplandicum*** **and** ***S. asperum*** **are very similar, and the flower colour of the first two is variable.** ***S. officinale*** **has strongly decussate stem leaves and a winged stem, the stem leaves of** ***S.*** **x** ***uplandicum*** **are scarcely decussate and the stem is hardly winged.**

Symphytum x *uplandicum* Nyman
RUSSIAN COMFREY
BLUE COMFREY
Probably arose as a result of hybridisation between *S. officinale* and *S. asperum*. It is the commonest comfrey of roadsides, hedgebanks, wood margins and waste ground on a wide range of soils throughout the British Isles but avoids the wet and waterside habitats frequented by *S. officinale*. Russian comfrey is widely cultivated on the Continent for cattle feed and was probably introduced to Britain. It occurs naturally in Russia where the distribution of the two parents overlap. A perennial, it flowers from June to August.

Symphytum asperum Lepech.
ROUGH COMFREY
Alien and a native of Iran and the Caucasus. It was widely cultivated in the 18th century for cattle food and has since become naturalised in waste places in a few scattered localities in England, Wales and Scotland. A perennial of up to 150 cm, it flowers during June and July.
❁ ***S. asperum*** **is distinguished by the shortly stalked, not sessile, upper stem leaves, blunt calyx teeth and flowers that are pink in bud, turning blue.**

Symphytum orientale L.
WHITE COMFREY
Alien and a native of Turkey. *S. orientale* is naturalised in hedge banks and rough grassy wasteland in a number of scattered localities, chiefly in eastern England but extending as far north as the Firth of Forth. Very rare in Wales and Ireland. A perennial of up to 70 cm, it flowers during April and May.
❁ ***S. orientale*** **is distinguished by the cordate basal leaves, white flowers and short calyx teeth (less than half the length of the calyx tube).**

❁ *Pulmonaria* **is distinguished by the calyx teeth being one-quarter to one-half the length of the calyx and the presence of five tufts of hair in the corolla, alternating with the stamens.** *P. longifolia* **and** *P. officinalis* **can be distinguished on leaf shape. The leaves of** *P. officinalis* **are not always spotted.**

Pulmonaria longifolia (Bast.) Bor.

NARROW-LEAVED LUNGWORT

Very local and confined to a small area of southern England around the Solent, where it is found in woodlands and scrub on the clays and marls of the Oligocene deposits of the New Forest and the Isle of Wight. It also occurs in one or two places in Dorset. A perennial of up to 40 cm, if flowers during April and May.

Pulmonaria officinalis L.

LUNGWORT

Alien but a native of central Europe from southern Sweden south to Albania and Bulgaria and east to the Caucasus. Widely cultivated, it is naturalised in a number of scattered localities throughout England, Wales and southern Scotland, but is absent from Ireland. It usually appears in woods and on hedge banks. A perennial growing up to 30 cm, it flowers from March to May.

Pulmonaria obscura L.

UNSPOTTED LUNGWORT

At present known only from three small woods on chalky boulder-clay in Suffolk. Almost certainly native and likely to be found in other woods in the area. (Not illustrated.)

❁ *P. obscura* **differs from** *P. officinalis* **in the unspotted basal leaves.**

Anchusa arvensis (L.) M. Bieb.

BUGLOSS

Distributed throughout the British Isles, but commoner in the east and with a markedly maritime distribution in the west, and in Ireland more or less restricted to the east coast. It occurs as a weed of arable crops, on roadsides, grass banks, in pits and disturbed ground on grassy heaths on dry, well-drained sandy or calcareous soils. An annual or perennial, it grows up to 50 cm and flowers from June to September.

❁ **The calyx of both** *Anchusa* **and** *Pentaglottis* **is divided almost to the base, and the throat of the corolla is closed by conspicuous white scales. The two can easily be distinguished by their leaf shapes.**

Pentaglottis sempervirens (L.) Tausch

GREEN ALKANET

Alien, but a native of south-west Europe from south-west France to Spain and Portugal. *P. sempervirens* appears completely naturalised throughout the British Isles to north Scotland, but is rather local except in south-west England where it is frequent. It occurs in shaded hedge banks and damp woodland borders, especially near buildings. A perennial up to 100 cm tall, it flowers during May and June.

❁ **The FORGET-ME-NOTS are a distinctive group but are not always easy to identify. In the water forget-me-nots and** *M. sicula*, **the calyx has appressed hairs or is glabrous; the other species have stiff, hooked hairs on the calyx.**

Myosotis scorpioides L.

WATER FORGET-ME-NOT

Common throughout the whole of the British Isles, except for parts of northern and western Scotland and western and southern Ireland. It is found around the margins of ponds, rivers, ditches, canals and streams in up to 0.5 m of water, most often on fertile, neutral or calcareous soils and reaching an altitude of 505 m in Scotland. A creeping perennial, it grows to up to 45 cm and flowers throughout the summer from May to September.

❁ **The flowers of** *M. scorpioides* **are 4-10 mm in diameter, the petals are flat and emarginate, and the fruit stalks are 1-2 times as long as the calyx. The flowers of** *M. laxa* **are 2-4 mm in diameter, the petals are rounded, and the fruit stalks are 2-3 times as long as the calyx.**

Myosotis laxa Lehm. subsp. *cespitosa* (Schultz) Hyl. (*M. cespitosa* Schultz)

TUFTED FORGET-ME-NOT

Generally distributed throughout the whole of the British Isles, but not as abundant as *M. scorpioides*. *M. laxa* grows in similar kinds of places to *M. scorpioides*, in marshes and along the margins of streams, dykes, canals, ponds and pools. An annual or biennial, it grows to a height of between 20 cm and 40 cm and flowers from May until August.

Myosotis sicula Guss. (*)

JERSEY FORGET-ME-NOT

Very rare, and confined in the British Isles to Jersey in the Channel Islands where it grows in damp areas in coastal dune slacks. A small annual species, usually no more than 10 cm tall, it flowers from May to June.

❁ *M. sicula* **has small flowers (2.5-3 mm diameter) and differs from** *M. laxa* **in the almost glabrous calyx and concave, not flat, petals.**

Myosotis secunda A. Murray

CREEPING FORGET-ME-NOT

Generally distributed and frequent in parts of south-west England, Wales, Scotland and western Ireland but rare in the lowlands except for the Weald and Hampshire. It is found in acid, calcium-deficient water, often on peaty soils. It appears to be tolerant of high iron concentrations and is shade-tolerant, often growing in woodland flushes at low altitudes. It is commoner in hilly areas than *M. scorpioides*, reaching 805 m in Wales. A perennial of up to 60 cm, it flowers from May to August.

❁ **The stems of** *M. secunda* **are covered by spreading hairs, and it differs from** *M. scorpioides* **in the leafy inflorescences and the longer fruit stalks (3-5 times as long as the calyx) and from** *M. laxa* **in the larger, emarginate petals.**

Myosotis stolonifera (DC.) Gay (*M. brevifolia* C.E. Salmon)

PALE FORGET-ME-NOT

Very local and confined to the hilly districts of northern England and a few areas in southern Scotland, occurring in Yorkshire, Durham, Cumbria, Peebleshire and Selkirkshire. It is found along the margins of mountain streams and in mountain flushes. An erect perennial, growing to a height of about 20 cm, it flowers from June to July.

❁ *M. stolonifera* **is distinguished from the other water forget-me-nots by the paler flowers and shorter, broader leaves, which are scarcely twice as long as broad.**

Myosotis sylvatica Hoffm.

WOOD FORGET-ME-NOT

A rather local species, distributed throughout most of England from the Scottish border south to a line from the Wash to the Severn and also in parts of the south-east, but absent from the south-west, Ireland and most of Wales and Scotland. It is a plant of damp woodlands, usually on heavy clay soils, and where it occurs it is often abundant. The garden forget-me-not is this species and it frequently becomes established as an escape from cultivation, obscuring its true native distribution. A perennial, it flowers during May and June.

❁ *M. sylvatica* **and** *M. alpestris* **both have flowers up to 8-10 mm in diameter and flat petals. The fruit stalks of** *M. sylvatica* **are 1.5-2 times as long as the calyx, and the lowest leaves are scarcely stalked. The fruit stalks of** *M. alpestris* **are about as long as the calyx and the lowest leaves are distinctly stalked.**

Myosotis alpestris Schmidt*

ALPINE FORGET-ME-NOT

Very rare and confined in Britain to four localities in Upper Teesdale in the northern Pennines and to about seven in the central Breadalbane mountains of Perthshire. In Upper Teesdale the plant grows in short, open turf on the Carboniferous limestone where it is often subject to sheep grazing. In the Breadalbanes it is a plant of steep, inaccessible mica-schist rock ledges. All British localities occur at altitudes in excess of 700 m and reaching to 1,180 m in Perthshire. The plants from the English populations are all smaller than those of the Scottish. A perennial, it flowers during June and July and is probably normally self-pollinated.

Myosotis arvensis (L.) Hill

FIELD FORGET-ME-NOT COMMON FORGET-ME-NOT

Common throughout the whole of the British Isles except for parts of northern and north-west Scotland. It is a plant of arable soils, roadsides, woodland rides, heath grassland and waste ground usually on dry, well-drained sandy or calcareous soils. An annual species growing to about 30 cm, it flowers throughout the summer from April to September.

❁ *M. arvensis* **differs from** *M. discolor* **and** *M. ramosissima* **in the large flowers (3-5 mm in diameter) and the fruit stalks being equal to or longer than the calyx.**

Myosotis discolor Pers.

CHANGING FORGET-ME-NOT YELLOW AND BLUE FORGET-ME-NOT

Distributed throughout the whole of the British Isles but rather scarce and local in parts of northern England, Wales and Ireland. It grows on bare ground in grass heathland, arable, woodland rides, road verges, banks and walls on dry, well-drained soils. An annual growing to a height of about 25 cm, it flowers from May to September.

❁ **The flowers of** *M. discolor* **and** *M. ramosissima* **are about 2 mm in diameter and the fruit stalks are shorter than the calyx. The flowers of** *M. discolor* **are yellow when first open, turning blue, and the corolla tube is longer than the calyx. The flowers of** *M. ramosissima* **are never yellow and the corolla tube is shorter than the calyx.**

Myosotis ramosissima Rochel

EARLY FORGET-ME-NOT

Distributed throughout most of the British Isles but scarce in the west or absent from most of Ireland and northern and western Scotland. It is found in open ground in arable fields, tracks, road verges, banks, heath grassland and mature sand dunes on dry, well-drained soils. A tiny annual, it flowers from April to June.

Trachystemon orientalis (L.) D. Don
ABRAHAM-ISAAC-JACOB
Alien, and a native of eastern Bulgaria, Asia Minor and the western Caucasus. It is established in a number of places in Devon, Kent, Surrey and Yorkshire, growing in damp woodland or along shaded streams and riverbanks. It was first introduced into British gardens about 1752, and is frequently planted for naturalising in shade. A perennial, it flowers from March to May.
❁ ***Trachystemon* is likely to be confused only with *Borago* (Plate 60). Both have symmetrical flowers with projecting stamens, but the stamens of *Trachystemon* are hairy with shorter anthers (2-3 times as long as broad), and those of *Borago* are glabrous with long anthers (8-10 times as long as broad).**

Lithospermum arvense L.
FIELD GROMWELL CORN GROMWELL BASTARD ALKANET
Widely distributed throughout lowland Britain south and east of a line from the Humber to the Severn, but scarce in the south-west and very rare elsewhere. It is primarily a weed of arable crops, being found on dry, well-drained acid or calcareous soils. An annual, it flowers from May to July.

❁ **The small white or yellowish flowers of *L. arvense* and *L. officinale* distinguish them from other members of the family.**

Lithospermum officinale L.
COMMON GROMWELL
A widely distributed but rather local plant of lowland Britain south and east of a line from the Tyne to the Severn, scarce in Wales and the south-west and very rare in Scotland and Ireland. It is a plant of wood borders, scrub and hedgerows almost always on calcareous or base-rich soils. A tall perennial of up to about 80 cm, it flowers during June and July.

Lithospermum purpurocaeruleum L.*
PURPLE GROMWELL
Very rare and now restricted as a native plant to about 13 localities on the limestone of Devon, Somerset, Glamorgan and Denbighshire. It is most abundant in the Mendips where some of the populations are very large. It usually grows at the margins of woods and in scrub but occasionally occurs in the deeper shade of the woodland itself. As well as its native localities, it occasionally appears as a casual elsewhere. A creeping perennial, it flowers from April to June.
❁ ***L. purpurocaeruleum* is distinguished from *Pulmonaria* (Plate 61) by the calyx being divided almost to the base and from *Pentaglottis* (Plate 61) and *Anchusa* (Plate 61) by the long, hairy folds in the throat of the corolla.**

Mertensia maritima (L.) S.F. Gray
OYSTERPLANT NORTHERN SHORE-WORT
A rare and decreasing plant of the coasts of northern Britain, now reaching no further south on the east coast than Berwickshire. On the west coast it still reaches as far south as north Wales, while in Ireland it occurs on the coasts of Donegal, Co. Antrim and Co. Down. It grows on both shingle and coarse sand within reach of winter storm tides and usually where there is some accumulation of rotting seaweed. A prostrate, fleshy perennial, it flowers from June to August and is normally self-pollinated .
❁ ***Mertensia* is unlikely to be confused with any other species. The prostrate habit and broad, glaucous, glabrous, rather succulent leaves are characteristic.**

❁ ***Echium* is distinguished by the corolla lobes being unequal and at least some of the stamens being longer than the corolla.**

Echium vulgare L.
VIPER'S-BUGLOSS
Distributed throughout the British Isles north to the Firth of Forth, but most frequent in the south and east. Further north it is confined to the east coast as far as the Moray Firth, while in Ireland it is confined to the east coast between Antrim and Wexford. It is a plant of open or disturbed ground in rough grassland, sea cliffs, shingle and sand dunes on light, well-drained calcareous or sandy soils. An erect perennial of up to 90 cm, it flowers from June to September and is pollinated by a wide variety of insects.

❁ **The leaves of *E. vulgare* are very rough and the basal leaves have a prominent midrib but obscure lateral veins. The flowers are pink in bud, and four of the stamens are longer than the corolla. The leaves of *E. plantagineum* are softer, with prominent lateral veins to the basal leaves; the flowers are red in bud, and only two of the stamens are longer than the corolla.**

Echium plantagineum L.*
PURPLE VIPER'S-BUGLOSS
Very rare and confined in Britain to a few coastal localities in south and west Cornwall, the Scilly Isles and Jersey, where it is found in rough ground, arable fields and on cliffs close to the sea on granite or sandy soils. Elsewhere it occasionally appears as a garden escape. A biennial species of up to about 60 cm, it flowers from June to August.

CUSCUTACEAE

Cuscuta L.
DODDER
The dodders are annual, parasitic herbs that are attached to their host plant by suckers. They have slender, twining stems with minute scale-like leaves.

Cuscuta europaea L.
GREATER DODDER
A rather local and declining species of lowland Britain, now frequent only in Surrey and Berkshire but also occurring in isolated localities in Cheshire, Cambridgeshire, Suffolk, Buckinghamshire, Bedfordshire, Somerset, Gloucestershire and Sussex. It is usually parasitic on nettles but also more rarely appears on hops. It flowers during August and September.

❁ ***C. europaea* is larger than *C. epithymum*; the styles are shorter than the ovary and the stamens not exserted, while the styles of *E. epithymum* are longer than the ovary and the stamens are exserted.**

Cuscuta epithymum (L.) L.
COMMON DODDER
Widespread but rather local in southern England south of the Thames-Severn and also in East Anglia. It is parasitic on heather and gorse and occasionally on wild thyme. It is most frequent on the heaths of the Weald, New Forest, Dorset and Dartmoor and the maritime heaths of north Norfolk and the south-west. Further north it occasionally occurs as a casual on various field crops. It flowers from July to September.

Cuscuta campestris Yuncker
YELLOW DODDER
Alien and a native of North America. It is reported quite frequently from different parts of southern Britain parasitising a variety of cultivated plants, including tomato and carrot as well as species of *Medicago* and *Trifolium*. It was originally introduced to Europe with agricultural seed in about 1900 and is now a weed in some parts of the Mediterranean.
❁ ***C. campestris* differs from *C. europaea* and *C. epithymum* in the orange-yellow, not reddish, stems and capitate, not elongate, stigmas.**

CONVOLVULACEAE

Convolvulus arvensis L.
FIELD BINDWEED
Widespread and abundant throughout most of England, but becoming scarce northwards and almost absent from northern Scotland and rather local in Ireland. It is a serious and persistent weed of arable crops and gardens, especially on neutral or calcareous soils. It is also found along roadside verges, railways and on wasteland as well as in short rough grassland close to the sea. A trailing or scrambling perennial, it flowers from June to September and is pollinated by a variety of long-tongued insects or self-pollinated.

❁ ***C. arvensis* is distinguished from *Calystegia* by the small bracteoles, which are set some distance back on the flower stalk from the calyx. The bracteoles of *Calystegia* are large and envelop the calyx.**

Calystegia soldanella (L.) R. Br.
SEA BINDWEED
A maritime species distributed around the British coast as far north as south Yorkshire on the east, with an isolated locality on the southern shore of the Firth of Forth, and as far north as South Uist and Moidart on the west. It is scattered all around the coast of Ireland but is rare in the north-west. It is a plant of sandy shores or fine shingle and of sand dunes, where it is found from the early marram-dominated stages through to the typical vegetation of 'fixed' dunes. A creeping, prostrate perennial, it flowers from June to August and is pollinated by bumble-bees or self-pollinated.

❁ ***C. soldanella* is distinguished from *C. septum* by the kidney-shaped leaves and the bracteoles, which are smaller than the calyx.**

Calystegia sepium (L.) R. Br.
HEDGE BINDWEED BELLBINE
Abundant and widespread throughout most of the British Isles but becoming scarce north of the Firth of Forth and absent from Shetland. It occurs in hedgerows, woodland borders, marshes, fen carr, river and canal banks and scrub and as a persistent and troublesome garden weed. A climbing herbaceous perennial, it flowers from July to September. The large showy flowers are self-incompatible and cross-pollination is effected by a variety of long-tongued insects, especially bumble-bees.

Calystegia silvatica (Kit. ex Schrader) Griseb.
(*C. sepium* subsp. *silvatica* (Kit.) Maire.)
LARGE BINDWEED
Alien and a native of southern Europe and north Africa from Spain to the Caspian Sea. It has a similar distribution in Britain to subsp. *sepium* but is probably commoner than the latter species in urban areas in the south-east. It also grows in similar habitats to subsp. *sepium* except that it does not favour the marsh and fen situations so characteristic of that species. It flowers from July to September and pollination is similar to subsp. *sepium*. Subsp. *silvatica* was recorded from Britain in 1867.

❁ ***C. silvatica* has large inflated bracteoles that overlap at the edges and completely obscure the calyx, while the bracteoles of *C. sepium* are neither inflated nor overlapping. *C. pulchra* has bright pink flowers and hairy leaf and flower stalks.**

continued on next page

Calystegia pulchra Brummitt & Heywood
(*C. sepium* subsp. *pulchra* (Brummitt & Heywood) Tutin)

HAIRY BINDWEED

An alien species whose origin is something of a mystery, but it probably appeared as a garden hybrid somewhere in Europe. A local plant, scattered throughout the British Isles, it is apparently most frequent in south-east and north-west England, where it usually appears close to gardens. It flowers from July to September. (Not illustrated.)

PLATE 63

SOLANACEAE • SCROPHULARIACEAE

(see illustrations page 136)

SOLANACEAE

Lycium barbarum L.
(*L. halimifolium* Mill.)

DUKE OF ARGYLL'S TEAPLANT

Alien and a native of China. It has been cultivated in English gardens since the 18th century as a hedging plant. It is widely used for seaside planting and the conspicuous berries are attractive to birds. It is widespread as a naturalised plant throughout most of England, but is scarce in Wales and the south-west and almost absent from Scotland and Ireland. It appears in hedgerows, growing over walls and on waste ground. A shrub of up to 2.5 m, it flowers from June to September.
❁ ***L. chinense* Miller is very similar but has broader leaves and a shorter tube to the corolla. It is also alien and occurs in similar habitats to *L. barbarum*.**

Atropa belladonna L.

DEADLY NIGHTSHADE

A rather local plant that is most frequent south and east of a line from the Tyne to the Severn with a few scattered localities only in Scotland, Ireland, Wales and the south-west. Deadly nightshade is primarily a plant of woodland clearings and paths, scrub and disused quarries on chalk or limestone soils. The most famous of British poisonous plants, it is nonetheless frequently confused with the much commoner and quite different woody nightshade, *Solanum dulcamara*. All parts of the plant are toxic, the most poisonous being the roots and seeds. The active principles are a number of alkaloids of which hyoscyamine is the most important. Atropine itself only occurs in very small quantities in the growing plant. A tall perennial, growing to about 150 cm, it flowers from June to August.

Hyoscyamus niger L.

HENBANE

Now a rather rare plant of spasmodic appearance throughout England and almost wholly coastal in Wales and in Scotland, where it is confined to the east, and very rare in Ireland. It is evident that henbane was once a common plant of waste ground, particularly where there was organic enrichment. Now it appears only occasionally in farmyards, around old buildings and in sandy places near the sea. All parts of the plant are highly poisonous due to the alkaloids hyoscyamine, atropine and scopolamine, and it was formerly widely cultivated for medicinal purposes. Its narcotic properties have been used throughout history as a cure for toothache. An annual or biennial, it grows to about 80 cm and flowers from June to August.

Datura stramonium L.

THORN-APPLE

Alien but widespread in temperate and sub-tropical latitudes of the northern hemisphere. It is an infrequent plant of southern and eastern England, where it appears as a casual of waste ground and cultivated soils. All parts of the plant are highly poisonous, containing the alkaloids atropine, hysocyamine and scopolamine. It was formerly widely cultivated for medicinal purposes, having a reputation as a cure for asthma. A tall annual of up to 1 m, it flowers from July to October.

Solanum villosum Miller
(*S. luteum* Miller)

Alien but a native of southern and central Europe; claims that it is native in Britain are mistaken. It appears as an infrequent casual of cultivated and waste ground in southern England. An annual of up to 50 cm, it flowers during late summer.

❁ ***S. villosum* differs from *S. nigrum* in the spreading, shaggy hairs and bright orange-red berries.**

Solanum nigrum L.

BLACK NIGHTSHADE

Widespread in England south and east of a line from the Humber to the Severn, but scarce in Wales and the south-west and absent from Ireland and Scotland. It is frequent and troublesome weed of arable crops on fertile soils in southern England. It also occurs in gardens, farmyards, around manure heaps and on waste ground with organic enrichment. An annual, it grows to about 60 cm and flowers from July to September. The plant contains the poisonous alkaloid solanine, and the shiny black berries bear a superficial resemblance to blackcurrants. The British plant is subsp. *nigrum*.

❁ ***S. sarachoides* differs from *S. nigrum* by the berries, which are green when ripe and enclosed by the enlarged calyx.**

Solanum sarachoides Sendtn.

GREEN NIGHTSHADE

Alien and a native of Brazil. It is established and apparently increasing in many parts of south-west, southern and eastern England. It occurs as a weed of arable crops, especially root crops and bulb fields, often on light sandy soils and also around rubbish dumps. An annual, it grows to about 40 cm, and flowers from July to September.

It is a rather variable species, apparently depending on the nature of the habitat.

Solanum dulcamara L.

BITTERSWEET
WOODY NIGHTSHADE

A widespread and common plant throughout England and Wales, except for parts of central Wales, but becoming scarce northwards and rare or absent from central and northern Scotland; it is local and scattered throughout Ireland. It is a plant of hedgerows, woodland borders and scrub, and also occurs in reed beds and fen carr on rich alluvial soils or calcareous peats. A distinct prostrate form is an early coloniser of bare shingle beaches. All parts of the plant contain the poisonous alkaloid solanine, and it is sometimes confused with the much less common deadly nightshade. A scrambling woody perennial, it grows to about 2 m, and flowers from June to September.

Solanum triflorum Nutt.

SMALL NIGHTSHADE

Alien and a native of western North America, it occasionally appears as a rare casual of arable soils in eastern England. In recent years it has been recorded from Norfolk and Lincolnshire. A large prostrate annual, it flowers during late summer.

Salpichroa origanifolia (Lam.) Thell.

COCK'S-EGGS

Alien and a native of east temperate South America. It is naturalised on waste ground in the Channel Islands and in scattered localities along the south coast to Kent. A scrambling woody perennial, it flowers during late summer.

SCROPHULARIACEAE

Antirrhinum majus L.

SNAPDRAGON

Alien but occasionally appearing naturalised mostly on old walls but also by railways and on waste ground scattered throughout England and Wales. The cultivated and naturalised plant usually belongs to subsp. *majus*, which is a native of and endemic to the eastern Pyrenees and the mountains of south central France and Majorca. A large number of cultivated colour varieties have been produced and, although a perennial, it is usually grown in British gardens as a half-hardy annual. It flowers from July to September and is pollinated by bumble-bees or self-pollinated.

❁ ***Antirrhinum* is distinguished from *Linaria* (Plate 65) by the absence of a spur to the corolla. *Antirrhinum* is a much larger plant than *Misopates*, with flowers 3-4 cm long and much longer than the calyx. The corolla of *Misopates* is 1-1.5 cm long and as long as or shorter than the calyx.**

Misopates orontium (L.) Rafin.
(*Antirrhinum orontium* L.)

LESSER SNAPDRAGON
WEASEL'S SNOUT

Only doubtfully native, and a rapidly diminishing species of southern Britain, it is a plant of arable fields on light, sandy well-drained soils. It is also found on roadsides and on waste ground and is most frequent on the sands of East Anglia, Surrey, Hampshire, Dorset, south-west England and south-west Wales.

Its decline is almost certainly attributable to the more widespread use of herbicides and to stubble-burning. A summer annual growing to about 30 cm, it flowers from July to October and is pollinated by bees or self-pollinated.

Limosella aquatica L.

MUDWORT

A rare and declining species scattered throughout England and Wales with a few isolated records from Scotland and Ireland. It is confined to drying mud at the edges of pools and is markedly intermittent in its occurrence, sometimes reappearing in large numbers after many years' absence. A small annual flowering from July to October, it produces copious amounts of seed, a property characteristic of plants of infrequently available habitats.

❁ **The leaves of *L. aquatica* are elliptic and the calyx is longer than the corolla tube; the leaves of *L. australis* are awl-shaped and the calyx is shorter than the corolla tube.**

Limosella australis R. Br.**
(*L. subulata* Ives)

WELSH MUDWORT

Very rare and confined to Britain to about five localities in Glamorgan, Merioneth and Caernarvonshire, where there are about eight populations in all. It grows in similar places to *L. aquatica* and flowers from June to October.

Verbascum pulverulentum Vill.
HOARY MULLEIN
Very rare. Almost confined to Norfolk from where it was first recorded around Norwich in 1745. It is now not infrequent in the rough grassland of roadside verges in the north of the county. There are also a few localities in Suffolk in similar places. A tall perennial growing to about 120 cm, it flowers during July and August.
❁ *V. pulverulentum* **is easily recognised by the thick, mealy white wool which covers the whole plant. It has smaller flowers (less than 2 cm diameter) than** *V. thapsus* **and differs from** *V. lychnitis,* **which has green upper surfaces to the leaves.**

Verbascum thapsus L.
GREAT MULLEIN AARON'S ROD
Widely distributed throughout England and Wales but becoming scarce northwards and rare or local in Scotland and Ireland and absent from the Hebrides, Orkney and Shetland. It is a frequent plant of rough grassland, hedge banks, roadsides and waste ground on warm, dry, sandy or calcareous soils. A tall biennial of up to 2 m, it flowers from June to August and is insect- or self-pollinated.
❁ *V. thapsus* **is covered by dense, soft white hairs, but differs from** *V. pulverulentum* **in the denser inflorescence and larger flowers (1.4-3 cm in diameter.)**

Verbascum lychnitis L.
WHITE MULLEIN
Rare and local. It has its headquarters on the North Downs in Kent where it grows on warm dry slopes, in old quarries, on railway banks, roadsides and in waste places on the chalk. It also occurs in the Arun valley in west Sussex and a yellow-flowered form grows near the coast in north Somerset. A biennial of up to about 150 cm tall, it flowers during July and August and is insect- or self-pollinated.
❁ *V. lychnitis* **can usually be distinguished by the white flowers. Yellow-flowered forms differ from** *V. pulverulentum* **in the angled stem and green, almost glabrous upper surface to the leaves.**

Verbascum nigrum L.
DARK MULLEIN
A frequent plant in lowland England, with some scattered localities in Wales, it also occurs as an introduction further north as far as the Firth of Forth. It is a plant of rough permanent grassland, roadsides and banks on warm, dry calcareous soils. A perennial, growing to a height of about 120 cm, it flowers from June to October and is cross-pollinated by a variety of insects.
❁ *V. nigrum* **is distinguished from** *V. blattaria* **and** *V. virgatum* **in being distinctly hairy. All three have purple, not white, hairs on the stamen filaments.**

Verbascum blattaria L.
MOTH MULLEIN
Alien and a native of central, eastern and southern Europe, the Near East and North Africa. It is a rapidly decreasing species of lowland Britain, where it occurs as a rare plant of waste ground. A biennial of up to 1 m, it flowers from June to October and is insect- or self-pollinated.

❁ *V. blattaria* **and** *V. virgatum* **are almost glabrous. The flowers of** *V. blattaria* **are solitary, and the pedicels are longer than the calyx; the flowers of** *V. virgatum* **are in small clusters and the pedicels are shorter than the calyx.**

Verbascum virgatum Stokes
TWIGGY MULLEIN
Very rare and confined as a native plant of Devon, Cornwall and the Isles of Scilly. Elsewhere it occasionally occurs on waste ground in southern England. A biennial growing to about 1 m, it flowers from June to October and is insect-or self-pollinated.

Scrophularia vernalis L.
YELLOW FIGWORT
Alien and a native of the mountains of central and southern Europe, now established in a number of scattered localities in England, Wales and Scotland as far north as Dundee. Not recorded from Ireland. It is found in shaded waste places and plantations. A biennial or perennial, it flowers early from April to June and is pollinated by bees.

Scrophularia scorodonia L.*
BALM-LEAVED FIGWORT
Very local, being confined to Devon, Cornwall, the Isles of Scilly and the Channel Islands, where it is sometimes abundant in hedgerows, roadsides, marshes and dune slacks. A perennial, growing to a height of 1 m, it flowers from June to August.
❁ *S. scorodonia* **differs from** *S. nodosa, S. auriculata* **and** *S. umbrosa* **in the downy stems and leaves.**

Scrophularia nodosa L.
COMMON FIGWORT
Widely distributed throughout the British Isles except for the Highlands and northern Scotland. It is a frequent plant of woodland rides, wood margins, hedgerows and shaded habitats usually on moist, fertile soils. A perennial growing to about 80 cm, it flowers in late summer from June to September. Pollination is effected primarily by wasps of the genus *Vespula*, the brownish-purple colour of the petals being typical of 'waspflowers'.
❁ *S. nodosa* **differs from** *S. auriculata* **and** *S. umbrosa* **in the four-angled, but unwinged, stem and the narrow scarious border to the sepals.**

Scrophularia auriculata L.
(*S. aquatica* L.)
WATER FIGWORT WATER BETONY
Widespread in England but rather local in the north, Wales and Ireland and absent from most of Scotland. It is a plant of river, canal, dyke and pond margins and marshes, fens and wet woods, usually on fertile, neutral soils. It occasionally occurs in drier conditions on calcareous soils. A perennial of up to 1 m, it flowers from June to September and, like *S. nodosa*, is pollinated chiefly by wasps.

❁ *S. auriculata* **and** *S. umbrosa* **both have winged stems and a distinct scarious border to the sepals (up to 1 mm wide). The leaves of** *S. auriculata* **are bluntly toothed and the staminode (a sterile stamen found under the upper lip of the corolla) is round or kidney-shaped. The leaves of** *S. umbrosa* **are sharply toothed and the staminode is distinctly two-lobed.**

Scrophularia umbrosa Dum.
GREEN FIGWORT
Rare and local, but increasing, scattered throughout England and Scotland as far north as the Moray Firth. Absent from Wales and the south-west and very rare in Ireland. It is found in damp woodland and shady marshes and fens. A perennial of up to 1 m in height, it flowers from July to September and is probably pollinated by wasps.

Kickxia spuria (L.) Dum.
ROUND-LEAVED FLUELLEN
Widely distributed in southern Britain south and east of a line from the Humber to the Severn, but scarce in the south-west. It is almost exclusively a weed of arable crops on light, well-drained soils. A trailing, summer-germinating annual, it is most characteristic of the late summer stubbles and, in common with several species of similar habitats, it has become much scarcer in recent years due to the increased frequency of stubble-burning. It flowers from July to October and is usually self-pollinated.
❁ *K. spuria* **and** *K. elatine* **can be separated on the shape of the leaves.**

Kickxia elatine (L.) Dum.
SHARP-LEAVED FLUELLEN
Has an almost identical distribution to *K. spuria*, but also occurs in north and west Wales and extends a little further north, but as a casual only. It is also found in similar habitats to *K. spuria* and is similarly suffering a marked decline due to the increased incidence of stubble-burning. A trailing annual, it flowers from July to October and is insect-pollinated.

❁ *Linaria* **and** *Chaenorrhinum* **differ from** *Antirrhinum* **in the spurred corolla.**

Linaria arenaria DC.
SAND TOADFLAX
Alien and a native of western France south to the Gironde. It is established on sand dunes at Braunton Burrows in north Devon. An annual growing to between 5 and 15 cm, it flowers from May to September.
❁ *L. arenaria* **is easily distinguished by the small yellow flowers (4-6 mm long) and dense covering of sticky, glandular hairs.**

Linaria supina (L.) Chaz.*
PROSTRATE TOADFLAX
Alien and a native of south-west Europe and Morocco. It is naturalised in a few places in Cornwall (where it is possibly native) and south Devon, where it grows in sandy ground and on old railway lines. A prostrate annual, it flowers from June to September and is insect-pollinated.

❁ *L. supina* **is distinguished from** *L. vulgaris* **by the prostrate habit and linear, obtuse sepals.** *L. vulgaris* **is erect and the sepals are ovate and acute.**

Linaria vulgaris Mill.
COMMON TOADFLAX
Widely distributed throughout England, Wales and southern Scotland but rare in northern and western Scotland and in Ireland, and absent from Orkney and Shetland. It is a frequent plant of hedge banks, roadsides, waste places and rough grassland, usually on dry, well-drained sandy or calcareous soils. A perennial growing to about 80 cm, it flowers from July to October and is pollinated chiefly by bumble-bees.

Linaria pelisseriana (L.) Mill.(*)
JERSEY TOADFLAX
Very rare (possibly extinct) and confined in the British Isles to the island of Jersey where it grows in dry heathy places. An erect annual of up to 30 cm, it flowers from May until July.

❁ *L. pelisseriana* **differs from** *L. purpurea* **and** *L. repens* **in the long, straight spur (almost as long as the rest of the corolla).**

Linaria purpurea (L.) Mill.
PURPLE TOADFLAX
Alien and a native of central and southern Italy and Sicily. It is commonly grown in gardens and has become naturalised in a large number of places throughout the British Isles, but most commonly in the south where it most often occurs on old walls, dry hedge banks and stony waste ground. A perennial of up to 90 cm, it flowers from June to August and is pollinated by bees.

❁ **The spur of** *L. purpurea* **and** *L. repens* **is short and curved.** *L. repens* **differs from** *L. purpurea* **in the whitish, purple-striped flowers and less dense inflorescence.**

Linaria repens (L.) Miller
PALE TOADFLAX
A rather local species scattered throughout England and Wales but very rare in Scotland and Ireland and absent from the Hebrides, Orkney and Shetland. It is most frequent in parts of west Wales and the Chilterns. It grows in arable fields and waste places on dry, well-drained, usually calcareous soils. A perennial growing to about 80 cm, it flowers from June to September and is pollinated by bees.

❁ *Chaenorhinum* **differs from** *Linaria* **in the axillary flowers.**

Chaenorhinum minus (L.) Lange
SMALL TOADFLAX
Generally distributed throughout the British Isles north to the Tay, with a few scattered localities on the east coast further north and commonest in southern England. It is a plant of waste places, disturbed ground in short permanent grassland and arable fields usually on dry, well-drained soils. It is particularly frequent along some railway lines, which seem to have facilitated its spread. A small annual, it is in flower from May until October and is probably self-pollinated.

Cymbalaria muralis Baumg.
IVY-LEAVED TOADFLAX
Alien and a native of southern Europe. It was first recorded in Britain in 1640 and now occurs commonly throughout almost the whole of the British Isles except for northern and north-west Scotland, Orkney, Shetland and the Outer Hebrides. It is found on old walls in both urban and rural situations and occasionally on rocks. A trailing perennial, it flowers from May to September and is pollinated by bees.

Mimulus moschatus Lindl.
MUSK
Alien and a native of western North America from British Columbia to California. It was first introduced in about 1826 and is commonly cultivated in gardens, and has become established in a number of scattered localities throughout the British Isles in wet places. A perennial growing to about 40 cm, it is in flower during July and August. The form with the characteristic musk scent now seems to have been lost from cultivation.

❁ *M. moschatus* **differs from** *M. luteus* **and** *M. guttatus* **in being covered all over by dense, sticky, glandular hairs.**

Mimulus luteus L.
BLOOD-DROP-EMLETS
Alien and a native of Chile. It has become naturalised in similar habitats to *M. guttatus* as an escape from garden cultivation, but is much less frequent. It mostly occurs in Scotland, with a few isolated records in England and Wales and none from Ireland. A perennial, it flowers from June to September and is pollinated chiefly by bees.

❁ *M. luteus* **and** *M. guttatus* **are distinguished by the colour of the corolla.** *M. guttatus* **has pubescent calyces and pedicels; in** *M. luteus* **they are glabrous.**

Mimulus guttatus DC.
MONKEYFLOWER
Alien and a native of western North America from Alaska south to New Mexico. It was first introduced to British gardens in 1826 and is now widespread throughout the British Isles except for parts of East Anglia, central Ireland and the Scottish Highlands. It grows completely naturalised in the wet marshy ground at the margins of rivers, streams and lakes. A perennial of up to 50 cm, it flowers from July to September and is pollinated by bees.

Sibthorpia europaea L.
CORNISH MONEYWORT
Has a remarkable south-western distribution in Britain, being almost confined to Devon and Cornwall with a few localities in Somerset, Dorset and south Wales. It is strangely rare in south-west Ireland, being confined to the Dingle peninsula, but in common with several other oceanic species it also occurs in the Weald of south-east England. It grows on wet rocks and soils and by streams in shady places on acid soils. A small creeping perennial, it flowers from July to October.

Parentucellia viscosa (L.) Caruel
YELLOW BARTSIA
Very local in Britain with distinct south-western distribution, occurring in south-west Ireland, Pembrokeshire, Devon, Cornwall and Dorset with a few isolated localities elsewhere in England. It usually grows in damp rough grassland, often close to the sea. An annual of up to 50 cm, it flowers from June to October.
❁ *Parentucellia* **is usually unbranched, and the whole plant is covered by sticky glandular hairs.**

Bartsia alpina L.*
ALPINE BARTSIA
Very rare and confined to only about 20 colonies in northern England and Scotland in Yorkshire, Durham, Cumbria, Perthshire and Argyll. It grows in wet alpine meadows, on rock ledges and in open alpine woodland on basic or calcareous soils from 240 m to 915 m. A perennial growing to about 20 cm, it flowers from June to August and is pollinated by bumble-bees.
❁ *B. alpina* **is hairy, and usually unbranched. The purplish-coloured bracts are characteristic.**

Odontites vernus (Bell.) Dum.
RED BARTSIA
Widely distributed throughout the British Isles. It is a frequent plant of field borders, roadsides, grassy pathsides, permanent pasture, meadows and waste ground on a wide range of different soils. An annual species that is partially parasitic on the roots of grasses, it flowers from June to August and is pollinated by bees.
There are three subspecies in Britain. Subsp. *vernus* is the commonest subspecies in northern Britain but local and infrequent in the south; subsp. *serotinus* (Syme) Corb. is common in southern England but rare or absent from Scotland; and subsp. *litoralis* (Fries) Nyman (subsp. *pumila* auct.) is a dwarf plant that is confined to coastal grassland in a few places in northern Scotland and the Outer Hebrides.
❁ *O. vernus* **subsp.** *vernus* **has more or less straight branches, leaving the stem at an angle of less than 45°, and distinctly toothed, lanceolate leaves with a rounded base. Subsp.** *serotinus* **has widely spreading branches that turn up at the tip and obscurely toothed, lanceolate leaves that taper gradually to the base. Subsp.** *litoralis* **is almost unbranched and the internodes are shorter than the leaves.**

❁ **The SPEEDWELLS are easily distinguished by the blue or, less often, pink flowers with four petals and two stamens. The four species of water or marsh speedwells have their flowers in axillary racemes.**

Veronica beccabunga L.
BROOKLIME
Distributed throughout the British Isles except for the central Highlands and northern and north-west Scotland, where it is rare and more or less restricted to the coast. It is a frequent plant of the shallow margins of ponds, pools, rivers, streams and dykes and in marshy patches in wet meadows, usually on fertile or calcareous soils. A creeping perennial, it flowers from May to September and is pollinated by small insects or self-pollinated.
❁ ***V. beccabunga* is distinguished from *V. anagallis-aquatica*, *V. catenata* and *V. scutellata* by the stalked and rounded leaves.**

Veronica anagallis-aquatica L.
BLUE WATER-SPEEDWELL
A frequent species in England south and east of a line from the Humber to the Exe but rare or local over the rest of the British Isles. It is a plant of the margins or shallow water of pools, ponds, drainage ditches and streams in still or slow-moving water, marshy meadows and wet mud. It is often one of the first species to reappear after dyke clearance. An annual or short-lived perennial growing to a height of about 30 cm, it flowers from June to August and is pollinated by flies or self-pollinated.
❁ ***V. anagallis-aquatica* has blue flowers; *V. catenata* has pink flowers.**

Veronica catenata Pennell
PINK WATER-SPEEDWELL
A locally frequent species of lowland England south and east of a line from the Humber to the Severn, but scattered throughout the rest of England and in Wales and Ireland. Very rare and wholly coastal in Scotland. It grows in similar places to *V. anagallis-aquatica*; they are often found together, and frequently hybridise. An annual or perennial, it flowers from June to August.

Veronica scutellata L.
MARSH SPEEDWELL
Widely distributed throughout the whole of the British Isles. It is found in the still or slow-moving water of the shallow margins of ponds, pools, ditches and drainage dykes and in marshy places in wet meadows, usually on rather infertile, acid or calcium-deficient soils. A creeping and ascending perennial, growing to a height of about 50 cm, it is in flower from June to August.
❁ ***V. scutellata* differs from *V. catenata* and *V. anagallis-aquatica* in the alternate racemes, i.e. one only from each pair of leaves.**

❁ ***V. officinalis*, *V. chamaedrys* and *V. montana* are distinguished by the axillary racemes.**

Veronica officinalis L.
HEATH SPEEDWELL
COMMON SPEEDWELL
Widely distributed throughout the whole of the British Isles. It is a common plant of grass heaths, woodland clearings and rides, commons and pastures on acid, well-drained soils. It also turns up on anthills in calcareous grassland. A perennial growing to about 25 cm, it flowers from May to August and is pollinated by a variety of small insects.
❁ ***V. officinalis* has rather dense racemes with the pedicels shorter than the bract and calyx.**

Veronica chamaedrys L.
GERMANDER SPEEDWELL
Common throughout the whole of the British Isles. It is a familiar plant of hedge banks, road and lane-sides, woodland borders, pasture, commons and rough grassland, usually on well-drained acid or calcareous soils. A prostrate perennial, it is in flower from March until July and is pollinated by small flies and Hymenoptera.

❁ ***V. chamaedrys* and *V. montana* have lax racemes and the pedicels are longer than the bract and calyx. *V. montana* has hairs all around the stem and stalked leaves; *V. chamaedrys* has hairs in two distinct rows down opposite sides of the stem, and almost sessile leaves.**

Veronica montana L.
WOOD SPEEDWELL
Widely distributed throughout England and Wales, but scarce in the less wooded parts of East Anglia and the east Midlands. In Ireland and Scotland it is very local and absent from Orkney, Shetland and the Outer Hebrides. It is a plant of damp woodlands, avoiding the most acid soils, and is often found in coppice. A creeping perennial, it flowers from April to July and is pollinated by small flies and Hymenoptera.

Veronica filiformis Sm.
SLENDER SPEEDWELL
Alien and a native of the mountains of Asia Minor and the Caucasus. It was first introduced to botanic gardens in Britain as rock garden plant in the early years of the last century but was not recorded as an established garden escape until 1927. Since then it has spread throughout the British Isles, being a frequent, troublesome and persistent weed of lawns in many areas. It also occurs on stream and riverbanks, roadside verges and in parks and churchyards. A creeping perennial, its normal flowering period is from April to June but occasionally as late as to August. It rarely sets seed in this country, its spread being almost completely vegetative.

❁ ***V. filiformis* is distinguished by the mat-like habit, small, regularly toothed, kidney-shaped leaves and solitary axillary flowers, with stems much longer than the leaves.**

Veronica spicata L.
SPIKED SPEEDWELL
In Britain *V. spicata* is usually separated into two subspecies.
Subsp. *spicata* **
Very rare and confined to the Breckland heaths of East Anglia, where it has now been reduced to four localities only. It grows in close-grazed turf on well-drained acid or calcareous sands. It is very tolerant of grazing and its decrease is attributable both to the conversion of land to arable and to the decline of the rabbit. A perennial, it grows to a height of about 30 cm and flowers from July to September.

Subsp. *hybrida* (L.) Gaudin.
A rare plant confined to western Britain, where it occurs in a few bare rocky habitats on the Carboniferous limestone of north Wales, Pembrokeshire, Carmarthenshire, Glamorgan, the Avon Gorge, west Yorkshire and Cumbria and on lime-rich dolerite in Radnorshire and Montgomeryshire. A perennial, it grows larger than subsp. *spicata*, reaching to about 60 cm, and flowers from July to September.
❁ ***V. spicata* is distinguished by the dense-flowered terminal racemes. The leaves of subsp. *spicata* are broadest near the middle, and gradually narrow to the petiole; the leaves of subsp. *hybrida* are broadest below the middle and more abruptly contracted to the petiole.**

Veronica peregrina L.
AMERICAN SPEEDWELL
Alien and a native of temperate America. It seems to have been in cultivation in Britain as early as 1680 but was not recorded as growing naturalised until 1836, when it was found in Co. Tyrone. It now occurs as a garden weed and on roadside verges in a number of scattered localities throughout the British Isles north as far as Dundee. An erect annual of up to 25 cm, it flowers from April to July, is self-pollinated and fruits freely.

❁ ***V. peregrina* is similar to *V. serpyllifolia* and is glabrous. It is distinguished by the pale inconspicuous flowers, the bracts that are much longer than the flowers, and the obscurely toothed leaves.**

Veronica serpyllifolia L.
THYME-LEAVED SPEEDWELL
Widespread and common throughout the British Isles. It grows in short grassland, grass heath, on woodland rides and commons and as a garden weed on acid, usually damp soils. A perennial, growing to about 15 cm, it flowers from March through to October and is pollinated by small flies.

There are two subspecies in Britain. The common plant is subsp. *serpyllifolia*. Subsp. *humifusa* (Dicks.) Syme, with rooting stems and broader, almost entire leaves and larger, bluer flowers is a plant of damp places in mountains.
❁ ***V. serpyllifolia* is distinguished by the glabrous and almost completely untoothed leaves and pale flowers. The bracts are longer than the pedicels, which are longer than the calyx.**

Veronica fruticans Jacq.*
ROCK SPEEDWELL
Very rare and confined to about 20 colonies in the mountains of Perthshire, Angus, Aberdeenshire and Inverness-shire. It grows on base-rich alpine rocks and ledges, usually of mica-schist, between 490 m and 915 m. A partially woody perennial growing to a height of about 20 cm, it flowers during July and August and is pollinated by small insects or self-pollinated.
❁ ***V. fruticans* is characteristically woody at the base, almost glabrous and with large deep bright blue flowers (about 1 cm diameter).**

Veronica alpina L.
ALPINE SPEEDWELL
A rare alpine species confined in Britain to the central and eastern Highlands of Scotland, where it grows on damp rock ledges between 490 m and 1,130 m. Although it occurs on both acid and basic mica-schist rocks, it is probably primarily a calcifuge plant. A perennial growing to about 15 cm, it flowers during July and August and is usually self-pollinated.
❁ ***V. alpina* is distinguished by the dense head-like inflorescence and dull blue flowers. It is glabrous below, with glandular hairs above.**

Veronica arvensis L.
WALL SPEEDWELL
Widespread throughout the whole of the British Isles. It is a common weed of arable crops and cultivated soils, but also occurs less often on disturbed and open ground in grassland, commons and heaths on dry, acid or calcareous soils. A small erect annual, it flowers from March to October and is pollinated by small insects or self-pollinated.
❁ ***V. arvensis* is distinguished by the small bright blue flowers, with petals shorter than the calyx, and pedicels shorter than the narrow untoothed bracts. The leaves are toothed and hairy.**

❁ *V. verna* **is similar to** *V. arvensis*, **from which it differs in the 3-7 lobed leaves.**

Veronica verna L.*

SPRING SPEEDWELL

A very rare species, confined to about eight localities in the Breckland heaths of East Anglia. It grows on the sides of tracks, in rabbit scratchings and around burrows and in bare parches in abandoned arable on dry, acid or calcareous sands. It is very intolerant of competition and its decline is due to a combination of a decrease in rabbit grazing and agricultural reclamation. A small annual, it is in flower from April to June.

❁ *V. triphyllos* **and** *V. praecox* **differ from** *V. arvensis* **and** *V. verna* **in the longer pedicels, which are longer than the calyx.** *V. triphyllos* **differs from** *V. praecox* **in the deeply divided leaves with 3-7 narrow lobes.**

Veronica triphyllos L.**

FINGERED SPEEDWELL

Very rare and now reduced to only three sites in the Breckland of East Anglia, and two of these are threatened. It grows on bare, acid or calcareous, rather coarse sands as a weed of arable crops, particularly lucerne. Open undisturbed conditions during spring are essential for its survival. A small annual, it flowers from March to June and is pollinated by small insects or self-pollinated.

Veronica praecox All.*

BRECKLAND SPEEDWELL

Probably introduced. A native of central, southern and western Europe, it was first recorded in Britain from Norfolk in 1933. It has always been very rare and is now known from only four localities in the Breckland of East Anglia, and is threatened in these by changes in agriculture. It grows in bare, loose, rather coarse, slightly acid or calcareous sand in fallow fields and field margins, on bare sandy roadsides and around rabbit scratchings. A small annual, it flowers from March to May. (Illustrated on Plate 102.)

❁ *V. hederifolia, V. persica, V. agrestis* **and** *V. polita* **all have solitary flowers in the axils of leaves that resemble the lowers stem leaves.**

Veronica hederifolia L.

IVY-LEAVED SPEEDWELL

Common in England south-east of a line from the Tyne to the Severn, widespread in the rest of England, Wales and south-east Scotland but local in the rest of Scotland and in Ireland. It is a weed of cultivated soils and arable crops but is perhaps most abundant in gardens. It is slightly shade-tolerant. A trailing annual, the main flowering period is during the spring but flowers can be found as late as August. It is pollinated by small insects or self-pollinated.

❁ *V. hederifolia* **is distinguished from** *V. persica, V. agrestis* **and** *V. polita* **by the lobed leaves. Subsp.** *lucorum* **(Klett & H. Richter) Hartl has 5-7 shallow lobes to the leaf, and the middle lobe is longer than it is wide. The petals are lilac with dark veins. Subsp.** *hederifolia* **has more deeply 3-5 lobed leaves and the middle lobe is wider than it is long. The petals are usually blue.**

Veronica persica Poir.

COMMON FIELD-SPEEDWELL
BUXBAUM'S SPEEDWELL

Alien and a native of south-west Asia. It was first recorded in Europe in about 1800 and in Britain from Berkshire in 1825. It is now thoroughly naturalised throughout the whole of the British Isles, being abundant in the south and east but scarce in northern and western Scotland and in northern Ireland. It grows as a persistent weed of arable crops, cultivated land and gardens. An annual, it flowers throughout the year from January to December and is insect- or self-pollinated.

❁ *V. persica* **differs from** *V. agrestis* **and** *V. polita* **by the larger flowers (8-12 mm diameter) and the divergent lobes of the fruit.**

Veronica polita Fries

GREY FIELD-SPEEDWELL
GREY SPEEDWELL

Distributed throughout the British Isles as far north as the Tay, common in the south but scattered and local further north and in Ireland. It is a weed of cultivated ground, arable crops, gardens and paths usually on dry soils. A spreading annual, growing to a height of about 15 cm, it flowers throughout the year from January to December and is self-pollinated.

❁ **The flowers of** *V. polita* **and** *V. agrestis* **are 4 -8 mm in diameter and the lobes of the fruit do not diverge. The flowers of** *V. polita* **are a uniform dark blue; but lower petal of** *V. agrestis* **is white.**

Veronica agrestis L.

GREEN FIELD-SPEEDWELL
FIELD SPEEDWELL

Widely distributed throughout the whole of the British Isles, frequent in parts of lowland England but often rather scattered and local in the north, west and in Ireland. It is a weed of cultivated ground and arable crops, usually on dry soils, and unlike the other species of similar habitats it seems to have become less frequent in recent years. An annual, it flowers throughout the year from January to December and is pollinated by small flies and Hymenoptera or self-pollinated.

Pedicularis palustris L.

MARSH LOUSEWORT
RED-RATTLE

Distributed throughout almost all the British Isles but very rare in central England and the south-east; common in the north and west. It is a plant of valley bogs, wet heaths, wet meadows, fens and hillside flushes, usually on rather acid soils to an altitude of 860 m. An annual, growing to about 70 cm, it flowers from May to September and is pollinated chiefly by bumble-bees. *P. palustris* is partially parasitic on the roots of other herbs. The British plant is subsp. *palustris*.

❁ **The calyx of** *P. palustris* **is pubescent and the upper lip of the corolla has four teeth; the calyx of** *P. sylvatica* **is glabrous, and the upper lip of the corolla has two teeth.**

Pedicularis sylvatica L.

LOUSEWORT

Frequent throughout the whole of the British Isles except for parts of the English Midlands, where it is scarce and local. It is a plant of grassy heathlands, commons, moorland, bogs, marshes and flushes on acid soils, reaching an altitude of 915 m. A perennial growing to about 25 cm, it is partially parasitic on the roots of other herbs. It flowers from April to July and is pollinated primarily by bumble-bees.

An endemic subspecies, *P. sylvatica* subsp. *hibernica* D.A. Webb, is widespread in western Ireland and differs from subsp. *sylvatica* in having the pedicels and calyces covered in long curly hairs. It also occurs occasionally in west Scotland.

Rhinanthus angustifolius C.C. Gmelin**
(*R. serotinus* (Schonh.) Oborny)

GREATER YELLOW-RATTLE

Very rare and now known from only about 10 places in Surrey, Lincolnshire, Yorkshire and Angus. It is found in arable fields, meadows, waste ground and occasionally on sand dunes. An annual, partial parasite, it flowers from June to September and is pollinated by bumble-bees or self-pollinated. The British plant is the subspecies *angustifolius*.

❁ *R. angustifolius* **differs from** *R. minor* **in the yellow-green bracts, upwardly curved corolla tube and the teeth of the upper lip of the corolla being twice as long as broad.**

Rhinanthus minor L.

YELLOW-RATTLE

Widely distributed throughout the whole of the British Isles. It is a frequent plant of permanent pastures, meadows, chalk and limestone grassland, fens and hill grassland. An annual, partial parasite on the roots of other plants, especially grasses, it flowers from May to August and is pollinated by bumble-bees or self-pollinated.

R. minor is a very variable species, the variation reflecting both the time of germination and flowering and the habitat. For instance, populations growing in mown meadows are often early-flowering. Several of these seasonal and habitat variations have been given separate names, although intermediates exist between them. Those usually named in Britain are: subsp. *minor* (early-flowering, meadows); subsp *calcareus* (late-flowering, chalk grassland in southern England); subsp. *stenophyllus* (late-flowering, fens); subsp. *monticola* (late-flowering, hills and mountains in England and Scotland); subsp. *borealis* (late-flowering, mountains in Scotland).

❁ **The bracts of** *R. minor* **are green, the corolla tube is straight and the teeth on the upper lip of the corolla are short and blunt, not longer than broad.**

Melampyrum cristatum L.

CRESTED COW-WHEAT

Very local, being confined to an area of eastern England centred on Cambridgeshire and Huntingdonshire and also occurring in Essex, Norfolk, Bedfordshire and Leicestershire. It is most commonly found growing on the edges of oak woodland and on roadside verges on chalky boulder-clay. An annual, growing to a height of about 60 cm, it flowers from June to October and is pollinated by bumble-bees or self-pollinated. In common with other species of the genus, it is a partial parasite on the roots of a range of other plants, including various grasses, bramble, privet and clover.

Melampyrum arvense L.**

FIELD COW-WHEAT

Very rare and now confined to about five localities in Wiltshire, the Isles of Wight, Essex and Bedfordshire. It is a cornfield weed, usually on calcareous or base-rich soils. It was formerly far more widespread and its decline is due to the intensification of agriculture, particularly the use of herbicides and stubble-burning. An annual, growing to about 50 cm, it flowers from June to September.

Melampyrum sylvaticum L.

SMALL COW-WHEAT
WOOD COW-WHEAT

Very rare and local. It occurs in a few localities in Yorkshire and the central and eastern Highlands of Scotland as far north as Inverness, where it grows in woodlands to an altitude of 395 m. An annual of up to about 30 cm, it flowers from June to August.

❁ *M. sylvaticum* **differs from** *M. pratense* **in the corolla tube being the same length or shorter than the calyx and the lower lip of the corolla being deflexed.**

continued on next page

Melampyrum pratense L.
COMMON COW-WHEAT
Distributed throughout the whole of the British Isles, but scarce and local in East Anglia, the east Midlands, north-east England, south-east Scotland and Ireland. It grows in three main kinds of habitat. It is found most commonly in rides, clearings and edges of heathy woodlands on acid soils. It also grows in scrub and hedgerows on calcareous soils in south and south-east England, and in northern Scotland it occurs in acid peat bogs. Cow-wheat, in common with other species of *Melampyrum*, is a partial parasite on the roots of other plants, usually trees, heather, bilberry or bog-myrtle. An annual, growing to about 60 cm, it flowers from May to October.

Two subspecies are recognised in Britain. Subsp. *pratense* is the widespread plant of acid soils, while subsp. *commutatum* (A. Kerner) C.E. Britton is confined to limestone soils in southern England.

PLATE 68
SCROPHULARIACEAE
(see illustrations page 146)

Euphrasia L.
EYEBRIGHT
The species of *Euphrasia* are very difficult to identify, and the treatment adopted here is based on the work of Dr P.F. Yeo.

Eyebrights are all annual, partial parasites on the roots of various grassland perennial herbs. The large-flowered species are pollinated by bees and hoverflies, while the small-flowered species are almost always self-pollinated. Most flower during the late summer, but some are out as early as May. All species exhibit great variability and most hybridise freely. However, they do have distinct geographical distributions and habitat preferences, such as between grazed and ungrazed grassland and between acid and calcareous soils. Descriptions and keys to the British species can be found in *New Flora of the British Isles*, *Flora Europaea* and in P.F. Yeo (1978) 'A taxonomic revision of *Euphrasia* in Europe', Botanical Journal of the Linnean Society, volume 77, pages 223-334.

Euphrasia salisburgensis Funck.
IRISH EYEBRIGHT
Confined in Britain to an area of western Ireland from Limerick north to Donegal where it is widespread. It occurs in open and grazed calcareous grassland and among limestone rocks. A dwarf species, reaching a height of about 12 cm, it flowers during July and August. The Irish plant belongs to the var. *hibernica* Pugsley.

Euphrasia rostkoviana Hayne
Subsp. *rostkoviana*
A local plant, scattered throughout Wales, northern England, southern Scotland and Ireland, but absent from northern Scotland, Orkney, Shetland and the Hebrides. Subsp. *rostkoviana* grows in rough pastures, hay meadows and roadsides in hilly country, often on damp or marshy soils. It flowers from June to August.

Subsp. *montana* (Jordan) Wettst.
(*E. montana* Jordan)
A much more local plant than subsp. *rostkoviana*, it is most frequent in northern England but also occurs rarely in southern Scotland. Subsp. *montana* grows in damp meadows and pastures in hilly or mountainous country, reaching higher altitudes than subsp. *rostkoviana*. It flowers from June to August, slightly earlier than the other subspecies.

Euphrasia rivularis Pugsley*
A very local species, endemic to the British Isles and confined to north Wales and the English Lake District, where it grows in damp mountain pastures and flushes and on rocky stream banks. It grows to about 10 cm and flowers early, from May to July.

Euphrasia anglica Pugsley
Widespread in southern Britain as far north as the Humber, and also appearing in the Lake District and the Isles of Man and scattered throughout Ireland. It is a plant of rough grassland, grazed pastures and heathland on both heavy and well-drained acid soils. It is in flower from May to late September and is probably endemic to the British Isles.

Euphrasia vigursii Davey*
Very local and confined to Devon and Cornwall, where it is now known from about 20 localities only. It is a plant of dry acid heathlands characterised by a mixture of *Ulex gallii* and the fine-leaved bent-grass, *Agrostis curtisii*. It is endemic to the British Isles and probably arose as a hybrid between *E. anglica* and *E. micrantha*. It flowers from June to September.

Euphrasia arctica Lange ex Rostrup
Subsp. *borealis* (Towns) P.F.Yeo
(*E. borealis*; *E. brevipila*)
Dr Yeo considers that all British plants previously named either *E. borealis* or *E. brevipila*, except for those included in *E. artica* subsp. *arctica*, belong to this subspecies. It is widespread throughout northern and western Britain as far north as Orkney, where it overlaps with subsp. *arctica*. A very variable plant, it is found in meadows, pastures and roadside verges, flowering from June to August.

Subsp. *arctica*
This plant, which was previously included in *E. borealis*, is confined to Orkney, Shetland and the Faroes, where it grows in hay meadows, pastures and dunes.

Euphrasia tetraquetra (Bréb.) Arrond.
(*E. occidentalis* Wettst.)
A plant of the short turf of sea cliffs and maritime dunes all along the south and west coasts of Britain and all Around the coast of Ireland. It is absent from north Scotland, the Outer Hebrides and eastern England south of Yorkshire. Inland it occurs in chalk and limestone pasture in Gloucestershire, Somerset, Dorset and Wiltshire. It flowers from May to August and grows to between 5 cm and 15 cm.

Euphrasia nemorosa (Pers.) Wallr.
The commonest and most widespread species of *Euphrasia* in lowland Britain, growing on grassy heaths, commons, chalk downs and dunes and in permanent pasture and woodland rides and clearings. In northern Scotland, Orkney, Shetland and the Outer Hebrides it is less frequent and more or less confined to coastal dunes. A very variable species, usually 10-20 cm tall, it flowers from July to September.

Euphrasia pseudokerneri Pugsley
A characteristic plant of the short grazed turf of the chalk downs of southern England, extending as far north as the Lincolnshire Wolds and as far west as the oolitic limestone of the Gloucestershire Cotswolds. In Norfolk it grows in calcareous fens and there are isolated populations in south Devon, Flintshire and the Burren of western Ireland. An attractive, large-flowered species, it is probably endemic to the British Isles and it flowers from July to September, slightly later than *E. nemorosa*, with which it often grows.

Euphrasia confusa Pugsley
A characteristic species of the short, grazed turf of cliffs, moors and dunes of western and northern Britain, being particularly frequent in south-west England, Wales and the Pennines. It is scattered throughout Scotland and the isles, where it becomes less branched, and a tall-growing form occurs in the Breckland of East Anglia. In Ireland it is local and almost always coastal. It is remarkably tolerant of heavy sheep gazing, and flowers from June to September.

Euphrasia cambrica Pugsley*
Confined to the mountains of Caernarvon and Merioneth, where it replaces *E. frigida*. It is known from about six localities only, growing on rock ledges, cliffs and grassy slopes. A dwarf species, it flowers during June and July and is endemic to the British Isles.

Euphrasia marshallii Pugsley *
Endemic to the British Isles and confined to the extreme north coast of Scotland, the island of Lewis in the Outer Hebrides and to Orkney and Shetland. It grows in the short turf of sea cliffs, mature sand dunes and the drier parts of salt marshes and occasionally on wet peat. It flowers during July and August and grows to a height of up to 12 cm.

Euphrasia rotundifolia Pugsley*
Very closely related to *E. marshallii*, with which it sometimes grows. It is confined to the extreme north of Scotland, Orkney and Shetland and the Outer Hebrides, where it grows in the short turf of sea cliffs and sand dunes. (Not illustrated.)

Euphrasia micrantha Reichb.
A widespread plant of northern and western Britain where it grows in acid heather-dominated heathlands, usually on dry soils but also occasionally in damp conditions. It grows to about 25 cm and flowers from July to September. It is probably a partial parasite on *Calluna* and *Erica*.

E. rhumica Pugsley* is probably a hybrid derived from *E. micrantha*. It is confined to the island of Rhum in the Outer Hebrides.

Euphrasia frigida Pugsley
Scattered throughout the Highlands of Scotland and extending as far south as the English Lake District, but absent from Orkney and Shetland. In Ireland it is more or less confined to a few localities on the west coast. It grows in mountain grassland and on damp rock ledges from 610 m to over 1,070 m, and flowers from June to August.

Euphrasia foulaensis Towns. ex Wettst.
A northern coastal species extending from the Moray Firth northwards to Orkney, Shetland and the Outer Hebrides. It is characteristic of coastal grassland, the upper parts of salt marshes and cliff tops. A dwarf species of up to about 6 cm, it flowers from June to August.

Euphrasia ostenfeldii (Pugsley) P.F. Yeo
A local maritime species of western and northern Britain, extending from north Wales to Orkney and Shetland but absent from the Outer Hebrides. It is a plant of coastal rock ledges, sandy and stony ground and short, open grassland near the sea. A small species of up to about 12 cm, it flowers from June to September.

Euphrasia campbelliae Pugsley*
A rare and local species confined to acid heathy grassland close to the sea on the Isles of Lewis in the Inner Hebrides. A dwarf plant of up to 10 cm, it flowers during July. It may have arisen as a hybrid between *E. marshallii* and *E. micrantha* or *E. scottica.*

Euphrasia scottica Wettst.
A widespread but local species of upland Britain, occurring in Wales, Ireland, northern England and Scotland north to Shetland. It grows on wet moorland and mountain flushes to an altitude of 915 m and flowers from June to August. Perhaps not distinct from *E. micrantha.*

Euphrasia heslop-harrisonii Pugsley*
A rare and local coastal species found only in the Isle of Rhum, Inverness, Ross, Sutherland, Orkney and Shetland. It grows in maritime grassland, marshes and on coastal cliffs, flowering during July and August. Perhaps not distinct from *E. micrantha.*

Erinus alpinus L.
FAIRY FOXGLOVE
Alien and a native of the mountains of southern and central Europe and North Africa. It is commonly cultivated as a rock garden plant, having been first introduced in 1739, and has been become naturalised on old walls and in rocky woodland in scattered localities throughout the British Isles. A small evergreen perennial, growing to about 25 cm, it has a long flowering period from March to October and is probably pollinated by Lepidoptera.

Digitalis purpurea L.
FOXGLOVE
The foxglove occurs throughout the whole of the British Isles with the exception of Shetland, but is scarce and local in the eastern counties of Cambridgeshire and Lincolnshire. It is a plant of woodland clearings, hedgebanks, wood margins, lane sides, open heathland and rocky hillsides to about 890 m on acid, well-drained soils. A biennial, or more rarely perennial, it flowers from June to September and is pollinated by bumble-bees. The whole plant is poisonous, containing a number of glycosides that act on the muscles of the heart, the most important of which is digitoxin. The dried and powdered leaves are known to medicine as 'digitalis'.

OROBANCHACEAE

Orobanche L.
The **BROOMRAPES** are herbaceous root-parasites of other flowering plants; the stem has brownish scale leaves which lack chlorophyll, and they obtain all their nourishment from the host plant. The *Orobanchaceae* is almost indistinguishable from the *Scrophulariaceae* , from which it is traditionally separated chiefly on the basis of the parasitic habit.

Orobanche differs from *Lathraea* (Plate 70) in the absence of a rhizome and in the laterally two-lipped corolla.

Orobanche ramosa L.
HEMP BROOMRAPE
BRANCHED BROOMRAPE
Alien, but native in southern and eastern Europe where it grows on a number of different species. In the early years of the century it was established in several places in eastern and southern England growing chiefly on hemp and tobacco. With the decline of the cultivation of hemp records have become very sporadic, the last appearing in 1928. It flowers from July to September and is probably self-pollinated.

❁ ***O. ramosa*** **is distinguished from other broomrapes by the branched habit.**

Orobanche purpurea Jacq.*
YARROW BROOMRAPE
PURPLE BROOMRAPE
Very rare and now known only from Lincolnshire, Norfolk, Hampshire, Dorset, the Isle of Wight and the Channel Islands. It is a parasite of yarrow, *Achillea millefolium*, and is usually found in rough grassland and pastures on dry well-drained soils. In the Channel Islands it also grows on walls. It flowers during June and July and is self-pollinated.
❁ ***O. purpurea*** **is distinguished by each flower having three bracts, one in front and two lateral (care must be taken to distinguish these from the calyx.) All other British species, except for** ***O. ramosa*****, have one bract to each flower.**

Orobanche alba Steph. ex. Willd.
THYME BROOMRAPE
RED BROOMRAPE
Very local, occurring in scattered localities in south-west Cornwall, western Scotland and the Inner and Outer Hebrides, around the northern coast of Ireland and in County Clare in the west. It is parasitic on wild thyme, *Thymus praecox*, and in Britain usually occurs on calcareous soils of maritime cliffs, slopes and scree. It flowers during June and August and is pollinated by bumble-bees.
❁ **The reddish-purple colour of the whole plant of** ***O. alba*** **distinguishes it from other species. It grows to about 25 cm, and the stigma lobes are reddish.**

❁ **The flowers of** ***O. reticulata, O. loricata, O. maritima*** **and** ***O. minor*** **(Plate 70) are 10-20 mm long, and the stigma lobes are purplish to reddish-brown.**

Orobanche reticulata Wallr.**
THISTLE BROOMRAPE
Very rare and now known from only four localities in Yorkshire, where it is declining and threatened by habitat damage and agricultural improvement. It is parasitic on various species of thistle, especially *Cirsium arvense* and *C. eriophorum* and flowers from June to August.

❁ ***O. reticulata*** **and** ***O. artemisiae-campestris*** **are very similar, with flowers 15-22 mm long. The filaments of** ***O. artemisiae-campestris*** **are densely hairy below and the corolla has pale glands. The filaments of** ***O. reticulata*** **are glabrous or only sparsely hairy below, and the corolla glands are dark purple.**

Orobanche artemisiae-campestris Vaucher ex Gaudin**
(*O. picridis* F.W. Schultz ex Koch, *O. loricata* Reichb.)
OXTONGUE BROOMRAPE
PICRIS BROOMRAPE
Very rare and now reduced to only about six localities in Sussex, Kent and the Isle of Wight, in some of which there are only single plants. The only thriving colony is one in east Kent. The plant is parasitic on species of *Picris* (oxtongue) and *Crepis* (hawk's-beard), especially *Picris hieracioides*, in dry calcareous grassland or more open rocky or cliff habitats. It flowers during June and July.

Orobanche minor Sm. var. *maritima* (Pugsley) Rumsey & Jury*
CARROT BROOMRAPE
Rare and confined to the south coast of England, occurring in east Kent, Hampshire, Devon, Cornwall and the Channel Islands. It grows in rough maritime grassland, parasitic on the wild carrot, *Daucus carota*, but has also been recorded on buck's-horn plantain, *Plantago coronopus*, and restharrow, *Ononis repens*. It flowers during June and July.
❁ ***O. minor*** **var.** ***maritima*** **is distinguished from** ***O. minor*** **subsp.** ***minor, O. reticulata*** **and** ***O. artemisiae-campestris*** **by the purplish stem and calyx shorter than the corolla tube.**

Orobanche minor Sm.
COMMON BROOMRAPE LESSER BROOMRAPE
The commonest British species of broomrape, it is widespread in England south and east of a line from the Wash to the Severn and in coastal parts of the south-west, and is rare and scattered in Ireland and absent from Scotland. It is parasitic mainly on *Trifolium* species and was once frequent in clover fields, but seems to be declining with the decline of the crop. It also occurs on various members of the Compositae, including *Crepis capillaris* and *Hypochaeris radicata*. *O. minor* grows to a height of about 50 cm, and flowers from June to September. It is a variable species which is now regarded as comprising a number of morphologically distinct varieties associated with different hosts. The common plant is var. *minor*. *O. minor* var. *flava* is confined to the Channel Islands.

❁ ***O. minor* has smaller flowers (10-16 mm long) than either *O. artemisiae-campestris* or *O. reticulata* (Plate 69), and the back of the flower is smoothly curved. In the other two species it is sharply curved at the base and then straight. The stem of var. *flava* is yellow.**

❁ ***O. elatior*, *O. rapum-genistae*, *O. hederae* and *O. minor* var. *flava* are distinguished from other species by the yellow stigma lobes.**

Orobanche hederae Duby
IVY BROOMRAPE
A local species with a mostly coastal distribution in the south and south-west from the Isle of Wight to north Wales, but also occurring in east Kent. It is rare and scattered throughout Ireland. *O. hederae* is parasitic on ivy and is chiefly found on old walls, cliffs and hedge banks. It grows to about 60 cm and flowers during June and July.
❁ ***O. hederae* and *O. minor* var. *flava* have small flowers, 10-22 mm long. *O. hederae* is distinguished by the reddish stem; the stem of *O. minor* var. *flava* is yellow.**

Orobanche elatior Sutton
KNAPWEED BROOMRAPE TALL BROOMRAPE
More or less confined to lowland England south and east of a line from the Humber to the Severn, where it has a rather local distribution centred on Hertfordshire and Cambridgeshire and Dorset and Wiltshire. It is parasitic on the greater knapweed, *Centaurea scabiosa*, and is found in rough grassland on the dry, shallow calcareous soils of the chalk. A tall species growing to about 70 cm, it flowers during June and July.
❁ ***O. elatior* and *O. rapum-genistae* have flowers 18-25 mm long. The upper lip of *O. elatior* is finely toothed and the filaments are attached well above the base of the corolla. The upper lip of *O. rapum-genistae* is attached close to the base of the corolla.**

Orobanche rapum-genistae Thuill.
GREATER BROOMRAPE
Once widely distributed throughout England and Wales and south-east Ireland, it has suffered a dramatic reduction during the last 50 years. It now occurs in a very few scattered, often coastal, localities within its former distribution. It is chiefly parasitic on gorse and broom, usually when growing in rough grassland on well-drained soils. A tall species, it grows to about 80 cm and flowers from May to July.

Orobanche caryophyllacea Sm.**
BEDSTRAW BROOMRAPE CLOVE-SCENTED BROOMRAPE
Very rare and now known from only two localities in east Kent where it grows in rough chalk grassland and on fixed sand dunes, parasitic on the hedge bedstraw, *Galium mollugo*. Its flowers are said to smell of cloves and they are attractive to bumble-bees. It grows to a height of 40 cm, and flowers during June and July.
❁ ***O. caryophyllacea* has purple stigma lobes but is distinguished from other species with dark-coloured stigma lobes by the larger flowers (20-30 mm long).**

Lathraea L.
TOOTHWORTS
The genus *Lathraea* should more properly be included in the *Scrophulariaceae*, from which it can only be distinguished by its parasitic habit. However, we are following here the convention adopted by most British floras by including it in the Orobanchaceae.

❁ ***Lathraea* differs from *Orobanche* in the scaly underground rhizome and equally four-lobed calyx.**

Lathraea squamaria L.
TOOTHWORT
Distributed throughout the British Isles north to Perthshire, but rare in Wales, the south-west and East Anglia, and in Ireland confined to the east. It is a rather local species, parasitic on the roots of various trees and shrubs, but chiefly hazel and elm, usually on moist fertile or calcareous soils. A perennial, growing to about 30 cm, it flowers during April and May and is pollinated by bumble-bees.

Lathraea clandestina L.
PURPLE TOOTHWORT
Alien and a native of Belgium, France, northern Spain and central and southern Italy. Introduced for naturalising in wild gardens, it is established in a number of localities in southern England where it grows parasitic on the roots of sallow, willow, popular and alder. The stems are wholly subterranean, so the clusters of large colourful flowers appear to arise directly from the soil. They are out during April and May and are pollinated by bumble-bees.

LENTIBULARIACEAE

The Lentibulariaceae is a family of insectivorous plants. *Pinguicula*, BUTTERWORT, catches its prey on the sticky glands of leaves and *Utricularia*, BLADDER-WORT, by an astonishingly sophisticated trap formed by the bladders on the submerged leaves.

Pinguicula lusitanica L.
PALE BUTTERWORT
Has a markedly western distribution in Britain, occurring in south-west England as far east as the New Forest, Pembrokeshire, western Scotland north to Orkney and in Ireland. It grows on wet moorland where the turf is short and often grazed. A small perennial growing to about 10 cm, it flowers from June to October and is self-pollinated.

❁ ***P. lusitanica* differs from *P. vulgaris* and *P. grandiflora* in the pale-coloured, small flowers (10 mm or less in length).**

Pinguicula grandiflora Lam.
LARGE-FLOWERED BUTTERWORT
Very local and restricted to the extreme south-west of Ireland, where it is almost confined to Co. Cork and Co. Kerry. Within that area it is a locally common plant of wet rocks and acid bogs to an altitude of 860 m. A perennial, it grows to about 20 cm, and flowers during May and June.

❁ ***P. grandiflora* has flowers 25-35 mm long; the flowers of *P. vulgaris* are 14-25 mm long.**

Pinguicula vulgaris L.
COMMON BUTTERWORT
Common and widespread throughout most of Scotland, northern England, Wales and Ireland except for the south. Very rare in the English lowlands except for parts of East Anglia. It grows on wet rocks, on bare wet acid peat, on wet heaths and moorland and in acid bogs to an altitude of about 980 m. A perennial, it grows to about 15 cm and flowers from May and July. It is pollinated by small bees.

Utricularia vulgaris L. and *U. australis* R. Br. (*U. neglecta* Lehm.)
GREATER BLADDERWORT
U. vulgaris and *U. australis* can only be distinguished with certainty while they are flowering, and as neither species produces flowers in northern Britain the distribution of the two is not fully known. The two species together occur scattered throughout the British Isles in lakes, pools, ditches and dykes in depths of up to 1 m. *U. vulgaris* is most frequent in fertile or calcareous water and is widespread in the Norfolk Broads and the East Anglian fens, but appears to be more or less absent from Wales and the south-west. *U. neglecta* is more characteristic of acid, infertile water, is absent from East Anglia and is the more frequent of the two species in Scotland, Wales and the south-west. Both are free-floating perennials, flowering during July and August and pollinated by bees.
❁ ***U. vulgaris* and *U. australis* have submerged stems all of one kind. The lower lip of the corolla of *U. vulgaris* has deflexed margins and the pedicels are 6-17 mm; the lower lip of *U. neglecta* is almost flat and undulate and the pedicels 11-26 mm.**

Utricularia minor L.
LESSER BLADDERWORT
A frequent species of western Britain from the Lake District northwards and throughout Ireland except for the south. Elsewhere almost confined to the heaths of Surrey, Dorset and the New Forest. It is a plant of small, shallow peaty acid pools and ditches to an altitude of about 700 m. A free-floating, submerged perennial, it flowers from June to September.

❁ ***U. minor* and *U. intermedia* have submerged stems of two kinds: stems with green floating leaves and colourless stems with much reduced leaves. The bladders in *U. intermedia* are confined to the colourless stems, while in *U. minor* the bladders are present on both green and colourless stems.**

Utricularia intermedia Hayne
INTERMEDIATE BLADDERWORT
A local species of northern Britain, south to the Lake District and rare and scattered throughout Ireland. Elsewhere very rare and restricted to a few localities in Norfolk, Hampshire, Dorset and Caernarvonshire. It is found in the acid peaty water of shallow, sheltered pools, lakes and ditches to an altitude of 990 m. A free-floating perennial, it flowers from July to September. Two other species, *U. stygia* Thor and *U. ochroleuca* R. Hartman, are very similar and much confused; *U. ochroleuca* may be the commonest of the three. See *New Flora of the British Isles*.

ACANTHACEAE

Acanthus mollis L.
BEAR'S-BREECHES
Alien and a native of southern Europe from Spain to Greece. It is one of several similar-looking species that are commonly grown in gardens and was first reported as a naturalised escape in 1820. It is now established in waste places in coastal areas of Devon, Cornwall, the Isles of Scilly and the Channel Islands. A perennial growing to about 1 m, it flowers from June to August and is pollinated by bumble-bees.

VERBENACEAE

Verbena officinalis L.
VERVAIN
A local plant of southern England, widespread north to the Wash with scattered localities as far north as Yorkshire. Also thinly distributed throughout Wales and south-east Ireland. Vervain is a plant of rough grassland, hedge banks, scrub and waste ground on well-drained, often calcareous soils. A perennial growing to about 60 cm, it flowers from July to September and is pollinated by hoverflies, small bees and butterflies or is self-pollinated.
❁ **Vervain looks like a member of the Labiatae, but the inflorescence is a simple leafless spike and the ovary is not deeply four-lobed.**

LAMIACEAE (= LABIATAE)

❁ The three British species of **THYME** are most readily separated by a careful examination of the stem. *T. pulegioides* is sharply angled with long hairs on the angles only; *T. polytrichus* is hairy on two opposite sides of the stem, while the stem of *T. serpyllum* is obscurely angled and hairy all round.

Thymus pulegioides L.
LARGE THYME
Distributed throughout southern England, south and east of a line from the Wash to the Severn with scattered localities as far north as Yorkshire. Very rare in Wales, Ireland and the south-west, it is a plant of the short turf of permanent grassland on dry, well-drained, usually south-facing slopes on calcareous soils and is most frequent on the chalk. More rarely it occurs on the sands and gravels of mildly acid heathland. A strongly smelling mat-like perennial, it flowers during July and August.

Thymus polytrichus A. Kerner ex Borbas subsp. *brittanicus* (Ronn. Kerguelen)
(*T. praecox* Opiz subsp. *arcticus* (Durnd.) Jalas) (*T. drucei* Ronn.)
WILD THYME
Distributed throughout the whole of the British Isles, but rather rare in parts of the English Midlands, East Anglia and central Ireland. It is a common plant of close-grazed permanent grassland, maritime and mountain heaths, cliffs, mature sand dunes, limestone pavements, scree and rocks on dry calcareous, basic or mildly acid soils, to altitudes of 1,200 m. In south-east England it is almost confined to the chalk; in dry pastures it is often a characteristic plant of ant-hills. A mat-like aromatic perennial, it flowers from May to July and is pollinated by a variety of insects, of which bees are the most important.

All three British species of *Thymus* are gynodioecious, having separate female and hermaphrodite flowers on different plants, and the female flowers are the smaller.

Thymus serpyllum L.*
BRECKLAND THYME
Very rare and confined to the Breckland heaths of Norfolk and Suffolk, where it is now known in about 18 places, and to a single locality on the chalk in Cambridgeshire. It grows in small bare patches in short open grassland disturbed by rabbit-scratching and occasionally on roadside verges, on dry coarse sandy soils. A prostrate, faintly aromatic perennial, it flowers during July and August.

Mentha L.
MINT
The mints are a difficult group of plants to identify due to the ease with which the different species hybridise and the frequency with which the numerous cultivated forms escape and cross with wild populations. The flowers are arranged in dense whorls, which may be axillary or form terminal heads or spikes. The degree of hairiness, shape of the calyx, length of the stamens and length of the petiole are all important.

Mentha pulegium L.**
PENNYROYAL
Now very rare and known from only about 14 localities in Leicestershire, Brecon, Berkshire, Cornwall, Devon, Dorset, Hampshire, Sussex, Surrey and Jersey. It is a plant of wet hollows on commons, pool and lake margins and damp grassland on sandy soils. Its decline seems to be associated with the decline of goose and duck grazing on commons and the drainage of lowland ponds. A prostrate perennial, it flowers from August to October.
❁ **The prostrate stems and small oval leaves, less than 1 cm broad, distinguish *M. pulegium* from other British mints.**

Mentha arvensis L.
CORN MINT
Distributed throughout the British Isles, but becoming scarce in northern Scotland and absent from Orkney and Shetland. It is a frequent plant of woodland rides and clearings, grassy roadsides and arable fields on acid or neutral soils, reaching an altitude of 370 m. A perennial, it flowers from May to October and is pollinated by various insects.
❁ **The flowers are all axillary, the calyx hairy, the stamens longer than the corolla and the leaves stalked.**

Mentha aquatica L.
WATER MINT
Common throughout almost all of the British Isles except for parts of the Scottish Highlands. It is a plant of stream, dyke, ditch, canal, pond and river margins, wet meadows, marshes, fens and swampy woodland on mildly acid to calcareous mineral or peaty soils. A perennial growing up to 90 cm, it flowers from July to October and is pollinated by various insects.
❁ **The flowers are in a terminal rounded head and also axillary; the leaves are stalked.**

Mentha x *verticillata* L.
(*M. aquatica* x *M. arvensis*)
WHORLED MINT
The commonest hybrid mint, occurring throughout the British Isles except for Orkney, Shetland and the Outer Hebrides. It occurs in similar habitats to the parents, but usually in wet conditions and often in the absence of one or both parents. (Illustrated on Plate 102.)
❁ **The flowers are all axillary, the calyx hairy, and the stamens shorter than the corolla.**

Mentha suaveolens Ehrh.
(*M. rotundifolia* auct.)
ROUND-LEAVED MINT APPLE-SCENTED MINT
A local species of southern and south-west England, Wales and Ireland with a few scattered localities in the south-east and as far north as Yorkshire, where it may not be native. It is found in ditches, roadsides, rough grassland and waste places. A perennial of up to 90 cm, it flowers during August and September. One of the most commonly cultivated culinary mints.
❁ **The flowers are in a spike, the leaves are not stalked, and are ovate and densely hairy.**

Mentha spicata L.
SPEAR MINT
Alien and a native of central Europe. It is the mint most commonly cultivated as a pot-herb and it has been recorded as established in the wild from all parts of the British Isles, but only rarely in Ireland. It is usually found by roadsides and in waste places on damp ground. A perennial of up to 90 cm, it flowers during August and September.
❁ **The flowers are in a spike; the leaves are not stalked, and are without hairs.**

Mentha longifolia (L.) Huds.
HORSE MINT
A native of central and southern Europe and western Siberia. Plants formerly named as this are now treated as pubescent forms of *M. spicata*; the true *M. longifolia* does not occur in Britain. (Illustrated on Plate 102.)
❁ **The flowers are in a spike; the leaves are not stalked, and are lanceolate and densely hairy.**

Mentha x *piperita* L.
(*M. aquatica* x *M. spicata*)
PEPPERMINT
Commonly cultivated as a pot-herb and frequently occurring as a garden escape as well as a wild plant. It occurs scattered throughout the British Isles, being found in ditches, damp roadsides and wet waste ground. It is a perennial and flowers from August to October.
❁ **The flowers are in a spike and the leaves are stalked.**

Mentha x *gracilis* Sole
(*M.* x *gentilis* auct., *M. arvensis* x *M. spicata*)
BUSHY MINT
This hybrid occurs throughout the British Isles, but is very rare in northern Scotland and absent from Orkney, Shetland and the Outer Hebrides. It is often found in the absence of the parents and occurs in ditches and damp waste ground. A variegated form is frequently cultivated in gardens. A very variable perennial, it grows to about 90 cm, and flowers from July to September.
❁ **The flowers are all axillary, the calyx is without hairs and the stamens are shorter than the corolla. The leaves are shortly stalked.**

Mentha x *smithiana* R.A. Graham
(*M. aquatica* x *M. arvensis* x *M. spicata*)
TALL MINT
A widespread hybrid in England and Wales but rare in Scotland and Ireland. It often occurs in the absence of *M. spicata* and is found in ditches, damp hedge banks and waste ground. *M.* x *smithiana* probably arose as a hybrid between *M.* x *verticillata* and *M. spicata*. A tall mint of up to 150 cm, it flowers from August to October.
❁ **The flowers are all axillary, the calyx is without hairs and the stamens are longer than the corolla. The leaves are shortly stalked.**

Lycopus europaeus L.
GIPSYWORT
A common species in England and thinly scattered in Ireland. Gipsywort is a plant of river, canal, dyke, pond and lake margins, marshes, fens and wet woodlands on moderately fertile mineral or peaty soils. A perennial of up to 1 m, it flowers from June to September and is pollinated by various small insects.

Origanum vulgare L.
MARJORAM
Distributed throughout the British Isles as far north as the Moray Firth; common in the south, but becoming scarce in northern England, East Anglia and Ireland and rare in Scotland. Marjoram is a plant of rough permanent grassland, hedge banks, scrub and roadsides on dry, usually calcareous soils. A perennial of up to 80 cm, it flowers from July to September and is attractive to a wide range of insects including butterflies and burnet moths.
✿ Marjoram can be distinguished from similar-looking plants by the longest stamens being longer than the longest petal.

Salvia pratensis L.**
MEADOW CLARY
Very rare and now restricted as a native to about 12 places in Wiltshire, Kent, Surrey, Berkshire, Oxfordshire, Gloucestershire and Monmouthshire, where it grows in old chalk or limestone grassland. It also occasionally turns up as a casual in scattered localities as far north as Lincolnshire. A perennial, growing to about 1 m, it flowers during June and July and is pollinated by bumble-bees.

✿ *S. pratensis* has flowers 15-25 mm long that are much longer than the shortly hairy calyx. *S. verbenaca* has smaller flowers, up to 15 mm long, some of which are shorter than the calyx, which is covered with long white hairs.

Salvia verbenaca L.
(*S. horminoides* Pourr.)
WILD CLARY
A local species of southern England, distributed south and east of a line from the Wash to the Severn with a few scattered localities further north as far as Yorkshire and north Wales, and very rare in Ireland. It is found in rough grassland, roadsides, old pastures and fixed dunes on dry, well-drained calcareous or sandy soils. A perennial, it grows to about 80 cm and flowers from May to August and is usually self-pollinated. It is a variable species containing numerous local forms, including a plant from sand dunes in Guernsey which is sometimes regarded as a distinct species.

Melittis melissophyllum L.
BASTARD BALM
Very local and more or less confined to Devon, Cornwall, Pembrokeshire and the New Forest where it grows in woodland and hedge banks. A perennial, it grows to about 50 cm, and flowers from May to July. It is pollinated by bumble-bees and hawk moths.

Prunella laciniata (L.) L.
CUT-LEAVED SELFHEAL
Alien and a native of central and southern Europe. It is naturalised in a number of scattered localities in southern England as far north as Lincolnshire, but is absent from Wales and the south-west. It occurs in dry calcareous grassland and flowers from June to August. A perennial, it grows to about 20 cm and is pollinated by bees.

Prunella vulgaris L.
SELFHEAL
Common throughout the whole of the British Isles. It is a ubiquitous plant of meadows, pastures, lawns, grassy commons, roadsides, woodland tracks and clearings, and waste ground up to altitudes of about 760 m. It avoids the more acid conditions, usually being found on neutral or calcareous soils. A perennial growing to about 25 cm, it flowers from June to September and is pollinated by bees.

Leonurus cardiaca L.
MOTHERWORT
Alien and a native of most of Europe except the north and parts of the Mediterranean. It was introduced into Britain during the Middle Ages as a medicinal plant in physic gardens and, as its vernacular name suggests, it was used to ease labour pains during childbirth. It occurs as a rare casual scattered through England and Wales in hedgerows, on walls and in waste places. A perennial, it grows to about 1 m, flowers from July to September and is pollinated by bees.

Ballota nigra L.
BLACK HOREHOUND
Widespread throughout England north to the Humber and extending northwards in the east as far as the Firth of Forth, and scarce in Wales except for the north and south coasts and very rare in Ireland. It is a frequent plant of hedgebanks, roadsides, waste places and tracksides on dry well-drained, usually neutral or calcareous soils. A perennial growing to about 70 cm, it flowers from June to October and is pollinated by bees.

The native British plant is the subspecies *foetida* (Vis.) Hayek. Subsp. *nigra* is a native of central and eastern Europe and occasionally turns up as a rare casual.
✿ *B. nigra* differs from similar-looking species in having a distinctly funnel-shaped calyx as opposed to a tubular or bell-shaped one, and by its distinctive and unpleasant smell. The British subspecies has very short, triangular calyx teeth.

✿ In *Clinopodium* the flowers are arranged in stalked cymes or dense whorls; the upper lip to the corolla is flat rather than concave.

Clinopodium vulgare L.
WILD BASIL
Distributed throughout most of the British Isles as far north as the Moray Firth, frequent in the south but becoming increasingly rare northwards and in Ireland only in a few isolated localities in the south-west. It is a plant of banks, hedgerows, scrub and rough grassland on dry, usually calcareous soils to an altitude of 400 m. A perennial, growing to about 50 cm, it flowers from July to September and is pollinated by bees, butterflies and moths.

Clinopodium acinos (L.) Kuntze
(*Acinos arvensis* (Lam.) Dandy)
BASIL THYME
A rather local species of lowland Britain distributed south and east of a line from the Tyne to the Severn with a few scattered localities in Scotland, Wales, Ireland and the south-west. It is found on bare patches in permanent grassland in arable fields, on rocks and waste ground on dry, well-drained calcareous soils. A small annual or short-lived perennial, it flowers from May to September and is pollinated by bees.

Clinopodium menthifolium (Host) Stace**
(*Calamintha sylvatica* Bromf. subsp. *sylvatica*)
WOOD CALAMINT
Very rare and restricted to a single locality in the Isle of Wight, where it has been known growing on a chalky bank since 1900. An erect perennial of up to 60 cm, it flowers during August and September. (Not illustrated.)

Clinopodium ascendens (Jordan) Samp.
(*Calamintha sylvatica* Bromf. subsp. *ascendens* (Jordan) P.W. Ball)
COMMON CALAMINT
A rather local plant, generally distributed in southern England south of a line from the Wash to the Severn and also in south-west Wales. Rare elsewhere as far north as Yorkshire and in southern Ireland. It grows in rough grassland, hedgerows, banks, and scrub on dry well-drained, usually calcareous but also sandy soils. A perennial of up to 60 cm, it flowers from July to September.

✿ *C. ascendens* and *C. calamintha* look rather similar. *C. ascendens* has long hairs on the calyx and the leaves are 2-4 cm long and green. *C. calamintha* has very short hairs on the calyx and the leaves are 1-2 cm long and grey-green.

Clinopodium calamintha (L.) Stace
(*Calamintha nepeta* auct.)
LESSER CALAMINT
A very local species with a restricted distribution centred around north Kent, Essex, Suffolk and south Cambridgeshire with a few scattered localities in Norfolk and elsewhere. It grows in rough grassland, on banks and in hedgerows, on dry, usually calcareous soils. A perennial of up to about 60 cm, it flowers from July to September and is pollinated chiefly by bees.

Lamiastrum galeobdolon (L.) Ehrend. & Polatschek
(*Galeobdolon luteum* Huds.; *Laminum galeobdolon* (L.) L.)
YELLOW ARCHANGEL
Widely distributed throughout England and Wales as far north as Yorkshire, but scarce in the south-west and western Wales and very rare in Ireland and Scotland where it may well not be native. It is a frequent plant of woodlands on heavy, neutral or calcareous soils and may be particularly abundant following coppicing. In the sparsely wooded countryside of eastern England it is particularly associated with ancient woodlands. A stoloniferous perennial, it grows to a height of about 45 cm, flowers during May and June and is pollinated by bees.

❁ The WOUNDWORTS (*Stachys*), DEAD-NETTLES (*Lamium*) and HEMP-NETTLES (*Galeopsis*) look very similar. In *Lamium* the lower lip of the flower is deeply notched with very small side lobes. The upper lip of the flower of *Galeopsis* is laterally compressed and helmet-shaped, and the calyx teeth end in long, fine points. The upper lip of *Stachys* is concave but not laterally compressed.

Stachys officinalis (L.) Trev. St Leon (*Betonica officinalis* L.)

BETONY

Widely distributed throughout England and Wales as far north as the Solway but scarce in East Anglia and very rare in Scotland and Ireland. It is a plant of permanent grassland, commons, heaths, banks, hedgerows and woodland paths, clearings and margins on light sandy soils. Less commonly it also occurs in rough calcareous grassland and scrub. A perennial, it grows to a height of about 60 cm, flowers from June to September and is pollinated by bees. Betony featured prominently in early medieval folklore, supposedly being invested with potent magical properties against all manner of evil.
❁ *S. officinalis* can be distinguished from all other species of *Stachys* by having a well-marked basal rosette of leaves.

Stachys alpina L.**

LIMESTONE WOUNDWORT

Very rare and now known from only two localitites in the British Isles: one on the oolitic limestone of the Cotswolds in Gloucestershire, the other from the Carboniferous limestone of north Wales in Denbighshire, where it is found in open woodland. A perennial of up to about 80 cm, it flowers from June to August.
❁ *S. alpina* is distinguished by the long bracteoles, which are as long as the calyx.

Stachys germanica L.**

DOWNY WOUNDWORT

Very rare and now known from about five localities in Oxfordshire, where it grows along the verges of ancient green lanes, wood edges and old quarries on the oolitic limestone; its numbers fluctuate from year to year. A perennial or biennial, growing to about 70 cm, it flowers during July and August and is pollinated by bees. (Illustrated on Plate 102.)
❁ The covering of long white hairs distinguishes *S. germanica* from other British species.

Stachys sylvatica L.

HEDGE WOUNDWORT

Ubiquitous throughout the British Isles, except for parts of the Scottish Highlands, where it is scarce. It is a common plant of hedge banks, woodlands and shaded gardens and waste places on fertile, mildly acid to calcareous soils to an altitude of 460 m. A perennial growing to about 70 cm, it flowers during July and August and is pollinated by bees.
❁ The long-stalked, ovate leaves distinguish *S. sylvatica* from *S. palustris*.

Stachys palustris L.

MARSH WOUNDWORT

Distributed throughout the whole of the British Isles, but scarce in the Scottish Highlands. It is a frequent plant of pond, lake, stream, dyke, canal and river margins, damp ditches, fens and marshes to an altitude of 460 m, usually on moderately fertile, mildly acid to calcareous soils. Occasionally it occurs as a weed of arable land. A perennial growing to about 1 m, it flowers from July to September and is mainly pollinated by bees.
❁ The shortly-stalked, lanceolate leaves distinguish *S. palustris* from *S. sylvatica*.

Stachys arvensis (L.) L.

FIELD WOUNDWORT

A rather local species distributed throughout the British Isles, commonest in the south and west and scarce in the north and east. In Ireland it is rare except in the south-east. It is primarily a weed of arable crops on light sandy soils. A small annual of up to 20 cm, it flowers from April to November and is self-pollinated.

Lamium album L.

WHITE DEAD-NETTLE

Common throughout most of the British Isles as far north as the Firth of Forth but scarce in south-west Scotland, north-west England, western Wales and Ireland except for the north-east. It is absent from northern and north-west Scotland. It is a plant of hedgerows, roadsides, waste ground and farmyards, usually on fertile soils. A perennial growing to about 50 cm, it flowers from May to December and is pollinated by bumble-bees.

❁ *Lamium purpureum* and *L. hybridum* differ from *L. amplexicaule* and *L. confertum* in having stalked, not sessile, upper bracts.

Lamium purpureum L.

RED DEAD-NETTLE

Ubiquitous throughout most of the British Isles except for parts of the Scottish Highlands and Ireland, where it is locally scarce. It is a common plant of gardens, arable fields, waste places and cultivated ground generally, usually on fertile soils. An annual growing to about 25 cm, it flowers from March to October and is pollinated by bees or self-pollinated.

❁ *L. purpureum* differs from *L. hybridum* in having regularly, not coarsely, toothed leaves and a conspicuous ring of hairs towards the base of the inside of the corolla.

Lamium hybridum Vill.

CUT-LEAVED DEAD-NEETLE

A rather local species distributed throughout the British Isles but rather scarce everywhere except for eastern England south of the Humber. It occurs as a weed of arable soils and cultivated land generally. An annual, growing to about 25 cm, it flowers from March to October and is usually pollinated by bees.

Lamium amplexicaule L.

HENBIT DEAD-NETTLE

Distributed throughout the British Isles, frequent in the east and south of a line from the Humber to the Severn but scarce and local elsewhere. It is rare in Ireland, where it is more or less confined to the south-east. It occurs chiefly as a weed of arable crops, usually on light sandy or calcareous soils. An annual, growing to about 20 cm, it flowers from April to August and is usually self-pollinated.

❁ The calyx of *L. amplexicaule* is densely covered by spreading hairs and the teeth are convergent in fruit, while the calyx of *L. confertum* has stiff appressed hairs and the teeth spread in fruit.

Lamium confertum Fries (*Lamium molucellifolium* auct.)

NORTHERN DEAD-NETTLE
INTERMEDIATE DEAD-NETTLE

A rather local species with something of a coastal distribution in Scotland, northern Ireland and the Isle of Man. It is most frequent on the east coast of Scotland from the southern side of the Moray Firth northwards. It occurs as a weed of arable crops, in waste places and on cultivated ground generally. An annual, it grows to about 25 cm and flowers from May to September.

Galeopsis segetum Necker*

DOWNY HEMP-NETTLE

Known as a native from a single locality in Caernarvonshire but now extinct. An annual weed of arable soil, its appearances are very erratic and are determined by the frequenty of ploughing. It flowers from July to October and is usually self-pollinated.

Galeopsis tetrahit L. (*G. bifida* Boenn.)

COMMON HEMP-NETTLE

The distribution of the two very similar species in the British Isles is not completely known. Together they occur throughout the whole of the British Isles and are frequent plants of field borders, arable crops, fens, marshes and woodland clearings on a wide range of different soils. They are annuals and grow to a height of about 1 m, flower from July to September and are usually self-pollinated.
❁ The two species can be separated by differences in the corolla. *G. bifida* (Bifid Hemp-nettle) as a deeply notched lip and a shorter corolla (13-16 mm), while the lip of *G. tetrahit* is entire and the corolla longer (13-20 mm.)

Galeopsis angustifolia Ehrh. ex Hoffm.

RED HEMP-NETTLE
NARROW-LEAVED HEMP-NETTLE

A rather local plant of southern and eastern England, distributed south and east of a line from the Tyne to the Severn. It is rare elsewhere and absent from Scotland. It grows as a weed of arable crops, usually on well-drained calcareous soils. It can also be found on the older parts of coastal shingle beaches. An annual, it grows to about 70 cm, flowers from July to October and is either insect- or self-pollinated.
❁ *G. angustifolia* can be distinguished from *G. tetrahit* and *G. bifida* in being sparsely, not coarsely, hairy and in the lanceolate, not ovate, leaves.

Galeopsis speciosa Mill.

LARGE-FLOWERED HEMP-NETTLE

A rather local species, distributed throughout most of the British Isles but rare or absent in the south-west, south Wales, most of Ireland and in northern and north-west Scotland. It is a weed of arable crops, often being associated with potatoes. It occurs on a wide range of soils, including those derived from fen peat in East Anglia. A large annual, it grows to about 1 m, flowers from July to September and is usually self-pollinated.

LAMIACEAE (= LABIATAE) *(see illustrations page 158)*

Phlomis fruticosa L.
JERUSALEM SAGE
Alien and a native of the eastern Mediterranean as far west as Sardinia. It has been cultivated in British gardens since the 16th century and has become naturalised in a few places in Somerset and Devon. A small evergreen shrub, growing to a height of about 130 cm, it flowers during June and July.

Nepeta cataria L.
CAT-MINT
A local and decreasing species scattered throughout England and Wales, but most frequent in eastern England. It is a plant of hedge banks and roadsides on dry calcareous soils, especially the chalk of the North Downs, Chilterns and East Anglia. A strongly aromatic perennial growing to about 75 cm, it flowers from July to September and is pollinated by bees.

Glechoma hederacea L.
GROUND-IVY
Ubiquitous throughout the British Isles except for the Scottish Highlands, northern Scotland, the Hebrides, Orkney and Shetland. It is a common plant of woodland rides, recent coppice, scrub, hedgerows, permanent grassland, waste ground and shady places in gardens usually on heavy, fertile or calcareous soils to an altitude of about 400 m. It is unusual in producing both hermaphrodite and female flowers on separate plants. A creeping perennial, it flowers from March to May and is pollinated by bees. Before the cultivation of hops in the 16th century, ground ivy was the chief source of bitter for flavouring beer.

Scutellaria galericulata L.
SKULLCAP
Distributed throughout the British Isles but scarce in Ireland, north-east England and eastern and northern Scotland and absent from Orkney and Shetland. Skullcap is a frequent plant of the margins of ponds, lakes, rivers, streams, dykes and canals and in fens and wet meadows to an altitude of 370 m, usually on fertile, neutral or calcareous soils. A perennial, growing to a height of about 50 cm, it flowers from June to September and is pollinated by a variety of small insects.

❁ ***S. galericulata* has shallowly-toothed leaves and blue-violet flowers, 10-20 mm long. The leaves of *S. minor* are virtually untoothed and the flowers a pale pinkish-purple, 6-10 mm long.**

Scutellaria minor Huds.
LESSER SKULLCAP
Has a distinctly western and southern distribution in Britain, being almost restricted to southern and south-east England south of the Thames, the south-west, Wales, north-west England, the west coast of Scotland from the Clyde to Skye and the Outer Hebrides. In Ireland it is common in the south-west and in parts of the south-east. It is a plant of woodland rides, pond margins, acid flushes and wet heaths on acid, peaty or mineral soils to an altitude of 460 m. A small perennial rarely more than 10 cm, it flowers from July to October.

Scutellaria altissima L.
SOMERSET SKULLCAP
Alien and a native of south-east Europe and central and southern Italy. A woodland species, it has become naturalised in a few places in Somerset and Surrey. It is a perennial and grows to a height of about 1 m.

Marrubium vulgare L.
WHITE HOREHOUND
As a native plant it is a rare and local species of the south and west coasts from Kent to north Wales. It grows on banks, roadsides and in dry grassland and waste places, usually on calcareous soils. It has been grown as a medicinal plant at least since Saxon times, and is still widely cultivated in cottage gardens throughout England and Wales and occasionally occurs naturalised as an escape from cultivation. A perennial, growing to about 50 cm, it flowers from June to November and is pollinated by bees or self-pollinated.

❁ **The flowers of *Teucrium* differ from all other British labiates in lacking an upper lip to the corolla.**

Teucrium scorodonia L.
WOOD SAGE
Distributed throughout the British Isles except for parts of the east Midlands and East Anglia and central Ireland, and absent from Shetland. It is a common plant of the less shaded parts of deciduous woodlands, wood margins, young conifer plantations, rough grassland, heaths and fixed sand dunes on dry well-drained, mineral, acid or calcareous soils to an altitude of 600 m. A perennial, growing to about 50 cm, it flowers from June to September and is usually insect-pollinated.

Teucrium scordium L.**
WATER GERMANDER
Very rare and now known from only two places in England: one in Cambridgeshire and the other in north Devon. It is still frequent in some parts of western Ireland, particularly around the River Shannon. It is found along river banks and in wet pits and fen ditches and in dune slacks on calcareous soils. A perennial, it flowers from July to October and is usually pollinated by bees. Its decline has been caused by land drainage and reclamation for agriculture.

❁ ***T. scordium* is most similar to *T. chamaedrys*, but the habitats are quite different. The flower whorls of *T. scordium* are well separated and the upper bracts are longer than the flowers. In *T. chamaedrys* the whorls are closer, forming a spike-like inflorescence, and the upper bracts are not longer than the flowers.**

Teucrium chamaedrys L.*
WALL GERMANDER
A widespread plant of central and southern Europe, it is generally regarded as an alien in Britain but has recently been found growing in old chalk downland turf in east Sussex, where it may well be native. It is commonly grown in gardens but is occasionally found naturalised on old walls in England and Wales. A perennial growing to about 25 cm, it flowers from July to September and is pollinated by bees or self-pollinated.

Teucrium botrys L.**
CUT-LEAVED GERMANDER
Very rare and now known from only eight places in southern England, in Kent, Surrey, Hampshire and Gloucestershire. It grows in open patches in permanent grassland and arable fields and on bare ground on steep, warm slopes on the chalk. An annual or biennial, it flowers from July to September and is pollinated by bees or self-pollinated.

Ajuga reptans L.
BUGLE
Ubiquitous throughout the British Isles except for the extreme north of Scotland and parts of central Ireland. It is a common plant of woodland clearings and rides, recent coppice, scrub, hedge banks, meadows and pastures usually on fairly fertile, damp, mildly acid to calcareous soils to an altitude of 670 m. A perennial, growing to about 25 cm, it flowers from May to July and is usually pollinated by bees, although self-pollination is possible.

Ajuga pyramidalis L.
PYRAMIDAL BUGLE
A local species of north-west Scotland and the Outer Hebrides, with one locality in England in Cumbria. It is usually found on bare, rocky banks and hillsides or in crevices on dry calcareous rocks to an altitude of 610 m. A perennial growing to about 25 cm, it flowers from May to July and is usually pollinated by bees.

❁ ***A. pyramidalis* differs from *A. reptans* in having stems that are hairy all round instead of on only two opposite sides, and in lacking stolons.**

Ajuga chamaepitys (L.) Schreb.**
GROUND-PINE
A very local species almost confined to Surrey, Kent and Hampshire with a few isolated localties in Suffolk, Hertfordshire and Sussex. Ground-pine is found in bare patches in short chalk grassland and around the edges of chalky arable fields. A small annual, rarely more than 10 cm in height, it flowers from May to September and is pollinated by bees.

PLANTAGINACEAE

Plantago media L.
HOARY PLANTAIN
Widely distributed throughout England, but rare in the south-west and also in Wales and southern Scotland; it is absent from northern and western Scotland and introduced into Ireland. It grows on permanent meadows, pastures and rough grassland to an altitude of 518m, usualy on well-drained calcareous soils but also occurring on base-rich clays and alluvium. It is particularly common in chalk and other limestone grassland, but is not found on arable land. A perennial, it flowers from June to October and is probably wind-pollinated, although the flowers are attractive to a wide range of insects.
❁ *P. media* **differs from** *P. major* **in the leaf blade being gradually narrowed into the very short stalk. The leaf blades of** *P. major* **are abruptly contracted into the stalk, which is almost as long as the blade.**

Plantago major L.
GREATER PLANTAIN
Ubiquitous throughout the whole of the British Isles. It is an abundant plant of disturbed ground and is particularly characteristic of paths, tracks and gateways, being remarkably tolerant of trampling. It is also common in waste places, roadsides and cultivated ground generally and is a troublesome weed of lawns. It occurs on almost all kinds of soils, except for acid peat and mountain grassland, to an altitude of about 625 m. A perennial usually growing to a height of about 15 cm, it flowers from June to August and is normally wind-pollinated, although self-pollination is possible.
❁ *P. major* **subsp.** *major* **has cordate leaves with 5-9 veins; the leaves of subsp.** *intermedia* **have 3-5 veins and the leaf blade narrows to the stalk.**

Plantago lanceolata L.
RIBWORT PLANTAIN
Ubiquitous throughout the whole of the British Isles. It is a common plant of meadows, pasture, grass heaths, rough grassland, roadside verges, maritime and dune grassland and cliff tops, reaching an altitude of 793 m in Scotland. It is found on most soils except for acid peat and in acidic uplands. It is less tolerant of trampling than *P. major* but is more palatable to sheep and cattle. A perennial, with an inflorescence stem of up to 45 cm, it flowers from June to August and is wind-pollinated.
❁ **Broad-leaved forms of** *P. lanceolata* **can be distinguished from narrow-leaved forms of** *P. media* **by the deeply-furrowed inflorescence stalk of** *P. lanceolata* **and the lilac, not white or buff, anthers of** *P. media.*

Plantago maritima L.
SEA PLANTAIN
Distributed all round the coasts of the British Isles and throughout the western and northern Highlands of Scotland and scattered throughout Snowdonia and the northern Pennines. It is a common plant of salt marshes, growing most characteristically as part of the general salt marsh vegetation but also occuring in the drier parts of salt marshes and in short brackish grassland. It also grows in the crevices of sea cliffs. Inland it occurs beside streams in the higher mountains and on limestone in western Ireland. A perennial, it flowers from June to August and is wind-pollinated.

Plantago coronopus L.
BUCK'S-HORN PLANTAIN
A mainly maritime species, distributed all around the coasts of the British Isles but also occurring inland in England, especially in East Anglia, the Thames basin and Hampshire and Dorset. It is a frequent plant of open grassland, waste ground, heaths, cliffs, cliff tops, sand dunes and maritime heath on dry sandy or gravelly soils. An annual or short-lived perennial, it flowers from May to July and is wind-pollinated.

Littorella uniflora (L.) Aschers.
SHORE-WEED
Distributed throughout the British Isles but most frequent in northern and western Scotland, the Lake District, Wales and the south-west and in northern and western Ireland. It is rare and decreasing in the lowlands. It grows around the margins of lakes, ponds and reservoirs in shallow water to depths of up to 4 m, or just exposed on sandy or shingly shores on mildly acid mineral soils. A turf-forming perennial, it flowers from June to August and only when the plant is exposed. Separate male and female flowers occur on the same plant and are wind-pollinated.
❁ **The leaves are 2-10 cm long and are half-cylindrical in section.**

CAMPANULACEAE

Wahlenbergia hederacea (L.) Reichb.
IVY-LEAVED BELLFLOWER
A species with a markedly western distribution in the British Isles, being almost confined to Wales and the south-west, where it is widespread, and to southern Ireland. In addition it occurs in the Central Weald of Kent and Sussex and in a few isolated localities elsewhere in the south. It is found in wet grassy flushes, spring and stream sides and woodland rides on acid, peaty or mineral soils. A small creeping perennial, it flowers during July and August.

Phyteuma orbiculare L. (*P. tenerum* R. Schulz)
ROUND-HEADED RAMPION
Very local and almost confined to south-east England, occurring on the chalk of Sussex, Surrey, Hampshire, Dorset and Wiltshire. It is most frequent on the South Downs where it is locally abundant in close-grazed to moderately rough permanent grassland on warm, dry, shallow chalk soils. A perennial, growing to about 50 cm, it flowers during July and August.
❁ *P. orbiculare* **is only likely to be confused with** *Jasione* **(Plate 76) or a scabious. It differs from** *Jasione* **in being glabrous, and from a scabious in the heads lacking a calyx-like involucre at the base.**

Phyteuma spicatum L.**
SPIKED RAMPION
Very rare and confined in Britain to a small area of the Central Weald in East Sussex, where it grows on wooded roadside verges, roadside banks and more rarely in woodland, on acid sandy soils. A tall perennial, growing to a height of about 80 cm, it flowers during July and August.

Campanula glomerata L.
CLUSTERED BELLFLOWER
Distributed throughout England except for the south-west and extending up the east coast as far north as Kincardine. Absent from the rest of Scotland, from Ireland and from Wales except for a few localities in the south. It is almost exclusively a plant of grazed or rough chalk grassland or open scrub, less frequently on limestone and on sea cliffs. A perennial, growing to about 25 cm, it flowers from June to September and is pollinated by bees or self-pollinated. The British plant is the subspecies *glomerata.*
❁ *C. glomerata* **is distinguished from other species by the sessile flowers.**

❁ *C. latifolia, C. trachelium* **and** *C. rapunculoides* **have ovate middle stem leaves.**

Campanula latifolia L.
GIANT BELLFLOWER
LARGE CAMPANULA
A widespread plant of northern England, the Welsh border and Scotland north to the Moray Firth but absent from most of the west coast of Scotland and from Ireland. It is a plant of woods and shady hedge banks usually on moist, calcareous or mildly acid soils. A tall perennial growing to more than 1 m, it flowers during July and August and is pollinated chiefly by bees or self-pollinated.

❁ *C. trachelium* **and** *C. latifolia* **both grow to about 1 m and have ovate, erect calyx teeth.** *C. trachelium* **has sharply-angled stems and cordate basal leaves;** *C. latifolia* **has bluntly angled stems and lower leaves with rounded or decurrent bases.**

Campanula trachelium L.
NETTLE-LEAVED BELLFLOWER
BATS-IN-THE-BELFRY
A plant of southern Britain extending as far north as the Humber and as far west as the Welsh border, Somerset and Dorset. Very rare in Ireland. It is found along woodland margins, in woodland clearings, scrub, hedgerows and shaded banks on neutral to basic clay, chalk or limestone soils. A tall perennial growing to up to 1 m, it flowers from July to September and is pollinated by bees or self-pollinated.

Campanula rapunculoides L.
CREEPING BELLFLOWER
CREEPING CAMPANULA
Alien but native throughout most of the rest of Europe. It is widely distributed as a naturalised plant throughout the British Isles, occurring in permanent grassland, grassy waste places, woodland margins and open woodland, often near buildings. A perennial, growing to about 50 cm, it flowers from July to September and is pollinated by bees or self-pollinated.
❁ *C. rapunculoides* **grows to about 50 cm and has narrow, spreading calyx teeth.**

Campanula persicifolia L.*
PEACH-LEAVED BELLFLOWER
Thought to have been possibly native in a few places in Surrey, Berkshire, Gloucestershire and Devon, but now extinct in all of these. A native throughout almost the whole of the rest of Europe except for the extreme north, it is frequently grown in gardens and has appeared as an occasional escape from cultivation in a number of localities in England, Wales, and Scotland. It is found in open woodland, commons, meadows and waste places. A perennial, growing to about 60 cm, it flowers from June to August and is pollinated by bees or self-pollinated. A white-flowered form occasionally appears.
❁ *C. persicifolia* **is distinguished by a combination of glabrous linear stem leaves and sub-erect, but not nodding, flowers.**

Campanula rotundifolia L.
HAREBELL
BLUEBELL (Scotland)
Generally distributed throughout England, Wales and Scotland, but strangely scarce in the south-west. Also scarce in Ireland except for coastal parts of the north and west. It is a common species of grassy hillsides, commons, heaths, downs, dunes, cliffs, and hedge banks on dry, well-drained acid or calcareous soils. A perennial growing to about 30 cm, it flowers from July to September and is pollinated by bees or self-pollinated.
❁ ***C. rotundifolia* is distinguished by the combination of linear stem leaves, rounded basal leaves and nodding flowers.**

Campanula patula L.*
SPREADING BELLFLOWER
A rare and declining species in England and Wales, now known from only seven counties, mostly around the Welsh border: Gloucestershire, Herefordshire, Shropshire, Radnorshire and also Warwickshire, Surrey and Berkshire. It is found in woods, commons, hedge banks and waste places. A biennial or short-lived perennial, it grows to about 50 cm and flowers from July to September. The reasons for its recent decline are not known.

❁ ***C. patula* and *C. rapunculus* have linear, hairy leaves. *C. patula* has numerous long inflorescence branches and bracteoles in the middle of the flower stalks. *C. rapunculus* has an almost unbranched inflorescence with bracteoles at the base of the flower stalks.**

Campanula rapunculus L.*
RAMPION BELLFLOWER
Alien but native throughout most of Europe from the Netherlands and central Russia southwards. It was once widely cultivated, the roots being used as a winter salad vegetable. It frequently occurred as an escape throughout most of England and southern Scotland, appearing thoroughly naturalised in fields, pastures and hedge banks on well-drained soils. It is now known in a few places only in Hampshire, Essex, Surrey and Berkshire. A biennial of up to about 50 cm, it flowers during July and August.

Campanula medium L.
CANTERBURY-BELLS
Alien and a native of northern and central Italy and south-east France. It is commonly grown in gardens and occasionally escapes and becomes established for a short time, particularly on railway banks, in southern England. A tall biennial, it flowers during May and June. Many cultivated forms and colour varieties have been produced.
❁ ***C. medium* is very distinctive, with broadly cordate, reflexed appendages between the calyx teeth.**

Campanula alliariifolia Willd.
CORNISH BELLFLOWER
Alien and a native of the Caucasus and central Turkey. It is naturalised in Cornwall and has occurred as a casual in several other places in southern England. A perennial, it flowers during July and August.

Legousia hybrida (L.) Delarb.
VENUS'S-LOOKING-GLASS
Widely distributed in England south and east of a line from the Tyne to the Severn, but very rare in the south-west and absent from Wales, Scotland and Ireland. It is a locally frequent weed of arable fields on light sandy or calcareous soils, although it is decreasing in some areas. An annual, it grows to about 20 cm and flowers from May to August.
❁ ***Legousia* differs from *Campanula* in the long ovary, at least three times as long as wide. The oblong leaves with a wavy margin, and the lilac petals shorter than the calyx, are characteristic.**

Jasione montana L.
SHEEP'S-BIT
Has a distinctly western distribution in the British Isles, being widespread in the south-west, Wales and in the north as far west as Skye and again in Scotland. Elsewhere it is frequent in Dorset, Hampshire and the Isle of Wight and in scattered localities over the rest of England. It occurs all around the coasts of Ireland but is absent from the centre. It is a characteristic plant of heaths, rough grassland, rocky hillsides, sea cliffs and maritime heaths on light acid soils. An annual or short-lived perennial, it flowers from May to August and is pollinated by a variety of insect including various wasps.
❁ ***Jasione* is only likely to be confused with *Phyteuma orbiculare*, from which it differs in being hairy. It differs from the scabious in the absence of a calyx-like involucre below the heads.**

Lobelia dortmanna L.
WATER LOBELIA
Widespread in the upland areas of north Wales, the Lake District, Scotland and western Ireland. It is a common plant of the sheltered shallow water at the margins of mountain tarns and lakes. It grows in depths of up to 3 m in acid or peaty water with a stony or gravelly bottom. A perennial, it flowers during July and August and is self-pollinated.

Lobelia urens L.*
HEATH LOBELIA
ACRID LOBELIA
Very rare and known from about 10 localities only in the southern counties of England from Sussex to Cornwall. It is a plant of grassy heathland and rough pastures on well-drained or damp, acid infertile soils. It is particularly susceptible to being shaded out by invading bracken. A perennial, growing to about 60 cm, it flowers from July to October and is pollinated by flies.

RUBIACEAE

Sherardia arvensis L.
FIELD MADDER
Widely distributed throughout the British Isles, but becoming scarcer northwards and rare and almost wholly coastal in Scotland north of a line from the Solway to the Firth of Forth. It is a common plant of arable fields, pathsides and waste ground on dry well-drained acid or calcareous soils to an altitude of 365 m. An annual growing to about 15 cm, it flowers from May to November and is pollinated by flies.
❁ ***Sherardia* is distinguished from other members of the Rubiaceae by its small heads of small lilac-coloured flowers surrounded by an involucre of leaf-like bracts.**

Asperula taurina L.
PINK WOODRUFF
Alien and native in southern Europe from Spain eastwards, it is established on waste ground in a few places in Leicestershire and Cumbria. A perennial, growing to a height of about 50 cm, it flowers during May and June and is pollinated by flies and bees.
❁ ***A. taurina* grows to about 50 cm, and has heads of white flowers surrounded by an involucre of leaf-like bracts.**

Asperula cynanchica L.
SQUINANCYWORT
Almost confined to the chalk and limestone soils of southern England and south Wales. It also occurs as far north as the southern shore of the Wash in East Anglia with scattered localities on the oolite in Lincolnshire, the Magnesian limestone in Yorkshire and the Carboniferous limestone at the head of Morecambe Bay, and is widespread on the Carboniferous limestone of the Burren district of Co. Clare in western Ireland. It is a common plant of the short grazed turf of dry, well-drained calcareous grassland and calcareous dunes. A small prostrate perennial, it flowers during June and July. Female and hermaphrodite flowers occur on separate plants and it is pollinated by small insects.
❁ ***A. cynanchica* differs from *Galium* (Plate 77) in having a funnel-shaped corolla with a tube at least as long as the corolla lobes. The flowers are white and pinkish on the outside.**

Rubia peregrina L.
WILD MADDER
Has a distinctly maritime distribution in south-west Britain from west Sussex to north Wales. Inland it occurs in Somerset. In Ireland it occurs around the south and west coast from Waterford to Galway. It is a plant of scrub, thickets, hedges and maritime heaths on cliffs, and stony hillsides, particularly on base-rich or calcareous rocks. A scrambling evergreen perennial, it flowers from June to August.

❁ ***Rubia* differs from *Galium* in having five, not four, corolla lobes.**

Cruciata laevipes Opiz
(*Galium cruciata* (L.) Scop)
CROSSWORT
Widely distributed throughout England, Wales and Scotland as far north as Angus, but scarce in the south-west, western Wales and south-west Scotland and absent from Ireland. Crosswort is a common plant of rough grassland, hedge banks, scrub and wood borders on basic or calcareous soils, to an altitude of 470 m in Wales. A perennial, growing to about 50 cm, it flowers during May and June and is pollinated by bees and flies. Separate male and hermaphrodite flowers are borne on the same plant.
❁ ***Cruciata* differs from *Galium* in the hairy, three-veined leaves in whorls of four, and the yellow flowers in dense axillary whorls.**

Galium
The BEDSTRAWS differ from *Asperula* in having a corolla tube that is shorter than the corolla lobes. They can be a little troublesome to identify, and particular attention should be paid to the number of 'leaves' in a whorl, the shape of the inflorescence, details of any stem and leaf prickles, and the surface of the fruits.

Galium boreale L.
NORTHERN BEDSTRAW
A plant of northern Britain from Yorkshire northwards, but absent from Orkney, Shetland and the Outer Hebrides. In Ireland it is scarce and restricted to the centre and north-west. It is found in rough grassland, rocky slopes, scree, cliffs, stream sides, shingle and stable sand dunes especially on base-rich or calcareous soils to 1,060 m in Scotland. A perennial, growing to about 40 cm, it flowers during July and August and is pollinated by a variety of small insects.
❁ *G. boreale* **is the only bedstraw with three-veined leaves in whorls of four, and white flowers.**

Galium odoratum (L.) Scop.
WOODRUFF
SWEET WOODRUFF
Widely distributed throughout the British Isles except for the Outer Hebrides, Orkney and Shetland. It is rather scarce in nothern Scotland and also in Ireland. Locally abundant in deciduous woodlands and coppice, especially on moist base-rich or calcareous soils. A fragrant perennial, it grows to about 30 cm, and flowers during May and June. It is pollinated by flies and bees.
❁ *G. odoratum* **differs from other bedstraws in the larger (up to 6 mm in diameter) funnel-shaped flowers, with the corolla tube only a little shorter than the corolla lobes.**

Galium verum L.
LADY'S BEDSTRAW
Distributed throughout almost the whole of the British Isles. It is a common plant of rough grassland, hedge banks, commons, grass heaths, downs, sand dunes and maritime heaths on dry, mildly acid to calcareous soils to an altitude of 655 m in Scotland. A perennial, it flowers during July and August and is pollinated chiefly by small flies. It was formerly used as a 'bed straw'; that is, for stuffing mattresses. It has a pleasant fragrance when dry and is said to have discouraged fleas.
❁ *G. verum* **is the only yellow-coloured bedstraw with the narrow, one-veined leaves (except for the hybrid** *G. verum* x *G. mollugo, G.* x *pomeranicum,* **which has the lower part of the stem four-angled, not smooth, and paler yellow flowers.**

Galium mollugo L. subsp. *mollugo*
HEDGE BEDSTRAW
Widely distributed throughout England but scarce in Wales, Scotland and Ireland and absent from the Outer Hebrides, Orkney and Shetland. It is a common plant in southern England of rough grassland, hedgerows, grassy banks, scrub and open woodland on dry calcareous or base-rich soils. It reaches an altitude of 365 m in Scotland. A perennial, it flowers from June to September and is pollinated by small flies.

❁ *G. mollugo* **subsp.** *mollugo* **and subsp.** *erectum* Syme **are large robust plants with dense inflorescences, almost smooth stems, and the leaves pointed and in whorls of 6-8.**

G. mollugo **subsp.** *mollugo* **has obovate leaves, flowers 2-3 mm in diameter and the lower inflorescence branches spreading widely in fruit.**

Subsp. *erectum* **is a more erect plant with narrower, almost linear leaves and larger flowers (3-5 mm diameter), and the basal inflorescence branches remain erect in fruit.**

Galium mollugo subsp. *erectum* Syme
UPRIGHT HEDGE BEDSTRAW
Occurs throughout most of lowland Britain, but is very rare in Ireland where it may not be native. It is a plant of rough grassland and permanent pastures on dry calcareous soils. A perennial, it flowers during midsummer and again in September, and is pollinated by small flies.

❁ *G. palustre* **and** *G. constrictum* **are distinguished by their blunt leaves in whorls of 4-6.**

Galium palustre L. subsp. *palustre*
COMMON MARSH-BEDSTRAW
Ubiquitous throughout the whole of the British Isles. It is a common plant of the margins of ponds, lakes, streams, dykes and ditches and of marshes, fens and wet woodlands, especially where water stands in winter. It is found on both acid and calcareous soils and reaches an altitude of 610 m. A slender perennial, it grows to 30-50 cm and flowers during June and July, two or three weeks earlier than subsp. *elongatum.*
❁ *G. palustre* **subsp.** *palustre* **rarely grows to more than 50 cm, and is less straggling than** *G. palustre* **subsp.** *elongatum*; **the leaves are 0.5-1.5 cm long, and the inflorescence branches are reflexed in fruit. Subsp.** *elongatum* **is a tall (up to more than 1 m) straggling plant with leaves 1.2-4 cm long, and the inflorescence branches spread in fruit.**

Galium palustre subsp. *elongatum* (C. Presl) Arcang.
GREAT MARSH-BEDSTRAW
Occurs throughout most of the British Isles and is most frequent in the tall vegetation of river and lake margins and reed-swamps, especially in standing water. It flowers during June and July, rather later than subsp *palustre,* and is pollinated chiefly by bees.

Galium constrictum Chaub.*
(*G. debile* Desv.)
SLENDER MARSH-BEDSTRAW
Very rare and now confined to the New Forest in Hampshire and to a single locality in south Devon. It grows in the short turf of damp hollows and around the margins of ponds on acid, sandy soils. A slender, more or less prostrate perennial, it flowers from May to July.
❁ *G. constrictum* **is more slender than** *G. palustre,* **with narrow linear leaves, smaller flowers (about 2.5 mm in diameter) and with erect branches to the inflorescence.**

❁ *G. saxatile, G. pumilum, G. sterneri* **and** *G. fleurotii* **are all small, prostrate, somewhat mat-forming plants with smooth stems and pointed leaves.**

Galium saxatile L.
HEATH BEDSTRAW
Widespread throughout the whole of the British Isles, except for parts of the east Midlands. It is a common plant of grass heaths, commons, hill grassland, moorland and open woodland usually on dry, well-drained, acid soils and reaches the tops of the highest Scottish mountains at about 1,310 m. A low, mat-forming perennial, it flowers from June to August and is pollinated by small insects, especially flies.
❁ *G. saxatile* **differs from** *G. pumilum, G. sterneri* **and** *G. fleurotii* **in the obovate, not lanceolate, leaves with forwardly directed prickles on the margin.**

Galium pumilum Murr.
SLENDER BEDSTRAW
Very local and restricted to chalk and limestone soils south and east of a line from the Humber to the Severn. It is most frequent on the North Downs of Surrey and Kent where it grows in short, herb-rich chalk downland turf, usually on warm south-facing slopes, but it is nowhere very common. A small prostrate perennial, it flowers during June and July and is pollinated chiefly by small flies.

❁ *G. pumilum* **is more loosely matted than** *G. sterneri,* **the leaves are usually in whorls of 8-9 and are 10-19 mm long, and the fruits are covered by low, rounded papillae.**

Galium sterneri Ehrend.
LIMESTONE BEDSTRAW
More or less restricted to the Carboniferous limestone of Brecon, Derbyshire, Yorkshire and Durham and western Ireland. It also occurs in scattered localities on other basic rocks in north Wales, Northumberland and Scotland. It is an abundant plant of permanent grazed grassland and rocky slopes on calcareous or basic soils to 915 m in Scotland. A prostrate perennial, it flowers during June and July and is pollinated by flies and other small insects.
❁ *G. sterneri* **forms a dense mat with many tangled, non-flowering shoots. The leaves on the flowering shoots are usually in whorls of 7-8 and are 7-12 mm long, and the fruits are covered by acute tubercles (a good hand lens is needed to see this character).**

Galium fleurotii Jord.*
Very rare and confined to a single locality at Cheddar in north Somerset where it grows on cliffs and scree of Carboniferous limestone. A prostrate mat-forming perennial, it flowers during June and July. Most recent opinion is that the Cheddar plants are a form of *G. pumilum* and not the true *G. fleurotii.*

❁ *G. uliginosum, G. tricornutum, G. aparine* **(Plate 78),** *G. spurium* **(Plate 78) and** *G. parisiense* **(Plate 78) all have pointed leaves and rough stems with prickles on the angles.**

Galium uliginosum L.
FEN BEDSTRAW
Distributed throughout the British Isles as far north as the Moray Firth, and scarce and local in Ireland. It is a characteristic and often abundant plant of fens and marshes on base-rich or calcareous peat or mineral soils to an altitude of 505 m. It flowers during July and August and is pollinated by small insects.
❁ *G. uliginosum* **is a rather scrambling plant with a many-flowered inflorescence, leaves 6-8 in a whorl and growing to about 50 cm.**

Galium tricornutum Dandy *
CORN CLEAVERS
ROUGH CORN BEDSTRAW
Alien but native throughout most of central, southern and western Europe. It was once widespread throughout lowland Britain but now it probably occurs in less than half a dozen places in Kent, Sussex, Cambridgeshire and Bedfordshire. A weed of cornfields and waste ground especially on calcareous soils, its decline has been caused by the use of cleaner seed corn and herbicides. A scrambling annual, it grows to about 40 cm, and flowers from June to September.
❁ *G. tricornutum* **is distinguished by the three-flowered axillary inflorescences, which are shorter than or just longer than the leaves, and the recurved fruit-stalks.**

❁ *Galium parisiense, G. aparine* **and** *G. spurium* **all differ from** *G. tricornutum* **in the axillary inflorescences all being distinctly longer than the subtending leaves.**

Galium parisiense L.
WALL BEDSTRAW
A rare and local species of south-east England and East Anglia, having been recorded from Hampshire, Sussex, Kent, Essex, Cambridgeshire, Suffolk and Norfolk. It is found on old walls, and in the Breckland of East Anglia it grows in the short turf of calcareous sands and also on bare areas of chalk rubble and old marl pits. A small prostrate annual, it flowers during June and July.
❁ *G. parisiense* **is a slender, often prostrate plant with small (0.5 mm diameter) greenish-white flowers and small forwardly-directed prickles along the margins of the leaves.**

Galium aparine L.
CLEAVERS GOOSEGRASS
Common throughout the whole of the Briitsh Isles, except for parts of the Scottish Highlands. It is an abundant plant of hedgerows, ditches, scrub, stream and river banks, limestone scree, shingle beaches and waste ground, usually on fertile soils. A scrambling annual, it flowers from June to August and is pollinated by small insects. The fruits are covered by hooked bristles which become attached to animals, so effecting dispersal. As its numerous vernacular names suggest, it was eaten by geese and fed chopped to young goslings.
❁ *G. aparine* **is a tall, scrambling plant with backwardly directed prickles along the margin of the leaf, flowers 2 mm in diameter, and fruits covered by stiff, hooked bristles.**

Galium spurium L.*
FALSE CLEAVERS
Alien, but native throughout most of the rest of Europe. It is very rare and now extinct in nearly all of its former localities except perhaps for one place in Essex. It is an annual weed of arable fields and waste ground and occasionally turns up as a casual. It flowers during July.
❁ *G. spurium* **is similar to** *G. aparine* **but with smaller greenish (not white) flowers (1 mm diameter) and only 2-3 bracts at the top of the inflorescence.**

CAPRIFOLIACEAE

Sambucus ebulus L.
DWARF ELDER DANEWORT
Danewort is only doubtfully native in Britain, although it is certainly long-established. It is native throughout most of the rest of Europe from the Netherlands to the Black Sea southwards. It occurs scattered throughout England, Wales and Ireland but is very rare in Scotland and is found in hedgerows, roadsides, waste places and churchyards. A perennial herb, not a woody shrub, it grows to a height of about 120 cm. It flowers during July and August and is pollinated by a variety of small insects. Danewort has featured in English legend since at least Saxon times and was probably first introduced as a medicinal plant or as the source of a blue dye.

❁ *S. ebulus* **grows to about 120 cm and differs from** *S. nigra* **in the herbaceous habit and large, conspicuous leaf stipules.**

Sambucus nigra L.
ELDER
Distributed throughout the British Isles, but introduced into Orkney and Shetland. Elder is a common plant of woods, scrub, hedgerows and waste ground. It is one of the first shrubs to colonise stable sand dunes and is particularly abundant around rabbit warrens. It is characteristic of disturbed ground and fertile, base-rich or calcareous soils, particularly where there has been some nitrogen enrichment. A deciduous shrub or small tree, growing to a height of about 10 m, it flowers during June and July and is pollinated by small flies. The black berries ripen during August and September. Elder has featured prominently in both folklore and medicine and much superstition still surrounds the plant in country areas.

Viburnum lantana L.
WAYFARING-TREE
Confined as a native to southern Britain, south and east of a line from the Wash to the Severn and extending westwards to Glamorgan and south Devon. Within this area it is a frequent plant of hedgerows, woodland margins and scrub on dry, calcareous soils. A deciduous shrub, it grows to a height of about 5 m, flowers during May and June and is pollinated by a variety of insects or self-pollinated. The black berries, which ripen during August and September, are not poisonous but have an unpleasant taste.

Viburnum opulus L.
GUELDER-ROSE
Widely distributed throughout England, Wales and Ireland and scattered throughout Scotland but absent from the Outer Hebrides, Orkney and Shetland. It is a characteristic plant of damp woodlands and fen carr on acid to calcareous mineral soils or peat. It also grows in scrub and hedgerows in similar conditions. A deciduous shrub, it grows to about 3 m, flowers during June and July and is pollinated by insects or self-pollinated. The popular garden form, often called 'snowball tree', belongs to the variety *roseum* and has sterile flowers.

Lonicera periclymenum L.
HONEYSUCKLE
Ubiquitous throughout the whole of the British Isles; a common plant of woodland, scrub and hedgerows on acid to calcareous soils. It avoids waterlogged conditions but occurs on clays as well as on more freely draining soils. It also grows on shaded rocks and cliffs up to an altitude of 610 m. A twining deciduous shrub climbing to 6 m, it flowers from June to September and is pollinated by night-flying moths, including hawk moths, and also by bumble-bees during the day.

Lonicera xylosteum L.*
FLY HONEYSUCKLE
Very rare. It is confined as a native plant to a short stretch of a north face of the South Downs in west Sussex, where it grows in scrub and open woodland on the shallow chalk soil. A deciduous shrub, it grows to a height of 2-3 m, flowers during May and June and is pollinated by bumble-bees. Occasionally cultivated, it occurs as an introduction or casual in a few scattered localities north to central Scotland.

Linnaea borealis L.
TWINFLOWER LINNAEA
Rare and local, being confined to eastern Scotland, chiefly in Aberdeenshire and Moray, where it grows on the floor of native pinewoods or on shaded rocky hillsides, reaching an altitude of 730 m. A small, creeping mat-forming evergreen shrub, it flowers from June to August and is pollinated by small insects.

ADOXACEAE

Adoxa moschatellina L.
MOSCHATEL TOWN-HALL CLOCK
Distributed throughout the British Isles as far north as the Moray Firth, but absent from Ireland. It is a frequent plant of woods, coppice, lane sides and hedge banks on a wide range of soils, but avoiding both very dry and very acid conditions. It also occurs on mountain rocks to altitudes of 1,095 m. A small perennial, growing to about 10 cm, it flowers during April and May and is pollinated by small insects or self-pollinated. The name 'town-hall clock' refers to the arrangement of the five flowers into four opposite faces with one on top.

VALERIANACEAE

Valerianella Mill.
CORNSALAD LAMB'S-LETTUCE
The five British species of *Valerianella* are all very similar in general appearance and can only be identified with any confidence by examining the ripe fruits. Full descriptions and keys can be found in the *New Flora of the British Isles*. The whole plant of *V. locusta*, the commonest species, is illustrated together with the fruits of each of the five.

Valerianella locusta (L.) Laterr.
COMMON CORNSALAD LAMB'S-LETTUCE
A rather local species distributed throughout the British Isles but rare and almost wholly coastal north of the Firth of Forth, and scattered in Ireland. It is a plant of arable fields, hedge banks, rocks, cliffs, walls and sand dunes on dry, well-drained sandy to calcareous soils. An annual, growing to about 20 cm, it flowers from April to June and is self-pollinated.

Valerianella dentata (L.) Poll.
NARROW-FRUITED CORNSALAD
Generally distributed throughout England north to the Tyne, but rare in Wales, Ireland and the south-west and almost absent from Scotland. It is a local and decreasing weed of cereal crops on light soils. An annual, growing to about 20 cm, it flowers during June and July and is self-pollinated.

Valerianella rimosa Bast.*
BROAD-FRUITED CORNSALAD
A rare and rapidly decreasing weed of cereal crops, now known from only six counties in the south and east: Dorset, Hampshire, Sussex, Berkshire, Bedfordshire and Leicestershire. An annual, growing to about 20 cm, it flowers later than any of the other *Valerianella* species, in July and August, and is self-pollinated.

Valerianella eriocarpa Desv.*
HAIRY-FRUITED CORNSALAD
Alien, and a native of the Mediterranean and North Africa. Very rare and now known from only a few scattered localities in England and Scotland in Cornwall, Dorset, Middlesex, Northamptonshire, Gloucestershire, Leicestershire and Moray and from Alderney in the Channel Isles. It occurs on banks, old walls, sand dunes and arable fields on dry, well-drained soils. An annual, it flowers during June and July.

Valerianella carinata Lois.
KEELED-FRUITED CORNSALAD
Very local and scattered throughout England north to Yorkshire, very rare in Wales and Ireland and absent from Scotland. It is most frequent in the south-west and occurs as weed of arable crops and on banks, walls and rock outcrops on dry, well-drained soils. An annual, it flowers from April to June.

continued on next page

Valerian officinalis L.
COMMON VALERIAN
Distributed throughout the whole of the British Isles except for Shetland. It is a frequent plant of the tall vegetation of marshes, fens, alpine meadows, wet woodlands and ditch sides and also in rough grassland on dry calcareous soils. A tall perennial, growing to about 120 cm, it flowers from June to August and is pollinated by various flies and Hymenoptera. Valerian was formerly an important medicinal plant.

❁ ***V. officinalis* is a much taller plant than *V. dioica*, growing to 120 cm, but the pinnate basal leaves will always separate it from the entire basal leaves of *V. dioica*, which rarely exceeds 25 cm.**

Valeriana pyrenaica L.
PYRENEAN VALERIAN
Alien; naturalised and frequent in southern Scotland but rare elsewhere. A perennial with large entire basal leaves with cordate bases, it occurs in damp woods and hedge banks. (Not illustrated.)

Valeriana dioica L.
MARSH VALERIAN
Distributed throughout England and Wales and north to a line from the Solway to the Firth of Forth and absent from Ireland. It is a frequent plant of marshes, fens, wet meadows and open areas in wet woodlands on mildly acid to calcareous, peaty or mineral soils. A perennial, growing to about 25 cm, it flowers during May and June and is pollinated chiefly by flies.

PLATE 79
VALERIANACEAE • DIPSACACEAE • ASTERACEAE (= COMPOSITAE)
(see illustrations page 168)

Centranthus ruber (L.) DC.
RED VALERIAN
Alien and a native in Europe in Portugal and the whole of the Mediterranean. It is commonly grown in gardens and occurs naturalised throughout the British Isles north to the Firth of Forth. It is most frequent in the south-west and coastal districts of Wales, growing on old walls, dry banks, along railways, and on cliffs and stony waste ground. A perennial, it grows to about 80 cm, flowers from June to August and is pollinated by Lepidoptera. Red, pink and white forms of the flowers occur.

DIPSACACEAE

Dipsacus fullonum L.
TEASEL
Widespread in England south and east of a line from the Humber to the Severn, also in the south-west and coastal districts of Wales but scarce elsewhere and absent north of the Firth of Forth. Very rare in Ireland. It occurs in rough grassland, along stream and river banks and roadsides, in open woods and on waste ground, especially on heavy, neutral clay soils. A tall biennial, growing to a height of up to 2 m, it flowers during July and August and is pollinated by bees and flies.
❁ ***D. sativus*, the fuller's teasel, differs from the wild *D. fullonum* (illustrated) in having the involucral bracts spreading horizontally and the receptacle bracts with spiny tips and longer than the flowers.**

Dipsacus pilosus L.
SMALL TEASEL
A very local species scattered throughout England and the Welsh border but absent from the south-west, Scotland and Ireland. It occurs in damp woods, ditches and hedge banks, especially on calcareous soils. A biennial, growing to about 1 m, it flowers during August and is probably pollinated by bees and flies.

Succisa pratensis Moench
DEVIL'S-BIT SCABIOUS
Ubiquitous throughout the whole of the British Isles. It is a common plant of wet meadows, marshes, fens, wet heathland, damp open woods and woodland rides on mildly acid to calcareous soils. It also occurs on drier soils in chalk and limestone grassland. A perennial, it grows to a height of 1 m, is in flower from June to October and is pollinated by bees and butterflies. The leaves are the foodplant of the larvae of the marsh fritillary butterfly, *Euphydryas aurinia*.

❁ ***Succisa* differs from *Scabiosa* and *Knautia* in the entire lower leaves.**

Scabiosa columbaria L.
SMALL SCABIOUS
Widespread in England and Wales but absent from Scotland, Ireland and the extreme south-west. It is a common and characteristic plant of short-grazed turf, rough grassland and grassy banks on shallow dry, well-drained calcareous soils, reaching an altitude of 610 m, in northern England. It is especially frequent on the chalk of southern England. A perennial, it grows to about 60 cm, is in flower during July and August and is pollinated by bees and Lepidoptera.

❁ ***Knautia* differs from *Scabiosa* in having ovate involucral bracts. The involucral bracts of *Scabiosa* are almost linear.**

Knautia arvensis (L.) Coulter
FIELD SCABIOUS
Distributed throughout the whole of the British Isles but rare in western and northern Scotland and northern Ireland. It is a frequent plant of roadsides, hedge banks and rough grassland and, less often, of cereal crops on dry, basic or calcareous soils, reaching to 365 m. A perennial growing to about 1 m, it flowers from July to September and is pollinated by bees and butterflies.

ASTERACEAE (= COMPOSITAE)

The Asteraceae is the largest family of flowering plants and includes some of the most taxonomically difficult genera, such as *Hieracium* (hawkweeds) and *Taraxacum* (dandelions). Even ignoring these, it usually takes a little time to become familiar with the family. The very small flowers (florets) are clustered together in flower-like heads (capitula) which are surrounded by a calyx-like involucre of bracts. The florets are of two main kinds: 'tubular' with the corolla tube crowned by five small teeth, or 'ligulate' with the corolla represented by a strap-shaped 'ligule'. The florets may be all of one kind, either all tubular or all ligulate, or the central florets may be tubular and the outer ligulate. The calyx is represented by small teeth, or by one or more rings of feathery hairs (the pappus). Occasionally it may be entirely absent.

Galinsoga parviflora Cav.
GALLANT-SOLDIER
Alien. It is a cosmopolitan weed whose country of origin is certainly in South America and probably Peru. It was first recorded from near Kew Gardens in 1861 and is now a frequent weed of gardens, waste ground and arable crops, particularly around London. An annual, it grows to about 75 cm and flowers from May to October.

A closely related South American species, *G. quadriradiata* Ruiz & Pavon (*G. ciliata* (Raf.) Blake), was first recorded in 1939 and is found in similar places, but is far less frequent.
❁ ***Galinsoga* is distinguished by the combination of white ray florets, yellow disc florets, opposite leaves and small heads. *G. quadriradiata* differs from *G. parviflora* in having the upper part of the stems densely covered by long, spreading hairs.**

Tephroseris integrifolia (L.) Holub subsp. *integrifolia* (*Senecio integrifolius* (L.) Clairv. subsp. *integrifolius*)
FIELD FLEAWORT
A very local plant confined to the chalk of southern England from Dorset to Sussex and Berkshire and along the Chilterns to Cambridgeshire. It also occurs in a few places on the oolitic limestone in Gloucestershire. It is restricted to short turf on dry, well-drained, shallow calcareous soils and usually grows near the tops of slopes, often in association with ancient earthworks. A biennial to perennial, it grows to a height of 30 cm, flowers during May and June and is pollinated by various insects.

Subsp. *maritima* (Syme) R. Nordenstam* is confined and endemic to north- and north-east-facing slopes of sea cliffs near the South Stack Lighthouse on Holyhead Island in north Wales. The basal leaves are more coarsely toothed and the flowering stems more leafy than in subsp. *integrifolius*. (Not illustrated.)
❁ ***Tephroseris* is distinguished from British species of *Senecio* by the rosette of entire ovate leaves.**

Senecio cineraria DC.
SILVER RAGWORT CINERARIA
Alien and a native of the western and central Mediterranean where it grows in rocky and sandy places. It is thoroughly naturalised on maritime cliffs in Devon and Cornwall and on chalk cliffs and shingle beaches in Kent. Elsewhere it occasionally appears as a casual escape from gardens. A dwarf shrub growing to about 50 cm, it flowers from June to August.
❁ ***S. cineraria* grows to about 50 cm and is easily distinguished by the white woolly stems and deeply dissected white woolly leaves.**

Senecio paludosus L.**
FEN RAGWORT
Very rare. It formerly grew in fen ditches in Cambridgeshire, Lincolnshire, Suffolk and Norfolk but became extinct towards the end of the 19th century as a result of the drainage of the fens. A small population was rediscovered in Cambridgeshire in 1972, where it is still thriving. A tall perennial growing up to 2 m, it flowers from May to July and is pollinated by various insects.

❁ ***S. paludosus* has white cottony hairs on the underside of the leaves and 10-20 ray florets. *S. fluviatilis* has glabrous leaves and 6-8 ray florets.**

Senecio fluviatilis Wallr.
BROAD-LEAVED RAGWORT
Alien and a native of central and eastern Europe west to the Netherlands. It is naturalised in damp meadows, fens, wet woods and stream sides in a number of places scattered throughout the British Isles north to central Scotland, and most frequently in Somerset. A tall perennial, growing to over 1 m, it flowers from July to September and is pollinated by bees and flies. It was originally introduced to Britain from the Netherlands or Germany in the 16th century as a medicinal plant for use as a wound herb.

❁ ***S. jacobaea*, *S. erucifolius*, *S. aquaticus* (Plate 80) and *S. squalidus* (Plate 80) all have conspicuous ray florets and deeply divided leaves.**

***S. jacobaea* and *S. erucifolius* have denser, flat-topped inflorescences; the inflorescences of *S. aquaticus* (Plate 80) and *S. squalidus* (Plate 80) are less dense and more irregular in shape.**

Senecio jacobaea L.
RAGWORT
Common throughout the British Isles and a troublesome weed of overgrazed grassland, roadsides

continued on next page

and disturbed ground on almost all kinds of soil except for the most acid peats and sands. It is a characteristic species of coastal sand dunes and also of some open woodlands, but is absent from waterlogged soils. It is extremely poisonous to cattle and horses, but is eaten by sheep. It is one of five plants scheduled in the Weed Act, 1974. An autumn-germinating biennial or short-lived perennial, it grows to about 120 cm and flowers from June to November. The flowers are attractive to many different insects.

Senecio erucifolius L.
HOARY RAGWORT
Widespread in England south and east of a line from the Tyne to the Severn, also in coastal districts of Wales and in the south-west, and very rare in Ireland. It is a plant of rough grassland, pastures, roadsides, hedge banks and shingle beaches especially on neutral to basic, clay or calcareous soils. A perennial, growing to about 1 m, it flowers from July to September and is pollinated by bees and flies.
❁ ***S. erucifolius* differs from *S. jacobaea* in the narrower leaflets and smaller terminal lobe. The lobes have white cottony hairs beneath and the margins are slightly revolute.**

PLATE 80
ASTERACEAE (= COMPOSITAE)
(see illustrations page 170)

Senecio squalidus L.
OXFORD RAGWORT
Alien and a native of the mountains of central and southern Europe. It is now a common plant of waste ground, railways, walls and roadsides throughout most of England and Wales although it is still very rare in Scotland and Ireland. It was first recorded growing on old walls in Oxford before the end of the 18th century, having almost certainly escaped from the Oxford Botanic Garden. From there it has spread throughout the country via the railway system, the plumed seeds being carried in the vortex of air behind the trains. An annual, it grows to about 25 cm, and flowers from May to December.

❁ ***S. squalidus* differs from *S. aquaticus* in the conspicuous black tips to the involucral bracts. The bracts of *S. aquaticus* have white margins.**

Senecio aquaticus Hill
MARSH RAGWORT
Generally distributed throughout the whole of the British Isles. It is a frequent plant of wet meadows and pastures, marshes, ditches, dykes and river and stream banks, usually on heavy, silty or alluvial soils, to an altitude of 460 m. A biennial, it grows to about 75 cm, flowers during July and August and is pollinated chiefly by flies.

❁ ***S. viscosus*, *S. vulgaris*, *S. sylvaticus* and *S. cambrensis* all have short or no ray florets.**

Senecio viscosus L.
STICKY GROUNSEL
STINKING GROUNDSEL
Doubtfully native in Britain, it is generally distributed throughout the British Isles as far north as the Firth of Forth. Elsewhere it is rare in northern Scotland, in Wales and the south-west and almost absent from Ireland. It is a frequent plant of waste ground, roadsides, railway tracks, sand dunes and shingle beaches. An annual, with a characteristic unpleasant smell and growing to about 50 cm, it flowers from July to September and is probably pollinated by bees and flies.
❁ ***S. viscosus* is densely covered by sticky glands.**

Senecio vulgaris L.
GROUNDSEL
Common throughout the whole of the British Isles except for some parts of the Scottish Highlands. Groundsel is a ubiquitous weed of arable, cultivated and disturbed ground of all kinds, gardens, waste places and sand dunes. It is most common on the heavier and moister soils and less frequent on well-drained sands and chalk. An annual, it flowers throughout the year and probably is usually self-pollinated.
❁ **Groundsel is a very variable plant and individuals possessing ray-florets are not infrequent, especially in coastal habitats. *S. vulgaris* normally has almost no ray florets; the heads are almost stalkless and are arranged in dense clusters.**

Senecio sylvaticus L.
HEATH GROUNDSEL
WOOD GROUNDSEL
Distributed throughout the British Isles north to Orkney but locally scarce in many areas, including western Scotland and Ireland. It is found in disturbed ground in heathland, open woodland and recent coppice, roadside verges and waste ground on dry, acid, usually well-drained sandy soils. It frequently appears in such places after a fire. A tall annual growing to about 70 cm, it flowers from July to September and is probably pollinated by small flies.
❁ ***S. sylvaticus* has characteristic yellow-green leaves and the heads are in large, open flat-topped inflorescences. All the heads are conspicuously stalked with distinct, but short, revolute ray florets.**

Senecio cambrensis Rosser*
WELSH GROUNDSEL
Very rare and endemic to the British Isles. It seems to have arisen as a result of a cross between *S. vulgaris* and *S. squalidus* and was first discovered on a roadside in Flintshire in 1948, where it still occurs. It has since been recorded from Denbighshire and Shropshire and seems to thrive best in open habitats such as gardens and roadsides. An annual, it flowers from May to October.
❁ ***S. cambrensis* is intermediate between *S. vulgaris* and *S. squalidus*. The ray florets are short, but longer than either *S. vulgaris* or *S. sylvaticus* (c. 5 mm).**

Bidens cernua L.
NODDING BUR-MARIGOLD
Occurs throughout the British Isles as far north as central Scotland but rather local and scarce in the south-west, Wales, northern England, southern Scotland and Ireland. It is a plant of wet meadows, ditch, dyke and stream sides and pond margins, especially where water stands in winter but disappears in summer. An annual, growing to about 50 cm, it flowers from July to September and is pollinated by bees and flies.

❁ ***Bidens* is distinguished by the opposite leaves and absence of ray florets. *B. cernua* has simple leaves and large drooping heads; *B. tripartita* has leaves deeply divided into lobes.**

Bidens tripartita L.
TRIFID BUR-MARIGOLD
Distributed throughout the British Isles as far north as the Dee, but rare north of the Humber and scarce in the south-west, Wales and Ireland. It is locally frequent in wet meadows and pastures and along the margins of streams, dykes, ditches, ponds and lakes usually on mildly acid to neutral or calcareous soils. An annual of up to 60 cm, it flowers from July to September and is pollinated by hoverflies and bees.

Doronicum pardalianches L.
LEOPARD'S-BANE
Alien; native to western Europe as far east as south-east Germany and Italy. It occurs naturalised in scattered localities throughout Britain but is absent from Ireland. It is particularly frequent in eastern Scotland and occurs in woods, plantations, roadsides and waste ground. It was formerly widely cultivated as a medicinal plant. A perennial, growing to about 75 cm, it flowers from May to July and is pollinated by various small insects.
❁ ***Doronicum* differs from *Senecio* in the larger heads (more than 4 cm diameter) and in the involucral bracts being in two rows rather than one.**

Tussilago farfara L.
COLT'S-FOOT
Distributed throughout the whole of the British Isles. It is a common plant of roadsides, hedge banks, arable fields and waste ground, especially on heavy calcareous clays. It is also found in chalk quarries, sand dunes, on stream-side shingle and hillside flushes to an altitude of 1,070 m in Scotland. A perennial, it flowers during March and April before the leaves appear; the central florets of the flower-heads are male, while the outer florets are female. The heads close up at night and in dull weather. Pollination is effected by bees and flies. The leaves were smoked as a cure for coughs and asthma.

Petasites fragrans (Vill.) Presl
WINTER HELIOTROPE
Alien but a native of the central Mediterranean. It was introduced to English gardens in 1806, since when it has become thoroughly naturalised throughout most of the British Isles except for Scotland, where it is very local. It is most abundant in southern England where it is a frequent plant of hedge banks, roadside verges, stream sides and waste ground. The flowers, which have a characteristic vanilla-like fragrance, appear at the same time as the leaves, and are pollinated by early flies and bees.

❁ ***P. fragrans* differs from the other species in that the flowers appear at the same time as the leaves, not before. The flowers of *P. hybridus*, *P. albus* and *P. japonicus* all appear before the leaves.**

Petasites hybridus (L.) Gaertn., May & Scherb.
BUTTERBUR
Widely distributed throughout England, Wales and Ireland and in most of Scotland, except for the eastern Highlands and the extreme north. It is a locally frequent plant of river and stream banks, wet meadows and damp open woodlands, reaching an altitude of 460 m. Male and female flowers are borne on separate plants and the female plants are more or less confined to parts of northern England from Leicestershire northwards, where the species is probably most abundant. The leaves were formerly used for wrapping butter, hence the vernacular name.
❁ **The violet flowers of *P. hybridus* distinguish it from both *P. albus* and *P. japonicus*.**

Petasites albus (L.) Gaertn.
WHITE BUTTERBUR
Alien, but native throughout most of central Europe. It is found scattered throughout England and Scotland, but is only at all frequent in eastern Scotland from the Firth of Forth to the Moray Firth. It occurs naturalised along roadsides, on waste ground and in woods and plantations. A perennial, it flowers before the leaves from March to May and is pollinated by various insects.

❁ **The leaves of *P. albus* are white and woolly beneath and up to 30 cm in diameter. The leaves of *P. japonicus* are huge, up to 1 m across, and almost glabrous beneath.**

Petasites japonicus (Sieb. & Zucc.) Schmidt.
GIANT BUTTERBUR
Alien and a native of Japan and Sakhalin. It is naturalised on stream banks as a garden escape in a few places in Devon, Buckinghamshire, Cheshire and Cumbria. The flowers appear before the leaves.

Homogyne alpina (L.) Cass.**
PURPLE COLT'S-FOOT
Almost certainly alien in Britain, but native in the mountains of most of central, western and southern Europe. It occurs in two localities only in the British Isles: one in Clova in Angus where there is a small population of about 20 plants at an altitude of 600 m, the other on South Uist in the Outer Hebrides. A perennial, growing to about 40 cm, it flowers from May to August.

❁ *Inula* **and** *Pulicaria* **both differ from** *Senecio* **in that the involucre consists of several rows of overlapping bracts instead of a single row.**

Inula helenium L.
ELECAMPANE
Alien and probably a native of parts of western and central Asia. It has been cultivated as a medicinal plant since early times and was certainly known to the Anglo-Saxons. It occurs as a naturalised escape from cultivation scattered throughout the British Isles in waste ground, old meadows, roadsides and old orchards. A tall perennial, it grows to about 150 cm, flowers during July and August and is pollinated by bees and hoverflies.
❁ *I. helenium* **is easily recognised by its large size, with heads up to 8 cm across.**

Inula salicina L.(*)
IRISH FLEABANE
WILLOW-LEAVED INULA
Very rare and confined in the British Isles to the stony limestone shores of Lough Derg in Galway and Tipperary, where it grows among tall fen vegetation. A perennial, it flowers during July and August. The Irish plant is subsp. *salicina*.
❁ *I. salicina* **grows to 50 cm and the leaves are almost glabrous.**

Inula conyzae (Griess.) Meikle (*I. conyza* DC.)
PLOUGHMAN'S-SPIKENARD
Distributed throughout most of England and Wales north to the Tees but absent from Scotland and Ireland. It is a frequent plant of rough grassland, scrub, cliffs and scree on dry, well-drained calcareous soils. A biennial or short-lived perennial, it grows to over 1 m and flowers from July to September.
❁ *I. conyza* **is distinguished by the foxglove-like leaves and narrow heads (about 1 cm).**

Inula crithmoides L.
GOLDEN SAMPHIRE
A very local species of the coasts of England, Wales and southern and eastern Ireland. It occurs in the upper parts of salt marshes in Essex, Kent and Hampshire, while on the south-west coasts and in south Wales and Anglesey it is a characteristic plant of sea cliffs and maritime rocks. More rarely it also grows on shingle beaches. A perennial growing to about 75 cm, it flowers during July and August.
❁ *I. crithmoides* **is easily recognised by its glabrous, succulent leaves.**

Pulicaria dysenterica (L.) Bernh.
COMMON FLEABANE
Generally distributed throughout England, Wales and most of Ireland but absent from Scotland except for a few places in the south. It is a frequent plant of damp roadsides, ditches, stream and river banks, marshes and wet meadows. A perennial growing up to 60 cm, it flowers during August and September and is attractive to a wide range of insects.
❁ *P. dysenterica* **can be distinguished from all** *Inula* **species by the softly and densely hairy cordate stem leaves.**

Pulicaria vulgaris Gaertn.**
SMALL FLEABANE
Very rare and now almost confined to the New Forest in Hampshire where it occurs in seven locations, growing in damp depressions and around the margins of ponds, particularly where water stands in winter, on old grazed sandy commons. Once widespread in southern and eastern England, its decline is probably attributable to the decline in the traditional grazing of village commons, especially by ducks and geese. An annual growing to about 30 cm, it flowers during August to September.
❁ *P. vulgaris* **is smaller than** *P. dysenterica*, **growing to about 30 cm; the stem leaves are not cordate, and it has short ray florets.**

❁ *Filago* **and** *Gnaphalium* **are rather similar in appearance, with woolly stems and leaves.** *Filago* **has small erect stem leaves and the outer involucral bracts are leaf-like in texture. The stem leaves of** *Gnaphalium* **are usually longer and spreading, and the involucral bracts are brown and papery.**

Filago gallica L.*
NARROW-LEAVED CUDWEED
Probably alien but native throughout most of western, southern and west central Europe. It was first recorded in Britain in 1696 and became established in dry gravelly grassland in a number of localities in south-eastern England and in the Channel Islands. It was well known in one place in Essex for over 100 years but is now probably extinct in the British Isles except for one locality on the island of Sark in the Channel Islands, although it has recently been reintroduced to its original Essex locality.

❁ *F. gallica* **and** *F. minima* **differ from the other species of** *Filago* **in that the inflorescence consists of clusters with few (usually less than eight) flower-heads.** *F. gallica* **has longer leaves (10-20 mm) than** *F. minima*, **which has leaves 5-10 mm long, and the flower clusters are overtopped by their basal leaves.**

Filago minima (Sm.) Pers.
SMALL CUDWEED
SLENDER CUDWEED
A local species distributed throughout the British Isles, but absent from Orkney, Shetland and the Hebrides and very rare in Ireland. It is most frequent in the south and in East Anglia, growing on open patches in heath grassland, commons and arable fields, along the edges of paths and in waste ground and pits on dry sandy or gravelly soils. Less often it may appear on calcareous soils. A small annual, growing to about 10 cm, it flowers from June to September.

Gnaphalium supinum L.
DWARF CUDWEED
Widespread in the Scottish Highlands from the central Highlands northwards, growing on cliffs and moraines on both acid and basic rocks at high altitudes. A small perennial growing to about 10 cm, it flowers during July.
❁ *G. supinum* **grows to about 10 cm, and is distinguished by its dwarf tufted habit.**

Gnaphalium sylvaticum L.
HEATH CUDWEED
WOOD CUDWEED
Distributed throughout the British Isles, but rare in the south-west, Wales and Ireland. It is a local plant of grassy heaths and commons and woodland rides, recent coppice and scrub on acid, well-drained sandy soils. A perennial, growing to about 40 cm, it flowers from July to September.

❁ **Both** *G. sylvaticum* **and** *G. norvegicum* **have spike-like inflorescences.** *G. sylvaticum* **is distinguished from** *G. norvegicum* **by the narrower one-veined leaves, which get progressively shorter from the base of the stem upwards.** *G. norvegicum* **has three-veined leaves which do not get shorter until well above the middle of the stem.**

Gnaphalium norvegicum Gunn.*
HIGHLAND CUDWEED
Very rare and confined to the Scottish Highlands where it is known at present from only eight places in Angus, Inverness-shire and Ross-shire growing at altitudes up to 1,100 m, usually on acid rocks. A perennial, growing to about 25 cm, it is in flower during August.

Gnaphalium luteoalbum L.**
JERSEY CUDWEED
Very rare, and probably only native in Norfolk and the Channel Islands, but it has probably disappeared from its Norfolk localities as it has not been seen since 1973. It is a species of open ground and bare patches of sandy fields, sand dunes and waste ground on dry, well-drained soils. Its decline is almost certainly the result of agricultural improvement. An annual, growing to about 30 cm, it flowers from June to August and is attractive to flies and bees.
❁ *G. luteo-album* **and** *G. uliginosum* **(Plate 82) both have the flower heads arranged in dense clusters, but the much-branched habit of** *G. uliginosum* **and the flower-heads overtopped by their basal leaves is distinctive.**

ASTERACEAE (= COMPOSITAE) *(see illustrations page 174)*

Gnaphalium uliginosum L.
(*Filaginella uliginosa* (L.) Opiz)
MARSH CUDWEED
Widespread and common throughout the British Isles but scarce in parts of northern Scotland and central Ireland. It is a plant of pond margins, woodland rides, arable fields, roadsides, heaths and gardens on damp or seasonally flooded clay or sandy soils. An annual, it grows to about 20 cm and flowers from July to September.

Filago vulgaris Lam.
(*F. germanica* L.)
COMMON CUDWEED
Widely distributed throughout England and Wales, but most frequent in the south and east. It is rare in Scotland north of the Firth of Forth and more or less confined to coastal areas in the east, reaching as far north as Sutherland and scattered in Ireland. It is a plant of heath grassland, commons, arable fields, roadsides, embankments and waste ground on light, acid sandy soils. An annual growing to about 25 cm, it flowers during July and August.
❁ *F. vulgaris* **is covered by white woolly hairs and differs from** *F. pyramidata* **and** *F. lutescens* **in the apical leaves not overtopping the flower heads, which are in clusters of 20-40. The apical leaves of** *F. pyramidata* **and** *F. lutescens* **overtop the flower heads, which are in clusters of 10-20.**

Filago lutescens Jord.**
(*F. apiculata* G.E. Sm.)
RED-TIPPED CUDWEED
Very rare and decreasing and now known only from Surrey, Sussex, Essex, Suffolk and Norfolk where it grows in arable fields, on the sides of tracks, on banks and in gravel pits on dry, well-drained sandy soils. An annual growing to about 20 cm, it flowers during July and August.
❁ *F. lutescens* **is covered by yellowish woolly hairs, and the bracts of the involucre have straight reddish tips.**

Filago pyramidata L.**
(*F. spathulata* C. Presl)
BROAD-LEAVED CUDWEED
SPATHULATE CUDWEED
Very rare and now known from only 11 places in Norfolk, Cambridgeshire, Hertfordshire, Berkshire, Kent, Surrey, Sussex and Hampshire. It is found at the edge of arable fields, on roadsides and in disturbed habitats on well-drained sandy or chalk soils. An annual growing to about 25 cm, it flowers during July and August.
❁ *F. pyramidata* **is an almost prostrate much-branched plant covered by white woolly hairs and the outer bracts of the involucre have a recurved yellowish tip.**

Anaphalis margaritacea (L.) Benth.
PEARLY EVERLASTING
Alien and a native of North America and north-east Asia, it has long been cultivated as an 'everlasting' in gardens and has become naturalised in a number of scattered localities throughout Britain but especially in parts of south Wales. It is found along river banks, in damp meadows and on walls and waste ground. A perennial, it flowers during August.
❁ *Anaphalis* **grows to almost 1 m, and is distinguished from** *Filago* **and** *Gnaphalium* **by its large size, umbel-like inflorescence and characteristic white shining tips to the bracts.**

Antennaria dioica (L.) Gaertn.
MOUNTAIN EVERLASTING
CAT'S-FOOT
Widely distributed throughout the upland areas of Britain, and common north of the Clyde and in parts of western Ireland. It is scattered elsewhere and rare or absent in the lowlands. It is found in mountain grassland, heaths and dry pastures, usually on calcareous or base-rich soils but often where there has been some surface acidification, to altitudes of about 915 m. A dioecious perennial, it grows to about 20 cm. It flowers during June and July and, although visited by various small insects, viable seeds are set without the flowers being pollinated (apomictic).

A form with broader leaves and with white hairs on both sides of the leaf, var. *hyperborea*, occurs in the Inner and Outer Hebrides.
❁ *Antennaria* **grows to about 15 cm and is recognised by its rosette of basal leaves and creeping stolons. The male flowers are usually white, the female pink.**

❁ *Aster* **differs from** *Erigeron* **(Plate 83) in having a single row of ray florets instead of several.**

Aster tripolium L.
SEA ASTER
A common plant of salt marshes all round the coasts of Britain and Ireland. In northern England and Scotland it is almost confined to estuaries and loch-heads, and it is absent from Shetland. Found on bare mobile mud at the lower end of salt marshes in association with *Salicornia* and *Spartina anglica*, and also as a less frequent constituent of the main salt marsh community. It is also a frequent plant of brackish grazing marshes and drainage dykes and is sometimes to be found growing on rocks and sea cliffs. A short-lived perennial growing to about 1 m, it flowers from July to October and is pollinated by a wide variety of insects.

A form without ray florets, var. *discoideus*, frequently occurs in the southern part of its range.
❁ *A. tripolium* **is distinguished from the other blue-flowered species by its fleshy, glabrous leaves and glabrous stems.**

Aster puniceus L.
Alien and a native of eastern North America. It was introduced to British gardens around the beginning of the 18th century with most of the other North American Michaelmas-daisies. It has become established in a number of localities in northern Britain, including Berwick, Dundee and Perth. A perennial, it flowers from July to October. The crushed leaves have a smell resembling juniper berries.

❁ *A. puniceus* **differs from** *A.* x *salignus* **and** *A. novi-belgii* **in its stiffly hairy stems and distinctly toothed leaves.**

Aster novi-belgii L.; *A. laevis* L.; *A. lanceolatus* Willd.
MICHAELMAS-DAISY
The most commonly cultivated Michaelmas-daisies are hybrids and cultivars of these three closely related species, of which *A. novi-belgii* is the most important. More than 70 different cultivars have been developed, including dwarf and double forms, the first double cultivar appearing in 1907.

All three are native to the eastern United States, *A. novi-belgii* being introduced into British gardens around 1710. Most of the more intensely coloured cultivars are derived from *A. novi-belgii*. *A. lanceolatus* is taller, with narrow, dark leaves and white flowers. Tall late-flowering cultivars are derived mostly from *A. laevis* and its hybrids.

Michaelmas-daisies commonly become established on waste ground, railway sidings and near houses. The most commonly encountered in such situations is *Aster* x *salignus* Willd., the hybrid between *A. novi-belgii* and *A. lanceolatus*. They are tall perennials, flowering from August to October.
❁ *Aster* x *salignus* **has dark green, narrow leaves that gradually taper to the base and do not clasp the stem, and pale flowers. The leaves of** *A. novi-belgii* **are broader and the base clasps the stem.**

A. novi-belgii **has a broad clasping base to the stem leaves. The leaves of** *A.* x *salignus* **are gradually tapered to the base and do not clasp the stem.**

Aster novae-angliae L.
HAIRY MICHAELMAS-DAISY
Alien. Like most of the Michaelmas-daisies, it is a native of North America. It was introduced to British gardens around 1710 and has become established in a number of localities. Several well-known 'cultivars' have been developed, but it is not so popular as *A. novi-belgii*. A tall perennial (taller than *A. novi-belgii*), it flowers during September and October and sometimes through to early November.

Aster linosyris (L.) Bernh.*
(*Linosyris vulgaris* Less.; *Crinitaria linosyris* (L.) Less.)
GOLDILOCKS ASTER
Very rare and confined to about seven localities on coastal limestone cliffs in south Devon, north Somerset, Glamorgan, Pembrokeshire, Caernarvonshire and Lancashire. Some of the colonies are very small and, although they are often inaccessible, the plant has suffered from collecting in the past. A woody perennial growing to about 50 cm, it flowers during August and September.

❁ *Erigeron* **differs from** *Aster* **(Plate 82) in having two or more rows of ray florets instead of one.**

Erigeron acer L.
BLUE FLEABANE
Widely distributed throughout England and Wales but scarce in the west except for coastal areas; it is rare in Ireland and absent from Scotland. It is a frequent plant of dry permanent grassland, mature sand dunes, banks and walls on dry well-drained, usually calcareous soils. An annual or biennial, it grows to about 30 cm, and flowers during July and August.

Erigeron borealis (Vierh.) Simmons**
ALPINE FLEABANE
BOREAL FLEABANE
Very rare, and now known only from Perthshire, Angus and Aberdeen. It was first discovered on Ben Lawers by James Dickson in 1789. About 10 colonies are now known, mostly growing on inaccessible basic mica-schist rock ledges between 730 m and 1,070 m. A perennial, growing to a height of about 15 cm, it is in flower during July and August.
❁ *E. borealis* **is distinguished from other species by the solitary heads.**

Erigeron karvinskianus DC.
(*E. mucronatus* DC.)
MEXICAN FLEABANE
Alien and a native of Mexico. It has been established on old walls in St Peter Port, Guernsey, since the end of the last century. It has since spread so that it is now common in similar places in the rest of the Channel Islands and in the Isles of Scilly, south Cornwall and south Devon, with isolated occurrences elsewhere in southern England and south Wales. A perennial, it flowers from July to September.
❁ **The heads of** *E. mucronatus* **are remarkably similar to those of the common daisy.**

Bellis perennis L.
DAISY
Common throughout the whole of the British Isles. Daisies are most familiarly associated with lawns, but there remains the question of where they grew before there were lawns. In semi-natural vegetation they are found in short grassland on a wide range of soils, from mildly acid to calcareous and from heavy to well-drained. They avoid the most acid conditions and are favoured by high fertility. The daisy is tolerant of both heavy grazing and trampling, and reaches an altitude of 900 m. A perennial, it flowers from January to October.

❁ **The six species of CHAMOMILES and rayed MAYWEEDS,** *Matricaria, Anthemis, Tripleurospermum* **and** *Chamaemelum,* **superficially all look very similar.**

Matricaria recutita L.
(*Chamomilla recutita* (L.) Rauschert)
SCENTED MAYWEED
WILD CHAMOMILE
Widely distributed throughout England, but scarce in the south-west and Wales and occurring only as a casual in Scotland and Ireland. It is a frequent weed of arable crops and waste ground, usually on sandy or loamy soils. An annual with a pleasant smell, it grows to about 40 cm and flowers during midsummer. It has been used in the past as a substitute for the true chamomile, *Chamaemelum nobile.*
❁ *M. recutita* **can be separated from** *Tripleurospermum* **by the conical, hollow receptacle, reflexed ray florets and usually smaller heads (1-2.5 cm diameter).**

Matricaria discoidea DC.
(*M. matricariodes* (Less.) Porter)
PINEAPPLE-WEED
RAYLESS MAYWEED
Alien and probably originally a native of north-east Asia, although it is now well established in North America, parts of South America, New Zealand and most of Europe. First found in 1871, it has since spread throughout the British Isles. It is a common weed of footpaths, gateways, cart-tracks, roadside verges and waste ground, and is very tolerant of trampling. Much of its rapid spread is thought to be due to the seeds being carried on car tyres. A strongly smelling annual, it flowers during midsummer.

❁ *Anthemis* **and** *Chamaemelum* **both have small colourless scales mixed among the florets; these are absent in** *Matricaria* **and** *Tripleurospermum.*

Anthemis arvensis L.
CORN CHAMOMILE
Scattered throughout England south and east of a line from the Humber to the Severn and rare in the west and in Scotland as far north as the Moray Firth, and absent from Ireland. It is a locally frequent weed of cereal crops on well-drained sandy or, more usually, calcareous soils. It is occasionally found in temporary grassland and on roadside verges. It is the least frequent of the four annual 'mayweeds' of cereal crops, *A. arvensis, A. cotula, Matricaria recutita* and *Tripleurospermum inodorum.*

❁ *A. arvensis* **can be distinguished from** *A. cotula* **and** *Chamaemelum nobile* **by the underside of the young leaves being covered by woolly hairs. The heads are larger (2-3 cm diameter) than those of** *A. cotula* **with longer stalks, and the plant has hardly any smell.**

Anthemis cotula L.
STINKING MAYWEED
A locally common plant in England and parts of Wales, but very rare in Scotland and Ireland. It is a weed of arable crops and farmyards, usually on heavy, base-rich clays or loams. Like all 'mayweeds' it is more or less resistant to the phenoxyacetic acids, but can be controlled by some more recently introduced herbicides. An autumn- and spring-germinating annual, it flowers from May to July and again in the stubble during September and October, and is pollinated chiefly by hoverflies.
❁ *A. cotula* **is sparsely hairy and the whole plant has a strong unpleasant smell. The heads are more shortly stalked than either** *A. arvensis* **or** *Chamaemelum.*

Chamaemelum nobile (L.) All.
CHAMOMILE
A species with a rather restricted distribution in southern England, East Anglia, south Wales and south-west Ireland. It is a local plant of grassy heaths, commons and roadsides on acid sandy soils. It has decreased considerably in recent years, mostly as a result of the reclamation or neglect of the old grazed village commons. This is the true 'chamomile' used in chamomile tea and traditionally in shampoo and poultices. A perennial, it flowers from June to August.
❁ *C. nobile* **differs from** *Anthemis* **in its perennial habit. It has a pleasant smell; the heads have relatively long stalks but the leaves are only sparsely hairy (cf** *A. arvensis*).

❁ *Tripleurospermum* **has a solid receptacle and spreading ray florets.** *T. maritimum* **has blunt, fleshy leaf segments and rather larger heads (3-5 cm diameter) than** *T. inodorum,* **which has non-fleshy, pointed leaf segments and heads 2-4 cm in diameter.**

Tripleurospermum maritimum (L.) Koch
(*Matricaria maritima* L.)
SEA MAYWEED
Occurs all round the coasts of the British Isles but is most frequent in Scotland, northern England, Wales and Ireland. It is a characteristic plant of shingle beaches and of the drift line at the foot of sand dunes, and cliffs, rocks and walls close to the sea. A prostrate biennial or perennial, it flowers during July and September.

Tripleurospermum inodorum (L.) Schultz-Bip.
(*Matricaria perforata* Merat)
SCENTLESS MAYWEED
Distributed throughout the British Isles but scarce in parts of the Scottish Highlands and in central Ireland. It is a common weed of arable, roadsides and waste ground on a wide range of soils, both heavy and well-drained and from mildly acid to calcareous. An annual growing to about 50 cm, it flowers from July to September.

Achillea ptarmica L.
SNEEZEWORT
Common throughout northern and western Britain but more local in the south and east. In Ireland it is common only in the north and west. It is a plant of meadows, commons, heaths, roadsides and stream banks on wet, acid to neutral, usually calcium-poor soils. A perennial, it flowers from July to September and is pollinated by bees and flies. The Elizabethan herbalist Gerard claimed that its smell caused sneezing. Double 'cultivars' are frequently grown in gardens.
❁ *A. ptarmica* **grows to about 50 cm and is unlikely to be confused with any other species. The undivided, toothed, almost glabrous stem-leaves are characteristic.**

Achillea millefolium L.
YARROW
MILFOIL
Distributed throughout the whole of the British Isles, yarrow is a common plant of all kinds of rough grassland, pastures, meadows, grass-heaths, lawns, roadside verges and hedge banks on mildly acid to calcareous soils, avoiding only the poorest, most acid conditions. It is absent from permanently waterlogged situations. A perennial growing to about 40 cm, it flowers throughout the summer and is pollinated by a great variety of insects. Yarrow was used as a wound-herb by the medieval herbalists; there are a few red-coloured garden 'cultivars'.

Otanthus maritimus (L.) Hoffmans & Link*
COTTONWEED
Extinct in Great Britain. It was first recorded from Essex in 1598 and subsequently from scattered localities all along the east and south coasts from Suffolk to north Devon and from Anglesey and the Channel Isles, but it is now restricted to a single site on the coast of Wexford in Ireland. A plant of fixed sand dunes and fine stable shingle, it is probable that its decline has been due to a change in climate as the British Isles are on the extreme northern edge of its range. A perennial, it flowers during August and September.

Chrysanthemum segetum L.
CORN MARIGOLD
Distributed throughout the British Isles. It is a locally common plant growing chiefly as a weed of root and cereal crops, especially barley, and is commonest on fertile, light acid sandy or loamy soils, especially those rich in nitrogen. It also occurs occasionally on waste and disturbed ground. Once a serious arable weed, it is now decreasing in all parts of the country due to increased liming and the use of herbicides. An annual, it flowers from June to August and is insect-pollinated.

Solidago virgaurea L.
GOLDENROD
Distributed throughout the whole of the British Isles but scarce in the Midlands, East Anglia and central Ireland. It is a common plant of dry woodland, hedge banks, scrub, rocky hillsides, stream sides and dunes on dry well-drained soils. It is more often found on acid than calcareous rocks, particularly in the south. In the uplands it reaches 1,085 m. A perennial, it flowers from July to September and is pollinated by bees and flies or self-pollinated.

Mountain forms with shorter stems, simpler inflorescences and larger heads have been distinguished as var. *cambrica* (Huds.) Sm.

❁ ***Solidago* grows up to 75 cm, and is similar to *Inula* (Plate 81), and *Pulicaria* (Plate 81), from which it is distinguished by the elongated inflorescence.**

Eupatorium cannabinum L.
HEMP-AGRIMONY
Widespread and common throughout most of England and Wales, but becoming scarcer northwards. In Scotland it is almost wholly coastal and is absent from Orkney, Shetland and the Outer Hebrides, and is scattered throughout Ireland. It is a plant of the tall vegetation of fens, marshes, clearings and rides in damp woods, river and pond sides and wet ditches on fertile, mildly acid to calcareous soils. It is also found on drier soils in calcareous woods and scrub. A tall perennial growing to about 120 cm, it flowers from July to September.

Conyza canadensis (L.) Cronq.
(*Erigeron canadensis* L.)
CANADIAN FLEABANE
Alien and a native of North America. It first appeared in this country at the beginning of the 18th century following its supposed introduction to Europe in the skin of a bird that had been stuffed with its seed plumes. It is now widespread in England south and east of a line from the Wash to the Isle of Wight and more scattered as far north as the Humber. It grows on old walls, waste ground, railway embankments, dunes and as a weed of cultivated ground on light, well-drained soils. An annual, it grows to about 60 cm, flowers during August and September and is pollinated by small insects.

❁ ***C. canadensis* is distinguished from species of *Erigeron* by the much-branched inflorescence consisting of small greenish-white heads.**

Tanacetum vulgare L.
(*Chrysanthemum vulgare* (L.) Bernh.)
TANSY
Distributed throughout the whole of the British Isles but rather scarce in parts of Scotland and in Ireland. It is a plant of roadsides, hedge banks, stream and river sides and waste ground on a wide range of soils, but avoiding the most acid conditions and reaching an altitude of 370 m in Scotland. A tall perennial, it flowers from July to September and is pollinated by a large variety of insects. It was once widely cultivated both as a pot-herb and as a medicinal plant for many purposes, including the prevention of miscarriages.

Tanacetum parthenium (L.) Shultz-Bip.
(*Chrysanthemum parthenium* (L.) Bernh.)
FEVERFEW
Alien and a native of the Balkan peninsula, where it grows in rocky mountain scrub. It has been cultivated for centuries and is established throughout the British Isles, but is scarce in northern Scotland and Ireland. It is a frequent plant of old walls, waste places and dry hedge banks, particularly near buildings. A strongly smelling perennial, it grows to about 50 cm, and flowers from July to September.

Feverfew was formerly used as a kind of herbalists' aspirin, and as its name suggests was regarded as a powerful relief for fever. Several garden cultivars have been developed, including double forms and varieties with yellow foliage.

Artemisia norvegica Fries**
NORWEGIAN MUGWORT
Very rare and confined to three localities in the mountains of north-west Scotland. It was discovered as a new British plant by Sir Christopher Cox in 1951, growing on a stony plateau of Torridonian sandstone at about 740 m in Wester Ross. A dwarf tufted perennial, it flowers between July and September. The British plant is the var. *scotica* Hulten.

❁ ***A. norvegica* only grows about 5 cm tall, and its small size, silky leaves and single head distinguish it from any other species.**

❁ **The leaflets of *A. verlotiorum*, *A. vulgaris* and *A. absinthium* are at least 2 mm wide; those of *A. campestris* and *Seriphidium maritimum* are narrower.**

Artemesia verlotiorum Lamotte
CHINESE MUGWORT
VERLOT'S MUGWORT
Alien and a native of China. It is established along roadsides and in waste places in an area of Kent, Surrey, Essex and Middlesex centred in the countryside around London. A tall perennial, it flowers during October and November.

❁ ***A. verlotiorum* and *A. vulgaris* both grow to over 1 m.**
***A. verlotiorum* differs from *A. vulgaris* in the densely hairy stems, more elongated terminal segments to the leaves, leafy inflorescence and narrow pith. The stems of *A. vulgaris* have a broad white pith and are only very sparsely hairy.**

Artemisia vulgaris L.
MUGWORT
Distributed throughout the British Isles, but almost wholly coastal in northern Scotland and less frequent in Ireland. It is a common plant of roadsides, hedge banks, riverbanks and waste ground on a wide variety of soils except for the most acid, and is perhaps most frequent on fertile or calcareous soils. A tall perennial, it flowers from July to September and is wind-pollinated. Mugwort featured prominently in medieval medicine and magic.

Artemisia absinthium L.
WORMWOOD
Distributed throughout England and Wales and scattered up the coasts of Scotland as far north as the Forth and the Clyde, and very rare in Ireland. It is a plant of roadsides and waste ground, and was a favourite plant of the medieval herbalists. A tall, strongly aromatic perennial, it flowers during July and August and is wind-pollinated.

❁ ***A. absinthium* is distinguished from *A. vulgaris* and *A. verlotiorum* by its covering of silky white hairs.**

Artemisia campestris L.**
FIELD WORMWOOD
FIELD SOUTHERNWOOD
Very rare and now confined to about two sites in the Breckland of East Anglia, in both of which the plant is vulnerable. Several transplants have been made to Breckland nature reserves in the hope of saving the species. It is found on road verges, on the edges of arable fields and in bare areas in abandoned arable and under conifer belts on calcareous or slightly acid, coarse sands. A much-branched perennial with a prostrate woody stem, it grows to about 60 cm, flowers during August and September and is wind-pollinated.

Seriphidium maritimum (L.) Polj.
(*Artemisia maritima* L.)
SEA WORMWOOD
Distributed all round the British coasts as far north as Kincardine on the east and Cumbria on the west, but most frequent on the south and east coasts from the Isle of Wight to the Humber and rare in Ireland. It is most characteristically a plant of the upper levels of salt and brackish marshes, but is also found on sea walls, sea cliffs and the drift line. A strongly aromatic perennial, it flowers during August and September and is wind-pollinated. The British species belongs to the subspecies *maritima.*

❁ ***S. maritimum* is distinguished from *A. campestris* by its strong, aromatic smell and woolly leaves.**

Leucanthemum vulgare Lam.
(*Chrysanthemum leucanthemum* L.)
OXEYE DAISY
MOON DAISY
MARGUERITE
DOG DAISY
Distributed throughout the whole of the British Isles but less frequent in Scotland. It is a common plant of rough grassland, roadsides, hedge banks and cliff grassland usually on dry, mildly acid to calcareous soils. It also grows on heavier ground that does not remain waterlogged throughout the year, and is most frequent on the more fertile soils. A perennial growing to about 60 cm, it flowers from June to August and is pollinated by a variety of insects.

Silybum marianum (L.) Gaertner
MILK THISTLE
Alien and a native of southern Europe, North Africa, the Caucasus and the Near East. It occurs naturalised in waste places and as a casual in scattered localities throughout the British Isles as far north as the Firth of Forth. An annual or biennial, it flowers from June to August and is probably pollinated by bees.

❁ ***Silybum* can be distinguished from other thistles by the conspicuously white-veined leaves.**

PLATE 85
ASTERACEAE
(= COMPOSITAE)
(see illustrations page 180)

Arctium lappa L.
GREATER BURDOCK
Generally distributed thoughout southern England, south and east of a line from the Humber to the Severn. It is scarce in the south-west and absent from most of Wales, except for parts of the centre and south, and is very rare in Ireland. It is a plant of roadsides, waste places and rough ground, and only occasionally appears in woodland. A tall perennial growing to about 150 cm, it flowers from July to September and is pollinated by bees and butterflies. The spiny fruiting heads are dispersed on the fur of animals.

❁ ***A. lappa* is distinguished from *A. minus* by the solid petioles and long-stalked (3-10 cm) larger heads (more than 35 mm diameter in fruit).**

continued on next page

Arctium minus (Hill) Bernh.

LESSER BURDOCK

Widely distributed throughout the British Isles except for parts of the Scottish Highlands. It is found along wood margins, in woodland clearings and rides, and on waste ground, roadsides and hedge banks on all but the most acid soils. A tall perennial growing to about 250 cm, it flowers from July to September and is pollinated by bees and butterflies.

A. minus is separated into three subspecies, but their distribution is incompletely known. Subspecies *minus* appears to be widespread in Britain, south of a line from Morecambe Bay to Flamborough Head; subsp. *nemorosum* (Lejeune) Syme is the most frequent subspecies; subsp. *pubens* (Bab.) Arenes is the commonest subspecies in the English Midlands.

❁ **The three subspecies are rather difficult to separate and numerous intermediates exist. Subsp. *minus* has a solitary terminal head to the inflorescence and the florets are longer than the involucre. Subspp. *pubens* and *nemorosum* have the terminal heads of the inflorescence in small clusters and the florets are as long as or shorter than the involucre. Subsp. *pubens* has longer peduncles (1.5-4 cm) than subsp. *nemorosum* (up to 1.5 cm). The involucre is pale-coloured, but green or purple in subsp. *nemorosum*.**

❁ **The two main THISTLE genera, *Carduus* and *Cirsium*, are technically distinguished on characters of the pappus; that of *Cirsium* is feathery, branched with fine lateral hairs that are visible to the naked eye when dry. The pappus of *Carduus* is unbranched or minutely toothed.**

Carduus nutans L.

MUSK THISTLE
NODDING THISTLE

Widespread throughout Britain as far north as the Solway and the Firth of Forth with a few scattered localities around the Moray Firth. It is rather scarce in Wales, and in Ireland is confined to a few coastal localities in Galway. It is a plant of roadsides, pastures, rough grassland, arable fields and waste ground, nearly always on well-drained calcareous soils and reaching 505 m in northern England. A biennial, it flowers from May to August. The flowers are supposed to have a scent resembling musk or almonds.

❁ ***C. nutans* is easily recognised by the large, solitary drooping heads and reflexed outer bracts. It grows up to 1 m.**

Carduus tenuiflorus Curtis

SLENDER THISTLE

Has a distinctly coastal distribution in Britain, reaching as far north as Ayrshire on the west and the Moray Firth on the east. It is a locally common plant of roadsides and waste ground close to the sea. Inland it is absent from Scotland, and scarce and local elsewhere. An annual or biennial growing to over 1 m, it flowers from June to August and is pollinated chiefly by bees.

❁ ***C. tenuiflorus* is distinguished from *C. crispus* by the stems being spiny-winged to just below the cylindrical heads. The heads of *C. acanthoides* are ovoid and the stems are unwinged beneath the flower-heads. Both species grow to over 1 m.**

Carduus crispus L.
(*C. acanthoides* L.)

WELTED THISTLE

Distributed throughout lowland Britain as far north as the Moray Firth but rare north of the Firth of Forth and rather scarce in the west and in Ireland. It is a plant of roadsides, hedgerows, stream sides, rough grassland, pastures and waste ground on fertile, often damp soils. A tall biennial, growing to about 120 cm, it flowers from June to August and is pollinated by a variety of bees, butterflies and hoverflies. The British plants belong to subsp. *multiflorus* (Gaudin) Franco.

Cirsium acaule (L.) Scop.

DWARF THISTLE
STEMLESS THISTLE

Widespread in England south and east of a line from north-east Yorkshire to the Severn. It is a locally common plant of the chalk and oolitic limestone of south-east England, with scattered localities on the Carboniferous limestone of Derbyshire, the Mendips, south Wales and the Welsh border and the chalk, oolite and Magnesian limestone of Yorkshire. It is a characteristic plant of short, grazed grassland on warm dry, shallow calcareous soils. Although favoured by grazing, it is intolerant of heavy trampling. A rosette-forming, long-lived perennial, it flowers from June to September and is pollinated primarily by bees.

❁ ***C. acaule* *is easily identified by its stemless heads.***

Cirsium eriophorum (L.)Scop.

WOOLLY THISTLE

Has a distinctive distribution in Britain, extending from Dorset and Somerset north to north-east Yorkshire following the outcrop of the Jurassic oolitic and liassic limestones. Elsewhere it occurs in scattered localities on the older limestone of south Wales, the Welsh borders and Derbyshire, the Magnesian limestone in south Yorkshire and the chalk of eastern England from east Kent to Yorkshire. It is a plant of rough grassland, roadsides, railway banks and scrub on dry, calcareous soils. A tall, handsome biennial, growing to 150 cm, it flowers from July to September and is pollinated by long-tongued bees and Lepidoptera. The British plant belongs to the subspecies *brittanicum* Petrak.

❁ ***C. eriophorum* is distinguished by the cottony heads and unwinged stems growing to 1.5 m.**

Cirsium vulgare (Savi) Ten.

SPEAR THISTLE

Abundant throughout the whole of the British Isles. It is a common weed of cultivated land, roadsides, waste land and disturbed ground, especially on fertile, base-rich or calcareous soils to an altitude of 625 m. It is less frequent in permanent pastures than *C. arvense*, but is similarly a scheduled injurious weed and can be controlled by the phenoxyacetic acid herbicides. An autumn-germinating biennial, it lacks the creeping thistle's means of vegetative spread. It flowers from July to October and is pollinated by long-tongued bees, flies and butterflies.

❁ ***C. vulgare* is distinguished by the leaves that are prickly and hairy on the upper surface wuth a long narrow terminal lobe and the spiny-winged stems. It grows to 1.5 m.**

Cirsium palustre (L.) Scop.

MARSH THISTLE

Common throughout the whole of the British Isles. It is a plant of damp woodland rides and clearings, shady roadsides, marshes and rough wet grassland on a wide variety of soils to an altitude of 760 m. A tall perennial, growing up to 150 cm, it flowers from July to September and is attractive to a large number of bees, flies and butterflies.

❁ ***C. palustre* is distinguished from *C. vulgare* by the hairy, not prickly, upper surface of the leaves which lack a long terminal lobe and the smaller, more crowded heads, and from *C. arvense* by the winged stem.**

Cirsium arvense (L.) Scop.

CREEPING THISTLE
FIELD THISTLE

Abundant throughout the whole of the British Isles. It is a common plant of meadows, pastures, arable, roadsides and waste places, especially on fertile ground. It is absent from the most acid soils but is tolerant of mildly saline conditions. A serious agricultural pest, it is one of the five species scheduled as injurious weeds under the Weeds Act of 1959. It can be successfully controlled by the phenoxyacetic acid herbicides. A perennial, capable of rapid vegetative spread by means of long underground stems, it flowers from July to September and the flowers are visited by a large variety of insects. Creeping thistle is normally dioecious, with separate male and female plants, although hermaphrodite plants do occur occasionally.

Cirsium heterophyllum (L.) Hill
(*C. heleniodes* auct.)

MELANCHOLY THISTLE

A widespread plant of northern Britain extending as far south as the Derbyshire and Staffordshire Pennines, and with a few scattered localities in north and mid Wales. It is a characteristic plant of open woodland, scrub, stream sides and rough hill pastures, often on calcareous or base-rich soils, between 90 m and 965 m. A tall perennial, it flowers during July and August and is pollinated chiefly by bees.

❁ ***C. heterophyllum* grows to over 1 m and is distinguished from *C. dissectum* and *C. tuberosum* by the larger heads (more than 3.5 cm diameter) and the densely white felted underside to the leaves.**

Cirsium dissectum (L.) Hill

MEADOW THISTLE

Widely distributed in lowland Britain south and east of a line from north-east Yorkshire to Pembrokeshire and throughout most of Ireland. It is a locally common plant of fens, marshes, wet heaths, bogs and flushes, often growing among moor-grass, *Molinia caerulea*, on wet, mildly acid to calcareous peats. A perennial, growing to about 75 cm, it flowers from June to August.

❁ **The leaves of *C. dissectum* have white cottony hairs on the undersides; those of *C. tuberosum* are green.**

Cirsium tuberosum (L.) All.*

TUBEROUS THISTLE

Very rare and more or less confined to a small area of the Wiltshire chalk, where it is known now in less than 20 places. It is also known in one locality on the chalk in Cambridgeshire, where it became extinct but has been reintroduced, and from a single site on the Carboniferous limestone in Glamorgan. It is a plant of chalk grassland and dry calcareous pastures, and its recent decline is due to a combination of ploughing and to hybridisation with *C. acaule*. A perennial, it flowers from June to August.

Cirsium oleraceum (L.) Scop.

CABBAGE THISTLE

Alien but native throughout most of Europe except for the extreme north and parts of the Mediterranean. It has become established in a few places in England and Scotland and is a plant of wet woods, stream sides, marshes and fens. A tall perennial growing to over 1 m, it flowers from July to September and is pollinated by bees and butterflies. (Not illustrated.

❁ ***C. oleraceum* has yellow heads.**

Carlina vulgaris L.

CARLINE THISTLE

Widely distributed throughout England and Wales, but scarce and almost wholly coastal in Scotland as far north as Skye and the Moray Firth; it is distributed throughout central Ireland but is rare in the north and south. It is a frequent and characteristic plant of dry, grazed calcareous grasslands and calcareous sand dunes. A biennial, growing to about 45 cm, it flowers from July to October and is pollinated by bees and hoverflies.

Onopordum acanthium L.

COTTON THISTLE
SCOTCH THISTLE

There is some doubt as to whether *O. acanthium* is a true native, but as it has certainly been in Britain since at least the Roman period the question is largely academic. It is widely distributed throughout England and Wales, but is more frequent in the eastern counties from Kent to the Wash, and is very rare in Scotland and Ireland. It is a plant of roadsides, hedge banks, waste ground and the edges of arable fields, usually on mildly acid to calcareous well-drained soils. A tall biennial, growing to about 150 cm, it flowers from July to September and is pollinated chiefly by bees. In spite of its vernacular name it is most unlikely that this is the thistle of Scottish heraldry, as it has always been very rare in that country.

❁ ***Onopordum* is distinguished from other thistles by the white, densely hariy leaves and stems.**

Centaurea scabiosa L.

GREATER KNAPWEED

Widely distributed in the lowlands throughout the British Isles as far north as the coast of Sutherland, but very rare and almost wholly coastal in Scotland. It is also coastal in most of north-west England, Wales and the south-west, and is widespread in west-central Ireland. It is a frequent plant of rough grassland, scrub, roadsides, hedge banks and cliffs on dry, usually calcareous soils. A perennial growing to about 85 cm, it flowers from July to September and is attractive to bees and flies.

Centaurea cyanus L.*

CORNFLOWER
BLUEBOTTLE

Cornflowers were once widely distributed throughout most of the British Isles up to an altitude of about 380 m. Formerly a serious weed of cornfields, especially on light, mildly acid soils, it was particularly associated with rye. The marked decline of the cornflower began in the 1920s with the advent of improved methods of cleaning seed-corn, and it is now rarely seen except as a casual or escape from cultivation. An annual, growing to about 75 cm, it flowers from June to August and is pollinated by flies and bees.

Centaurea jacea L.

BROWN KNAPWEED

A rare alien but a native of almost the whole of the rest of Europe. In the past it has become established in a number of places in southern England, mostly in Middlesex, Surrey and Sussex, but it rarely persists. It hybridises freely with *C. nigra*, producing hybrid swarms from which *C. jacea* soon disappears. It is a plant of rough grassland, golf links, roadsides and waste ground. A perennial growing to about 60 cm, it flowers during August and September and is pollinated by various bees, flies and butterflies.

❁ ***C. jacea* is distinguished from *C. nigra* by the thin, pale brown, shortly toothed tips to the bracts. The tips of the bracts of *C. nigra* are dark brown or black and deeply and finely toothed.**

Centaurea nigra L.

KNAPWEED

Common throughout the whole of the British Isles except in Scotland, where it has been introduced. A perennial growing to about 60 cm, it flowers from June to September and is pollinated by a variety of insects.

Two subspecies are sometimes recognised in Britain.

Centaurea nigra subsp. *nigra*

COMMON KNAPWEED
HARDHEADS

Occurs throughout the British Isles and is apparently the only subspecies in northern England and Scotland. It is a plant of rough grassland, meadows, pastures and roadsides to an altitude of 560 m. In the south it is most frequent on the heavier and wetter soils.

Centaurea nigra subsp. *nemoralis* (Jord.) Gugler (*C. debeauxii* Gren. & Gordon)

SLENDER KNAPWEED

Widespread in England south and east of a line from the Humber to the Severn, with a few mostly coastal localities in Wales and the south-west. Subsp. *nemoralis* is most frequent in rough grassland and on cliffs on well-drained chalk and limestone soils.

❁ **The two subspecies of *C. nigra* are not always easy to separate and intermediates exist between them. For this reason most botanists now feel that there is little justification in distinguishing them. Subsp. *nigra* has toothed or shallowly lobed leaves and the stems are conspicuously swollen beneath the heads. Subsp. *nemoralis* is more branching than subsp. *nigra*, the leaves are almost entire and the stems are hardly swollen beneath the heads.**

Centaurea calcitrapa L.*

RED STAR-THISTLE
STAR THISTLE

Very rare and almost certainly introduced. It occurs in a number of scattered localities along the Sussex coast, from where it was first recorded by Gilbert White in 1765. It grows in rough grazed grassland on dry chalk or sandy soils close to the sea. It has been recorded as a casual from a number of other scattered localities in England north to Lancashire and probably originates as an impurity in lucerne and clover seed. A biennial, it grows to about 50 cm, flowers from July to September and is pollinated by bees and flies.

❁ ***C. calcitrapa* and *C. aspera* have spiny tips to the bracts. The bracts of *C. calcitrapa* have a long terminal spine with shorter laterals, those of *C. aspera* have 3-5 equal-lengthened spines.**

Centaurea aspera L.*

ROUGH STAR-THISTLE

Very rare and only doubtfully native. It is established on sand dunes and waste ground in Jersey and Guernsey in the Channel Islands, and is naturalised in Glamorgan. A perennial growing to 90 cm, it flowers from July to September.

Centaurea solstitialis L.

YELLOW STAR-THISTLE
ST BARNABY'S THISTLE

Alien and a native of southern Europe. It was formerly established as a weed of lucerne and sainfoin fields on dry soils in southern and eastern England, but has now become very rare with the decline in those crops. An annual growing to about 50 cm, it flowers from July to September and is pollinated chiefly by bees.

Saussurea alpina (L.) DC.

ALPINE SAW-WORT
ALPINE SAUSSUREA

An alpine species almost confined to Scotland from the central highlands northwards, but with scattered localities in the southern uplands, the Lake District, Snowdonia and coastal areas of northern and western Ireland. It grows on sheltered alpine and maritime cliffs and ledges, usually on calcareous or base-rich rock, between 45 m and 1,190 m. A stoloniferous perennial, producing flowering stems up to about 40 cm tall, it flowers during August and September and is pollinated by flies and bees.

❁ ***Saussurea* is distinguished from the thistles by the lack of spines and from the knapweeds by the absence of appendages on the tips of the bracts.**

Serratula tinctoria L.

SAW-WORT

Widely distributed throughout England and Wales and north to the north shore of the Solway. In Ireland there is one locality only in the south-east. It is a plant of rough permanent grassland, commons, heaths and woodland margins and grassy clearings and rides up to 380 m. In southern and south-east England it is usually found on damp acid soils and peat, but further north and west it also grows to about 80 cm. Saw-wort is normally dioecious, with separate male and female plants, flowers from July to September and is pollinated by flies and bees.

❁ ***Serratula* is readily identified by the characteristic leaves. White-flowered forms occasionally occur.**

Cichorium intybus L.

CHICORY
WILD SUCCORY

Distributed throughout the British Isles but scarce and possibly not native in Scotland and Ireland. It is most frequent in lowland England. A plant of rough grassland, roadsides verges and waste ground, usually on dry, calcareous soils, it reaches 275 m in Scotland. A perennial growing to about 1 m, it flowers from July to October and is pollinated chiefly by bees and hoverflies. Chicory was formely widely cultivated as a medicinal plant and more recently as a coffee substitute.

❁ **The yellow-flowered composites with dandelion-like flower heads consisting only of ligulate florets are those that usually give most trouble with identification. With the exception of the dandelions (*Taraxacum*) and hawkweeds (*Hieracium*), most species are readily recognised with practice, providing attention is paid to the important characters such as the arrangement of the receptacle bracts, the presence of scales among the florets and, in some cases, details of the fruit and pappus.**

Lapsana communis L.

NIPPLEWORT

Distributed throughout the whole of the British Isles except for parts of the Scottish Highlands and the extreme north of Scotland. It is a common plant of hedgerows, roadsides, walls, wood borders, gardens and waste ground on mildly acid to calcareous soils. An annual growing to about 75 cm, it flowers from July to September and is pollinated by small bees and flies. The vernacular name refers to the nipple-like shape of the flower buds.

❁ ***Lapsana* is easily recognised by the leafy stems and absence of a pappus.**

❁ *Hypochaeris*, **CAT'S-EARS, lack normal stem leaves, but small scale-like bracts may be present on the stems. The flower-heads have numerous pale scale-like bracts mixed up among the florets.**

Hypochaeris glabra L.
SMOOTH CAT'S-EAR
Widely distributed throughout lowland England east of the Isle of Wight, but scarce in the west and Wales. In Scotland it is confined to the southern shore of the Moray Firth and absent from Ireland. A rather local and declining species of open habitats such as abandoned arable fields, grass heaths, commons, road verges, tracks, waste ground and fixed dunes on warm, light sandy soils. An annual, growing to about 25 cm, it flowers from June to October. The flower heads, which only open widely in full sunlight in the morning, are attractive to a variety of small insects.
❁ *H. glabra* **is recognised by its glabrous leaves, small heads and florets only about as long as the involucre.**

Hypochaeris radicata L.
CAT'S-EAR
Common throughout the whole of the British Isles. It is found in pastures, meadows, lawns, commons, grass-heaths, roadsides and fixed dunes. It has a distinct preference for mildly acid sands and clays, avoiding calcareous and base-rich soils, and reaches an altitude of 610 m. A perennial, it flowers from June to September and is pollinated by a variety of insects.
❁ **The leaves of** *H. radicata* **are covered by rough, unbranched hairs and the stems are branched, with several conspicuous scale-like bracts.**

Hypochaeris maculata L.*
SPOTTED CAT'S-EAR
Very rare and now known from less than 12 places in England, Wales and the Channel Islands. In eastern England it occurs in grazed or ungrazed calcareous grassland in five localities on the chalk and oolitic limestone in Herefordshire, Bedfordshire, Cambridgeshire, Suffolk and Northamptonshire, often associated with ancient earthworks or old quarry workings. In western Britain it grows on maritime cliffs of the Carboniferous limestone at Humphrey Head in Lancashire and the Great Orme in Caernarvonshire, on the serpentine at Kynance Cove in Cornwall and on soil derived from granite on coastal cliffs in Jersey. A perennial, it flowers during June and July and is pollinated by bees and hoverflies.
❁ *H. maculata* **is recognised by the large, broad, purple-blotched basal leaves and the rather large, usually solitary, flower heads.**

❁ *Leontodon* (**HAWKBIT**) **lacks normal stem-leaves and the flower-heads do not have scale-like bracts mixed up among the florets (cf.** *Hypochaeris*).

Leontodon autumnalis L.
AUTUMN HAWKBIT
Common throughout the whole of the British Isles. It is a grassland plant occuring in meadows, pastures, grass heaths, commons, roadsides and scree. It grows in a wide range of soils but is characteristic of calcareous grassland. In the mountains it reaches 975 m. A perennial, the flowering stems grow to about 50 cm. It flowers from June to October and is insect- or self-pollinated.
❁ *L. autumnalis* **has branched stems and deeply-lobed basal leaves.**

Leontodon hispidus L.
ROUGH HAWKBIT
Common throughout England and Wales and widespread in Scotland as far north as the Firth of Forth and on Islay, and scattered throughout central Ireland. It is a grassland plant found in meadows, pastures, rough grazings and roadside verges, usually on well-drained calcareous soils. A perennial, it flowers from June to September and is pollinated chiefly by bees and flies.

❁ *L. hispidus* **and** *L. saxatilis* **both have unbranched stems and the basal leaves are covered with small Y-shaped hairs (cf.** *Hypochaeris radicata*). *L. hispidus* **has densely hairy stems, especially in the upper half, larger heads (25-40 mm diameter), and the outer florets may be reddish or orange beneath.** *L. saxatilis* **has almost glabrous stems, especially in the upper half, smaller heads (20 mm or less diameter) and the outer florets are usually greyish beneath.**

Leontodon saxatilis Lam.
(*L. taraxacoides* (Vill.) Merat)
LESSER HAWKBIT
HAIRY HAWKBIT
Widely distributed throughout most of England, Wales and Ireland, but becoming scarce northwards and in Scotland more or less confined to the east coast as far as the Firth of Forth. It is a characteristic grassland plant of heaths, commons, rough grazings, roadsides, banks and stable dunes on well-drained, calcareous or sandy soils. A short-lived perennial, it is in flower from June to September.

Arnoseris minima (L.) Schweigg. & Koerte.*
LAMB'S SUCCORY
SWINE'S SUCCORY
Very rare and now extinct. It was formerly a widespread but local species of eastern England occurring in arable fields on sandy soils. In spite of attempts to re-find it, it has not been seen in any of its old sites since 1971. A small annual, it flowers from June to August and is probably pollinated by flies.
❁ *Arnoseris* **is readily recognised by the absence of stem leaves, the thickened stems beneath the heads, and no pappus.**

Picris hieracioides L.
HAWKWEED OXTONGUE
Widespread in southern England but becomes scarce northwards, is almost absent from Scotland and Ireland and almost wholly coastal in Wales and the south-west. It is a plant of rough grassland, grassy field borders and roadsides, usually on dry calcareous soils. A biennial or short-lived perennial, it flowers from July to September.
❁ *P. hieracioides* **has bristly hairs on the leaves and the receptacle bracts are in several overlapping rows, the outer ones more or less spreading.**

Picris echioides L.
BRISTLY OXTONGUE
Probably introduced to Britain but native throughout southern Europe. It is widespread in lowland England but becomes scarce northwards and is more or less absent from Scotland and Ireland, and almost wholly coastal in Wales and the south-west. It occurs on roadsides, riverbanks, hedgerows, field borders and waste ground on heavy calcareous soils. An annual or biennial, it is in flower from June to October.
❁ *P. echioides* **is distinguished by its densely bristly leaves, the bristles growing on a pale-coloured pimple and the broad leaf-like outer bracts.**

Mycelis muralis (L.) Dum.
WALL LETTUCE
Widely distributed throughout England and Wales as far north as the Solway, but scarce in the south-west, the east Midlands and East Anglia and also in Scotland and Ireland. It is a frequent plant of walls, hedge banks and rocky woodlands, especially on calcareous or base-rich soils on chalk or limestone. A perennial, growing to about 1 m, it flowers from July to September.
❁ *Mycelis* **is distinguished by its spreading branches and narrow involucre consisting of two rows of bracts, the outer shorter than the inner. The involucral bracts of** *Lactuca* **are in several overlapping rows.**

❁ *Lactuca* **and** *Sonchus* **(Plate 88) both have their involucral bracts arranged in several overlapping rows and the broken stems exude a milky juice (latex).**
Lactuca **differs from** *Sonchus* **in its narrower receptacle and elongated inflorescence. The fruits of** *Lactuca* **are 'beaked', i.e. there is a short stalk between the tip of the fruit and the base of the pappus.**

Lactuca saligna L.**
LEAST LETTUCE
Very rare, and now confined to four coastal localities in East Sussex and the Thames Estuary. The Kent and Essex sites are all on sea walls, where the plant seems to be dependent upon patches of bare ground produced by cattle poaching for successful germination and seedling establishment. In east Sussex a small population persists on shingle near Rye. A winter- and spring-germinating annual, it flowers during July and August.

Lactuca virosa L.
GREAT LETTUCE
Widely distributed in eastern England south and east of a line from the Tyne to the Severn, but most frequent around the Thames estuary and in north Norfolk. It is a plant of disturbed ground and open habitats occurring on roadside verges and canal banks and around gravel workings and quarries as well as on sand dunes and cliff ledges, and occasionally on woodland margins. An annual or biennial growing to 2 m, it flowers from July to September.

❁ *L. serriola* **and** *L. virosa* **are rather similar. The stem leaves of** *L. serriola* **are held vertically, usually in the north-south plane, and the bracts at the base of the flower-head stalks have spreading basal lobes. The leaves of** *L. virosa* **are held horizontally and the bracts have appressed basal lobes.**

Lactuca serriola L.
PRICKLY LETTUCE
A species almost wholly confined to eastern England, east of a line from the Wash to the Isle of Wight with a few scattered localities further west and north but absent from Scotland, Wales and Ireland. It most often occurs on disturbed ground such as the verges of new roads and building sites, but is also found in other, more natural well-drained, open habitats such as sand dunes. An annual or winter annual growing to 150 cm, it flowers from July and September and is usually self-pollinated.

Tragopogon pratensis L.
GOAT'S-BEARD
JACK-GO-TO-BED-AT-NOON
Generally distributed throughout most of England, Wales and southern Scotland, but scarce in the west and in Ireland and absent from most of Scotland north of the Firth of Forth. It is a plant of rough grassland, roadside verges, hedge banks, meadows, pastures and sand dunes, reaching 370 m in the Pennines. An annual or short-lived perennial, it flowers during June and July and is insect- or self-pollinated.

Three subspecies occur in Britain. Subsp. *minor* (Mill.) Wahlenb. is the commonest, and possibly the only native subspecies in Britain. Subsp. *pratensis* is much less common than subsp. *minor*, and is probably not native. Subsp. *orientalis* (L.) Celak. is alien and a native of central and eastern Europe, occurring only as a casual in Britain.
❁ *Tragopogon* **is readily recognised by its grass-like basal leaves. The florets of** *T. pratensis* **subsp.** *minor* **are about half as long as the involucral bracts. The florets of subsp.** *pratensis* **about equal the involucral bracts. Subsp.** *orientalis*

continued on next page

has golden-yellow florets that equal or exceed the involucral bracts.

T. porrifolius, **SALSIFY, has purple florets. (Not illustrated.)**

Scorzonera humilis L.**

VIPER'S-GRASS
DWARF SCORZONERA

Very rare and now confined to a single locality in Dorset, where a population of several thousand plants grows in a rough marshy field on acid soil. The site is managed as a nature reserve. A perennial growing to about 50 cm, it flowers from May to July and is insect- or self-pollinated.

✽ *Scorzonera* **is only likely to be confused with** *Tragopogon*, **from which it differs in the involucral bracts being arranged in many overlapping rows (one row in** *Tragopogon*).

PLATE 88

ASTERACEAE (= COMPOSITAE)

(see illustrations page 186)

✽ *Sonchus* **differs from** *Lactuca* **(Plate 87) in its broader receptacle and more or less flat-topped inflorescence. The fruits of** *Sonchus* **are not beaked.**

Sonchus arvensis L.

PERENNIAL SOW-THISTLE
FIELD MILK-THISTLE

Distributed throughout the lowlands of the British Isles, but becoming scarce northwards and absent from large areas of the Scottish Highlands. It is a common plant of stream and river banks, arable land, sea walls and the drift line of brackish and salt marshes on mildly acid to basic soils. A perennial growing to about 150 cm, it flowers from July to October and is pollinated by a variety of insects.

✽ *S. arvensis* **and** *S. palustris* **are both tall perennials with heads 4 cm more in diameter.** *S. arvensis* **has rounded lobes at the base of the stem leaves and orange-coloured hairs on the receptacle;** *S. palustris* **has pointed lobes on the stem leaves and black hairs on the receptacle.**

Sonchus palustris L.

MARSH SOW-THISTLE

Very local and now more or less confined to three areas of eastern England: the Norfolk Broads, parts of east Suffolk and the lower Medway Valley in Kent. Within these areas it is still locally quite frequent, growing in marshes, fens and along river and stream sides in base-rich, alluvial or peaty soils. A tall perennial growing to about 3 m, it flowers from July to September.

Sonchus asper (L.) Hill

PRICKLY SOW-THISTLE
SPINY MILK-THISTLE

Distributed throughout the British Isles except for parts of the Scottish Highlands and northern Scotland. It is a common weed of gardens, arable, roadsides and waste ground on fertile, mildly acid to calcareous soils. An annual, or overwintering annual growing to about 1 m, it flowers from June to August and is pollinated chiefly by bees and hoverflies.

✽ *S. asper* **differs from** *S. oleraceus* **in the prickly stem leaves with rounded basal lobes;** *S. oleraceus* **has pointed lobes to the stem leaves.**

Sonchus oleraceus L.

SMOOTH SOW-THISTLE
MILK-THISTLE

Distributed throughout the British Isles except for parts of the Scottish Highlands. It is a common weed of gardens, arable, burnt ground, waste places, roadsides and disturbed ground on fertile, mildly acid to calcareous soils. An annual, or overwintering annual, it flowers from June to August and is pollinated chiefly by bees and hoverflies.

Cicerbita alpina (l.) Wallr.**

ALPINE SOW-THISTLE
BLUE SOW-THISTLE

Very rare. It is now known from only about 10 localities in the Scottish Highlands in Angus and Aberdeenshire. It grows on moist inaccessible rock ledges, usually on acid soil derived from granite, and typically among luxuriant herbaceous vegetation out of reach of grazing animals. A tall, handsome plant growing to about 2 m, it flowers from July to September.

✽ *Crepis* **(HAWK'S-BEARD) has leafy stems, the involucre consists of two rows of bracts (the outer much shorter than the inner), and it has a pappus.**

Crepis mollis (Jacq.) Asch.

NORTHERN HAWK'S-BEARD
SOFT HAWK'S-BEARD

A rare and decreasing plant of northern England and Scotland, now more or less confined to parts of Yorkshire, Cumbria, Northumberland, Perth and Aberdeenshire. It is a plant of hilly stream sides, fens and woodlands on calcareous or base-rich soils to an altitude of 370 m. A perennial, it flowers during July and August and is pollinated chiefly by bees.

✽ *C. mollis* **and** *C. paludosa* **both have entire or toothed, but not lobed, leaves. The leaves of** *C. paludosa* **are strongly toothed and the pappus a yellowish-white; the leaves of** *C. mollis* **are untoothed or remotely toothed and the pappus is pure white.**

The other species of *Crepis* **all have deeply lobed leaves.**

Crepis paludosa (L.) Moench

MARSH HAWK'S-BEARD

Widespread throughout northern Britain and north Wales, and northern and north-west Ireland. It is a plant of wet meadows and pastures, stream sides, fens, marshes and wet woodland to an altitude of 915 m. A perennial, it flowers from July to September and is pollinated chiefly by flies and bees.

Crepis setosa Haller f.

BRISTLY HAWK'S-BEARD

Alien but a native of southern and south-central Europe. It is a rare casual of disturbed ground, roadsides and refuse tips. It was formerly more frequent as a weed of clover crops and was probably introduced as an impurity with the seed. An annual or biennial, it flowers from July to September.

✽ *C. setosa* **is distinguished by the spiny bristles on the upper parts of the stem and the involucre.**

Crepis biennis L.

ROUGH HAWK'S-BEARD

A rather local plant, scattered throughout England and most frequent in the south-east, but rare in the south-west, Wales and Ireland more or less absent from Scotland. It occurs in waste places, roadsides, wood margins and arable fields, especially on calcareous soils. It was formerly more frequent as a weed of clover and lucerne. A biennial, it flowers during June and July and is pollinated chiefly by bees and hoverflies.

✽ *C. biennis* **is recognised by its large heads (2.5-3.5 cm diameter), unbeaked fruits (see under** *Lactuca*, **Plate 87) and non-clasping stem leaves.**

Crepis capillaris (L.) Wallr.

SMOOTH HAWK'S-BEARD

Distributed throughout the whole of the British Isles. It is a common plant of grassland, roadsides, heaths, commons, waste places and old walls, usually on dry soils to an altitude of about 445 m. An annual, or more rarely a biennial, it is in flower from June to September and is pollinated chiefly by flies and bees.

✽ *C. capillaris* **has small heads (1-1.5 cm diameter), clasping stem leaves and unbeaked fruits.**

Crepis vesicaria L.

BEAKED HAWK'S-BEARD

Alien but native throughout most of central, southern and western Europe. It was first recorded in Britain in 1713. It spread rapidly during 19th century and is now widespread south and east of a line from the Humber to the Severn, and scattered throughout Wales and central Ireland. It is a frequent plant of roadsides, railway banks, waste ground and walls and, less often, of cultivated fields, especially on dry calcareous soils. A biennial, it flowers from May to July. The British plant belongs to the subspecies *taraxacifolia* (Thuill.) Thell. (subsp. *haenseleri* (Boiss. ex DC.) Sell).

✽ *C. vesicaria* **has heads 1.5-2.5 cm in diameter that are erect in bud, finely hairy basal leaves, clasping stem-leaves and beaked fruits.**

Crepis foetida L.**

STINKING HAWK'S-BEARD

Very rare and now probably confined to the Dungeness area of Kent, where it grows on shingle. It was formerly more widespread in southern England on waste ground on both chalk and shingle. An annual or biennial, it flowers from June to August.

✽ *C. foetida* **has beaked fruits, but differs from** *C. vesicaria* **in its strong unpleasant smell, densely hairy basal leaves and heads that are nodding in bud.**

Taraxacum Weber

DANDELION

The dandelions are an extremely complicated group of plants. All the British species are regularly apomictic; that is, they set viable seed without fertilisation, the pollen being defective. About 220 'micro-species' have been described from Britain, falling into nine more or less clearly defined groups.

Representative plants of four of the groups are illustrated. Full descriptions and details of the distribution and ecology of most of the British species, together with keys to their identification, can be found in Richards, A.J. and Dudman, A.A. (1997) *Dandelioins of Britain and Ireland* (B.S.B.I.)

Taraxacum (section *Ruderalia)* (section *Vulgaria*; *Taraxacum officinale* Wigg. *sensu lato)*

DANDELION

Common throughout the British Isles in meadows, pastures, lawns, roadsides and waste ground to an altitude of 1,175 m. They are perennial and flower from March to October.

✽ **Most British dandelions belong to this group. They are usually robust plants with the outer bracts recurved or spreading and with no small scale-like appendage on the outer side of the tip.**

Taraxacum (section *Palustria)* (Dahlst.) Dahlst.

NARROW-LEAVED MARSH DANDELION

Distributed throughout the British Isles, but local and declining everywhere. Dandelions of the *Palustria* group are plants of fens, wet grazing marsh, winter flooded meadows and stream sides to an altitude of 915 m. Widespread agricultural drainage is the chief reason for its decline. It is a perennial, and flowers from April to June.

✽ **Dandelions of this group have linear, often unlobed, leaves and the broad involucral bracts have a wide, pale border and are appressed, not recurved or spreading.**

Taraxacum (section *Spectabilia)* (Dahlst.) Dahlst.
Most frequent in hilly districts of northern Britain in wet grassland, along roadsides, stream banks and wet rock ledges on calcareous or base-rich soils. Some forms are also common in southern Britain. They are perennials and flower from April to June.
❁ **Dandelions belonging to this section are usually robust plants with lobed, often spotted leaves with reddish midribs and spreading or appressed involucral bracts.**

Taraxacum (section *Obliqua)* Dahlst.
These are very local plants of sand dunes, dune slacks and machair in western Scotland.
❁ **Plants belonging to this section differ in the deeper coloured heads, often with the florets turned inwards. (Not illustrated.)**

Taraxacum (section *Erythrosperma)* (Lindb. f.) Dahlst.

LESSER DANDELION

Found throughout the British Isles, but apparently rare in central and western Scotland. Dandelions of the *Erythrosperma* group are characteristic of dry, well-drained grassland, downs, dunes, heaths, cliffs, walls and rocky habitats. They are perennials and flower from April to June.
❁ **Dandelions belonging to this section are usually small plants with deeply divided leaves; the outer involucral bracts have a small lobe on the outerside of the tip.**

❁ ***Pilosella*** **is readily recognised by its rosettes of oval-shaped leaves covered by a dense felt of white hairs beneath, long stolons and leafless stems. It is sometimes treated as a section of** ***Hieracium.***

Pilosella officinarum F. Schultz & Schultz-Bip.
(*Hieracium pilosella* L.)

MOUSE-EAR HAWKWEED

Distributed throughout the British Isles, but scarce in the East Anglian fens and parts of northern Scotland and absent from Shetland. It is a common plant of the short turf of pastures, grass heaths, commons, hillsides, stabilised dunes, banks and walls on dry well-drained, acid or calcareous soils. A perennial, stoloniferous herb, it flowers from May to August.

Hieracium L.

HAWKWEED

About 245 different species of *Hieracium* have been named from the British Isles. They are an extremely complicated and difficult group to identify, and almost all the British species are apomictic; that is they set viable seed without fertilisation. The pollen is nearly always sterile. Representatives from each of the sections into which the native British species are usually divided are illustrated. All the British species appear in the account by P.D. Sell and C. West in volume 4 of *Flora Europaea.* The *Critical Supplement to the Atlas of the British Flora* contains a complete set of distribution maps and a text also by Sell and West. Descriptions of the more common species can be found in *Excursion Flora of the British Isles.* The following notes are based on the work of these authorities.

Hieracium (section *Alpina)* (18 species)

Hieracium holosericeum Backhouse
A frequent plant throughout the Scottish Highlands, and also occuring more locally in the southern uplands, the English Lake District and in north Wales. It grows on high mountain ledges, grassy slopes and scree on acid or base-rich rock at altitudes above 650 m and flowers during July and August.
❁ **Hawkweeds of section** ***Alpina*** **are small plants with a basal rosette of leaves with a few glandular hairs along the margins, no or few stem leaves, and usually solitary heads with densely hairy and shaggy involucres.**

Hieracium (section *Subalpina)* (30 species)

Hieracium lingulatum Backhouse
Confined to the Highlands of Scotland where it is widespread, growing by rocky stream sides and on rock ledges above 450 m. It flowers from June to August.
❁ **Hawkweeds of section** ***Subalpina*** **are similar to those of section** ***Alpina,*** **except that they have fewer rosette leaves and are generally taller plants with 2-5 flower heads.**

Hieracium (section *Cerinthoidea)* (10 species)

Hieracium anglicum Fries
Widely distributed throughout the upland areas of England, Scotland and Ireland but very rare in Wales. It is a characteristic plant of rocky stream sides and cliff ledges, usually on calcareous or base-rich rocks. It flowers from May to October.
❁ **Hawkweeds belonging to the section** ***Cerinthoidea*** **are generally robust plants growing to about 35 cm with a basal rosette of leaves and up to seven bluish-green, clasping stem leaves.**

Hieracium (section *Oreadea)* (44 species)

Hieracium britannicum F.J. Hanbury
Confined to the Carboniferous limestone of the Derbyshire and Staffordshire Dales where, however, it is abundant. It flowers during May and June.

Hieracium decolor W.R. Linton
(*H. subcyaneum* W.R. Linton)
A common plant of the Carboniferous limestone of the Derbyshire Dales and north-west England. It flowers from May to September.

Hieracium caledonicum F.J. Hanbury
Widespread on the limestone of the Pennines of central and northern England and in north Wales, Scotland and northern Ireland.
❁ **Hawkweeds belonging to the section** ***Oreadea*** **have a basal rosette of bluish-green, often purplish or spotted, bristly leaves and no or few non-clasping stem leaves. The involucral bracts are erect in bud and covered by stiff glandular hairs.**

Hieracium (section *Vulgata)* (82 species)

Hieracium orcadense W.R. Linton
Scattered throughout western and northern Britain from Brecon to Orkney and rare and nearly always coastal in Ireland. It is a plant of rocky and grassy habitats, usually on basic soils, and grows from sea level to over 900 m.

Hieracium vulgatum Fries
Distributed throughout northern England, north Wales, Scotland and north-west Ireland, with a few localities further south in England, but absent from Orkney and Shetland. It is a characteristic plant of rocky grassland at all altitudes and is the commonest hawkweed in northern Britain. It flowers from June to August.

Hieracium acuminatum Jordan
Widely distributed throughout England and Wales, with isolated localities in Scotland and Ireland. In upland areas it occurs in rocky habitats, but in the English lowlands, where it is one of the commonest hawkweeds, it grows on roadsides, railway banks, walls and in rough grassland. It flowers during June and July.

❁ **Hawkweeds of the section** ***Vulgata*** **have a basal rosette of leaves but differ from those of section** ***Oreadea*** **in the hairy, but not bristly, leaves, the involucre being covered by a down of stellate hairs and by the bracts incurved in bud. The plants are very varied in size.**

Hieracium (section *Alpestria)* (18 species)

Hieracium dewarii Syme
A widespread but local species of central and western Scotland, but absent from the extreme north. It is found on stream banks and less often on rocky ledges, and flowers during July and August.
❁ **Hawkweeds of the section** ***Alpestria*** **have few stem leaves, the middle ones more or less clasping; the basal leaves usually wither before flowering, and the involucral bracts have a few glandular and white hairs. The plants grow to about 1 m.**

Hieracium (section *Prenanthoidea)*
(2 species)
Hieracium prenanthoides Vill.
A locally common plant of northern England, south Wales and parts of central Scotland, with a single locality in north-east Ireland. It grows on grassy banks, stream sides and rocky ground, and flowers during July and August.
❁ **Hawkweeds of the section *Prenanthoidea* have no rosette leaves and the stem leaves are strongly reticulate and rather constricted just above the broad clasping base. The involucre is glandular and covered by a down of soft, stellate hairs.**

Hieracium (section *Tridentata)*
(21 species)

Hieracium trichocaulon (Dahlst.) Johans.
A widespread and common plant in south and south-east England, with isolated localities in Lincolnshire and in north and south Wales. It is found on sandy heaths, in woodland rides and clearings and on roadsides on sandy soils. It flowers during July and August.
❁ **Hawkweeds of the section *Tridentata* have no true rosette leaves, the lower part of the stem is often reddish and the stem leaves are rather narrow, tapering to a non-clasping base. The plants grow to about 1 m.**

Hieracium (section *Foliosa)*
(10 species)

Hieracium latobrigorum (Zahn) Roffey
A rather common species in Scotland and occurring less frequently in Orkney, northern England and eastern Ireland with isolated localities in north Wales. *H. latobrigorum* is found in rocky and grassy places in hilly country but does not reach high altitudes. It flowers during July and August.
❁ **Hawkweeds of the section *Foliosa* have no rosette leaves but rather numerous broad-based, somewhat clasping stem leaves. The stems are often reddish and grow to over 1 m.**

Hieracium (section *Sabauda)*
(5 species)

Hieracium sabaudum L.
Distributed throughout England, Wales and Scotland but absent from the islands and in Ireland confined to the south-east. It is a frequent species of heaths and open woods on sandy soils. It flowers from July to September.
❁ **Hawkweeds of the section *Sabauda* are robust plants growing to over 1 m. They have no rosette leaves but numerous stem leaves (up to 50), the lower of which are shortly-stalked and the upper sessile.**

Hieracium (section *Umbellata)*
(1 species)

Hieracium umbellatum L.
Distributed throughout lowland England and Wales, but local and scattered in northern England and Scotland and absent from Orkney and Shetland and mostly coastal in Ireland. It is found on heaths, dunes, rough grassland, rocky ground and in open woodland on sandy soils. It flowers during July and August.
❁ ***Hieracium umbellatum* grows to about 75 cm, and is easily distinguished by the lack of rosette leaves and numerous dark green, narrow, rough-edged stem leaves.**

ALISMATACEAE

Baldellia ranunculoides (L.) Parl.
LESSER WATER-PLANTAIN
A local and declining species scattered throughout the lowlands of the British Isles. It grows in wet ground or shallow water beside slow-moving streams, dykes, drainage ditches, pools and ponds on fertile, usually base- or calcium-rich mineral soils. A perennial, it flowers from May to August.

❁ ***Baldellia* differs from *Alisma* in the inflorescence consisting of two whorls of branches or of a single umbel-like whorl. The plant grows to between 5 and 20 cm and the flowers are up to 15 mm in diameter.**

Alisma lanceolatum With.
NARROW-LEAVED WATER-PLANTAIN
A very local species scattered throughout lowland England and Wales from Lancashire southwards; it is rare in Ireland and has one isolated locality in Scotland. It grows in similar habitats to *A. plantago-aquatica,* and in the south-east the two may occur together. A perennial, it flowers from June to August.

❁ ***A. lanceolatum* has darker flowers than *A. plantago-aquatica,* the base of the leaf tapers into the stalk, the style arises above the middle of the fruit, and the flowers are open in the morning. *A. plantago-aquatica* has a rounded base to the leaf-blade, the styles arise below the middle of the fruit, and the flowers are open in the afternoon and evening.**

Alisma plantago-aquatica L.
WATER-PLANTAIN
Distributed throughout the British Isles but rare in northern Scotland and absent from Orkney, Shetland and the Hebrides. It is a frequent plant of the marginal vegetation of ponds, lakes, canals and slow-flowing rivers, ditches and drainage dykes, growing in wet fertile muds or in up to 0.75 m of water. A perennial, it flowers from June to August.

Alisma gramineum Lejeune**
RIBBON-LEAVED WATER-PLANTAIN
Very rare and now confined to a single site near Droitwich in Worcestershire, from where it was first recorded in 1920. Until recently it was also known in Norfolk, Cambridgeshire and Lincolnshire. It grows in the shallow water of ponds, dykes and streams, usually on fertile muddy soils. It has recently been suggested that it is introduced into Britain from Europe by migrating wildfowl, which would explain the temporary nature of the records. A perennial, it flowers from June to August.
❁ ***A. gramineum* differs from *Baldellia* in the more branched inflorescence and smaller flowers (about 6 mm diameter), which open in the evening.**

Luronium natans (L.) Rafin.**
FLOATING WATER-PLANTAIN
A local and declining species more or less confined to north Wales, Shropshire, Cheshire, and Lancashire. It is found in ponds, lakes and tarns and slow-moving canals in acid water of varying fertility. A submerged and free-floating perennial, it flowers during July and August. It has been introduced into Norfolk.
❁ ***Luronium* is distinguished by the broad, blunt floating leaves and stems and large (12-15 diameter), usually single flowers.**

Damasonium alisma Miller**
STARFRUIT THRUMWORT
Very rare and now probably extinct in its last known sites: a single pond in Surrey and two localities in Buckinghamshire. It was once a widespread plant in lowland England, especially in the south-east, growing in the shallow water of acid ponds and ditches, usually on sandy or gravelly soils and often on village commons. The reasons for extinction are a combination of infilling, drainage and pollution. It has recently been reintroduced to a pond in Buckinghamshire. A submerged and floating aquatic annual, it flowers from June to August.
❁ ***Damasonium* gets its English name from the star-shaped arrangement of the fruits. The leaves are floating or submerged and the flowers are small, about 6 mm diameter.**

Sagittaria sagittifolia L.
ARROWHEAD
Widely distributed throughout England, north to the Tyne, but very rare in Wales and the south-west and infrequent and local in Ireland. It is a characteristic plant of the shallow, unpolluted water of ponds, canals, dykes, ditches, streams and slow-flowing rivers, usually on fertile clays and loams. It grows as a submerged, floating or emergent aquatic perennial and flowers during July and August.

BUTOMACEAE

Butomus umbellatus L.
FLOWERING-RUSH
A rather local species distributed throughout England, but very rare in Wales (except for Anglesey) and the south-west. It is rare in Ireland and introduced into southern Scotland. It grows in the shallow water of slow-moving rivers, streams, dykes, canals and pond margins on fertile clay or alluvial soils. A tall, beautiful, emergent aquatic perennial, it flowers from July to September.

HYDROCHARITACEAE

Hydrocharis morsus-ranae L.
FROGBIT
A locally frequent plant of the Norfolk Broads, East Anglian fens, the Somerset Levels and the coastal levels of Kent and Sussex. It is rare and decreasing elsewhere as far north as the Tyne and is rare and scattered in Ireland. It is a plant of pools, ponds and slow-flowing ditches, canals and dykes, growing in fertile, calcium-rich water on clay, peat or alluvial soils. A free-floating stoloniferous aquatic, it perennates by means of overwintering 'turions' which sink to the mud in the autumn. The flowers, which are unisexual, are out in July and August.

Stratiotes aloides L.

WATER-SOLDIER

Very local; probably only truly native in the Norfolk Broads and a few other scattered localities in central England as far north as the Humber, but widely introduced into other parts of England and southern Scotland. It is found in the shallow water of ponds, lakes, broads, dykes and ditches on fertile, calcareous muds and peat, and is very sensitive to pollution. A submerged aquatic, the large rosettes of spiny leaves rise to the surface at the time of flowering, from June to August. It is dioecious, the male plant being very rare, and fruit is never produced in Britain.

Elodea nuttallii (Planchon) St John

NUTTALL'S WATERWEED

Alien; a native of North America. It seems to have appeared in Britain quite recently, and in some parts of southern England is increasing rapidly. At Amberley Wild Brooks in west Sussex it now dominates several of the alluvial drainage dykes, suppressing other submerged species, including *E. canadensis*. The plant is dioecious, but the male flowers are very rare in Britain.

❁ ***E. nuttallii*** **can be distinguished from** ***E. canadensis*** **by the longer (about 1.5 cm), narrower, more recurved, sharp-pointed leaves. The leaves of** ***E. canadensis*** **are about 1 cm long and rounded at the tip.**

Elodea canadensis Mich.

CANADIAN PONDWEED

Alien and a native of North America. It was first recorded from County Down in 1836, was reported from Scotland in 1842 and its first English locality was Foxton Reservoir in Leicestershire in 1847. It is now widespread throughout the British Isles as far north as the Moray Firth, but is rare throughout most of central Scotland. It can be found in most kinds of ponds, canals, dykes, rivers and streams on fine, alluvial or peat soils where the water is of at least moderate fertility. On first colonising a new site it frequently increases very fast by vegetative spread before declining to a more normal level of abundance. The plant is dioecious, the flowers being carried to the surface by the slender, elongated perianth tube. Male plants are very rare in Britain and flowering is from May to October.

Hydrilla verticillata (L.f.) Royle*

ESTHWAITE WATERWEED

Very rare. First recorded by W.H. Pearsall from Esthwaite Water in the Lake District in 1914, but as it has not been seen since 1934 it may now be extinct in England. In 1934 Pearsall recorded the same species from Rusheenduff Lough in Co. Galway, a small lake separated from the sea by a shingle bar, where it still occurs. *Hydrilla* is a dioecious submerged perennial that overwinters by means of dormant buds that are detached in the early autumn. Flowering has never been recorded in the wild in the British Isles, but plants taken into cultivation at the National Botanical Gardens in Dublin in 1974 produced female flowers. (Illustrated on Plate 102).

❁ ***Hydrilla*** **can only be distinguished from** ***Elodea*** **with certainty by the male flowers. However, it differs from** ***E. nuttallii*** **in its more slender habit, paler green colour, leaves faintly toothed at the tips and in whorls of 4-5 in the middle of the stem, and the stipules being fringed with orange-brown hairs.**

Vallisneria spiralis L.

TAPE-GRASS

Alien but widely distributed throughout the warmer latitudes, and reaching as far north in Europe as central France. It is commonly grown in tropical aquaria and is established in several places in western and northern England, where the water is warmed by industrial effluents. Like other members of the family it is dioecious, the male flowers being produced at the base of the plant and breaking off to float to the surface where wind and currents bring them into contact with the stalked female flowers. It flowers from June to October.

SCHEUCHZERIACEAE

Scheuchzeria palustris L.*

RANNOCH-RUSH

Very rare and now confined to Rannoch Moor in Perthshire. It formerly occurred in one or two other places in Scotland and in isolated sites in Shropshire, Cheshire and Yorkshire. It has also disappeared from its single Irish locality. It grows in acid pools in wet *Sphagnum* bogs, often with the bog-sedge, *Carex limosa*. Its decline is due to a combination of drainage, peat-cutting and afforestation. A perennial, it flowers from June to August.

❁ ***Scheuchzeria*** **grows to between 10 cm and 20 cm and has six persistent yellow-green perianth segments and hermaphrodite flowers.**

JUNCAGINACEAE

Triglochin palustre L.

MARSH ARROWGRASS

A rather local species that is widely distributed throughout the whole of the British Isles, but markedly more frequent in northern England, Scotland and western Ireland. It is a plant of marshes, fens and grassy stream sides on wet, mildly acid to calcareous, rather infertile soils. It is often found in places that are rough-grazed. A perennial, it flowers from June to August and is wind-pollinated.

❁ ***T. palustris*** **differs from** ***T. maritimum*** **in its more slender habit, the fruits remaining appressed to the stem, and the leaves up to 2 mm wide (up to 4 mm in** ***T. maritimum.***

Triglochin maritimum L.

SEA ARROWGRASS

Common in suitable habitats all round the coasts of the British Isles. It is a characteristic plant of the middle levels of coastal and estuarine salt marshes. It also grows in brackish meadows, along the margins of brackish drainage dykes and in grassy spots on rocky shores. A perennial growing to about 50 cm, it flowers from July to September and is wind-pollinated.

ZOSTERACEAE

Zostera L.

EELGRASS

The eelgrasses belong to a family of submerged marine perennials, one of the very few groups of truly marine flowering plants known. They are monoecious, with the separate male and female flowers borne alternately on the same inflorescence surrounded by a protective sheath. The pollen grains are thread-like and liberated into the sea in masses. On contact they curl around the stigmas of the female flowers. In Britain eelgrass provides important grazing for wintering flocks of Brent geese.

Zostera marina L.

EELGRASS
GRASS-WRACK

A local species scattered all around the British coasts as far north as Orkney and Shetland. Until 1933 it was most frequent in the south from Norfolk to the coasts of Devon and Cornwall. Its subsequent decline appears to have been due to disease, but there is some evidence that it is now reappearing in a few of its former localities. It grows on fine gravel, sand or mud from low water spring tides down to about 4 m. Occasionally it occurs in estuaries. A perennial, it flowers from June to September.

❁ ***Z. marina*** **differs from both** ***Z. noltii*** **and** ***Z. angustifolia*** **in its large size, with leaves between 5 mm and 10 mm wide.**

Zostera angustifolia (Hornem.) Reichb.

NARROW-LEAVED EELGRASS

A local species, scattered around the British coast as far north as the Tay on the east and Anglesey on the west, and very rare in Ireland. It grows on the bare mud of coastal flats and estuaries from mid-tide to low-water spings and occasionally down to 4 m, and will tolerate salinities ranging from 25 to 42 parts per thousand (S $^{0}/_{00}$). A perennial, it flowers from June to November.

❁ **The flower stems of** ***Z. angustifolia*** **are branched and the leaves 1-2 mm wide and 15-30 cm long; the flower stems of** ***Z. noltii*** **are unbranched and the leaves up to 12 cm long and 1.5 mm wide.**

Zostera noltii Hornem.

DWARF EELGRASS

A local species scattered around the coasts of Britain as far north as the Moray Firth; in Ireland it is confined to the east coast. It grows in similar kinds of places to *Z. angustifolia*, on the mud banks of estuaries from mid-tide to low-tide level. A perennial, it flowers from June to October.

POTAMOGETONACEAE

Potamogeton L.

PONDWEED

The pondweeds are a group of perennial submerged aquatics, some of which have floating leaves. They perennate by means of their rhizomes or by special overwintering buds, 'turions', that develop either on the rhizomes or the leafy shoots. The pondweeds prefer clear, unpolluted water and nearly all are sensitive to any kind of nutrient enrichment, toxicity or turbidity. Many species are declining due to land drainage and pollution.

The 21 British species are not easy to identify. Several show considerable morphological variation depending upon conditions, and hybrids are frequent. Comprehensive keys and descriptions can be found in *Flora of the British Isles*, in Haslam, Sinker and Wolseley (1975) 'British Water Plants' *Field Studies* 4, 243-351 and in 'Pondweeds of Great Britain and Ireland', by C.D. Preston (BSBI Handbook No. 8) 1995. Particular attention should be paid to the venation of the leaves and the structure of the leaf stipules.

Potamogeton natans L.

BROAD-LEAVED PONDWEED

Generally distributed throughout the British Isles. It is a common plant of ponds, lakes and slow-moving streams and drainage dykes in depths of about 1 m. It grows in clear, mildly acid to calcareous water of moderate fertility, often on organic soils. It flowers from May to September.

❁ ***P. natans*** **differs from other species with floating leaves in having linear submerged leaves. The stalks of the floating leaves have a flexible 'bend' towards the top.**

❁ ***P. polygonifolius, P. coloratus*** **and** ***P. nodosus*** **all have stalked submerged leaves, if present.**

Potamogeton coloratus Hornem.

FEN PONDWEED

A local species scattered throughout Britain as far north as the Firth of Forth, but only at all frequent in the fenlands of East Anglia. It is a characteristic plant of pools, ponds, dykes and streams in fen peat, growing in clear, shallow, calcium-rich water of moderate fertility. It flowers during June and July.

❁ ***P. coloratus*** **is distinguished from** ***P. polygonifolius*** **and** ***P. nodosus*** **by**

continued on next page

both the floating and submerged leaves being thin and translucent, the floating leaves of the other two species being thick and opaque.

Potamogeton nodosus Poiret*
LODDON PONDWEED
A rare plant now known from only three rivers in lowland England: the Bristol Avon, the Dorset Stour and the Berkshire Loddon. Formerly it also occurred in the Thames, where it was last collected in 1941 and is now probably extinct. It grows in gravelly shallows or on a silty bottom at greater depths in slow-flowing, calcareous water. It flowers during August and September.

✽ *P. nodosus* **is distinguished from** *P. polygonifolius* **by the conspicuously net-veined submerged leaves.**

Potamogeton polygonifolius Pourret
BOG PONDWEED
Widespread throughout upland and western Britain, but less common in the lowlands except for the heaths of south-east and southern England. It is a common plant of small ponds, bog pools, drainage dykes, spring heads and streams, growing in shallow, acid, infertile, often peaty water to an altitude of 700 m. It flowers from May to October.

PLATE 92
POTAMOGETONACEAE
(see illustrations page 194)

Potamogeton epihydrus Rafin.*
AMERICAN PONDWEED
LEAFY PONDWEED
Very rare. It is confined as a native plant to the shallow water of three small calcareous lochs set among maritime sand deposits on the island of South Uist in the Outer Hebrides. It has also long been known as an introduction in Lancashire and Yorkshire, where it still occurs in five localities in the River Calder and in canals around Halifax. It flowers from June to August.
✽ *P. epihydrus* **has both floating and submerged leaves and is distinguished by its flattened stem and narrow (less than 8 mm wide) strap-shaped submerged leaves.**

Potamogeton gramineus L.
VARIOUS-LEAVED PONDWEED
A rather local species that is widespread throughout northern and eastern England, Scotland and Ireland, reaching an altitude of 700 m, but very rare elsewhere. It occurs in depths of up to 3 m in slow-flowing streams and canals and in lakes and pools, usually in mildly acid, rather infertile water. It is rather more tolerant of low levels of pollution than most of the species. It flowers from June to September.
✽ *P. gramineus* **has both floating and submerged leaves and the tips of the submerged leaves are pointed, not blunt, with minutely toothed margins. Floating leaves may be absent.**

Potamogeton lucens L.
SHINING PONDWEED
Local but widespread in lowland England reaching an altitude of 380 m in Yorkshire, but absent from the south-west and very rare in Scotland, Wales and Ireland. It occurs in lakes and ponds and in slow-flowing canals, streams and rivers with a muddy bottom, often over limestone. It prefers clear, fertile, calcium-rich water and will grow in depths of up to 4 m. It flowers from June to September.
✽ *P. lucens* **is distinguished by its large leaves with tapering non-clasping bases and pointed tips.**

Potamogeton alpinus Balbis
RED PONDWEED
A rather local species scattered throughout the British Isles but rare in Wales, the south-west and much of central England. It is found in lakes, ponds, dykes, canals and streams to altitudes of over 1,000 m. It prefers clear, mildly acid water of moderate fertility and is often found in streams subject to spate. It flowers from June to September.
✽ *P. alpinus* **has blunt-tipped, usually reddish-tinged submerged leaves which distinguishes it from** *P. lucens* **when floating leaves are absent.**

Potamogeton perfoliatus L.
PERFOLIATE PONDWEED
Widely distributed throughout the British Isles but scarce in parts of northern Scotland, Wales, south-west England and Ireland. It grows in clear, moderately fertile, mildly acid to neutral water in depths of up to about 1 m and is found in lakes, ponds, canals and slow-flowing streams and drainage dykes. A predominantly lowland species, it reaches an altitude of about 700 m in Scotland.
✽ *P. perfoliatus* **is easily recognised by the broad, clasping leaves.**

Potamogeton praelongus Wulfen
LONG-STALKED PONDWEED
A rather local species scattered throughout the British Isles from the Thames valley north to Shetland. It is most frequent in suitable habitats in the Norfolk Broads, the East Anglian fens and in parts of central and eastern Scotland, where it reaches 900 m, and is rare in Wales and Ireland. It grows in the fertile, calcium-rich water of lakes and slow-flowing rivers, dykes, canals and streams in depths of between 1 m and 6 m. It flowers from May to August.
✽ **The leaves of** *P. praelongus* **have a distinctly hooded tip and the bases are more or less clasping.**

Potamogeton friesii Rupr.
FLAT-STALKED PONDWEED
A rather local species scattered throughout lowland England, but rare in Scotland and Ireland and more or less absent from northern England, Wales and the south-west. It grows in fertile, usually calcium-rich waters of lakes, ponds, drainage dykes and canals with a muddy or peaty bottom in depths of up to 2 m. It flowers from June to August.
✽ *P. friesii* **is distinguished by the free stipules, flattened stems and leaves 2-3 mm wide with five veins, the laterals closer to the margin than to the midrib.**

Potamogeton rutilus Wolfg.*
SHETLAND PONDWEED
Very rare. It is confined to a small number of scattered localities on Shetland, the Inner and Outer Hebrides, Ross and Inverness-shire. It is a plant of mildly acid, exposed lochs and flowers during August.
✽ *P. rutilus* **has very narrow (0.5-1 mm wide), finely pointed leaves with strongly veined persistent stipules that are tubular at the base.**

Potamogeton pusillus L.
LESSER PONDWEED
A rather local species, but widely distributed throughout the British Isles as far north as Shetland. It is scarce in much of northern Scotland, Wales, Ireland and the south-west. Found in lakes, pools, canals, ditches, dykes and streams, usually with a muddy bottom, it grows in depths of up to 2 m, usually in fertile, calcium-rich water, and is tolerant of mildly brackish conditions. It flowers from June to September.
✽ *P. pusillus* **has abruptly pointed leaves less than 2 mm wide, with faintly veined stipules that are tubular for about two-thirds of their length.**

Potamogeton obtusifolius Mert & Koch
BLUNT-LEAVED PONDWEED
GRASSY PONDWEED
Scattered throughout the British Isles as far north as the Moray Firth but very rare in west-central Scotland, Wales and the south-west, and scarce in Ireland. It is a lowland species found in lakes, ponds, canals, dykes and streams with a muddy or peaty bottom. It grows in depths of up to 3 m in moderately fertile, mildly acid to neutral water and flowers from June to September.
✽ **The leaves of** *P. obtusifolius* **are 2-4 mm wide, blunt-tipped, with indistinct lateral veins and overlapping, not tubular, stipules.**

Potamogeton berchtoldii Fieb.
SMALL PONDWEED
Distributed throughout the British Isles, but scarce in parts of the Scottish Highlands and Ireland. It is one of the most widespread and frequent of the 'grass-leaved' pondweeds. It is found in lakes, ponds, canals, drainage dykes and streams with a sandy, silty, muddy or peaty bottom. It grows in depths of up to 1 m in both acid and calcareous water of varying fertility and flowers from June to September.
✽ *P. berchtoldii* **has leaves about 2 mm wide, tapered towards the base, with three veins and stipules that are overlapping, not tubular, at the base.**

Potamogeton trichoides Cham. & Schlecht.
HAIR-LIKE PONDWEED
A very local species more or less confined to the English lowlands, perhaps increasing in some areas. It grows in lakes, ponds, canals and drainage dykes with a silty, muddy or peaty bottom. It prefers shallow, mildly acid to neutral water of moderate fertility and flowers from June to September.
✽ *P. trichoides* **has very narrow (0.5-1 mm wide) finely pointed leaves with a prominent midrib and open stipules.**

Potamogeton compressus L.
GRASS-WRACK PONDWEED
A local species of central and eastern England with a few isolated localities in Wales and Scotland. It is found in lakes, ponds, canals, dykes and slow-flowing streams with a muddy or peaty bottom. It prefers shallow, fertile, calcium-rich water and flowers from June to September.
✽ *P. compressus* **is distinguished by its very flattened stems, leaves about 3 mm wide, with five prominent veins with numerous fine intermediate strands, and blunt tips.**

Potamogeton acutifolius Link
SHARP-LEAVED PONDWEED
A very rare and declining species now more or less confined to the Norfolk Broads and the Sussex coastal levels. It is found in slow-flowing streams, ditches and drainage dykes with a muddy or peaty bottom. It grows in depths of up to 1 m, usually in clear, fertile, mildly acid to calcareous water. It flowers during June and July.
✽ *P. acutifolius* **has flattened stems and finely pointed leaves, 2-3 mm wide with three prominent veins and fine intermediate strands.**

PLATE 93
POTAMOGETONACEAE • RUPPIACEAE • ZANNICHELLIACEAE • NAJADACEAE • ERIOCAULACEAE • LILIACEAE
(see illustrations page 196)

Potamogeton pectinatus L.
FENNEL PONDWEED
Widespread throughout England, but mostly coastal in Scotland north to Shetland and in Wales and the south-west and scattered throughout Ireland. It is found in ponds, lakes, canals, streams and drainage dykes with a silty or muddy bottom. It usually grows in depths between 0.5 m and 2.5 m in fertile, neutral or calcareous water. In coastal areas it is tolerant of quite high levels of salinity and

continued on next page

is more tolerant than other species of mild pollution and turbidity. It flowers from May to September.

❁ *P. pectinatus* **has a much-branched stem with long, fine leaves composed of two hollow tubes and stipules joined to the leaf base forming an open leaf sheath encircling the stem below the leaf insertion.**

❁ *P. filiformis* **is distinguished from** *P. pectinatus* **by the closed leaf sheath and the shape of the fruit.**

Potamogeton filiformis Pers.

SLENDER-LEAVED PONDWEED

A local species chiefly of coastal areas in Scotland and the Scottish islands; it also occurs scattered throughout northern and western Ireland and in Anglesey. It most commonly grows in the shallow water around the exposed shores of lakes, pools and streams, preferring nutrient-rich water, and where growing close to the shore is tolerant of brackish conditions. It flowers from May to August.

Potamogeton crispus L.

CURLED PONDWEED

Widely distributed throughout the British Isles as far north as Orkney but absent from much of northern Scotland and western Wales. It is a frequent plant of lakes, ponds, streams, canals and drainage dykes with a silty, muddy or peaty botttom. A lowland species reaching about 400 m in Scotland, it grows in depths of up to 1 m in clear, mildly acid to calcareous water and flowers from May to October.

❁ *P. crispus* **is easily recognised by the finely toothed leaves with curled margins.**

Groenlandia densa (L.) Fourr.

OPPOSITE-LEAVED PONDWEED

Widely distributed but declining throughout the English lowlands, and very rare in the south-west and in Scotland, Wales and Ireland. It most often occurs in dykes and streams with a slow to moderate rate of flow. It prefers shallow, clear, fertile, calcium-rich water with a sandy or silty bottom and flowers from May to September.

❁ *Groenlandia* **is easily distinguished from other pondweeds by its broad opposite leaves.**

RUPPIACEAE

❁ *Ruppia* **has mostly opposite leaves (cf.** *Potamogeton***) with sheathing bases.** *R. cirrhosa* **differs from** *R. maritima* **in the more inflated leaf sheaths and the peduncles much longer than the pedicels.**

Ruppia maritima L.

BEAKED TASSELWEED

A local species, scattered all around the coasts of the British Isles as far north as Shetland and most frequent in the south-east and in parts of north Wales. It is found in salt marsh pools and in brackish dykes, ditches and lagoons close to the sea. A submerged perennial, it flowers from July to September. The pollen is released into air bubbles which burst, scattering the pollen over the surface where pollination occurs.

Ruppia cirrhosa (Petagna) Grande

SPIRAL TASSELWEED

A rare and declining species scattered around the east and south coasts as far north as the Humber, with a few scattered localities on the west coast, the Scottish islands and Ireland. It is found in brackish ditches and lagoons near the sea. A submerged perennial, it flowers from July to September.

ZANNICHELLIACEAE

Zannichellia palustris L.

HORNED PONDWEED

Widely distributed throughout the British lowlands but scarce and almost wholly coastal in the south-west, Wales and Scotland, and rare and scattered throughout Ireland. It is found in lakes, ponds, ditches and streams with a silty, muddy or peaty bottom. It grows in depths of up to 2 m in fertile, mildly acid to calcareous water; near the coast it is found in brackish dykes and lagoons. A submerged perennial, it flowers from May to August. The flowers are unisexual, male and female occurring on the same plant, and pollination takes place under water.

❁ *Zannichellia* **is a much-branched pondweed with opposite leaves (cf.** *Potamogeton***), which is distinguished from** *Ruppia* **by the axillary flowers.**

NAJADACEAE

Najas marina L.*

HOLLY-LEAVED NAIAD

Very rare and confined to a few of the Norfolk Broads, where it has declined dramatically in recent years due to turbulence and pollution. It grows in slightly brackish water with a muddy or peaty bottom. A submerged aquatic, it flowers during July and August. The flowers are unisexual, male and female flowers usually being borne on the same plant.

❁ **The opposite spiny-toothed leaves of** *N. marina* **will distinguish it from all other aquatic plants.**

Najas flexilis (Willd.) Rostk.& Schmidt*

SLENDER NAIAD

Very rare and confined to a few lakes in north Lancashire, Kirkcudbrightshire, Perthshire, Kintyre and the Inner and Outer Hebrides. It also occurs in a number of localities scattered along the west coast of Ireland. A submerged annual, it flowers during August and September.

❁ *N. flexilis* **can be distinguished from similar-looking aquatics by the minutely toothed leaves arranged in whorls of two or three.**

ERIOCAULACEAE

Eriocaulon aquaticum (Hill) Druce*

PIPEWORT

Widespread and locally abundant in western Ireland from Kerry to West Donegal. In Scotland it is known from about 19 localities in Inverness-shire and the Inner Hebrides from Coll to Skye, in some of which it is locally abundant. It forms mats on bare, wet peaty ground, or in the shallow water around the margins of acid peaty lochs. A creeping perennial, it flowers from July to September. The flowers are unisexual, male and female being mixed in the same heads.

LILIACEAE

Tofieldia pusilla (Mich.) Pers.

SCOTTISH ASPHODEL

Widespread on the Scottish mainland north of a line from the Clyde to Aberdeen, with a few isolated localities in the Inner Hebrides. In England it is confined to Upper Teesdale. It is a local plant of wet hillside flushes and the sides of mountain streams and springs between 215 m and 915 m. A perennial, it flowers from June to August and is pollinated by small insects or is self-pollinated.

Narthecium ossifragum (L.) Hudson

BOG ASPHODEL

Widely distributed throughout northern and western Britain but local in the lowlands, being confined to areas of acid heaths in Dorset, the New Forest, the Weald and north Norfolk. It is often an abundant plant of blanket bogs, raised bogs, valley bogs and acid flushes reaching 1,130 m in Scotland. It grows best in acid peats in areas of ground-water movement. A perennial, it flowers during July and August and is pollinated by a variety of insects or self-pollinated.

Simethis planifolia (L.) Gren.*

KERRY LILY

Very rare and confined to an area of about 14 km by 3 km near Derrynane in Kerry, where it grows among rough gorse in rocky coastal heath. It grows among pines near Bournemouth in Dorset, where it was probably introduced with maritime pines. A perennial, it flowers from May to July.

Maianthemum bifolium (L.) F.W. Schmidt*

MAY LILY

Very rare and confined to a few places in Durham, Yorkshire, Lincolnshire and Norfolk. It forms extensive colonies on the floor of deciduous woodlands on acid soils. It is possible that it is not native in Norfolk, but was introduced with exotic conifers. A creeping perennial, it flowers during May and June and is pollinated by small insects or self-pollinated.

PLATE 94

LILIACEAE *(see illustrations page 198)*

Convallaria majalis L.

LILY-OF-THE-VALLEY

Widespread but local and declining throughout England, rare in Scotland, Wales and the south-west and absent from Ireland. It is typically a plant of dry woodlands, especially ash, on the older limestones and is also a frequent plant of limestone pavements in northern England. It occurs less commonly in old deciduous woodlands on sandstone, particularly in the south. Commonly cultivated since the Middle Ages and a traditional cottage garden plant, it also appears as an escape near houses. All parts of the plant are poisonous, containing two glycosides, convallamarin and convallarin. A perennial, it flowers during May and June and is pollinated by insects or self-pollinated.

Polygonatum verticillatum (L.) All.**

WHORLED SOLOMON'S-SEAL

Very rare. It now seems to be confined to two areas of mountain woodland in Perthshire. It was previously known in Angus and Northumberland, but has long been extinct in both these places. A perennial, it flowers during June and July and is pollinated by bees or self-pollinated.

Polygonatum odoratum (Miller) Druce

ANGULAR SOLOMON'S-SEAL

A very local species with a distribution restricted to three main areas of England: the oolitic limestone of the Gloucestershire Cotswolds, the Carboniferous limestone of the Staffordshire and Derbyshire Dales and the Yorkshire Dales, Lancashire and Cumbria. In addition there are isolated localities on the Carboniferous limestone in the Mendips (Somerset), Breconshire and Pembrokeshire. It is found in open deciduous limestone woodland, especially ash, and in northern England it also grows in the grikes of limestone pavement. A perennial, it flowers during June and July and is pollinated by bumble-bees or self-pollinated.

❁ *P. odoratum* **is distinguished from** *P. multiflorum* **by the angled stem and cylindrical flowers arranged in groups of two. The stem of** *P. multiflorum* **is smooth, and the flowers are contracted in the middle and arranged in groups of up to five.**

Polygonatum multiflorum (L.) All.

SOLOMON'S-SEAL

A local species with a distribution centred on Hampshire, Wiltshire, south Berkshire and Somerset, and scattered elsewhere in England and Wales north to Cumbria. It is characteristically

continued on next page

a plant of dry woodlands, especially on chalk and limestone, although it also occasionally occurs on acid soils. A perennial, it flowers during June and July and is pollinated by bumble-bees or self-pollinated. Its true native distribution is obscured by the frequency of escapes from cultivation, which have been recorded as far as the Moray Firth in Scotland. The usual garden plant is the hybrid *P. multiflorum* x *P. odoratum* = *P.* x *hybridum* Brügg.

Asparagus officinalis L.
ASPARAGUS
Two subspecies occur in Britain.

A. officinalis subsp. *officinalis*
Introduced to the British Isles, but a native of Europe, this is the well-known cultivated vegetable. Its true native distribution is difficult to determine as a result of frequent escapes from cultivation and bird-dispersal of the fruits and seeds. A perennial, it has long been established in the wild and is naturalised in a number of places throughout lowland England and south Wales in waste places and on coastal sand dunes. It flowers from June to September and is pollinated by insects.

A. officinalis subsp. *prostratus* (Dum.) Corbière*
Very rare and declining, and only recorded in recent years from Cornwall, Pembrokeshire, the Channel Islands and Counties Waterford, Wexford and Wicklow in south-east Ireland. It grows on grassy sea cliffs and coastal sands, and in some localities the populations consist of between 20 and 30 plants. A prostrate, creeping perennial, it flowers from June to September.

Ruscus aculeatus L.
BUTCHER'S-BROOM
Almost confined as a native plant to an area of southern England south of a line from Essex to the Lizard, but also occurring in Norfolk, Suffolk and Dyfed (Pembrokeshire and Carmarthenshire). It is most characteristically a plant of old woodlands on well-drained soils. It seems to be indifferent to soil reaction, being found on both chalk and acid sands and gravels. Near the coast it also grows in more exposed and open conditions. In other parts of the country it often occurs as an escape from cultivation. A low shrub, growing to a height of about 80 cm, it has no leaves, the leaf-like structures being flattened shoots or cladodes on which the unisexual flowers are borne. The plant is dioecious and is in flower from January to April.

Lilium martagon L.
MARTAGON LILY
A native of the mountains of central and southern Europe, it was introduced to British gardens towards the end of the 16th century. It occurs in a number of scattered localities throughout Britain as far north as the Firth of Forth, but is undoubtedly an escape from cultivation in most of them. However, it may be native in a few places on the North Downs in Surrey, in the Cotswolds in Gloucestershire and in the Wye Valley. In each of these areas, it is growing in chalk or limestone woodland and is particularly abundant following coppicing. A tall, beautiful perennial, it flowers during August and September and is pollinated by butterflies and moths or self-pollinated.

Lilium pyrenaicum L.
PYRENEAN LILY
Alien and a native of the Pyrenees. It is widely grown in gardens, and has become established as an escape of cultivation in hedge banks in north Devon and elsewhere. A tall perennial, it flowers from May to July.

Fritillaria meleagris L.
FRITILLARY
Rare and very local. In the early years of the century, fritillaries were frequent plants of damp meadows throughout central and eastern England. Today they are restricted to no more than about 24 localities, mostly in the Thames valley above Oxford. The decline is a result of agricultural improvement and drainage of the old meadows and pastures in which they grew. It has long been cultivated and naturalised in old orchards, and no doubt in many of its old localities, especially in the south, it may well be an escape. A bulbous perennial, it flowers during April and May and is pollinated by bumble-bees or self-pollinated. As well as the familiar dull-purple chequered flower, a creamy-white form occasionally appears.

Tulipa sylvestris L.
WILD TULIP
Alien, but native throughout most of Europe where it is particularly characteristic of vineyards and orchards. It was one of the first of the wild species tulips to be cultivated in British gardens, having been introduced towards the end of the 18th century. It was first reported as naturalised in the wild in 1790, and by the beginning of this century was widespread in meadows and orchards throughout most of central and eastern England. In recent years it has declined dramatically as a result of agricultural improvement and is now both rare and local. It flowers during April and May and is pollinated by small insects or self-pollinated.

Scilla autumnalis L.
AUTUMN SQUILL
Very local and almost wholly confined to dry maritime grassland in Devon, Cornwall and the Channel Islands, with isolated localities in the Isle of Wight, the London area and north Somerset. It is most often found in short, dry turf close to the sea on a wide range of soils including sands, serpentine and limestone. In some places the plants can be numbered in thousands. A small bulbous perennial, it flowers from July to September.

❁ *S. autumnalis* **is distinguished from** *S. verna* **by the absence of bracts. The bracts of** *S. verna* **are longer than the pedicels.**

Scilla verna Hudson
SPRING SQUILL
A local species distributed all round the west coast of the British Isles from south Devon to Orkney and Shetland, with scattered localities in the east in Northumberland, Berwickshire and from Aberdeen to Moray. It also occurs along the north east coast of Ireland from Co. Wicklow to Co. Londonderry. It is a plant of short, dry grassland close to the sea on a wide range of soils, including sands, limestone and serpentine. A small bulbous perennial, it flowers during April and May and is pollinated by insects.

Gagea bohemica (Zauschner) J.A. & J.H. Schultes*
EARLY STAR-OF-BETHLEHEM
Very rare and confined to a single site in Wales. It was first found in 1965, but owing to the absence of adequate flowers was incorrectly identified as *Lloydia serotina*. Its true identity was eventually established in 1978. It grows in pockets of shallow soils on south- and east-facing cliffs of dolerite in Radnorshire. The population is large, but only a few plants flower each year. Flowering is early, from mid-January to March. The site is protected as a nature reserve.

❁ *G. bohemica* **differs from** *G. lutea* **by its smaller size and two, not one, filiform basal leaves. The leaves of** *G. lutea* **are broader, 7-12 mm wide.**

Gagea lutea (L.) Ker-Gawl.
YELLOW STAR-OF-BETHLEHEM
Very local but scattered throughout England and southern Scotland north to the Tay. *Gagea lutea* most often occurs in damp woodlands on deep, rich calcareous loams. It is most frequent on the oolitic limestone and is found from the southern edge of the Cotswolds around Bath, through Oxfordshire to north-east Yorkshire, and also in a few localities on the Carboniferous limestone of the north Pennines. More rarely it grows in damp calcareous pastures. A bulbous perennial, it flowers from March to May and is pollinated by insects.

PLATE 95
LILIACEAE (see illustrations page 200)

Hyacinthoides non-scripta (L.) Chouard ex Rothm.
(*Endymion non-scriptus* (L.) Garcke)
BLUEBELL
WILD HYACINTH
Widely distributed and common throughout almost the whole of the British Isles except for the unwooded parts of East Anglia, the Scottish Highlands and Ireland, and absent from Orkney and Shetland. It has a markedly Atlantic distribution in Europe, and bluebell woods are among the most distinctly British of all plant communities. They are most characteristic of acid, sandy loams, although they may also be abundant on both heavier and calcareous soils. Bluebells flower most freely in light shade and following coppicing, and in the west are commonly found in hedge banks and in open moorland and heathland. They flower from April to early June and are pollinated by insects.

Lloydia serotina (L.) Reichb.**
SNOWDON LILY
LLOYDIA
Very rare. It is confined in Britain to about five populations in the Snowdonia range in Caernarvonshire, north Wales, where it grows on narrow, inaccessible ledges of basic rock and in small vertical fissures on steep cliff faces of north- and east-facing corries between 640 m and 730 m. Collecting has caused its disappearance from a number of localities in recent years, and several of the remaining populations consist of only single plants. A small bulbous perennial, it flowers from mid-June to early July and is pollinated by a variety of small wasps and flies or self-pollinated. The plant is named in honour of its discoverer in the 17th century, Edward Lloyd.

Muscari neglectum Guss. ex Ten.*
(*M. racemosum, M. atlanticum*)
GRAPE HYACINTH
Very rare and now confined to Cambridgeshire and the Suffolk Breckland, where about 12 localities still exist. It grows on the grassy verges of roadsides and tracks on low sand banks under Scots pines, and on roadside and field banks in coarse calcareous sand. It is eliminated by competition from more vigorous species and by the lack of rabbit-grazing. A bulbous perennial, it flowers during April and May.

❁ **The inflorescence of the ONIONS and LEEKS,** *Allium,* **is initially enclosed in a thin sheath, the spathe, which splits on flowering to form one or two bracts.**

❁ *A. schoenoprasum, A. sphaerocephalon, A. vineale* **and** *A. oleraceum* **have hollow cylindrical or half-cylindrical leaves.**

Allium schoenoprasum L.
CHIVES
Very local and found only in Cornwall, Brecon, Radnorshire, Pembrokeshire, Cumbria and Northumberland. It grows in rocky, hilly pastures usually on limestone in the north of England and in coastal grassland in Cornwall and west Wales. It is a tufted perennial and flowers during June and July. A variable

species, it is commonly cultivated for flavouring and as a garnish for salads and sauces, and occasionally occurs as a garden escape.

❁ *A. schoenoprasum* **differs from** *A. sphaerocephalon* **in its blue-green cylindrical leaves, spreading perianth and non-protruding stamens.** *A. sphaerocephalon* **has green, half-cylindrical leaves, erect perianth segments and protruding stamens.**

Allium sphaerocephalon L.**

ROUND-HEADED LEEK

Very rare. It occurs in two places only in the British Isles, growing on rocks of the Carboniferous limestone at St Vincent's Rocks in the Avon Gorge near Bristol and at St Aubin's Bay in Jersey. A bulbous perennial, it flowers from June to August and is pollinated by insects or self-pollinated.

Allium vineale L.

WILD ONION
CROW GARLIC

Widespread and frequent in England south and east of a line from the Wash to the Severn, and scattered elsewhere as far north as Aberdeen; rare and scattered in Ireland. It grows on rough grassland, permanent pastures, arable, roadsides, riversides, dry grassy banks and fixed dunes on sandy and clay soils, reaching to 460 m. In parts of the Midlands and East Anglia it can be a troublesome pasture weed. A bulbous perennial, it flowers during June and July and is insect-pollinated.

❁ *A. oleraceum* **differs from** *A. vineale* **in the spathe consisting of two long-pointed bracts that are longer than the flowers and the non-protruding stamens. The spathe of** *A. vineale* **consists of a single bract that is no longer than the flowers, and the stamens protrude.**

Allium oleraceum L.

FIELD GARLIC

Scattered throughout England, but rare in Scotland, Wales and the south-west and declining, especially in the south. It is a plant of dry, rough grassland, usually on limestone, being found in the Mendips on the oolite, the Magnesian limestone in Yorkshire and in the Derbyshire and Yorkshire Dales. A bulbous perennial, it flowers during July and August.

❁ *A. ampeloprasum*, *A. scorodoprasum*, *A. roseum*, **and** *A. carinatum* **have flat leaves.**

Allium ampeloprasum L.
There are two varieties in Britain.

Allium ampeloprasum var. *ampeloprasum**

WILD LEEK

Very rare and now confined to Cornwall, Steep Holm and Flat Holm in the Bristol Channel and to Guernsey and Herm in the Channel Islands. It grows in rocky and waste places close to the sea, and on Guernsey it still appears to be spreading. A perennial, it flowers during July and August.

A. ampeloprasum var. *babingtonii* (Borrer) Syme* (*A. babingtonii* Borzer)

BABINGTON'S LEEK

Very rare and endemic to the British Isles. It is now found only in Cornwall, Dorset, the Isles of Scilly and in Galway and Mayo on the west coast of Ireland. It grows on cliffs, in rock clefts, on sand dunes and in hedge banks close to the sea. A perennial, it flowers during July and August. (Not illustrated.)

❁ *A. ampeloprasum* **is a tall robust plant growing up to 2 m tall, with stout stems and umbels 7-10 cm in diameter.**

Allium carinatum L.

KEELED GARLIC

Alien and a native of much of central Europe. Cultivated in British gardens since the 17th century, it is naturalised in a number of scattered localities from Cornwall to the Moray Firth and in north-east Ireland. It is a bulbous perennial and flowers during August.

❁ *A. carinatum* **differs from** *A. roseum* **and** *A. scorodoprasum* **in its protruding stamens and spathe consisting of two long bracts. It differs from** *A. oleraceum* **in its flat leaves and pink flowers with protruding stamens.**

❁ *A. scorodoprasum* **and** *A. roseum* **both have short spathes and non-protruding stamens.** *A. scorodoprasum* **has keeled, rough-edged leaves and reddish-purple flowers.** *A. roseum* **has unkeeled, smooth-edged leaves and pink flowers.**

Allium scorodoprasum L.

SAND LEEK

A local species of northern England south to Derbyshire with a few scattered localities in southern Scotland. It is a plant of rough grassland and scrub on dry soils. A bulbous perennial, it flowers from May to August.

Allium roseum L.

ROSY GARLIC

Alien and a native of the whole of the Mediterranean region and the Azores, where it grows in dry open woodland and in rocky ground. Cultivated in British gardens since 1752, it has become naturalised in a number of places in the milder parts of the country. A bulbous perennial, it flowers during May and June.

Allium triquetrum L.

THREE-CORNERED LEEK
TRIQUETROUS GARLIC

Alien and a native of the western Mediterranean from Portugal and Morocco to Italy and Tunisia where it grows in damp shady places, often by streams. It has been cultivated in British gardens since about 1752 and is now thoroughly naturalised in hedge banks, roadside verges and waste places in Cornwall, the Channel Islands, the Scillies and coastal areas of Devon, Wales and southern Ireland. It is completely hardy only in the milder parts of the country. A bulbous perennial, it flowers from April to June and the seeds are dispersed by ants.

Allium paradoxum (Bieb.) G. Don

FEW-FLOWERED LEEK

Alien and a native to the Caucasus and northern Iran, where it grows in forests from sea level to 2,300 m. It is easily cultivated in shady conditions and has become thoroughly naturalised in a number of places in England and Scotland, most frequently in the south-east. It flowers during April and May. (Not illustrated.)

Allium ursinum L.

RAMSONS

Widely distributed throughout the British Isles but scarce in northern and north-east Scotland, absent from Orkney and Shetland and rather local and scattered in Ireland. It is a common plant of damp woodlands on rich loamy, mildly acid to calcareous soils throughout England and Wales. It often occurs along stream banks but avoids waterlogged conditions. In the wetter western parts of the country it grows in hedge banks and also in the grikes of limestone pavement. A bulbous perennial, it flowers from April to June and is probably normally self-pollinated.

Colchicum autumnale L.

MEADOW SAFFRON
AUTUMN CROCUS

A lowland species most frequent from Oxfordshire west to Somerset and the Welsh borders, and scattered northwards to Cumbria. It is locally abundant in damp permanent meadows and open woodlands on basic or neutral soils, but it has disappeared from many areas due to agricultural improvement. All parts of the plant are extremely poisonous, containing the cumulative toxin colchicine. A perennial, it flowers from August to October after the leaves have withered. The fruit ripens during the following April and May surrounded by the new leaves. The plant is pollinated by insects or self-pollinated.

❁ *Colchicum* **superficially resembles a** *Crocus*, **but has the superior ovary of the Liliaceae and six, not three, stamens.**

PLATE 96
LILIACEAE • IRIDACEAE

(see illustrations page 202)

Ornithogalum angustifolium Boreau

STAR-OF-BETHLEHEM

Scattered throughout the British Isles; perhaps native only in southern and eastern England where it grows in dry sandy grasslands, road verges, waste ground and in woodland. The larger *O. umbellatum* L. (illustrated), with petals up to 30 mm (not 12-20 mm) and up to 20 flowers (not 4-12) is cultivated in gardens and may be naturalised. The species are easily confused and there is doubt as to the range of both of them.

❁ *O. angustifolium* **differs from both** *O. nutans* **and** *O. pyrenaicum* **in the flat-topped inflorescence with the lower flower stalks much longer than the upper.**

Ornithogalum nutans L.

DROOPING STAR-OF-BETHLEHEM

Alien and a native of southern and eastern Europe and Asia Minor. It has become more or less naturalised in the past in grassy habitats in a number of scattered localities throughout southern, central and eastern England, but is now very scarce. A bulbous perennial, it flowers during May and June and is insect- or self-pollinated.

❁ *O. nutans* **grows to 25-60 cm and is distinguished from** *O. pyrenaicum* **by the large flowers (15-30 mm) and leaves with a central white stripe.** *O. pyrenaicum* **grows to 1 m and the flowers are 10 mm or less.**

Ornithogalum pyrenaicum L.

SPIKED STAR-OF-BETHLEHEM
BATH ASPARAGUS

Very local and restricted as a native plant to the counties of Somerset, Wiltshire, Gloucestershire, Berkshire, Bedfordshire and Cambridgeshire (Huntingdonshire). It is most frequent in open woodlands, scrub and on banks on the oolitic limestone around Frome and Bath. It occasionally appears as a casual elsewhere in southern England. The young shoots used to be sold in Bath as 'Bath Asparagus'. A tall bulbous perennial, it flowers during June and July.

Paris quadrifolia L.

HERB PARIS

A locally frequent species distributed throughout most of England, but rare in Wales and Scotland and absent from south-west England and Ireland. It is a species of damp woodlands on rich, calcareous loams reaching to 360 m in northern England. It often grows with *Mercurialis perennis*, is very shade-tolerant and in eastern England is confined to ancient woodland. A perennial, it flowers from May to August and is pollinated by small flies or self-pollinated. It is the only British member of the Trilliaceae, which includes the often cultivated North American *Trilliums*.

Leucojum aestivum L.*

SUMMER SNOWFLAKE
LODDON LILY

Very local and restricted to two main areas of lowland England: along the Thames and the lower reaches of the Loddon between Reading and Windsor, and further upstream between Goring and Abingdon. In addition there are one or two isolated occurrences by the Rivers Avon and Bourne in Wiltshire.

A recent survey revealed that there are 48 native colonies of the plant in England with a total of

continued on next page

about 13,000 plants. It usually grows in dense willow carr or on islands in the river and less often in woodland margins and hedgerows. A bulbous perennial, it flowers during April and May and is pollinated by bees. It is commonly grown in gardens and occasionally appears as an escape from cultivation.

✽ *L. vernum* grows to 20 cm and is distinguished from *L. aestivum* by the solitary flowers. *L. aestivum* grows to 30-60 cm.

Leucojum vernum L.*

SPRING SNOWFLAKE

Very rare and possibly native in only two localities in south-west England: one in Dorset and the other in Somerset. It grows in damp scrub, hedge banks and by stream sides, and both populations are large and flourishing. A bulbous perennial, it flowers from February to April and is pollinated chiefly by bees. The seeds are dispersed by ants. *L. vernum* is frequently grown in gardens but only rarely appears as an escape of cultivation. (Illustrated on Plate 102).

✽ *L. vernum* differs from *Galanthus* by the perianth segments all being of the same size.

Narcissus pseudonarcissus L. subsp. *pseudonarcissus*

WILD DAFFODIL
LENT LILY

Widely distributed in southern and western England as far north as the Solway, it is rare in the east and in most of Wales and absent as a native plant from Scotland and Ireland. It is a locally abundant plant of damp open woodlands, heathland, commons and meadows, usually on mildly acid soils. A bulbous perennial, it flowers from February to April and is pollinated by bumble-bees or self-pollinated.

✽ Subsp. *pseudonarcissus* is distinguished from both subsp. *obvallaris* and subsp. *hispanicus* by the corona being darker than the perianth.

Narcissus pseudonarcissus subsp. *major* (Curtis) Baker (*N. hispanicus* Gouan)

SPANISH DAFFODIL

Alien but formerly much grown in gardens and naturalised in grassy places in a number of localities. Now replaced in cultivation by larger-flowered hybrids. It is a native of Spain, Portugal and southern France.

✽ Subsp. *major* is distinguished from subsp. *obvallaris* by the larger flowers (5-6 cm across), twisted perianth segments, and longer pedicels (25-35 mm). The flowers of subsp. *obvallaris* are 3.5-4.5 cm across and the pedicels are 1-15 mm long.

Narcissus pseudonarcissus subsp. *obvallaris* (Salisb.) Fernandes* (*N. obvallaris* Salisb.)

TENBY DAFFODIL

First discovered growing in pastures around Tenby in south Wales, it is not known anywhere else in the wild and its origin is a mystery, although it may well have arisen in cultivation. It has also been reported from Shropshire and Carmarthenshire but has since disappeared from both these places. No truly wild population appears to remain and the plant is maintained in gardens in the area in which it originated. It flowers during April.

Narcissus poeticus subsp. *poeticus* (*N. majalis* Curt.)

PHEASANT'S-EYE

Alien but naturalised in a number of places. Formerly much grown in gardens, but now less popular. It is a native of the mountains of central and southern Europe, where it grows in damp meadows. It flowers during May and is pollinated by butterflies and moths or self-pollinated.

Narcissus x *medioluteus* Miller (*N. poeticus* x *N. tazetta*)

PRIMROSE-PEERLESS

Locally naturalised in grassy places throughout England, Wales and southern Ireland and in Midlothian and Jersey, and native in southern France. It is the most frequent daffodil to be found in the wild, after *N. pseudonarcissus*. It flowers during April and May.

Galanthus nivalis L.

SNOWDROP

Although cultivated in gardens since the 16th century, snowdrops were not recorded from the wild until the 1770s in Gloucestershire and Worcestershire. They frequently become naturalised as escapes from cultivation, so that there is speculation as to whether they are truly native anywhere in Britain, although they may be wild in parts of the west and Wales. They are found growing in damp woods and by streams throughout the British Isles as far north as the Moray Firth but are absent from Ireland. Snowdrops are in flower from January to March and are pollinated by bees.

IRIDACEAE

Sisyrinchium bermudiana L.

BLUE-EYED-GRASS

First discovered near Woodford in Co. Galway in 1845 by the Reverend J. Lynam. The Irish plant is identical with the one that is widespread in the eastern United States, and its status in Ireland has been questioned; however, there seems little doubt that it is native. It is unlikely to have originated as a garden escape as the blue-eyed-grass widely cultivated in Europe is *S. montanum*. *S. bermudiana* is locally abundant in marshy meadows, on river banks and gravelly lake shores in most parts of western Ireland from Co. Cork to Co. Donegal. A perennial, it flowers during July and is insect- or self-pollinated.

Crocus vernus (L.) Hill* (*C. purpureus* Weston)

SPRING CROCUS
PURPLE CROCUS

Alien and a native of southern Europe from Italy eastwards, where it grows in mountain meadows, scrub and open woodland. It is frequently grown in gardens and has become naturalised in old meadows, pastures and churchyards, sometimes in thousands, in a number of scattered localities in central, southern and eastern England and in a single locality in south-east Ireland. A perennial, it flowers during March and April with the leaves or shortly after they appear.

Crocus nudiflorus Sm.

AUTUMN CROCUS

Alien and a native of Spain and south-west France, where it grows in meadows. Widely cultivated and naturalised in grass, it has become established in a number of scattered localities, especially in north-west England. A perennial, it flowers during November and October long before the leaves appear.

PLATE 97
IRIDACEAE • DIOSCOREACEAE • ORCHIDACEAE

(see illustrations page 204)

Iris foetidissima L.

STINKING IRIS
GLADDON

Widely distributed throughout southern England, south of a line from the Wash to Pembrokeshire with scattered localities in north Wales and absent from Ireland except for introductions. It is a frequent plant of hedge banks, open woods, scrub and sea cliffs, usually on well-drained calcareous or base-rich soils. The crushed leaves have a distinctive smell of raw beef, and the plant was much used by medieval herbalists as a purgative. A tufted perennial, it flowers from May to July. The ripe seeds which are exposed when the capsule dehisces are a bright orange-red.

✽ *I. foetidissima* differs from *I. spuria* and *I. versicolor* in the dark green, evergreen leaves and purplish-yellow flowers.

Iris spuria L.*

BLUE IRIS

Widespread throughout Europe from Denmark to Spain and North Africa, and eastwards to the Causasus. It is almost certainly not native in Britain, but has been known for more than 100 years beside fen ditches in Lincolshire, where only one locality now remains. A population of about 100 plants also survives in old grassland in Dorset. A perennial, it flowers during June.

✽ *I. spuria* differs from *I. versicolor* in the flower colour, and the broad terminal part of the outer petal round with the basal part of the petal twice as long. The terminal part of the outer petals of *I. versicolor* is gradually narrowed at the base, and the narrow basal part of the petals is about as long as the broad part.

Iris versicolor L.*

PURPLE IRIS

Alien and a native of North America. It has long been known as naturalised in reed swamp at the edge of Ullswater in Cumbria, and has become established in marshy ground at the edge of lakes, ponds and streams in about seven other localities in Essex, Kirkcudbrightshire, Inverness-shire and the Outer Hebrides. A tall perennial, it flowers during June and July.

Iris pseudacorus L.

YELLOW IRIS
YELLOW FLAG

Distributed throughout the whole of the British Isles except for parts of the Scottish Highlands. It is a common plant of marshes, fens, wet woods and fen carr and the shallow water of the margins of ponds, lakes, canals, dykes, rivers and streams on muddy or peaty, mildly acid to calcareous soils. A tall perennial, it flowers from May to July. The rhizomes were formerly used to produce a black dye and black ink.

Romulea columnae Sebastiani & Mauri*

SAND CROCUS

Confined in the British Isles to the Channel Islands, where it is frequent and widespread, and to a single locality in south Devon. It grows in short, dry grassland on sandy ground close to the sea. In Devon the population extends over a large area of golf course and is maintained by the mowing and grazing of the turf. A small perennial, it is in flower from March to May.

Crocosmia x *crocosmiiflora* (Lemoine) N.E. Br. (*Tritonia* x *crocosmiiflora* (Lemoine) Nicholson)

MONTBRETIA

Montbretia was raised by Victor Lemoine at Nancy in France towards the end of the last century by crossing the South African *T. pottsii* and *T. aurea*. It is now commonly naturalised as an escape from cultivation throughout the whole of the western parts of the British Isles, and is particularly abundant in the south-west, western Ireland and western Scotland. It grows in hedge banks and wood margins and by the sides of lakes, rivers and ditches. A perennial, it flowers during July and August.

Gladiolus illyricus Koch**

WILD GLADIOLUS

Very rare. It was first discovered growing in the New Forest near Lyndhurst in 1856. It is still confined to the New Forest, a colony on the Isle of Wight having become extinct in 1897. About

continued on next page

populations are known, growing among bracken on rough heathland. Although protected by law, it suffers from heavy picking. It is a perennial and flowers from June to August.

DIOSCOREACEAE

Tamus communis L.

BLACK BRYONY

Distributed throughout almost the whole of England and Wales as far north as the Tyne; it is common in the south, but scarce in parts of the north-west and central Wales. It is primarily a plant of hedgerows, but is also found in scrub and wood margins on moist, well-drained fertile soils to an altitude of about 245 m. It is the only British member of the Dioscoreaceae, the family which contains the tropical yams. A climbing perennial, with a large stem tuber and annual twining stems, it flowers from May to July and is pollinated by various small insects. The plant is dioecious, with male and female flowers on separate plants. The pale red berries are extremely poisonous, containing the toxic glucoside saponin.

ORCHIDACEAE

Cypripedium calceolus L.**

LADY'S-SLIPPER

Very rare and now known from only a single locality on the Carboniferous limestone in Yorkshire. This lovely plant was first discovered in Helks Wood near Ingleborough in 1640 and was formerly widespread, although always local and never common, on the Carboniferous, Magnesian and Corallian limestones of Derbyshire, Yorkshire, Durham and Cumbria. It grows in open limestone grassland. Its virtual extinction is the result of picking and uprooting by gardeners and botanists since the 18th century and the surviving population is heavily protected. It flowers during May and June and is pollinated by small bees.

Cephalanthera longifolia (L.) Fritsch

NARROW-LEAVED HELLEBORINE LONG-LEAVED HELLEBORINE

Rare, local and declining. It occurs in scattered localities in Kent, Sussex, Hampshire and Oxfordshire, in the Welsh borders and along the west coast from Cardigan to Sutherland. There are also about 10 localities in southern Ireland. It most frequently occurs in chalk and limestone woodland, but it is less shade-tolerant than *C. damasonium* and may also grow in calcareous maritime sands. It flowers during May and is pollinated by small bees.

❁ *C. longifolia* **differs from** *C. damasonium* **in the narrow lanceolate leaves and bracts shorter than the ovary.**

Cephalanthera damasonium (Miller) Druce

WHITE HELLEBORINE

Widespread on the chalk and oolitic limestone of southern England, it is a frequent plant of beechwoods on the South and North Downs, the Chilterns as far north as Cambridgeshire, in Hampshire, Wiltshire and Dorset and on the Cotswolds in Gloucestershire. It is very shade-tolerant and is often found growing with *Epipactis helleborine* and *Neottia*. It flowers during May and June and is usually self-pollinated.

Cephalanthera rubra (L.) Rich.**

RED HELLEBORINE

Very rare. It is now confined to a single locality in beech woodland in the Chilterns, and to two localities in beechwoods in the Cotswolds in Gloucestershire. In addition, it has recently been discovered in Hampshire. It has always been rare in Britain but there are old records for Somerset, Sussex and Kent. Flowering, which is sporadic and unpredictable, occurs during June and July and pollination is effected by small bees.

Spiranthes romanzoffiana Cham.*

IRISH LADY'S-TRESSES

Has a peculiarly fragmented distribution in western Britain. It was first discovered in 1810 in Cork and Kerry, and it also grows around the shores and streams of Lough Neagh in Northern Ireland. It is known from four localities in the Inner Hebrides and on the Scottish mainland it occurs in about seven places in Argyll and Inverness-shire, while a population in south Devon was destroyed recently by agricultural drainage. It is one of the few British plants which occurs on both sides of the Atlantic, having the centre of its distribution in the eastern United States and Canada. It is a plant of marshy meadows and pastures near rivers and streams and of seasonally wet ground on the shore of lakes and rivers. Flowering, which occurs during July and August, is erratic, with large numbers in some years and very few in others.

❁ *S. romanzoffiana* **differs from** *S. spiralis* **in the leafy stem and flowers in three spirally twisted rows rather than one.**

Spiranthes spiralis (L.) Chevall.

AUTUMN LADY'S-TRESSES

Widely distributed throughout southern England and around the west coast as far north as Morecambe Bay. In Ireland it is scattered in the west and around the south and south-east coasts. It is a plant of the short turf of old grassland, pastures, cliff tops, grassy coastal dunes and lawns on calcareous or base-rich soils. It has declined greatly in recent years as a result of agricultural improvement, but some colonies still consist of thousands of plants. It flowers during August and September and is pollinated by bumble-bees. The leaf rosette develops in September, overwinters and withers before flowering.

Spiranthes aestivalis (Poiret) Richard*

SUMMER LADY'S-TRESSES

Now extinct in Britain. It was first recorded in 1840 growing in a bog in the New Forest, but by 1959 it had disappeared from the last of its four known localities. It was last seen in Guernsey in 1914 and in Jersey in 1926, both sites having been lost due to over-collecting. (Not illustrated.)

PLATE 98

ORCHIDACEAE

(see illustrations page 206)

❁ **Most species of** *Epipactis* **have rather inconspicuous flowers with the lip divided into two parts, a basal cup-shaped 'hypochile' and a terminal triangular or rounded lobe, the 'epichile'.**

Epipactis palustris (L.) Crantz

MARSH HELLEBORINE

A local species scattered throughout Britain as far north as the Firth of Forth and throughout central and western Ireland. It is a plant of calcium-rich fens and marshes and is especially characteristic of wet calcium-rich coastal dune slacks. Exceptionally, it also occurs in dry chalk grassland. It flowers from July to early September and is pollinated by solitary wasps.

❁ *E. helleborine* **and** *E. purpurata* **are distinguished from** *E. leptochila, E. phyllanthes* **and** *E. dunensis* **by the spirally arranged leaves. The other three species have the leaves in two opposite rows.**

Epipatis helleborine (L.) Crantz

BROAD-LEAVED HELLEBORINE

The commonest and the most widespread of the British species of *Epipactis*, it occurs throughout the British Isles as far north as the Firth of Tay on the east; in the west it extends up the coast to Sutherland. It is scattered throughout Ireland. It is a plant of woods and wood margins, most often on calcareous or base-rich soils. In the north it also grows among limestone scree and on limestone pavement. It flowers from July to September and is pollinated by wasps.

❁ *E. purpurata* **usually grows in clumps of five or more stems and the lower bracts are longer than the flowers.** *E. helleborine* **rarely occurs with more than three stems together and the lower bracts are about as long as the flowers.**

Epipactis purpurata Sm.

VIOLET HELLEBORINE

A rather local species that is most frequent on the chalk of south-east England and the Chilterns, but extending as far north and west as the limestone of the Welsh Border in Herefordshire and Shropshire. Although typically a plant of beechwoods on chalk or limestone, it also occurs in woods on base-rich clays and sands. It is more shade tolerant than *E. helleborine*, with which it sometimes grows, and flowers about a fortnight later in August and September. It is pollinated by wasps.

❁ *E. phyllanthes* **differs from** *E. leptochila* **and** *E. dunensis* **in the pendulous flowers, almost glabrous stems, and greenish-white inside to the hypochile.**

Epipactis phyllanthes G.E. Sm.

GREEN-FLOWERED HELLEBORINE

A local species that is most frequent on the chalk of Hampshire and Wiltshire, but with scattered localities in East Kent, West Sussex, the Isle of Wight, the Chilterns and the Cotswolds. It also occurs in coastal sites in south Wales, Lancashire and Cumbria and in isolated localities in north Wales, Yorkshire, Northumberland and Ireland. A very variable species, it grows in a range of habitats, most usually in chalk woodland but also in woodland on base-rich sands or clays, in coastal sand dunes and in Northumberland in birch woodland on lead-contaminated gravels. It flowers from June to September, according to locality, and is self-pollinated.

Epipactis leptochila (Godfery) Godfery

Two varieties occur in the British Isles.

Epipactis leptochila var. *leptochila*

NARROW-LIPPED HELLEBORINE

An uncommon species that is locally frequent on the escarpments of the Chilterns and the Cotswolds, with a number of scattered localities on the North and South Downs, on the Hampshire chalk, the Carboniferous limestone of the Mendips and the Wye Valley, in south Devon and Northumberland. It is primarily a plant of beech woods on the chalk and oolite and is more shade-tolerant than *E. helleborine*, with which it often grows. It occasionally occurs in woodland on sand, and in Northumberland it grows in birch scrub on heavy-metal-contaminated gravels by the River Tyne. It flowers from the end of June to the beginning of August and is self-pollinated.

❁ **The distal part of the lip of var.** *leptochila* **is longer than wide; the distal part of the lip of var.** *dunensis* **is reflexed and wider than long.**

Epipactis leptochila var. *dunensis* T. & T.A. Stephenson*
(*E. dunensis* (T. & T.A. Stephenson) Godfery*

DUNE HELLEBORINE

Very rare and apparently endemic to the British Isles; known from about 10 localities in Anglesey, Lancashire and Northumberland, where it grows in stabilised coastal sand dunes, often among bushes of the creeping willow *Salix repens.* A dull-looking plant, it flowers during June and July and is self-pollinated.

Epipactis youngiana A.J. Richards and A.F. Porter*

YELLOW HELLEBORINE

First described as a species new to science in 1982, having been discovered in two localities in Northumberland during 1976 and 1977 by A.J. Richards and A.F. Porter. In one it grows in an oak wood on a mildly acid clay soil, and in the other among regenerating woodland and a young pine plantation on contaminated soils around a disused lead mine. It flowers during July and August and is self-pollinated. Richards and Porter suggest that it may have originated as a hybrid between another self-pollinated species and *E. helleborine.* (Not illustrated.)

Epipactis atrorubens (Hoffm.) Besser

DARK-RED HELLEBORINE

A very local species confined to the harder limestones of northern and western Britain. It occurs on the Carboniferous limestone of Derbyshire, West Yorkshire, the southern Lake District, north Wales and in the Burren of Galway and Co. Clare in western Ireland. In northern and western Scotland it is found on the Durness limestone of Sutherland and in scattered localities in Wester Ross and on Skye. Typically, it grows in exposed situations in the grikes of limestone pavement, in cracks in limestone cliffs and among scree and boulders. It flowers during June and July and is pollinated by bees, wasps and hoverflies.

Epipogium aphyllum Swartz**

GHOST ORCHID
SPURRED CORAL-ROOT

One of the rarest of all British plants. It is apparently now confined to one or two beechwoods in the Chilterns in Buckinghamshire and Oxfordshire, where it grows in dense shade among the deep litter of decaying beech leaves. The plant is saprophytic, completely lacking chlorophyll. There are no roots, but the underground rhizome is a much-lobed coral-like structure which produces thread-like runners that give rise to new plants. Flowering is very erratic and may not occur at all for several years, and then usually follows a wet spring. The flowers, which can appear at any time from the end of May to the beginning of September, are pollinated by bumble-bees, but seed is rarely set.

Listera ovata (L.) R. Br.

TWAYBLADE

Distributed throughout the British Isles as far north as Orkney, but scarce in most of northern Scotland except for the north coast. It may be locally abundant in rough grassland, scrub, moist woods and lane sides on calcareous or base-rich soils. It also occurs on heaths and commons on acid sandy soils and in damp coastal dune slacks. It flowers from May to August according to locality and season, and is pollinated chiefly by small flies and parasitic wasps.

Listera cordata (L.) R. Br.

LESSER TWAYBLADE

A plant of northern Britain, being most frequent in central and northern Scotland but scattered as far south as the Humber and north Wales with isolated localities in Somerset and Hampshire, and scattered throughout most of Ireland. It is found in wet open moorland and on acid bogs, often growing in *Sphagnum* moss or among the carpet of moss at the base of heather and bilberry. A small, inconspicuous plant, it is in flower from the end of May and is pollinated by small flies and parasitic wasps.

Neottia nidus-avis (L.) Rich.

BIRD'S-NEST ORCHID

Widely distributed in England south and east of a line from the Wash to the Severn, and scattered throughout the rest of the British Isles as far north as the Moray Firth; rare and scattered in Ireland. It occurs most frequently in the deep shade of beechwoods on calcareous, humus-rich soils. It also occurs less commonly in deciduous woodlands on base-rich clays and sands. The plant is saprophytic, being wholly without chlorophyll, and the underground rhizome is surrounded by a tangle of fleshy roots resembling an untidy bird's nest. It flowers from May to July and is pollinated by a variety of small insects or is self-pollinated.

Goodyera repens (L.) R. Br.

CREEPING LADY'S-TRESSES

Primarily a plant of the ancient pine woods of the Eastern Highlands of Scotland, where it grows among deep layers of rotting pine needles and moss. It is occasionally found in birch woods and in moist areas in old coastal sand-dunes. Further south there are isolated localities in southern Scotland and Cumbria and, more surprisingly, it is flourishing in some pine plantations in north Norfolk, where presumably it has been introduced with sapling pines from Scotland. The plant spreads vegetatively by means of creeping underground rhizomes. It flowers during July and August and is pollinated by bumble-bees.

❁ **The stoloniferous habit and net-veined leaves distinguish *Goodyera* from *Spiranthes* (Plate 97). It can be separated from both *Pseudorchis* (Plate 100) and *Neotinea* (Plate 100) by the lack of a spur to the flowers.**

Hammarbya paludosa (L.) O. Kuntze *

BOG ORCHID

Rare and local. It is now more or less confined to western Scotland and the New Forest in Hampshire, with isolated localities in south Devon, Dorset, west Wales, Cumbria and eastern Ireland. It was formerly more widespread but has declined as its habitat has been destroyed by drainage. It is a plant of wet, acid *Sphagnum* bogs, usually growing in rather exposed situations in the surface of the *Sphagnum* carpet. A small, inconspicuous orchid, it is easily overlooked. Flowering, which is erratic, is from July to September, and it is pollinated by small flies.

❁ **The lip of the flower (labellum) in both *Hammarbya* and *Liparis* is on the upper side of the flower and pointing upwards. All other similar-looking species have the flowers orientated in the normal way.**

Liparis loeselii (L.) Rich.**

FEN ORCHID

Very rare and declining. It once occurred in about 30 localities in East Anglia and south Wales, but is now known from only eight in Norfolk, Glamorgan and Carmarthenshire, with an isolated locality in Devon. In East Anglia, where drainage has brought it to the verge of extinction, it usually grows around the margins of pools in calcareous fens, and flowers most freely in years following reed and sedge cutting. In south Wales it grows in wet, calcareous coastal dune slacks, often among creeping willow, *Salix repens.* It flowers during June and July, but it is unclear whether the plant is insect-pollinated or self-pollinated.

The dune form from south Wales differs from the typical fenland plant in having broader leaves, and is sometimes separated as the var. *ovata.*

PLATE 99
ORCHIDACEAE

(see illustrations page 208)

Corallorhiza trifida Chatel.

CORALROOT ORCHID

A rare and local plant of northern Britain, where it is most frequent along the south side of the Moray Firth. It extends southwards in a number of scattered localities as far as Yorkshire, growing in damp, peaty, mossy pine or mixed pine and birch woods and in dense willow and alder scrub. Alternatively it can be found in the more open conditions of damp coastal dune slacks. A saprophytic species in which the rhizome develops into a coral-like mass with no true roots, it flowers erratically during June and July and is probably insect-pollinated.

Herminium monorchis (L.) R. Br.

MUSK ORCHID

The musk orchid is a rare and local plant of the chalk hills of southern England, being found in the Chilterns, the North and South Downs of Kent, Surrey and Sussex and in Hampshire and Wiltshire. It also occurs further west in Somerset and in the Gloucestershire Cotswolds. It is found in short turf in exposed conditions, sometimes in old quarry spoil heaps or the sides of paths and often in large numbers. A small, rather inconspicuous orchid, it flowers during June and July and is pollinated by small flies and parasitic wasps. In spite of its name the flower does not smell of musk.

❁ ***Herminium* is only likely to be confused with *Hammarbya* (Plate 98), but the habitat is quite different. It lacks the basal 'bulb' of *Hammarbya* and the flowers are orientated in the normal way.**

Coeloglossum viride (L.) Hartman

FROG ORCHID

Distributed throughout the whole of the British Isles, it is a local species which is declining in much of lowland England. It grows in the short turf of chalk and limestone pastures, in mountain grassland and on damp rock ledges up to an altitude of 1,000 m. It also occurs in areas of damp turf in old coastal sand dunes. A rather inconspicuous orchid, it flowers from June to August and is insect-pollinated.

Ophrys insectifera L.

FLY ORCHID

A local species distributed throughout England as far north as Cumbria and north-east Yorkshire, but most frequent on the chalk and oolite of the south and very rare in the south-west and in Wales, where it is restricted to Anglesey and Denbighshire. In Ireland it is more or less confined to the Burren of Galway and Co. Clare. It is shade-tolerant and is usually found in woods and scrub on chalk and limestone. It occasionally occurs on open downland and field borders and more rarely in fens. The flowers, which bear an obvious resemblance to an insect, are pollinated by male wasps of the genus *Gorytes* and are out from May to July.

Ophrys sphegodes Miller**

EARLY SPIDER-ORCHID

Rare and local. It is now confined to Dorset, Wiltshire, Sussex and Kent, where it grows in the short turf of old, unimproved chalk grassland, often close to the sea. There are now probably less than 30 localities left, but some of the colonies consist of several thousand plants. Although the flower bears an obvious resemblance to a bee (rather than a spider), the actual species most responsible for pollination is not known. It flowers early, from the end of April to the beginning of June, but flowering success is very erratic from year to year.

continued on next page

Ophrys fuciflora (Crantz) Moench**

LATE SPIDER-ORCHID

Very rare. It is confined in Britain to about 10 localities on the North Downs in east Kent, where it grows in the short turf of old chalk grassland on steep slopes and banks. As its English name implies, it flowers later than *O. sphegodes*, from late June to mid-July. Pollination has not been observed in this country, but on the Continent males of the bee *Eucera tuberculata* have been seen to visit the flowers, and this insect does occur in Britain.

❁ ***O. fuciflora*** **differs from** ***O. apifera*** **in the broader-tipped, flat, differently-patterned labellum. The little lobe that projects out from the tip of the labellum is distinctive and absent in** ***O. apifera.***

Ophrys apifera Hudson

BEE ORCHID

Widespread in England as far north as the Border, but rare in the north-west, Wales and the south-west. In Ireland it is scattered throughout the Central Plain and in the Burren. The bee orchid is the commonest of the four British species of *Ophrys*, and is usually found in the short, dry turf of unimproved chalk and limestone grassland. It also occurs in old chalk quarries and railway cuttings, and on the coast will grow in the moist hollows of calcareous sand dunes. Occasional plants may appear in almost any short neutral to calcareous grassland. It only rarely grows in shade. It flowers during June and July, but is very variable in its appearance from year to year. Insect pollination is rare in Britain, the plant being almost always self-pollinated.

❁ **Orchids of the genus** ***Orchis*** **differ from** ***Dactylorhiza*** **(Plate 100) in their small membranous bracts, while the bracts of** ***Dactylorhiza*** **are leaf-like.**

Orchis mascula (L.) L.

EARLY PURPLE ORCHID

Widely distributed throughout the British Isles, common in the south, but becoming scarcer northwards and absent from Shetland. It grows in a great variety of different habitats. It is commonly found in deciduous woodland on base-rich loams, in hedge banks and road verges and in open chalk grassland and chalk scrub. In northern Britain it grows on open hillsides to an altitude of 880 m and is also found on grassy clifftops in the west. It flowers from late April to June and is pollinated by bees.

❁ ***O. mascula*** **and** ***O. laxiflora*** **differ from the other** ***Orchis*** **species in that the upper sepals and petals do not come together to form a 'helmet' over the rest of the flower.**

O. mascula **occasionally occurs with unspotted leaves. The spur of** ***O. mascula*** **is as long as or longer than the ovary; the spur of** ***O. laxiflora*** **is shorter than the ovary.**

Orchis laxiflora (Lam.) (*)

LOOSE-FLOWERED ORCHID
JERSEY ORCHID

Confined in the British Isles to Jersey and Guernsey in the Channel Islands, where it is frequent in wet meadows and marshy fields. It flowers during May and June.

Orchis morio L.

GREEN-WINGED ORCHID

Widely distributed throughout England as far north as the border, but most frequent in the south and scarce in the north-west, Wales and the south-west. In Ireland it is scattered from the east coast, through the Central Plain to the Burren. It is a plant of old unimproved meadows and pastures and also churchyards, on damp calcareous soils or base-rich sands and clays. In some places it still appears in large numbers, but agricultural improvement and drainage has resulted in a severe decline in the number of localities in recent years. It flowers from late April to early June and is pollinated by bees.

❁ **The flower colour of** ***O. morio*** **is very variable, but the dark-striped sepals are always distinctive.**

Orchis ustulata L.

BURNT ORCHID

A local species distributed throughout England except for the south-west. It is also absent from Scotland, Wales and Ireland. It is a plant of the short turf of old, undisturbed dry chalk grassland in Kent, Sussex, Hampshire, Wiltshire, Berkshire and Bedfordshire and the oolite in Gloucestershire. In northern England it is a scarce plant of limestone grassland in Derbyshire, Lincolnshire, Yorkshire and Cumbria. Although it still appears in large numbers in some localities in a good year, it is declining everywhere. It normally flowers during May and June but some populations flower late, in July.

Orchis militaris L.**

MILITARY ORCHID
SOLDIER ORCHID

Very rare. By 1914 the military orchid was thought to be extinct in Britain, but it was rediscovered in the Chilterns in Buckinghamshire in 1947 and in 1954 a second locality was discovered in Suffolk. It grows at the edges of woods, clearings and among scrub on the chalk. The colonies are strictly protected as both have suffered from careless and over-enthusiastic visitors in the past. It flowers from mid-May to mid-June.

❁ **The 'legs' of the flower of** ***O. militaris*** **are shorter and broader than the 'arms'. The 'legs' and 'arms' of** ***O. simia*** **are both very narrow and the helmet is paler than in** ***O. militaris.***

Orchis simia Lam.**

MONKEY ORCHID

Very rare and now restricted to only five sites in Britain: two on the North Downs in east Kent, two in the Chilterns in Oxfordshire and one in Yorkshire. All the surviving populations are strictly protected and are flourishing as a result of careful habitat management and artificial pollination. The monkey orchid is a species of rough chalk grassland, often thriving under moderate shade. It flowers during May and June and is pollinated by a variety of insects.

Orchis purpurea Hudson

LADY ORCHID

Confined in Britain to the North Downs in Kent where it occurs in more than 60 localities in beechwoods, coppiced woodland and scrub on the chalk. The populations to the east of the River Stour differ in the structure of the inflorescence and in the shape and colour of the flower from those to the west between the Stour and the Darent. A tall, handsome orchid, it flowers from mid-May to early June and is pollinated by small flies.

❁ **The heavily coloured helmet of** ***O. purpurea*** **is distinctive.**

PLATE 100
ORCHIDACEAE

(see illustrations page 210)

Gymnadenia conopsea (L.) R. Br.

FRAGRANT ORCHID

Distributed throughout the whole of the British Isles. In southern England the fragrant orchid is primarily a plant of dry, unimproved chalk and limestone grassland where it can occur in huge numbers. In northern Britain it grows in hill pastures on calcareous, base-rich or, less commonly, mildly acid soils, reaching an altitude of 640 m. In the south it flowers during June and July, but in the north it extends into August. The plant is pollinated chiefly by moths.

A distinct form, subsp. *densiflora* (Wahlenb.) Camus, Bergon & A. Camus occurs in calcareous and base-rich fens and marshes. It is most frequent in East Anglia and southern England, but occurs in scattered localities throughout the range of the species.

In Scotland the commonest subspecies is subsp. *borealis* (Drace) F. Rose, where it grows in hill pasture, heathland and on road verges. It also occurs in scattered localities in similar habitats in Ireland, Wales, northern England, Cornwall, Hampshire and Essex.

❁ **The flowers of** ***Gymnadenia*** **are rather similar to those of** ***Anacamptis,*** **but lack the two raised 'pollen guides' that occur on the labellum of** ***Anacamptis.*** **The shape of the inflorescences is characteristic.**

Anacamptis pyramidalis (L.) Rich.

PYRAMIDAL ORCHID

Widespread in southern and eastern Britain as far north as the Firth of Forth and along the western seaboard as far as the Solway with scattered localities as far north as Barra in the Outer Hebrides, and distributed throughout most of Ireland. It is a frequent plant of rough unimproved chalk and limestone grassland and of fixed dry calcareous coastal sand dunes. It flowers from June to August and is pollinated by butterflies and moths.

Neotinea maculata (Desf.) Stearn* (*N. intacta* (Link) Reichb. f.)

DENSE-FLOWERED ORCHID

Almost confined to the Burren district of Co. Clare and Co. Galway, where it was first recorded in 1864. It grows in the crevices of limestone pavement, in hill grassland, old pastures and on road verges. More recently it has been recorded from Co. Mayo, Co. Roscommon, Offaly, East Cork and the Arran Isles. In 1966 a small population was discovered growing on calcareous coastal dunes in the Isle of Man. It flowers for a short period during May and is usually self-pollinated.

❁ **The flowers of** ***Neotinea*** **and** ***Pseudorchis*** **both have spurs which distinguish them from** ***Goodyera*** **(Plate 98) and** ***Spiranthes*** **(Plate 97).**

The flowers of ***Pseudorchis*** **are yellowish-white; those of** ***Neotinea*** **are white or pinkish.**

Pseudorchis albida (L.) A. & D. Löve (*Leucorchis albida* (L.) E. Mey)

SMALL-WHITE ORCHID

Widely distributed throughout Scotland north of a line from the Clyde to Aberdeen, but common in the west. There are scattered localities further south as far as Derbyshire, in central Wales and throughout Ireland. It grows in hilly pastures, mountain grassland and on rock ledges on dry acid or calcareous soils to an altitude of 610 m. It flowers from the end of May to July and is pollinated by butterflies, day-flying moths and bees.

Platanthera bifolia (L.) Rich.

LESSER BUTTERFLY-ORCHID

Distributed throughout the British Isles but absent from the Channel Islands, Orkney and Shetland. It is most frequent in the north and west, where it grows in hill grassland, moorland and heathland, often among bracken and heath, on a wide variety of soils and reaching to 385 m. In the south it is more frequent on calcareous soils, appearing in woodlands following felling and on chalk downs as well as on more acid soils. It flowers from May to July and is pollinated at night by moths.

❁ **The flowers of** ***P. bifolia*** **are generally smaller than those of** ***P. chlorantha*** **and the spike paler, but the most reliable difference between the two butterfly orchids are the two pollen-masses or 'pollinia'. Those of** ***P. bifolia*** **lie parallel, while those of** ***P. chlorantha*** **diverge downwards.**

continued on next page

Platanthera chlorantha (Custer) Reichb.

GREATER BUTTERFLY-ORCHID

A local species, distributed throughout the British Isles but absent from the Channel Islands, Orkney and Shetland. It is most frequent in central and southern England and parts of western Scotland and is found in pastures, meadows and hill grassland to an altitude of 460 m, sometimes with *P. bifolia*. It also occurs in woods and scrub on calcareous soils or base-rich clays. It flowers from May to July and is pollinated by night-flying moths.

Himantoglossum hircinum (L.) Sprengel**

LIZARD ORCHID

Very rare and erratic in its appearance. In recent years it has been recorded from Kent, Sussex, Berkshire, Oxfordshire, Cambridgeshire, Suffolk and Somerset. The lizard orchid occurs in rough calcareous grassland, field borders, scrub and woodland clearings on chalk or limestone soils and on fixed calcareous sand-dunes. The flowers, which have a strong smell of goats, are out in June and July and are pollinated by a variety of flies, wasps and bees.

Aceras anthropophorum (L.) Aiton f.

MAN ORCHID

Very local with a distribution centred on the North Downs in Kent and Surrey and extending as far north as Lincolnshire and with scattered localities as far west as Somerset. It is almost exclusively a plant of rough, unimproved chalk grassland, often growing among sparse scrub or in abandoned chalk quarries. It flowers during June and July and is pollinated by small insects.

Dactylorhiza Nevski

SPOTTED AND MARSH ORCHIDS

The spotted and marsh orchids belonging to the genus *Dactylorhiza* are an exceedingly complex group. Most of the species are very variable and hybridise freely with each other. Not surprisingly, different authors have treated the group in different ways, and the arrangement used here follows that of the *New Flora of the British Isles*.

❁ **Orchids of the genus *Dactylorhiza* differ from *Orchis* (Plate 99) in their leaf-like, rather than scale-like, bracts. The colour, shape and marking of the labellum is especially important for correct identification.**

Dactylorhiza fuchsii (Druce) Soó (*Dactylorchis fuchsii* (Druce) Vermeul.)

COMMON SPOTTED-ORCHID

Widespread throughout the whole of the British Isles; commonest in the south and scarce in parts of the south-west and in central, northern and eastern Scotland. It is a common plant of meadows, pastures, unimproved grassland, roadside verges, marshes, fens, moist dune-slacks and woodland clearings on calcareous or base-rich soils and reaching an altitude of 370 m. It flowers from June to August and is pollinated by bees and hoverflies.

Three subspecies or varieties of *D. fuchsii* are generally recognised in the British Isles. Subsp. *fuchsii* is the common and widespread subspecies; subsp. *hebridensis* (Wilmott) Soó largely replaces subsp. *fuchsii* in the Outer Hebrides and on Tiree, Jura and Islay, where it occurs in large numbers on the machair; subsp. *okellyi* (Druce) Soó is the commonest subspecies in northern and western Ireland, especially in the cracks and crevices of limestone pavement, and also occurring in parts of north-west Scotland and in the Isle of Man.

❁ ***D. fuchsii* and *D. maculata* differ from the other species in the presence of a few small transitional leaves between the leaves and bracts and in the lower bracts being no longer than the flowers.**

The basal leaves of *D. fuchsii* are blunt and the labellum of the flower consists of three almost equal lobes, the central lobe often longer than the laterals. The basal leaves of *D. maculata* are pointed and the central lobe of the labellum is much smaller than the broad, rounded lateral lobes.

Dactylorhiza maculata (L.) Soó (*Dactylorchis maculata* (L.) Vermeul.)

HEATH SPOTTED-ORCHID
MOORLAND SPOTTED-ORCHID

Distributed throughout the British Isles and common in the north and west and on heathlands in the south. It is a plant of heaths and moorland on acid, peaty or mineral soils reaching an altitude of 915 m in Scotland. It tolerates a range of soil moistures from dry, sandy heathland to wet springlines among moor-grass, *Molinia*, although it is less common on wet, open *Sphagnum* bogs. It flowers from June to August and is pollinated by bees and flies. The British plant belongs to the subsp. *ericetorum* (Linton) P.F. Hunt & Summerhayes.

Dactylorhiza incarnata (L.) Soó (*Dactylorchis incarnata* (L.) Vermeul.)

EARLY MARSH-ORCHID

Occurs throughout the whole of the British Isles in wet meadows, marshes, fens, bogs and wet dune-slacks. It flowers during May and June and is probably pollinated by bees. A very variable species, *D. incarnata* has been separated into five subspecies in the British Isles.

Subsp. *incarnata* occurs throughout the British Isles in fens, marshes and wet meadows, usually on base-rich or calcareous soils.

Subsp. *pulchella* (Druce) Soó occurs throughout the British Isles but is perhaps most frequent in the north and west. It replaces subsp. *incarnata* in acid *Sphagnum* bogs.

Subsp. *coccinea* (Pugsley) Soó is a plant of wet coastal dune slacks, where in some localities it grows in thousands. It is known in north and south Wales, the Isle of Man, Norfolk, Co. Durham, the Outer Hebrides and in several places around the coast of Ireland.

Subsp. *cruenta* (O.F. Muell.) P.D. Sell is restricted to the lake area of Co. Clare, Co. Galway and Co. Mayo in the limestone region of western Ireland where it grows in turloughs.

Subsp. *ochroleuca* (Bell) Hunt & Summerhayes is restricted to a few calcareous fens in Norfolk, Suffolk, Cambridgeshire, Surrey and south Wales.

❁ ***D. incarnata* is distinguished by its yellow-green, keeled leaves with hooded tips. The sides of the labellum are usually bent back. Flowers of the various subspecies are separately illustrated. Subsp. *cruenta* has the leaves spotted on both sides.**

Dactylorhiza purpurella (T. & T.A. Steph.) Soó (*Dactylorchis purpurella* (T. & T.A. Steph.) Vermuel., *Dactylorhiza majalis* subsp. *purpurella*)

NORTHERN MARSH-ORCHID

Widespread throughout northern England and Scotland, in north Wales and northern, north-west and south-east Ireland. There is also a single locality in the New Forest in Hampshire. The distribution is almost the complete opposite to that of *D. praetermissa. D. purpurella* is found in fens, marshes and wet meadows usually on calcareous or base-rich soils to an altitude of 450 m. It flowers during June and July and is insect-pollinated.

❁ ***D. purpurella* has short leaves and a rather square-topped inflorescence. It differs from the other species in the broadly diamond-shaped, almost unlobed labellum.**

Dactylorhiza traunsteineri (Sauter) Soó (*Dactylorchis traunsteineri* (Sauter) Vermeul.)

NARROW-LEAVED MARSH-ORCHID

A rare and local species confined to East Anglia and to scattered localities in Berkshire, Hampshire, Yorkshire, Anglesey, Caernarvonshire and the west coast of Scotland. In Ireland there are a number of widely scattered localities in the Central Plain. *D. traunsteineri* is confined to wet, rich, calcareous fens, often growing on the edges of reed beds and flowering most profusely in the years following reed-cutting. It also occurs in wet, calcareous flushes and dune slacks. It flowers during May and June and is probably pollinated by bees.

❁ ***D. traunsteineri* is distinguished by the narrow leaves, usually no more than 1.5 cm wide, long brownish-purple tinged bracts, and a rather long, narrow middle lobe to the lip.**

Dactylorhiza praetermissa (Druce) Soó (*D. praetermissa* (Druce) Vermeul., *Dactylorchis majalis* subsp. *praetermissa*)

SOUTHERN MARSH-ORCHID

Widely distributed throughout southern Britain as far north as a line from Pembrokeshire to the Humber, with a few scattered localities further north as far as Co. Durham, and absent from Ireland. It has a distribution that is almost perfectly complementary to that of *D. purpurella*. It grows in calcareous or base-rich marshes, fens, wet-meadows and dune slacks, and flowers from mid-June to the end of July.

A plant with spots and ring-marks on the leaves, sometimes called the Leopard Marsh-orchid, is probably either a form of *D. praetermissa* or a hybrid between *D. praetermissa* and *D. fuchsii*.

❁ ***D. praetermissa* and *D. majalis* are similar, some botanists considering them to be subspecies of the same species.**

***D. praetermissa* has unspotted leaves, the lip is often concave and almost unlobed, and the spots are mostly confined to the basal part of the lip. The leaves of *D. majalis* are either spotted or unspotted, the lip is three-lobed and flat and the dark spots almost reach the tip.**

Dactylorhiza majalis (Reichb.) P.F. Hunt & Summerhayes

WESTERN MARSH-ORCHID

D. majalis consists of three subspecies in the British Isles. Subsp. *occidentalis* (Pugsley) Sell Endemic to the British Isles and widespread in west and south-west Ireland. It occurs in damp coastal dune slacks, fens, marshes and wet meadows and flowers early, during May and June.

Subsp. *cambrensis* (R.H. Roberts) R.H. Roberts
Known only from a few localities in north Wales and Yorkshire, it flowers later than subsp. *occidentalis* in June and July. Plants growing on the machair of North Uist have been separated as subsp. *scotica*.

❁ ***D. majalis* subsp. *occidentalis* usually has heavily spotted leaves.**

Dactylorhiza lapponica (Hartman) Soó**

LAPLAND MARSH-ORCHID

Recognised as a species new to the British Isles in 1988, it is confined to the west coast of Scotland, South Harris and Rhum where it grows in base-rich hillside flushes from sea level to 300 m. It flowers from May to July. (Not illustrated.)

❁ **The leaves of *D. lapponica* are usually heavily spotted and the bracts purplish-tinged. The lip is strongly marked and the mid-lobe pointed and longer than the side-lobes.**

ARACEAE

Arum maculatum L.
LORDS-AND-LADIES
CUCKOO-PINT

Distributed throughout the whole of the British Isles as far north as the Firth of Forth and throughout Ireland. It is a common plant of hedgerows, hedge banks, woodland margins, scrub, wooded cliffs and gardens on moist humus-rich mildly acid, base-rich or calcareous loams to an altitude of 410 m. The inflorescence consists of a basal ring of female flowers surmounted by a ring of male flowers, the whole enclosed in the base of the spathe. The inflorescence axis terminates in the purple spadix which heats up and emits an odour attracting small flies, known as owl-midges, of the genus *Psychoda* (usually *P. phalaenoides*.) The midges enter the floral chamber, passing a ring of stiff bristles which prevent them from escaping, and pollinate the female flowers. The stamens then ripen, dusting the midges with pollen, which are then able to escape as the ring of bristles wilts. A perennial, it flowers during April and May and the conspicuous red, poisonous berries ripen in July and August. Geoffrey Grigson in 'The Englishman's Flora' lists 100 local and vernacular names for the plant.

Arum italicum Miller
ITALIAN LORDS-AND-LADIES

A local species of the south coast of England, extending from Kent to Cornwall with an isolated locality in Glamorgan. It is a plant of scrub, wood margins and hedge banks on stony ground, usually close to the sea. A perennial, it flowers during April and May, but rather later than *A. maculatum*.

❁ ***A. italicum*** **differs from *A. maculatum* in the yellow spadix, one-third of the length of the spathe. The leaves develop in December. The spadix of *A. maculatum* is rarely yellow but is half as long as the spathe, and the leaves develop in the spring.**

Acorus calamus L.
SWEET-FLAG

Alien and a native of Asia and central and western North America. It was introduced to Britain from Asia during the middle of the 16th century and was growing wild by 1666. It is found throughout England as far north as Yorkshire, with scattered localities further north and in Wales, Ireland and the south-west. It grows in shallow nutrient-rich or calcareous water at the margins of lakes, ponds, canals and river on muddy soils. A tall perennial, growing to a height of 1 m, it flowers from May to July.
❁ **The leaves of *Acorus* can be distinguished from similar-looking sedge-like plants by their bright green colour, crinkly edges and strong smell of tangerines when crushed.**

LEMNACEAE

Wolffia arrhiza (L.) Wimmer
ROOTLESS DUCKWEED

Very local and decreasing; now almost confined to the Romney Marsh area of the Kent-Sussex border and to the Somerset Levels. It is found in the still water of nutrient-rich, sometimes mildly brackish, drainage dykes on alluvial or muddy soils. A minute, free-floating aquatic, with fronds of between 0.5 and 1.0 mm in diameter, it is the smallest British flowering plant, although the flowers are unknown in Europe. Its decline is due to agricultural drainage schemes.

❁ ***Wolffia*** **differs from *Lemna* in its smaller size (less than 1 mm) and absence of roots.**

Lemna trisulca L.
IVY-LEAVED DUCKWEED

Widely distributed throughout England but rare in Scotland, Wales and the south-west. It is frequent in north-east Ireland but scattered in the rest of the country. It is a common plant of the still waters of ponds, dykes and canals in lowland England, and it flowers from May to July.
❁ **The fronds of *L. trisulca* are thin and taper to a stalk at their base. Several are usually joined together and it floats beneath the surface.**

Lemna gibba L.
FAT DUCKWEED
GIBBOUS DUCKWEED

Locally common in lowland England, but absent from Scotland and most of Wales and the south-west; rare in Ireland. It occurs in the still water of nutrient-rich ponds, dykes and streams. It flowers during June and July.
❁ ***L. gibba*** **is recognised by its convex upper surface and white, swollen lower surface. The fronds often go reddish in late summer.**

Lemna minor L.
COMMON DUCKWEED

Distributed throughout the British Isles, but rare in northern Scotland. A very common plant of ponds, ditches, dykes, canals and slow-flowing rivers and streams, growing in both nutrient-poor and fertile water. It flowers during June and July.
❁ **The fronds of *L. minor* each have a single root and three indistinct longitudinal veins.**

Lemna minuta Kunth
(*L. minuscula* Herter)
LEAST DUCKWEED

Alien and a native of North and South America. First collected from a ditch in Cambridge in 1977 and has since been recorded from more than 20 localities in south-east and eastern England and north Wales, and will probably be found elsewhere. It occurs in ponds, ditches, canals and rivers, usually in association with other species of duckweeds. (Not illustrated.)
❁ ***L. minuta*** **can only certainly be distinguished from *L. minor* microscopically. *L. minuta* has a single faint vein in the frond; *L. minor* has three. In addition, the frond of *L. minuta* is smaller, more pointed, a paler green and more translucent and symmetrical than that of *L. minor*, but these characters should only be regarded as guides.**

Spirodela polyrhiza (L.) Schleiden
(= *Lemna polyrhiza* L.)
GREATER DUCKWEED

A rather local species of lowland England, but very rare in Scotland, Wales, Ireland and south-west England. It occurs in ponds, drainage dykes and canals with a muddy or peaty bottom. It flowers during July, but only rarely in England.
❁ ***Spirodela*** **is distinguished from *Lemna* by its larger fronds (up to 8 mm), each with several roots.**

SPARGANIACEAE

Sparganium erectum L.
BRANCHED BUR-REED

Distributed throughout the British Isles, common in the lowlands but scarce in northern Scotland and absent from Shetland. It grows in the shallow water of the margins of lakes, ponds, rivers, canals, dykes and streams on fertile, silty, muddy or peaty soils. A tall perennial, growing to a height of 1.5 m, it flowers from June to August and is wind-pollinated.

S. erectum is separated into four subspecies in Britain, but little is known about their respective distributions and apparently they differ very little in habitat. They are distinguished by differences in the shape and size of the fruit. The subspecies are subsp. *erectum*, subsp. *microcarpum* (Neuman) Domin, subsp. *neglectum* (Beeby) Schinz & Thell., and subsp. *oocarpum* (Celak.). Domin (which may be the hybrid between subsp. *erectum* and subsp. *neglectum*.)
❁ ***S. erectum*** **is distinguished from the other species of bur-reed by its branched stems. The four subspecies are separated on the basis of the shape and size of the fruits. Details can be found in** *New Flora of the British Isles*.

Sparganium emersum Rehmann
UNBRANCHED BUR-REED

A rather local species, distributed throughout the whole of the British Isles but scarce in Scotland, Wales, Ireland and south-west England. It grows in the shallow, fertile water of rivers, canals, streams, lakes and ponds with a silty, clayey or peaty bottom. An erect or floating perennial of between 20 cm and 60 cm, it flowers during June and July and is wind-pollinated.
❁ ***S. emersum*** **usually has no floating leaves or if they are present they are distinctly keeled at the base. It has more than three male heads.**

Sparganium angustifolium Mich.
FLOATING BUR-REED

A local species, frequent in western Scotland, Orkney, Shetland and the Hebrides and scarce in north-west England, west Wales and Ireland, and absent elsewhere. It is a plant of acid, peaty mountain lochs and pools. A slender floating perennial, it flowers during August and September and is wind-pollinated.
❁ ***S. angustifolium*** **has floating leaves that are semicircular in section, and no more than three male heads.**

Sparganium natans L.
(*S. minimum* Wallr.)
LEAST BUR-REED
SMALL BUR-REED

A local species, scattered throughout Scotland, northern England, East Anglia and Ireland but very rare elsewhere. It is found in acid or calcareous lakes, and pools with a peaty bottom. A floating perennial, it flowers during June and July and is wind-pollinated.
❁ ***S. natans*** **has floating stems and leaves. The leaves are thin and flat and there is only a single male head.**

TYPHACEAE

Typha latifolia L.
BULRUSH
GREAT REEDMACE
CAT'S-TAIL

Widespread and common throughout lowland Britain, but scarce in Scotland and absent from Orkney, Shetland and the Hebrides, and rather local in Wales and Ireland. It grows in the shallow water of the margins of lakes, ponds, canals, dykes and slow-flowing rivers and streams, where it often forms extensive pure stands on a silty or clayey bottom. It prefers fertile water and is tolerant of low levels of organic pollution. A tall perennial growing to a height of 1.5 m to 2.5 m, it flowers during June and July and is wind-pollinated.

❁ ***T. angustifolia*** **differs from *T. latifolia* in the narrow leaves (4 mm wide), and the male and female parts of the inflorescence are separated by a short length of bare stem. The leaves of *T. latifolia* are about 15 mm wide.**

Typha angustifolia L.
LESSER BULRUSH
LESSER REEDMACE

A rather local plant that is frequent in parts of lowland England but rare or absent in northern England, Scotland, Wales, the south-west and Ireland. It grows in the shallow water of the margins of lakes, ponds, canals, dykes and slow-flowing rivers with a clayey or organic-rich bottom. It is most frequent in nutrient-rich water but is intolerant of pollution. A tall perennial, growing to a height of up to 3 m, it flowers in June and July and is wind-pollinated.

GLOSSARY

acid Applied to soil or water. An acid soil is 'sour' and often deficient in essential plant nutrients. Strictly it has a pH below 7.0, although plants typical of acid soils (calcifuges) do not usually appear until the pH is less than 6.0

acute Referring to a leaf: tapering gradually to a fine sharp point.

alien A plant thought to have been introduced originally to the British Isles either deliberately or accidentally by man

alternate Usually referring to the arrangement of leaves on a stem: in two rows, but the individual leaves not in opposite pairs

annual Completing the life-cycle from germination to seed production and death in 12 months

anther The apical part of the stamen, containing the pollen grains

apomixis (adj. **apomictic**) Producing viable seed without fertilisation

appressed Held close to another part of the plant, but not joined to it

ascending Usually referring to a stem: curving upwards

axil The angle between the steam and the leaf or bract

axillary Arising in the axil of a leaf or bract

basal Referring to a leaf: arising from the base of the stem or the rhizome

base-rich Referring to soils: relatively rich in metals like calcium and magnesium and usually with a fairly high pH

basic Referring to soils: not acid, strictly with pH in excess of 7.0

beak Narrow projection at the tip of a fruit

berry A fleshy fruit, usually containing several seeds

biennial Completing the life-cycle from germination to seed production within two years, and not flowering in the first year

blanket bog Bog developed in the uplands where climate is so cool and wet that peat builds up directly on underlying rock

bog A plant community developed on wet, acid peat

bract Small, often leaf-like appendage arising at base of flower-stalk or main branch of inflorescence

bracteole A bract arising at the base of a secondary branch of an inflorescence

bulb An onion-shaped underground organ composed of colourless overlapping fleshy leaves enclosing next year's bud.

bulbil A small bulb developing in the axil of a leaf or on the inflorescence

calcicole A plant normally restricted to soils rich in calcium carbonate, such as those derived from chalk or limestone

calcifuge A plant normally restricted to soils deficient in calcium such as acid sands and peats

calyx All the sepals of a flower together comprise the calyx

capsule A dry fruit that opens to shed the seed when ripe

casual An introduced plant that persists for only a short time in the wild and does not become established

clints The blocks of limestone in limestone pavement, separated by fissures (grikes)

compound Referring to a leaf: made up of a number of distinct leaflets

cordate Referring to a leaf: heart-shaped

corolla All the petals of a flower together comprise the corolla

crisped Curled at the edges

cyme A repeatedly branched inflorescence, where each growing point ends in a flower

deciduous Shedding its leaves in the autumn

decumbent Referring to stems: lying on the ground and growing upwards at the tips

decurrent Referring to leaves: having the bases prolonged down the stem as wings

decussate Referring to leaves: in opposite pairs, but with each successive pair orientated at right angles to each other

deflexed Bent sharply downwards

dioecious With male and female flowers on separate plants, i.e. with separate male and female plants

diploid Having two basic sets of chromosomes

dominant A plant that is so common in a particular habitat that it gives to the plant community its characteristic appearance

ecotype A population of a species that is genetically distinct from other populations of the same species in physiological or morphological characteristics

emarginate With a notch in the tip

endemic Confined as a native to a particular country or other restricted geographical area

entire Referring to a leaf: without teeth or lobes

epicalyx A calyx-like structure outside, but usually appressed to, the true calyx

escape A plant growing outside a garden, having escaped from cultivation, but not well established

exserted Protruding (usually refers to the stamens or stigmas)

fen A plant community developed on wet calcareous peat

fertile A soil or water rich in the essential plant nutrients, especially nitrogen, phosphorus and potassium

filament The stalk of the anther, the two together forming the stamen

floret Small individual flower of the condensed inflorescence of the Compositae

flaccid Limp, drooping

flush Wet ground, usually on a hillside, but always with flowing or seeping water but not in a definite channel

fruit The ripe seeds together with the structures surrounding or enclosing them

glabrous Without hairs

gland A small, usually shining globular vesicle containing oil or some other liquid on the surface of some part of the plant

glandular Covered with glands

glandular hair A stalked gland

glaucous Bluish

globose Globe-shaped

grikes The fissures in limestone pavement

heath A lowland plant community on acid sandy soils dominated by dwarf shrubs belonging to the Ericaceae

herb Any non-woody plant

herbaceous Green, with a leaf-like texture

hermaphrodite Having male and female organs (stamens and ovary) in the same flower

heterostyly Condition found in those species where the style is of two or three different lengths, relative to other parts of the flower, in different plants

hybrid Plant resulting from the fertilisation of one species by another species

Hymenoptera The order of insects that includes the bees, wasps and ants

included Not protruding; usually refers to stamens or stigmas

inferior Referring to the ovary: with the petals and sepals inserted around the top of the ovary

inflorescence That part of the stem carrying the flowers and above the uppermost stem leaf, a flowering branch

internode Part of the stem between two nodes

introduced Thought to have been brought to Britain either deliberately or accidentally by man; not native

involucre A calyx-like structure composed of bracts surrounding the base of a head of flowers or condensed inflorescence, especially in the Compositae

keel The lower petal of a flower when shaped like the keel of a boat e.g. in the Leguminosae and Fumariaceae

labellum The enlarged lower petal of a flower, e.g. in many orchids

lanceolate Referring to a leaf: long, narrow and tapering to a fine point.

latex A milky juice

Lepidoptera The order of insects comprising the butterflies and moths

ligule Referring to the Compositae: the narrow strap-shaped corolla of the ray-florets

limb The flattened and expanded tip of a petal that has a tubular base

linear Referring to a leaf: long, very narrow and parallel-sided

lip Two or more petals close together and clearly separated from the rest of the corolla and forming an 'upper lip' or a 'lower lip'

marsh Plant community developed on a wet mineral soil

meadow Grassy field cut for hay

monoecious Having separate male and female flowers on the same plant

moor Upland plant community developed on dry or damp peat, often dominated by heather

native Natural to a particular geographical area; not known to have been introduced

nectary Structure of the flower containing nectar

nerve A strand of strengthening or conducting tissue running through a leaf

neutral Referring to a soil: neither very acid nor very basic

node Point on a stem from which one or more leaves arise

nutrient-rich Referring to a soil or water: fertile, rich in essential plant nutrients, especially nitrogen, phosphorus and potassium

oblong Referring to a leaf: long, broad and parallel-sided

obovate Referring to the leaf shape: oval, with the widest part above the middle

obtuse Blunt

opposite Referring to the leaves: two leaves arising from opposite sides of the same point on the stem

ovary Swollen basal part of the female part of the flower containing the ovules and surmounted by the styles and stigmas

ovate Referring to the leaf-shape: oval, with the widest part at or below the middle

pappus Tuft of hairs at apex of seeds of many Compositae (e.g. as in dandelion clock)

parasite A plant that derives its food wholly or partly (semi-parasite) from other living plants to which it is attached

pasture A grassy field grazed during the summer

peat Accumulated partially-decayed remains of dead plants; develops in cool, wet and waterlogged conditions

pedicel The stalk of a single flower

peduncle The stalk of an inflorescence or partial inflorescence

perennial A plant that lives for more than two years, and usually flowering each year

perianth All of the floral leaves of the flower; the petals and sepals together if they are different

petal A member of the inner ring of floral-leaves of the flower if they are distinguished from the outer ring (sepals), especially if they are brightly coloured

petiole The stalk of a leaf

pH Referring to soil and water: the scale of 1-14 by which the degree of acidity is measured. Strictly, a pH below 7.0 is acid, and above 7.0 basic or alkaline. Most plants characteristic of acid soils occur at a pH below 5.5-6.0

pinnate A leaf composed of more than three leaflets arranged in pairs down each side of the main stalk

pubescent Shortly and softly hairy

raceme An unbranched inflorescence in which each individual flower has a distinct stalk

ray The stalk of a partial umbel, i.e. of a secondary umbel in a compound umbel, as in most members of the Umbelliferae

ray-floret A floret (individual flower) of a member of the Compositae with the corolla that is a ligule

receptacle The swollen, flattened or cup-shaped upper part of a stem to which the parts of the flower are attached

recurved Referring to petal, bract or leaf: curved back

revolute Referring to leaf or petal: rolled under (usually along the margin)

rhizome An underground stem living for more than one year

ruderal Plant growing on open disturbed ground of a temporary nature: a smart name for a weed

salt-marsh A community of flowering plants developed on soft, inter-tidal mud on a sheltered shore

saprophyte A plant deriving its food wholly or partially from dead organic matter

scarious Usually referring to bracts or sepals; thin and colourless (not green) with a papery texture

scabrid Rough to the touch

scrub A plant community dominated by shrubs

seed The unique reproductive unit of the seed-plants resulting from the fertilised ovule and containing the embryo protected by a thick seed-coat

sepal A member of the outer ring of floral-leaves of the flower, usually green and leaf-like and distinguished from the coloured petals

sessile Without a stalk

shrub A woody plant, usually much branched from the base and not reaching a height of much more than 5 m when mature

simple Referring to a leaf: not compound

spathes Large leaf-like sheath enclosing and protecting flowers of *Arum*

spur A hollow tubular projection from the base of a petal

stamen One of the male reproductive structures of the flower, consisting of the filament (stalk) and anther (containing the pollen grains)

sterile Referring to stamens: not producing viable pollen. Referring to seed: not capable of germination

stigma The apex of the female reproductive structure of the flower to which the pollen adheres

stipule A scale-like or leaf-like appendage at the base of the petiole, and sometimes partly adhering to it

stolon A creeping overground stem produced by a plant with a central rosette

tepal Individual part of the perianth, used when petals and sepals not differentiated

tendril A climbing organ, most often the terminal part of a leaf, but sometimes formed from part of the stem

ternate A compound leaf divided into three more or less equal leaflets joined at a common point

tetraploid Having double the diploid number of chromosomes

truncate Usually refers to the base of a leaf: squared off at right-angles to the petiole. Referring to fruit: squared off at the apex

tuber Swollen portion of a root of one year's duration

turion Detached overwintering bud of a water plant

umbel An umbrella-shaped inflorescence

compound umbel A compound inflorescence which has secondary or partial umbels arising from the ends of the branches of the main umbel

vein A strand of strengthening or conducting tissue in the leaf

INDEX

PLATE NUMBERS IN **BOLD** ARE FOLLOWED BY THE PAGE NUMBER ON WHICH THE CORRESPONDING TEXT APPEARS

A

B

D

E

F

G

H

I

R

S

T